Case Studies in Biomedical Ethics

Case Studies in Biomedical Ethics

Decision-Making, Principles, and Cases

ROBERT M. VEATCH

The Kennedy Institute of Ethics
Georgetown University

AMY M. HADDAD

Center for Health Policy and Ethics
Creighton University

DAN C. ENGLISH

Center for Clinical Bioethics
Georgetown University

New York   Oxford
OXFORD UNIVERSITY PRESS
2010

Oxford University Press, Inc., publishes works that further Oxford University's
objective of excellence in research, scholarship, and education.

Oxford New York
Auckland Cape Town Dar es Salaam Hong Kong Karachi
Kuala Lumpur Madrid Melbourne Mexico City Nairobi
New Delhi Shanghai Taipei Toronto

With offices in
Argentina Austria Brazil Chile Czech Republic France Greece
Guatemala Hungary Italy Japan Poland Portugal Singapore
South Korea Switzerland Thailand Turkey Ukraine Vietnam

Published by Oxford University Press, Inc.
198 Madison Avenue, New York, New York 10016
http://www.oup.com

Oxford is a registered trademark of Oxford University Press

Library of Congress Cataloging-in-Publication Data

Veatch, Robert M.
  Case studies in biomedical ethics : decision-making, principles, and cases /
Robert M. Veatch, Amy M. Haddad, Dan C. English.
    p. ; cm.
  Includes bibliographical references and index.
  ISBN 978-0-19-530972-0 (alk. paper)
 1. Medical ethics—Case studies.   I. Haddad, Amy Marie.   II. English,
Dan C.   III. Title.
  [DNLM: 1. Bioethical Issues—Case Reports.   2. Decision Making—Case
Reports.   WB 60 V394c 2010]
  R724.V3985 2010
  174.2—dc22

                                                          2008052687

Printing number: 9 8 7 6 5 4 3 2 1

Printed in the United States of America
on acid-free paper

TABLE OF CONTENTS

DETAILED TABLE OF CONTENTS

LIST OF CASES

LIST OF TABLES

PREFACE

We are living in the era of the biological revolution. Controversy surrounds topics such as artificial organs and abortions, gene therapy and brain circuitry, euthanasia and eugenics—medicine is remaking humans. At the same time, it is posing problems to be pondered by patients and professionals alike. One of the most provocative ways of studying these dilemmas is by using actual cases from the clinic or the court room. In the early days of what has become known as the era of bioethics, those working in the field began collecting cases. The first collection of these cases appeared in print in 1977 when the original edition of *Case Studies in Medical Ethics* was published.

Much has happened in the field of medical ethics since that time. Starting with Louise Brown in 1978, babies have been born using in vitro fertilization, patients such as Karen Quinlan and Terri Schiavo have died when nutrition was stopped; new genes have been implanted—and such experiments have led to the deaths of Jesse Gelsinger and Jolee Mohr. On other fronts, a man named Nushawn J. Williams was accused of intentionally exposing sexual partners with HIV, a disease that did not exist when the original collection of cases appeared. In a noble effort, a man named Ash Falkingham offered one of his kidneys to a total stranger in a foreign country. A former governor of Pennsylvania named Bob Casey received a simultaneous transplant of a heart and a liver. And little Lorie Ann Cardosa died, after being trapped in an old refrigerator, when an ambulance drove her from one hospital to another trying to find a place that would take her because she did not have any insurance.

Stories like these and many more have been collected for a new and completely revised edition of this volume. Like these cases, some included in this volume come from public sources, from the courts and from news accounts. In these cases, which are identified with sources, real names are used and real events described. These cases and their sources are listed in the "List of Cases from Public Sources" at the back of the book. Most of the cases collected here, however, come from real events that have occurred behind the closed doors of hospitals, doctors' offices, and family bedrooms. In these cases, names and details have been changed to provide anonymity and clarity of issues. Each case, however, whether public or private, is based on some real-life story that presented some ethical dilemma.

Sometimes ethical controversies in health care involve moral positions that are connected to specific religious stances. This is particularly true of some of the difficult and well-known moral issues: abortion, sterilization, euthanasia, and refusal of medical treatments such as blood transfusion. Several of the cases in this volume and the commentaries associated with them include discussion of positions articulated in specifically religious terms. This is true, in part, because some religious groups have well-developed positions on moral issues in medicine, some of which are difficult to understand outside of the religious tradition involved. We include several cases in which one or more of the participants are articulating explicit religious views—Roman Catholic, Methodist, Baptist, Lutheran, Jehovah's Witness, Muslim, and more sectarian views all put in an appearance. We do this because in the real world of medical ethics, these issues arise with regularity and both lay people and professionals in health care should be prepared to deal with them. Although religious perspectives often lead to opposition to certain medical procedures (such as abortion or blood transfusion), we note that in several of these cases in this volume, the parties making religious appeals do so in such a way that controversial procedures (such as withdrawing nutrition and hydration) are supported. The authors of this volume do not present any one religious perspective. In fact, 90 percent of the cases involve no explicit religious dimension at all, and the authors have never discussed their personal religious commitments among themselves. Our objective has been to include a reasonable sampling of some of the standard moral arguments including those only comprehensible by noting their religious sources.

The editors of this collection have worked together in various capacities over many years. Two of us have previously published two editions of a companion collection, *Case Studies in Pharmacy Ethics*. These are part of a series of case study volumes that have appeared since the original volume. Case collections in nursing,[1] dentistry,[2] and allied health[3] have also been published in addition to pharmacy[4] and broader areas of health care.[5] While giving attention to these volumes oriented to specific professions in health care, we had not returned to the original broader collection covering the full range of health care until now. Since we were working simultaneously on a new edition of *Case Studies in Pharmacy Ethics*, also for Oxford University Press, we proposed that we draw on some of the introductory material and analysis from that volume to prepare this new collection of cases covering the range of medical ethical issues including decisions by various health professions and lay people. This new edition includes almost entirely new cases and, just as important, a much more sophisticated structure than the original 1977 volume.

We know that this volume (as well as its companion volumes) will often be used in classrooms where teachers want to provide a systematic approach based in normative ethical theory. Thus, we start in Part 1 with basic questions (often called *metaethics*) of separating evaluative questions from questions of fact, distinguishing ethical from nonethical evaluations, and identifying the source or grounding of ethical judgments. We then devote the chapters of Part 2 to six standard ethical principles—beneficence, nonmaleficence, justice, respect for autonomy, fidelity, veracity, and avoidance of killing. These two parts contain cases that will help understand these basic issues and concepts. Then, in Part 3, we present cases in the major topical areas in health care. Since the cases in the earlier parts often deal with issues in these topical areas, each chapter begins with a list of cases from other chapters that the reader may also find relevant.

In developing a book of cases, we rely on many health professionals and lay people to provide us the stories told here. Some have chosen to remain anonymous, and we thank them without disclosing their identity. Others are acknowledged in notes attached to particular cases. Some have agreed to permit us to thank them without attaching their names to specific cases. In particular, we thank Maurice Bernstein, MD, Assistant Clinical Professor of Medicine, University of Southern California School of Medicine. We are also grateful to six scholars who reviewed the manuscript: Daniel Berthold of Bard College; William H. Bruening of Indiana-Purdue University at Fort Wayne; Karey Harwood of North Carolina State University; Daniel Palmer of Kent State University; Susan M. Purviance of the University of Toledo; and Laurie Zoloth of Northwestern University. They have all agreed to let us identify them, which gives us the opportunity to express our appreciation for the careful reading they gave the manuscript. We have given careful consideration to their many constructive suggestions and in almost all cases have incorporated their ideas into the final manuscript.

We are also indebted to many colleagues who have provided many kinds of help. Robert Veatch relied on his colleagues at the Kennedy Institute of Ethics at Georgetown, especially LeRoy Walters, who helped clarify details of many of the cases. He thanks Avi Craimer, a graduate student in philosophy at Georgetown, who provided research on several of the cases, and Stephanie P. Wilson, an intern at the Institute, who provided research as well. He also acknowledges the enormous help of the very special staff of professional librarians at the Kennedy Institute's National Reference Center for Bioethics Literature and Linda Powell, Moheba Hanif, and Sally Schofield of the Kennedy Institute staff.

Amy Haddad wishes to acknowledge the support of Rebecca Crowell and Chris Jorgenson both staff members at the Center for Health Policy and Ethics at Creighton University.

Dan English wishes to acknowledge N. Perryman Collins, MD, thoracic surgeon; Don G. Hunt, MD, vascular surgeon; Warren Levinson, MD, PhD, Professor of Microbiology, University of California at San Francisco; Steven Z. Pantilat, MD, Asssociate Professor of Medicine, University of California at San Francisco; Laura and Don Stemmle, MDs, pediatricians; and other anonymous physicians.

We all appreciate the cooperation of Robert Miller, our editor at Oxford, as well as Peter Ohlin our editor at Oxford for *Case Studies in Pharmacy Ethics.*

Robert M. Veatch, Washington, DC
Amy M. Haddad, Omaha, NE
Dan C. English, Alexandria, VA

NOTES

[1] Veatch, Robert M. and Sara T. Fry. *Case Studies in Nursing Ethics*. Philadelphia, PA: Lippincott, 1987; reprinted, Boston, MA: Jones and Bartlett, 1995; second edition 2000; third edition, 2006.

[2] Rule, James T. and Robert M. Veatch. *Ethical Questions in Dentistry*. Chicago, IL: Quintessence Books, 1993; second edition 2004.

[3] Veatch, Robert M. and Harley E. Flack. *Case Studies in Allied Health Ethics*. Upper Saddle River, NJ: Prentice-Hall, Inc., 1997.

[4] Veatch, Robert M. and Amy Haddad. *Case Studies in Pharmacy Ethics*. New York: Oxford University Press, 1999; second edition, 2008.

[5] Veatch, Robert M. *Case Studies in Medical Ethics*. Cambridge, MA: Harvard University Press, 1977; Levine, Carol and Robert M. Veatch, editors. *Cases in Bioethics from the Hastings Center Report*. Hastings-on-Hudson, New York: The Hastings Center, 1982; English, Dan. *Bioethics: A Clinical Guide for Medical Students*. New York: W. W. Norton, 1994. Haddad, Amy M. and Marshall Kapp. *Ethical and Legal Issues in Home Health Care: Case Studies and Analysis*. Norwalk, CT: Appleton and Lange, 1991.

Case Studies in Biomedical Ethics

INTRODUCTION

_・◦_

Four Questions of Ethics

Biomedical ethics as a field presents a fundamental problem. As a branch of applied ethics, biomedical ethics becomes interesting and relevant only when it abandons the ephemeral realm of theory and abstract speculation and gets down to practical questions raised by real, everyday problems of health and illness. Much of biomedical ethics, especially as practiced within the health professions, is indeed oriented to the practical questions of what should be done in a particular case. Yet if those who must resolve the ever-increasing ethical dilemmas in health care treat every case as something entirely novel, they will lose perhaps the best way of reaching a solution, that is, by understanding the general principles of ethics and facing each new situation from a systematic ethical stance.

This is a volume of case studies in medical ethics. It begins by recognizing the fact that one cannot do any ethics, especially health care ethics, in the abstract. It is only in real-life, flesh-and-blood situations that fundamental ethical questions are raised. This volume also acknowledges that a general framework is needed from which to resolve the dilemmas of ethics, whether one is practicing one's profession or confronting the issues as a lay person, trying to determine what to do to take care of one's health or that of some person for which one is responsible. The chapters and the issues discussed within the chapters are therefore arranged in order to work systematically through the questions of ethics. Since the main purpose of this book is to provide a collection of case studies from which to build a more comprehensive scheme for health care ethics, the first few pages are addressed to the more theoretical issues. The object is to construct a framework of the basic questions that must be answered in any complete and systematic bioethical system. In Chapter 1, we will present a model that can be used for analyzing cases. Before we turn to that model, however, it will be useful to outline the range of questions that can arise in any case.

We suggest that four fundamental questions must be answered in order for someone to take a complete and systematic ethical position. Each question has several plausible answers that have emerged over 2,000 years of Western thought. For normal, day-to-day decisions made by the health professional, it is not necessary to consider each of these questions. In fact, to do so would paralyze the decision-maker. Most decisions are quite ordinary—such as deciding what tests should be performed, what treatments to try, or which diet and exercise regimen to follow. They do not always demand full ethical analysis. Other decisions, as in the case of emergency intervention, are not ordinary at all. Still, in both ordinary and emergency situations it is only possible to act without becoming immobilized by ethical or other value concerns because some general rules or guidelines have emerged from previous experience and reflection. If ethical conflict is serious enough, it will be necessary to address, at least implicitly, all four of the fundamental questions of ethics: (1) What are the source, meaning, and justification of ethical claims?; (2) What kinds of acts are right?; (3) How do rules apply to specific situations?; and (4) What ought to be done in specific situations?

WHAT ARE THE SOURCE, MEANING, AND JUSTIFICATION OF ETHICAL CLAIMS?

At the most general level, which ethicists call the level of *metaethics*, the first question is the following: what are the source, meaning, and justification of ethical claims? What is it about a judgment that makes it an ethical judgment? Metaethics does not focus directly on what actions are right or wrong, but rather on such questions as where it is that ethical judgments are grounded (in God's will or in reason, for example). Metaethics also takes up what it means for a judgment to be an ethical one rather than some other kind of judgment.

It may not at first be obvious what counts as an ethical problem in health care. Physicians, other health care professionals, patients, and other lay people all can easily recognize ethical issues in abortion, euthanasia, test-tube babies, and gene manipulation. They can understand the moral crisis in deciding whether to turn away a patient who cannot afford to pay for needed treatment or deciding which of two needy patients should get a single heart available for transplant. These situations clearly involve ethical problems. Yet it is not immediately evident why we call these problems ethical, while other choices faced more commonly in the routine medical practice are not. We need to be clear on the difference between matters of ethics on the one hand and law, customs, aesthetics, or personal tastes on the other.

To make ethical problems obvious, several steps should be followed:

Distinguish between Evaluative Statements and Statements Presenting Nonevaluative Facts

Ethics involves making evaluations; therefore, it is a normative enterprise. Moving from the judgment that we *can* do something to the one that we *ought to* do something involves incorporating a set of norms—of judgments of value, rights, duties, and responsibilities. Thus, in order to be ethically responsible in medical decision-making, it is important to develop the ability to recognize evaluations or value judgments as they are made.

Table 1 Steps in Identifying Ethical Judgments

Distinguish between evaluative statements and statements presenting nonevaluative facts.
Distinguish between moral and nonmoral evaluations.
Determine who ought to decide.

These judgments are made by both health care professionals and lay people. Health professionals may believe that normally their professional practice does not involve any evaluations, but that is not really accurate. Value judgments are sometimes hard to recognize, especially when they are not controversial. To develop the ability to identify an evaluation, try the following: Select an experience that at first seems not to involve any particular value judgments such as providing counseling to a patient about a healthy lifestyle. Then begin to describe what occurred, keeping watch for evaluative words. Every time a word expressing value is encountered, note it. Among the words to watch out for are such verbs as *want, desire, prefer, should,* or *ought.* The physician who says the patient should get thirty minutes of exercise three times a week is making a value judgment. The word "should" is a signal of it. These evaluations may also be expressed as nouns, such as *benefit, harm, duty, responsibility, right,* or *obligation,* or in related adjectival forms, such as *good* and *bad, right* and *wrong, responsible, fitting,* and the like. Saying the patient will benefit from five servings of vegetables a day contains the evaluative term "benefit."

Table 2 Terms Signaling Normative Evaluations

Verbs	Nouns	Adjectives
Want	Benefit	Good
Desire	Harm	Bad
Prefer	Duty	Right
Should	Responsibility	Wrong
Feel Obliged	Right	Responsible
Ought	Obligation	Fitting

Sometimes evaluations are made in terms that are not literal, direct expressions of opinion but nonetheless clearly function as value judgments. When the Hippocratic Oath has the physician pledge, "I will not give to a woman an abortive remedy," this is not a mere description of the physician's behavior; it is a statement of how the physician ought to act.[1] By this statement, the writer of the Oath could be describing the way all physicians actually behave. Obviously, however, this is not what the statement describes. Rather it is saying that the physician who practices medicine according to Hippocratic norms ought to avoid participating in abortions or, more precisely, avoid providing abortive remedies. Of course, other codes of conduct do not necessarily accept this normative judgment.

Distinguish between Ethical and Nonethical Evaluations

Normative judgments take several forms. We need to distinguish *ethical* from *nonethical* normative judgments. (Some would refer to this as the distinction between *moral* and *nonmoral* evaluations. For our purposes, we will refer to "ethical" and "moral" interchangeably although some would consider the term "moral" to refer to more concrete judgments.) This process of distinguishing between ethical and nonethical evaluations can be much harder because often the difference cannot be discerned from the language itself. If one says that the physician did a good job responding to a dying patient's request for assistance in ending his life, the statement could express many kinds of evaluations. It could mean the physician did a good job legally, that the physician fulfilled the law, for example, refusing to engage in providing assistance to the patient to take steps to commit suicide. This statement would have to be evaluated by the laws of the jurisdiction. Its accuracy would depend on whether the physician was in Oregon or the Netherlands or some other jurisdiction. It could also mean the physician did a good job psychologically, that the job was done in a way that produced a good psychological impact on the patient. It could mean the physician did a good job technically, that the instructions to the patient were technically correct. Or it could mean the physician did a good job ethically, that the physician did what was morally required. Conceivably, doing a good job legally or technically could still leave open the question of whether the physician fulfilled every ethical obligation. For example, as we shall see in Chapter 9, the physician could fulfill all the laws of the jurisdiction and state by helping the patient kill himself in exactly the ways the law of Oregon prescribes but still violate some set of ethical standards.

Sometimes value judgments in health care simply express nonethical evaluations. Saying that the patient ate well does not express an ethical evaluation of the way the patient consumed his or her food. Saying that another day of hospitalization will be good for the patient may mean only that the patient will be helped physically or psychologically, not morally.

Even these apparently nonethical judgments about benefits and harms, however, may quickly lead one into the sphere of ethics. When the patient's judgment of what will be beneficial, for example, differs from the health professional's judgment, ethical dilemmas may emerge. A health professional who is committed morally to doing what will benefit the patient will choose one course while the one who is committed to preserving patient autonomy may reluctantly choose the other.

Ethical or moral evaluations are judgments of what is good or bad, right or wrong, having certain characteristics that separate them from evaluations that are not moral in content, such as aesthetic judgments, personal preferences, beliefs, or matters of taste. The difference between ethical and nonethical evaluations lies in the grounds on, or the reasons for which, they are being made.[2]

Ethical evaluations possess certain characteristics. They are evaluations of human actions, practices, or character traits rather than of inanimate objects, such as paintings or architectural structures. Not all evaluations of human actions are ethical evaluations, however. We may say that a physician is a good administrator or a good clinician without making a moral evaluation. To be considered ethical, an evaluation must have additional characteristics. Three characteristics are often mentioned as the distinctive features of ethical evaluations. First, the evaluations must be ultimate. They must have a certain preemptive quality, meaning that other values or human ends cannot, as a rule, override them.[3] Second, they must possess universality. Moral evaluations are thought of as reflecting a standpoint that applies to everyone. They are evaluations that everyone in principle ought to be able to make and understand (even if some in fact do not do so).[4] Finally, many add a third, more material, condition: that moral evaluations must treat the good of everyone alike. They must be general in the sense that they avoid giving a special place to one's own welfare. They must have an "other-regarding" focus or, at least, consider one's own welfare no more important than that of another.[5]

Table 3 Characteristics of Ethical Evaluations

---

1. The evaluations must be ultimate or beyond any further appeal.
2. The evaluations must possess universality. All persons ought to agree (even if they do not).
3. The evaluations must treat the good of everyone alike. One's own welfare should get no special consideration.

Ethical judgments possessing these characteristics can sometimes conflict with one another. Conflicts over whether the health care professional ought to care for a patient in the way thought to be most beneficial or most respecting of the patient's autonomy (even though harm may result) can involve conflicts between moral characteristics. Or the caregiver may be faced with the choice between preserving the patient's welfare or that of someone else. He or she may have to choose whether to keep a promise of confidentiality or provide needed assistance for a patient even though a confidence would have to be broken. The caregiver may have to decide whether to protect the interests of colleagues or the institution, whether to serve future patients by striking for better conditions or serve present patients by refusing to strike. These are moral conflicts faced by health care professionals. Chapter 2 presents a series of cases in which both moral and nonmoral evaluations are made in what appear to be quite ordinary health care situations faced by both health professionals and lay people.

The main task is to discern the value dimensions and to separate them from physiological, psychological, and other facts.

Determine Who Ought to Decide

A closely related problem that depends on the question of the source, meaning, and justification of ethical claims is who ought to decide? This is the focus of Chapter 3. Having learned to recognize the difference between the factual and evaluative dimensions of a case in health care ethics, one will constantly encounter the problem of who ought to decide or where the locus of decision-making ought to rest. The answer will depend, of course, on deciding from where morals come. Chapter 3 presents cases considering a range of sources of moral authority, from professional organizations, health care institutions, patients, families, physicians, and administrators to professional committees and the general public.

The choice among these decision-makers depends, at least in part, on what it is that ethical terms mean, or more generally, what it is that makes right acts right. Several answers to this question have been offered. One answer recognizes that different societies seem to reach different conclusions about whether a given act is right or wrong. From this perspective, to say that an act is morally right means nothing more than that it is in accord with the values of the group to which the speaker belongs or simply that it is approved by the speaker's group. This position, called social relativism, explains rightness or wrongness on the basis of whether the act fits within the social customs, mores, and folkways of the group. One problem with this view is that it seems to make sense to say that sometimes an act is morally wrong even though it is approved by the speaker's group. That would be impossible if moral judgments were based simply on the values of the speaker's group. The relation between ethics and the opinions of a social or cultural group are particularly crucial in cases in which the patient and the health care professional come from different cultures.

A second answer to the question of what makes right acts right attempts to correct this problem. According to this position, to say that an act is right means that it is approved by the speaker. This position, called personal relativism, reduces ethical meaning to personal preference. Of course, according to this position, behavior thought to be immoral by some is approved by others. Some say that the reason this can happen is that moral judgments are merely expressions of the speaker's preference.

Such differences in judgment, however, may have another explanation other than that ethical terms refer to the speaker's own preferences. Those disagreeing might simply not be working with the same facts. To claim that two people are in moral disagreement simply because the same act is seen as right by one person or group and wrong by another requires proof that both see the facts in the same way. Differences of circumstances, perspective, or belief about the facts could easily account for many moral differences. For example, two people may disagree about whether to allow an apparently unconscious person die, but they may disagree only because one believes that the person is permanently without any mental capacity, while the other believes that the individual really remains conscious. They could agree about all the ethical issues—that it is acceptable to let irreversibly unconscious people die, for instance—and still disagree about a particular case if they disagree about the medical facts.

In contrast with social and personal relativism, there is a third group of answers to the question of what makes right acts right. These positions, collectively called universalism or sometimes absolutism, hold that, in principle, acts that are called morally right or wrong are right or wrong independent of social or personal views. Certainly some choices merely involve personal taste: flavors of ice cream or hair lengths vary from time to time, place to place, and person to person. But these are matters of preference, not morality. Other evaluations appeal beyond the standards of social and personal taste to a more universal, more ultimate frame of reference. When these are concerned with acts of human conduct or character traits—as opposed to, say, paintings or music—they are thought of as moral evaluations.

However, the nature of the universal standard is often disputed. For the theologically oriented, it may be a single divine standard as we see in the monotheistic religions. According to this view, calling it right to disconnect a respirator that is keeping a terminally ill, comatose patient alive is to say that God would approve of the act or that it is in accord with God's will. This position is sometimes called theological absolutism or theological universalism.

Still another view among universalists takes empirical observation as the model. The standard in this case is nature or external reality. The problem of knowing whether an act is right or wrong is then the problem of knowing what is in nature. Empirical absolutism, as the view is sometimes called, sees the problem of knowing right and wrong as analogous to knowing scientific facts.[6] While astronomers try to discern the real nature of the universe of stars, and chemists the real nature of atoms as ordered in nature, ethics, according to this view, is an effort to discern rightness and wrongness as ordered in nature. The position sometimes takes the form of a natural law position. As with the physicist's law of gravity, moral laws are thought to be rooted in nature. Natural law positions may be secular or may have a theological foundation, such as in the ethics of Thomas Aquinas and traditional Catholic moral theology.

Still another form of universalism or absolutism rejects both the theological and the empirical models. It supposes that right and wrong are not empirically knowable, but are nonnatural properties known only by intuition. Thus, the position is sometimes called intuitionism or nonnaturalism.[7] Although for the intuitionist or nonnaturalist, right and wrong are not empirically knowable, they are still universal. All persons should in principle have the same intuitions about a particular act, provided they are intuiting properly. Still others, sometimes called rationalists, hold that reason can determine what is ethically required.[8]

There are other answers to the question of what makes right acts right. One view—in various forms called noncognitivism, emotivism, or prescriptivism—which ascended to popularity during the mid-twentieth century, perceived ethical utterances as evincing feelings about a particular act.[9]

A full exploration of the answers to the question of the source, meaning, and justification of ethical claims—this most abstract of ethical questions—is not possible here.[10] Ultimately, however, if an ethical dispute growing out of a case is serious enough and cannot be resolved at any other level, this question must be faced. If one says that it is wrong to participate in an abortion and another says that it is right to do so in the same circumstances, some way must be found of adjudicating the dispute between the two views. If the dispute is a moral one, the act cannot be both right and wrong at the same time. One must ask what it is that makes right acts right, how conflicts can be resolved, what the final authority is for morality, and whose judgment about what is right should prevail.

WHAT KINDS OF ACTS ARE RIGHT?

A second fundamental question of ethics moves beyond determining what makes right acts right to ask: What kinds of acts are right? This is the realm of *normative ethics*. The main question at this level is whether there are any general principles or norms describing the characteristics that make actions right or wrong.

Consequentialism

Two major schools of thought dominate Western thought regarding general ethical principles. One position looks at the consequences of acts; the other, at what is taken to be inherently right or wrong. The first position claims that acts are right to the extent that they produce good consequences and wrong to the extent that they produce bad consequences. The two principles of consequentialist ethics are referred to as beneficence (the idea that actions are right insofar as they produce benefits) and nonmaleficence (the idea that actions are wrong insofar as they produce bad consequences). The key evaluative terms for this position, known in various forms as utilitarianism or consequentialism, are good and bad. The focus is on the consequences or ends of action. This is the position of John Stuart Mill and Jeremy Bentham as well as of Epicurus, Thomas Aquinas, and capitalist economics. Aquinas, for example, argued that the first principle of the natural law is that "good is to be done and promoted and evil is to be avoided."[11]

Since Aquinas stands at the center of the Roman Catholic natural law tradition, he illustrates that natural law thinking (which is one answer to the first question of what makes right acts right) is not incompatible with consequentialism. The two positions are answers to two different questions. While natural law thinkers are not always consequentialists, they can be.

Classical utilitarianism determines what kinds of acts are right by figuring the net of good consequences minus bad ones for each person affected and then adding up to find the total net good.[12] The certainty and duration of the benefits and harms are taken into account. This form of consequentialism is indifferent to who obtains the benefits and harms. Thus, if the total net benefits of providing expensive drug therapy for a relatively healthy but powerful figure are thought to be greater than those of providing the same to a sicker Medicare recipient, the healthy and powerful ought to be given the care without further ethical debate.

Traditional health professional ethics is oriented to benefiting patients. This tradition combines the utilitarian answer to the question of what kinds of acts are right with a particular answer to the question of to whom moral duty is owed. Loyalty is to the patient, and the goal is toward what will produce the most benefit and avoid the most harm to the patient.

The ethics of the medical profession has traditionally held that the health professional's primary commitment is to the patient's care and safety. Some interpret this as giving first priority to protecting the patient from harm rather than to benefiting the patient. Like the principle of physician ethics, *primum non nocere* or "first of all do no harm," this view gives special weight to avoiding harm over and above the weight given to goods that can be produced.

Among some health professionals, the principle of doing no harm is often interpreted conservatively. When a potentially risky intervention is contemplated, harm may be avoided by refusing to intervene. That way no harm is done (although the health care provider thereby avoids doing any good that the intervention could have brought). This form of consequentialism, which gives priority to avoiding harm, needs to be distinguished from classical utilitarianism, which counts goods and harms for all affected people in calculating the net benefit of an action.

Problems arise from tension between classical utilitarianism (which counts benefits to all in society equally) and traditional, or Hippocratic, health care ethics. Hippocratic ethics, referring to the ethics of the Oath named after the father of Western medicine, focuses on the individual patient and sometimes gives special weight to avoiding harms through the prescriptive duty of advocacy. These issues are raised in the cases presented in Chapter 4.

Deontological or "Duty-Based" Ethics

Over against these positions that are oriented to consequences, the other major group of answers to the question of what kinds of acts are right asserts that rightness and wrongness are inherent in the act itself, independent of the consequences. These positions, collectively known as formalism or deontologism, hold that right- and wrong-making characteristics may be independent of consequences, that morality is a matter of duty rather than of merely evaluating consequences. Hence this approach can be called "duty-based" ethics. Kant stated the position most starkly.[13] It is based on ethical principles that express these duties, the duty to respect autonomy or to avoid killing being possible examples.

Chapter 5 takes up problems of health care delivery and, in doing so, poses probably the most significant challenge to the consequentialist ethic. Today some of the most challenging ethical problems in health care arise in cases in which physicians and other health professionals have so many demands placed on them that they cannot do everything they would like for their patients. One approach is to simply determine which course of action will do the most good overall. That, however, could mean leaving some patients virtually without care. It seems unfair or unjust (even if it turns out to be efficient in maximizing the total good done). One principle that is sometimes thought to restrain the production of overall good is the principle of justice. Taken in the sense of fairness in distributing goods and harms, justice is held by many to be an ethical right-making characteristic even if the consequences are not the best.

The problem is whether it is morally preferable to have a higher net total of benefits in society even if unevenly distributed or to have a somewhat lower total good but to have that good more equally distributed. This issue will be the focus of the cases in Chapter 5. Utilitarians may acknowledge that the distribution of the good is relevant but only because the net benefits tend to be greater when benefits are distributed more evenly. The benefits may be larger because of decreasing marginal utility—that is, because the more benefits one possesses, the less valuable each marginal additional benefit is. They claim that the only reason to distribute goods, such as health care, more evenly is to maximize the total good. However, the formalist who holds that justice is a right-making characteristic independent of utility does not require an item-by-item calculation of benefits and harms before concluding that the unequal distribution of goods is wrong with regard to fairness. (When we consider a single dimension of rightness or wrongness, such as focusing only on justice as an independent right-making characteristic, we sometimes say the action is *prima facie* right or wrong with regard to this aspect of the action.)

Another major challenge to consequentialism comes from the principle of respect for autonomy. Classical utilitarianism demands noninterference with the autonomy of others in society only when this produces greater net benefits. By contrast, Kantian formalism leads to the moral demand that persons and their beliefs be respected even if doing so will not produce the most good. Conflicts between the health care professional's nonconsequentialist duties to respect the autonomy or self-determination of individual patients and his or her consequentialist duties to produce benefit are discussed in Chapter 6.

Another ethical principle that many formalists hold to be independent of consequences is that of veracity or truth-telling. As with the other principles, utilitarians argue that truth-telling is an operational principle designed to guarantee maximum benefit. When truth-telling does more harm than good, according to the utilitarians, there is no obligation to tell the truth. To them, telling the dying patient of his condition can be cruel and therefore wrong. In contrast, to one who holds that truth-telling is a right-making ethical principle in itself, the problem of what the dying patient would be told is much more complex. Telling a lie is wrong in itself even if telling the lie does more good than telling the truth. This problem of what the patient would be told is the subject of Chapter 7.

Another principle that many formalists believe to be right-making independent of consequences is fidelity, especially the keeping of promises. Those who include the principle of fidelity in their normative ethics hold that people owe to others certain acts based on commitments they have made. Keeping these commitments is morally obligatory, even if the consequences would be better if they were not kept. Kant and others have held that breaking a promise is wrong independent of the consequences. The utilitarian points out that breaking a promise often has bad consequences. For them, we usually should keep our promises, but only because of the bad consequences if we do not. The formalist, although granting this danger, argues that there is something more intrinsically wrong in breaking a promise and that, to know this, one need not even go on to look at the consequences. The formalist might, with the utilitarian, grant that to look at consequences may reveal even more reasons to oppose promise-breaking, but this is not necessary to know that promise-breaking is *prima facie* wrong.

The professional–patient relationship can be viewed essentially as one involving promises or contracts or, to use a term with fewer legalistic implications, covenants. The relationship is founded on implied and sometimes explicit promises. One of these promises is that information disclosed in the professional–patient relationship is confidential, that it will not be disclosed by the health care provider without the patient's permission. In Chapter 8, cases present the various problems growing out of the ethical principle of fidelity.

The cases of Chapter 9 introduce a final principle that can be included in a general ethical system: the avoidance of killing. All societies have some kind of prohibition on killing. The Buddhists make it one of their five basic precepts. Those in the Judeo-Christian tradition recognize it as one of the Ten Commandments. The moral foundation of the prohibition on killing is not always clear, however. For some people, who base their ethic on doing good and avoiding evil, prohibiting killing is simply a rule summarizing the obvious conclusion that it usually harms people to kill them. If that is the full foundation of the prohibition on killing, then killing is just an example of a way that one can do harm.

This presents a problem, however. Many people believe they are aware of special cases where killing someone may actually do good, on balance. It will stop a greater evil that the one killed would otherwise have committed, or it will, in health care, possibly relieve a terminally ill patient of otherwise intractable pain. Is killing a human being always morally a characteristic of actions that tends to make them wrong, or is it wrong only when more harm than good results from the killing? For those who hold that killing is always a wrong-making characteristic, avoiding killing takes on a life as an independent principle, much like veracity or autonomy or fidelity. The health professional is increasingly being asked to become involved in decisions that could result in terminating a human life. Physician-assisted suicide is now legal in Oregon. Direct killing of patients by physicians is now legal in the Netherlands and Belgium, and may arise outside the law in other jurisdictions. The cases of Chapter 9 explore these questions.

Other Issues of Normative Ethics

In health care ethics over the past thirty years, the major issue in normative ethics has been the debate over what are the principles of morally right action. The two consequence-oriented principles of benefiting the patient (beneficence) and protecting the patient from harm (nonmaleficence) have been contrasted with the duty-based principles, such as justice, respecting autonomy, avoiding killing, veracity, and fidelity. Sometimes ethical controversy involves other issues, however. Here it is important to get the terminology straight. Ethicists distinguish principles from virtues and values. When they speak precisely, these terms refer to different aspects of normative ethics.

Principles, as we have seen, are general criteria that make human actions morally right or wrong. They refer to the actions (or groups of actions) rather than to the character of the actors. Hence, a physician with a despicable character could, theoretically, fulfill all the moral principles. He or she might do so even though it was done for selfish reasons or bad motives. Sometimes ethical evaluations address the character of the actor rather than the nature of the behavior. When we assess the character of an actor, we use the terms *virtue* and *vice*. In our everyday interactions with others, we make the distinction between character and actions. For example, when a generally unpleasant colleague does something nice, our reaction could easily be one of suspicion regarding this seemingly out-of-character action. Virtues are praiseworthy traits of character, and vices are blameworthy ones. Among the virtues often arising in health care ethics are compassion, humaneness, and caring. A health professional might fulfill the principle of veracity without showing any of these virtues (or violate the principle of veracity while being compassionate, humane, or caring). Principles refer to the actions; virtues, to the disposition or character of the actor. In this volume we will focus primarily on principles of right action, though sometimes we may want to assess the character of the health professional or patient as well.

For normative ethics that are concerned about consequences, there is still another dimension of normative ethics. If producing good consequences or avoiding harmful ones is seen as important in ethics, then we need to ask what outcomes count as good or bad consequences. We will use the term *value* to refer to a good outcome and *intrinsic value* to refer to whatever counts as an outcome that is good in itself. Money is valued by most people but usually because it enables us to buy things we consider valuable. Money and similar goods can be thought of as *instrumentally valuable*. Those things that are good in themselves are *intrinsically valuable*. One branch of normative ethics is devoted to "value theory," that is, the theory of what is intrinsically valuable. Among the goods often seen as intrinsically valuable are knowledge, aesthetic beauty, happiness, and health. Health is, of course, particularly important to health care professionals.

We will use the word *principle* to refer to general characteristics of actions that make them morally right (independent of the character of the actor) and *virtue* to refer to persistent dispositions or traits of people that are considered praiseworthy (independent of whether the behavior of those people always conforms to ethical principles). We will reserve the word *value* to refer to those things that are considered good or beneficial.

HOW DO RULES APPLY TO SPECIFIC SITUATIONS?

A third question that also is important in providing a full ethical evaluation of conduct stems from the fact that each case raising an ethical problem is at least in some ways situationally unique. The ethical principles of beneficence (producing benefit), justice, autonomy, veracity, fidelity, and avoidance of killing are extremely broad. They constitute a small set of criteria that make up the most general right-making characteristics of actions or practices. The question is: how do the general principles apply to specific situations?

As a bridge to the specific case, an intermediate, more specific set of rules is often used. These intermediate rules probably cause more problems in ethics than any other component of ethical theory. At the same time, they probably are more helpful than anything else as guides to day-to-day ethical behavior.

The problems arise in part because of a misunderstanding of the nature and function of these rules. Rules may have two functions. They may simply serve as guidelines summarizing conclusions we tend to reach in moral problems of a certain kind. When rules have the function of simply summarizing experiences from similar situations of the past, they are called guiding rules or summary rules.

In contrast, rules may function to specify behavior that is required independent of individual judgment about a specific situation. The rules against abortion of a viable fetus or against killing a dying patient are examples of rules that are often directly linked to right-making characteristics. Sometimes this kind of rule is called a rule of practice. The rule specifies a practice that, in turn, is justified by the general principles. For example, a rule of the practice of medicine has been that the health professional should not cooperate in the active, intentional killing of patients. Even if the patient is terminally ill and suffering, intentional killing has been considered to be ethically unacceptable. According to this rules-of-practice view, it is unacceptable to overturn a general practice simply because the outcome in a particular case would be better.

The conflict between those who believe that the rules themselves should be the defining factor and those who consider the situation itself to be the most critical determinant of moral rightness led to a major ethical controversy in the mid-twentieth century. It is sometimes called the rules–situation debate.[14] At one extreme is the rigorist who insists that rules should never be violated. At the other is the antinomian (literally "against rules") who claims that rules never apply because every situation is unique. Probably both positions taken to the extreme lead to absurdity. Rigorists are immobilized when two of their rules conflict. Antinomians are immobilized when they treat a situation as so brand new that no moral help can be gained from past experience.

Between these two extremes are two more complex but more plausible views. A situationalist is one who considers every situation as unique and will not legalistically apply rules but is willing to be guided by the moral rules. Those rules are seen as summarizing past experience in similar situations, as guidelines, but not as rules to be followed blindly. A second intermediate position is closer to the rigorist end of the spectrum. Those endorsing what is called the "rules-of-practice" view take moral rules very seriously. They hold that normally the rules should just be applied rather than each case evaluated from scratch. Nevertheless, holders of the "rules-of-practice" position are willing, in special situations, to reassess the rules to see if the rules should be reformulated to reflect more accurately the requirements of the moral principles. Sometimes an analogy to the game of baseball is cited by defenders of the rules-of-practice position. On the one hand, they claim that, in baseball, the rules cannot be changed in the middle of the game—that it is inappropriate to propose in the late innings that it should take four strikes to make the batter out. On the other hand, also in baseball, there are special moments when those in charge get together to reassess the rules, for example, at the annual meetings of the baseball team owners. So, likewise, defenders of the rules-of-practice view claim that at special moments in history moral rules may be reevaluated in order to formulate a more accurate specification of the general principles. Society has reassessed certain practices in health care such that the moral rules have changed. Fifty years ago, health care professionals were generally not supposed to tell patients the name of the drugs they were taking because of concern that patients would misunderstand and suffer psychological harm. For example, taking a pharmaceutical that had many uses might lead a patient mistakenly to believe that he or she had some condition other than the one for which the drug was dispensed. Over the years the rule against disclosing the name of a drug has changed. The rules-of-practice view accepts these changes in the rules—perhaps expressed in a change in the code of ethics of the professional association, while it does not accept the notion that the health professional should decide in the individual case whether the rule applies. The situationalist is more willing to reassess the rules on a case-by-case basis.

This difference over how seriously rules should be taken cuts across the answers to the question of what kinds of action are right. One can be a utilitarian, who assesses the consequences case by case (a situational- or act-utilitarian), or a *rule-utilitarian*, someone who believes in the rules-of-practice view, holding that rules should govern individual moral choices but that the rules should be chosen based on their expected consequences. Likewise, someone who is a *deontologist*, who believes there are certain inherent right-making characteristics of actions independent of the consequences, can either apply the general principles (such as respect for autonomy or veracity) directly to individual situations or use them to generate a set of rules, which are then applied to individual cases. The former would be an *act-deontologist*; the latter, a *rule-deontologist*.

Rules can be difficult to apply to individual cases for two distinct reasons. First, because rules are rather general, it can be difficult to determine how the rule applies to the individual case. It may be hard to determine, for example, whether the rule against killing applies to forgoing life support. Second, rules may come into conflict with other rules. The rule requiring respect for patient refusal of consent may conflict with the rule to preserve life. Either problem may lead to controversy over the application of rules in ethics.

The rules–situation debate does not lend itself to special cases grouped together. The problem arises continually throughout the cases in this volume. The final question we address is: what ought to be done in specific cases? This question requires special chapters with cases selected to examine the problems raised.

WHAT OUGHT TO BE DONE IN SPECIFIC CASES?

After the determination of the source and meaning of ethical judgments, what kinds of actions are right, and how rules apply to specific situations, there are still a large number of specific situations that make up the bulk of problems in pharmacy ethics. The question remains, what ought to be done in a specific case or kind of case? Health care professionals, being particularly oriented to case problems, are given to organizing ethical problems around specific kinds of cases.

The first two parts of this volume emphasize the overarching problems of how to relate facts to values, of who ought to decide, of respecting autonomy, veracity, fidelity, of avoiding killing, and of delivering health care in a just manner. These are among the larger questions of biomedical ethics. Part 3 shifts to cases involving specific problem areas. Cases in Chapter 10 raise the problems of abortion, sterilization, and conception control. Chapter 11 moves to the related problems of genetic counseling and engineering and of intervention in the prenatal period. The next chapters take up in turn the problems of mental health and the control of human behavior; confidentiality, organ transplantation, health insurance, and health system planning, human experimentation; consent and the right to refuse medical treatment; and finally, death and dying.

The answer to the question of what ought to be done in a specific case requires the integration of the answers to all of the other questions, if a thorough analysis and justification is to be given. The first line of moral defense will probably be a set of moral rules and rights thought to apply to the case.

In abortion, the right to control one's body and the right of the health care professional to practice his or her profession are pitted against the right to life. In human experimentation, the rules of informed consent pertain. Among the dying, rules concerning euthanasia conflict with the right to pursue happiness, and the right to refuse medical treatment conflicts with the rule that the health care provider ought to do everything possible to preserve life.

In many cases in which the tension between conflicting rules cannot be resolved, the analysis escalates from an issue of moral rules and rights to the higher, more abstract level of ethical principle. It must be determined, for example, whether informed consent is designed to maximize benefits to the experimental subject or to facilitate the subject's freedom of self-determination. It must also be explored whether harm to the patient justifies withholding information from the patient or whether the formalist truth-telling principle justifies disclosure.

Table 4 The Levels of Ethical Analysis

Metaethics: The Source, Meaning, and Justification of Ethical Claims

↕

Normative Ethics: Principles, Virtues, and Values

↕

Rules and Rights

↕

Specific Cases

Solving the problem of what ought to be done in a specific case also requires a great deal of information beyond what is moral. It requires considerable empirical data. Value-relevant biological and psychological facts have developed around many case problems in biomedical ethics. The predictive capacity of a flat electroencephalogram may be important for the definition of death. The legal facts are relevant for the refusal of treatment. Basic religious and philosophical beliefs of the patient may be critical for resolving some cases in health care ethics. It is impossible to present all of the relevant facts such as medical, genetic, legal, cultural practices, and psychological that are necessary for a complete analysis of any case, but it is possible to present the major facts required for understanding. Readers will have to supplement these facts for a fuller understanding of the cases, just as they will have to supplement their reading in ethical theory for a fuller understanding of the basic questions of ethics.

NOTES

[1] Edelstein, Ludwig. "The Hippocratic Oath: Text, Translation and Interpretation." In *Ancient Medicine: Selected Papers of Ludwig Edelstein*. Owsei Temkin and

C. Lilian Temkin, editors. Baltimore, MD: The Johns Hopkins Press, 1967, p. 6 (pp. 3–64).

2 Frankena, William. *Ethics*, 2nd ed. Englewood Cliffs, NJ: Prentice-Hall, 1973, p. 62.

3 Beauchamp, Tom L. and James F. Childress, editors. *Principles of Biomedical Ethics*, 3rd ed. New York: Oxford University Press, 1989, p. 18.

4 Fried, Charles. *Right and Wrong*. Cambridge, MA: Harvard University Press, 1978, p. 12.

5 Beauchamp and Childress, *Principles of Biomedical Ethics*, pp. 20–21; Also see Rawls, John. *A Theory of Justice*. Cambridge, MA: Harvard University Press, 1971, pp. 131–136; Baier, Kurt. *The Moral View*. New York: Random House, 1965, pp. 106–109.

6 Firth, Roderick. "Ethical Absolutism and the Ideal Observer Theory." *Philosophy and Phenomonological Research* 12 (1952):317–345; Broad, C. D. "Some Reflections on Moral-Sense Theories in Ethics." *Proceedings, the Aristotelian Society* (1944–1945):131–166.

7 Ross, W. D. *The Right and the Good*. Oxford: Oxford University Press, 1939.

8 Kant, Immanuel. *Groundwork of the Metaphysic of Morals*. H. J. Paton, Translator. New York: Harper and Row, 1964.

9 Ayer, A. J. *Language, Truth, and Logic*. London: Victor Gollancz Ltd., 1948; Stevenson, C. L. *Ethics and Language*. New Haven, CT: Yale University Press, 1944; Hare, R. M. *The Language of Morals*. Oxford: Clarendon, 1952.

10 For classical basic surveys of ethical theory see Frankena, *Ethics*, and Warnock, G. J. *Contemporary Moral Philosophy*. New York: St. Martin's, 1967. For more detailed introductions see Brandt, Richard B. *Ethical Theory: The Problems of Normative and Critical Ethics*. Englewood Cliffs, NJ: Prentice-Hall, 1959; Beauchamp, Tom L. *Philosophical Ethics: An Introduction to Moral Philosophy*. New York: McGraw-Hill Book Co., 1982; Feldman, Fred. *Introductory Ethics*. Englewood Cliffs, NJ: Prentice-Hall, 1978; and Taylor, Paul W. *Principles of Ethics: An Introduction*. Encino, CA: Dickenson Publishing Co., 1975. For works containing classical sources see Brandt, Richard B. *Value and Obligation: Systematic Readings in Ethics*. New York: Harcourt, Brace, & World, 1961; and Melden, A. I., editor. *Ethical Theories: A Book of Readings*, 2nd ed. Englewood Cliffs, NJ: Prentice-Hall, 1967. For more recent discussions of ethical theory see Kagan, Shelly. *Normative Ethics*. Boulder, CO: Westview Press, 1998, and Shafer-Landau, Russ, editor. *Ethical Theory: An Anthology*. Malden, MA: Blackwell, 2007.

11 Thomas Aquinas. *Summa theologica* I–II, A. 94, Art. 2. Fathers of the English Dominican Province, editors. London: R & T Washbourne Ltd., 1915.

12 Bentham, Jeremy. "An Introduction to the Principles of Morals and Legislation." In Melden, *Ethical Theories*, pp. 367–390.

13 Kant, *Groundwork of the Metaphysic of Morals*.

14 Rawls, John. "Two Concepts of Rules." *Philosophical Review* 44 (1955): 3–32; Fletcher, Joseph. *Situation Ethics: The New Morality*. Philadelphia, PA: Westminster, 1966; Ramsey, Paul. *Deeds and Rules in Christian Ethics*. New York: Charles Scribner's Sons, 1967; and Bayles, Michael D., editor. *Contemporary Utilitarianism*. Garden City, NY: Doubleday, 1968.

PART 1

❧

Ethics and Values in Medical Cases

CHAPTER 1

✦◯

A Model for Ethical Problem Solving

After the determination of the source and meaning of ethical judgments, what kinds of actions are right, and how rules apply to specific situations, the question remains: what ought to be done in a specific case or situation? Physicians and other health professionals often go through the process of determining the correct action in a specific case unconsciously. Furthermore, if asked, they would be hard pressed to articulate just what steps they went through to arrive at a sound and justifiable decision. There are many normative models for resolving ethical problems in the health science literature,[1] but all require critical thinking and should result in a choice that is morally justifiable. Decision-making, whether in ethics or any other area of life, is often thought of entirely in terms of its anatomy or structure, that is, the steps one should follow and the component parts of each step. However, ethical decision-making is more than just following steps, it involves an appreciation of the complexity of the components of each step such as what really comprises gathering information and how the steps relate to each other. The majority of the volume addresses the "function" of how general ethical principles apply to ethical problems in health care. Here, a framework is offered that includes those principles and a stepwise process to systematically resolve ethical problems in particular cases.

THE FIVE-STEP MODEL

The five steps provide the structure for the decision-making process and are linear: that is, they should be carried out in the order listed below:

1. Respond to the "sense" or feeling that something is wrong.
2. Gather information/assessment.
3. Identify the ethical problem/moral diagnosis.
4. Seek a resolution.
5. Work with others to determine a course of action.

The steps in the model outline a process, a way of making judgments about what should be done in a particular situation. Additional steps could be added and much elaboration could be included within each step. But, the basic framework is sufficient to focus moral judgments and simple enough to recall and apply in actual clinical practice.

APPLICATION OF THE MODEL

The five-step structure will be applied to Case 1-1 to illustrate the process of decision-making.

CASE 1-1

Disclosure of a Terminal Diagnosis

Richard Dossey, a 68-year-old architect, was admitted to the oncology service after having an emergency operation in another state. According to Mr. Dossey, the surgeon at the hospital told him that he had gastric cancer, but assured him that, "Two or three cycles of chemotherapy and the cancer should clear up."

Sashi Jajoura, MD, the oncologist who was now attending Mr. Dossey, read the surgical report and was shocked to discover that there were significant lymph node metastases. She knew that surgical removal was the only potentially curative treatment for gastric cancer.[2] Most patients who have advanced disease have an extremely poor prognosis. In essence, the gastric cancer was inoperable and consequently incurable. The information in the pathology report in Mr. Dossey's clinical records from the hospital did not mesh with his reported understanding of his prognosis. Meanwhile, as Dr. Jajoura determined the best course of palliative treatment for Mr. Dossey, he developed acute renal failure. A sonogram revealed a bilateral hydronephrosis, probably caused by the primary tumor that had extended to the ureters. During this crisis, Dr. Jajoura informed Mr. Dossey that he was acutely ill as a result of kidney failure. She also informed him that the probable reason for his kidney failure was the cancer that was inoperable.

Dr. Jajoura then discussed the plan of treatment with Mr. Dossey proposing that catheters be placed into the ureters through small bilateral incisions and a presurgical CAT scan. She explained that, postoperatively, he would be a candidate for radiation therapy and chemotherapy that would include a drug regimen including 5-fluorouracil and cisplatin. Also, because Mr. Dossey's creatinine and blood urea nitrogen (BUN) levels were rising quickly, she asked him if he had prepared any advance directive and if he had specifically thought about a do-not-resuscitate order should his heart stop beating or if he should stop breathing.

Though stunned, Mr. Dossey said he would like to talk to his wife, his adult son, and the pastor at his church about his prognosis and the proposed treatment. He then angrily burst out, "That surgeon lied to me!"

The next day, Mr. Dossey told the clinical nurse specialist and the staff nurses that he wanted to go home that day without treatment and without any more diagnostic tests, saying, "I know the doctors aren't going to agree with me, but I want to leave anyway." When the nurses asked his wife and son about Mr. Dossey's decision, both responded in unison, "He has always made his own decisions. We support him in this decision." Dr. Jajoura asked Mr. Dossey to consent to the CAT scan to determine the extent of the cancer, but he refused and stood by his request to be discharged.[3]

COMMENTARY

This case is complex, but reveals potential ethical concerns. As the physician involved in the case, Dr. Jajoura will need to decide what she should do and why. The five-step model can help Dr. Jajoura and the other members of the health care team involved in Mr. Dossey's care to work toward a justifiable resolution.

1. Respond to the Sense that Something Is Wrong

The first step in the ethical decision-making process is to respond to the intuitive sense that something is wrong in a given situation. Unlike obvious physical signs and symptoms that clinicians are used to looking for in patients to determine what is wrong, such as a change in breathing pattern or a rise in BUN or creatinine, there are no objective signs that one is involved in an ethical problem. It is obvious that urgent care areas such as the emergency department and intensive care units can be fraught with stress and emotion. It is obvious that Mr. Dossey's case is fraught with emotion: He was described as stunned, angry, and determined. Dr. Jajoura was "shocked." Do these emotional signs indicate that an ethical problem is in progress? The answer, as is often the case in ethics, is yes and no. Just because people are emotionally upset with each other or under a lot of stress does not necessarily mean that an ethical problem is involved. However, heightened emotional sensitivity—along with "stress and tension intrapersonally or interpersonally; and ineffective communication patterns such as avoidance, nagging, or silence"[4]—are often warning signs that one is involved in an ethical problem.

In Mr. Dossey's case, Dr. Jajoura responded to her feeling that something was not right as soon as she saw the discrepancy between his optimistic statement that "the cancer should clear up" and the grim reality of his diagnosis. She proposed an operation to correct the acute renal failure, and Mr. Dossey wanted to be discharged without treatment. Dr. Jajoura may also feel angry and frustrated with her surgical colleague who seems to have withheld the bad news from Mr. Dossey about his prognosis. These negative emotions and interpersonal conflicts are indications that an ethical problem may be present. This first step in the decision-making process merely requires one to respond to the feeling that something is wrong. One should then move on to the next step.

2. Gather Information

There is an old saw in ethics: "Good ethics begins with good facts." Clearly, to make an informed decision, one must have the facts. To organize the numerous facts in the situation in which Dr. Jajoura is involved, one can classify them into clinical and situational information.[5]

Clinical information deals with the relevant clinical data in the case in question. The following types of clinical questions are relevant when reviewing a case: What is the medical status of the patient or patients involved in the situation? Medical history? Diagnosis? Prognosis? What drugs are involved and what are their actions, side effects, and so on? What is the patient's probable life expectancy and general condition if treatment is given? What is the patient's probable life expectancy and general condition if treatment is not given? What are the risks and side effects of the proposed treatment?

In Mr. Dossey's case, the clinical information appeared to be unambiguous. His cancer was inoperable; it had metastasized and was now causing acute renal failure—a life-threatening condition. Because of the acute problem, Dr. Jajoura asked him if she could perform a diagnostic test, a CAT scan, to determine the extent of the cancer. However, this information would not change his poor prognosis and would only assist in determining appropriate treatment for the renal failure. Mr. Dossey will certainly die in the immediate future if he does not receive treatment to relieve the blockage of the ureters— the cause of the acute renal failure. The risks of performing an operation to relieve the blockage would also have to be considered. Even if the odds that the treatment to relieve the immediate problem were great, the underlying condition would not change. At that point, Mr. Dossey would have to consider the risks and burdens of radiation and chemotherapy treatment options.

As much as possible, it is important to clarify the relevant clinical information in the case before moving on to a more in-depth analysis of the moral relevance of these facts.

Situational information includes data regarding the values and perspectives of the principals involved; their authority; verbal and nonverbal communication including language barriers; cultural and religious factors; setting and time constraints; and the relationships of those immediately involved in the case. In other words, even if the clinical "facts" of a case are held constant, changes in the situational or contextual factors such as the values of a key principle in the case could change the ethical focus or intensity of the ethical conflict. Of all the situational data mentioned, the most important is the identification and understanding of the value judgments involved in a case. An extensive discussion of value judgments is in Chapter 2.

The main players in this case are Mr. Dossey, his wife and son, Dr. Jajoura, members of the nursing staff and, from a distance, the surgeon who first cared for Mr. Dossey and supplied the less than honest news about his prognosis. All the individuals involved in the case possess values about many things including values about health, honesty, professional competence, and loyalty, to name a few.

We know that Mr. Dossey has a wife and son. Did they completely understand the seriousness of Mr. Dossey's condition? What were their positions? Did they agree with one another? What are the views of the other individuals involved in the case such as the nursing staff or Mr. Dossey's pastor? How do these views compare and contrast?

We know that responsibility for the care of Mr. Dossey rested with various members of the health care team. Each member's responsibilities are distinct, yet overlap. As part of the information gathering step, it is important to sort out the various responsibilities, not for blame-placing but for identifying moral accountability. For example, Dr. Jajoura may not be the one who presented the less than accurate view of Mr. Dossey's diagnosis, but she is the one who has to break the bad news at this point if she wants to honestly present treatment options to her patient and obtain valid consent. These are only some of the facts that impact an ethical decision from all of the information provided in the case. Once the facts are outlined, one can examine them to see whether the case has the characteristics of an ethical problem.

3. Identify the Ethical Problem/Moral Diagnosis

As has been noted in the introduction, ethics deals with a wide range of imperatives and obligations regarding human dignity and conduct. The distinct characteristics of moral evaluation, also mentioned earlier in the introduction, apply to this third step of the five-step model, that is, they must be ultimate, possess universality, and treat the good of everyone alike. Ethical principles are relevant sources of ethical guidance and can serve as a guideline to identify the types of ethical problems in a case. The values, rights, duties, or principles that are in conflict should be identified. The ethical principles most often involved in complex cases such as Dr. Jajoura's situation are (1) respect for patient autonomy, (2) beneficence and nonmaleficence, and (3) veracity. In this volume we will treat justice, fidelity, and avoidance of killing as possible principles as well. Separate chapters are presented in Part 2 of this book to develop each of these principles.

The principles that are in conflict in the case at a minimum are respect for autonomy, which, in this case, implies the patient's right to make an informed decision about his treatment, and veracity, nonmaleficence, and beneficence, raising the question of the obligations of the physician to be honest and to prevent harm and do good when possible. Because the patient's preferences or wishes take priority over other parties involved, his wishes should be considered first. Generally, the wishes of competent, informed patients should be respected and followed, that is, the implication of the principle of respect for autonomy. Therefore, ascertaining the patient's competency is important. Is Mr. Dossey capable of making decisions? The fact that his creatinine and BUN levels were rising quickly may have affected his central nervous system and affected his ability to make a competent decision. Though determination of competency is a legal determination, the parties involved with Mr. Dossey could have informally validated his ability to understand the information presented to him, to appreciate that the information applied to his case, to state the benefits and burdens of treatment and nontreatment options presented, and to demonstrate a logical coherence between his wishes and the predictable outcomes. For example, it would be illogical for Mr. Dossey to say, "I really want to be discharged without any treatment, but I want to do everything to prevent my death." A competent person would understand that discharge without treatment is tantamount to death.

Nonmaleficence is the principle underlying the original surgeon's decision to withhold the truth from Mr. Dossey. He wanted to avoid the psychological trauma that the bad news would bring. Nonmaleficence also motivates Dr. Jajoura's conviction that she should strive to protect Mr. Dossey from unnecessary harms. The immediate harm from acute renal failure is of greatest concern especially since it is a harm that can probably be corrected. The long-term harms from metastatic disease can be ameliorated but not eliminated. Assuming she was not willing, like the original surgeon, to treat Mr. Dossey without informing him of his situation, the duty to protect her patient from harm could lead Dr. Jajoura to try one more time to reach Mr. Dossey about the seriousness of his present status. Perhaps she would even consider seeking the family's support in convincing him about the treatability of the acute renal failure. At a minimum, treatment of the acute problem could buy more time for the family and the patient to grasp the poor prognosis and determine if palliative radiation or chemotherapy is worth the benefits and burdens involved or if hospice care is the right choice at this time.

Also at stake is the principle of veracity, the moral notion that one is obligated to speak truthfully, especially in situations in which one is in a role in which one cannot keep silent. This principle separates Dr. Jajoura and the original treating physician. Mr. Dossey was not adequately informed about his prognosis and treatment options. Clearly, the surgeon who initially treated him was not honest about his diagnosis and prognosis. Dr. Jajoura did offer information about the prognosis, but did Mr. Dossey really hear anything after that? When Mr. Dossey fully grasped the truth, he became angry. Furthermore, the revelation about the gravity of his diagnosis and the deception might have caused him to mistrust other health care professionals including Dr. Jajoura. She believes that she is obligated to tell the truth to Mr. Dossey about his diagnosis and prognosis so that she can propose treatment options to him. She may also believe that Mr. Dossey will benefit from open discussion of his prognosis. It could avoid anxiety from not knowing his situation. In that case, the principle of beneficence would support disclosure even if Dr. Jajoura did not accept the principle of veracity.

At this point, we can move to the fourth step in the solving of the problem at hand by exploring various courses of action, which requires both determining which principles are involved and what their implications are.

4. Seek a Resolution

The working phase of decision-making is, indeed, proposing more than one course of action and examining the ethical justification of various actions. Many people try to avoid this step in the decision-making process and at the same time reduce stress by settling for the first option that comes to mind or what at first appears to be the safe choice.

Some of the courses of action that are open to Dr. Jajoura are (1) if she faces her moral choice before she has revealed his true situation, she could continue the original plan of deceiving him; (2) she could, by declaring him incompetent or simply ignoring his competence, treat him against his will to eliminate the risk of life-threatening renal failure; (3) she could let Mr. Dossey leave and call the next day to see if he has changed his mind keeping the door open to treatment of the acute renal failure; (4) she could propose hospice care for Mr. Dossey in his home thereby honoring his wishes. The actions actually fall into the categories of directly overriding Mr. Dossey's autonomy, treating him as nonautonomous, honoring Mr. Dossey's autonomy but still trying to change his mind, completely honoring his decision by ordering hospice services, thus confirming the decision to stop curative treatment for the acute renal failure, and offering symptom management and assistance with end-of-life care.

To determine which options are morally justifiable, one must project the probable consequences of each action and the underlying intention of the action as well as whether there are moral duties that prevail independent of the consequences. This process involves the application of the ethical principles presented earlier and the ethical theories described below. By following this process, one can reject some options immediately because they would result in harm or would conflict with another basic ethical principle.

Choosing the first option would be hard to reconcile with the principle of veracity, but could be supported by more consequence-oriented ethics that stress beneficence and nonmaleficence.

Two major versions of consequence-oriented ethics were presented in the introduction: utilitarianism and Hippocratic ethics. Hippocratic ethics would focus on the principles of beneficence and nonmaleficence, but only insofar as the action affects the patient.

Utilitarianism differs from Hippocratic ethics not in focusing on the principles of beneficence and nonmaleficence, but in which consequences are relevant. It holds we should choose the option that would bring about the greatest good for the greatest number. For example, if Dr. Jajoura were a utilitarian, she might agree with the original surgeon that Mr. Dossey would be better off if he were deceived, but she might still fear that others (including his family) would learn from this experience that doctors lie to patients. If she was worried that the long-term bad consequences for other patients—developing fear that doctors cannot be trusted—would outweigh any benefits for Mr. Dossey, she might decide against the first option.

By contrast, the Hippocratic form of consequentialism factors in only the consequences for the individual patient. She might still reject the first option if she thought Mr. Dossey himself would be harmed by the continuing deception, if, for example, she feared he would soon find out he was getting worse and faced the additional problem of not being able to talk openly with his doctor and family about his impending death.

Thus, consequentialists—those who focus only on principles of beneficence and nonmaleficence—can either accept or reject the first option depending on how they assess the consequences and whose consequences they include.

Option two may involve a variation on option one—ignoring respect for autonomy. In some cultures, physicians have had the power simply to treat a patient in the way that they think is best for the patient, ignoring the patient's autonomy. If Dr. Jajoura is driven by beneficence for the patient, she might conclude that this is a viable strategy. It could solve the renal failure problem, but could make Mr. Dossey upset. It would also be illegal in our society, assuming Mr. Dossey was competent to consent or refuse consent. On the other hand, if Dr. Jajoura really believed Mr. Dossey was incompetent to consent, she could pursue the course of trying to get him declared incompetent, thus acting on the principle of beneficence, which may be the only relevant principle left for one who, lacking competence, has no possibility of autonomous decision-making. Dr. Jajoura should realize, however, that, if Mr. Dossey is declared incompetent, someone will be appointed his guardian—probably his wife or son—and they may make the same choice for him that he was going to make.

Options three and four both follow a different strategy, one based on a belief that Mr. Dossey is an autonomous agent and that his autonomy must be respected. Respect for autonomy is a principle that leaves patients free to follow their own life plans even if sometimes doing so does not result in what is best for the patient. The principle of veracity also supports some version of open disclosure. Respecting autonomy and the related principle of veracity will prohibit deception in Mr. Dossey's case. Such respect, however, does not rule out reasonable attempts to persuade a patient to follow a course that the doctor believes to be best. One could leave Mr. Dossey to his own choice and still follow-up at sometime in the near future to see if he has changed his mind. At that time, one could again offer hospice care, which would be consistent with respecting autonomy and veracity. This might also avoid some harm due to other courses and lead to giving Mr. Dossey as much benefit as possible. It is possible, however, that the conflict between such respect for autonomy and the more consequence-oriented principles of beneficence and nonmaleficence cannot be resolved. In that case, Dr. Jajoura will have to decide whether she is to be guided by a consequence-oriented ethic or one that holds that in the end the duty to respect the patient's autonomy must prevail.

We have at this point identified several possible courses of action and the implications of various ethical principles for each of those courses.

5. Work with Others to Choose a Course of Action

No one makes decisions alone in a health care setting. The same is true for ethical decisions. A better decision can be reached if the people who are legitimately involved have the opportunity to discuss their perceptions, values, and concerns openly. Referring back to the first step of the decision-making model, the response to the sense that something is wrong is a subjective one that is limited by one's intuition and is informed by many factors such as culture, gender, class, race, and ethnicity to name a few. To help broaden our limited perspectives, it is important to share views and insights with others involved in a case. Who should be part of the team or group to resolve ethical problems? In an acute care setting, that will usually involve members of the health care team who provide direct care to a patient and family. A care conference or other form of team meeting in which goals of treatment are discussed could be the place where collaborative decisions are made and concerns aired even if those concerns are not specifically labeled as ethical ones. In a complex case such as this, Dr. Jajoura should also call on the input of the institutional ethics committee that usually has representatives from a variety of disciplines such as nursing, social services, pastoral care, and medicine. One should seek the counsel of an ethics committee when the goals of care are confused or there is a sense of conflicting duties, or when those involved would benefit from a facilitated discussion. By soliciting different points of view and discussing concerns in a mutually respectful environment where all voices can be heard, they can reach a more comprehensive decision that is ethically justifiable.

It is apparent that the duty-based principles such as respect for autonomy and veracity, push us very hard to disclose Mr. Dossey's diagnosis and honor his decision if it is indeed substantially autonomous. On the other hand, the Hippocratic form of a consequence-based ethic provides the most plausible basis for overriding his decision to refuse treatment for an acute health problem that could probably be reversed. There are many cases in ethics that lead to relatively clear resolutions. At times, reasonable people can reason to the same resolution but support their decision with entirely different principles or theories. Mr. Dossey's case, however, does not lead to a definitive resolution because of the facts of the case and the individuals involved. Health professionals encounter all of these types of ethical problems from the clear-cut to the vague and messy. The decision-making model is one tool to help determine justifiable options whether the case is simple or complex.

NOTES

[1] Purtilo, Ruth. *Ethical Dimensions in the Health Professions*, 3rd ed. Philadelphia, PA: W.B. Saunders, 2005; Fletcher, John C. (editor) *Fletcher's Introduction to Clinical Ethics*, 2nd ed. Frederick, MD: University Publishing Group, 2005; Haddad, A.

and M. Kapp. *Ethical and Legal Problems in Home Health Care*, Norwalk, CT: Appleton and Lange, 1991; Rule, James T. and Robert M. Veatch. *Ethical Questions in Dentistry*, 2nd ed. Chicago, IL: Quintessence Books, 2004.

[2] Leong, Trevor. "Chemotherapy and Radiotherapy in the Management of Gastric Cancer." *Current Opinions in Gastroenterology* 21 (2005):673–678.

[3] Haddad, Amy. "The Anatomy and Physiology of Ethical Decision Making in Oncology." *Journal of Psychosocial Oncology* 11(1) (1993):69–82.

[4] Salladay, Susan and Amy Haddad. "Point–Counterpoint Technique in Assessing Hidden Agendas." *Dimensions of Critical Care Nursing* 5(4) (1986):238–243.

[5] Haddad and Kapp. *Ethical and Legal Problems in Home Health Care*, p. 13.

CHAPTER 2

❦

Values in Health and Illness

At first it might appear that ethical and other value problems arise infrequently in medical decision-making. Although the health professional and patient are increasingly seen as confronting such issues—in decisions about abortion, euthanasia, test-tube baby cases, and genetics, for example—most medical choices seem at first to be more technical or scientific. They seem like straightforward problems of how to best prevent or cure problems with our bodies.

While the morally conspicuous controversies in medicine are on the rise, it is important to realize that even the most routine medical choices involve a set of value judgments and that some of those value judgments involve moral choices.

Before turning to specific topics such as the ethics of abortion, genetics, informed consent, and death and dying, some preliminary work must be done. We must first be sure we can recognize ethical and other value issues when they arise. This is the focus of this second chapter. The cases in this first chapter are selected to help identify the value dimensions in medical choices and to distinguish moral from nonmoral value judgments.

IDENTIFYING VALUE JUDGMENTS IN MEDICINE

The first task in analyzing the ethics of cases is making sure the normative judgments (or what are sometimes called value judgments) are identified when they occur. In fact, normative judgments occur constantly in all health care decisions. It is impossible to get to a clinical conclusion—to prescribe or take a drug, use an over-the-counter medication, pick between a trade name and generic medication, begin an exercise program, or enter a hospice—without making a normative judgment as well. Whenever someone decides to act (or refrain from acting), some evaluation has taken place. A decision is made that a particular course is the *right* one. It is *better* than available alternatives. It is what one *ought* to do.

One key to learning to recognize that evaluative judgments have taken place is to watch for value terms. Words such as *right*, *better*, and *ought* all signal a process of evaluation. It is the nature of all professional clinical roles—being a physician, nurse, pharmacist, dentist, or allied health professional—that one constantly makes these evaluations. Just as important, people in roles outside the professional medical realm—in the role of patient, family member, judge and legislator, or citizen—make evaluative choices in medicine as well. They decide they have a problem that needs a physician's attention; they give their children aspirin, authorize a physician and family to withdraw life support, pass a law legalizing physician-assisted suicide, or vote for a politician who favors or opposes a new health insurance plan.

Case 2-1 does not raise a dramatic or grave ethical issue. It may not raise any ethical issue at all. It does involve a number of evaluations, however. It involves a patient confronted with a choice about how to manage his cholesterol and a physician who has to decide when to prescribe an anticholesterol medication. These are important choices, ones that patients and doctors must face daily, but they do not present obvious or dramatic ethical problems. This case helps us recognize value choices when they occur in medicine.

CASE 2-1

Exercise, Diet, or Drugs to Control Cholesterol

Jake knew he had a problem. He was thirty-seven years old. At 5'10" and 230 pounds, he was heavier than his doctor liked. His sedentary life style as an information technology specialist at a major accounting firm meant he did not get the exercise that his wife and his physician thought he should. His physical exams over the past several years showed a nagging increase in total cholesterol levels (237 mg/dl); the low-density lipoprotein (LDL; "bad") was too high and the good high-density lipoprotein (HDL) was too low. His physician had twice recommended exercise at least three days a week and some dietary modification to get the cholesterol lower. Jake went part way. He cut down on eggs for breakfast. He did not like them much anyway. He intentionally signed up for the cheaper parking lot at work so he would be forced to walk about three blocks to his office. He knew, however, that this was not exactly what his physician had in mind.

Now at a routine trip to his HMO, his doctor nagged him again about diet and exercise. The physician continued to worry about the cholesterol, pointing out that the treatment protocol at the HMO indicated that diet and exercise should bring the cholesterol into line. If not, Jake was going to have to go on one of the new cholesterol-lowering medications called "statins."

The effect on Jake was not what the physician had expected. A question occurred to Jake. He said to himself, "Do you mean I could get the same cholesterol reduction by simply taking the pill and still eat what I have been eating and not sign up for the plan at the local gym?" Jake considered his options: (1) ask the doctor to put him on a statin drug right now, (2) intentionally avoid the diet and exercise regimen until his next physical exam when the physician would discover that his cholesterol was still too high and, on his own, write the prescription for the statin drug, or (3) attempt to follow more faithfully the physician's recommendation about diet and exercise to see if the cholesterol problem will be taken care of. Of course, there was a fourth option—take his chances and continue with a high cholesterol level, unmedicated and uncontrolled by either diet or exercise.

COMMENTARY

At first this case may appear to raise no evaluative issues at all. The physician was giving standard medical advice and was following a treatment protocol endorsed by the HMO and widely accepted in the medical community.

Searching for the value terms, however, reveals a number of judgments that are clearly in the realm of values. They begin to appear in the very first line. Jake recognized he had what he called a "problem." That is already an evaluative judgment. To say that one has a problem is to say that there is something bad about the situation. In the next sentence we see that the physician was not happy with the patient's weight. That is a judgment on the doctor's part that something is wrong. In the third sentence the word "should" signals that both the physician and the patient's wife are making value judgments. In the next sentence, high-density and low-density lipids are classified as "good" and "bad." They both thought his life would be better if he got more exercise. This is followed by a recommendation from the physician that Jake begin a regimen of exercise and diet. Any "recommendation" conveys that the one making it evaluates the proposed course of action positively.

Jake's responses involved further evaluation. He changed his behavior—at least modestly. He cut down on eggs, which he did not like much anyway, and signed up for a parking lot that would force him to walk some each day. The parking lot choice involves a rather complicated set of value judgments: he no doubt valued the money he would save but did not like the extra walking. Up until this time, he apparently believed that spending the extra money to get the more convenient parking was worth it, but with his reevaluation taking into account the newly appreciated value of some extra walking, he apparently decided the combined benefits of the saving and the exercise outweighed the inconvenience of the extra walking.

These evaluations are all preliminary to the main focus of the case. The physician seems convinced that the cholesterol is higher than it should be; that is, that bad things are more likely to happen with continued high cholesterol levels. Moreover, he recognizes that there are at least two possible strategies to lower the cholesterol—either a combined plan of diet and exercise or the use of statin drugs. Finally, he seems to accept the value judgment of the writers of the HMO protocol that diet and exercise should be tried first, that they offer better chance of overall benefit.

That judgment is so commonly held among medical professionals that many are likely to assume that somehow it is a fact of medicine that diet and exercise are a better first approach to the problem of high cholesterol. That turns out to be a category mistake. It is not a fact that diet and exercise are better than drugs. It may turn out to be a widely held value judgment, but it is a value judgment nonetheless. Diet and exercise are cheaper than drugs; they do not pose the risk of side effects that the statin drugs do; and they have some other features that appeal to many people. They are thought of as "natural" rather than as "artificial" or "chemical" interventions. All of these considerations lead many people to evaluate diet and exercise as preferable at least as a first response to high cholesterol.

Even though many people are concerned about the pharmacological risks of statin drugs (they can cause liver toxicity, for example), and they are attracted to the economic and philosophical features of interventions that they consider "natural," there are also problems with the diet and exercise approach. Jake is clearly among those who do not find exercise particularly enjoyable. He apparently likes foods that contribute to his cholesterol problem rather than those that would help reduce it. This leaves Jake in a bind. He perceives disvalue in the diet and exercise regimen. He seems to evaluate that regimen differently than the doctor and his colleagues. He may also evaluate the benefits and risks of the statin drugs differently. Surely, taking the drug is easier, perhaps much easier in Jake's opinion. He may also judge the pharmacological risks differently. He may not adequately appreciate the problems statin drugs can cause. On the other hand, he may fully understand and simply make the value judgment that the small risk of a serious liver problem from the statin drug is less onerous than the certain disvalue of the diet and exercise program.

It seems like this patient and physician simply have different assessments of the benefits and risks of the options that are available. They have made different value judgments. Is there any way that one could claim that the physician has made the correct evaluation? It should be clear that there is no amount of medical science that could prove whether the physician's evaluation was correct. If Jake were ignoring the risk of the statin drugs, if he had not been told about the liver toxicity risk, then the physician would have been working with a different set of facts. He would have failed to inform his patient. But, assuming that the doctor adequately informed the patient, there is no way that medical science can prove that the risks of the drug outweigh the negatives of the diet and exercise. Even if all physicians believed the drug's risks were more weighty, that would not constitute proof. It would merely show that doctors evaluate the options in a particular way. A double-blind, controlled study with large numbers of patients would be convincing evidence of what the effects of the two approaches would be. It could identify the risks and benefits of each alternative but still could not prove which set of risks and benefits would be better. That is a value choice not amenable to medical science.

Some philosophers hold that some value judgments—perhaps the one comparing the risks of drugs and of diet and exercise can be held to some objective standard. They claim that, at least in the ideal, there are objective lists of right and wrong evaluations. In aesthetics, for example, they might hold that Van Cliburn is "objectively" a better pianist than Liberace. People who hold this position are sometimes called "objective list theorists."[1] Others hold that value judgments are inherently subjective, that there is no external objective standard of what is good and what is bad.

For purposes of medical ethical decisions, however, we need not settle this difficult question. Even if there is some objectively correct answer to the question of which set of risks and benefits among alternative medical treatments is preferable, this is surely not a question that medical science can answer. For evaluations such as this, increasingly patients' value judgments are seen as requiring respect. These are not matter of ethics. These are what could be called nonmoral value judgments. For these, either there are no objective standards of good and bad or, if there are, they are not matters of medical science. Many health professionals and, in fact, many lay people may agree with the doctor that the risks and benefits of diet and exercise are more attractive as a first line of therapy, but, if they do, it is an evaluative judgment, not a medical fact. Unless one can develop a definitive list of objective values for such choices, it will not be possible to prove that one choice or the other is superior.

Case 2-2 presents another opportunity to identify the evaluations taking place in a conversation between a health professional and a patient. In this case, try to identify the value judgments made.

CASE 2-2

Treating Breast Cancer: Finding the Value Judgments

It seemed to May Bachman that she had never been confronted with so many important decisions in such a short time-frame in her life. Just two short weeks ago, when she went in for annual mammography, she learned that the microcalcifications in her right breast (the radiologist had been monitoring) had changed in their appearance from the last year's film. Ms. Bachman had dense breast tissue with numerous microcalcifications, so she knew that annual mammography was in order. She had been told by her radiologist that the calcifications could be a sign of ductal carcinoma in situ (DCIS). It was still a shock to hear that the changes in the mammography films required more diagnostic tests; a breast biopsy was needed to ascertain the actual pathology.

The results from the core needle biopsy showed that the lesion was invasive cancer. There was no palpable mass in the breast, but only further operation would determine the size of the tumor and whether it had invaded the lymph nodes. In a whirlwind of appointments, Ms. Bachman met with a surgeon to learn about what options were available. Breast conserving therapy (BCT), also called lumpectomy, was one option as was a simple mastectomy (excision of the breast, nipple, areola, and most of the overlying skin). Ms. Bachman also met with an oncologist who said that further treatment decisions would be based on the stage of the disease and her age. For example, if the tumor was small, from 2 to 5 cm, and had invaded the lymph nodes, then she would be a candidate for chemotherapy (doxorubicin and cyclophosphamide) followed by tamoxifen. Moreover, whether the tumor was estrogen-receptor positive or negative played a significant role on how aggressive treatment should be.

Depending on how many lymph nodes were involved, the oncologist might recommend radiation therapy, noting that some studies suggested that postmastectomy radiation therapy was indicated even for patients with T1–2 (tumor of 1–2 cm) breast cancer with 0–3 positive nodes. The chemotherapy had significant side effects such as nausea, vomiting, fatigue, cognitive changes, alopecia, insomnia, and constipation. Another serious side effect was ovarian toxicity. Since Ms. Bachman was thirty-seven years old and premenopausal, this was of concern to her. It was likely that chemotherapy would result in amenorrhea and premature menopause. The surgeon and oncologist stated that if the cancer was in an early stage, they would recommend BCT and aggressive chemotherapy and radiation for the best survival outcomes. Ms. Bachman knew, from looking at sites on the Internet, that there was controversy over what was the best course of action. She felt pressured by the surgeon to choose BCT even though she thought she would feel safer with a more radical removal of breast tissue, but she was not sure. She had so little time to weigh the benefits and risks of all the different treatment options that were presented to her, she felt overwhelmed.

COMMENTARY

As in Case 2-1 the issues in this case are not conspicuously matters of ethical controversy. The subject matter may be more momentous—matters potentially involving life and death—but most probably would not consider this an ethics case. Nevertheless, the account contains many evaluations. Most would agree with the judgment opening sentence that the decisions Ms. Bachman would face were important. That in itself is a value judgment even if it is one that would be widely shared.

Further in that first paragraph we learn that annual mammography was "in order." The value choice here may be less apparent. Presumably, Ms. Bachman "knew" this because she had been told about it by her clinicians. That was apparently the common consensus among clinicians. The phrase "in order" is a less obvious way of conveying the evaluation, but it is an evaluation nonetheless. Clinicians had considered the medical facts about the possible risks of microcalcifications that show up on mammography films, the difference between DCIS (not cancer) and cancer, the importance of detection while the tumor is at an early stage, and the potentially terrible consequences if the tumor metastasizes.

If those were the only considerations, however, they might recommend testing more often than once a year. They must also have considered the costs of the mammography, the risks of radiation exposure, and the inconvenience to the patient in coming up with the recommendation that yearly exams were right. It should be obvious, however, that different patients in different circumstances might make these evaluations differently. A woman who is particularly anxious about the risk of DCIS leading to invasive cancer might want the mammography more often. Someone with very good insurance or great wealth would worry less about costs. Those with great fear of radiation might prefer somewhat less frequent exams. Weekly mammography would pose such costs, risks, and inconvenience that virtually no woman would seriously consider it. Going without any further testing similarly poses extreme risks that most women would reject (although in some cultures mammography is beyond the economic reach of many citizens). Different patients with different evaluations would no doubt prefer somewhat more or less frequent retesting.

Once the test results show invasive cancer, the evaluations become even more conspicuous. The first issue was presented as a choice between two treatment options: BCT (lumpectomy) or a simple mastectomy. The first option would remove only a small portion of the breast; the second would remove the entire breast. Choosing between them would, of course, depend on the current scientific evidence regarding survival rates. That literature is, unfortunately, somewhat ambiguous. Some sources indicate that breast conservation should be attempted when possible and desired. If the lesion is large, a simple mastectomy may be necessary. There are differences of opinion on radiation treatment depending on the size of the tumor.[2] Ms. Bachman may also feel that common sense would support the belief that, when it comes to survival, the removal of more of the breast would give her greater confidence. Thus, if she is worried about removing as much of the cancer as possible, she may prefer the more total procedure even if current medical science does not provide clear evidence of superiority. On the other hand, the more worried she is about the psychological and social aspects of preserving as much of her breast as possible, the more she might be inclined toward the lumpectomy. It would not be irrational to take some degree of risk with survival in order to gain these more psychological benefits.

At the other extreme one could choose no operation at all. While that would be more likely to have fatal consequences if in fact Ms. Bachman has invasive cancer, someone without insurance or someone with extreme fear of operative procedures might consider it. Although these options would be considered only for people with unusual values or unusual economic situations, one cannot rule them out in all circumstances, even if, for most people, they would make little sense.

Finally, we come to the postsurgical therapy. Here the options are greater and the choices more subtle. The value judgments are more complex. The case includes the provocative sentence, "the oncologist might recommend radiation therapy noting that some studies suggested that postmastectomy radiation therapy was indicated even for patients with T1–2 breast cancer with 0–3 positive nodes." Note first that the "oncologist *might* recommend radiation." This reveals that different oncologists might evaluate the radiation option differently even for medically identical patients with identical lymph node involvement. Even more provocative is the claim that some studies suggest radiation therapy is "indicated" for patients with T1–2 breast cancer with 0–3 positive nodes. If nodes are involved, the cancer may have spread beyond the breast, but with a small number of nodes involved, that risk is not great.

The choice is a complex one. It involves not only the estimate of the risk of cancer beyond the breast but also assumptions about how much risk to take with the radiation. To claim that radiation therapy is "indicated" begs the question of what this strange word means here. Many clinicians understand it to mean that the evidence shows that radiation ought to be used in these cases. That, of course, is something that evidence cannot show. The evidence can show that the risk of a secondary cancer is less with the combination treatment of BCT and radiation.[3] Almost no one would reject radiation if the difference in expected survival with and without the radiation were great. With small numbers of nodes involved, however, the difference will be rather small (although even with radiation survival is not absolutely guaranteed). It seems that different patients with different concerns about radiation and about secondary cancer would evaluate the radiation option differently. Certainly, studies cannot definitively tell us exactly when radiation should be provided. That is why different oncologists will see the choices differently.

Chemotherapy following operation poses similar value choices. Many of the negative effects of the chemotherapy are subjective: Nausea, vomiting, fatigue, cognitive changes, alopecia, insomnia, and constipation are all unpleasant to almost everyone, but deciding how much unpleasantness is worth enduring for the potential gains from the chemotherapy requires subtle trade-offs that patients and physicians may make differently. Ms. Bachman also learns that the drugs could produce a premature menopause—an effect that women would perceive differently depending on whether they want to have future children or have unbearable menstrual cycles.

Although her physicians seem to hold values that support BCT (the lumpectomy) and radiation therapy, Ms. Bachman reveals values that seem to incline her toward the simple mastectomy. Is there any reason why Ms. Bachman would be mistaken if she chose the more invasive procedure?

Case 2-1 and Case 2-2 each pose value issues that do not seem to involve ethical questions. The choice between the lifestyle option and drugs for controlling cholesterol would not normally be seen as a moral choice, nor would the choice between lumpectomy and mastectomy. It is conceivable that someone would insist that it is immoral to use drugs when lifestyle will accomplish similar results. Some minority cultural group might believe it is unethical to choose less than the most certain strategy for preserving life but most probably would see these as nonmoral value judgments. They are usually perceived as matters of personal or cultural preference rather than as matters of morality. In the second half of this chapter we look at two cases that force us to identify clearly what makes normative judgments moral judgments.

SEPARATING ETHICAL AND OTHER EVALUATIONS

We have seen that evaluative judgments arise constantly in medicine, not just in the ethically dramatic cases, but in routine judgments about whether an effect is good or bad, whose good or bad it is, and whether it is worth taking the risk of a procedure, diagnostic test, or medication, given the alternatives available. Not all evaluations are *ethical* judgments, however. This section examines the relation between ethical and other kinds of evaluations.

In order for an evaluation to be an ethical evaluation, certain criteria must be met. First, the judgment must be about a human action or character or about norms generally governing actions or character. When we say that a painting is good, we do not make an ethical judgment; we make an aesthetic one. When we say a person is good, however, we can mean many things. If we say he or she is a good runner, we probably mean the person is technically proficient; we are still not making a moral judgment. We may mean, however, that the person is morally good.

In that case we are judging the person's character or conduct. Moreover, we are judging it by what we take to be a certain standard, an ultimate or final standard from which no further appeal is possible. By contrast, a person may be good according to the standards of the local community or the culture. Or he may be good according to a legal standard. In these cases we might agree that the person is approved of by the local community or culture or law, but still ask meaningfully whether the person or the person's actions are ethical.

An ethical evaluation is one that is made according to the most ultimate standard. For religious people that standard may be the will of God. For secular people it may be reason or natural law or some similar standard. Since the standard is ultimate, it is universal. We believe that everyone ought to reach the same conclusion. If there is one ultimate standard, it would be contradictory for some people to claim that the behavior conforms to the standard and others to claim it does not. Of course, in the real world finite humans disagree about ethical evaluations. The point, however, is that if two people disagree about what they take to be matters of ethics, logically, at least one of them must be wrong.

This is not to suggest that moral norms have to be so rigidly applied that ethics can be reduced to simple, general rules. It is not that all mercy killings or all breaches of confidentiality or all research without consent of the subject is wrong no matter what the circumstances. Rather it is that if two people are debating a particular instance of mercy killing or breaching confidentiality or conducting research without consent and one of them claims that instance is unethical while the other claims it is ethical, there is an understanding that at least one of them must be wrong. They must be wrong because they agree that they are debating whether this instance conforms to some single, universal standard—the approval of a deity or reason or some set of laws of nature. The deity or reason might well approve of some breaches of confidence and disapprove of others. It cannot simultaneously approve and disapprove of a particular case in a particular circumstance. One of the chief characteristics of an ethical evaluation is the presumption that the evaluation is based not on mere personal or social or cultural standards, but some universal authority.

The following cases provide an opportunity to try to separate ethical judgments from other kinds of evaluations. It deals with a couple making decisions about infertility treatment. The substantive issues of this case will be covered in the cases in Chapter 11. Here the focus should be on identifying the evaluative judgments. In reading them, try to identify the issues you consider to be ethical and those that involve nonethical evaluations.

CASE 2-3

Infertility Treatment: God's Will?

Bette Sass had struggled with obesity most of her adult life. She lost and gained 100 pounds at least twice. When she finally found a healthy combination of diet and exercise, she was almost thirty. A year later she met Gino, the man she would marry. For the past six years Bette and Gino have tried to conceive. Both were fully evaluated at an infertility center. Test results indicated that the Sasses have unexplained infertility although Bette's age and weight gain since her marriage were risk factors in the development of infertility.

As a practicing Catholic, Bette had spoken with her priest, who said there were no church objections to drugs to induce ovarian hyperstimulation (OH) or timed intercourse. In vitro fertilization (IVF) and intrauterine insemination (IUI) were not permitted. If any treatment resulted in multiple pregnancies, reduction of the number of embryos, a common recommendation, would be forbidden as it would be seen as abortion according to Church teaching.

Bette began OH treatment but did not become pregnant during her first cycle. She was discouraged because of her efforts and of the significant expense. A friend who was going through the same treatment decided to terminate further treatment after IVF failure. She told Bette, "You just have to accept the reality that technology doesn't work all the time."

With Gino's encouragement, Bette decided to continue treatment. The next month, hope loomed on the horizon. Studies showed there were multiple mature follicles indicating a good chance of a multifetal pregnancy thus increasing the risks to the fetuses and herself if she carried all of the babies to delivery.

She felt like time was running out so she opted to proceed saying to herself that whatever happened was God's will.

COMMENTARY

New technologies that modify the conception and birth process present many evaluative issues that are often considered to be moral. This case presents the opportunity to try to tease out the moral from the nonmoral judgments. This case begins with a couple who desire to have a child. That desire clearly represents a value judgment on their part. Most people would view the desire for children to be a matter of personal preference. Some couples may prefer not to have children, but desiring to have them does not automatically raise ethical issues (at least if the couple is married and the number they desire is modest). No matter how strongly the couple or members of their family desire for the birth of offspring, typically bearing children is not considered a moral duty. Bette's friend who opted out of continuing with fertility treatments apparently did not see having a biological child as a moral duty.

In some traditions, Judaism, for example, the bearing of children can be considered not merely desirable, but one's moral duty. The issue here is what the difference is between mere desires and moral duties. If bearing children is merely a matter of personal desire, no sense of obligation is attached. Others who similarly view childbearing as a matter of personal preference might feel sorry for the childless couple, but they would not render a judgment that they have failed in their obligation. By contrast, if childbearing were perceived as obligatory, then others who share that perception would feel justified in judging them as having failed in some duty.

The source of that obligation is critical. Not all obligations are moral. We can also have obligations grounded in law, for example. A legal obligation differs from a moral one in part because the source of the legal duty is a cultural institution such as a state legislature or court that has acted to create a duty. In the case of an ethical obligation, the perceived requiredness comes not from the act of a state legislature, that is, from a political group, but from some more ultimate source. For most ethical theories there is a single, ultimate source. For religious people, this could be the will or command of the deity. For secular people, the ultimate, universal source could be reason, intuition of moral law, or some other commonly shared source. Since there is believed to be a single, universal source for grounding moral judgment, there is a shared perception that actions can be judged right or wrong. In the case of personal preference, we might say that there is no duty to act in a particular way. It is merely a matter of taste. Our first task is to clarify whether Bette and Gino have a duty to have a child or merely a desire.

Turning to the means they consider for having this child, we learn that, as Roman Catholics, they believe that certain means of conception are morally controversial. Catholics believe that there are natural ends of beings (including humans) and of social institutions such as marriage. They believe that moral duties can be gleaned from these natural ends. Specifically, marriage and sexual relations are believed to have both "unitive" and "procreative" ends, that is, such relations should both express the union of the couple and be open to production of offspring.[4]

Since Catholics believe that these matters of procreation are governed by universal divine moral laws of nature, such as the natural ends of marriage and of sexual relations, for Bette and Gino how they have children is, at least in part, a moral matter. While many Catholics would consider bearing children by IVF or IUI to be a violation of these natural laws, Bette and Gino have apparently concluded some components of fertility treatment are acceptable (OH) and others not (IVF or IUI). While for many people, deciding for or against IVF is merely a matter of personal preference or aesthetic judgment; for others it presents moral choice.

Having one way or another concluded that it is acceptable to manipulate the hormones in order to increase or decrease the number of egg cells and thus the number of possible embryos, they now face the possibility of a multifetal pregnancy. They have already decided that they will not selectively reduce the number of embryos. Some people would see no moral issues raised. Destroying the extra embryos would be at most a matter of preference. For others, it would be a serious moral offense, the equivalent of a homicide.

The choices throughout the events leading to technologically assisted pregnancy require evaluative judgments. For some these will be mere expressions of preference; for others, matters of critical moral decision.

The evaluative choices in Case 2-3 presented an opportunity to attempt to distinguish between personal and social preferences, on the one hand, and moral evaluations, on the other. Moral obligations involve obligations while personal preferences do not. Not all obligations are moral, however. The next case explores the boundaries between moral and legal evaluations.

CASE 2-4

Baby Doe: Legal and Moral Options

On April 9, 1982, a baby was born in Bloomington, Indiana, who would eventually be referred to as "Baby Doe."[5] He had an esophageal atresia (a blockage of the tube that carries food to the stomach) and associated tracheo-esophageal fistula (an opening between the esophagus and the trachea that would permit food to pass into the lungs rather than the stomach). The baby had other physical anomalies as well, including reportedly an opening between the chambers of the heart. He also had a genetic condition known as Down syndrome. The Down syndrome would leave the boy with some undetermined level of mental retardation even if his anatomical problems were corrected, but, according to published reports, the child would have a high probability of surviving, albeit with the Down syndrome, if his only medical problems were the surgically correctable fistula and atresia.

The attending obstetrician, Walter Owens, informed the parents that, even with the operation, the child would still not be normal. He would "have all the problems that even the best of them have." He added that "some of these children...are mere blobs." {cited in U.S. Commission on Civil Rights, p. 22.}

On the basis of this information, the parents decided not to permit operation to correct the fistula. The parents were trained as teachers and had experience teaching handicapped and retarded children. They had two other children without Down syndrome.

Some reports indicated that the baby also had a cardiac septal defect, a serious malformation of the heart that would require operative repair. That possibility might explain why some claims were made that the child had only a 50-50 chance of survival even with operation.[6]

When nurses protested the decision of the parents not to treat, the hospital sought judicial intervention. In the lower court, Judge John G. Baker supported the parental decision finding that the parents, after being fully informed, "have the right to choose a medically recommended course of treatment for their child in the present circumstances." The Indiana Supreme Court refused to get involved, thus upholding the lower court's decision.

Those opposing the parents sought appeal to U.S. Supreme Court, but that appeal was made moot by death of the baby on April 15. Two weeks later President Reagan asked the Attorney General and Sec. of Health and Human Services (HHS)_ to become involved, noting that federal law prohibits discrimination against the handicapped. This led to issuing of a notice that it was illegal to discriminate against infants solely on the basis of handicap. While this notice was rejected by the courts, eventually a law was passed classifying withholding of life support in cases such as this as child abuse.[7]

COMMENTARY

In this case, many evaluative judgments were made. Some of them were like the judgments in the previous cases. They were expressions of matters of preference. Sometimes those judgments were presented as statements of fact, but they clearly contained value implications. They were expressed in value-loaded statements, such as referring to some people with Down syndrome as "blobs," claiming that they had a "high probability" of survival.

For our purposes, we should focus on the evaluations that go beyond these personal opinions to note the interplay in this case between the law and morality. The nurses and other hospital personnel who intervened to seek court review clearly thought that this baby's treatment was more than a matter of personal preferences. They no doubt were convinced that it was morally wrong to allow a child to die who could survive regardless of the underlying Down syndrome. They discovered, however, that regardless of their ethical judgments, the Indiana courts concluded there were no grounds for intervening. The parents, according to Judge, John G. Baker, had a right to control medical decisions for their infant.

We thus have a situation in which allowing the infant to die from lack of surgical intervention was ethically unacceptable to many people even though doing so was deemed not to be illegal. There are many cases in which ethics and law part company. The law is the product of a political entity. It is a crude device and refrains from speaking about many behaviors that seem clearly unethical. The law permits, indeed requires, public enforcement of a normative standard enacted by a political group. Ethics normally does not have available a formal enforcement mechanism and is grounded in a more ultimate, universal standard of reference.

For example, lying to a spouse is, in the normal circumstance, a violation of the norms of morality yet almost never would such unethical behavior be subject to legal sanction. Especially, in cases in which the ultimate standard for judging is controversial and hard to access, we may simultaneously recognize that a behavior is immoral but should not be made illegal. Some medical ethical decisions fall into this category. Not everything that people believe is unethical will be a violation of the law.

As this case evolved, a rather unusual reversal occurred. As the Reagan administration began a national assessment of Baby Doe decisions, it concluded that allowing infants to die from lack of potentially effective medical treatment was a violation of the law. On grounds of both discrimination against the handicapped, and child abuse and neglect, arguments were made that existing law made what these parents decided illegal. New legislation eventually clarified the law so that it is now recognized in the United States that forgoing of life support for infants is illegal. The only exceptions are cases in which the infant is inevitably dying regardless of treatment, will remain in a permanent coma, or in which treatment will be virtually futile in prolonging life and will be inhumane. Even in these cases, "appropriate nutrition and hydration" must be provided. Hence, what these parents did in 1982 would now almost universally be considered illegal.

This suggests an interesting possibility. Although withholding life support is illegal, not everyone believes it would always be unethical. It could be that we are witnessing a kind of reversal in which what once was thought to be legal but unethical is now thought by some to be illegal but ethical. For example, moral theologians as well as secular thinkers hold that it is ethically acceptable to withhold life support under certain circumstances. They hold that, as long as the death of the patient is not the direct intention, it is acceptable to withhold life support when the expected burdens exceed the expected benefits. (The details will be outlined in Chapter 15.) Sometimes this might be the case even when the patient is not comatose, inevitably dying, or even suffering from a condition in which treatment is "virtually futile" for prolonging life. A patient could be suffering terribly from a treatment even though it could prolong life. The patient could be an infant in a case governed by the Baby Doe regulations. If so, even those who hold conservative views on matters of life and death might support the ethics of a decision to forgo life support. If the patient were an infant (but oddly not if it were an older child), withholding such treatment would be deemed illegal in current American law. This could be a case in which withholding life support was illegal even though it was deemed ethical by a group normally strongly opposed to hastening death. What is ethical and what is legal are often separate issues. In analyzing cases in the remaining chapters of this book, personal preferences and desires must be distinguished from obligations and, among obligations, the legal must be kept sharply separate from the ethical.

In Chapter 3 we turn to cases that will permit us to examine how we can know what is ethical. The role of the health professions in deciding and articulating ethical norms will be addressed as well as the role of religious authorities, the state, the administration of a hospital, and the individual conscience.

NOTES

1 Parfit, Derek. "What Makes Someone's Life Go Best." *Reasons and Persons*. Oxford: Clarendon Press, 1984, pp. 493–503; Gert, Bernard. "Rationality, Human Nature, and Lists." *Ethics* 100 (1990):279–300; DeGrazia, David. "Value Theory and the Best Interests Standard." *Bioethics* 9 (1995):50–61.

2 Golhirsch, Aron, John H. Glick, Richard D. Gelber, Alan S. Coates, and Hans-Jorg Senn. "Meeting Highlights: International Consensus Panel on the Treatment of Primary Breast Cancer." *Journal of Clinical Oncology* 19 (No. 18, 2001):3817–3827; Fisher, B., J. Dognam, E. Tan-Chui, et al. "Pathological Findings from the National Surgical Adjuvant Breast Project (NSABP) Eight-Year Update of Protocol B-17: Intraductal Carcinoma." *Cancer* 86 (1999):429–438; Silverstein, M. J., M. D. Lagios, S. Groshen, et al. "The Influence of Margin Width on Local Control of Ductal Carcinoma In Situ of the Breast." *New England Journal of Medicine* 340 (1999):1455–1461; Early Breast Cancer Trialists' Collaborative Group. "Favourable and Unfavourable Effects on Long-Term Survival of Radiotherapy for Early Breast Cancer." *Lancet* 355 (2000):1757–1770.

3 Obedian, Edwards, Diana B. Fischer, and Bruce Haffty. "Second Malignancies after Treatment of Early-Stage Breast Cancer: Lumpectomy and Radiation Therapy versus Mastectomy." *Journal of Clinical Oncology* 18 (No. 12, 2000):2406–2412.

4 United States Conference of Catholic Bishops. *Ethical and Religious Directives for Catholic Health Care Services*. Washington, DC, United States Catholic Conference, 2001, see especially directive 38.

5 This case is based on events in Bloomington, Indiana, in 1982. The medical and some court records are sealed, but considerable information was made public at the time. Names, insofar as they are used in this case, are real. This account is based on *re* Infant Doe, No. GU 8204-00 (Cir. Ct. Monroe County, Ind. April 12, 1982, *writ of mandamus dismissed sub nom.* State *ex rel.* Infant Doe v. Baker, No. 482 S 140 (Indiana Supreme Ct., May 27, 1982). (Case mooted by child's death.); "The Demise of 'Infant Doe': Permitted Death Gives New Life to an Old Debate." *Washington Post*, April 17, 1982, pp. A1; and United States Commission on Civil Rights. *Medical Discrimination against Children with Disabilities: A Report*

of the U.S. Commission on Civil Rights. Washington, DC: U.S. Commission on Civil Rights, 1989, pp. 21–22.

[6] "The Demise of 'Infant Doe'."

[7] U.S. Department of Health and Human Services. "Child Abuse and Neglect Prevention and Treatment Program: Final Rule: 45 CFR 1340." *Federal Register: Rules and Regulations* 50 (No. 72, April 15, 1985):14878–14892.

CHAPTER 3

⤙⟳

What Is the Source of Moral Judgments?

Other Cases Involving the Sources of Moral Judgments

4-7: For the Welfare of the Profession: Should Nurses Strike?
12-8: The Interrogation of Guantanamo Prisoner Mohammed al-Qahtani
13-1: Warning: Premarital Sex May Be Dangerous to Your Health
18-8: Demands for Futile Care

Once ethical and other evaluative judgments are identified, the next question is where one should look to determine what is moral. Health professionals often believe the problem of what is moral to be a matter of "professional ethics." They might turn to the code of ethics of their profession. For physicians this might mean consulting the American Medical Association's (AMA's) *Code of Medical Ethics*.[1] Members of the other health professions have similar codes that their members can consult. For pharmacists this might be the current *Code of Ethics for Pharmacists* of the American Pharmacists Association (APhA); for nurses, the American Nurses Association's *Code of Ethics for Nurses*;[2] for dentists, the American Dental Association's *Principles of Ethics and Code of Professional Conduct*.[3] All of the healing professions have such codes that are often taken as definitive moral authority for their members when it comes to professional conduct. Someone might wonder, however, whether a health professional's conduct is always correct just because it conforms to the professional society's code of ethics.

A number of problems arise. These are codes for American professional associations. Other nations have analogous codes, and they do not always agree. Some members of a health profession are not members of their professional society. Some have refused to join because they do not agree with their profession's stance on some issues. In the 1940s, for example, some more liberal physicians objected to the AMA's opposition to government-sponsored health insurance. Other physicians with more conservative leanings have withheld support from the AMA for its refusal explicitly to condemn abortion. Sometimes problems arise when one professional organization's code disagrees with another profession's position.

While the authority of professional codes can be challenged by those of other health professions and by individual members of a profession who disagree with the organization's stance, a more basic problem also arises. Some may ask why a professional group should have the authority to determine what is ethical for its members in the first place. Other sources of moral authority may compete for attention.

For example, a physician working in a hospital may have to contend not only with the physician's professional ethical code but also with the code of the hospital. The hospital may have a locally generated code of conduct or may be subject to ethical positions taken by its sponsor or of the American Hospital Association. Should the health professional consider his or her professional code of ethics to be authoritative or the local hospital's code of conduct?

If the hospital is sponsored by a religious organization, the hospital's ethical code may be derived from the theological ethical commitments of the religious group. For Catholic hospitals in the United States, for instance, this would be the Ethical and Religious Directives for Catholic Health Care Services.

The health professional himself (or herself) may stand in some religious tradition, which may or may not be the same as the sponsoring hospital. Should a religious tradition be treated as being an authoritative source for knowing what is ethical? If so, should it be the hospital's tradition or the health professional's? And how should either of these be weighed in relation to the professional code?

Finally, the health professional will often confront ethical dilemmas involving a particular patient who also has moral standards that he or she feels should be the foundation of moral judgments involving his or her treatment. Is the patient's ethical stance a defensible basis for grounding the ethical positions taken by a health professional? In this chapter, cases are presented that provide an opportunity to examine alternative ways of grounding moral judgments. In each case, the important problem on which to focus is not so much what is the right thing to do, but rather what is the source of moral authority and on what authority the health professional's behavior should be shaped.

GROUNDING ETHICS IN THE PROFESSIONAL CODE

A health professional confronting an ethical problem that poses a significant difficulty may want to turn to the professional code of ethics to determine what it says regarding the issue at stake. Often the professional code will provide insight based on years of collective experience of the members of the professional group.

Sometimes the apparent answer from the code seems so appropriate that no further consideration is necessary. But in other cases it may not be obvious to the individual health professional that the profession's collective wisdom is morally definitive. One problem arises because the professional group's code can change over the years. The AMA code, for example, was originally adopted in 1847 and published a year later,[4] but it has been revised many times since then. Major changes occurred in 1903, 1912, 1947, and 1957, and then dramatic changes were adopted in 1980 and published the following year.[5] Some of the differences are substantial. The early versions, for example, said nothing about informed consent. Their understanding of confidentiality was radically different from that of the most recent versions. Changes are reflected not only in the norms for right conduct, but also in the character traits that the codes hold out as praiseworthy. In the most recent principles, a physician is, according to the AMA, supposed to provide medical service with compassion and respect for human dignity; in 1847 the traits of character for the physician were tenderness, steadiness, condescension, and authority.[6] Similar changes have occurred in the codes of the other professions. The American Pharmaceutical Association's code was first written in 1852[7] but was revised in 1922[8] and again in 1952[9] and 1969. Modest changes were made in 1975, 1981, and 1985.[10] Finally, in 1994 a completely revised code was adopted.[11] Each time the code changed, did the ethically correct behavior for pharmacists really change or was it only what the APhA members believed was the correct behavior?

What about health professionals who are not members of their professional associations or who immigrate to the United States from other countries that may have codes that differ? Does this professional code determine what is ethically correct for those who are not members or only for those who are members? Can what is ethically correct for health professionals change, depending on whether they are members of their professional association? And what about health professionals in other nations? Does the American professional code or does their own professional organization's code determine what is right for these persons? It seems odd that what is right could depend on the country in which they practice and when they practice. The following case asks what the role of a professional code should be in determining what is ethically correct conduct.

CASE 3-1

Withholding Nutrition: The AMA, the Government, and the Church in Disagreement

Infant Jimmy McCarthy was born at thirty-four weeks gestation at a rural hospital. The obstetrician, Dr. Herman Nolan, immediately recognized gross abnormalities. The child was determined to have trisomy 21 (Down syndrome), partial duodenal atresia, monosomy 18, liver pathology (which was possibly transient and reversible), and a cardiac septal defect (which was potentially surgically correctable, but could require several operations). He was immediately transferred to St. Luke's

Catholic hospital, a tertiary care hospital in a major city with a high-level neonatal care department capable of caring for the most severely impaired newborns.

When the infant arrived at St. Luke's, an immediate assessment was made by a complex care team. The surgeon considered operation on the duodenal atresia too risky on a premature infant that small. He recommended IV and nasogastric feeding for at least four weeks, waiting to see if the child grew sufficiently to make a surgical procedure possible. He also recommended an immediate consult with a pediatric cardiac surgeon.

The geneticist had never seen convergence of trisomy 21 and monosomy 18 in one infant and could find none in the literature. The trisomy 21 without the other complications could lead to many years of life, if the anatomical problems were corrected. It would leave the child with some undetermined degree of mental retardation.

The monosomy 18 was much rarer. Isolated cases of years of survival were reported in the literature, but it inevitably would involve severe retardation and institutionalization. The best judgment was that the child would be permanently bedridden with severe physical and mental impairment.

The care team believed that the medical problems presented in this combination were synergistic. No one would necessarily be fatal, but combined they all believed the child will not live more than weeks or a few years at best. He would be in discomfort from repeated operations and cardiac complications. On the basis of this prognosis, the care team identified three options. One alternative was "full court press" including correction of the atresia as soon as it was feasible, as well as eventual cardiac procedures necessary to correct the septal defect. A second option was intravenous nutrition and hydration for a period to see if the infant survived long enough for the operation to be performed. The third alternative was immediate cessation of all interventions to sustain life—including omission of the nasogastric feeding, even though it would mean the rapid decline and death of the infant. The team decided to recommend temporary intravenous nutrition and hydration feeding to see if the infant thrived so that the duodenal atresia could be corrected. They also recommended a do-not-attempt-resuscitation (DNAR) order in the interim. Although combining a DNAR order with a plan for eventual surgical intervention was unusual, in this case they believed that, if the infant suffered a cardiac or respiratory arrest before an operation could be performed, it would foretell severe problems for the child.

The care team knew that this was a complex and potentially controversial case. It occurred at a time when the Baby Doe controversies were at their peak. In order to assess the options further, the St. Luke's Ethics Committee was convened. The parents were asked to attend the meeting. The mother was distraught, but she understood the situation. She was quiet and turned to her husband when the chairman asked any questions of them. The father, dressed in a business suit, was a teacher in a local high school.

After exploring the options, the father spoke saying he and his wife were deeply committed Catholics, and they believed there was a message from God here. The committee members feared that the father would demand maximal life support, an option they considered inhumane to a child that was likely to die soon, regardless of medical treatment.

The father began by saying that all life is precious no matter what the intelligence. He said, "Jimmy has been a blessing to us. God will provide." He added that he had consulted with experts at the National Institutes of Health (NIH), a lawyer specializing in treatment decisions for critically ill infants, and their parish priest. He then shocked them by saying, "God's place for Jimmy is in heaven." He wanted all treatment including intravenous nutrition and hydration stopped. He claimed that any suffering in the short term from withholding nutrition and hydration would be more than offset by being spared the pain and suffering of many operations and hospitalizations. He added that the parish priest said that a treatment is morally expendable when it involves grave burden. He was sure that any of the treatments, even the intravenous nutrition feeding, would eventually lead to terrible suffering. The inevitable result of the feeding was, according to the father, at least two major operations, which, if successful, would lead to possible further operations, possible liver failure, residual cardiac problems, and a short life bedridden in a hospital with severe mental and physical impairments.

At least one priest on the hospital's ethics committee confirmed that the church's position was that life support could be forgone if it presented grave burden, if the burdens exceeded the expected benefits. He stressed that the church's position was generally pro-life, but the Vatican had acknowledged that in extraordinary circumstances, treatments could be omitted.

The surgeon was troubled by this. He stressed that the traditional duty of the physician was to preserve life. He was particularly concerned about withholding or withdrawing medically supplied nutrition. He cited the current American Medical Association position:

> Unless it is clearly established that the patient is terminally ill or irreversibly comatose, a physician should not be deterred from appropriately aggressive treatment of a patient.[12]

The surgeon pointed out that Jimmy McCarthy was clearly not irreversibly comatose and that he was not really terminally ill either. He felt morally obliged to continue providing nutrition and hydration.

The hospital ethics committee knew that it was legally obligated to follow federal regulations called the Baby Doe Rule. This required that life support be provided unless a baby was inevitably dying regardless of treatment, irreversibly comatose, or the treatment was virtually futile in prolonging life and inhumane. The members all agreed that Jimmy McCarthy was not comatose and was not inevitably dying regardless of treatment. Some members thought that he could fall into the category of patients for whom treatment was "virtually futile" in prolonging life and also inhumane. They recognized that the burden of the future treatments would be great, possibly sufficient to call the treatment "inhumane." They were divided, however, over whether they could claim that the treatments would be virtually futile in preserving life. Furthermore, the regulations state that, even if the proposed treatment falls under one of the three exceptions, it is still necessary to provide what the regulations called "appropriate treatment."

The committee was left with a dilemma. The regulations seemed to require providing the nutrition and hydration against the parents' wishes and the surgeon was convinced that the AMA Code also required providing them. Nevertheless, the

parents were refusing to consent and the priest on this Catholic hospital's committee held that such treatments were morally expendable according to the teachings
of the authorities that sponsored the hospital.

COMMENTARY

The substantive issues of the ethics of withholding medically supplied nutrition and hydration from a patient will be discussed in Chapters 9 and 15 when
we examine the ethics of terminal care and of surrogate decision-making.
The focus here is on what the parties of this case—the parents, the surgeon,
the priest, and the members of the ethics committee—should rely on as their
source of moral norms.

Those involved in this decision have several options: a professional code,
a hospital ethics committee consensus, government regulations, church teachings, and individual conscience. The surgeon appears to place authority in the
position of his professional association.

The problem raised here is whether the professional association code is
necessarily always the definitive authority for determining what is ethical for
physicians or other health professionals. It seems to make sense to consult the
code in difficult cases, but is that because the code *defines* what is right for
the health professional or is it because the code simply summarizes the judgment of the health professional's colleagues who have faced somewhat similar
situations?

It could be that what is the right behavior for a health professional is whatever the code says. If the code literally defines what is ethical for members
of the profession, then it is logically impossible for it to be wrong. Moreover,
whenever the code is changed, then what is right for the health professional
changes.

In this case, the AMA had during the 1980s adopted a position that held
that patients should be treated with aggressive life support. The 1986 code held
that the preference of the patient should prevail if the patient were terminally
ill, but that if the patient is neither terminally ill nor irreversibly comatose then
"appropriately aggressive treatment" should be provided. Apparently, at this
point in the evolution of AMA thinking on these matters, the patient's refusal
of life support would not govern the physician's choice if the patient were not
terminal or comatose. By 1994 the AMA's position had changed substantially.
At that time it held:

Even if the patient is not terminally ill or permanently unconscious, it is
not unethical to discontinue all means of life-sustaining medical treatment in
accordance with a proper substituted judgment or best interest analysis.[13]

This remains the current AMA position. The problem is whether the surgeon in this case needs to feel bound by his professional association's position
and, if so, why. The implication seems to be that the foundation for ethics

within the practice of medicine is the consensus of the professional association or, alternatively, that the professional association is in the best position to know what is ethically required in the practice of medicine. If the professional association is authoritative because what is ethical is simply whatever the group agrees is morally required, then some puzzles are created. This would seem to imply that there is no deeper, more fundamental basis for ethical judgment than group consensus. Moreover, there would seem to be no reason why different professional groups could not reach different judgments or that the same group could not change what is right and wrong from time to time. In this case, the surgeon would seem locked in to the view that withholding nutrition and hydration for a baby who was not terminally ill was unacceptable in the 1980s, but became acceptable in 1994. Thus, even if one ignores the perspective of the patient and family (and the related informed consent requirements), ambiguity exists within the professional codes.

The reliance on a consensus expressed in a professional code also poses serious problems for members of other health professions and for medical lay people. Other members of the health care team—nurses, social workers, pharmacists, and allied health professionals—all are members of professional associations that have written codes of ethics for their professions. If what is ethical is determined by the consensus of the professional group, different members of the health care team might be faced with conflicting ethical requirements if their professional association reached a different consensus.

One of the criteria for a norm to be a matter of ethics (rather than mere personal or social preference) is that the norm has its foundation in some ultimate standard—divine authority or reason, for example (depending on whether one's ethics is theologically or secularly grounded). Mere consensus of a professional group does not meet this standard. It could be that those, like this surgeon, who turn to a professional code have a somewhat different view. They may hold that ethical requirements for practice of the profession are not based merely on professional consensus, but that the professional group is the most authoritative in knowing the moral norms for practices within the profession. This poses problems as well, however. It implies that being a member of the profession gives one special knowledge in the area of ethics. This is a controversial position, however. If one's ethics is theological, it implies that becoming a member of a health profession gives one special authority in knowing the divine will or divine law—an odd position to say the least. If, on the other hand, one's ethics is secular, it implies that becoming a member of a health profession gives one special authority in knowing the moral laws of nature or what reason requires in health professional settings. No doubt, being a member of a profession gives one some kinds of expertise—knowledge of medical science, for example, but it is hard to imagine why it would give one expertise in knowing what morality requires, in knowing, for example, whether it is acceptable to forgo nutrition and hydration in a conscious, but critically ill baby like Jimmy McCarthy. There must be some alternative foundation for ethics.

One alternative is that the foundation for ethics in health care is something more basic than the current professional agreement or professional knowledge. For example, for those standing in a religious tradition, what is ethically right and wrong might be determined by the approval or will of the deity. For some secular thinkers what is right is determined by reason, by the moral laws of nature, or by other fundamental standards. The idea is that the standard for ethics is the most ultimate appeal one can make, the point beyond which no further appeal is possible.

Some people have given up hope of recognizing the will of a deity, the moral laws of nature, or what reason requires. They may be convinced that the standard of ethics is a societal one. In that view, an act is right if one's society says it is. In the case of Jimmy McCarthy that might suggest that the current government regulations express a moral consensus of the society—that life support can only be forgone if the infant is terminally ill or permanently unconscious or if the treatment would be inhumane and simultaneously virtually futile. Even in these situations, if we follow the federal Baby Doe regulations, appropriate nutrition and hydration must be provided.

If the moral foundation is a societal consensus, this leaves open the possibility that for other people in other societies some other behavior would be ethical (because in their society some other behavior is approved).

This raises the question of whether ethics is seen as being grounded in some foundation beyond either professional or societal agreement. Both the parish priest and the priest on the ethics committee in Jimmy McCarthy's case seem to believe that ethics is a matter of divine authority and that some complex combination of scripture, tradition, hierarchical authority, and religious revelation provide the standard for moral judgment. They have reached the surprising conclusion that morality accepts the forgoing of life support in cases such as this one, provided the treatment would result in a disproportionately grave burden for the patient. In this conclusion, they are consistent with important teachings of their tradition. The Vatican in 1980 summarized a long tradition within Catholic moral theology that opposes all intentional active euthanasia, but accepts forgoing life support on what is referred to as proportionality grounds.[14] While there is a strong commitment within that tradition to providing nutrition and hydration when these offer net benefit, even those within that tradition, who are quite conservative on matters of medical ethics, acknowledge that there are special cases in which continuing nutrition and hydration offer grave burden with very little benefit.[15] It appears that was the conclusion reached by the priests and the parents in this case. It is an odd set of circumstances in which the AMA and the federal government both were insisting on continued treatment while the church that informed the parents' views as well as those of the hospital would be more permissive. Only by determining the relative importance of the professional code, the government's stance, and the teachings of the church will we know what is ethical in this case. Even then we may be left with the possibility that what is ethical may not be legal.

GROUNDING ETHICS IN THE PHYSICIAN'S ORDERS

In some situations, patients and caregivers are presented with ethical decisions that seem to be grounded not so much in either public policy or professional codes, but in the beliefs of practicing physicians. Of course, the physician in reaching his or her moral conclusion may have to decide how important the physician's professional code is, but by the time the physician has decided on a course of action, others involved may be presented only with the doctor's order. The following case raises the question of whether the implicit moral judgments incorporated into the physician's instructions provide a grounding of moral positions taken in the practice of medicine.

CASE 3-2

The Case of the Meddling Clergyman

Rev. Geoffrey Kerman, the minister at Wesley Methodist Church, visited the hospital to call on two parishioners. When he reached the hospital he found the name of Mrs. Olive Patterson on the admissions list. She was a woman in her sixties who was a long-term member of Wesley Methodist Church. She had been hospitalized 2–3 times in the past five years for abdominal cancer, but Rev. Kerman had not been aware of the current hospitalization.

He decided to visit Mrs. Patterson's room. He found her in some pain and groggy. She had pain in her legs over the past month and also lost bladder control. She had come to the hospital over the past weekend and was now complaining about all the tests they were running. She said to Rev. Kerman, "I know I'm dying but I don't know why I can't go out awake. I can hardly keep my eyes open. There must be a way to keep the pain under control without knocking me out."

Her physician, Dr. Gordon Simweiler, had told her that the only way to control the pain was to "knock her out." Rev. Kerman offered a brief prayer and left the room.

Rev. Kerman met Dr. Simweiler at the nurse's station. Dr. Simweiler commented, "She doesn't look good. We'll have to increase her pain medication."

Rev. Kerman felt certain that Mrs. Patterson would not want to be "knocked out" further. He knew that, since the days their church's founder, John Wesley, had run clinics in eighteenth-century England, their denomination had stood firmly for the active involvement of the patient in choosing appropriate medical care including care for cancer and other critical illnesses. The church's position is that

> We encourage the use of medical technologies to provide palliative care at the end of life when life-sustaining treatments no longer support the goals of life, and when they have reached their limits. There is no moral or religious obligation to use these when they impose undue burdens or only extend the process of dying. Dying persons and their families are free to discontinue treatments when they cease to be of benefit to the patient.[16]

The church's position is that patients have a responsibility to prepare for their own deaths working with their physicians, their families, their friends, and their faith community. Rev. Kerman was concerned that Mrs. Patterson was not being given this opportunity regarding her pain management. At the same time, he was aware that she had not asked him to intervene; in fact, she had not even told him she was in the hospital. Should Rev. Kerman take steps to question Dr. Simweiler's orders for pain medication?

COMMENTARY

This case leaves the clergyman having to evaluate the moral judgments of a physician. Rev. Kerman recognizes that Dr. Simweiler's choice of pain medication and his decision that appears to minimize the patient's involvement in the treatment decisions involve moral choices. At the same time, Rev. Kerman is aware that he is in an awkward position. He is on the doctor's turf and has not even been invited into the case by Mrs. Patterson.

Rev. Kerman is also aware that traditional medical ethics has long presumed that the physician has the right and the responsibility to formulate a treatment plan including making judgments about what is morally right conduct in a doctor/patient relationship. The Hippocratic Oath, for example, has the physician pledge to "benefit the sick according to my ability and judgment." This Hippocratic foundation has evolved into a presumption that a doctor's orders should prevail in the clinic.

At the same time, Rev. Kerman knows that he is a member of a profession that has historically often assumed moral decision-making authority for parishioners. At least the clergy have traditionally provided moral advice and interpretation of church teachings. Thus we have a case of members of two professions colliding in which both are accustomed to acting on behalf of lay people rendering judgments about their welfare and what is morally appropriate for them.

What is at stake here is not only a choice of treatment options, but also a question of the proper style for doing one's dying. One strategy attempts to spare the patient the burden of direct confrontation with some technically complex and psychologically difficult choices. The other holds that the patient has not only the right but also the duty to confront them.

One approach to this case is to ask whether either of these professional actors has any legitimate claim to make moral choices for these patients. Is there any skill or status inherent in the roles that would authorize either Dr. Simweiler or Rev. Kerman to decide how Mrs. Patterson should deal with her pain and eventual death? While physicians are sometimes placed in a position in which it is assumed that they are the medical experts and therefore have authority to make choices in the doctor/patient relation, that assumption is now being examined more closely.

Surely, on technical matters, the physician has a special expertise. While Dr. Simweiler might not be a world authority on pain management options for his patients, he surely is in a position of relative expertise. He is the authority among all the players on the scene.

The issue here, however, is not primarily over technical matters of Mrs. Patterson's pain management. Rather the issues here involve moral questions: how much Mrs. Patterson should be told about her options and how active a role she should play in choosing a pain management regimen. Choices must be made about steps to be taken to prepare for what is likely to be a long and difficult process that could eventually lead to her death.

Rev. Kerman also is in a profession that has traditionally claimed expertise in dealing with these normative issues. Moreover, as a clergyman, he is in a profession that has assumed responsibility for teaching and guidance on matters moral. While Dr. Simweiler's expertise seems to prepare him poorly for providing moral and spiritual counsel to Mrs. Patterson, clergy are often assumed to be uniquely prepared for that role, especially for those parishioners who have voluntarily chosen to be members of their congregations. Thus, the clergy are recognized by members of their congregations to have a role in expounding on moral norms within their communities.

Rev. Kerman is within a church that has not emphasized the teaching and moral guidance role of the clergy as much as some other traditions. Roman Catholic and Jewish traditions, for example, explicitly recognize the teaching authority of their clerical professionals. Nevertheless, Rev. Kerman seems to be standing in a relation to Mrs. Patterson that is different from that of Dr. Simweiler. At the same time, although Mrs. Patterson is a member of Rev. Kerman's church, she has not asked him to become involved. Can either Dr. Simweiler or Rev. Kerman claim authority to establish the moral norms for Mrs. Patterson's care. If so, under what conditions?

GROUNDING ETHICS IN INSTITUTIONAL POLICY

If we cannot automatically ground ethical judgments in a physician's moral views, societal opinion, or professional beliefs about what is ethically correct, can the institution in which health professionals work provide that grounding? Many health professionals work in hospitals or other health care institutions that may have codes of ethics of their own. These codes may come from large public or private organizations that sponsor the hospital or the local institution that, through its board of trustees or its medical board, may have formally adopted a statement or code of conduct about what is believed to be ethical. To what extent should health professionals working within such institutions feel bound by such statements? To what extent is the institution the "source" of the ethical obligation?

CASE 3-3

Providing Less-than-Optimal Services

The number of clients referred to the out-client rehabilitation clinic of Centerview Medical Center seemed to increase every week. The clinic was the best in the area for rehabilitation of serious injuries. Occupational therapist, Jonathan Petty, OTR/L, enjoyed the busy pace and the variety of clients he saw in the clinic. Jonathon was assigned a new client, Alberto Modesto, a 28-year-old automobile manufacturing worker, who had sustained a severe crush injury of his hand on the job. Mr. Petty noted that there were orders to "evaluate and begin treatment." As he read further in Mr. Modesto's medical record, he saw that the insurance company responsible for paying for the care would reimburse only a certified hand therapist's (CHT) services. Mr. Petty was not a CHT, so he approached his supervisor, Charlotte Cunningham, to discuss the problem. Mr. Petty explained that only a CHT would be reimbursed by the insurer.

"How soon can Mr. Modesto see the CHT?" he asked his supervisor.

"She's just too busy to take any new clients," Ms. Cunningham responded. "I'll tell you what to do. I would hate to lose this case and hate to have the patient wait. It looks like it will take at least a year of service to rehabilitate Mr. Modesto, and he needs to begin right away. It is part of our hospital's officially adopted code of ethics that we must work always for the good of the patient. Why do not you just go ahead and provide services to him and have the CHT sign the notes? She can check to make sure that your treatment plan is appropriate. Who will know the difference?" Ms. Cunningham stated and walked away.

Jonathan Petty was left standing in the middle of the hallway with the patient's chart in his hand and a perplexed look on his face. Provide services to a client and have someone else sign off on them? On the face of it, that seemed very wrong. Yet he, too, would hate to lose this interesting case, and he knew that Mr. Modesto needed to start therapy as soon as possible. He was convinced that the therapy the patient would receive would be superior to any alternatives available. He had briefly met Mr. Modesto and instantly liked him. Would anyone really know the difference if he provided the care or if the CHT did? Mr. Petty wondered what the right thing was to do.[17]

COMMENTARY

In this case, the rehabilitation clinic's policy seems controversial. One could easily suggest it is grounded in self-interest. It could be in serious legal trouble if the patient learned of the substitution of a lesser skilled professional than indicated in the clinical record. Assume, however, for purposes of discussion that Mr. Petty is convinced that the clinic's policy is, in fact, believed by his supervisor and the administrators to be justified as the best way to get the patient high-quality therapy—that they really are concerned that patient would have to wait for the CHT to provide treatment and delaying therapy would jeopardize Mr. Modesto's well-being. This, after all, is a long-standing interpretation of the Hippocratic Oath's imperative to do whatever is believed to benefit that patient. (The text of the Hippocratic Oath is included as an appendix to this volume.)

If the clinic's position is intended to have a moral purpose, then there is a real conflict between the holders of two ethical perspectives. One focuses on the dishonesty or deception in having the CHT sign-off on treatment she did not provide; the other on the traditional moral imperative to do what is best for the patient. Here the issue is whether an occupational therapist should treat the clinic and its supervisory staff as the legitimate source of morality for choosing between these two options. Presumably Mr. Petty made at least an implied commitment to the clinic to abide by its norms when he accepted employment there. To what extent does that commitment imply agreeing to accept clinic policy as a source of moral authority?

In some ways, the problem is similar to the conflict in Case 3-1, the case in which physicians and parents have to factor into their reasoning the moral obligation to obey the Baby Doe regulations. In this case, however, Mr. Petty has real reason to believe the clinic's policy is unacceptable and to question whether what amounts to fraud is moral just because the clinic policy writers have concluded it is. There is no reason to assume that a policy is moral just because it is incorporated into clinic policy or the interpretations of that policy by the supervisory staff. Can Mr. Petty, at the same time, acknowledge his general obligation to conform to clinic policy and still claim that there is a source of moral obligation beyond the clinic where he works?

GROUNDING ETHICS IN THE PATIENT'S VALUES

The patient is another possibility for the source of the ethical and other evaluations that are incorporated into the medical practice. It is sometimes believed that, since there are so many different ethical positions possible on controversial issues, every person should have the right to choose his or her own ethics. A slightly different view, referred to by philosophers as *personal relativism*, is that to say something is ethical literally means nothing more than that it is the position approved by the speaker. According to this view, if one believes an action is morally right, it literally is right, that is, the final standard. However, someone else may have a quite different perspective. For the other person, the same action could, for him or her, be wrong. There is no further appeal beyond the individual.

When medical choices are made by lay people outside the context of relationship with a medical professional, no direct conflict with the ethics of the professional will arise. Nevertheless, many find it implausible to claim that ethics is literally nothing more than one's personally chosen standards. In relations with a physician or other health professional, personal relativism presents an even more difficult problem. A physician–patient relationship could exist in which a patient holds a certain treatment course (e.g., actively ending a patient's life for mercy) is ethical while the physician holds it to be unethical. The following case, poses the problem of whether a physician-researcher and an institutional review board (IRB) regulating human subjects research should treat the patient as the source of moral standards.

CASE 3-4

The Eager Research Subject: Justifying External Moral Standards

Dr. Laura Bollinger was a 62-year-old former college professor of biology who had taken early retirement when she developed macular degeneration that produced blindness. Over the years in which her sight was deteriorating, she began researching the causes and potential therapies for blindness. She had been a patient in the NIH's Age-related Eye Disease study and had developed a friendship with NIH scientists at the National Eye Institute. In particular, she came to know and became friends with Dr. Anton Hakola, one of the leading researchers in the vision restoration lab.

From that friendship she learned of some avant-garde research that was arousing the interest of the research ophthalmology community. With the development of microcircuity electronics, some scientists believed that eventually the technology would be developed that could produce an artificial eye. In effect, it would be a miniature camera that converted images into electrical impulses that could be fed directly into the occipital lobe of the brain, thus by-passing a damaged eye. At the point Dr. Bollinger heard about these ideas, the research was in its earliest stages. Very few animal studies had been completed. She knew that eventually researchers would want to attempt the development of this technology in humans who could give much more precise feedback on the placing of the electrodes into the brain.

After extensive research on the safety and potential effectiveness of this line of research, Dr. Bollinger gradually came to the conclusion that she would be the ideal research subject. She was blind; had a deep interest in developing such technology; and had the scientific capacity to understand the risks and to cooperate with the investigators. She also had large amounts of time available. She offered her services to Dr. Hakola.

At first he was hesitant but came to believe that Dr. Bollinger understood exactly what she was doing and could, in fact, be a significant contributor to the research. She understood that the research would involve cutting a half-dollar-sized hole in her skull through which researchers could pass electrodes. Similar work had been done over the years to map the location of motor and sensory areas of the brain, but these experiments were often done on patients who needed to have their skulls opened for some therapeutic purpose. This project would involve a much larger hole, and it would be undertaken solely for research purposes.

A protocol was developed and presented to an internal IRB a hospital board responsible for reviewing research to assure subjects are protected. Several members of that board questioned the research on the grounds that it posed risks that were too great and that the research must first be developed in lower animal species before being tried in humans. After extensive debate the IRB refused to approve the proposal until further animal studies were completed. These could take 2–3 years.

Dr. Bollinger was disturbed, indeed annoyed, at the IRB decision. She understood that she was very unlikely to benefit from the study. Surely the first results would produce nothing more than a crude visual image of light and dark patterns, and that could take many years. She was unlikely to live long enough for the technology to be perfected. On the other hand, she felt a close identification with the community of the visually impaired and felt she had a moral right to make her unique contribution as long as scientists were willing to accept her as a research subject. She was willing to sign any legal release from liability that seemed necessary. If Dr. Bollinger and Dr. Hakola both find this research at this time to be moral and the informed consent is impeccable, are there moral standards to which the IRB can appeal that would justify delaying the research?

COMMENTARY

The question raised by Dr. Bollinger's offer to volunteer for avant-garde research deals with the substantive questions of the ethics of human subjects research as well as the ethics of informed consent. These will be explored further in the cases in Chapters 16 and 17, respectively. Here the problem needing attention is where the parties should turn to find the source of his moral obligation in this case.

The patient is making a moral claim. She feels a moral right and perhaps even an obligation to contribute to a community of people with whom she shares a special interest in therapies to overcome blindness. Dr. Hakola is probably similarly motivated by compassion for those who could benefit from his research. The IRB seems to have concluded that, even with impeccable consent from an ideally informed subject who is a member of the class of patients who will eventually benefit from the research, it has a duty to impose moral standards on the research.

In some cases, committees such as IRBs may feel obliged to impose restrictions on research to protect the institution from lawsuits or news stories that could damage the institution's reputation. If this was what was driving the IRB, their appeal would not be a moral one. Moral appeals require a more ultimate grounding, not merely to the legal or financial interests of the institution. In this case, the IRB seems to believe that it is immoral, not merely imprudent, to permit a human subject to undertake risky research unrelated to therapy before adequate laboratory and nonhuman animal studies have been done.

Two counter-positions seem possible. One is that ethics is merely a matter of personal judgment about what is right or wrong so that, if Dr. Bollinger and Dr. Hakola both find moving directly to human studies acceptable, there is no basis for objecting provided they have an adequate understanding of their decision. Since the potential subject and the investigators are both well-trained scientists with considerable experience in this line of research, there can, in principle, be no moral objection to their proceeding.

The other possibility is to concede that morality is not merely a matter of personal judgment; it rests in some definitive, objective external standard. It could be, however, that in cases like this the general moral rule against moving to risky research on human subjects before animal studies have been completed needs a sophisticated qualifier that takes into account the moral perspectives of the potential subject, her moral commitment to her group, and her unusual level of knowledge and understanding. It could be that a carefully crafted moral rule would allow for this particular subject to volunteer, perhaps even acknowledge that she is morally obligated to volunteer. That is a conclusion quite different from the claim that morality can be reduced to personal preference or judgment.

GROUNDING ETHICS IN RELIGIOUS OR PHILOSOPHICAL PERSPECTIVES

Health professionals sometimes find that they or the people with whom they are interacting claim they are grounding their ethical positions not in professional codes, public policy, or the opinions of physicians, hospitals, or patients, but see them as coming from certain religious or philosophical perspectives. The problem can be especially acute when, as in the following case, one's own religious or philosophical perspective may conflict with the codified ethic of the profession or one's institution.

CASE 3-5

Abortion in a Catholic Hospital

Natasha Jones was a 34-year-old, unmarried black woman pregnant for the fourth time. She was being seen in the prenatal clinic at the community's only tertiary care Catholic hospital because she had a history of three previous episodes of ruptured uterus that had resulted in the deaths of her previous fetuses. She was currently in her twentieth week of pregnancy. She was a member of a local Baptist church.

Dr. Lakisha Nevitt, her attending physician, was very concerned because ultrasound revealed a portion of Ms. Jones's uterine wall was no more than a millimeter in thickness. She was convinced it would soon rupture ending the life of the fetus and posing a serious risk to Ms. Jones's life. It was her opinion that with virtual certainty the uterus would rupture before the fetus could reach full term.

Dr. Nevitt knew that, since the hospital had a Roman Catholic affiliation, abortion could not be performed there. Even though Dr. Nevitt was herself not Catholic, she accepted this stance when she went to work at this hospital. Even if an exception could be made in this case to preserve the life of the mother, no one in the hospital's obstetrics department had enough experience with abortion to perform one safely. The real issue was whether they should advise Ms. Jones of the seriousness of her situation and recommend that she be transferred to City Hospital, which was only a mile away and had a staff with considerable experience with abortion.

Dr. Nevitt asked for a hospital ethics committee meeting to try to sort out the options. There was a quick consensus among the medical people on the committee that this was a life-threatening situation and that Ms. Jones's uterus would almost certainly rupture well before a full-term birth. The ethics committee included two Catholic chaplains, both of whom emphasized that since they were in a Catholic institution, they must begin with the presumption that all life, including fetal life, is sacred and cannot be intentionally terminated. The "Ethical and Religious Directives for Catholic Health Care Services" was cited, which states categorically, "Abortion (that is, the directly intended termination of pregnancy before viability or the directly intended destruction of a viable fetus) is never permitted."[18]

One of the committee members raised the question of whether an exception can be made for preserving the life of the mother. He pointed out that it seems sad to condone the death of both mother and fetus when at least the mother could be saved. Since this was an extremely rare case where there was virtual certainty that the mother could not survive the rupture and that, if this occurred, the fetus would die as well, he urged making an exception by informing the woman that their committee recommend that she be transferred to a secular hospital such as City Hospital.

One of the chaplains responded pointing out that the prohibition was exceptionless. The only possibility would be to interpret the intervention as an "indirect" killing of the fetus, which would be acceptable for proportionally good reasons. This, he indicated, was the reasoning used in cases in which a pregnant woman has cancer of the uterus. In such cases a hysterectomy is permitted to remove the cancer even though the fetus would die in the process. He suggested that perhaps a hysterectomy could be acceptable in this case as well since the weakness in the uterine wall would pose a threat to the woman not only in this pregnancy but in any future pregnancies as well. He acknowledged that this reasoning was controversial, but thought it would justify a recommendation from the committee that the patient be directed to the City Hospital. He noted that legally the hospital was not required to have staff to perform abortions, but that they were required to inform the patient of treatment options—including transferring to another hospital that would offer abortion services.

The committee members recognized that, if this case had arisen in any other hospital without an institutional commitment opposing all direct abortions, a recommendation for terminating this pregnancy would be reached by easy consensus.

The dilemma here is how the moral stance of the sponsors of the hospital should shape the way medicine is practiced in this institution.

COMMENTARY

The substantive issues of abortion will be taken up in the cases of Chapter 10.

Here the problem is what role the hospital ethical commitment and the moral framework of a religious community should play in deciding how to handle a controversial case. In almost all hospitals this patient would receive a strong recommendation to terminate the pregnancy in order to save the patient's life. This seems to be the rare case in which medical science can present no good alternatives if the risk to the woman is to be avoided.

That the Catholic Church has a well-developed position on abortion is widely known. When the church operates hospitals, it insists on its right to rely on its moral stance in operating an obstetrics department. Most people understand this and accept it even if they do not agree substantively with the church's stance. The problem here is to what extent that stance can shape the behavior of the staff including presentation of options to patients.

Those who developed and run this hospital presumably accept the main tenets of the church's teachings. This includes the metaethics, that is, the general theory of how one can know what is morally right and wrong. In the case of the Catholic Church, its teachings hold that morality can be known by reason aided by revelation, by reflection on the moral laws of nature. Moral authority resides with the scripture, tradition, the Pope, and church councils, all of which aid reason in discerning the content of the natural law. Those in the Catholic tradition acknowledge these sources of moral knowledge, which get reflected in teachings from the Vatican as well as national bodies such as the American Council of Bishops, the group responsible for the "Ethical and Religious Directives for Catholic Health Care Services," the source cited in the ethics committee meeting. Since those committed to the moral tradition around which this hospital is organized accept this metaethical view, there is reason why it would be reflected in the policies of the hospital and its ethics committee.

The professional staff of the hospital, including Dr. Nevitt, should be made aware when they accept employment at a hospital that it is committed to a particular medical ethical tradition. This seems rather different from entering a profession such as medicine. When one chooses to go to medical school and become a physician, one usually does not think of these choices as committing to a metaethical theory about where ethical norms are grounded. Committing to a religious tradition, in contrast, seems to imply a general acceptance of that tradition's views about the foundation of ethics (even if individuals may conscientiously depart from those views on some occasions). Working or receiving care in a religiously sponsored institution carries with it some implication that one is willing, to some extent, to accept that view of moral norms. In this particular case, the religiously sponsored institution may confront some legal requirements—the requirement of adequately informed consent including presentation of reasonable alternatives for treatment—that conflict with the institutional understanding of what is morally required.

The patient may be left in an awkward position. In this case, Ms. Jones became a patient at this hospital for prenatal care. When patients become involved with a hospital they may or may not understand that they are committing to an institution that operates based on a moral tradition of its sponsors.

Follow-up: Ms. Jones was informed by Dr. Nevitt that her pregnancy posed a very serious threat to her life. She was informed that this hospital was sponsored by the Catholic Church and therefore could not endorse an abortion even though her condition was life threatening. In conformity with legal requirements, she was told that abortion services were available at City Hospital and that she was free to transfer to that institution.

When she learned of this, Ms. Jones appeared deeply disturbed. She told them she had no principled objections to abortion, but that she had chosen a Catholic hospital because she knew this was her last chance at having a baby. She was going to carry this child through to a live birth or die trying.

Once the clinical team understood the strength of her commitment, they reoriented to the task of providing carefully monitored support for her as an inpatient. On the basis of careful review they determined that she could probably carry the pregnancy until between thirty and thirty-two weeks, at which time they could deliver the baby by Caesarian section. They explained to her that the longer they waited, the better it would be for the baby, but the greater the risk to the mother. They eventually agreed to attempt to wait until the 30–32-week period before intervening.

NOTES

[1] American Medical Association. Council on Ethical and Judicial Affairs. *Code of Medical Ethics: Current Opinions with Annotations*, 2006–2007. Chicago, IL: AMA Press, 2006.

[2] American Nurses Association. *Code of Ethics for Nurses with Interpretive Statements*. Washington, DC: American Nurses Association, 2001.

[3] American Dental Association Council on Ethics, Bylaws and Judicial Affairs. *ADA Principles of Ethics and Code of Professional Conduct*. Chicago, IL: American Dental Association, 1994.

[4] American Medical Association. *Code of Medical Ethics: Adopted by the American Medical Association at Philadelphia, May, 1847, and by the New York Academy of Medicine in October, 1847*. New York: H. Ludwig and Company, 1848.

[5]   American Medical Association. *Current Opinion of the Judicial Council of the American Medical Association.* Chicago, IL: American Medical Association, 1981.

[6]   American Medical Association. *Code of Medical Ethics: Adopted by the American Medical Association at Philadelphia*, p. 13.

[7]   "Code of Ethics of the American Pharmaceutical Association." *Proceedings of the National Pharmaceutical Convention, Held at Philadelphia, October 6th, 1852.* 2nd ed. Philadelphia, PA: Merrihew & Son, 1865, pp. 24–26.

[8]   "Code of Ethics of the American Pharmaceutical Association (Adopted August 17, 1922)." *Journal of the American Pharmaceutical Association* 11 (No. 9, 1922):728–729.

[9]   "Code of Ethics of the American Pharmaceutical Association, 1952." *Journal of the American Pharmaceutical Association* 13 (1952):721–723.

[10] The texts of these and previous editions of the APhA codes appear in Buerki, Robert A. and Louis D. Vottero. *Ethical Responsibility in Pharmacy Practice*, 2nd ed. Madison, WI: American Institute of the History of Pharmacy, 2002.

[11] American Pharmaceutical Association. *Code of Ethics for Pharmacists.* Washington, DC: American Pharmaceutical Association, 1995.

[12] American Medical Association. *Current Opinions of the Council on Ethical and Judicial Affairs of the American Medical Association—1986: Including the Principles of Medical Ethics and Rules of the Council on Ethical and Judicial Affairs.* Chicago, IL: American Medical Association, 1986, section 2.19, page 13.

[13] American Medical Association. *Council on Ethical and Judicial Affairs. Code of Medical Ethics: Current Opinions with Annotations*, Chicago, IL: American Medical Association, 1994, section 2.20, p. 37.

[14] Sacred Congregation for the Doctrine of the Faith. *Declaration on Euthanasia.* Rome: Sacred Congregation for the Doctrine of the Faith, May 5, 1980.

[15] May, William E., Robert Barry, Orville Griese, et al. "Feeding and Hydrating the Permanently Unconscious and Other Vulnerable Persons." *Issues in Law and Medicine* 3 (No. 3, 1987):203–217.

[16] The United Methodist Church. "Faithful care of Dying Persons," *Social Principles.* Available on the internet at http://archives.umc.org/interior.asp?ptid=1&mid=1734, accessed August 30, 2006.

[17] This case is adapted from Haddad, Amy. "Ethical Issues Related to Splinting." In *Introduction to Splinting: A Clinical Reasoning and Problem Solving Approach*, 3rd ed. Brenda Coppard and Helene Lohman, editors. St. Louis, MO: Mosby, 2008, pp. 436–446. Case is on page 442.

[18] United States Conference of Catholic Bishops. *Ethical and Religious Directives for Catholic Health Care Services.* Washington, DC: United States Catholic Conference, 2001, directive 45.

PART 2

Ethical Principles in Medical Ethics

CHAPTER 4

⌒

Benefiting the Patient and Others: The Duty to Do Good and Avoid Harm

Other Cases Involving Benefit–Harm Issues

One way to approach medical ethical decision-making is to examine principles that describe general characteristics of actions that tend to make them morally right. In the introduction, the principles of beneficence (doing good), non-maleficence (avoiding harm), fidelity, respect for autonomy, veracity, avoiding killing, and justice are mentioned. Ethical problems in medicine often involve conflicts between these principles. In other cases, the moral problem arises over the interpretation of one of these principles.

The idea that it is ethically right to do good, especially good for the patient, is one of the most obvious in health care ethics. The Hippocratic Oath has the physician pledge to "benefit the patient according to [the physician's] ability and judgment."[1] The Declaration of Geneva, the modern rewrite of the Hippocratic Oath by the World Medical Association, limits benefit to "health" but similarly commits to patient benefit stating that "the health of my patient will be my first consideration."[2] The other health professions contain similar commitments to patient welfare. The 1994 American Pharmaceutical Association Code of

Ethics says that "A pharmacist promotes the good of every patient in a caring, compassionate, and confidential manner."[3] The American Nurses Association in 2001 adopted a revised version of its Code of Ethics holding that "the nurse's primary commitment is to the health, well-being, and safety of the patient...."[4] These are all versions of the principle of doing good for the patient. While this seems so obvious as to be platitudinous, in fact, many serious moral problems arise over the interpretation of this principle.

First, even if it is agreed that the benefits and harms that ought to be the focus of the health professional's concern are the patient's, there is still considerable room for controversy. The concepts of benefit and harm, themselves are controversial. Sometimes these are defined in a way that is purely subjective, in which case a benefit or a harm may be whatever the individual finds valuable. In other views, a benefit or a harm may be thought to be objective so that, for example, we might say that a patient suffers a harm even though the patient does not see it that way. The first group of cases provides an opportunity to sort out exactly what it means to benefit the patient and protect the patient from harm.

Equally controversial is the question of whether the health professional should limit his or her concern to benefits and harms that accrue to the patient alone. For example, what if protecting the patient will come at considerable risk of harm to society in general or to specific identifiable people who are not patients? What if the interests of the profession conflict with those of the patient? Or what if doing what is necessary to help the patient conflicts with the interests of the health professional's family? Is it obvious that the health professional should always place the patient's interest above those of his or her family? These are the problems of the cases in this chapter.

BENEFITING THE PATIENT

Assume for the time being that it is agreed that an important moral principle is that the health professional should act so as to benefit the patient. Even limiting our concern to this apparently simple principle turns out to raise serious problems of interpretation. For example, many ethical systems take as their goal producing good results for people. The first case in this section forces the health professional to decide what should happen when nonhealth benefits might outweigh the health risks of a medication. Later cases examine the relation between producing good and avoiding harm for the patient and between determining the good produced by various rules rather than the good in individual cases.

Health in Conflict with Other Goods

Health professionals are normally committed to restoring, maintaining, or improving the health of patients. Health is viewed by virtually everyone as good, as something intrinsically desirable. Yet there are many other goods that rational people desire as well. These include knowledge, aesthetic beauty, and psychological and material well-being. Often, unfortunately, these various goods that people want to pursue compete for scarce resources including time, money, and energy. Deciding what mix of goods is the proper one is a complex and highly individual decision. Normally, however, rational people would not choose to give absolute priority to one of these goods over another. Just as people constantly sacrifice their future material well-being for pleasures of the moment, so they also make some compromise with their health for other goods they consider important. The reasonable goal is not maximum well-being in any one sphere (including health), but maximum well-being across all kinds of possible goods.

This poses a problem for health professionals. They are experts, at most, in the good of health. Normally, they cannot claim to be expert in how to help people in other areas such as their finances, art appreciation, or social well-being. At best, they can advise how to maximize health. The Declaration of Geneva—a code of ethics written by the World Medical Association, a collection of professional organizations—commits the physician to promote the patient's "health" while the Hippocratic Oath commits him or her to the patient's "benefit" (not limiting attention to health). The current code of the American Pharmacists Association (1994) commits the pharmacist to the patient's well-being while the earlier 1981 version limited attention to the patient's "health and safety." The current code of the American Nurses Association (2001) at one point speaks of the nurse's primary commitment being to the patient's "health, well-being, and safety," thus identifying both the narrower "health" and the more expansive "well-being" as legitimate objectives for the nurse.[5] Part of the problem is that health professionals will not normally be in a position to advise about what really benefits patients, only, at most, about what serves their health. But rational people would not normally want to maximize their health; they would want to maximize their overall well-being. Thus if health professionals are committed first of all to the health and safety of patients, their patients should normally have somewhat broader interests (their total well-being even if it somewhat risks health and safety). On the other hand, if the health professional is committed to the overall well-being or "good" of the patient, he or she is going beyond his or her sphere of expertise. The following case illustrates the problem.

CASE 4-1

Stimulants as Performance Enhancer

Michael Chadwell was a 22-year-old medical student studying for his final exams in the first semester of his first year. He had been struggling all semester to keep up with the amount of reading and studying that was required. He had particular problems with pathophysiology and knew he was "on the bubble". He needed the best grade he could possibly get on the final to avoid a failing grade.

He simply had to cram for the exam day and night. About a month ago, Michael noticed that one of his classmates, Sheila Tan, always seemed to be alert and full of energy when the other members of their study group were flagging. When he asked how she had so much energy, she told him, "I take Xenadrine that you can get over-the-counter at any drugstore and phentermine which I can get on the internet." He asked her about the possibility of detection of the drugs because the university was a "drug free" environment and they had agreed to this when entering medical school. Sheila responded, "I was worried about that, but you would have to take a bucket of this stuff to have it show up in your urine." At the end of their conversation, Sheila had given him some of the phentermine to try. Michael had also bought some Xenadrine. He had not used either of them yet, but if there was ever a time he might need help in making it through the week, he reasoned, this was it.

He had never taken either of these drugs, so he was not sure of the effect. He was a little concerned that they might be more potent than Sheila let on because he had noticed lately that she had gotten quite thin and haggard looking. She told him, "I am only sleeping about 3 hours a night. I cannot wake up without these pills." He is not sure how much she is taking, though, and did not plan on taking more than a few pills a day to get him through this week of studying. Without it he felt sure he would not do well on the exam; with the drugs he might do well. He thought he had little to lose and an entire career to gain.

Should he take the Xenadrine and phentermine even though he knows there could be some serious side effects? What if it is discovered that he has broken the "drug free" policy of the School of Medicine?

COMMENTARY

Most cases in this volume involve ethical issues arising in a relationship between a health professional, but many medical choices are made outside of such relations. People choose whether to follow a regimen of exercise and diet, self-medicate for headache or muscle pain, or call for an appointment with a health professional. All of these are medical choices made daily by lay people. Some of them can involve important moral dimensions.

Michael Chadwell, the college student in this case, is facing such a choice. He faces a decision that poses some undeniable medical risk. Although Xenadrine is available over the counter, it is not without side effects. It once contained ephedrine but was reformulated after its toxicity became apparent. Its label now claims that it contains "natural herbs and amino acids." It includes caffeine. Phentermine, one of the ingredients in the diet combination known as "phen-fen," is still available, but restricted to prescription use. Nevertheless, it is available on the Internet without any direct contact with a physician. It can cause irritability, nausea, vomiting, and occasionally more serious cardiac problems as well as dependency. The benefits are essentially non-medical—a possible increased alertness that could produce improvement in performance on a critical medical school exam.

The common wisdom in both the medical professional and lay communities is that Michael's proposed plan is too dangerous. Deciding whether the risks are worth it is a complex issue, however. Michael does not have direct experience with the medication, but he is aware of a classmate who is pleased with its effects. He has heard of her experience, which appears to him to be worth the risks. Assessing risks and benefits of any medical treatment is inherently subjective. Not only does Michael know some things about how the drug affects him; he is also in a unique position regarding the benefits. He realizes the huge potential benefit—the difference between remaining in medical school and failing. For him, the risks seem worth the relatively large benefits. A physician is in a good position to assess the medical risks of a drug such as phentermine but is not well placed to assess the non-medical benefit and how that benefit compares with the medical risks.

Some medical ethicists claim that medicine should be used only to pursue medical benefit. They object to any interventions not designed to improve the patient's health, to cosmetic surgery, abortion and infertility treatment, and drugs for intentional euthanasia, for example. The idea is that there is an "internal morality" in medicine.[6] Its purpose is to promote health, not to strive for general human happiness.

Critics of this "internal morality" thesis reject the idea that medicine can only be used for promoting health. They claim there is no reason why medical science should not be used for promoting human well-being outside the realm of health. Goals external to medicine are also legitimate.[7] In that case, the choice facing Michael (and already faced by Sheila) becomes a matter of judgment about whether the great potential benefits justify the risks of taking the drug.

In addition to the risk–benefit questions in this case, there are some more subtle questions relating morality to law and social fairness. Sometimes, as in this case, the use of drugs for performance enhancement raises questions of legality. Drugs are bought on the black market rather than conforming to laws requiring that they be prescribed by a physician. Others might ask whether using drugs for performance enhancement amounts to cheating. The athlete who clandestinely uses steroids gains a competitive advantage that is reflected directly in having a different winner in a sports contest. Most would see this as raising questions of fairness. Whether Michael's use of these stimulants gives him an unfair competitive advantage over other medical students is a more complicated question. One might argue that he is already at a competitive disadvantage compared with Sheila, who is already using these stimulants. On the other hand, if some students use chemical stimulants, all others will be forced to use them or stand in a relatively disadvantaged place. The problem is similar to sports in which some competitors use chemical performance enhancers.

Finally, we should consider how Michael's physician should respond if he or she learns of Michael's use of the phentermine without his physician's involvement. We could even consider whether she should cooperate if Michael were to ask her to prescribe the phentermine for his new purpose. Although studying for exams is not a labeled use, it is not illegal for a physician to prescribe a legal drug for "off-label" use. Almost no physician would be willing to cooperate in this case, however. The more difficult question is what the physician should do if he or she discovers that Michael is using phentermine in this way. Surely, she should counsel Michael about the risks. She should realize, however, that her counsel could well be influenced by the fact that she is professionally committed to focus on the medical dimensions of drug use. Since there is essentially no medical benefit and very real medical risks, her counsel is likely to reflect how one sided the judgment is from a medical perspective. On the other hand, she would have no special expertise in evaluating the educational risks and benefits. She might consider reporting her patient, but it is not clear on what basis she could provide anything more than advice and counsel.

We are left with something of a dilemma for a medical ethic that strives, as the Hippocratic Oath does, to produce benefit for the patient. Not all benefits are health related. Some people may have goals in mind that are not primarily health related. They may be willing to take some risks with their health in order to try for non-medical benefits. Whether we pursue health-related benefit or total overall well-being will make a big difference. These are issues not only for these stimulants, but also for steroids, growth hormones, and other medications used for performance enhancement.

Conflicts among Health-Related Benefits

Many physicians faced with the tension between medical and non-medical benefits such as those in Case 4-1 decide that, since total well-being, including non-medical benefits, is well beyond the physician's expertise, they will limit their attention to the medical sphere. They conclude that at least in the medical realm they can determine what will benefit the patient. They may recognize that it will be up to the patient to determine whether to accept the doctor's recommendation about what is medically beneficial or reject that advice in favor of some non-medical good. They, in effect, adopt a more modest ambition of focusing on the narrower sphere of medical benefit. Even here, however, controversy can arise. Several kinds of medical benefit can be pursued. In the mid-twentieth century the assumed goal was to preserve life, even preserve life at all costs, but since then other goals have been considered as well, goals such as curing disease, relieving suffering, or preserving health. The next case requires a choice among these medical goals.

CASE 4-2

Is an Operation a Benefit for a Hospice Patient?

Ms. Helen Heyn, a 40-year-old woman, was HIV+ for many years before she developed multicentric lymphoma of the brain, cytomegalic inclusion retinitis, and disseminated Kaposi's sarcoma of the thigh and groin that was treated with irradiation. On referral to Hurley Hospital, she was considered terminally ill. Ms. Heyn was transferred to a local hospice. Two months later, on the order of the hospice physician, Erwin Billings, MD, she was transported to the surgical E.D. at Hurley for treatment of deep vein thrombosis (clot formation) of the left thigh. Such a thrombosis can result in a large clot breaking off and moving to the lungs, a fatal result in some cases. The E.D. physician, Christine Vaughn, agreed with the diagnosis but did not agree that Ms. Heyn should be admitted, particularly since such a patient can be treated with anticoagulants rather than by operation. She referred her back for hospice care. Dr. Vaughn disagreed with Dr. Billings's assessment that treating the deep vein thrombosis would count as a benefit. Dr. Vaughn reasoned that she would suffer less from a fatal embolism to the lungs (that was not certain to happen) than from the lingering experience of AIDS sequelae or from convulsive seizures due to the brain cancer. How should these physicians resolve their disagreement?

COMMENTARY

In this case two physicians, the medical director of the hospice and the E.D. doctor who received the patient back from the hospice appear to be in something of a dispute about what is best for Ms Heyn. Each is focusing on what most people would recognize as medical benefits. They are not extending their assessment of patient benefit to educational, financial, legal, or other spheres of her well-being. Nevertheless, they are not in agreement about what is best.

When she entered the hospice, her diagnosis was a terminal one—HIV, multicentric lymphoma of the brain, and a Kaposi's sarcoma. The definition of "terminal illness" is remarkably difficult to pin down. It implies a medical condition from which one is declining relatively rapidly toward death regardless of medical intervention, but there is no agreement on exactly how long "rapidly" is or when one should be placed in the category of the terminally ill. For hospice benefit purposes, the prognosis should be one of less than six months to live. Few would disagree that Ms. Heyn is terminally ill. Nevertheless, it does not automatically follow that Ms. Heyn is ready for hospice care, which implies she should receive only palliative care rather than interventions designed to prolong life. Many would accept the conclusion, however, that, if they were in Ms. Heyn's situation, they would prefer hospice-type treatments.

Even though Dr. Billings is the medical director of a hospice, he seems to have a different assessment of what would be in the best interest of Ms. Heyn. Since she has developed a potentially lethal thrombosis that could be treated by clot removal, he believes she should be transported back to the hospital in order to have the procedure. Let us assume that having the operation would increase the chances that Ms. Heyn would survive longer but leave her facing her terminal prognosis from the HIV, lymphoma, and sarcoma. She will still be expected to live less than six months, although she increases the chance of living more of those six months if she has the surgical intervention.

Dr. Vaughn, the E.D. physician, accepts the diagnosis, but disagrees with the decision to operate on the thrombosis. She points to the option of treatment with anticoagulants. It should be apparent that the physicians do not share the same view about what would count as a medical benefit. One option, the one preferred by the hospice medical director, Dr. Billings, is designed to maximize life expectancy (even though that life postoperatively would still be relatively short). Dr. Billings seems to interpret medical benefit to be measured in terms of maximizing life prolongation. Dr. Vaughn interprets medical benefit in terms of maximizing comfort including avoiding discomfort that will come from AIDS sequelae and brain cancer.

There are several different goals of medical intervention including prolonging life, relieving suffering, curing disease, and maintaining health. In this case maintaining health and curing disease are beyond the capacity of medicine. There are real trade-offs, however, between prolonging life (for a while) and avoiding suffering. Both doctors seem to believe that there is some objective basis for making these trade-offs. It is not clear to what medical science they could appeal to resolve this dispute. Many would argue that there is no definitive, objective basis for deciding priorities among these goods, even within the medical sphere.

From the available information, we do not know whether Ms. Heyn was consulted with and/or understood the choice either to be transferred to the hospital or to be admitted to the hospital for possible surgical treatment of the blood clot in the thigh. Presumably, she did understand her basic condition and "terminal" state. If there is no objective, scientific basis for deciding how to balance life prolongation and avoidance of suffering, it is understandable that physicians might disagree just as lay people could. In such cases, the question arises of whether the patient should be given the authority to determine what would produce the most good from her point of view rather than having a physician consider "quality of life" in deciding on appropriate care for her.

Deciding what will benefit a patient is difficult (some would say impossible) for a physician to do objectively even when the benefit is limited to the medical outcome. It becomes a more complicated question if non-medical costs to the patient are included or if one should factor in those needs of others who would be denied access to needed treatment if limited resources are devoted to Ms. Heyn. These problems of relating patient benefit to the welfare of others will arise in the last four cases in this chapter as well as in the resource allocation cases of Chapter 5. Before turning to that problem, we need to address another dimension of the duty to benefit patients and avoid harm to them: how assessment of benefit should relate to anticipated harms.

Relating Benefits and Harms

After the problem of relating health benefits to overall benefits is solved, a second question needs to be addressed if the health professionals and patients are to figure out what it means to do what will benefit the patient. Often the intervention that offers the greatest prospect for benefit is also most risky; it offers not only the greatest good but also the greatest risk for harm. How is one to relate the benefits and harms in attempting to determine what will produce the most good?

One possibility is to approach the problem arithmetically. The benefits could be viewed as "pluses" and the harms as "minuses" on a common scale. According to this view, the harms are subtracted from the goods to determine what course will do the most "net" good. This is the position of many utilitarian philosophers. It is sometimes identified with the great nineteenth-century British utilitarian Jeremy Bentham.[8] In carrying out such mental calculations, one has to factor in the probability of each envisioned benefit or harm. Some of these benefits and harms are rather easily quantifiable, such as expected numbers of years of life added with an intervention. Others, such as pain and suffering or the benefit of getting to see a loved one, can, at best, be approximated. Policy analysts have developed sophisticated strategies for estimating such benefits and harms. For example, the quality-adjusted life year (QALY) method is designed to take into account not only number of years of life but also the quality of the years.[9]

It is not obvious morally that it is correct to pursue the course of action that is expected to produce the greatest net good. Many believe there are moral constraints on such actions based on other moral principles, which are to be explored in cases in later chapters. But even for those who limit their ethics to beneficence and nonmaleficence, to doing good and avoiding evil, there are problems.

For example, one might try to maximize the benefit/harm ratio rather than maximize the net goods. This approaches the problem of relating benefits and harms geometrically rather than arithmetically. If one imagines two courses, the second of which has twice the expected benefit and twice the expected harm, according to the ratios method there is no difference between the two, but according to the method of subtracting harms from benefits, the option with twice the benefits and twice the harms would produce a net gain that is twice as large as the alternative. According to the arithmetic method, one is always obliged to choose the high-gain/high-risk option, while according to the ratios approach the two options would be treated as equally attractive.

Still another way of relating benefits to harms is to give nonmaleficence, the duty to avoid harming, a moral priority over beneficence. According to this view, the duty to not harm is more stringent than the duty to help. One is morally free to try to help only when one is sure that harm will not be done. In contrast to the approaches that calculate net good done or ratios, giving priority to avoiding harm gives a preference to the more cautious course. In fact, if carried to an extreme, it would always lead to doing nothing. In that case, at least one will have avoided harming (even though one would also have missed opportunities to do good and to prevent harm). The following case provides an opportunity to compare different ways of weighing benefits and harms of alternative courses of action.

CASE 4-3

The Benefits and Harms of High-Risk Chemotherapy

Joe Cavanaugh, a 58-year-old professor of economics, was diagnosed with chronic myelogenous leukemia (CML) several months ago. Though this particular type of leukemia is somewhat less responsive to chemotherapy, Dr. Cavanaugh responded well to a course of busulfan and hydroxyurea, which he took orally shortly after his diagnosis. Dr. Cavanaugh's last blood count indicated that his white blood count was greatly reduced. During the course of his chemotherapy, Dr. Cavanaugh had become close to Heather Eyberg, Pharm.D., the clinical pharmacist in the cancer treatment center.

After a follow-up visit with the oncologist, Dr. Cavanaugh stopped by Dr. Eyberg's office. Dr. Cavanaugh said,

> The doctor has suggested several possibilities regarding my treatment. I trust you, and I would appreciate your opinion on my options. The doctor said that now that I have finished taking the oral chemotherapy, I could start interferon alpha or, if I want to be "cured," I should think about a stem cell transplant. The type of leukemia I have can rapidly change from this chronic phase into acute leukemia. If that happens, it is unlikely that anything would help, and I would not have long to live. The doctor wants me to think about a stem cell transplant. He said I could remain in this latent phase for years, but there is no way of knowing. Or I could have high-dose chemotherapy and stem cell transplant. What do you think?

Dr. Eyberg respects Dr. Cavanaugh and his capacity to understand the risks and benefits involved regarding stem cell transplantation. She knows that allogenic hematopoietic stem cell transplantation (HSCT) is the only therapy proven to cure CML. If Dr. Cavanaugh has a sibling that is a match and has the HSCT within the first year of his diagnosis, he has a better five-year survival rate than those who undergo HSCT after the first year of diagnosis. The two options presented to Dr. Cavanaugh are essentially: watch, wait, take the interferon alpha and hope that the disease never progresses to the blastic phase or take a chance on HSCT now. The risks of HSCT are substantial. The possibility of infection and other complications is very high. It is not inconceivable that Dr. Cavanaugh could die from the HSCT itself.

Since Dr. Eyberg is part of the cancer treatment team, she is unsure of where her moral commitment should lie. Should she counsel Dr. Cavanaugh to choose the least harmful course of therapy? The conservative route would probably be to watch and wait and take the interferon alpha. Yet, if the disease progresses to acute leukemia, there is little anyone could do to help Dr. Cavanaugh. However, Dr. Cavanaugh could be in the percentage of patients who never progress to this fatal phase of the disease. Even if he eventually did change to the blastic phase, Dr. Cavanaugh might have many good years with his wife and children until then.

Dr. Eyberg could also counsel Dr. Cavanaugh to choose that option which maximizes the benefit for him. It is hard in this situation to determine which course of action will do the most good in the long run. Clearly, HSCT holds greater risk in the short run, but offers the potential for a cure of Dr. Cavanaugh's leukemia in the long run.

Finally, Dr. Eyberg is troubled by the memory of another patient with a similar diagnosis who recently chose the option of HSCT and did not survive the procedure. Given all of these considerations, Dr. Eyberg is not sure where to begin.

COMMENTARY

The issue in this case is whether there is a *moral* reason to prefer one course or the other. The health professional and the patient can consider the potential benefits and potential harms of the options. They would take into account not only the amount of benefit and harm, but also the probability that they will occur. Sometimes this is hard to do; often one can only estimate quantity and likelihood.

One approach favored by some ethical theories is to give a moral priority to avoiding harm, even to oneself. Sometimes this is expressed with the slogan *primum non nocere*, that is, first do no harm. Many assume this slogan comes from the Hippocratic Oath, but it does not. In fact, it is not found in ancient medical ethical writing that is known to modern scholars. The fact that it is in Latin is a clue that it is not from the Oath, which was written in Greek. Why it is normally rendered in Latin remains a mystery.

If there is a moral duty to give priority to avoiding harm (to the principle of nonmaleficence to use the technical term), then the correct moral advice would be to take the "safer" course and avoid the transplant. No one would then engage in a risky action that could be directly responsible for harming Dr. Cavanaugh, even causing his death. That might, of course, also mean losing a chance at producing great benefit, but those who give priority to not harming are willing to accept that consequence.

This suggests a second approach. Consider the possibility that Dr. Cavanaugh not only estimates the risk of the stem cell therapy greater, but also estimates the benefit greater in the same proportion. It could be that in comparing benefits and harms, the correct approach is to compare ratios of benefits and harms and choose the course that has the greatest ratio of benefit to harm. If the ratios were the same, then based on ratios one would be morally indifferent between the two choices. It would be a matter of taste.

A third approach is also possible. One could attempt to calculate the *net* benefit from the alternative courses. If Dr Eyberg or Dr. Cavanaugh feel that the chance of doing harm was greater with the transplant, but that the risk of harm was offset by the proportionally greater increase in benefit then the ratios would be the same, but instead of looking at the ratios, one could calculate the net benefit by subtracting the estimated harms from the estimated benefits. If the ratios were the same but the stem cell transplant posed both greater benefits and greater risk of harm, then the net difference (subtracting the harms from the benefits) would be greater for the stem cell transplant. If one were a Benthamite utilitarian, this would be the favored approach. One would be *morally* obliged to choose the course that would produce more net good, that is, the stem cell transplant.

Dr. Cavanaugh will favor the conservative therapy if he gives priority to not causing harm; he will favor the more experimental stem cell transplant if he looks at the net benefit; and he will be indifferent between the two if he focuses on the ratio of benefit to harm. In order for Dr. Eyberg to know how to advise Dr. Cavanaugh, she needs to know what the correct approach is to relating the benefits and the harms.

Benefits of Rules and Benefits in Specific Cases

Even if the health professional and patient solve the problem of relating benefits to harms as well as the problem of relating health to nonhealth benefits, there is still another difficulty in figuring out what will benefit the patient. Some people who calculate consequences do so with reference to the specific case considered in isolation. They look only at the effects of alternative actions in the specific case. Others are equally focused on consequences, but they are interested in the consequences of alternative rules. Those people, who were referred to as "rule utilitarians" in the introduction, hold that one should look at the consequences of alternative rules and choose the rule that produces consequences as good or better than any alternative. Then, once the rule is adopted, morality requires that it be followed without reassessment in specific cases. Only at the stage of adopting rules do consequences count according to this view. Some rule utilitarians oppose case-by-case calculations either for pragmatic reasons—because they think there is too much room for error in the heat of a crisis and is too time consuming. Others oppose case-by-case calculations for theoretical reasons—because morality is simply a matter of playing by the rules once they have been adopted. The following case illustrates how these two approaches to calculating consequences affect a physician's moral choices.

CASE 4-4

Physician Assistance in an ALS Patient's Suicide

Dr. Jim Witcher was a 57-year-old retired veterinarian who owned a horse farm in Louisiana.[10] He had amyotrophic lateral sclerosis (ALS—sometimes called Lou Gehrig's disease) that was gradually causing him to lose muscle control. He had been active on his farm and enjoyed caring for his horses but was now wheel-chair bound in a power-assisted chair. He could, with assistance, get out on his farm, but was losing the ability to feed himself. He worried about his gradual decline and loss of control. He also worried about the enormous costs that were depleting the resources set aside to support him and his wife during their retirement.

His wife provided around-the-clock care. She resisted suggestions that she place Dr. Witcher in a nursing home or even hire help for his care. Their children were grown and occupied, raising their own families. Dr. Witcher knew the burdens on his wife were enormous.

Dr. Witcher realized that he would soon lose all ability to consume food and medicine unaided and anticipated the day when he would not be able to hold his grandchild or even breathe on his own. He knew what he did when one of the horses under his care developed incurable disability. One day during a routine visit with his internist, he raised the question of why humans could not get similar assistance to quickly end their misery when their suffering and disability became unbearable.

His doctor told Dr. Witcher what he already knew. Physician assistance in suicide was illegal and violated the traditional norms of the physician's medical ethics. His physician pointed out that highly skilled and compassionate hospice care was available that would make his inevitable deterioration as comfortable as possible, but that he could not legally or ethically assist by prescribing or administering a lethal drug.

Dr. Witcher acknowledged that what he desired was illegal, but asked why the law could not be changed.

COMMENTARY

This case involves the ethics of physician-assisted suicide. A complete analysis must carefully differentiate it from the ethics of suicide that does not involve a physician's assistance as well as from physician euthanasia, what could be called "homicide on request." This moral and linguistic analysis will occur in detail in the cases of Chapter 9, which examines the ethics of medical killing. Here our focus is on how the assessment of benefits and harms should be handled in such cases.

Dr. Witcher is of the opinion that the burdens he and his family will suffer under any legal strategy for his terminal care will exceed the benefits. He believes that an active, intentional termination of his life at a point before the burdens become unbearable and the family resources are depleted will be, on balance, better than any alternative including compassionate hospice care. With ALS he is completely lucid mentally and has had many months to contemplate his alternatives. He has a stable, ongoing relationship with a personal physician. He would like for that physician to be able to actively assist in ending his life at the proper moment either by prescribing medication and instructing Dr. Witcher on how to use it (physician-assisted suicide) or actually administering a lethal injection (intentional mercy killing).

Many controversies could take place over whether Dr. Witcher has calculated the consequences properly. For discussion purposes, let us give him the benefit of any doubt and assume he has calculated correctly what will produce the best possible consequences for him and his family. It is possible that, even if he has correctly determined that assisted suicide is better for him than any alternative, it is still morally the wrong course.

One possibility that will be discussed in Chapter 9 is that intentional killing of a human, even for mercy, is simply a violation of some moral norm that prohibits such behavior—some principle of avoiding killing or the sacredness of life. Another possibility is that we cannot decide morality directly by analyzing the consequences on a case-by-case basis.

The real issue needing attention at this time is whether it is morally acceptable for Dr. Witcher and his physician to consider the benefits and harms of this specific act in isolation. If Dr. Witcher concludes that physician-assisted suicide would be morally right in this case, he seems to be claiming that whatever will produce the best consequences in an individual case determines what is moral. Judging the ethics of a decision by calculating the consequences of the individual action is what is sometimes called "act-utilitarianism."

Others, even some who believe ethics should be based on consequences, might conclude that, on balance, even though in this case it would be better for Dr. Witcher to have access to physician assistance in ending his life, the practice of permitting physicians to provide such assistance, whenever they thought the consequences justified it, would have such a bad result that it is better to affirm the rule, "physicians should never intentionally kill their patients even if they believe the consequences would be better than any alternative course…." If he took that position, he would be a rule-utilitarian.

Some support rule-utilitarianism on the practical grounds that the consequences of rigidly following some rules may be better in the long run than permitting individuals to decide on a case-by-case basis. Humans are fallible; they may miscalculate. Particularly, for irreversible decisions of such momentous importance as terminating human life, it may be better to follow a simple rule prohibiting intentional killing. Others may defend rule-utilitarianism on more theoretical grounds. It may simply be a matter that morality requires playing the "game" of life by a set of rules, moral rules in this case. Either way, those who are rule-utilitarian will choose the rule or set of rules that will produce the best consequences in the long run rather than applying calculations of benefit and harm to make decisions directly in the individual case.

While this might sound legalistic, it need not be viewed as a totally exceptionless position. A rule-utilitarian may tolerate exceptions in extreme cases. One might even build exception clauses into the rules. An exception clause might require that the consequences of violating the rule be overwhelming in order to justify making an exception.

The problem facing Dr. Witcher and his doctor is one of deciding whether they will calculate the consequences looking only at the specific case or whether they will calculate consequences of alternative rules and choose the rule that has the best consequences.

Benefiting Society and Individuals
Who Are Not Patients

The focus of benefit in the cases thus far in this chapter is the patient. Occasionally benefits to others emerged in the cases, but it was usually in a very marginal way. In other situations, the health professional appears caught between doing what will benefit the patient and doing something else that will have much greater benefit on other parties.

According to the classical Hippocratic ethic, the health professional was, in such cases, to choose to benefit the patient. The modern paraphrase of the Oath, The Declaration of Geneva, is not quite as unilaterally focused on the patient, but it has the physician pledge that "the health of my patient will be my first consideration."

As early as the nineteenth century, the writers of the professional codes began to realize that sometimes the moral obligation of the health professional extended beyond the individual patient. The emergence of public health in the nineteenth century made code writers realize that sometimes the health professional had to consider the welfare of the population as a whole. More recently, health professionals have recognized ethical tensions created by their obligation to others such as the family of patients, the profession as a whole, or to their own families. These cases raise this conflict between benefits to the patient and to others.

Benefits to Society

During the past century, health professionals have gradually reached the conclusion that they bear responsibilities not only to individual patients but also to the community. When the American Medical Association was first formed in 1847, it wrote a code of ethics that included a very brief final section that recognized the duty of the profession to society. Physicians were urged to be "ever vigilant for the welfare of the community."[11] The primary focus, however, was on the welfare of the patient. The revision of 1903 retained essentially the same wording. By 1957, when there was a major rewrite, the tenth of ten provisions seems to give slightly greater weight to the professional's obligation to society stating that "the responsibilities of the physician extend not only to the individual, but also to society...."[12] In the revision of 1980, the seventh and final principle held that "A physician shall recognize a responsibility to participate in activities contributing to an improved community."[13] In the most recent revision, in 2001, the association saw fit to reemphasize the primacy of the duty to the patient. The new eighth principle states, "A physician shall, while caring for a patient, regard responsibility to the patient as paramount."[14] Thus the pattern is one of organized American medicine struggling with the tension between a duty to benefit the individual patient, which is recognized as paramount, at least when dealing with the patient, and a duty to the broader society that persists in a secondary position. Many other codes of the health professions have incorporated similar notions of the health professional's duty to the community in addition to the individual patient.

The ethically difficult issue is what should happen when the health professional's opportunity to serve the public comes at the expense of the individual patient. They are variously asked to participate in medical research for the purpose of creating generalizable knowledge, in public health campaigns, and in cost containment efforts. None of these is ethically possible on strictly Hippocratic (individual patient welfare) grounds. The next case forces a physician to choose between serving a community of patients and an individual patient.

CASE 4-5

Blocking Transplant for an HMO Patient with Liver Cancer: Serving the Patient and Serving the Community

Rafael Villanueva was a 38-year-old venture capitalist with a serious liver problem. He had been diagnosed with a primary tumor of the liver at the HMO where he was a member. Mr. Villanueva had been asymptomatic during the early stages of the tumor's development. When he was diagnosed the tumor had grown to 5 cm in diameter, which meant it had developed to the point that it was beginning to pose a serious risk of metastasis. He was informed by his HMO heptologist, Dr. Edwards, that the only possible therapy was a liver transplant, but given the size of the tumor, it was not medically appropriate.

Dr. Edwards had researched the options. He discovered that the liver transplant center with which the HMO had a contract would not accept patients once the tumor size had reached 5 cm. They reasoned that the chances of metastatic disease were sufficiently great that the transplant was unlikely to succeed. On that basis, Dr. Edwards had told his patient that the transplant was not medically indicated.

Mr. Villanueva gradually realized that this was a death sentence. The liver cancer would continue to develop until it took his life. He began researching the treatment options. He had amassed a sizable estate and traveled internationally reviewing start-up enterprises in which he could invest. He discovered that there was general agreement in the transplant world that liver grafts should not be attempted once the tumor had reached this size, but that two centers in the United States and one in Sweden were performing transplants on an experimental basis.

On the basis of this discovery Mr. Villanueva returned to his HMO and asked if he could once again be considered, given the fact that death was the certain alternative. He expressed concern that his wife and small child would be left without a father and income provider, should he die. When Dr. Edwards again refused to recommend him for transplant, Mr. Villanueva discovered that he could appeal his clinician's decision.

The case was appealed to the Medical Director, the final HMO authority in such cases. The Medical Director, Dr. Florence Cunningham, received

Mr. Villanueva's appeal. After a week to investigate the facts, she again denied his request, citing both the clinical judgment that the transplant was not medically appropriate and the fact that one-year cancer-free survival following transplant in the programs doing experimental grafts for primary liver tumors was only 5–15 percent. If the tumor has not metastasized, the transplant will remove the cancer, but in most cases cancer cells will already have migrated beyond the liver. She also noted that livers for transplant were very scarce, life-saving resources and should not be used for patients who have such a small chance of successful transplant.

COMMENTARY

Two physicians at the HMO are involved in deciding that Mr. Villanueva should not be listed for a liver transplant. Their moral roles need to be analyzed separately. Dr. Edwards, the internist, would traditionally have been seen as having a Hippocratic duty to do what he thinks will benefit the patient. That may be what Dr. Edwards did in this case. He advised his patient that the transplant was not "medically indicated."

Part of the problem in this case is that the term "medically indicated" is vague and sometimes misleading. Sometimes it is used to mean that the treatment will produce an effect. Saying a treatment is not medically indicated can therefore mean it will not be effective for the patient's condition. When physicians say that antibiotics are not medically indicated for a viral infection, they mean the antibiotic will not have an effect on the virus. If the liver transplant would have no effect on Mr. Villanueva's cancer, the term could be used in this way. However, the transplant does have a chance of being effective; it has a 5–15 percent chance of producing a 1-year cancer-free survival. Nevertheless, that means an 85–95 percent chance that the transplant will not overcome the cancer. Moreover, transplant combined with immunosuppression therapy produces serious, burdensome side effects. Dr. Edwards could mean when he says that the transplant is not "indicated" that, even though the transplant has a small chance of working, he believes that the burdensome side effects outweigh any chance of benefit. The original Hippocratic Oath holds that benefit to the patient is to be determined by the physician's "ability and judgment." If Dr. Edwards believes that the burdens outweigh the benefits, this could be what he means by saying the transplant is not indicated.

Of course, Mr. Villanueva may have a different evaluation of the risks and benefits of the transplant. He may believe the 5–15 percent chance of success make the burdens worth it. If benefits and burdens are inevitably subjective, some would hold that it is the patient's judgment that should count.

There is another possible explanation of Dr. Edwards' claim that the transplant is not indicated. The internist never mentions that livers for transplant are a scarce, life-saving resource and that listing Mr. Villanueva for transplant could lead to using up a liver that otherwise could be used for another patient who would have a much better chance of a successful graft. Although clinicians are traditionally committed to focus exclusively on the welfare of their patients, they are increasingly pressured to consider the interests of other patients. Some interpretations of professional ethics summarize the clinician's duty as servicing the interest of "patients" rather than the single, isolated patient with whom the clinician is presently interacting. If the patient population as a whole is the proper target of clinician concern, then refraining from listing Mr. Villanueva in order to save the organ for some other needy patient would be more defensible. If that is Dr. Edwards' reasoning, he needs to face the question of what he conveys to Mr. Villanueva. He could plausibly be obligated to tell him that he bases his recommendation on his judgment about the interests of other patients as well as Mr. Villanueva.

The case also involves a second physician, the medical director, Dr. Florence Cunningham. It was to her that Mr. Villanueva appealed when he was denied a transplant listing. Dr. Cunningham is in a different position than that of the primary physician, Dr. Edwards. As medical director, she has responsibility for the joint welfare of all her patients, not just the one who is making an appeal. She may also be thought of as having responsibility to the HMO management and board of directors. Hence, she needs to take into account the welfare of all patients and maybe the economic interests of the HMO as well.

She never mentions the economic interest of the HMO in denying Mr. Villnueva's appeal. The cost of the transplant would have been about $200,000. Since the transplant has only about a 10 percent chance of success, she could have reasoned that it would cost $2,000,000 for one life saved. While medical people do not like to think in dollar terms, that is a very large amount to spend to save one life. Most insurers who understand medical economics would not be willing to spend that amount to save a life. Looked at from the point of view of the subscribers to the HMO, if they expected such expenditures, their premiums would be unacceptably high. Spending the same money on other life-saving interventions such as highway safety and health maintenance programs would be a much wiser investment.

Given these facts, all health insurers, including HMOs, have to set some implied limit on what they would be willing to pay for a chance at saving a life. Unless subscribers were willing to pay extremely large premiums, they should expect some decision-maker within the insuring organization to cap the longshot, expensive efforts at saving life. Had Dr. Cunningham, overtly said she was blocking the transplant because it would cost too much given the probability of saving a life, would she have been justified?

In fact, she did not appeal to this cost. She appealed to the fact that livers were scarce and that other lives could be saved if Mr. Villanueva were not listed. That raises the question of whether the medical director (or any gatekeeper within a health insurance system or HMO) has any moral responsibility to sacrifice patients' interest for the benefit of the society, in this case; the group of liver transplant candidates who would stand to benefit from having Mr. Villanueva excluded from the list. The lawyers who eventually represented Mr. Villanueva' wife after he died from a lack of a transplant argued that the medical director would be within her rights to claim that the economic interests of subscribers would justify not listing the patient, but that a medical director has no responsibility to sacrifice her patients for the good of others in society. In fact, the United Network for Organ Sharing, the national body responsible for organ allocation, has policies that control who should be listed and who should be excluded. The attorneys claimed that it would be their responsibility to decide whether Mr. Villanueva should be listed. In fact, he would have qualified for listing and, given his urgent medical situation, would have been given high priority for a transplant at any center willing to perform it.

Benefits to Specific Nonpatients

A variant on the problem in the previous case arises when the health professional can promote the interests of those other than the patient, and those others are specific, identifiable nonpatients. For example, the other person might be a member of the patient's family. Others in the family could have their psychological or economic interests jeopardized by offering an expensive experimental procedure to a patient when that procedure is very unlikely to work. A parent, in fact, may prefer that his or her own interests be subordinated to those of other family members. In other cases, the patient's interest may directly conflict with the interest of someone who is not a patient of the health professional. The patient may, as in the following case, threaten violence or an exposure to AIDS.

CASE 4-6

Intentional Exposure of Unknowing
Sexual Partners to HIV

In 1997 Nushawn J. Williams was twenty years old.[15] He was publicly identified by name as a drug dealer who in upstate New York and New York City had intentionally had unprotected sexual relations with as many as 300 women and adolescent girls, one as young as thirteen years of age. At least thirteen of them had since been found infected with HIV. Mr. Williams had learned of his HIV status the previous September while in Chautauqua County jail on a charge of stealing a car. He continued to be sexually active after being told by a public health nurse of his HIV status.

Mr. Williams kept a list of his sexual partners. Thus, it would be possible to identify them, contact them, and offer testing. In the case of pregnancies, treatment could be provided lowering the probability that the newborns would retain the infection. Mr. Williams, who claimed he suffered from schizophrenia, had many contacts with health professionals while in jail after being prosecuted by Chautauqua Country District Attorney, James Subjack. Although it has never been made public whether the diagnosis of schizophrenia has been confirmed, his claim provides a reason why his contacts with health professionals were so extensive.

Traditionally, health professionals owe a strict duty of confidentiality to their patients or clients. The World Medical Association's Declaration of Geneva states bluntly, "I will respect the secrets that are confided in me." It also states that "the health of my patient will be my first consideration."[16]

Other traditional codes require that the health professional remain dedicated to the welfare of the patient. In this case, however, the health professional who learns of Mr. Williams's aggressive and dangerous behavior would be aware that his sexual partners are at serious risk from his activity. Moreover, should they become pregnant, their children could receive life-saving benefit if the women are informed, diagnosed, and treated. Their future sexual partners also have a direct interest in learning of their situation. It is plausible that Mr. Williams has a legal, financial, and psychological interest in not letting this information be passed to the women he has exposed. If a health professional becomes aware of Mr. Williams's behavior and knows he has a list of the women he has exposed, is that professional's duty exclusively to serve the patient's interest or must he or she in determining their moral duty also take into account the interests of the women and those associated with them?

COMMENTARY

The underlying substantive moral issue in this case is the ethics of confidentiality. That topic will be addressed in detail in Chapter 13. In that chapter we will see that there are two moral arguments that could lead a health professional to consider breaching confidentiality: to serve the welfare of the patient and to protect others from the patient. Some patients may be engaging in behavior that is dangerous to themselves, which could plausibly be stopped only if confidentiality were broken. In other cases, the patient's interest will be served by maintaining confidentiality, but others could be helped dramatically if they were warned or treated.

We will examine these issues in the forthcoming chapter. Here we confront the more general underlying issue: is the health professional's duty to the patient and the patient exclusively, or do other parties have a claim on the health professional's attention? Here a nurse and perhaps others could have had an opportunity to intervene; by learning the identity of the sexual partners, they could be warned, tested, and treated. In turn, their further sexual partners and offspring could be protected. If, however, the first, primary, or sole duty of a clinical professional is to serve the patient's interests, then these other parties are off the agenda. Unless it could be argued successfully that it is in Mr. Williams's interest to have the sexual partners warned, the physician or nurse should keep quiet even if she learns of the partners' identity.

The question is whether the professional's duty is solely to the patient as the Hippocratic tradition suggests and is expressed in the modern paraphrase of the Oath in the World Medical Association's Declaration of Geneva, or, alternatively, whether physicians and other health professionals also have to take into account the interests of others.

In Case 4-5, we faced a similar problem, but there the potential beneficiaries if the physician cast a gaze beyond the patient was some unidentified person—the one who would gain an organ that would otherwise go to the patient with liver cancer and the ones who would pay smaller premiums if the money were saved that could be spent on the transplant. In the present case, a group of specific women and girls are the potential beneficiaries. Sometimes, in public health, the nurse or physician will claim that these identifiable people are really patients even though they are not interacting directly with the public health officer. The issue is whether the fact that they are identifiable individuals who are or could be some health professional's patients makes a moral difference.

This problem is sometimes referred to as the "statistical" lives problem. If a public health officer knows that statistically a hundred people will benefit from a public health campaign but has no idea who these beneficiaries are, is that morally different from the case of the public health officer who learns the specific identity of Mr. Williams' victims? If the clinical health professional's duty is to serve the patient, does the identifying of the patient—by name, age, and gender—change the nature of the moral relationship?

Benefit to the Profession

One of the possible groups other than patients that could command the attention of the health professionals is their professional group. Professionals often perceive that they have an obligation to the professional group, which commands loyalty that requires certain sacrifices on the part of the individual. This is sometimes thought to include an obligation to conform to the moral standards of the profession, a problem addressed in the cases of the previous chapter. It also is sometimes believed to include a duty to promote the good of the profession. Since physicians and other health professionals are traditionally thought to have a duty to promote the good of the patient, this raises an interesting problem when the good of the profession conflicts with the good of the patient. The following case poses the problem dramatically.

CASE 4-7

For the Welfare of the Profession:
Should Nurses Strike?

The nurses at University Hospital were showing all the signs of professional burnout—irritability, fatigue, and impatience. Owing to the worst nursing shortage in history, increasingly ill and fragile patients, and the "aging" of the nursing staff as a whole resulting in a number of retirements, the nurses who were left at the bedside were stretched beyond their limits. A large number of the hospital's 220 nurses met to discuss their dilemma.

One of the nurses, Anne Roberts, R.N., stated,

> We are at the point where our exhaustion is going to affect patient welfare. Additionally, I don't think any of us can continue to take this much stress. I think we have to take a stand, demand a salary increase commensurate with the work we are being asked to do, and ask for an increase in full time positions on the busiest units.

Another nurse added, "If we have to, I think we should go on strike." After considerable discussion, the majority of the nurses concurred. Ms. Roberts was not as certain about the strike as were her colleagues.

The union presented their demands to the hospital administration. The hospital administration was quite concerned about the nurses' threat to strike if their demands were not met. Although the nurses were required by law to give the hospital ten days notice to prepare for a strike, that was not a lot of time to transfer the hospital's sickest patients. Ms. Roberts watched with growing concern as it appeared a strike was imminent. She thought a strike might or might not be effective in changing the administration's mind. In other states where nurses had "walked out," the hospitals had merely hired registered nurses who were willing to cross the strike zone. She had heard that these replacement nurses sometimes made upwards of $5,000 per week. She knew of one strike that lasted more than a month. One thing was certain: the strike had the potential of exposing a substantial number of patients to inconvenience and perhaps even considerable risk. However, things could not continue the way they had been going. Ms. Roberts was not certain what she would do—stay or strike.

COMMENTARY

This case raises the question of whether the consequences should be used to evaluate a rule or should be applied directly to the individual case, an issue raised earlier in this chapter. The case is presented here, however, to examine what appears to be a conflict between the welfare of patients and the interests of the profession. The conflict Anne Roberts faces has the appearance of a conflict between the interests of patients in getting proper care and the interests of her professional colleagues in having tolerable working conditions. In fact she will have to do considerable work to sort out whose interests are in conflict here. The most obvious patient welfare issue is the interest of the patients who may need to be moved to other facilities during the strike. Other patient interests are at stake as well, however.

We might also ask if there are ways in which patients' interests would be served by the strike. In the longer run, the nurses could argue that they are really pursuing patients' interests by striking. After all, if the acuity of patients and short staffing increases, it is the patients who could be injured. Hence, in some ways this is a case of pitting one group of patients against another.

From another perspective, however, it might be that the interests of the profession and its members are in conflict with those of patients. On the one hand, the profession has traditionally claimed that its first interest was the well-being of patients. If that is so, then striking might be simultaneously a professional obligation and in the interest of those patients who will eventually benefit from the strike. On the other hand, the strike can be seen as serving the interests of the nurses, whose working conditions would eventually be made better (at the expense of those patients whose care will at a minimum be disrupted during the strike). It appears that the interests of the employees, then, does conflict with the interests of at least some patients.

This raises the question of whether "the interests of the profession" can be taken to equal the sum of the personal interests of the members of the profession. Is it possible that there is something called a professional interest beyond this interest of individual nurses? For instance, if nurses were objecting to a hospital's staffing policy that risked the quality of the nursing care in order to save money, would that count as a true "professional" interest that differs from the self-interest of nurses? If so, would that be legitimately on the nurse's agenda if this professional interest conflicted with those of the patient?

Benefit to the Health Professional and the Health Professional's Family

There is one final group of interests that could conflict with those of the patient: those of the health professional and his or her family. In the traditional Hippocratic health professional ethic, the only welfare that counted was that of the patient. There was never a formal recognition that the interests of the health professional could ever legitimately compete with those of the patient. Of course, health professionals have always recognized some limits to serving the patient. The following case explores those limits.

CASE 4-8

A Physician Choosing between His Patient and His Own Family

William Peters, a general surgeon in a small practice that included three general surgeons, two obstetricians, and two general practitioners, was on call on a weekend. His daughter, Suzy, was a high school senior who was scheduled to sing a solo in a major musical production that Saturday afternoon. Dr. Peters, perhaps unduly optimistic that he would not be called, failed to change the schedule with one of the other surgeons. Unfortunately, he was called to the phone just before Suzy was to make her debut. The call was from the emergency room: a 7-year-old boy who

Dr. Peters had seen a year earlier for appendicitis had sustained a full thickness laceration of the face, obviously requiring repair.

Dr. Peters immediately realized his dilemma: if he went to the hospital, he would miss being present for his daughter's long-practiced performance. He considered one of the other general surgeons in the practice but that seemed unfair to the colleague and would mean the boy would see a stranger rather than someone he would remember from their previous contact.

He guiltily stayed for her introduction and heard a few notes she sang, then left the auditorium. As he drove to the hospital, his frustration and disappointment grew. On arrival, the nursing staff had done the basic preparation; he briefly introduced himself and gave minimal information to the parents and to the child. As he repaired the injury, he complained about his personal sacrifice of the experience at the performance. Instructions were given for care of the wound and follow-up for office removal of the sutures. The father of the child later called Dr. Peters's office to notify the doctor that the child would not be brought back to him for further care.

COMMENTARY

Dr. Peters is challenged to find out whether he literally believes that the physician always works for the well-being of the patient. It is hard to see what else he could do, but miss his daughter's singing debut if his only concern is his patient's welfare. Presumably if that were his only concern, he would keep responding to emergency calls day and night until he became so stressed from ignoring his family that his patients' interests were jeopardized. Yet no health professional really would do this.

Dr. Peters also lives other roles in life. He is husband, father, neighbor, and citizen. He has made commitments in these other roles to work for the welfare of others in his life. He is also a person in his own right and has an interest in his own welfare. A utilitarian would resolve such conflicts by asking which course would do the most good taking into account the effects of all parties— his patient, his children, and everyone else including himself. Is this the way Dr. Peters should decide whenever he is on call on a weekend?

Suppose that Dr. Peters realizes that there are occasions in which he could do more good overall if he simply ignored his patients and did something good for a stranger. According to utilitarian reasoning, he should abandon his patient in such cases. What is the difference between Dr. Skinner's duty to his children, his patient, his colleagues, and strangers?

Dr. Peters faces an interesting set of choices. He could completely ignore his daughter and his interest in hearing her sing. He could completely ignore his patient and stay for her entire concert. He could also make some compromise. One would be to call a colleague. This would provide competent care for the boy even if it was not psychologically ideal since the boy would see a stranger rather than a surgeon who was an acquaintance. This would also be an inconvenience to the colleague and would test Dr. Peters's relation with him. The most interesting option is the one Dr. Peters chose—a compromise in which he attends some of his daughter's performance and yet provides adequate, if not ideal, attention to his patient. Dr. Peters could mentally calculate the benefits and harms of each of these options, but they do not all seem to have the same moral weight. For example, the inconvenience to his surgical colleague might not have the same claim as the interests of the patient. If he did not already have an existing relation with the patient, disrupting the colleague's weekend would be an option to consider.

One possibility is that these conflicts cannot be resolved ethically solely by looking at which course will do the most good. Perhaps one has to take into account other moral obligations grounded in principles other than beneficence and nonmaleficence, principles calling for distributing goods justly, respecting autonomy, telling the truth, keeping commitments, and avoiding taking human life as well as the amount of good that is done. Dr. Peters has special commitments to both his patients and his family. The problem in this case is that those special commitments conflict. The resolution may require abandoning the traditional maxim that health professionals owe to their patients a literal commitment to doing what is best for them. An intriguing feature of this case is that Dr. Peters can choose to balance the commitments to his patient and his daughter by picking the proportion of the performance he will see (and thereby determining how much time he will devote to his patient). In the next five chapters we shall examine how these moral principles other than beneficence and nonmaleficence are factored into moral decisions confronting health professionals.

NOTES

1   Edelstein, Ludwig. "The Hippocratic Oath: Text, Translation and Interpretation." In *Ancient Medicine: Selected Papers of Ludwig Edelstein*. Owsei Temkin and C. Lilian Temkin, editors. Baltimore, MD: The Johns Hopkins Press, 1967, p. 6.

2   World Medical Association. "Declaration of Geneva." Adopted by the 2nd General Assembly of the World Medical Association, Geneva, Switzerland, September 1948, revised periodically, most recently at the 173rd Council Session, Divonne-les-Bains, France, May 2006. http://www.wma.net/e/policy/c8.htm, accessed September 8, 2006.

3   American Pharmaceutical Association. *Code of Ethics for Pharmacists*. Washington, DC: American Pharmaceutical Association, 1995.

4   American Nurses Association. *Code of Ethics for Nurses with Interpretive Statements*. Washington, DC: American Nurses Association, 2001, p. 14. http://www.ana.org/ethics/code/protected_nwcoe303.htm, accessed September 8, 2006.

5 Ibid.
6 Pellegrino, Edmund D. "The Internal Morality of Clinical Medicine: A Paradigm for the Ethics of the Helping and Healing Professions." *Journal of Medicine and Philosophy* 26 (No. 6, 2001):559–579.
7 Beauchamp, Tom L. "Internal and External Standards for Medical Morality." *Journal of Medicine and Philosophy* 26 (No.6, 2001):601–619; Veatch, Robert M. "The Impossibility of a Morality Internal to Medicine." *Journal of Medicine and Philosophy* 26 (2001):621–664.
8 Bentham, Jeremy. "An Introduction to the Principles of Morals and Legislation." In *Ethical Theories: A Book of Readings.* A. I. Melden, editor. Englewood Cliffs, NJ: Prentice-Hall, Inc., 1967, pp. 367–390.
9 Weinstein, Milton C. and William B. Stason. "Foundations of Cost-Effectiveness Analysis for Health and Medical Practices." *New England Journal of Medicine* 296 (1977):716–721; Kaplan, R. M. and J. W. Bush. "Health-Related Quality of Life Measurement for Evaluation Research and Policy Analysis." *Health Psychology* 11 (1982):61–80; Mehrez, Abraham, and Amiram Gafni. "Quality-Adjusted Life Years, Utility Theory, and Healthy-Years Equivalents." *Medical Decision Making* 9 (1989):142–149.
10 This case is based on the PBS documentary, "On Our Own Terms: Moyers on Dying," which first aired September 10–13, 2000. More information and a study guide are available at http://www.pbs.org/wnet/onourownterms/about/index.html (accessed September 19, 2007).
11 American Medical Association. *Code of Medical Ethics: Adopted by the American Medical Association at Philadelphia, May, 1847, and by the New York Academy of Medicine in October, 1847.* New York: H. Ludwig and Company, 1848, p. 23.
12 American Medical Association. "Principles of Medical Ethics of the American Medical Association." *Journal of the American Medical Association* 164 (1957):1119–1120.
13 American Medical Association. *Current Opinion of the Judicial Council of the American Medical Association.* Chicago, IL: American Medical Association, 1981.
14 American Medical Association, Council on Ethical and Judicial Affairs. *Code of Medical Ethics: Current Opinions with Annotations, 2002–2003 Edition.* Chicago, IL: American Medical Association, 2002.
15 http://query.nytimes.com/gst/fullpage.html?res=9B06E1DC173AF93AA15752 C0A96E958260&sec=health&pagewanted=print, accessed September 15, 2006.
16 World Medical Association. "Declaration of Geneva," Adopted by the 2nd General Assembly of the World Medical Association, Geneva, Switzerland, September 1948, revised periodically, most recently at the 173rd Council Session, Divonne-les-Bains, France, May 2006. http://www.wma.net/e/policy/c8.htm, accessed September 8, 2006.

CHAPTER 5

~◯

Justice: The Allocation of Health Resources

Other Cases Involving Justice and Resource Allocation

In the previous chapter, the principles of beneficence and nonmaleficence—of doing good and avoiding harm—were introduced. One of the problems raised was the conflict between the welfare of the patient and the welfare of other parties. The utilitarian solution to this problem is to strive to maximize the total amount of good that was done regardless of the beneficiary. We saw that sometimes the utilitarian approach conflicted with the Hippocratic ethic, which requires that the health professional focus exclusively on the welfare of the patient.

Physicians and other health professionals often find themselves in situations in which the interests of their patients are in conflict. The care professional must choose between patients or between a patient and those who are not patients. Whether to provide health care services for those who cannot pay the full costs and shift the costs onto those who can is one example.

The Hippocratic mandate to serve the interests of the patient (in the singular) does not help. However, it seems ethically crass simply to count up the total amounts of good and harm and choose the course that maximizes total social outcome regardless of the impact on the individuals affected. That could lead, for instance, to refusing to provide services to those who are not useful to society or to those who can benefit only modestly from health care services.

Some ethical theories introduce a new ethical principle to deal with this problem—the principle of justice. While beneficence and nonmaleficence are devoted, respectively, simply to producing as much good and preventing as much harm as possible, justice is concerned with how the goods and harms are distributed. Justice is concerned with the equity or fairness of the patterns of the benefits and harm.

Among those who hold that there is a principle of justice that is concerned about the ways goods and harms are distributed, many schools of thought exist regarding what counts as a just or equitable distribution. The just distribution might focus on the effort of the various parties (even if sometimes those exerting great effort do not produce beneficial outcomes). Others, especially in health care, look at the need of the parties. In health care, those who are in the greatest need (usually those who are the sickest) may not be the most efficient to treat. In such cases, a choice must be made between using health care services in the way that will do the most good (sometimes treating healthier, more stable patients) and treating those with the greatest need. Any ethical principle that focuses on maximizing the good done for patients would tolerate—indeed require—that those with the greatest need be sacrificed. However, a principle of justice that focuses on need would accept the inefficiencies of an allocation of health resources that concentrates on the neediest.

Transplanting human organs is an example of a good in health care that is inevitably scarce. Often we face the question of whether to give the organ to someone who will get a great deal of benefit, even though that person may be healthy enough that he does not need the organ right away. The alternative might be to give the organ to someone who is so sick she will die soon without the organ. That second person may, however, be so ill that it can be predicted that she will get less benefit from the organ. In this case, the principle of beneficence would favor the less needy person who will predictably get more benefit while justice might favor the more needy person even if she cannot benefit as much. The cases in this chapter look at various problems of health resource allocation and the conflict between maximizing efficiency, called for by the principles of beneficence and nonmaleficence, and distributing resources equitably, called for by the principle of justice.

JUSTICE AMONG PATIENTS

Some physicians accept the traditional Hippocratic ethic that limits the focus of the clinician's ethical responsibility to the welfare of the patient. They hold that it is simply outside the moral scope of the health professional's role to worry about saving society money, catching welfare cheaters, or serving other societal interests.

Even the Hippocratic physician sometimes still must allocate resources. He or she may face a direct conflict between the interests of different patients. The next two cases raise such conflicts.

CASE 5-1

Under the Gun: Staying on Schedule in the HMO

A key concern of an HMO is efficiency (production) by the professionals, rather than allowing the MDs, physician's assistants, and nurse practitioners to spend whatever time they think is appropriate with individual patients. At a major HMO, patients are scheduled at fifteen-minute intervals. Dr. Daniel Hamilton was seeing Stephanie Wanzer, a 58-year-old high school teacher, for a routine sixth-month visit during which he monitored her high blood pressure and chronic sinus infections. He repeated the blood pressure readings that had already been taken by the nurse and began an examination of the head and neck. The blood pressure readings were a bit high, 150/90, and he confirmed Ms. Wanzer's complaint that her sinuses were giving her trouble. He reviewed her medications—an ace inhibitor and an antihistamine—and determined that they could be refilled. He adjusted the ace inhibitor dose, increasing it slightly.

At this point, Ms. Wanzer took out a piece of paper indicating she had several concerns she wanted to raise. She had heard there was a new antihistamine on the market she wanted to ask about. She was also concerned about difficulty sleeping and about a rash that had recently appeared on her upper thigh. This was a pattern Dr. Hamilton had come to expect from her. He enjoyed having her as a patient. She often had a long list of questions. She was intelligent and took notes on Dr. Hamilton's responses. At the same time, Dr. Hamilton realized he was slipping behind on his schedule. The examination had already consumed ten minutes. He needed the time for evaluation of the symptoms, exploration, and clarification of the physical exam. He had had to wait for the nurse to return as a chaperone for the examination of the rash. He needed the remaining five minutes for ordering tests and recording notes on the computer. He needed to allow time to write the new prescriptions and complete the patient's chart notes. The result was no health education and no consideration of prevention. He felt that he was becoming a test-orderer and prescription writer, usually completed by rapid judgment or reasonable guess. This behavior, he believed, was driven by the market system and merely "first aid," far beneath what was owed to a patient in a professional setting. As the fifteen-minute mark passed Ms. Wanzer was still making her way down her list.

Dr. Hamilton's next patient had arrived fifteen minutes early. She was an 84-year-old patient with metastatic cancer of the breast and was declining rapidly. She was very sick, but Dr. Hamilton feared there was not much he could do but comfort her, although he knew well that part of his obligation to patients is to spend time with them in any way that might serve their needs for understanding and for emotional support, even if treatment success was not possible. Should Dr. Hamilton terminate the session with Ms. Wanzer or steal some time from the next patient?

CASE 5-2

Unfunded Dialysis at the Expense of Other Patients

Tilly Hawthorne was a 77-year-old Jamaican in chronic renal failure. She was a non-resident alien living in a large East Coast American city. Dialysis, which she received three times a week at the hospital dialysis program, improved her condition, but it left her physically weak and largely home-bound at a single-room occupancy hotel where she lived. She had no health insurance and was ineligible for Medicaid. Dr. Jeffrey Morsch, her primary care physician, had taken her case two months earlier and was responsible for her treatment at the clinic where she was an out-patient. He knew that, given her serious medical condition and desperate financial situation, she was unlikely to thrive. She had no one to care for her in the hotel room and was not eating well. Her treatment costs were being absorbed by the hospital, which meant they were being passed on to Dr. Morsch's other patients in the form of higher fees for their dialysis. This practice is sometimes referred to as "cost-shifting." Dr. Morsch knew that if Ms. Hawthorne and similar nonpaying patients continued receiving unfunded dialysis at the clinic, other services for other patients, some of which Dr. Morsch believed would be more beneficial, would have to be forgone. He was also the physician-in-charge for these other patients.

The alternative for Dr. Morsch was to discharge Ms. Hawthorne and urge her to return to Jamaica where her family could provide better support. He had no idea whether she would receive dialysis once she got home. Since Ms. Hawthorne is not doing well on the clinic's dialysis program and could find a more supportive environment in Jamaica, does Dr. Morsch owe it to his other patients to discharge her?

COMMENTARY

Case 5-1 and Case 5-2 both present problems that the doctor cannot escape even if his approach is purely Hippocratic; that is, if the doctor is committed to the welfare of his patients. Some might argue that the real problem here is that the health care institution—the hospital or the HMO—is not providing adequate resources so that clinicians can do what is best for all their patients. This could mean enough time for both Ms. Wanzer and the woman with the breast mass. It could mean dialyzing all patients in need. There are two issues raised by that response. First, in the real world, physicians will have to continue practicing medicine in settings in which they are constrained by their institutions, not getting the resources they would like for their patients. Second, some would claim that in reality it would not be good for institutions to provide such unlimited resources to their physicians and patients. The institutions must obtain funding from somewhere—from fees charged from patients, from HMO subscriber fees, from charitable contributions, or government budgets. Since resources are inevitably scarce, providing all the funds desired by clinicians would necessarily come at the expense of other worthwhile purposes. Subscribers and taxpayers would in all likelihood protest if budgets were funded at a level at which there were no constraints at all on staff. It may well be that funding is not adequate and that more resources should be made available by increasing subscriber premiums or taxes or by decreasing profits in the case of profit-making health care institutions, but even if this were to occur, there would still be scarcity. Let us assume for the remainder of this discussion that Drs. Hamilton and Morsch will inevitably find themselves confronted with pressures of time and budget.

In Case 5-1 Dr. Hamilton may insist that his only concern is to benefit his patient, but here more than one of his patients is in need of his attention. He cannot give his sole attention to both at the same time.

First, consider what Dr. Hamilton would do if he were only acting on the basis of the more social version of an ethic of beneficence and nonmaleficence, if his only goal were to do as much good as possible considering the sum of the effects on both his first patient, the high school teacher, and the patient in the waiting room with the metastatic cancer of the breast. He would have to calculate the benefits and harms much as was done in the cases in Chapter 4, asking what the relevant effects would be of giving attention to each of these patients. It would appear that Dr. Hamilton has considerable help to offer Ms. Wanzer. She has real questions and will adjust her life according to the advice given. She understands the complexities of medicine and could gain from further discussion. The cancer patient, on the other hand, presents a case in which calculating benefit will be very difficult. Dr. Hamilton can offer little for her medically, although comforting her could prove important. A strong case can be made that, even though Ms. Wanzer is clearly much better off medically than the patient with breast cancer, she will probably benefit more from some extra minutes with Dr. Hamilton than the cancer patient would benefit from those minutes. If that is true, then one who is focusing exclusively on the benefit that can be offered to the patients would support giving more time to Ms. Wanzer.

Now consider what else Dr. Hamilton might take into account other than the sum of the benefits and harms. It is plausible to conclude that more good would come from giving extra time to Ms. Wanzer, but it seems clear that the cancer patient is sicker. This raises the question of whether worse off patients have a special moral claim on a clinician. The ethical principle of justice may come into play here, potentially competing with considerations of how much net benefit is done, that is, the consideration of the principles of beneficence and nonmaleficence.

The principle of justice focuses on the pattern of the distribution of benefit and harm. One pattern that emerges in health care is distribution of health resources according to who is sickest. In Case 5-1 the cancer patient is clearly sicker than Ms. Wanzer. The morally intriguing case is the one in which one use of Dr. Hamilton's time would produce the greatest good (spending extra time with Ms. Wanzer) while another use would provide benefit to the sickest patient (the cancer patient) even though less good is likely to be done.

Another pattern that arises in discussions of the principle of justice is one based on equality. In some areas of life equal treatment seems to require equality. The most clear example of this would be the maxim of "one person, one vote." One might consider having an HMO give equal fifteen-minute slots to all patients, but that makes little sense at least at the point of scheduling. Some patients can be known in advance to require longer appointments, others shorter times. There is no good reason to hold that all patients deserve equal time simply. In this case, however, the two patients have been scheduled, rightly or wrongly, for equal fifteen-minute appointments. Is that a reason why Dr. Hamilton should stop his conversation with Ms. Wanzer? Whether this should be thought of as a kind of promise that could influence Dr. Hamilton's decision will be considered in the cases of Chapter 8.

In Case 5-2, Dr. Morsch's dilemma about whether to continue caring for the dialysis patient, similar problems arise when the costs of Tilly Hawthorne's care are shifted to other patients. The approach based on consideration of benefit and harm would require Dr. Morsch to estimate the amount of good the other patients collectively could do with the funds involved and compare that with the good using those funds for Ms. Hawthorne's care. This would, of course, be a difficult calculation for Dr. Morsch to make. He would have no way of knowing how the other patients, once a surcharge for unfunded care was imposed, would otherwise spend those resources. He would not even know for sure whether the costs would be passed on to other patients or could be taken from profits that would otherwise go to shareholders in the hospital. This calculation would even be difficult for administrators who might more appropriately be expected to make the decision about continued provision of unfunded treatment for Ms. Hawthorne.

If the principle of justice were introduced, the calculation would still be difficult, but the question would be somewhat different. Dr. Morsch would need to ask not what the relative benefit and harm would be from providing Ms. Hawthorne's dialysis and discharging her to fend for herself in Jamaica; rather, he would ask whether Ms. Hawthorne or the others who would end up funding her care have a greater claim of justice to the resources. If justice claims are based on who would be worse off, Ms. Hawthorne's case would seem to be a strong one, but the judgment would require making some estimate of how poorly off the other patients (or the owners of the hospital) would be if they ended up providing the funds for Ms. Hawthrone's treatment.

Another principle of ethics might also come into play in this case. Some people might argue that the other patients are the legitimate "owners" of the funds that they would be required to pay if Ms. Hawthorne's care were funded by cost-shifting, by a surcharge on the care of other patients. Is there something unfair about a health care institution including a surcharge to generate the funds needed to pay for the care of those not otherwise able to pay?

JUSTICE BETWEEN PATIENTS AND OTHERS

In both of the previous cases, patients were competing among themselves for scarce resources—two patients for a physician's time in the first case, the funds to support dialysis in the second. Sometimes, however, a physician must choose between the patient and others. Of course, in purely Hippocratic ethics, the patient is the only interest that is morally relevant. Neither other patients nor those who are not patients count morally. Either way, the health professional has a duty to totally ignore the interests of others. The following cases make clear that sometimes that is hard to do.

CASE 5-3

Antibiotic for a Child's Otitis Media

Mrs. Linda Beauclair brought her 2-year-old son, Tommy, to the pediatrician for an unscheduled visit because he had suffered ear pain and fever for two days. He had screamed most of the night, leading her to call Dr. Richard Rust early the next morning. He was able to work Tommy into his schedule at the end of the afternoon appointments.

Just as he had suspected, Dr. Rust found a case of otitis media, typical of young children. Dr. Rust was certain that it was a common viral infection that would resolve in a few days. The medical evidence had accumulated, showing no long-term ill effects of what can be an unpleasant, but relatively benign infection. He urged Mrs. Beauclair to keep Tommy away from other children but offered no medication.

Mrs. Beauclair asked rather aggressively if Tommy could have an antibiotic. She wanted to do something for him.

Dr. Rust explained that antibiotics were only effective against bacterial infections and that there was almost no chance that Tommy's ear problems were caused by bacteria. He also explained that extensive use of antibiotics when they are not necessary can lead to the development of resistant strains of bacteria. This could eventually mean that some child will develop an infection from the resistant strain and suffer consequences much more serious than Tommy's earache because antibiotics had been used too often to attempt to treat minor infections, especially those that the antibiotic is very unlikely to help.

Mrs. Beauclair responded by stating rather angrily that she was Tommy's mother, not the mother of all the children in the future. She pressed Dr. Rust on whether there was any chance—even a small one—that Tommy's infection was from a bacterium that could respond to the antibiotic. She wanted to do everything possible to make sure Tommy did not spend another night like he had spent the previous one.

Dr. Rust had always accepted the common wisdom that antibiotics were being overused and should be avoided except in cases in which they are necessary to avoid serious medical problems. The antibiotics, he believed, should be saved for the truly most needy cases. Still, he acknowledged to himself that the risks of today's antibiotics are very low and that there was some small mathematical chance that Tommy had a bacterial infection that would respond to the antibiotic. He realized that, if he focused solely on his patient, Mrs. Beauclair was making a good case. Mrs. Beauclair made him realize that, as a physician who had always believed in the Hippocratic Oath, his job was really more to serve the interests of his patient, just as a mother's job is to protect her child. Neither was in a role in which they were supposed to pursue the best interests of some imagined needy hypothetical persons in the more distant future. Should Dr. Rust consider these more needy people or remain committed to maximizing Tommy's welfare?

COMMENTARY

This case raises issues that are similar to the two previous cases. Dr. Rust seems to concede that Mrs. Beauclair might be right that the potential benefit of an antibiotic for her son, however, remote, may exist. Furthermore, given the relative safety of today's antibiotics, the risk is small. From the point of view of the welfare of the patient, Tommy, a case can be made that he has a little to gain and very little to lose with the antibiotic. Not all clinicians would necessarily reach that conclusion. The risks of some antibiotics have to be taken into account, but if Dr. Rust ends up sharing Mrs. Beauclair's opinion that the benefits to Tommy outweigh the risks, and if he is Hippocratically committed to working only for the welfare of his patient, he seems to be locked into a conclusion that he ought to prescribe the antibiotic. However, the physician is also expected to follow professional standards of care in such frequently occurring problems. The harms to some future, hypothetical people who would be infected with drug-resistant strains of bacteria are off the table.

Not all medical ethics would resolve this case in that way, however. Some are more classically utilitarian. They would consider the benefits and harms not only to Tommy but also to all people affected by Tommy's prescription. In a vague, but very real sense, some people in the future will be put at very serious risk if Dr. Rust and other pediatricians prescribe antibiotics every time a child has otitis media and his or her mother insists on a prescription. If Dr. Rust is permitted to include the effects on all future users of antibiotics in his calculation, he may reach a different conclusion.

There is another moral dimension to this case. While Tommy is uncomfortable and his mother feels compelled to do whatever she can to promote his well-being regardless of the impact on others, Dr. Rust might consider taking into account something more than the aggregate benefit to all those in the future who would be subject to drug-resistant strains of bacteria. The aggregate total of benefit to all future people is an unimaginably large benefit because the number of people is potentially enormous. But there is another factor as well. The future people who will be put at risk by the indiscriminate use of antibiotics is not only very large in number; those people are potentially much worse off than Tommy.

Many ethicists resist utilitarian appeals to aggregating benefits across all future generations. They consider such mathematics unfair. Those committed to the principle of justice will focus not on the aggregate effect but on those persons who are worst off. In this case, the future people in need of antibiotics may not only be harmed greatly in aggregate, they may also include very poorly off persons—persons much worse off than Tommy. Should Dr. Rust remain Hippocratic and work only for the welfare of his patient or should he consider future sufferers from bacterial infection as well? If he should consider future sufferers, is it the total amount of benefit that is morally relevant or the fact that some of those future sufferers are potentially much worse off than Tommy?

Finally, what difference, if any, does it make that one of the parties is a patient while the others are not? Is the difference morally relevant for Dr. Rust in deciding when to prescribe antibiotics?

JUSTICE IN PUBLIC POLICY

The questions of justice in the allocation of resources arise not only in clinical situations but also in matters of policy. A key difference is that the health professional facing policy decisions does not have a specific patient or patients in mind whose interests can be served. If a specific patient's case is debated, it is as an example of a more general policy question in which the interests of a group are at stake, as the HMO subscribers in the following case, or in a community whose interests must be treated fairly. The pharmacist in such cases is not so much acting as an agent for the specific patient as for the entire group.

CASE 5-4

Dental Sealants for Children's Teeth: Justice or Utility?

Some years ago, a new technology in dentistry was developed that permits placing a resin sealant on the teeth of children, greatly reducing the risk of dental cavities.[1] A National Institutes of Health consensus development panel quickly concluded that the sealants were both safe and effective.[2] Moreover, sealants significantly reduced the costs of dental care. For maximum efficiency the sealants should be placed on the teeth of children at about six years of age when their first set of teeth is complete and at twelve when adult dentition is in place.

Although the long-term cost-effectiveness is clear, a community-wide campaign to provide sealants for all eligible children would be costly. Some counties have decided to provide pilot programs for low-income children, identifying certain political districts for initial funding. The problem faced by public health officials is how to select the communities for the pilot program.

In one such county, some communities are on water systems that are fluoridated, while other communities obtained water from private wells or from non-fluoridated community water systems. An initial proposal suggested basing the decision about which children should receive the sealants during the pilot project on the basis of whether their communities fluoridated their central water supplies. The issue of moral controversy was over whether the children who already receive community-based fluoridated water deserve the highest or lower priority for the sealants. Fluoride is especially effective in reducing caries on proximal surfaces while the sealants protect what are called "pit and fissure" areas (the crevices on the biting surfaces of the teeth). This leads to an unexpected moral puzzle. The sealants are more efficient on children who also have the protection of fluoride. This is because the children need fewer restorations in the areas given the protection from fluoride, so the sealant will be damaged less often. This means that fewer sealants will be destroyed.

Thus, public health officers committed to maximizing the efficiency of the sealant program and getting as much protection as possible with the limited funds available for the program are advocating that the sealants be used in communities that already fluoridate.

This had the effect of providing the benefit of the sealants to the very children who are already better off in terms of their dental health. They have the protection of fluoride, which would qualify them for additional protection from the sealants.

Others criticized this approach arguing that it is precisely the children who do not have the fluoride protection and thus have the worst dental health who deserve the benefit of the sealant program.

The advocates of allocating the initial funds to the communities without fluoride faced several issues. Do the families that have chosen not to fluoridate deserve priority because they have made a choice that is contrary to the dental well-being of their children? Is not this unfair, at least to the children in families in which the parents had advocated fluoridation and had lost the political struggle? A community-wide program that either includes or excludes sealants will mean that some children in the communities that do not fluoridate will suffer even though their parents have voted in favor of fluoridation and may even provide fluoridation through individual application using fluoridated toothpaste, vitamins, or direct application to the teeth. The advocates for children in the communities that did not fluoridate on a community-wide basis in the water supply argued that at least the children who were getting fluoride applications deserved to have their teeth sealed. Opponents responded, however, that efficiency for a pilot program required that, in order to maximize the benefit, the program decisions had to be made on a community-wide basis. Should the county pilot program be directed to the communities that use community-fluoridated water, thus maximizing efficiency from the budget for dental sealants, or should it be directed to the communities that do not fluoridate in order to give these children, who statistically would have worse dental health, an opportunity for the protection the sealants would provide? However, the program would be less efficient because the seals would in some cases have to be destroyed to repair the teeth damaged from lack of fluoride.

CASE 5-5

Allocating Livers for Transplant

In the late 1990s, controversy arose over the national policy in the United States for allocating livers obtained from deceased donors. Such livers are very scarce and offer life-saving benefit to those patients in liver failure who are chosen to receive them. At the point that the controversy erupted, livers were allocated first to the organ procurement organization (OPO) in the metropolitan area in which the liver was procured. There are approximately sixty such OPOs in the country. Within the OPO, the liver was assigned first to the sickest patient who was a suitable match for size and blood type. Those near death, normally in the intensive care unit, got first priority. Next priority were the patients in the area who were less sick but still hospitalized, after which home-bound patients even less sick were selected. Only if no local patients could use the liver would it pass beyond the local OPO to another area of the country. This was the policy even if the liver could have gone to a patient in some other area who was in desperate need and near death for lack of a liver. The relatively healthy local patients got priority over the most urgent cases beyond the local area.

The federal officials in the Department of Health and Human Services (DHHS) challenged this policy, demanding that there be greater equity or fairness in the allocation of livers. A rule was established requiring the United Network for Organ Sharing (UNOS), the organ procurement and transplantation network controlling all organ allocation in the United States, to develop a policy that would spread livers more fairly.[3]

Officials at UNOS resisted the rule.[4] They did not deny that livers were more readily available in some communities than others and that the result was that some people who were very ill had a high probability of being transplanted, while equally sick people in other communities had a much lower chance of getting an organ. They argued, however, that there were significant benefits of the "locals-first" policy that led to greater overall good being done than if livers were transported to the sickest patients in other communities. First, they noted that the transportation of the livers itself meant livers suffered potential damage from greater "cold-ischemia time," that is, time when the livers were not receiving blood. Second, they argued that the sickest patients were often the most difficult to treat. They had less of a chance of surviving with a donated liver than the healthier local patients currently receiving the organs. Finally, they claimed that a locals-first policy had the effect of increasing willingness of grieving families to donate a loved-one's organs. If "locals" believed it was going to help a neighbor, transplant personnel believed this would increase the likelihood of donation. In short, at least three reasons supported a policy of keeping the organs locally unless there was no one locally who could use them, even if the recipients were relatively healthy.

The government officials, led by then-Secretary of HHS Donna Shalala, pressed for a more fair system even if the impact was a decrease in the number of life years expected per organ transplanted and a decrease in the supply of organs. Officials at DHHS challenged the claim that locals-first would increase the rate of donation. They claimed there were no data to support this belief, but insisted that, even if this were true, the moral mandate had to be to produce an organ allocation system that was fair. This, they said, meant equally sick patients throughout the United States should have an equal chance of getting an organ. This could be accomplished only by transporting organs to other OPOs when necessary. Should the liver allocation system be maximally fair or maximally efficient at producing added years of life from organ transplant?[5]

COMMENTARY

In neither of these cases is the moral choice one that can be made by individual clinicians at the bedside. The questions are for policy-makers to decide—the county public health officers deciding how to allocate their scarce funds for a pilot program involving dental sealants and the national officials responsible for setting policy for allocating donated livers for organ transplant. Local dentists and transplant surgeons are not in a position where they can make these choices. In fact, if they attempted to make them, they would quickly find themselves in a conflict of interest. Historically, their moral duty has been to be advocates for their patients. Transplant surgeons asked to decide whether an organ should go to their own patients or to some stranger in some other community would face the traditional commitment of health professionals to work always for the benefit of their patients. The result could be that the allocation was neither fair nor efficient in allocating organs.

Thus, surgeons responsible for patients and dentists responsible for the dentition of their pediatric patients are in a particularly bad position to make resource allocation decisions. These choices are made at the level of public policy, by professional organizations or by government health policy officials.

In both of these cases, Case 5-4 and Case 5-5, the policy-makers are presented with a choice between an option that will be maximally efficient at producing benefit from the use of a scarce resource (maximizing the number of dental cavities prevented per dollar invested in Case 5-4 and maximizing the number of life year's expected in Case 5-5) or distributing the resource so that the benefits are distributed more fairly even if the aggregate amount of good produced is somewhat less. Giving the sealants to the children without the benefits of fluoride and giving the organs to the sickest was defended as the policy required by an ethical principle of justice, one that favors allocating scarce resources so that they benefit the worst off members of the relevant community (even if the aggregate benefit is less).

The moral principle of justice is concerned about the pattern of the distribution of the benefit—to the worst off patients—while the policy that would produce the most aggregate benefit would be the one favored by the moral principles of beneficence and nonmaleficence (doing good and avoiding harm). Neither principle is consistent with the classical Hippocratic notion of doing as much good as possible for the individual patient. That seems beside the point when the policy question is whether to do as much good for the population as a whole or to spread the benefit fairly among members of the community.

Case 5-5 raises another interesting problem. The debate was stimulated because the members of the Clinton administration, a more liberal Democratic administration oriented to greater fairness issued a rule requiring greater fairness, while the UNOS, dominated by members of the medical profession, was strongly committed to maximizing efficient production of benefit. Here is a case in which public officials seemed to favor one moral principle, justice, while the medical profession favored another, beneficence. This repeats a pattern that is seen in other circumstances and is consistent with a profession that has long maintained an ethic driven by beneficence and nonmaleficence—producing good and avoiding evil—rather than concern growing out of the principle of justice, a principle that has been absent from professional codes of ethics, at least until very recently. What should happen when public officials favor one ethical principle and health professionals support another?

JUSTICE AND OTHER ETHICAL PRINCIPLES

We have, throughout this chapter, been examining how the principle of justice relates to the principles of beneficence and nonmaleficence. Nonutilitarians hold that right-making characteristics of actions other than the net amount of good produced are morally relevant. Justice, that is, some morally right pattern of the distribution of benefits and burdens, is just one such principle of rightness. In later chapters, other principles that are sometimes identified as right-making characteristics will be discussed. These include respect for autonomy, truth-telling, fidelity to promises, and the duty to avoid killing (the topics of Chapters 6–9). We shall see that sometimes these principles come into conflict. When they do, a full ethic will have to have some method for resolving the conflict. One approach is to view the various principles (the right-making characteristics) as elements that identify characteristics that will tend to make actions right. Then considering only the single dimension, the action can be said to be right. It would be right if there were no conflicting considerations pulling in the other direction. If ethical principles are used to identify these right-making elements, they are sometimes called *prima facie* principles. They identify characteristics that would make an action right "other things being equal." In the following case, we can identify what justice requires but might also have to take into account that other principles pull the decision-maker in another direction. Here is an example of a conflict between the principles of justice and other ethical principles—beneficence and autonomy.

CASE 5-6

Dialysis in an End-Stage HIV+ Patient: Justice, Benefit, and Patient Autonomy

Ron Beato, a 30-year-old male, was admitted to hospital with severe weight loss (he weighed 119 pounds), severe shortness of breath, fever, chills, and generalized fluid retention. A crack and cocaine user, admitting to multiple sex partners, he was married and father of one child. Examination confirmed renal and/or heart failure, and lab studies determined he was indeed in kidney failure. His diagnoses were terminal AIDS, end-stage renal disease, chronic anemia, and possible bloodstream infection (sepsis).

He refused additional diagnostic procedures and blood transfusion. Antibiotic therapy was instituted. Generally, he was poorly compliant with medical advice. He also had spells of crying and apparent depression. The physicians assessed his mental competency as adequate for decision-making and discussed with him and his family options for advance directives, including cardiopulmonary resuscitation (CPR), which he declined. Hemodialysis was not offered as a treatment option because it would be of "no benefit to life expectancy." (The nephrology consultant agreed.) After three days of hospitalization, he was transferred to a hospice program.

COMMENTARY

The central question here is whether not offering dialysis was fair to Ron Beato. The moral principle of justice requires a fair allocation of resources; that is, an allocation that distributes resources following a pattern that gives people their due. Most contemporary theories of justice when applied to health care understand a fair pattern for health care to be one that orients to who is the worst off. Mr. Beato surely is among the worst off of patients. He is suffering from a fatal disease with awful symptoms. Thus, from the point of view of the principle of justice, one might conclude that he has a high priority claim on the hospital's resources.

Even though this seems to be what the principle of justice requires, there are complexities. First, even if Mr. Beato, as one among the worst off of patients, has the highest priority claim on any resources that could benefit him, the principle of justice is a principle that distributes benefits. If dialysis is of no benefit, no purpose would be served in providing it to Mr. Beato, and it therefore need not be provided.

Matters of treatment options, including no treatment ("don't just do something, stand there") are often debatable, particularly in end of life situations. It is common for competent, thoughtful clinicians and patients to disagree. The primary responsibility of professional decision-making is that of the attending physician, unless he or she refers the patient to a consultant. The patient in this case appears not to have been consulted about whether he thinks dialysis would be beneficial.

This raises the question of whether the physicians in this case can know, objectively, that dialysis is of "no benefit." There are cases in which dialyzing a patient who is near death will temporarily extend life in a manner in which many people would claim that this temporary extension is of no benefit. Others, however, might believe that even temporary extension of life is an important benefit (so that relatives may gather, for example). Even if the dialysis is determined not to extend life at all, it may provide other benefits—keeping the patient lucid at the end, for example.[6] Thus, the claim of the physicians that they can know that the dialysis would be of "no benefit" is controversial.

One interesting possibility is that the dialysis would be seen by the patient to be somewhat beneficial. We probably cannot know without asking him. It is possible that the patient could reasonably reach conclusion that the dialysis offers some benefit even if all the physicians saw it to be of no value from their perspective. If the dialysis were deemed beneficial, even marginally beneficial, a principle of justice would support giving the treatment to the patient. Assuming he is among the worst off, the standard interpretation of the principle requires arranging resources to benefit him.

Even though this seems to be what the principle of justice requires, several other moral principles may come into play in this case. These other principles may have implications that conflict with the principle of justice. One might ask if the principle of justice should prevail in such a circumstance. Particularly, if the patient saw the benefit as small—as giving him only a short additional time or making him only slightly more comfortable—some might ask if the dialysis would be worth it. If the same resources could be used to produce significantly more benefit for some other patient who is ill, but better off than Mr. Beato, we have a classic conflict between the principle of justice and the principles of beneficence and nonmaleficence. Justice (understood as requiring distribution of resources so as to benefit the worst off) would require one allocation; beneficence and nonmaleficence would require a different one. Utilitarians—those who hold that the principles of beneficence and nonmaleficence should prevail—would withhold the resources from Mr. Beato if those resources would do more good some place else. This decision would then depend on whether the principle of justice or the utility maximizing principles of beneficence and nonmaleficence should take priority.

There is still another dimension to this case. Mr. Beato has a history of noncompliance. This introduces consideration of how another ethical principle—the principle of respect for autonomy—should come into play. This principle holds that competent persons should be free from interference in leading their lives according to their own life-plans. That could include the choice to be noncompliant with medical recommendations or to refuse medical treatments being offered such as CPR or other means of life support. Respect for autonomy will be the focus of the cases in the following chapter, but in this case we need to understand how this principle intersects with the principles of justice, beneficence, and nonmaleficence. For starters, we should recognize that Mr. Beato would surely retain the right to refuse dialysis if it were offered. Since he has already refused other treatment proposals, he might also refuse the dialysis. That would eliminate any moral controversy in the case.

Assuming he did not decline the dialysis, respect for autonomy introduces another issue. Does his autonomously chosen decision to be noncompliant negate his claim of justice to receive the dialysis? Some would argue that justice requires that persons who are among the worst off be given opportunities for benefit. If, however, Mr. Beato has had opportunities to be better off, but has rejected them, this could leave him in a morally different position from those who are among the worst off without having had such opportunities. Does autonomously chosen noncompliance lessen Mr. Beato's claim of justice? That will depend on one's interpretation of the principle of respect for autonomy, the principle to which we now turn.

NOTES

[1] Proceedings of a Symposium on Pit-and-Fissure Sealants. "Is It Time for a New Initiative?" *Journal of Public Health Dentistry* 42 (Fall 1982):295–336.

[2] National Institutes of Health. "Consensus Development Conference Statement: Dental Sealants in the Prevention of Tooth Decay." *Journal of Dental Education* 48 (Supplement, February 1984):126–131.

[3] U.S. Department of Health and Human Services, Health Resources and Services Administration. "Organ Procurement and Transplantation Network; Final Rule." *Federal Register* 42 CFR Part 121 (20 October 1999):5650–5661.

[4] Heiney, Douglas A. Director, Department of Membership, UNOS, "Memorandum: Proposed Liver Allocation Policy Development Plan for Public Comment." Richmond, VA: UNOS, February 15, 2000.

[5] Veatch, Robert M. "A New Basis for Allocating Livers for Transplant." *The Kennedy Institute of Ethics Journal* 10 (March 2000):75–80.

[6] Cohen, L. M., M. J. Germain, D. M. Poppel, A. L. Woods, P. S. Pekow, C. M. Kjellstranc. (2000). "Dying Well after Discontinuing the Life-Support Treatment of Dialysis." *Archives of Internal Medicine* 160 (September 11):2513–2518.

CHAPTER 6

◦

Autonomy

Other Cases Involving Autonomy

In the previous chapter we saw that in social ethics the principles of beneficence and nonmaleficence (maximizing aggregate total net benefits) may not be the only morally relevant consideration. The principle of justice affirms that certain patterns of distribution of the good, such as distribution based on medical need, may also be morally relevant. Justice , when it is considered a principle of fair distribution, is not the only moral consideration that can provide a check on the principles of beneficence and nonmaleficence. In this and the following chapters we shall explore several other moral principles—respect for autonomy, veracity, fidelity, and avoiding killing—principles that all, in one way or another, refer to right-making elements or actions or practices that do not focus on maximizing the net good produced.

Justice is concerned with the distribution of goods in morally preferred patterns. It, therefore, always involves more than one person who is the potential beneficiary. The remaining principles are relevant, however, even if there is only one person our actions affect. Thus these principles are particularly important in traditional clinical health care ethics in which the professional is thought of as acting on one and only one patient. In fact, we increasingly recognize that, even in these clinical situations, many people are affected by the clinician's actions. There is not only one patient but also other patients whom the clinician could be treating. Family members of the patient, friends, and citizens may be affected by each treatment decision, as well as fellow health professionals.

Nevertheless, many ethical decisions in health care can be analyzed as if there were only one party who is principally affected. When we contemplate violating a patient's autonomy, lying to a patient, breaking a promise such as the promise of confidentiality, or acting in a way that will kill a patient, it is the patient's moral interests that are primarily affected. Other people's interests are much more indirect. Therefore, while remembering the important ethical issues raised by the principle of justice in the previous chapter, the cases in this and the following chapters in this part of the book will focus primarily on the more individual ethical concerns. These begin with the moral principle of autonomy.[1] This principle is more accurately referred to as the principle of respect for autonomy, since it does not require that people act autonomously, only that their autonomy be respected.

Autonomy is both a psychological and a moral term. Psychologically, autonomy is a term describing the mental state of persons who are free to choose their own life plans and act on those plans substantially independent of internal or external constraints. One leads the life of an autonomous person to the extent one is free to be "self-legislating." Autonomy means creating one's own legislation. As such being autonomous is always a matter of degree. No one is "fully autonomous" in the sense of being totally free from internal and external constraints. Some people may be totally lacking in autonomy— infants and the comatose are examples. Many people whom we call nonautonomous, however, possess some limited capacity to make their own choices. Small children, the mentally retarded, the mentally ill, and the senile all may be able to make limited choices based on their own beliefs and values and yet are hardly autonomous enough to be called self-determining in any meaningful way. Thus being autonomous is decision-specific as well as a matter of degree. We treat those persons who have a sufficient degree of autonomy as being essentially self-determining; we call them "substantially autonomous persons." For purposes of public policy, we assume that persons below the age of majority, usually eighteen, are lacking sufficient autonomy for a range of publicly significant decisions unless proven otherwise. We admit that some 16-year-old may have both the internal knowledge and intellectual capacity and be sufficiently free from external constraints to be as autonomous as some adults. The courts will occasionally recognize such minors as "mature" for purposes of making medical decisions on their own. But the working presumption is that minors lack competence to make many substantially autonomous decisions.

By contrast, those who have reached the age of majority are presumed to be substantially autonomous unless there is adequate evidence to the contrary. One type of evidence comes from a judicial determination of lack of competence. There is a striking problem with patients who are clearly unconscious. They are obviously not capable of making autonomous decisions, yet they have never been declared incompetent through any formal proceedings such as in a court. One approach is to require that, if a clinician or a family member believes such persons are totally lacking in competence, he or she must take reasonable steps to inform the patient of that belief. Of course, if the patient is unconscious, no such action would be necessary, but if the patient is capable of disagreement and the patient coherently expresses that disagreement, then he or she should be presumed to be competent until adjudicated otherwise. If he or she fails to disagree, then a presumption of lack of capacity to make substantially autonomous choices seems reasonable.[2]

This, however, does not mean automatically that a clinical care giver is free to do what seems reasonable to those who are not substantially autonomous. In the case of children, we presume that only parents and those designated by the courts are free to act as surrogate decision-makers. In the case of adults, even if the presumption of lack of autonomy is warranted, we still need to determine who is authorized to speak for the individual. The health professional—physician, nurse, pharmacist, or other health worker—does not automatically have that authority.

Even if one is believed to be substantially autonomous, it does not necessarily follow that he or she should be free to make all decisions about his or her actions. If one's actions are likely to harm others, we routinely accept the idea that they can be restrained. This might be supported on what can be called the "harm to others" principle. From the time of John Stuart Mill, this limit on action has been well recognized, even among defenders of human liberty.[3]

The principle of justice might also be a basis for constraining actions that affect others. That is, we may want to control people because of the effect of their action on the distribution of goods as well as because of the total amount of harm one's actions will bring to others. Still others believe that it is acceptable to constrain people who we believe are substantially autonomous in order to produce a greater good for society. Constraining someone in order to produce good for others is, however, more controversial than constraining to protect others from harm or to promote justice. Finally, some people believe it is acceptable to constrain those who are substantially autonomous in order to produce good for those individuals themselves. This is what is called *paternalism*.

If a person's substantially autonomous actions have no appreciable effect on other people, it is an open question whether it is ethically right for others to constrain his or her behavior, that is, to act paternalistically. Even if their free choices only affect themselves, some people have held that it is morally appropriate to constrain actions. Laws requiring motorcycle riders to wear helmets, laws restricting access to drugs with dangerous side effects, and, in some cases, laws authorizing restraint of persons who are of danger to themselves have all been defended as justifiable infringements on personal freedom. When these restraints are imposed on substantially autonomous persons, such laws are paternalistic.

This is where autonomy surfaces as a *moral* principle. The moral principle of respect for autonomy holds that an action or practice is morally wrong insofar as it attempts to control the actions of substantially autonomous persons on the basis of a concern for their own welfare.

Classical Hippocratic ethics in the health care professions has been committed to the principle that the health care worker should do whatever is necessary to benefit the patient. This has been understood to include violating the autonomy of the patient. Physicians in the name of Hippocratic paternalism have refused to tell patients their diagnoses, prescribed placebos, refused to prescribe drugs believed dangerous, and have engaged in all manner of violations of the autonomous choices of patients. They have done so not out of a concern to protect the welfare of others or to promote justice, but rather out of concern that the patient would hurt himself or herself. Classical Hippocratic professional ethics contains no moral principle of respect for autonomy.

By contrast, the moral principle of autonomy says that patients have a right to be self-determining insofar as their actions affect only themselves. The principle of autonomy poses increasingly difficult moral problems for health professionals, first in determining whether patients really are sufficiently autonomous so that the principle of respect for autonomy applies, second, in deciding whether persons who are, in principle, sufficiently autonomous are being constrained by external forces that control their choices, and finally in deciding whether it is morally appropriate to override autonomy in order to protect the patient's welfare. The following cases confront these issues.

DETERMINING WHETHER A PATIENT IS AUTONOMOUS

Some persons may lack the capacity to make many substantially autonomous decisions. They may, through age or brain pathology, lack the neurological development to process information necessary for making choices. They may suffer from severe mental impairments, delusions, or errors in understanding.

In the easy cases, this capacity is totally lacking. In these cases, such as in small children, we presume by public policy that autonomy is absent and designate someone as a surrogate, such as a parent or court-appointed guardian. In adults in whom autonomy appears to be totally lacking, matters are more complex. First, the adult may have made choices while competent that are thought to be still relevant. Second, public policy does not automatically designate any adults incompetent (as with someone under the age of majority). It is here that we are still striving to develop legal and public policy mechanisms for transferring decision-making authority.[4] Presently no clear legal authority exists for health professionals, on their own, to declare incompetency and assume the role of surrogate decision-maker. Competence is a legal term that can only be determined by the courts.

Since adults are normally presumed competent until adjudicated otherwise, there is a real problem for adults in need of medical treatment who appear to lack the capacity for making autonomous choices and yet need medical treatment immediately. Legally, consent is presumed in cases of emergency.[5] That presumption is not valid, however, for situations that are not emergencies. For instance, if a physician is planning to write a medical order not to resuscitate a patient in the case of a cardiac arrest, it normally is not an emergency.

The presumption of incompetency is also probably not valid for emergencies in which the patient is coherent enough to demand not to be treated. As a society we are moving toward a consensus that in cases in which the patient is so lacking in capacity that he or she cannot respond coherently to a declaration of incompetency, the transfer of decision-making to the appropriate surrogate is acceptable, even without a formal court review.

That presumption of incompetency leaves open the question of who the appropriate surrogate should be. Normally, we would want as a surrogate someone committed to looking out for our interests and, if possible, someone who knows our particular values. These criteria point in the direction of someone who knows the full range of our values and interests, such as a family member, but we would also want to guard against someone who has a conflict of interest. The pattern emerging seems to be that it is the next-of-kin, rather than the health professional, who is in charge.

In cases in which the patient can respond to a declaration of lack of capacity by the care provider, it is much less clear what should be done. If the patient acknowledges that he or she cannot make decisions and accepts the suggestion that the next-of-kin take on that role, it seems reasonable to proceed, but if the patient claims to be able to make his or her own decisions, no clear policy guides health professionals on what to do. If there is enough time, it is probably best to seek informal help from an ethics committee or a formal, legally binding review from a court. If there is not enough time, it is far less clear what should be done.

CASE 6-1

Borderline Competency: Deciding About Major Heart Surgery

William Maxwell was admitted to the hospital with chest pain, intermittently severe, poorly relieved by nitroglycerin. He was sixty-nine years old, moderately obese, hypertensive, and diabetic. Initial evaluations indicated severe ischemic heart disease, believed to be life threatening. A recent diagnosis of dementia had been made, but his competency to make autonomous decisions was variable. Dr. Nina Sandstedt considered cardiac catheterization necessary before any cardiac operative procedure could be planned.

On evaluation by Dr. Sandstedt and consultants, Mr. Maxwell was noted to be awake, showing capacity for pleasure and pain, but disoriented. He could state his name but did not know what city he was in. Family members were available and his wife, Esther, was available to act as a surrogate. He could identify her by name.

Evaluation of surgical mortality of coronary artery bypass surgery (CABG) for him suggested he had approximately a 10 percent chance of not surviving the procedure. Postoperative pain following placement of coronary bypass grafts would be considerable but could be controlled with medication. Pneumonia and other complications could occur.

The professional dilemmas included satisfactory assessment of Mr. Maxwell's mental capacity for decision-making, and successive discussions with him or surrogates as options for surgical treatment were clarified. A hospital administrator did not assess the possible procedures as extraordinary in cost or in use of personnel and equipment. Dr. Sandstedt believed that the procedure would be a major trauma for a patient in Mr. Maxwell's condition, but she believed that, if it were she, she would opt for the operation if the catheterization showed evidence that an operation would be beneficial. There was general agreement that the probable benefits of surgical intervention outweighed his risks and possible complications. On the other hand, she knew some patients with Mr. Maxwell's degree of chronic heart impairment who had refused such procedures. When Mr. Maxwell was asked, he seemed to resist the proposal of an operation, but his capacity to refuse consent was questionable. Dr. Sandstedt knew she could not operate without a valid operative permit. Mr. Maxwell had not discussed questions of life-prolonging treatment prior to the development of his dementia. Should she rely on Mr. Maxwell's apparent refusal? Should she invite Esther Maxwell to function as his surrogate? What if she also refused what Dr. Sandstedt believed was a reasonable recommendation to proceed with the procedure?

CASE 6-2

A Mature 12-Year-Old Who Refuses a Heart Transplant

Twelve-year-old Emma Ogden had suffered all her life from a congenital heart defect that had led to over forty operations during her short life. Still, she was not doing well. She suffered cardiac episodes periodically while in school or on the street leading to repeated calls to the emergency medical services (EMS) personnel. Up to this point, they had always been able to resuscitate her and transport her to the emergency room (ER) where eventually her condition was stabilized.

Now Dr. Abdul Hamid, the transplant surgeon at the hospital, had informed Emma and her parents that her only long-term hope was a heart transplant. The child's condition was so severe that she would not survive much longer without the operation. Even with a transplant, her prognosis was not good: no more than 10–20 percent chance of five-year survival with likely repeated crises related to her damaged lungs and circulatory system.

Emma was a remarkable young woman. She had recently been conducting class sessions in school trying to help her classmates understand what was happening when she would lose consciousness in school, leading to rescue personnel rushing in and her fellow students being evacuated from the classroom until she could be removed. She had written an essay published in their local community newspaper describing her situation. The teachers had told her parents that, in spite of her many missed school days over the years, she tested three years above her grade level.

She had read everything she could find about her condition. She knew her chances of survival were not good. She had had about all she could take of hospitals, operations, and medical crises. After considerable thought she came to the conclusion that the transplant was not worth it. She knew the alternative was certain death in the near future. She had also come to understand that an adult in this position would have the legal right to refuse consent for the procedure. She told Dr. Hamid that she did not want the transplant.

She had discussed the matter at length with her parents who had reluctantly come to understand her position. They would support her if that is what she wanted to do.

Dr. Hamid was taken aback. In all his years of cardiac transplant surgery, he had never had a case like this one. Occasionally, an elderly patient who was rapidly declining and had been advised that he or she was unlikely to survive heart transplant had accepted his advice and declined the extreme procedure, but never before had he been confronted with a 12-year-old who could potentially survive many years if everything worked just right.

Dr. Hamid considered the possibility to getting consent from her parents but realized that they might also refuse. He turned to an ethics committee, who explained to him that some adolescent minors were considered sufficiently mature that they had the authority to make medical decisions on their own behalf. (Some pregnant adolescents have consented to abortion on this basis, for instance.) On the other hand, the committee members had never invoked the mature minor rule on someone as young as twelve and for a decision as momentous as a life-ending transplant refusal. Their alternative was to treat her as other 12-year-olds, some of whom might express resistance to needed medical procedures. Parental consent is normally acceptable in such cases. Dr. Hamid knew, however, that the parents might themselves refuse, which would leave him the only option of seeking a court order to operate against the wishes of both the girl and her parents. Should he accept the girl's refusal, rely on the parents' judgment, or attempt to get the court order?

COMMENTARY

Case 6-1 and 6-2 both raise questions of the mental competence of patients to make crucial medical choices. Had Mr. Maxwell been more severely impaired, the ethical and clinical problem posed by the first of these cases would have disappeared or been changed significantly. Had Emma Ogden been five years old and refusing a major operation, we would have no difficulty disqualifying her from any role in deciding about her transplant.

Both of these patients show some signs of mental capacity to understand the decisions that need to be made. In Case 6-1, Mr. Maxwell shows signs of dementia and had no documented record of his views about life prolongation prior to his current illness. Dr. Sandstedt seems to be of the view that operation might be warranted and that catheterization should be performed to provide a more reliable basis for making that decision. Clearly, if Mr. Maxwell has the capacity to consent or refuse consent, the catheterization would be pointless if he knew he would not give that consent.

Assessment of capacity to consent is not a precise science. Dr. Sandstedt, perhaps with the help of a psychiatric consultant, could initiate such an assessment leading to a judgment on her part of whether Mr. Maxwell is sufficiently autonomous that she should rely on his consent or refusal. In the past, some physicians have determined competency on the basis of the plausibility of the patient's choice. The reasoning is, "Refusing a life-saving operation would be crazy; the patient is refusing so I should treat him as lacking the capacity to consent because of his unreasonable refusal." This determination of capacity to consent on the basis of the reasonableness of the patient's choices is not generally considered acceptable. An independent assessment is called for, based on whether the patient understands the nature of the choice and the likely effects of various options. If the patient is found to have capacity to understand and is not coerced or otherwise constrained in the choice he makes, then respect for patient autonomy requires respecting the choice made, at least if the patient's welfare would be the basis for overruling the patient.

If Dr. Sandstedt and those assisting her in the assessment of Mr. Maxwell's capacity decide he has sufficient capacity to consent and she accepts the moral principle of respect for autonomy, she seems locked into the conclusion that she should not do the catheterization even though she might herself find it the better choice. Only if Dr. Sandstedt remained committed to a more Hippocratic perspective based on the principle of beneficence, with a more paternalistic imposition of the physician's choice on the patient, would she consider overriding Mr. Maxwell's decision.

If she finds Mr. Maxwell lacking in the capacity to understand the choice he might be asked to make, Dr. Sandstedt is in a more complex position. That would still not lead to giving her the authority to make the decision on her patient's behalf. It is possible that she and her patient could disagree on his capacity to decide. It is for cases like this that some now recommend informing the patient of the physician's decision that the capacity is lacking. The patient might concur, leading to agreement that some other decision-maker would have to be found. If the patient disagreed, then further work would be in order. Dr. Sandstedt might seek additional consultation, might ask for an ethics committee's review, or might, in an extreme case, seek to have Mr. Maxwell declared incompetent by a court.

If she proceeds, based on a decision that Mr. Maxwell lacks capacity, then a valid surrogate is needed. Esther, the patient's wife, seems like the obvious candidate here. Technically, there is some ambiguity in the law. Whether the law specifically authorizes it as it does in some states, most clinicians work on the presumption that the next-of-kin is the legitimate and valid surrogate. In a case such as this one in which there is even difference of opinion among competent clinicians, it seems reasonable to accept the surrogate's choice as long as it is within reason. That could include the possibility that Esther Maxwell would, after taking into account what she knows about her husband's values, decide against an operation.

In cases such as this, in which a questionably competent patient and surrogate presumed to be valid agree on the course to be followed, the clinician may not have to spend a great deal of time and energy sorting out whether the decision comes from the patient or the surrogate, but Dr. Sandstedt should realize that potentially down the road Mr. Maxwell and his wife may reach a choice about which they do not agree. At that point Dr. Sandstedt would have to be clear on which person really has the authority.

In Case 6-2, we also have a case in which a physician, Dr. Hamid, needs to know whether he will treat the patient herself as the agent with the capacity to make medical decisions or will rely on a valid surrogate. Normally for children as young as twelve, there is no doubt that they lack sufficient capacity, especially for momentous life-and-death choices such as heart transplant. The parents would be presumed to be surrogates in a legitimate position to consent to the treatment. In this case, however, Emma has shown remarkable capacity to understand. She has extensive experience with being a surgical patient and with coping with her condition. She has the unusual maturity to have thought long about her options and to have taught and written about her situation.

Although we begin with the presumption that anyone under the age of majority lacks capacity to make critical medical decisions, there are exceptions. Minors may be classified as "mature," that is, capable of sufficient autonomy to make their own choices. This occurs with some frequency for older teenagers, especially when faced with a decision such as birth control in which, for confidentiality reasons, they might resist getting parents involved. Some minors are also treated as "emancipated" even though they may lack sufficient maturity to make their own choices. De facto, emancipated minors become their own decision-makers if they are married, living independently, or otherwise emancipated from their parents.

Emma Ogden is not emancipated, but a case can be made that she is sufficiently mature to make her own medical choices, even a major life-and-death crisis. If she is deemed mature, then the views of her parents are technically irrelevant (except as they might serve as advice to their daughter). There remains controversy over whether clinicians can, on their own, declare a minor to be sufficiently mature or whether they need a declaration by a court before relying on the minor's consent or refusal. If the clinicians unilaterally decide to treat a minor as mature, their action could be challenged by the parents, relatives, or by other health professionals.

If a minor is not emancipated or classified as mature for purposes of medical decision-making, then the parents are the surrogates with responsibility to make medical choices until the time that they are disqualified by a court. If Emma were not deemed mature, they would clearly have the right to consent to the transplant even in the face of their daughter's objection.

In this case, the parents seemed to concur in Emma's choice to refuse the transplant. Dr. Hamid faces additional decisions at that point. He could honor Emma's own choice on the grounds that he deems her a mature minor. He might do so without the determination by a court of her status. Alternatively, he could classify her as not sufficiently autonomous to make such a major decision and rely on the parents' decision. If he follows this course, however, he could run into an additional problem. While patients deemed sufficiently autonomous have an almost unlimited right to refuse medical treatment, parents acting as surrogates have somewhat less freedom. We know Jehovah's Witness and Christian Science parents can be overruled on grounds of patient welfare, even though the parents are acting in good faith.

It is theoretically possible that Emma, a mature minor, has the authority to refuse the transplant but that her parents could be challenged as not being sufficiently reasonable if they are the ones asked to consent or refuse. In that case, Dr. Sandstedt would have to be clear on whether she was relying on the patient's own refusal (on grounds that she was a mature minor) or on parental surrogate decision-making.

In both of these cases the patient's authority to refuse consent to potentially life-saving treatment is made complicated by constraints on the capacity of the patient to make substantially autonomous decisions. In Mr. Maxwell's case, the problem was his dementia; in Emma's case it was her age. In either case, however, clinicians could confront a choice between treating the patient as possessing sufficient capacity to consent or treating the patient as lacking that capacity, thus relying on a familial surrogate. The policies and limits of decisional authority differ in the two courses. The constraints, insofar as they exist, are what is sometimes called "internal" in both these cases. They are problems with the capacity of the patient related to some condition that exists within the patient. In the following cases we examine limits on autonomy based on external constraints.

External Constraints on Autonomy

Persons may be substantially autonomous in the sense that they have the neurological and mental capacity as well as adequate knowledge but still be constrained for specific choices by external forces. Persons in special institutions, sometimes called "total" institutions, such as prisons, boarding schools, or the military may be subject to forces that exert substantial control on their choices. Persons may also be under the threat of physical force. One interesting problem in this area is whether persons have their autonomy violated when they are pressured by "irresistibly attractive offers." For example, if an imprisoned sexual offender is offered release if, and only if, he agrees to an implant of a long-acting hormone that is expected to control his sexual aggression, is such a person able to autonomously choose to accept or reject the offer? If not, is it because the offer is made while he is in prison or is it because the option seems so attractive compared to the alternative? Ethical problems of respect for autonomy can be created by the external forces such as these. The following case illustrates the problem.

═══════════ **CASE 6-3** ═══════════

Readdicting a Heroin User: Are Prisoners Free to Consent to Research?

Forty-eight-year-old Harry Henning was in the fifth year of a twenty-year sentence in the state prison for a third offense of possession of heroin and attempting to sell.

He had been convicted within a few years of completing college. Since entering the prison he had been drug free, but often recalled the "rush" of his drug of choice. The state prison was notoriously overcrowded, with three prisoners per cell and limited time for exercise or recreation.

Marc Turner, MD, was a research pharmacologist who had devoted his career to problems of addiction. For the past five years he had been doing research on a new agent that was a specific heroin receptor cell blocker. The drug, which could be administered by an implant, was designed to provide long-term blocking of the effects of heroin. It had been tested in mice and in three other species of animals and was now ready for initial trials in humans.

Dr. Turner turned to the state prison to find research subjects for a phase-one trial of his new compound. On the basis of animal studies, he had good reason to believe it would be safe in humans and effective in blocking the addiction response by interfering with the site at which heroin binds in the brain. He proposed to recruit former heroin addicts, administer the implant, and then administer heroin to study the response.

State regulations permitted the use of certain prisoners for research, but prohibited payment of undue compensation, defined as any amount significantly different from what prisoners could earn in other prison employment. Dr. Turner realized that, if his study went as planned, the subjects would experience none of the traditional pleasures of heroin. Nevertheless, in case the drug did not work as hoped, he wanted to make the initial trial of the drug on persons whose environment would be tightly controlled for many years. Furthermore, he needed to control the environment of the subjects tightly during the research period.

In order to provide this control, he proposed to do the research on prisoners with long enough sentences that they would have many years to recover should something go wrong with the experiment. To provide adequate control of the environment during the research, he proposed to move the prisoner subjects to the hospital ward of the prison where the prisoner would be placed in a private room with bath. Each prison hospital room had a TV and easy chair as well as a hospital bed.

When Harry Henning saw the notice recruiting subjects, he figured he was an ideal candidate. He had had his life destroyed by his uncontrollable addiction and would like to make a contribution to society to prevent similar problems with others in the future. The private room was also appealing. Should the institutional review board responsible for approving research in the prison permit prisoners such as Mr. Henning to volunteer for this research? If so, can a prisoner in this environment give an adequately free and informed consent?

COMMENTARY

Former drug addict, Harry Henning, has become a candidate for a research project, a clinical trial of a new narcotic antagonist that potentially could treat heroin addicts by blocking the effects of that drug. The general questions of the ethics of clinical trials will be discussed in Chapter 16 and those of informed consent in Chapter 17. Here, the issue of debate is whether Harry Henning is a substantially autonomous person for the purposes of deciding whether to participate in the proposed research and whether the institutional review board (IRB) should approve the study.

There is no reason to believe that Mr. Henning lacks the innate capacity to understand the information presented during the consent conversation or process it. He lacks none of the factors inherently necessary to be an autonomous person. He is not mentally ill, retarded, or ill to the point that he cannot think clearly. The real problem is whether his environment provides such external constraints that his decisions in this setting cannot be substantially autonomous ones.

There is evidence in the case that Mr. Henning probably would not (or should not) consent to be part of this study if he were not incarcerated. He is a former addict, and the study poses a real if small risk of readdicting him or producing other side effects. It seems clear that the main reason Mr. Henning would agree to participate is because he is incarcerated. (The other possibility is that he realizes that the drug designed to attach to the same receptor that binds heroin could actually produce the heroin-like euphoria he remembers so vividly. The drug is designed to attach to the site in such a way that it blocks the heroin from the receptor, but does not itself trigger the heroin response, but there is a chance that this would not be the result in humans so that a heroin euphoria could result from the drug and he would be readdicted.)

Does the incarceration present external constraints on his behavior that make his choice nonvoluntary? Mr. Henning is presented with two options, returning to his present life in the crowded cell block or moving to the new, more comfortable surroundings and taking a chance he will get the medication that is harmful. Is that an unacceptable offer? If so, is it simply because it is irresistibly attractive?

Consider someone who is dying from cancer who is told the only chance she has of a cure is to agree to a nauseatingly unpleasant chemotherapeutic agent. Presumably that agent is at least as unattractive to the cancer patient as the narcotic antagonist medication is to Mr. Henning. Yet the offer must appear to be irresistibly attractive considering the alternative (which is death in the case of the cancer patient). Yet we do not normally argue that the cancer patient cannot consent to the chemotherapy because the offer is so attractive. If someone tried to ban the offer because it is so attractive we would probably protest—precisely because the offer is so attractive. People should have access to very attractive options even when their choices are very limited.

What is the difference between the prisoner's case and the cancer patient's? The prisoner's choices are "artificially constrained" by the incarceration. Yet let us assume that Mr. Henning is justifiably imprisoned. Should he not be allowed to make limited choices, say between two different work details, even though his environment is artificially confining? If so, should he not be allowed to choose a "work" option of being a research subject, even if the offer is terribly attractive? Is he less autonomous if he is given the additional option that is very attractive? Would it be more ethical to conduct the research if the living conditions were made much worse, say, as bad as those in which he would otherwise be living?

Overriding the Choices of Autonomous Persons

Up to this point, this chapter has dealt with persons whose autonomy is debated, either because of inherent lack of the internal capacity to make substantially autonomous choices or because of external constraints that could make specific choices nonautonomous. Some persons, however, are substantially autonomous. They possess both the internal capacity to make choices according to their life plan and are in an environment that offers them reasonable freedom to choose without external constraints. Still the choices they make may seem to be very foolish. They may seem to offer risks of harms that far exceed any benefits that could be gained. Assuming a person is substantially autonomous, is there ever a time when it is ethically justified to constrain his or her actions for the individual's own good or does respect for autonomy always win out, requiring that the autonomous individual's own choices be respected insofar as it is only that individual whose interests are jeopardized?

The answer will depend on how one's ethical theory handles cases of conflict among principles. In these situations involving clearly autonomous people constrained neither by internal nor external factors, if the principle of autonomy holds sway, then no interference can be justified even to provide great benefit or prevent great harm, as long as the benefit and harm involved are those of the person who would be the target of such intervention. On the other hand, some ethical theories balance competing claims when two principles come into conflict. In that case, if the principle involved other than autonomy becomes weighty enough, autonomy may lose out. The most common case is one in which beneficence and nonmaleficence conflict with respect for autonomy as in the following cases.

CASE 6-4

A Diabetic Who Refuses Treatment for an Infection

Horace Johnson is a 60-year-old, wheel-chair limited patient suffering from insulin dependent diabetes mellitus (IDDM) of ten-year's duration. He has an infected, draining toe with bone exposed, cellulitis, and x-ray evidence of osteomyelitis brought on by the poor arterial circulation related to his IDDM. He is noncompliant in visits to the outpatient clinic for care of his infection, has no insurance coverage, refuses social worker and psychiatric consults, and now is refusing further debridement of the decaying tissue around the infection.

Mr. Johnson had on previous visits been seen by a consulting psychiatrist who found him to be eccentric, a semiretired man who had done janitorial work and odd jobs through his adult life. The psychiatrist had found some depression, but no evidence of mental illness that would have made it possible to declare him incompetent.

Dr. Maria Garcia was very concerned about the infection. She was afraid that he would lose the toe or worse, the foot, from gangrene if Mr. Johnson did not receive aggressive treatment.

She contemplated hospitalizing him and using sedation in order to treat the foot. She could not imagine his losing a toe or foot simply because he was so stubborn he would not agree to her recommendation.

COMMENTARY

Mr. Johnson has made a choice that most of us would find strange. He refuses a treatment that any physician would consider essential to avoid an amputation. To be sure, the physician's recommendation for debridement involves a value judgment—that it is better to suffer the discomfort of the aggressive treatment including debridement than to lose a toe or foot, but the value judgment seems so obviously right that most would be tempted to claim it is a "fact." Many would be tempted to say that anyone such as Mr. Johnson who would choose to take the very real risk of losing the toe or foot has simply made a mistake. Either the person has very strange values or is mentally ill and unable to make a rational evaluation of the options.

Dr. Garcia had previously followed a reasonable course of asking for a psychiatric consultation, learning that at that time Mr. Johnson was not a candidate for a declaration of incompetency. Had that been possible, the ethical problems related to the principle of respect for autonomy would have vanished. If Mr. Johnson were not competent, his autonomy would not be violated if he were treated against his will. He would not have sufficient autonomy for the principle to come into play. On the basis of the previous consult, however, Mr. Johnson has been treated as possessing enough autonomy that treating him against his wishes would be considered a violation of that autonomy. It could, of course, be that his mental condition has deteriorated since the psychiatric consultation. Dr. Garcia could seek to have him declared incompetent so that a guardian could be appointed to authorize treating him. She seems to understand, however, that she would likely fail in trying to get a declaration of incompetency. Mr. Johnson, whatever his strange behavior, does not appear sufficiently deranged to warrant such a declaration.

That leaves Dr. Garcia with two stark choices: respect his autonomy by letting his infection go without the needed treatment, or invoke the principle of beneficence—the moral imperative to benefit the patient—as a justification for admitting him to the hospital, sedating him, and treating him without his consent. Is this a case in which beneficence should triumph over respect for autonomy?

```
┌─────────────────── CASE 6–5 ───────────────────┐
```

Brought to the ER after a Suicide Attempt

Max Perrin, a 55-year-old male, was brought to the ER by the local rescue squad following a suicide attempt by means of consuming rat poison. The ER physician, Dr. Christopher LeMarke, recognized him immediately, as did the ER nurses. He had been a regular in the facility, having visited for his primary medical care and for two previous suicide attempts within the past eighteen months. During the previous visits his history had been explored completely. He was divorced, alienated from his adult children, and chronically depressed, but was not considered sufficiently impaired that he could be declared incompetent.

On the basis of state law, such patients could be held for up to seventy-two hours on the signature of two physicians, if they were deemed dangerous to themselves or others. Mr. Perrin, had never before engaged in any behavior that would suggest he was dangerous to others, but he surely was a danger to himself. He had on past admissions received short-term psychotherapy and prescriptions for antidepressant drugs, but he had stopped taking them because he said they made him feel sleepy.

He was now in the ER, incoherent and semiconscious. Should Dr. LeMarke sign the involuntary commitment and initiate another round of therapy?

COMMENTARY

This patient is certainly facing a serious crisis. He is suicidal and will die if not treated. Dr. LeMarke has the legal authority to commit him involuntarily and treat his medical problems that result from his suicide attempt. If Mr. Perrin were sufficiently mentally ill as to be treated as incompetent, as not sufficiently autonomous to make his own medical choices, the case would be relatively straightforward from the point of view of the ethics involved. He could be committed and treated without violating the ethical principle of respect for autonomy.

Mr. Perrin has previously been evaluated by a psychiatric consultant, however, and has been found to be sufficiently in touch with reality that he cannot be considered lacking in capacity. He seems to understand what he is doing. He has merely reached the conclusion he would, in his circumstances, rather die than live. Given his chronic depression that has not responded adequately to previous therapy, his isolation from his family, and his continuing problems, he has made the choice that life is not worth living. He is what some would call "rationally suicidal," that is, suicidal while having an understanding of his situation and capable of understanding the choices available to him.

Most commitment laws still permit retaining persons who are deemed dangerous to themselves or others. Committing those who are dangerous to others seems relatively uncontroversial. No matter how competent and rational, it is unacceptable to pose a serious, credible threat to others. Retaining such persons does not involve paternalism because paternalism requires that the action be undertaken for the good of the one who is restrained.

Committing those who are dangerous to themselves is more complicated. These laws were written in an era in which it was widely assumed that anyone who contemplated suicide was either mentally ill or morally wrong. While that is often the case, the interesting situations are the ones in which mental illness is ruled out or is at least of such a mild degree that the person cannot be declared incompetent.

This presents a group of cases of people who are of danger only to themselves and not sufficiently mentally ill to warrant restraint on the grounds that they are unable to know or control what they are doing. They are suicidal, but mentally competent, and only of danger to themselves. Restraining such persons using state laws permitting such restraint is paternalism in its most robust sense.

This poses an unexpectedly complicated problem. On the one hand, we generally accept the right of adults not only to hold any belief they choose, but also to act on those beliefs, provided their actions do not have an unacceptable impact on others. This might lead us to challenge Dr. LeMarke if he decided to use the existing paternalistic provisions of the current state law. On the other hand, the physician historically has been committed to preserving life. Especially in a case like this one, in which a life can be preserved for the foreseeable future (until a suicide attempt is successful), many doctors will feel morally obliged to take advantage of the present state law and commit the patient even if he is sufficiently mentally competent to understand what he is doing.

Competent adults generally have the legal and moral right to refuse life-saving treatment once they are determined to be mentally competent. Is there any reason why an exception should be made in the case of suicide?

CASE 6-6

Ignoring a Daughter's Do-Not-Resuscitate (DNR) Decision

This 88-year-old Hispanic man, Roberto Gonzalez, was admitted to Jefferson White Hospital Emergency Department with a diagnosis of cerebral hemorrhage and coma. Before Mr. Gonzalez's daughter could get to the hospital the consultant pulmonologist, Melanie Caldarone, administered cardiopulmonary resuscitation (CPR) and admitted him to the intensive care unit (ICU). Upon Ms. Gonzalez's arrival at the hospital, she explained that she did not want CPR or other life-sustaining measures based on past communication with her father. She showed them a letter from Mr. Gonzalez stating his concern about a friend who ended up "helpless on machines." There was no formal advance directive, however, just this one example

of Mr. Gonzalez's worry about his friend. The family physician and consultant neurologist had authorized extubation and removal of the respirator but did not insist
on that course because of the pulmonologist's insistence that Mr. Gonzalez was
"not brain dead." He was maintained on support for three days and then expired.

The insurance department of the HMO funding Mr. Gonzalez's hospitalization refused to pay for the ICU expenses because of the family's decision for DNR,
charging that the hospital and staff had overused the facilities and nursing staff and
for which the HMO accepted no financial responsibility.

COMMENTARY

Perhaps reflective of a fear of criticism from those who believed physicians have
a duty to use their skills to preserve life or perhaps out of intimidation by the
pulmonary consultant's specialty credentials and aggressive stance, the attending physician essentially relinquished his professional and moral authority by
taking the strange step of authorizing, but not insisting on, removal of the tube
and withdrawal of the respirator. Perhaps the attending physician did not want
to alienate this colleague. This is not good medical practice. Usually, disagreement among staff physicians does not cause lasting estrangement. The case is
further complicated by the mistaken belief on the part of the pulmonologist
that only "brain death" justifies withdrawal of respirators. This is a confusion
of the question of whether a patient can be pronounced dead with the question
of when a treatment becomes futile in the sense of not offering benefits to the
patient. We shall examine in Chapters 9 and 18 these questions of the relation
between brain death and decisions to forgo life support. Here our focus is on
the question of the principle of respect for autonomy and how it impacts decisions to attempt resuscitation.

If Mr. Gonzalez were the author of the instruction to his physicians not
to attempt resuscitation and he had given the instruction (in writing or orally)
when he was clearly competent, this case would be relatively straightforward.
Competent persons currently have the legal and moral right to refuse any
medical treatments whatsoever, provided they are offered for their own good.
This includes end-of-life support with devices such as respirators. The principle
of respect for autonomy is taken to require respect for the substantially autonomous decisions of persons including refusals of life-supporting medical care.

The case is made more complex by the fact that Mr. Gonzalez is not competent; he is in a coma. Moreover, the only evidence we have is a letter with
indirect reference to his wishes. It is his daughter who interpreted the letter to
mean that her father would not want to be resuscitated. She did so in her presumed capacity as Mr. Gonzalez's surrogate decision-maker.

This raises the question of how such decisions relate to the principle of
autonomy. As we shall see in more detail in the cases of Chapter 18, surrogates

who step in to make medical decisions for formerly competent adults such as Mr. Gonzalez must first attempt to do what the patient would have wanted, based on what is known about the patient's beliefs and values. If the patient has explicitly stated his desires, this could be relatively easy. If the patient had signed a written advance directive refusing respirators or other means of resuscitation in these circumstances, we would be respecting the patient's autonomy. In a very real sense, autonomy of the patient can be extended into the period of incompetency in this way.

If, however, his daughter has no direct evidence of what her father would have wanted for his own care, extending patient autonomy is impossible. She then takes on the surrogate role, guided at most by her general knowledge of her father's life choices, beliefs, and values. As the degree of certainty about her father's wishes decreases, the possibility of patient autonomy being the basis of the choice decreases as well. In the limiting case, familial surrogates may have to make choices based entirely on what they believe is best for the patient, unguided by the patient's own beliefs, values, and preferences. What, then, is the place of the principle of respect for autonomy in such cases?

In such cases, the question arises of why the daughter has any authority to make choices at all. Some defend her role because they believe that the one who knows the patient best will be the one who has the best chance of choosing what the patient would have wanted. In Mr. Gonzalez's case, this may be true, but that certainly does not provide a reason for familial surrogate decision-making in the case when the patient is an infant or a severely impaired older person who has never formulated beliefs about terminal care. Even in these cases, however, we generally favor giving the next-of-kin the role of surrogate. Until such time that the next-of-kin is shown to be too foolish, too malicious, or simply unwilling to serve in this role, the familial surrogate is given the responsibility of deciding what is best for the patient.

In this role, family members may well retain some discretion in choosing what they think is best based on the family's beliefs and values rather than those of the patient. To the extent that this is done, we may see something that can be called "familial autonomy." On the basis of an analogy to the respect shown for the decisions of autonomous individuals, those who believe in some role of special importance for the family hold that the family unit, represented by the next-of-kin, has a special place in choosing what is best for the patient whose own views cannot be determined. In this sense, they have some range of discretion, some autonomy, in deciding on the plan that is best for the patient.

Clearly, family discretion is more limited than that given to competent and formerly competent patients. Family surrogates can go beyond reason. This notion will be explored further in Chapter 18. What is critical here is that the principle of respecting autonomy may have a place not only in requiring respect for substantially autonomous individual decisions but also in giving a family unit some space in making choices consistent with the family's beliefs and values.

There is a final question raised by this case: whether the HMO insurance staff was justified in denying coverage for those last three days That question will be addressed in Chapter 15.

NOTES

[1] For good discussions of the principle of autonomy and related concepts see Feinberg, Joel. "Legal Paternalism." In his *Rights, Justice, and the Bounds of Liberty: Essays in Social Philosophy*. Princeton, NJ: Princeton University Press, 1980, pp. 110–129; Dworkin, Gerald. "Moral Autonomy." In *Morals, Science, and Society*. H. Tristram Engelhardt and Daniel Callahan, editors. Hastings-on-Hudson, NY: The Hastings Center, 1978, pp. 156–171; Faden, Ruth, and Tom L. Beauchamp in collaboration with Nancy N. P. King. *A History and Theory of Informed Consent*. New York: Oxford University Press, 1986; and Beauchamp, Tom L. and James F. Childress, editors. *Principles of Biomedical Ethics*, 4th ed. New York: Oxford University Press, 1994, pp. 120–188.

[2] See the extended discussion of this approach in The Hastings Center. *Guidelines on the Termination of Life-Sustaining Treatment and the Care of the Dying*. Briarcliff Manor, New York: The Hastings Center, 1987, pp. 20–29.

[3] Mill, John Stuart. *On Liberty*. New York: The Liberal Arts Press, 1956.

[4] Areen, Judith. "The Legal Status of Consent Obtained from Families of Adult Patients to Withhold or Withdraw Treatment." *Journal of the American Medical Association* 258 (No. 2, July 10, 1987):229–235; Veatch, Robert M. "Limits of Guardian Treatment Refusal: A Reasonableness Standard." *American Journal of Law and Medicine* 9 (4, Winter 1984):427–468.

[5] Appelbaum, Paul S., Charles W. Lidz, and Alan Meisel. *Informed Consent: Legal Theory and Clinical Practice*. New York: Oxford University Press, 1987, pp. 66–69.

CHAPTER 7

＊○

Veracity: Honesty with Patients

Other Cases Involving Veracity

1-1: Disclosure of a Terminal Diagnosis
17-1: Therapeutic Privilege: Scaring the Patient to Death
with News about Risks

In the previous chapter, health professionals were in positions in which they had to choose between doing what they thought was best for patients and respecting the patient's autonomy. The moral principle of autonomy was in conflict with the principle of beneficence. We saw that some people held that respect for autonomy can take precedence over doing good for the patient.

Respect for autonomy is an element of a more general moral concept of respect for persons. Respect for persons, according to this view, sometimes requires moral choices that do not maximize the patient's well-being.

Another element of respect for persons deals with honest disclosure. Traditional ethics holds that it is simply wrong morally to lie to people, even if it is expedient to do so, even if greater good will come from the lie. According to this view, lying to people is morally wrong in that it shows lack of respect for them. Expressed as a moral principle, holders of this view claim that veracity or honesty or truth-telling is a moral principle. The principle conveys that dishonesty in actions or practices is an element that makes them wrong. As with justice and autonomy, there may also be other dimensions that tend toward making actions right. For example, the fact that a lie produces good results would tend to make it right. However, holders of this view maintain that, nevertheless, the lie itself is an element that makes the action wrong. It is, according to this approach, *prima facie* wrong, that is, wrong insofar as the lying dimension is considered.

It is striking that even though many common moral systems treat lying as wrong in and of itself, traditional professional health care ethics has not. Thus the Hippocratic Oath does not require that physicians deal honestly with patients.

Many health professionals have, in fact, maintained that it is right for them to lie to a patient when doing so will spare the patient agony. In this sense, professional medical ethics has focused on the consequences of actions, not on any inherent moral elements whether it be respecting autonomy or telling the truth.

Benevolent dishonesty by physicians was accepted (or at least not directly condemned) by organized medicine for centuries. That changed in the United States in 1980 with a major rewriting of the American Medical Association's (AMA's) *Code of Ethics*. In that code, an entirely new provision was included reading, "A physician shall deal honesty with patients and colleagues...."[1] The medical professional group, for the first time, explicitly endorsed honesty. The AMA position remained until what is generally taken to be a minor revision in 2001. At that time this provision was softened to read, "A physician shall...be honest in all professional interactions...." Some have suggested that this made the text more ambiguous leaving open the possibility that the injunction to honesty is only to apply to physician interaction with other health professionals. While the AMA's statement of principles has become more ambiguous, the more detailed opinions and annotation retain the earlier wording: holding that "a physician should at all times deal honestly and openly with patients."[2]

The other health professions have taken somewhat different positions on veracity. The code of the American Pharmacists Association (APhA) has for many years considered truthfulness as part of the essential character of the pharmacist. The 1969 version of the APhA *Code of Ethics* states that "A Pharmacist should strive to provide information to patients regarding professional services truthfully, accurately, and fully and should avoid misleading patients regarding the nature, cost, or value of these professional services."[3] The 1995 revised code states, "A pharmacist acts with honesty and integrity in professional relationships." This provision is followed with an interpretation that reads, "A pharmacist has a duty to tell the truth and to act with conviction of conscience."[4]

The American Nurses Association does not speak directly of honesty among nurses, but does hold that "Patients have the moral and legal right...to be given accurate, complete, and understandable information in a manner that facilitates an informed judgment."[5]

Ethics that focus on consequences, such as the Hippocratic Oath, accept lies when they produce more good than harm. Classical utilitarian ethics assesses the acceptability of a lie based on the total consequences. It considers the benefits and harms for all parties.[6] By contrast, traditional health professional ethics looks only at the consequences for the patient.[7] For example, in the era when health professionals were expected to be paternalistic, if they were asked by a patient on the purpose of a medication they might give an evasive answer trying to avoid alarming the patient. If the patient said, "Isn't it true that I am taking this because I have advanced cancer?," the physician would have at least considered telling a benevolent "white lie" or misleading reference to some other name for the tumor. Likewise, physicians sometimes prescribed placebos. If asked the ingredient in the prescription, the physician would probably have dishonestly told the patient the name of the medication that the placebo was mimicking. The cases in this chapter present situations in which health professionals believe that they can benefit their patients by lying or at least withholding the truth.

While ethics that focus on consequences evaluate whether to lie by trying to determine whether a lie will produce benefit, the ethics that emphasize features other than consequences, such as respect for persons, hold that there is something simply wrong about lying. Immanuel Kant, the eighteenth-century philosopher, is most closely identified with this view.[8] Twentieth-century thinkers outside of medicine agreed.[9] By contrast, most physicians traditionally accepted the legitimacy of lying to patients in order to protect them. This was still the case as late as the early 1960s.[10] There were some exceptions. In the middle of the nineteenth century, physician Worthington Hooker argued for honesty because he thought the consequences of failing to be truthful would be harmful, an argument also used by physician Richard Cabot in the early twentieth century.[11] More recent developments, as seen in a survey of physicians in the late 1970s, suggest that physicians are changing, giving greater emphasis on the patient's right to the truth.[12]

The cases in this chapter begin with the special problem of what patients should be told when health professionals themselves are not yet sure what the facts are. Then a series of cases involving the problem of lying to patients in order to benefit them will be explored, followed by cases in which the health professional considers lying to the patient in order to benefit others. The chapter will then take up two special situations involving veracity: cases in which first the patient and then the patient's family asks not to be told. Finally, a case explores disclosure to patients who ask to see their medical record.

THE CONDITION OF DOUBT

Before discussing the ethics of disclosure, it is important to get some sense of exactly what it is that might be disclosed. In health care, a problem arises frequently that can be referred to as the "condition of doubt." It arises when the health care professional is in real doubt about what the facts are.

The confusion may be in regard to a diagnosis about which the health care professional has only a preliminary suspicion. The doubt may arise when innovative therapies are contemplated and the physician is not clear about what the effects of the treatment will be. He or she may not even know whether the doubt is from personal ignorance of the current literature or because even the leading authorities are unclear.

Consulting physicians and specialists as well as nurses and members of other health professions may have only limited knowledge about a patient's condition. Someone else on the health care team may be better informed. In these cases, even one who is in principle militantly committed to dealing honestly with the patient may not know exactly what should be said. The first case in this chapter raises this problem.

═══════ **CASE 7–1** ═══════

A Routine Mole or an Early Case of Skin Cancer: The Duty to Disclose Doubtful Information

During routine physical examination, the skin of 46-year-old Betty Harris was examined by her internist, Daniel Newlander. The examination was part of Dr. Newlander's standard procedure to look for any dermatological problems. On Ms. Harris's back, Dr. Newlander saw a brown, mole-like spot that alarmed him. The color was varied; the edges ragged. He could not recall seeing it before.

Dr. Newlander's first thought was that it looked rather like it could be melanoma. Of course, he would not know without excising the tissue and getting a report from the lab. He wanted the tissue removed as soon as possible and asked Ms. Harris to schedule an appointment. Dr. Newlander suggested an opening in his schedule later in the week.

Ms. Harris asked him what the hurry was. She asked him, "Do you think it is cancer or something?" That was precisely Dr. Newlander's concern, but he did not wish to alarm her and, in fact, could not know without the lab results. He was strongly committed to dealing honestly with patients, but knew that he did not know the full answer to her question. How should he respond to her question?

COMMENTARY

Even though Dr. Newlander is committed to honesty, there are several possible honest responses. One would be simply to say that he did not know what the tissue was. Another would be to say that he did not know, but he was concerned it could be skin cancer. He could go even further and convey that the growth had many characteristics of skin cancer. Or he might say that he does not think it is cancer, but he would not know for sure until the lab results are back. All of these responses are approximately honest, yet they convey very different impressions. The last response may stretch the truth, especially if he really is quite concerned.

If the lab results had come back and had shown that the tissue either was or was not cancerous, then Dr. Newlander would have no difficulty in deciding what Ms. Harris should be told. But Dr. Newlander's situation is quite different. The real problem here seems to be that Dr. Newlander is confronted with a situation in which he really does not know what the cells are. He has a concern, in fact, a serious worry, but lacks any basis for a firm opinion.

Many people who generally believe there is a moral duty to tell the truth also recognize that there are situations in which it is too early to tell what the truth is. If a physician sees a patient who is a smoker and who had a persistent cough, laryngitis, and fever, the diagnosis of lung cancer may enter her mind, but that does not mean she should blurt out to the patient immediately that she may have lung cancer. Not only is there real doubt about the diagnosis at this point but also there is doubt about who should be the one to raise the issue.

Dr. Newlander must decide what counts as truthful, meaningful communication about a preliminary concern that the growth looks like it could be cancerous. It should be clear that no one wants what could be called the "full truth." There is an infinite number of things that could be said. No reasonable patient wants to know everything: the technical names of the possible tumor, the names of the tests to be performed and how those tests were developed, the statistical probabilities of the various results, and so forth. There are many facts that most patients would not be interested in knowing.

What is usually expected is information that is "reasonably meaningful." The problem in this case is that it is not clear exactly what is reasonably meaningful. Surely some suggestions in the literature are so tenuous and the effects so trivial that patients would not consider them meaningful. In fact, supplying too much trivial, unneeded information will actually make the consent process more confusing and therefore less adequate.

Dr. Newlander's problem is compounded because he faces two different kinds of uncertainty. First, there is the uncertainty inherent in the lack of information. Even the best dermatologist in the world may lack certainty with a preliminary examination of a mole. Second, there is here doubt about whether an internist like Dr. Newlander knows adequately what the best dermatologists can know at this point. He probably does not remember the exact details of everything he has read and been taught about diagnosing a malignant skin growth. Even if he did, he would never know for sure whether newer, more definitive studies had appeared in the literature that he simply had not seen. If he did an exhaustive search of the literature—something he cannot realistically do for the special conditions of each patient presenting in the doctor's office, he still would not know whether he had covered all the data. He will have to learn to live with the uncertainty.[13] He simply responds by saying he can not know what the growth is until the lab results are back. These are questions that arise in the consent context, which we will be discussed in more detail in Chapter 17.

LYING IN ORDER TO BENEFIT

Resolving doubt about "what is the truth" is not all that is at stake in the ethics of truth-telling. In some cases, the health care professional may know the truth, but fear that disclosing it to the patient will do the patient or someone else significant harm. Often it turns out that telling the truth is also beneficial, but the interesting moral cases are those in which honesty involves risk of hurting someone. In such cases, is there still a moral duty to tell the truth or is it right to be honest only in those cases in which telling the truth is expected to be beneficial? The following cases are ones in which someone is worried about hurting another person by being honest.

Protecting the Patient by Lying

Often it is the patient who could be injured—psychologically or physically—if the medical professional is completely honest. Among the issues presented in the following case are (1) is avoiding the truth any different morally than telling an outright lie, (2) how can the physician know what the consequences will be, (3) can the problem be avoided by referring the patient to another physician for disclosure, and (4) what is the nature of the duty to be honest?

CASE 7–2

Placebos for Addiction Withdrawal

Seventy-four-year-old Mrs. Abraham had been getting the prescription filled for years. She had a malignancy of the colon 4 years previously. An operation had corrected the problem, but in the emotional and physical distress that followed, Mrs. Abraham had a terrible time sleeping. She had received a prescription from her internist, Dr. Raymond Siemens for Seconal® to help her sleep and continued taking them to the point at which she could not sleep without them. Her physician, after several months, realized that he had caused her to become addicted and felt that it was his duty to help her break her habit. He had arranged with the pharmacist to take Seconal® capsules and gradually replace more and more of the active ingredient, until some months later she was on pure lactose packaged in the distinctive Seconal® capsules. She still claimed, however, that she could not sleep without her sleeping pills.

Dr. Siemens firmly believed that it was in his patient's best interest, but he felt uncomfortable about the placebo prescription he was writing. He was concerned about potential legal implications of lack of informed consent. (He surely had not informed his patient of the treatment strategy and the risks and benefits of the "drug" he was now prescribing.) Furthermore, he was asking the pharmacist to mislabel the prescription, placing the drug name on the prescription label when, in fact, it contained nothing but inert lactose. Mislabeling was against the law. He was concerned about the fact that Mrs. Abraham was paying monthly for the prescription that contained no active ingredients. The charge was modest, barely covering the cost of the capsules' ingredients which were being discarded, surely not compensating the pharmacist for the extra time involved in emptying the capsules and refilling them. But most of all he was concerned about whether he was being dishonest. Do placebo prescriptions such as Mrs. Abraham's involve lying and, if so, are they morally wrong?

COMMENTARY

Dr. Siemens is facing the classical ethical dilemma of the conflict between medical paternalism and the principle of veracity. According to the traditional ethical health care ethics based on the duty to be beneficent to the patient, placebos were considered an important therapy in the armamentarium of the health care professional. Patients in situations such as Mrs. Abraham's occasionally become addicted. If the physician were convinced that the drugs were doing more harm than good and had tried other more direct methods of withdrawing his patient without success, then the graded reduction in dosage, often done without the patient's knowledge, was judged to be the best course for the patient.

In this case, when a physician reaches this conclusion and his action is to write a placebo prescription, then the pharmacist, if he fills the prescription, is willy-nilly brought into the act as well. Thus two health professionals face a moral issue. A first level of problem might arise in deciding whether a placebo for addiction withdrawal is the best course. Other treatment options, such as referral to a psychiatrist or a plan for decreasing dosage involving the full knowledge of the patient could be alternatives. One problem with the placebo option is that there is some chance that the patient could find out what the physician has done, potentially undercutting the trust that is critical in the doctor–patient relation. Is there any reason to assume that the physician's judgment about the placebo being the best course should prevail?

There is a deeper level of controversy in this case. Critics may agree that the placebo is in Mrs. Abraham's best interest but feel that the physician is still doing her wrong if he continues to prescribe an inert substance when he comes to believe that the active drug is no longer needed. The placebo prescription clearly generates costs for Mrs. Abraham, but that may not be the main concern. Some would be concerned that it is simply dishonest to imply to the patient that she is getting something that she really is not. Some, including those who reason like eighteenth-century philosopher, Immanuel Kant, believe that there is simply something unethical about telling such lies—even when everyone is better off for the lie being told. People who hold such a view believe there is a moral principle that it is wrong to lie regardless of the consequences. This principle, sometimes called the principle of veracity, identifies all knowing wrongful statements as unethical, at least in regard to the lie.

The pharmacist in this case may see the dispensing as an implicit lie. He may consider the labeling an outright lie as well as a legally suspect practice. First, consider the distinction often drawn between lying and failing to tell the truth. Can Dr. Siemens reason that prescribing, if it did not contain directly false statements to the patient, was not lying, but merely withholding the truth about the placebo? Could he say, for instance, that "This prescription will help you sleep" without explicitly saying that he is continuing to prescribe Seconal®?

Even if all outright dishonest statements are morally wrong, no one has a moral duty to say everything he knows to other people. Could Dr. Siemens solve his ethical dilemma by omitting the directly false information?

Outright lying is different morally from simply failing to tell the whole truth. In normal human interactions, out of courtesy we sometimes fail to tell the whole truth—for instance about the appearance of someone who is not terribly attractive. Lying always involves failing to respect persons in a way that merely withholding part of the truth does not.

At the same time, health professionals have a duty to make sure patients are adequately informed so that they can make autonomous choices about the treatment options. Informed consent requires that patients get relevant information truthfully. A health professional is in a fiduciary relation with a patient in which truthful information is expected. Once a relationship is established, that relationship implies not merely a duty to avoid outright lies but also a duty to provide certain information. This suggests that health professionals have an obligation to disclose relevant information, even if ordinary citizens do not always have such obligations. Here the duty of veracity is interconnected with the principle of fidelity. Those who are committed to the respect-for-persons perspective would probably claim in this case that the health professionals— the physician and the pharmacist—owe to the patient, with whom there is a bond of fidelity or loyalty, not only refraining from false statements but also providing all potentially relevant information honestly. Holders of this view might even reach that conclusion when it conflicts with the duty to do what the provider believes is best for the patient.

Protecting the Welfare of Others

In the previous case, a medical professional contemplated lying or withholding the truth because he thought it would be better for the patient not to know. Sometimes it is not the patient, but someone else—a colleague or friend— whose welfare could be protected if the truth were withheld. In the following cases, health professionals are asked to lie to protect others.

CASE 7–3

Confessing an Error in Judgment: Is It Necessary?

Emilia Hedges is a 68-year-old woman who saw her primary care physician, Lawrence Aleman, soon after experiencing sudden slurring of speech and brief weakness in the right upper arm. She reported the episode lasted about thirty minutes, with clearing of all symptoms. Dr. Aleman prescribed an aspirin and asked her to report back if any similar symptoms returned.

Three days later, she was hospitalized with a major left-sided stroke (CVA). An ultrasound examination of the left carotid artery revealed a 98% narrowing (called a "pinpoint"). On the Neurology service, Ms. Hedges was treated with anticoagulants (blood thinners). A month later, an operation was performed to remove the clot (a procedure called an endarterectomy). She subsequently was left with marked weakness of the right upper arm and some impairment of her speech.

Dr. Aleman was terribly distressed by this outcome. He felt guilt from missing the signs of a transient ischemic attack that indicated a severe obstruction of blood flow to the left side of the brain, affecting the right arm and the speech center. He realized there were more things he could have done during Ms. Hedges's initial visit such as listening to the carotid arteries with a stethoscope. Hearing a murmur suggesting blockage is clinically helpful, even if it is not definitive.

Now he faces the dilemma of whether he should say something to Ms. Hedges about the fact that he realizes he could have, probably should have, done more for her. Primary care physicians are frequently placed in a position in which they are not sure whether they ought to refer a patient to a specialist. That comes with the territory of being a general internist or primary care doctor. Dr. Aleman's question is whether, when he realizes he made the wrong judgment, he should say something to his patient about it. At this point, there is really nothing that can be done to reverse his error in judgment. Telling Ms. Hedges will necessarily destroy the trust and confidence that she has in him. It will be an embarrassing and unpleasant experience for him and arguably will not do anything to help Ms. Hedges correct the effects of Dr. Aleman's error.

COMMENTARY

Like the previous cases, this situation poses a conflict between following the principles of beneficence and nonmaleficence on the one hand and the principle of veracity on the other. The difference here is that there is little reason to believe that the patient, Ms. Hedges, will benefit from the disclosure of Dr. Aleman's bad judgment. In fact, she could plausibly be harmed in the sense that she will experience a strain in her relation with her physician. It is possible that, with the information about his error, she might take action to protect herself in the future—by changing primary care doctors, for example. Nevertheless, if the case were to be decided on Hippocratic grounds of patient benefit, an argument could be made that having Dr. Aleman keep his mistake to himself does Ms. Hedges more good than harm.

The real issue is whether that is the ground on which this case should be decided. There are two other grounds. Still working within the framework of beneficence and nonmaleficence, there are benefits and harms to other parties that some consequentialist ethics would take into account. Utilitarianism differs from Hippocratic ethics in that it considers potential benefits and harms to all parties impacted by an action.

There are two other elements of benefit and harm that one might want to consider. First, the disclosure of errors in judgment by health care professionals potentially could affect future patients. The disclosure might lead to corrective action—further education or development of checks on decision-making that could eventually benefit patients down the road. Hippocratic ethics would not necessarily take these effects into account, at least if that tradition is interpreted as requiring that only benefits and harms to the present patient count morally. Still a utilitarian would consider these less direct consequences to be morally relevant.

The other party who could be affected is Dr. Aleman himself. He has interests at stake. He surely will feel more comfortable if he can avoid disclosing to his patient that he has failed to perform tests and make a referral and that these judgments are directly related to Ms. Hedges's present medical problems. If a utilitarian would take into account all parties affected by a decision about whether to disclose, then presumably Dr. Aleman can add into the calculation, the benefits and harms not only for Ms. Hedges and future patients, but also for himself, his family, and anyone else who will be influenced by his disclosure decision.

Many analysts of this case will call into question whether consequences alone should be the basis for settling the issue. The principle of veracity holds that actions are morally right in so far as they involve speaking truthfully to patients. This includes admitting to patients one's lack of competency to respond to a given problem and to see that such expertise is obtained. When serious errors of judgment occur, this at minimum would require answering a patient's questions about the error truthfully. In the previous commentary, we saw that the structure of some relationships requires not only speaking truthfully but also disclosing information, even embarrassing and painful information, when the relationship is a fiduciary one in which such communication is expected. Do benefits for Ms. Hedges or for Dr. Aleman justify withholding what he knows about Ms. Hedges's medical problems?

CASE 7–4

Scanning for Money: Increasing Imaging to Enhance Practice Finances

In a small, independent group practice, comprised primarily of internists and general practitioners, the business manager asked for one of the clinicians to bring a financial issue before the members of the group, at the regular meeting of the physicians. The current chairman, Dr. Bryan Turner, conducted the meeting after clinical hours and most of the physicians attended. Under the heading of "new business," the chairman began a discussion about the recent use of radioisotopes rented by the group.

With obvious embarrassment, Dr. Turner admitted his discomfort about the subject: "Our income from the use of the isotopes is not paying for the expense of their use. Obviously, if we are to continue this practice, more of these screening tests will have to be done". The small, general hospital in the city did provide the services provided by the isotopes, if a bit less conveniently for both patients and physicians. In essence, the clinicians were being asked to order more tests.

Dr. Turner also knew, however, that there were patients seen by the group who were not presently being scanned who could gain from scanning, at least marginally to rule out more obscure diagnoses. He believed there were enough cases seen by their group in which a legitimate case could be put forward to defend the scans—at least cases that were strong enough that they would pass muster with the insurance companies that would be asked to pay for the procedures.

It seemed to be that the bottom line was a factor in trying to stimulate increased use of the isotopes, but some patient would probably gain something along the way. If physicians in the practice increased the orders for scanning, what should they say to patients?

COMMENTARY

Historically, quality control of laboratory and radiologic services has been erratic in the various arrangements of physician ownership or interest in such services. Only in 1992 was the Clinical Laboratory Improvement Act (CLIA) activated, regulating proficiency and quality assurance procedures. Even so, the implementation of inspections or other evaluations has been sporadic and of variable quality. An obvious conflict of interests exists, in a highly commercialized culture, when diagnostic activities are not done only in the best interest of patients.

In this case, clearly the individual physicians were not intending to ask patients to undergo invasive tests for the beneficial profit ratio of the medical group. It seemed possible, however, to encourage the use of the tests more often so that each clinician would be more inclined to order tests when there was even a remote possibility of benefit. On the other hand, to attempt to obfuscate that motive is to become dishonest with those being served. In this case, the group of physicians had the obvious option to reduce financial expense: refer those patients with clinical indications for such tests to the hospital radiology department.

In April of 1989, a study of the U.S. Department of Health and Human Services (HHS) was published, showing correlation of doctor ownership with increased tests for patients. Specifically, when doctors owned shares in labs outside their offices, their Medicare patients were billed for up to 45% more tests than the patients of other doctors.[14]

Given the data showing increased use of diagnostic imaging and similar testing when physicians own the equipment and the argument that some marginal benefit may accrue to patients from the additional testing, the question arises of what patients need to be told about the ownership arrangement and the discussion at this meeting stimulated by a business officer whose agenda was not solely that of patient benefit. Must patients be told about the ownership arrangement and the economic interest of the group in maximal use of the scanning? Must they be told of risks and benefits of the scanning? Must they be told of the meeting and how the subject came up?

SPECIAL CASES OF TRUTH-TELLING

Although the usual cases of truth-telling involve situations in which the physician contemplates lying or withholding the truth in order to benefit the patient or benefit someone else, some special cases occur in which lies, deceptions, or withholdings of information are motivated by other concerns such as respect for someone who is believed to have authority to decide that the truth should be withheld. These include cases in which the patient or some member of the family requests that the truth be withheld.

Patients Who Do Not Want to Be Told

Sometimes a patient is said to fear bad news or, for other reasons, desires not to know some of the aspects of his or her condition. When being seen for a diagnosis of a potentially fatal disease, the patient himself or herself may explicitly ask the provider to avoid disclosing the bad news. A physician may, as in the following case, contemplate a plan of care including informing the patient of his diagnosis only to discover that the patient does not want the information.

CASE 7–5

Refusing to Learn about Cancer

Wesley Crossman was a 43-year-old real estate broker who had just been hospitalized for persistent pain in the bone of his hips. At first he thought he must have pulled a muscle, but the pain gradually became more severe. About 6 months ago, after he had had the pain for almost a month, he went to his family physician, who made a tentative diagnosis of arthritis. After several months of treatment with indomethacin, an antiarthritic drug, during which time the pain became unbearable, referral was made to an orthopedic specialist for further tests.

Mr. Crossman was the proprietor of a small agency in a suburb of Phoenix, Arizona, in the path of urban growth. Although only marginally successful, he earned enough to support his wife and three children who were now 18, 14, and 12. The rapid development of the area gave him new hope for a financial bonanza. With one child in college and two more in line, he could use the money. He had recently sold a tract of land to a local group, including a physician and two lawyers, who were planning to build a shopping center. After overcoming his wife's reservations ("She's always too hesitant to take a chance"), he invested $20,000 from their savings account in the project. It would take a few years to payoff, but he was tired of making fortunes on land for everyone else while he and his family put their savings into a bank which added only a dribble of interest twice a year.

Mr. Crossman felt tense when he went to the appointment with Dr. Marvin Greenblatt, the orthopedic specialist. He had not said anything explicit to his wife, but they were both thinking about the neighbor who had succumbed to bone cancer. During the examination, Mr. Crossman remarked that he was a busy man who did not have time for a lot of conversation. "Doctor, you do what you have to do to get rid of this pain," he said. "Put me in the hospital if you have to, but don't trouble me with all the details. Do what you think is best. Even if it's awful, I'd just as soon not know." Both Mr. Crossman and Dr. Greenblatt knew that "cancer" was the word he would not or could not say.

Dr. Greenblatt had seen patients like Mr. Crossman before. Some patients give signals, just as clear as can be, that a diagnosis of a terminal illness would be more than they could handle psychologically. Dr. Greenblatt asked himself, however, "Does he have a right not to know the truth?"

COMMENTARY

This case leads to conclusions that are atypical of most truth-telling cases. Whereas in most cases the principle of patient self-determination would lead to a decision to disclose a diagnosis or prognosis, and the consideration of consequences for the patient would support nondisclosure, at least from some points of view, in this case these arguments seem to lead to the reverse conclusions. If patient freedom and self-determination are dominant, then the clearly expressed wishes of the patient not to be bothered with the details certainly support nondisclosure, even if the physician feels Mr. Crossman would be better-off knowing.

On the contrary, if Dr. Greenblatt considers the consequences, he might conclude that Mr. Crossman ought to be told. If he limits the relevant consequences to those related to the patient, he might consider the therapeutic advantages as well as psychological adjustment that can be made over the next few months if the patient knows his condition. These consequences alone, however, probably will not be decisive in a decision to disclose because of the consequences. If, however, Dr. Greenblatt considers the consequences for Mr. Crossman's three teenage children of having a father speculate with the family's modest savings in a venture that will not payoff for several years, he might well conclude that the total consequences will be better if he tells Mr. Crossman of his condition. Even if he limits his concern only to patient-related consequences, this might be relevant. If Mr. Crossman will later be disturbed at the realization that he has squandered the resources his children need, then the consequences for Mr. Crossman himself might more decisively justify the disclosure.

The case can be approached from another perspective. Instead of asking what Dr. Greenblatt ought to do, one can ask what Mr. Crossman ought to have done. While the principle of patient self-determination might well justify the physician's agreement with the request of the patient not to disclose, it is irrelevant to the patient-centered question. Assuming that Mr. Crossman has the freedom to request nondisclosure, ought he to do so? While the consequences for the family must be excluded from the physician's judgment if he follows the principle of doing what he thinks will benefit his patient, those familial consequences certainly are not irrelevant to Mr. Crossman's own moral decision-making. He has an obligation to provide for his family and presumably an interest in their welfare as well. From the standpoint of consequences it seems that he has a strong obligation to have the important information about his future.

What, however, if there were no family members in the picture? Would there then be any obligation to accept the information if he would rather not be troubled with it? While the freedom of choice of the competent patient might justify his right to refuse the information, some would nevertheless hold that such refusal is still not ethically the best course. According to this view, a mature adult has an obligation as well as a right to make decisions about his own medical care. The fact that avoiding unpleasant information makes life more comfortable would not necessarily make it right. Some would make the case that Mr. Crossman ought not to have requested the nondisclosure even if the interests of his children were excluded from the case.

Family Members Who Insist the Patient Not Be Told

A second kind of special case involves a patient whose family insists the patient should not be told or that the consequences of telling would be so bad that the physician should refrain. Now it is the family member who is claiming the authority to waive the right to know. In some cases, such as the two that follow, it can be argued that the patient would be hurt, psychologically or physically, if he or she knew the threatening information. Some families might also be concerned that the patient could not understand the information, that he or she might really not want to know, or that the patient would be better off not knowing. Nevertheless, the question persists whether there is anyone who has the authority to overturn the patient's claim on the information. The first of the cases in this section involves a patient from a culture where nondisclosure is the norm. In this case, there is no reason to believe that the patient is mentally impaired and, in the United States, nondisclosure would appear to constitute treating without consent. In the second case, the patient may well not be mentally competent, in which case the next-of-kin is normally the presumed surrogate. The issue becomes one of whether the valid surrogate can decide that the patient should not be informed.

CASE 7–6

A Clash of Cultures: A Japanese Family Asks that Their Father Not Be Told of Cancer

The surgeon, Dr. Phyllis Rollins, had just examined the patient after referral from an internist. Dr. Rollins was part of a large oncology practice in a large West Coast

American city. Mr. Nikki previously had endoscopy and biopsy of the stomach confirming a very large cancer. Since Mr. Nikki spoke little English, his son came into the
room to help. The patient's wife took the patient into another room beyond hearing
distance. Then the surgeon fully explained the nature of the malignancy, that operation is clearly indicated, and that the father must be given that information, including
the process of preparation, the prognosis, the risks, probable outcomes, and other
details so that truly informed consent may be obtained. Abruptly, the son replied
that if his father were told the diagnosis, "he will wither up and die." Dr. Rollins
replied that she cannot proceed with surgical care of Mr. Nikki without his understanding of and agreement to a major operation. "You just don't understand 'the
Japanese way'—in Japan, the word 'cancer' cannot be mentioned," said the son. He
proposed that Dr. Rollins tell Mr. Nikki nothing, and prepare for surgical treatment
secretly. Dr. Rollins withdrew from the case, providing some other surgeons' names
to the family. Later, she learned that the patient had been operated upon at another
hospital, presumably without being told of his diagnosis.

COMMENTARY

Given the facts as presented, the initial surgeon felt bound by important ethical principles and the law requiring that patients be told truthfully of their
condition as part of the consent process. Failure to disclose would mean that
consent is not adequately informed, which would constitute an assault against
the patient. In this case, Dr. Rollins withdrew from the care of the patient by
referral. The net result was that, as far as Dr. Rollins knew, the patient was
treated without being fully informed.

It could be claimed that Mr. Nikki delegated decision-making authority
to his family, who aggressively acted for him in their understanding of his best
interest. He could have done so explicitly (although there is no evidence of this).
Some patients, particularly those in stressful medical situations, may explicitly
acknowledge that they do not feel capable of handling decision-making and
may waive their right to be informed. That was the issue in the previous case.

This case presents a more complicated problem. Assuming that Mr. Nikki
did not explicitly waive his right to be informed and consent to his medical
treatment, could it be argued that, given that he was part of the traditional
Japanese culture in which disclosure to the family rather than to the patient
was the usual custom?[15]

There are problems with the presumption that Mr. Nikki would consent
to having his family take over decision-making. Even in Japan there are people
who reject the traditional view. They insist that they would want to be informed
of their diagnosis and retain decision-making authority. Since there is no way
to determine whether a specific patient is in this group who would want to
retain his or her decision-making authority (and patients cannot be asked without arising suspicion of some serious medical problem), showing respect for

the unidentified group who are not willing to let their family play this role is a serious problem in Japan. From the point of view of those who believe there is a moral right to truthful disclosure, this right cannot be waived by majority vote even if it can be shown that the patient is from a culture that generally follows a pattern of nondisclosure.

In the United States, the issue is even more complicated. There is an increasing moral consensus in favor of truthful disclosure of diagnosis. The duty of honesty is even incorporated into the AMA *Code of Ethics*. Hence in the United States, where Mr. Nikki is being treated, both law and ethical principle support a duty of disclosure. Although that duty might be overridden in the case in which a competent patient explicitly authorizes nondisclosure, it is hard to imagine the justification based solely on the instruction of the family.

The physician who accepted the case under the reported "don't tell" stipulations of the Japanese culture did so even though there was no evidence that the patient was incompetent. Postoperative care might well be compromised by complications, need for reoperation and/or intensive care, and so on.

The issue of familial request for nondisclosure is even more complex in the case in which there is doubt about the mental competency of the patient. That is the situation in the next case.

CASE 7–7

Disclosing Cancer to a Mentally Compromised Patient

A 64-year-old man, David Younis, was brought to the emergency room (ER) after his wife found him suddenly disoriented and incoherent. Mr. Younis was known at the hospital for alcohol dependence, with cirrhosis of the liver. Examination revealed liver enlargement including a mass (CT scan). He was admitted to the hospital and a biopsy of the mass was scheduled. Mr. Younis's mental status improved; his wife requested that he not be told if the diagnosis is malignant. Mrs. Younis said that if he learns he has cancer, he will kill himself. Dr. Andre Caldarone, the hepatologist (liver specialist), then cancels the biopsy procedure.

COMMENTARY

This case resembles Case 7-6 in many ways. Both cases involve family requesting that a patient not be told of a diagnosis on grounds that it would be contrary to the best interest of the patient to disclose. The present case differs, however, not only because the potential harm to the patient appears more severe—a purported risk of suicide—but also because that patient has been disoriented and incoherent. The moral principle of veracity and its related notion of informed consent clearly applies to patients who are mentally competent. Whether it also applies to mentally compromised patients is difficult to determine.

If Mr. Younis is not mentally competent, the doctrine of informed consent does not apply directly. Consent is related to the rights derived from the principle of autonomy. As such it only applies to substantially autonomous persons. If Mr. Younis is incompetent, his wife is his presumed surrogate. She would retain the right to determine how much he should be told based on her assessment of his best interest. This is the same approach used in informing young children, who are also mentally not competent to consent to medical treatment.

Not all mentally compromised patients are sufficiently lacking in autonomy that they should be treated as incompetent. Thus the first problem for Dr. Caldarone is a determination of Mr. Younis's competence. This could involve a psychiatric consultation and, especially if the matter is in dispute, potentially a judicial determination of whether the patient is competent, and, if not, who should be his surrogate or guardian.

If Mr. Younis is found to be incompetent, his wife would plausibly become the moral and legal surrogate. The obligation to benefit the patient clinically would prevail unless she knows his wishes about how he would want to be treated. A good utilitarian argument could be made that the greatest good is preservation of life, which calls for proper clinical diagnosis and treatment of a potential life-threatening illness as well as avoiding the threatened suicide. This could lead to a biopsy diagnosis and then truth-telling in careful but honest terms, with promise of and support/care of the patient afterward. The attending physician will require virtues of interpersonal skills, professional skills of evaluation and decision-making, and great sensitivity in truly caring for this patient.

The abrupt canceling of the biopsy raises additional moral issues. While it is true that that physician cannot legally operate without a valid consent, either consent from the next-of-kin under the presumption that the patient was not competent or a further discussion with the wife if the patient is determined to be competent would seem to be in order.

THE RIGHT OF ACCESS TO MEDICAL RECORDS

Closely related to the ethics of truth-telling is the question of the right of access of a patient to his or her medical records. This is a problem for medical records administrators and also for all other health care professionals, especially those in a hospital setting. If the patient has the right to be told all that is potentially meaningful about his or her medical condition and treatment, does that also imply a right to see his or her medical records or at least to know what they contain?

Traditional medical ethics and law presumed that patients had no right of access to their medical records. They were presumed to be the property of the treating health professional. Concern was expressed based on Hippocratic concern for patient well-being that if patients saw their records, they could learn things that would be upsetting. Moreover, they might misunderstand the content of the record causing psychological distress and confusion.

More recently as medical ethics has shifted from more paternalistic consequentialism to a more rights-oriented ethic, patients are seen as having a right
of access as part of their more general right to be truthfully informed of their
medical condition.[16]

CASE 7–8

A Psychiatric Patient's Right to See
Her Medical Record

Claire Mowry was a 38-year-old, never-married woman who had worked intermittently over the past ten years as a secretary. She had had difficulty keeping jobs
because she would regularly engage in disputes with fellow employees accusing
them of not carrying their load of the office work, criticizing her work, and in one
case reporting her to the supervisor for consistently showing up late for work.

By the end of her fourth visit with Dr. Gaskell, Ms. Mowry had become convinced that Dr. Gaskell did not like her. She thought he seemed to be implying that

Currently out of work, she was seeing Martin Gaskell, a psychiatrist working
with the mental health clinic of the HMO of her previous employer. Ms. Mowry was
currently paying out-of-pocket so her HMO coverage could continue.

Dr. Gaskell had now had four appointments with Ms. Mowry. He had identified patterns of what appeared to be paranoid thinking and had generally come to
find her an unpleasant, difficult patient. She clearly did not have a major psychiatric
disorder. She was not psychotic—a paranoid schizophrenic—but she had personal-
ity traits that were causing her problems.

By the end of her fourth visit with Dr. Gaskell, Ms. Mowry had become convinced that Dr. Gaskell did not like her. She thought he seemed to be implying that
her employment problems were her own fault and that she needed further therapy
to address these issues. Ms. Mowry suspected that Dr. Gaskell was keeping notes
on her that would reflect his poor opinion of her. She asked to see her medical
record.

When Dr. Gaskell hesitated, she indicated she would report him to the management of the HMO. The law is currently in flux regarding the right of patients to
see their medical records. Moral uncertainty also exists. In particular, many physicians, especially psychiatrists, are concerned that granting patients the right to see
their records may harm patients as well as violate the privacy rights of the provider.
Regardless of the law in the jurisdiction of this case, what is an ethically appropriate
decision by Dr. Gaskell?

COMMENTARY

In the era of Hippocratic medicine, it was assumed that medical records were
not for the patient to see. They were the property of the physician. A patient
would not be able to understand the physician's documentation and could be
harmed by any misunderstanding. Psychiatric records were particularly subject

to the claim that disclosing of contents could do more harm than good. If the patient were mentally incompetent—a child, an adult adjudicated to be incompetent, or perhaps even an adult who has not formally been found incompetent but is deemed to lack sufficient mental capacity for autonomous medical decision-making, there is good reason why records might not be disclosed, but cases of mentally competent adults, including those who have some psychiatric problems, pose the question of whether they ought to be given access to their records, whether the information in some sense belongs to them.

In more recent times, the assumption that patient access to medical records will cause harm to the patient has been called into question. Some claim that seeing the record will actually help the patient understand his or her condition and clarify matters not adequately presented by the physician. Seeing the record of the physician or the hospital is considered an additional source of information to help the patient understand the diagnosis and treatment as well as clarify any miscommunication from the provider. In addition, the patient is sometimes believed to have a right to information about the physician's views of the patient's problem.

Those concerned that the record could be misunderstood have suggested that the patient who asks to see his or her record should have access with the professional present to clarify any issues that are not clear. Others have suggested that the patient should be given an oral summary rather than the printed text.

Ms. Mowry has revealed sufficient signs of paranoid thought that she probably would not be satisfied with an oral summary. She might well believe that the psychiatrist was not presenting his written notes accurately.

A traditional consequentialist would ask whether the information would, on balance, be beneficial to the patient. The answer in this case is not obvious. There is information at stake that is potentially important to her current health care and peace of mind. On the other hand, the physician or other members of the health care team may have entered notes about the patient's mental state or other potentially embarrassing information they did not expect the patient to see. Basing an assessment just on the consequences, it may not be clear whether the patient will, on balance, be helped or hurt by seeing her record.

Now look at the case from the point of view of the rights of the patient. Assuming she has the right to information that is potentially meaningful in making medical decisions, from this point of view she would have a right to the information even if it is, on balance, likely to harm her.

Increasingly, courts are granting the right of patients to see medical records[17] and many state legislatures now have passed laws granting patients the right to see their records.[18] Patient advocacy groups are pressing for a right of access.[19] Physicians and others examining the psychological and medical effects of granting a right of access are increasingly more positive about such access.[20] Most laws require a written request to the physician and the physician has a certain amount of time to comply. In California, for example, the physician does not have to give the actual copy of the record; he or she can provide a written summary of the information in the record. Would that be an acceptable policy in this case?

This completes the exploration of the cases dealing with the ethical principle of veracity. Autonomy and veracity, the issues of the previous chapter and this one, were the first two principles related to respect for persons. We now turn to the third such principle: fidelity.

NOTES

1 American Medical Association. *Current Opinion of the Judicial Council of the American Medical Association*. Chicago, IL: American Medical Association, 1981, p. ix.
2 American Medical Association. Council on Ethical and Judicial Affairs. *Code of Medical Ethics: Current Opinions with Annotations*, 2004–2005. Chicago, IL: AMA Press, 2004, p. 229.
3 American Pharmaceutical Association. *Code of Ethics*. Washington, DC: American Pharmaceutical Association, 1969. This provision was not changed in the amendments of 1975 or the revision of 1981.
4 It continues, however, with a possible opening to the more traditional Hippocratic paternalism when it adds that, "A pharmacist avoids…actions that compromise dedication to the best interests of patients." See American Pharmaceutical Association. *Code of Ethics for Pharmacists*. Washington, DC: American Pharmaceutical Association, 1995.
5 American Nurses Association. *Code of Ethics for Nurses with Interpretive Statements*. Washington, DC: American Nurses Association, 2001, p. 8.
6 Sidgwick, Henry. *The Methods of Ethics*. New York: Dover Publications, Inc., 1966, [1874].
7 Meyer, Bernard. "Truth and the Physician." In *Ethical Issues in Medicine*. E. Fuller Torrey, editor. Boston, MA: Little Brown, 1968, pp. 159–177.
8 Kant, Immanuel. "On the Supposed Right to Tell Lies from Benevolent Motives." Translated by Thomas Kingsmill Abbott and reprinted in Kant's *Critique of Practical Reason and Other Works on the Theory of Ethics*. London: Longmans, 1909 [1797], pp. 361–365.
9 Ross, W. D. *The Right and the Good*. Oxford: Oxford University Press, 1939.
10 Oken, Donald. "What to Tell Cancer Patients: A Study of Medical Attitudes." *Journal of the American Medical Association* 175 (April 1, 1961):1120–1128.
11 Hooker, Worthington. *Physician and Patient: Or, a Practical View of the Mutual Duties, Relations and Interests of the Medical Profession and the Community*. New York: Baker & Scribner, 1849; Cabot, Richard Clarke. *Honesty*. New York: The Macmillan Company, 1938.
12 Novack, Dennis H., Robin Plumer, Raymond L. Smith, Herbert Ochitill, Gary R. Morrow, and John M. Bennett. "Changes in Physicians' Attitudes Toward Telling the Cancer Patient." *Journal of the American Medical Association* 241 (March 2, 1979):897–900.
13 Good discussions of the problems of uncertainty faced by health professionals are Fox, Renée C. "Training for Uncertainty." In *The Student-Physician*. Robert

K. Merton, George Reader, and Patricia L. Kendall, editors. Cambridge, MA: Harvard University Press, 1957, pp. 207–241; Fox, Renée C., "Medical Uncertainty." *Second-Opinion* (Nov 1987):91–105; and Bosk, Charles, *Forgive and Remember: Managing Medical Failure*. Chicago, IL: University of Chicago Press, 1979.

14 [Kusserow, Rickard P., Inspector General], "Financial Arrangements Between Physicians and Health Care Business: Report to Congress." May, 1989. Office of Analysis and Inspections] OAI-12-88-01410. Available on the Internet at http:// oig.hhs.gov/oei/reports/oai-12-88-01410.pdf, accessed August 21, 2007.

15 Akabayashi, Akira, Michael D. Fetters, and Todd S. Elwyn. "Family Consent, Communication, and Advance Directives for Cancer Disclosure: A Japanese Case and Discussion." *Journal of Medical Ethics* 25 (1999):296–301; Okamura, Hitoshi, Yosuke Uchitomi, Mitsuru Sasako, Kenji Eguchi, and Tadao Kakizoe. "Guidelines for Telling the Truth to Cancer Patients." *Japanese Journal of Clinical Oncology* 28 (1, 1998):1–4; Hamajima, Nobuyuki, Kazuo Tajima, Mayumi Morishita, Chigusa Hyodo, Noriko Sakakibara, Chisato Kawai, and Shigeko Moritaka. "Patients' Expectations of Information Provided at Cancer Hospitals in Japan." *Japanese Journal of Clinical Oncology* 26 (5, 1996):362–367.

16 Bruce, Jo Anne Czecowski. "Access of Patient to Health Records." In her *Privacy and Confidentiality of Health Care Information*, 2nd ed. Chicago, IL: American Hospital Publishing; 1988, pp. 161–182; Kirby, Brian J. "Patient Access to Medical Records." *Journal of the Royal College of Physicians of London* 25 (July 1991):240–242; Gilhooly, Mary L. M., Sarah M. McGhee. "Medical Records: Practicalities and Principles of Patient Possession." *Journal of Medical Ethics* 17 (September, 1991):138–143; de Klerk, Anton. "Should a Patient Have Access to His Medical Records?" *Medicine and Law* 8 (1989):475–483; Rosenman, Hayley. "Patients' Rights to Access Their Medical Records: An Argument for Uniform Recognition of a Right of Access in the United States and Australia." *Fordham International Law Journal* 21 (No. 4, April 1998): 1500–1557; Davies, Jackie. "Patients' Rights of Access to Their Health Records." *Medical Law International* 2(No. 3, 1996): 189–213; Kirby, Michael D. "A Patient's Right of Access to Medical Records." *Journal of Contemporary Health Law and Policy* 12(No. 1, 1995 Fall): 93–111.

17 McLaren, Paul. "The Right to Know: Patients' Records Should Be Understandable by Patients, Too." *British Medical Journal* 303 (October 19, 1991, No. 6808): 937–938; Bruce, Jo Anne Czecowski. "Access of Patient to Health Records." In her *Privacy and Confidentiality of Health Care Information*, 2nd ed. Chicago, IL: American Hospital Publishing, 1988, pp. 161–182; Kirby. "Patient Access to Medical Records"; Gilhooly and McGhee. "Medical Records"; de-Klerk. "Should a Patient Have Access to His Medical Records?"; Klugman, Ellen. "Toward a Uniform Right to Medical Records: a Proposal for a Model Patient Access and Information Practices Statute." *UCLA Law Review* 30 (August 1983):1349–1385; Fox, Lloyd A. "Medical and Prescription Records—Patient Access and Confidentiality." *U.S. Pharmacist* 4 (No. 2, 1979):15–16+.

18 "Summary of Selected Statutes Concerning Confidentiality of and Patient Access to Medical Records." *State Health Legislation Report* 9 (No. 1, May 1981):13–23;

Annas, George J., Daryl B. Matthews, and Leonard H. Glantz. "Patient Access to Medical Records." *Medicolegal News* 8 (No. 2, April 1980):17–18.

19   Public Citizen Health Research Group. *Medical Records: Getting Yours.* Washington, DC: Public Citizen Research Health Research Group, 1986.

20   Schade, Hugh I. "My Patients Take Their Medical Records with Them." *Medical Economics* (March 8, 1976): 75–81; Giglio, R., B. Spears, David Rumpf, and Nancy Eddy. "Encouraging Behavior Changes by Use of Client-Held Health Records." *Medical Care* 16 (1978):757–764; Shenkin, Budd N., and David C. Warner. "Giving the Patient His Medical Record: A Proposal to Improve the System." *New England Journal of Medicine* 289 (1973): 688–692.

CHAPTER 8

✒

Fidelity: Promise-Keeping, Loyalty to Patients, and Impaired Professionals

Other Cases Involving Fidelity

16-4: Surveying Illegal Immigrants
16-5: Homicide in Research: A Duty to Breach Confidentiality?
Also see the cases of Chapter 13 dealing with confidentiality

The cases in the previous chapter included a number of situations in which health professionals did not propose to overtly lie to patients, but nevertheless contemplated withholding the truth. We noted that the principle of veracity treated the intentional telling of false information as a moral infringement, but that it was less clear how to treat withholding of information. No one has a duty to tell all the truth to anyone who happens along. At the same time, certain people have a duty not only to avoid lying, but also to tell certain things to others. In general, physicians who are in an ongoing relation with a patient or patients have a duty to disclose what they would reasonably want to know or find meaningful in making a decision related to care.

We might attribute such a duty to the principle of veracity (truthfulness, honesty, correctness, and accuracy), but it can also be associated with what we will call the *principle of fidelity*. When people exist in special relations with others, they take on special duties. Parents have duties to their children, spouses to each other that they do not have with other people. Likewise, when a health care professional enters a special relation with a patient, certain special obligations are created. This relation is more than a legal contract: it is not just a matter of a business relation. A moral contract is established generating mutual obligations. This contract is sometimes referred to as a "covenant."[1] As part of the contract or "covenant" that establishes the relation, commitments are made that generate new and special mutual obligations and rights.[2] The duty to disclose potentially meaningful information is one such duty, but there are many others.

In general, when one party promises something to another, such a special relation is established. That promise can take the form of a routine promise to return something that has been borrowed or it can take the form of establishing a relation between provider and patient. Usually, promise-making is reciprocal. Each party offers something and agrees to be bound by mutual agreement. In health care, promises are made in scheduling appointments, agreeing to fee schedules, and in keeping records. More fundamentally, promises are made when a patient–provider relation is established that includes a provider's pledge of loyalty to the patient—to abide by a code of ethics and to stay with the patient in time of need. Among the promises made is the promise to keep information confidential, a subject that will be the focus of Chapter 13.

All promises are made with implicit or explicit limits. The commitment to establish a provider–patient relation normally carries with it an implied limit that either party can break the relation under certain conditions: adequate notice, justifiable reason, and—in the case of the health care professional—arrangement for a colleague to assume responsibility.

The contract, covenant, commitment, or promise that establishes the relation between provider and patient rests, in part, on the ethics of keeping promises. The principle underlying the idea that one has a duty—other things being equal—to keep a commitment once it is made is sometimes called the principle of fidelity. The cases in this chapter look at situations in which health care professionals are faced with problems of what the moral limits are on keeping commitments once they are made. In particular, we will face cases in which the physician or other health professional has made some sort of commitment and later discovers that, in the physician's estimate, the patient or someone else would be better off if the commitment were not kept. The general problem is, thus, one of conflict between the principle of beneficence and the principle of fidelity.

The first cases involve general notions of fidelity to explicit and implicit promises. The second section of the chapter deals with the obligation of loyalty to patients in the face of financial and other conflicts of interest. Finally, we look at fidelity in terms of professional obligations and loyalty when dealing with incompetent, impaired, or dishonest colleagues.

THE ETHICS OF PROMISES: EXPLICIT AND IMPLICIT

We all learn very young that it is immoral to break a promise. Unfortunately, soon thereafter we also learn that there are cases when one can give strong reasons why promises should not always be kept. There are promises that are in one's self-interest to break. Normally, however, we do not confuse self-interest with ethics. The interesting case is the one in which a promise has been made, but one comes to believe that it will serve the welfare of others to break it. These other-regarding reasons for breaking promises may pose legitimate moral dilemmas.

Sometimes, as in the first case in this section, the promise is explicit and yet the one to whom the promise is made will be hurt only modestly if the promise is not kept, and someone else will benefit enormously if it is violated. The question raised here is whether that counts as an acceptable reason to break the promise. Sometimes patterns emerge in clinical practice that are so much a part of a practitioner's routine that he or she may even fail to grasp that a commitment has been made to a patient. One example is the making of an appointment with a patient.

CASE 8-1

Keeping a Patient Waiting

Fifty-eight-year-old Judy Anderson had accepted the only appointment available with her internist, Anthony Fantaw, a member of one of the adult care teams at a major East Coast HMO. She had been diagnosed a month ago with hypertension (175/95). Dr. Fantaw had prescribed the generic for Microzide, (hydrochlorothiazide) and Prinivil (lisinopril) and told her to schedule an appointment for follow-up.

Ms. Anderson had been bothered by jitteriness and loss of appetite since taking the medication, so she was eager to discuss these problems with Dr. Fantaw to see if they might be related to her medication. She had accepted a 1:30 p.m. appointment, which was the only one available even though she was responsible for picking up her grandson after school at 3 p.m. Since the HMO placed its physicians on a regimen of ten minutes per patient for such routine follow-up appointments, Ms. Anderson figured she would be done in plenty of time.

Ms. Anderson arrived at 1:15 p.m. She registered, paid her co-payment, and took a seat in the waiting room with about ten others. By 1:40 p.m. she had not been called by the nurse and was beginning to get nervous. By 1:50 p.m. she was more uncomfortable since her grandson's school was about a half hour away from the HMO offices. No one had said anything to her about the delay so she asked the receptionist what was happening.

The receptionist said that Dr. Fantaw had been running behind all day, a rather common pattern for him. He had spent twenty-five minutes with a patient that morning who had an unusually complicated set of problems. As a clinician deeply committed to high-quality medical care for his patients, he often found himself pressured to go a bit over the ten-minute time period. By this point in the afternoon he was running about forty-five minutes behind.

Ms. Anderson wondered why the receptionist had not told her all of this when she registered. She also wondered why, if this was a common pattern for Dr. Fantaw, some action was not taken to address the issue of his regular inability to stay on time.

COMMENTARY

This is a troublesome case of a physician creating problems for a patient by faithfully fulfilling his commitment to provide high-quality care to his patients, which, in turn, requires that he break his commitment to see patients at the scheduled time.

The pattern of physicians keeping patients waiting for appointments beyond their scheduled time is so common that some doctors may not even perceive this as breaking a promise. Nevertheless, there is a sense in which an appointment with a patient is a promise made to the patient. That promise is reciprocated when the patient commits to be there on time or call to cancel. Ms. Anderson kept her part of the "bargain." She went further. She showed up fifteen minutes early.

It is not that Dr. Fantaw is irresponsibly lacking in concern for his patients. In fact, it is his concern about them that gets him behind. In the interest of serving his patients and providing thorough patient care he often falls into a pattern of slipping behind his appointment schedule. In this case, he took more than double the allotted time for a patient earlier in the day who had an unusually complicated set of problems. This is precisely what our stereotype of an ideal physician would be. Moreover, he has taken extra minutes with other patients to the point that, by the time he reaches Ms. Anderson's time slot, he is forty-five minutes behind.

In the language of moral philosophy, Dr. Fantaw has gotten behind by pursuing the principle of beneficence—maximizing each patient's best interest—and has manifested loyalty to his earlier patients—an implication of the principle of fidelity. In doing so, however, he has violated another implication of the principle of fidelity—the idea that once a commitment has been made to a patient, that commitment should be kept. Appointments are commitments—promises—and Dr. Fantaw has broken one of his promises.

Looked at strictly from the perspective of the principle of beneficence, Dr. Fantaw may have done exactly what was required. His beneficence-based duty would be to benefit the patient. In this case, his duty is made more complicated by the fact that he has not one patient, but many. One of the problems with a strictly Hippocratic form of beneficence is that it assumes there is only one patient. Some Hippocratic physicians address this problem by serving the best interest of the patient with whom they are dealing at the moment. That may be precisely what Dr. Fantaw did—pursue the interest of the patient in front of him one at a time until he reached the end of his list of patients for the day.

Hippocratic beneficence presents some problems. First, it seems unlikely that the twenty-five minutes he spent with the earlier patient with the complicated problems was literally what was *best* for that patient. No doubt, he could have spent even more time with her and helped her at least somewhat more. Doing what is best for the current patient probably would put such high demands on the physician's schedule that he could see only a fraction of his scheduled patients each day.

Some critics of HMOs might argue that the fault lies with the health management for permitting only ten-minute appointment windows. Perhaps twenty- or thirty-minute windows would permit the physicians to come closer to the Hippocratic ideal with each patient. That strategy presents serious problems, however. If appointment slots are longer, physicians will see fewer patients. More physicians or other primary care providers such as nurse practitioners (NPs) or physician's assistants (PAs) will be required to cover the same number of patients. The cost of the health premium would go up proportionally (somewhat less so if NPs and PAs were used instead of MDs), an implication that may not be in the interest of patients. Would subscribers be willing to pay 100 percent more for twenty-minute slots with their physicians than they presently pay for the ten-minute windows?

Not all ethics that adopt the principle of beneficence do so Hippocratically. Utilitarian ethics also relies exclusively on beneficence, but takes into account all the consequences for all parties impacted by an action. In this case, a utilitarian would set the time slots based on what was best for patients overall and would allocate Dr. Fantaw's time on that basis. He would give some patients more time, others less than the typical slot.

Most critically from the point of view of ethics, the mere fact that a commitment had been made to Ms. Anderson would not count in determining what was ethical in Dr. Fantaw's time allocation. He would stay on schedule or slip behind solely on the basis of what was best overall. Of course, sophisticated utilitarians would have to take into account all of the indirect consequences of scheduling—the fact that Ms. Anderson might be late picking up her grandson and might lower her opinion of Dr. Fantaw as one who does not keep his word. It gradually should become clear that Dr. Fantaw is not in a good position to calculate whether the overall consequences of taking twenty-five minutes with his morning patient is utility maximizing or not. He simply cannot know whether later patients will need more or less time and cannot determine very easily what the indirect impacts will be on his or his institution's reputation if he fails to keep his scheduling commitments.

The fact that consequences are so difficult to determine makes it even more imperative that we also consider the principle of fidelity in this case. In particular, Dr. Fantaw has made a commitment to patients that he will see them at a certain time. They have organized their time accordingly and the responsible ones have kept their part of the agreement by showing up on time (or early). Is the fact that a commitment was made relevant to the ethical analysis of this case? Defenders of the principle of fidelity hold that, independent of considerations of consequences, the fact that a commitment was made influences what is morally required of Dr. Fantaw. They hold that fidelity to commitments made is morally important even if the consequences are not better when one does so.

Ethical theorists attempt to make this point by asking us to imagine two possible actions one can take that will produce exactly the same amount of good consequences. They then add the fact that one has promised to do one of the actions, but not the other. The pure consequentialist, the one who works only with the principle of beneficence, should feel indifferent between the two actions. However, most people feel that if one has promised to do one of them, then that one is morally preferred. Really sophisticated analysts will eliminate the indirect consequences on one's reputation if one were to fail to do what one had promised by imagining a situation in which no one who can see which action is performed even knew that the promise was made (e.g., if the one to whom the promise was made had died or was in a position in which she could not learn which action were chosen). In these cases, if one feels morally obliged to pursue what one has promised rather than an equally beneficial action that one had not promised to do, then there must be something other than consequences shaping the judgment.

In Dr. Fantaw's case, Ms. Anderson and the other patients on the schedule for the day will know whether the doctor has kept his word about the appointment. That could tarnish his reputation and might be a reason some would conclude he should keep to his schedule. Consider the case, however, in which Dr. Fantaw takes all of this into account and discovers that he believes his early patient with a complicated case will benefit just enough more to offset the harm to his reputation if he gets off schedule. If he is a utilitarian, he will be indifferent as to whether he keeps his schedule. If he gives weight to the principle of fidelity, he will have a reason to keep his commitments, at least to the point that the benefits to the patient with the complicated case get so overwhelming that they outweigh the force of the principle of fidelity. Defenders of that principle will at least claim that there is a moral issue when appointments are not kept. How much benefit is required to a patient with a complicated case to override the promises made to the other patients is a matter of dispute.

Here is another case in which a physician considers breaking a commitment made to a patient because he can do more good for another patient by breaking the promise.

CASE 8-2

I Will Be There for You at the End:
A Promise Broken?

Mabel Dacosta, an 80-year-old, was an end-stage cancer patient who had been admitted twelve days earlier to the inpatient hospice unit at City Hospital. She was now in the last stages of her illness under the care of the hospice team including Chris Humphries, MD, and Lois Kiger, RN, the primary nurse. She had also been visited regularly by the chaplain, a social worker, and a hospice volunteer. Her needs were met well even though she had no immediate family or friends who called upon her.

Ms. Dacosta had been quite depressed and nervous when under the care of her oncologist, but the transfer to the hospice unit had been reassuring. One of her key concerns was that she did not want to die alone. She repeatedly expressed her concern to Dr. Humphries, the hospice medical director, who said the team would be there to keep her comfortable twenty-four hours a day. She asked Dr. Humphries if he personally would be there when she died. He pointed out that he could not be present twenty-four hours a day, seven days a week, but he said, if he possibly could, he would be at her bedside when the time came.

As Ms. Dacosta declined, she spent most of her time sleeping. She appeared to recognize none of the staff when she was awake. When the day came when the team realized she would probably not last long, Dr. Humphries remembered his commitment. He completed his rounds and stopped at Ms. Dacosta's room. She did not appear to recognize him, but he sat in the chair near her. He was able to complete his notes for the charts of other patients. After some time, Ms. Kiger appeared at the door. Another patient was in serious pain and needed his attention. She offered to stay with Ms. Dacosta, but Dr. Humphries remembered his commitment to her.

He realized that she would not know whether he was actually present at her death and that no one else had heard him make the commitment to stay with her. He knew that Ms. Kiger was an excellent nurse who could do everything that could assist Ms. Dacosta at least as well or better than he could, but that he was the best person to work up the patient who needed a new pain regimen. He realized that he could do more good for his two patients if he broke his promise to Ms. Dacosta and that he had explicitly mentioned to her that he could not be present twenty-four hours a day. At the same time he knew he had promised her his presence. A resident on the hospice unit could work up the patient in pain and give him a report on what she recommended. Did he make a promise and should he break it?

COMMENTARY

There seems little doubt that Dr. Humphries could do more good overall if he went back on his word and left Ms. Dacosta's room to care for the other patient. She would, in all likelihood, not even know whether he was present. Moreover, in this case (in contrast with Case 8-1), literally no one would know that he was breaking a commitment he had made since Ms. Dacosta had been the only one who heard him make it, and she was not conscious enough now to know who was present. From the point of view of the principle of beneficence, leaving to care for the patient in pain is the only defensible option.

The moral problem is that Dr. Humphries, in some sense, made a promise to be present at her dying if he possibly could. One way out of his dilemma would be to claim that he had not made an absolutely firm commitment. He said he would be present if he could be. He could try to convince himself that he could not possibly be present because another patient was in need.

This is a case in which almost certainly more good would be done for patients overall if he breaks his commitment. Only the principle of fidelity should lead him to consider staying with Ms. Dacosta. Since the other patient will receive adequate, if not ideal care, should he keep his promise?

In Case 8-1 the patient was conscientious in keeping the commitment she made to her physician. In Case 8-2 likewise it is the physician whose commitment is in question. In other cases, the moral limits on loyalty in the patient–physician relation are questioned because the patient fails to keep his or her part of an agreement. This could involve failing to follow the recommendations given by the clinician (as was the issue in Case 6-4). It can also arise, as in the next case, if the patient fails to keep a commitment to pay bills.

CASE 8-3

Continuing Treatment of a Patient Who Will Not Pay Her Bills

A thoracic surgeon, Beau Schenker, MD, was called to the Emergency Department to evaluate and treat Nelda Thomas, a 40-year-old female who had chest pain of sudden onset. Her history pointed to lung disease, not cardiac problems. The exam revealed decreased breath sounds in the left chest and x-rays confirmed free air in the chest that had collapsed the left lung. Dr. Schenker determined that the patient had a spontaneous pneumothorax. He discussed with Ms. Thomas the well-established treatment: a chest tube. Dr. Schenken stated, "We will need to insert a small tube into your chest to withdraw the air and allow the lung to re-expand." Ms. Thomas and her husband were relieved to learn that the chest pain was not the result of a heart problem and agreed quickly to the procedure, which was successful.

During the brief hospital stay, Dr. Schenker and Mr. Thomas, the patient's husband, reminisced about their days in high school since they coincidentally attended the same school. Ms. Thomas was seen several times for appropriate follow-up in Dr. Schenker's office after her hospitalization. Several months later, Dr. Schenker's business manager reported that the balance of Ms. Thomas' bill had not been paid. Since Dr. Schenker's office had a policy of not using collection companies, Dr. Schenker said "write the bill off."

Two years later, Ms. Thomas was once again in the emergency room (ER) for recurrence of the same problem. She requested to be seen by Dr. Schenker. When the Emergency Department paged Dr. Schenker, he advised the staff to call another available thoracic surgeon to see Ms. Thomas. A few minutes later, Mr. Thomas called Dr. Schenker directly at his office. Mr. Thomas admitted he had not paid the earlier bill (although Dr. Schenker had not brought up the matter) and promised to pay the old balance and then pre-pay for the costs of his wife's current needs. Dr. Schenken replied, "It's not about the money but about mutual respect. I am sorry but I cannot take care of your wife at this time. Another thoracic surgeon will take the case so you have nothing to worry about." Ms. Thomas was treated successfully by another physician. Should Dr. Schenker have relented and taken the case the second time?

COMMENTARY

In this case it is the patient who is threatening the trust of the patient–physician relationship. Much has been written about professional obligations in the relationship with patients, less about patient obligations. Once an ongoing clinical relation is established, physicians and other health professionals are obligated not to abandon the patient. Even if the patient is difficult, fails to follow the physician's recommendations, or, as in this case, fails to pay bills, the physician continues to have responsibility for the medical welfare of the patient. Only after a competent colleague agrees to take over a case, can an initial physician withdraw from the case.

This case is complicated by the fact that, in a real sense, the patient–physician relationship had ended when Ms. Thomas's follow-up care from the first episode was completed. There is no ethical responsibility for either party to resume a prior relationship if a new acute medical problem occurs and a competent alternative professional is available to serve the patient's needs. In this case, the initial thoracic surgeon, Dr. Schenker, might have agreed to resume care under the conditions the husband offered, but he apparently valued the relationship itself as one of mutual trust and respect and preferred not to be involved further. As long as it is legitimate to conceptualize this set of events as an attempt by Ms. Thomas to reestablish a relationship that had ended and a competent colleague is available, Dr. Schenker seems to be within his rights.

FIDELITY AND CONFLICTS OF INTEREST

Another aspect of the principle of fidelity in the patient–physician relationship is the problem of conflict of interest. The principle of fidelity calls for loyalty of the health professional to the patient and that loyalty can be challenged when other interests are on the agenda of the clinician. Physicians, like all human beings, have economic and other interests. Some of the conflicts of interest are overtly financial. A physician may, but should not be tempted to, prescribe a drug manufactured by a pharmaceutical company in which the physician owns stock. Health care specialists feel a need to maintain good relations with internists who have the power to refer patients. These conflicts of interest are ubiquitous in life, but pose special problems in health care because providers are in a fiduciary (trust) relation with patients who count on their professionals to make honest, unbiased treatment recommendations in areas in which the patient is not expected to have expertise. A recommendation for an expensive diagnostic procedure or for an extensive treatment regimen must be received by the patient on faith, but provider income will be impacted by such recommendations. The following three cases all pose economic conflict of interest issues. These are followed by cases involving other, more subtle conflicts of interest.

CASE 8-4

A GP Assisting in Surgical Operations: Stealing Business and Harming Patients?

After completing a lengthy, if prestigious, residency program, the young surgeon, Diane Daemer, began the difficult process of establishing a solo practice. She took frequent call from the ERs, did insurance physical exams, went to all hospital staff meetings, did not take vacation, and so on. The practice grew slowly, and she was gratified when a busy general practitioner, David Parish, referred a patient with lung cancer for her evaluation. When operation was recommended, the referring doctor asked to assist in the procedure, a custom not unusual in her community. She agreed and the procedure subsequently went well, after her usual meticulous preoperative care and communication with all parties.

Three weeks later, the same GP referred a patient who needed a partial resection of the stomach. Again, Dr. Parish assisted in the operation. Further operative cases followed. Then Dr. Parish spoke of his interest in doing "simple operations like hernia repairs and appendectomies" with Dr. Daemer assisting him. She politely refused, feeling manipulated because of the referrals and was unwilling to "cover" the lack of surgical credentials of the other. The surgeon came to believe that the arrangement was a deception, clearly not in the interest of the patients.

CASE 8-5

Profiting from Unnecessary Angioplasty

A 70-year-old man with known peripheral vascular disease complained of increasing claudication (cramping of leg muscles when walking). Further evaluation was done by angiogram of the blood vessels of the leg, and these films revealed no useful blood flow below the knee. Vascular consultation was obtained, with the assessment that no operative procedure was feasible or technically possible. On the basis of the patient's request, the primary care physician, Marshall Fitzpatrick, obtained a second opinion from a cardiologist, Ivonne Keys, who suggested an angioplasty and stent procedure, which he performed. The symptoms did not change and the disease course was not altered. The cost of this procedure was $12,000, including a $3,000 fee to the cardiologist.

=========================== **CASE 8-6** ===========================

Profiting from Self-Referral for MRIs

For many years internist Jonathan Birch had performed x-rays on his patients in his private office. He billed them a reasonable charge for the time and materials involved including enough to amortize the costs of the equipment. By the late 1980s Dr. Birch was making increased use of more sophisticated imaging techniques such as magnetic resonance imaging (MRI) and CT-scans. By comparison, this equipment was extremely expensive and would not be utilized sufficiently to justify having the equipment in his office. He began referring patients needing this type of diagnostic test to an imaging center at the local hospital. Patients were billed directly by the hospital. This had the effect of reducing Dr. Birch's income that he used to derive from the simpler in-office procedures.

In 1989 Dr. Birch was approached by Imaging Resources, Inc., about a new free-standing imaging facility it was launching. Dr. Birch was invited to visit the facility and inspect its state-of-the-art equipment. Dr. Birch was impressed. He considered it better than the hospital's facility and was considering shifting his referrals to the new center.

The director of the center then presented an offer to Dr. Birch. He was invited to invest in the center. He could buy a 1 percent interest in the facility with income on the investment projected as 12 percent. Furthermore, the facility would loan Dr. Birch the money he needed to make the investment at 6 percent interest with the interest and principal paid off with the earnings on the investment. As soon as the investment was paid off, Dr. Birch would own his share in the company and would receive profits on his ownership.

Dr. Birch realized that the more patients he referred the better the imaging business would do. In effect, he would be able to recoup some of the income he had lost when he shifted from x-rays in his office to the use of the outside imaging facility at the hospital. Dr. Birch was vaguely uncomfortable with the offer he received. It could be interpreted as giving him an ownership interest in order to influence his decisions about when to order imaging and what facility to recommend. He was made more uncomfortable when he learned that only physicians were being offered the favorable investment terms. He learned that only colleagues who did substantial amounts of referral for imaging were approached. Even so, Dr. Birch accepted the offer and the loan.

Follow-up:

By 1991 the U.S. Department of Health and Human Services was taking action against some of these joint venture investment schemes that gave the appearance of being designed to provide financial incentives to physicians to channel business to certain imaging centers.[3] There were accusations of kickbacks. In response, the government issued regulations that provided "safe harbors," provisions which, if met, would give physicians assurance that they would not be guilty of violating anti-kickback laws. The original provisions made clear that investment in large, public corporations was acceptable (such as drug companies), that physicians could provide services to joint ventures for a reasonable fee, and that investment terms (such as the loan received by Dr. Birch) had to be available to all investors, not just doctors who referred patients.[4] Later amendments clarified these provisions, but they remain in place essentially as originally promulgated.

As a result of these regulations, Dr. Birch decided to repay the loan and made an effort to assure that the company made a good faith effort to conform to all the provisions of the safe harbor regulations. He was convinced that the company, of which he was now a minority owner, was the best facility in town and that he would never refer a patient in order to increase the profits of the company. Still, he was concerned about whether this arrangement was ethical.

COMMENTARY

All three of these cases raise questions about fidelity to patients and potential economic conflicts of interest. In many such cases, patient-well-being as well as the economic interests of the provider are at stake.

In Case 8-4 involving a GP who wants to assist in surgery both the surgeon, Dr. Daemer, and the GP, Dr. Parish, could claim that their concerns were for the welfare of patients. Dr. Daemer was concerned that a physician without proper training in surgery was posing a risk to patients while Dr. Parish could cite continuity of care and long-term knowledge of the patient as a reason why his presence as an assistant in the surgery could help the patient. He might also point to eventual lower costs if he performs minor surgical procedures himself rather than referring to a more expensive surgeon. In spite of the potential patient-centered agendas for each of these physicians, there were also concerns of economic self-interest. Dr. Parish seems to be pursuing a course that will permit him to retain his patients for surgical procedures and capture some additional income. On the other hand, the surgeon might be concerned about losing a potential source of patient referrals.

Case 8-5 seems, at least at first, to be a more straightforward example of a physician who performed a procedure for the economic gain it would generate rather than for the well-being of the patient. It is, of course, possible that the cardiologist, Dr. Keys, really believed that the angioplasty and stent procedure had some chance of benefiting the patient. It could be that Dr. Keys and Dr. Fitzpatrick simply disagreed on how large a chance of success is needed to justify the procedure. That, of course, is not really a scientific question. The patient would appropriately be the one who could decide. More likely, this is a case in which a surgeon believes a cardiologist is performing unnecessary and useless operations with an eye toward the profits for the hospital and cardiologist. It is also possible that the surgeon is concerned about losing the patient.

Moral concerns in this case include issues of subjection of a patient to unnecessary anesthesia (after a vascular surgeon failed to advise operation), and performance of the procedure by a cardiologist who was paid a fee of $3,000. The acceptance of a cardiology consult (in general, cardiologists have less expertise in peripheral vascular disease than do vascular surgeons) raises the question "why not a third opinion, at least to break the tie?"

Case 8-6 escalates the conflict of interest to the institutional level. An entire arrangement between a physician with potential to generate lucrative referrals and the for-profit imaging center smacks of conflict of interest. Dr. Birch seems honestly to believe that the center in which he has invested and to which he steers patients is the best available. On the other hand, the economic arrangement, at least as it was originally established, seems clearly to be designed to induce Dr. Birch to generate business for the imaging center. Kickback is not an inappropriate term for such an arrangement. The adjustments following the development of federal safe-harbor provisions make the moral problem more subtle. The investment terms and the profits generated are now more reasonable, but still Dr. Birch will gain income from his inclination to point patients toward this particular center. Does the fact that he profited without controversy from the in-office x-rays provide a basis for justifying his income from the imaging center? Would fidelity to patients require an absolute prohibition on any such financial interests? If so, why should physicians be able to charge for in-office procedures and tests? How would physicians generate any income?

INCOMPETENT AND DISHONEST COLLEAGUES

The principle of fidelity has thus far been applied to the areas of the making and breaking of promises and conflicts of interest. Those who recognize an independent principle of fidelity believe that there is something intrinsically immoral about breaking a promise or commitment, including a commitment to the patient's well-being.

There are other implications of the principle of fidelity. One of the most significant regards loyalty to colleagues, especially when it conflicts with loyalty to the profession as a whole or loyalty to the patient. Many of the professional codes require reporting of incompetent or dishonest practices. This seems consistent with serving the welfare of patients as well as showing loyalty to the profession of which one is a member. However, we are also expected in life to be loyal to our friends and colleagues. If a colleague appears to be incompetent or dishonest, as in the following cases, the health care worker is often put in a situation of conflict.

CASE 8-7

Incompetent Colleagues: A Response to a Surgical Complication

William Harris had been having increasingly frequent symptoms of what he termed "water brash" or "heartburn after meals." He was fifty-seven years old, with no significant chronic illnesses or disabilities. He finally sought the advice of his general practice physician, Dr. Trent, who first tried treatment with antacid medications; these were only mildly effective. Subsequently, an x-ray evaluation of the esophagus and stomach outlined a large, hiatal hernia (herniation of the upper stomach into the lower chest cavity, above the diaphragm). This condition does not improve with medication, since acid from the stomach easily enters the esophagus and inflames its lining, producing the symptoms of "burning." If not treated effectively, serious changes will occur in the lining of the esophagus, leading to strictures or other serious problems. Only about 10 percent of patients with this problem require operative treatment.

A surgeon, Dr. Alfred Sievers, was consulted, the nature of the mechanical problem was explained, and the expectation of patient and surgeon was that replacement of the stomach in the abdomen and repair of the defect in the diaphragm would be successful.

In the recovery room, one of the surgeons responded to changes in Mr. Harris's pulse rate by checking the breath sounds and finding them greatly diminished on one side of the chest. A needle inserted into the chest cavity released free air, almost certainly indicating a rupture of the esophagus. A thoracic surgeon, James Fisher, was immediately called in consultation. He arrived within an hour, having been busy with another patient, and he inserted a drainage tube into the chest and began antibiotic treatment. This surprised Dr. Sievers, the general surgeon; he thought he remembered from his residency training that such patients should be immediately operated through the chest so that a tear could be repaired directly. However, he deferred to the specific expertise of the thoracic surgeon and was reluctant to question his decision.

Dr. Fisher's conservative treatment (drain and antibiotics) of Mr. Harris failed; esophageal leakage continued, infection became severe, and he died two weeks later.

COMMENTARY

This tragic case demonstrates the potential seriousness of major surgical procedures, however appropriate for the patient's condition and well intended. The mortality rate in such a case after reoperation and repair of the esophageal leak is approximately 5 percent; when only chest drainage and antibiotic therapy are used, the mortality rate exceeds 50 percent. It is not only an example of an error in technical judgment to only drain the chest, but it raises ethical questions as well.

Most codes of ethics for health professionals include a provision that the clinician has a duty to maintain professional competence. This includes obligations for continuing education and staying current on new developments in one's field. For example, the American Medical Association's (AMA's) principles include the provision that

The physician shall continue to study, apply, and advance scientific knowledge, maintain a commitment to medical education, make relevant information available to patients, colleagues, and the public and obtain consultation and use the talents of other health professionals when indicated.[5]

Recent codifications have been more explicit in requiring maintenance of competence. The more complex moral issue is what obligations, if any, the one observing the error of a colleague bears. In this case, Dr. Sievers, the general surgeon, thought he recognized an inappropriately conservative response on Dr. Fisher's part. The case, then, can be seen as involving an ethical failure of one of the other physicians to question a colleague's judgment directly. There was time to consult the literature or even to call another thoracic surgeon and to obtain another opinion. If this had not been persuasive, the attending surgeon in the case could have actually called for another thoracic consultation at the bedside of Mr. Harris, however awkward or uncomfortable for the physicians involved. Further, if the thoracic surgeon was too busy in his practice to do the more extensive procedure, while knowing that reoperation should be done, he failed in his obligation by not referring the case to another thoracic surgeon.

The good of the patient was sacrificed to professional interests in avoiding conflict based on different perceptions of appropriate response to this complication. The generalist failed that good, by deferring to the specialist without discussion.

The more controversial aspect of this case is what, if anything, Dr. Sievers should have said to the patient or family. No doubt informing them of the error would strain professional relations with Dr. Fisher, but at least in the days immediately following the events, it is possible that speaking up could have led to corrective intervention. The family no doubt would have legal, financial, and psychological reasons for wanting to know the reasons underlying their loved one's death. The recent AMA *Code of Medical Ethics*, for example, states that the initial report of an incompetent colleague should be made "to the appropriate clinical authority."[6] Oddly, it also states that incompetence that poses an immediate threat to the health of patients "should be reported to the state licensing board."[7] There is no suggestion in this section that patients or families need be informed. In an earlier section, however, the code states that "When patient harm has been caused by an error, physicians should offer a general explanation regarding the nature of the error and measures being taken to prevent similar occurrences in the future."[8] Should Dr. Sievers have said something to the patient and family as well as to the relevant health care professionals?

CASE 8-8

Dishonest Colleagues: Intentionally Shorting Tablet Counts

After Lorine Lance, Pharm.D., counseled Ferris Janowski, an elderly patient, about his three cardiac maintenance medications, she was surprised by Mr. Janowski's final question, "Would you please open these prescriptions and count them for me so that I know I'm getting what I paid for? There was a letter in my favorite advice column last night that told about how you can get shorted on your prescriptions, so I just want to make sure all the pills are there. No offense meant, you understand. I just can't afford to pay for pills and not get them."

Mr. Janowski's prescriptions had been filled by the owner of the pharmacy, Glen Battin, R.Ph., who would not be in for several hours. Dr. Lance decided to humor Mr. Janowski and opened the first bottle. To her dismay, the prescription was four tablets short. She made up the difference. The remaining two prescriptions were also short by the same amount—four pills each. Dr. Lance remedied the shortage in these two and returned all three prescriptions to Mr. Janowski. "I guarantee you that these are filled accurately and fully," Dr. Lance told Mr. Janowski as she handed him his medications.

Mr. Janowski was not the only patient with concerns about shortages that day. Evidently, several patients were prompted by the newspaper article to count their pills and found less than there should have been. Dr. Lance took numerous calls from angry patients and tried to determine if the caller might have miscounted, lost a pill, or took more than they should have, all reasons that the prescriptions could appear short. She noted that all of the prescriptions that patients claimed were shorted were for maintenance drugs and that Mr. Battin had filled them.

When Mr. Battin arrived at the pharmacy, an exhausted Dr. Lance told him about what she had discovered and the number of dissatisfied patients that called to complain about shortages. She was certain Mr. Battin would have a reasonable explanation. He stated, "It's really a shame that advice column printed that letter. We'll have to stop shorting maintenance prescriptions for a while until people get over the excitement and the need to count every prescription."

Dr. Lance could not believe what she was hearing. "You mean that you *have* been shorting prescriptions?" Mr. Battin shrugged, "Just the maintenance prescriptions and only on the higher-end products. People don't miss three or four pills a month and the pharmacy recoups a steady amount. Besides, they always come in for a refill before they run out, so the patients aren't harmed."

Dr. Lance had always admired Mr. Battin, but his nonchalant admission of guilt instantly changed her appraisal of her employer. She had never knowingly shorted a prescription. How could she work for someone who did it as a matter of course? Furthermore, what should she do about this dishonest behavior?

COMMENTARY

Glen Battin, the owner of the pharmacy who is routinely shorting patients on their medication, spares us the problem we had encountered in the previous case of determining whether the practitioner understands and is responsible for what he is doing. He nonchalantly acknowledges to Lorine Lance what he is doing. He seems to think that as long as he limits his practice to maintenance prescriptions and his patients get them refilled before they run out, he is not causing any harm and that his behavior is tolerable.

Of course, patients can be injured financially as well as medically. They are here being cheated out of four tablets for which they are paying. Even if it is an insurer that is bearing the extra costs, someone is paying for something the patient is not getting. Mr. Battin also needs to take into account the fact that his dispensing practice constitutes a deception to the patient if not an outright lie. If ethics is a matter of keeping faith with patients as well as making sure that their interests are served, there is at minimum a challenge to fidelity in the pharmacist–patient relation with this practice.

The more subtle ethical issue raised by this case is what the implications of the principle of fidelity are for his employee, Dr. Lance. If she is operating strictly on the Hippocratic principle of protecting the patient's interests (especially if it is an insurer who is paying the bills), she might conclude that her employer's practice is not hurting the patient. No harm, no foul. However, she may understand her responsibilities to be more complex. Even if Mr. Janowski is not paying directly for the medication, he may pay indirectly in the form of extra premiums required to support Mr. Battin's practice (and other similar practices to which the insurer is exposed). Moreover, even if Mr. Janowski is insured through a public Medicare or Medicaid program for which he bears essentially no financial burden, somebody is paying the costs of this practice. If Dr. Lance is a utilitarian concerned about burdens to others as well as to her patient, she will have cause for concern.

Most critically, Dr. Lance may feel that she has an obligation to maintain trust with her patient. There is a sense in which the trust of the community in the profession of pharmacy is jeopardized by Mr. Battin's practice. If there are duties of fidelity incumbent upon a pharmacist, Dr. Lance owes it to her profession and patients in general to challenge the dishonest practice of one of the profession's members.

Pharmacists also have some kind of duty of fidelity to colleagues. A collegial relationship commands loyalty that is grounded in the principle of fidelity. Is there any sense in which a colleague's duties of loyalty require remaining silent about dishonest practices, especially those that seem not to jeopardize a patient's welfare in any dramatic and direct way? Is there any case to be made for remaining silent in the face of impaired, incompetent, and dishonest practices such as those in these last two cases? If not, what action can Dr. Lance take?

NOTES

[1] May, William F. "Code, Covenant, Contract, or Philanthropy?" *Hastings Center Report* 5 (December 1975):29–38; Master, Roger D. "Is Contract an Adequate Basis for Medical Ethics?" *Hastings Center Report* 5 (December 1975):24–28; Veatch, Robert M. "The Case for Contract in Medical Ethics." In *The Clinical Encounter: The Moral Fabric of the Patient–Physician Relationship.* Earl E. Shelp,

editor. Dordrecht, Holland: D. Reidel Publishing Co., 1983, pp. 105–112; Brody, Howard. "The Physician–Patient Contract: Legal and Ethical Aspects." *The Journal of Legal Medicine* (July/August 1976), pp. 25–29.

2 Benjamin, Martin. "Lay Obligations in Professional Relations." *Journal of Medicine and Philosophy* 10 (1985):85–103.

3 Crane, Thomas S. "The Problem of Physician Self-Referral Under the Medicare and Medicaid Antikickback Statute." *Journal of the American Medical Association* 268 (No. 1, July 1, 1992):85–91.

4 Department of Health and Human Services, Office of Inspector General, 42 CFR Part 1001, RIN 0991-AA49, Medicare and State Health Care Programs: Fraud and Abuse; OIG Anti-Kickback Provisions, Monday, July 29, 1991 (56 FR 35952) available on the Internet at http://www.oig.hhs.gov/fraud/docs/safeharborregulations/072991.htm (accessed Dec. 7, 2006).

5 American Medical Association. Council on Ethical and Judicial Affairs. *Code of Medical Ethics: Current Opinions with Annotations*, 2004–2005. Chicago, IL: AMA Press, 2004, p. xiv.

6 Ibid., p. 261.

7 Ibid.

8 Ibid., p. 231

CHAPTER 9

᠅

Avoidance of Killing

Other Cases Involving Issues of Killing

4-4: Physician Assistance in an ALS Patient's Suicide
6-5: Brought to the ER after a Suicide Attempt
12-1: Guilt Over Suicidal Thoughts
14-4: Treating Donors to Optimize Organ Quality
Also see the cases of Chapter 18

═══════════

The principles examined in the preceding chapters—beneficence, nonmaleficence, justice, respect for autonomy, veracity, and fidelity—cover most of the moral considerations that arise in one-on-one personal moral decisions in health care. But before turning to some special topical areas in Part 3, we should look at one additional important moral consideration. Many moral controversies in health care hinge on claims that are variously based on the notion that human life is sacred or that killing of a human is morally wrong. In this chapter, we look at cases involving health professionals who are put in positions in which they need to know exactly what is implied by these notions. With the emergence of the legalization of physician-assisted suicide, health professionals will increasingly be put in a position in which they will be parties to patient suicides. At least in Oregon and Washington, patients who meet certain criteria, including mental competence, can now legally get prescriptions filled for the explicit purpose of killing themselves. In this chapter we explore the ethical implications of this emerging practice.

For all of us killing of another person is usually wrong if for no other reason than that normally people want to live. Killing people normally violates their autonomy. Killing also does people harm in a dramatic way. The principle of nonmaleficence (not harming) counts strongly against killing in most cases. But there are special cases when people may consent to being killed or when it is not as obvious that killing would be perceived as a harm by the individual. Some patients are suicidal. While many suicidal persons are so seriously depressed that they are not mentally competent, others may have an accurate grasp of their life prospects and may have decided that their future will, on balance, offer more burdens than benefits. Others are so racked with the pain of a chronic, perhaps terminal, illness that they would plead to be killed or to be aided in dying.

Killing is a complex and ambiguous term. Some people imply when they use the word that the term always conveys a negative moral judgment—that to say something is a killing is to say that it is morally wrong. However, we sometimes speak of *justified killings*, such as in cases of justified war, police actions, self-defense, and perhaps merciful euthanasia. There are many ways in which society, both secular and religious, has condoned the taking of another person's life, some of these against that person's will. The wide prevalence of the death penalty, ethnic cleansing, jihads, and even assassinations makes clear that many throughout human history have at least believed that killings can be justified.

It seems that not all behavior that is causally related to the shortening of life is classified as killing. For example, as we see in this chapter, most do not consider refusal of life support to be a killing, even though such refusal will lead to death. Moreover, even if some action is deemed a *killing*, the use of that term does not automatically imply that the action is morally wrong. For example, accidental killings, such as from a lethal idiosyncratic reaction to anesthesia or a prescription, are not always morally wrong.

Even among actions that are directly intended to terminate the life of another, we can distinguish killing for merciful motive from other kinds of killing. We can also distinguish self-killing (suicide) from the killing of another (homicide). We can distinguish killing with the consent of the one killed from those that are involuntary (against the victim's wishes) and those that are nonvoluntary (without the approval or disapproval of the one who is killed). Finally, we can distinguish homicide on request (in which the care provider or other acquaintance of the patient will kill on the patient's request) from assisted suicide (in which the health professional supplies information or materials, such as medication, but patients themselves take the last decisive step in ending their own lives).

Our traditional religious and secular values have dictated that even in cases in which the motive is merciful and the patient requests the action, it is wrong to kill. But why? If the killing relieves severe suffering, especially if it is requested by a competent patient, can it not count as a good and noble thing to help those who are suffering end it?

We have seen that some people hold that in ethics the consequences are the only morally relevant factor. Utilitarians, for example, hold this view. So do those who subscribe to the Hippocratic principle, which requires the health professional to always act only so as to benefit the patient. Although many health professionals do not realize it, the Hippocratic principle by itself could permit or even require him or her to cooperate in killing a patient when it would, on balance, do more good than harm.

However, the Hippocratic Oath also contains a specific provision that is usually interpreted as prohibiting active killing. Technically it proscribes "giving a deadly drug, even if asked." But usually in modern readings, that is taken to prohibit any physician participation in killing. Insofar as the Oath can be extended to all health professionals, it would prohibit pharmacists, nurses, and other health professionals from participating as well. Since health professionals other than physicians are not normally in positions where they would seriously contemplate mercifully killing patients on their own, the codes for these other health professions often do not mention a prohibition on killing, but one can assume that such actions would be opposed by the traditional organizations.

The interesting problem is why such a prohibition on killing exists if the goal of the professional is always to benefit the patient. One possibility, of course, would be that the authors of the Oath considered it always a net harm to the patient to end the patient's life. Many people, however, are willing to concede that, at least in rare cases, the patient may be worse off if he or she continues to live. Normally, that would involve cases of intractable, severe suffering. If some patients occasionally would actually be "better off dead," then there are two other possible justifications for proscribing merciful killings.

First, as we have seen in previous chapters, some people who base moral judgments on consequences do not believe it is right to directly calculate the consequences in each individual case. Instead they consider possible alternative moral rules or policies. They assess the net consequences of the alternative rules or policies and choose the rule or policy that they believe will do more good than any alternative. These people are called *rule-utilitarians*.[1] Rule-utilitarians sometimes hold that the policy of prohibiting killing will, over time, produce better consequences than any other rule even if occasionally a particular merciful killing does more good than harm.

They may do this for a number of reasons. First, some are worried about the risk of error if individuals were permitted to make the calculations on the spot for each case. Especially in highly emotionally charged situations where rapid decisions have to be made and when those doing the calculating may not know the individuals affected very well, the danger of miscalculation may be great. These critics of merciful killing believe that in the long run more good may be done (and more harm prevented) if we simply apply the rule against killing because, on balance, it will produce more good than any alternative.

Second, some people, not necessarily persuaded that the risk of error is this great, may still hold that it is just the nature of morality that practices are established by evaluating alternative rules or policies and choosing the set that produces the greatest net good.[2] They may favor a rule against merciful killing because they consider it the utility-maximizing rule; that is, they may believe that the rule prohibiting such killing produces more good outcomes than any other rule they can imagine. For either of these reasons, some consequentialists, those who are rule consequentialists, may favor a rule that prohibits the participation of health professionals in killing.

There is a second reason why the Hippocratic Oath may prohibit active killings for mercy. As we have seen in previous chapters, there may be moral principles other than beneficence and nonmaleficence that determine whether an act is right or wrong. We have noted that some people hold that respect for autonomy, veracity, and fidelity to promises help determine the rightness of actions regardless of the consequences. Is it possible that killing is just inherently wrong—even if the one who is killed is better off than if he or she had lived? If so, avoidance of killing could be an independent principle that helps shape the rightness and wrongness of human conduct. We might refer to it simply as the *principle of avoidance of killing*. It is not clear whether the writer of the Hippocratic Oath believed this. If he did, then he was not a pure consequentialist.

Whether the Hippocratic author believed that killing people was inherently wrong, clearly other moral traditions are committed to this view. Judaism considers life to be sacred, a gift from God. Killing a human, at least an innocent human, is always wrong. In fact, Judaism has even gone beyond the view that killing, at least killing of the innocent is wrong, to the view that all human life is sacred. According to this perspective, it is always wrong for humans to make decisions, such as deciding to withdraw life support, which will predictably shorten a patient's life.

Catholicism considers killing an intrinsic wrong, but, as we shall see, this tradition does not extend its condemnation to all actions that will shorten life. It accepts certain forgoing of life support. Other moral traditions, both religious and secular, condemn killing as well.[3] They at least view it as *prima facie* wrong, that is, wrong insofar as the action involves killing (although that wrongness might, on occasion, be offset by other moral considerations). If killing is always a wrong-making characteristic of an action, then avoidance of killing can be thought of as another moral principle that must hold beneficence and nonmaleficence in check.[4] The cases in this chapter help clarify how lay people and health professionals should evaluate possible attempts to relieve patients of their misery by putting them to death. In later sections of the chapter, participation in active merciful killing will be compared and contrasted with decisions to forgo treatment (to withhold or withdraw treatment).

ACTIVE KILLING VERSUS LETTING DIE

Both religious and secular traditions in the West have held that it is always morally wrong to actively kill a human being even if the killing is done for a merciful motive. For example, some terminally ill patients appear to be in pain. They may be inevitably dying rapidly and could be spared the misery of the dying if someone simply actively intervened with an injection of a drug to hasten the death. Some argue that such intervention would be the humane and moral thing to do, but others claim that there is something intrinsically wrong with killing—that life is sacred and to be preserved or that at least it should not be ended directly by human hand. The following case, raises the question of whether there is any significant moral difference between actively killing someone who is dying and simply stepping aside and letting nature take its course.

CASE 9-1

Jack Kevorkian: Merciful Homicide, Suicide, and Forgoing Life Support

Fifty-two-year-old Thomas Youk suffered from amyotrophic lateral sclerosis (ALS, sometimes called Lou Gehrig's Disease). In the fall of 1998 he was having difficulty breathing and swallowing. He contacted Jack Kevorkian, known as "Dr. Death." Dr. Kevorkian, a pathologist whose license to practice medicine had been revoked, had through the 1990s assisted in the suicides of over 100 people who had requested help in ending their lives. Prior to the case of Mr. Youk, apparently all of the deaths in which he had been involved were suicides. Dr. Kevorkian provided counsel and then helped the individuals by inserting an IV or attaching a mask. Harmless saline or air was initially flowing through the equipment. In these cases, the patients themselves took the last step in the chain of events that led to their deaths. They turned a stopcock or control so that lethal potassium chloride or carbon monoxide began to flow, the eventual cause of the deaths.

Since the patients themselves took the action responsible for their deaths, these were considered assisted suicides rather than homicides. Even assisting in a suicide has generally been considered illegal. Dr. Kevorkian was prosecuted no fewer than three times. In each of these cases he was acquitted. The jurors, perhaps out of sympathy for his actions, found some reason for finding him not guilty. Problems in proving his involvement, in establishing the jurisdiction, or other technicalities were sometimes cited.

In Thomas Youk's case, he was suffering from a disease that caused paralysis while leaving him mentally lucid. He requested Dr. Kevorkian's assistance in ending his life but was physically not able to take the final action leading to his death. He requested that Dr. Kevorkian inject a lethal substance to end his life.

Dr. Kevorkian had long been attempting to change the law about intentional merciful killing. To force the issue before the courts and general public, he videotaped the final moments of Mr. Youk's life and released the video to the CBS television program, "60 Minutes."

On September 15 Dr. Kevorkian went to Mr. Youk's home to discuss his situation. The interaction was videotaped showing Mr. Youk requesting help in "ending his suffering." Dr. Kevorkian indicated that Youk needed to agree to a statement: a consent to "direct injection." The statement to which he agreed read:

"I, Thomas Youk, the undersigned, entirely voluntarily, without any reservation, external persuasion, pressure, or duress, and after prolonged a thorough deliberation, hereby consent to the following medical procedure of my own choosing, and that you have chosen direct injection, or what they call active euthanasia, to be administered by a competent medical professional, in order to end with certainty my intolerable and hopelessly incurable suffering."

On September 16, 1998, at 9:49 p.m., Dr. Kevorkian again videotaped his interaction with Mr. Youk. After asking Mr. Youk to reaffirm his desire to go through with the plan, Dr. Kevorkian injected Anectine and Seconal before injecting potassium chloride. Most people who have viewed the videotape have no doubt that Mr. Youk knew exactly what was happening, was mentally lucid, and desired to have the injection.

Dr. Kevorkian was tried before the Oakland County, Michigan, Circuit Court, found guilty of second degree murder, and sentenced to 10–25 years in jail. He was paroled on June 1, 2007.[*]

COMMENTARY

There is now little doubt that what Dr. Kevorkian did was illegal. The moral question is whether it ought to be illegal and, if so, whether this kind of intentional direct, active killing differs in any morally significant way from various other actions and omissions that can lead to a human's death.

First, we need to be clear about terminology. Active killing is typically distinguished from omissions of life-supporting medical interventions that lead to death. The former has traditionally been considered unethical while the latter is morally acceptable in many, but not all, ethical traditions. Active killing can be done intentionally or accidentally. Accidental killings occur from time to time in medicine and outside of it. Assuming the one who did the killing was not reckless or negligent, some accidental killings are morally tolerable. In medicine, for example, an anesthesia accident may actively kill a patient on the operating table. It is active, but surely not intended. Assuming there was adequate consent for the administration of the anesthetic and a contraindication was not negligently overlooked, the one administering it will be excused. The killing was not expected and the one administering it will be exonerated.

Mr. Youk's death was the result of an intentional action taken by Dr. Kevorkian. If the one who dies has had to take a critical last step in the causal chain leading to the death (such as turning a stopcock to start the flow of a lethal agent or swallowing a pill), this will be deemed a suicide. The one providing education, counsel, equipment, or support assists in the suicide but is not deemed to have committed a homicide. Nevertheless, assisting in a suicide is generally considered to be illegal. Dr. Kevorkian assisted in the hundred or

[*]This case is based on People v. Kevorkian, 248 Mich. App. 373, 639 N.W.2d 291 (Mich. Ct. App. 2001) and related material. The videotape of the interaction between Mr. Youk and Dr. Kevorkian is entitled "Death by Doctor." It aired on 60 Minutes on November 22, 1998, and is available by calling CBS Video at 800-848-3256. The item number is SM81122A. The cost for rental is $29.95 plus shipping and handling.

so cases of suicide involving either a lethal drug or carbon monoxide. In some cases he inserted an IV administering saline, but with a control so that the patient could switch to a lethal drug. In other cases he attached a respirator mask through which oxygen was administered, but with a control that would permit the patient to switch to carbon monoxide. Either would count as suicide with physician assistance. Dr. Kevorkian was tried for three of these cases and found not guilty by the juries. This cannot be taken as the overturning of laws prohibiting physician assistance. It is more like "jury nullification," the practice by which a sympathetic jury refuses to convict someone even though what he did was a legal violation.

What Dr. Kevorkian did in Mr. Youk's case was not assistance in suicide. It was what could be called "homicide on request." Dr. Kevorkian took the steps that led to Mr. Youk's death.

Ethically, four factors are potentially relevant to evaluating what Dr. Kevorkian did. First is the difference between assistance in suicide and homicide on request. In either case, the intention is to bring about a death. The most that could be said for a difference is that in the case of assisting in suicide, we have some degree of additional evidence that the deceased really wanted to end his or her life (since he or she actually did something, but for which the death would not have occurred). Still in Mr. Youk's case, the videotape provides convincing evidence of Mr. Youk's desire, probably more evidence than we have in some of the assisted suicide cases in which Dr. Kevorkian was involved.

This suggests a second factor in the evaluating of Dr. Kevorkian's action: he claims to have the consent of the one who was killed, a claim that seems supported by the videotape. Legally, consent does not provide a justification for the killing. Ethically, if the only offense in killing is the depriving of someone of his autonomy, then a valid consent from a substantially autonomous person might be taken as providing a justification. Nevertheless, some would view autonomy as inalienable, that is, incapable of being surrendered voluntarily. Since consenting to one's own death necessarily renders one nonautonomous, one reason to oppose assisting in a suicide or homicide is that it can destroy autonomy.

This brings us to the third factor in evaluating Dr. Kevorkian's action. Consequentialists hold that the feature that makes most killings morally wrong is that it harms the "victim." Since some would argue that Mr. Youk was not harmed by this killing, no violation of the principle of nonmaleficence occurred. Figuring out whether harm occurred is a complex task. It seems clear that Mr. Youk did not consider himself to be harmed. To the contrary, he saw the action as removing the harm of the intractable suffering he would otherwise endure. Nevertheless, some might consider the taking of a life, especially a human life, as objectively a harm. Something of intrinsic value, a human life, is removed from the earth. If life is objectively good (regardless of the suffering involved), one might argue that killing is always a harm.

If killing of Mr. Youk, with his substantially voluntary consent, does not violate his autonomy and cannot be interpreted as producing an objective harm, then the only other option for supporting the claim that this merciful killing is immoral would be to hold that killing of a human (and according to some perhaps some nonhuman animals) is an intrinsic moral wrong. Even if it does not violate the principles of autonomy and nonmaleficence, it might violate a principle of avoiding killing—the idea that is simply intrinsically wrong to kill. Just like it is seen by some as intrinsically wrong to lie or break promises or violate the autonomy of others, so it might be wrong to kill.

If avoiding killing is a separate moral principle, then we must understand exactly what is proscribed. It is common to omit life support, especially if the patient or surrogate refuses consent for it. If patients die following such an omission, we need to determine whether a killing has occurred and, if so, whether the killing was immoral. Some hold that in the case of actions that result in death, the one taking the action did the killing, but in the case of an omission, no human agent caused the death—an underlying disease caused it.

Some find this sufficient reason to hold that active killings are always morally wrong (at least *prima facie*), but that omissions are not immoral. The problem with this is that sometimes it really is immoral to omit life support. If a physician withheld cardiopulmonary resuscitation (CPR) because she was mad at the patient and as a result the patient dies, the physician should be guilty of a killing.

One difficulty with omissions is that it is sometimes hard to determine who is responsible for an omission, while it is usually quite clear if someone took an action that caused a death. In the case of omission, every person in the world failed to act, yet surely not everyone is guilty of homicide when a death results. We normally limit killings by omission to cases in which there was a clear-cut duty to act and the one with that duty failed to do so.

Where justified or not, it is very common to hold that actions that kill, at least kill intentionally, are immoral while omissions are not unless there was a duty to act. Since a valid refusal of treatment by a patient or surrogate prohibits action even by a physician who would like to provide life support, omissions that lead to death following valid refusal of consent are generally considered acceptable and are not normally described as killings.

In order to further clarify these issues, we still need to examine the intermediate case of withdrawing life support once it is begun.

WITHHOLDING VERSUS WITHDRAWING TREATMENT

While the distinction between killing and simply omitting life-sustaining treatment in order to let the patient die has a long history and is well understood by most clinicians, there is an intermediate case that has generated confusion. If a therapy is once begun, its withdrawal would seem to be morally similar to not providing it in the first place, and yet, psychologically, it may feel to many care providers much closer to actively doing something to the patient to cause the patient's death. One of the most famous cases in all of bioethics was that of Karen Ann Quinlan, a 21-year-old young woman in a persistent vegetative state and on a ventilator following a respiratory arrest. Her physician resisted her parents' insistence upon stopping the ventilator. This case is taken from the court records.[†]

CASE 9-2

Karen Quinlan: The Case of Withdrawing a Ventilator

On the night of April 15, 1975, friends of 21-year-old Karen Quinlan summoned the local police and emergency rescue squad, and she was taken to Newton Memorial Hospital. The precise events leading up to her admission to Newton Memorial Hospital are unclear. She apparently ceased breathing for at least two fifteen-minute periods. Mouth to mouth resuscitation was applied by her friends the first time and by a police respirator the second time. The exact amount of time she was without spontaneous respiration is unknown.

Upon her admission to Newton Memorial, urine and blood tests indicated the presence of quinine, aspirin, barbiturates in normal range as well as traces of valium and Librium. Dr. Robert Morse, the neurologist in charge of her care found the drugs to be in the therapeutic range and the quinine consistent with mixing in drinks like soda water. The interruption in respiration apparently caused anoxia—insufficient supply of oxygen in the blood—resulting in her present condition.

At 10 p.m. on April 16, 1975, Dr. Morse again examined Karen. He found her in a coma with evidence of what he called *decortication* indicating an altered level of consciousness. She required the respirator for assistance. She did not breathe spontaneously.

Karen was transferred to the intensive care unit (ICU) of St. Clare's Hospital, under the care of Dr. Morse. At the time of her transfer, she was still unconscious, still on a respirator, a catheter was inserted into her bladder; and a tracheostomy had been performed.

Dr. Morse testified Karen changed from a sleeping comatose condition to a sleep–awake type comatose condition but described this as normal in comatose patients and not any indication of improvement. He indicated that during the awake cycle, she was still unconscious. He claimed that Karen was not brain dead and would not return to a level of cognitive function.

[†]The details of this case are adapted from the lower court opinion, In *re* Quinlan, 137 N.J. super 227 (1975). While that court ruled that the physicians could continue life support against the parents' wishes, that opinion was later overturned by the New Jersey Supreme Court: In *re* Quinlan, 70 N.J. 10, 355 A. 2d 647 (1976), *cert. denied* sub nom., Garger v. New Jersey, 429 U.S. 922 (1976), overruled in part, In *re* Conroy, 98 N.J. 321, 486 A.2d 1209 (1985). See also Quinlan, Joseph and Julia with Phyllis Battelle. *Karen Ann*. Garden City, New York: Doubleday, 1977.

Karen was examined by several experts for the various parties. All agree she was in a persistent vegetative state. She had irreversible brain damage; no cognitive or cerebral functioning; chances for useful sapient life or return of discriminative functioning were considered remote.

Karen's parents, Joseph and Julia Quinlan, assumed responsibility for the care of their daughter. The decision to request that she be removed from the respirator, understandably, came tortuously, arduously to the Quinlans. At the outset, they authorized Dr. Morse to do everything he could to keep her alive, believing she would recover. They participated in a constant vigil over her with other family members. They were in constant contact with the doctors, particularly Dr. Morse, receiving day by day reports concerning her prognosis which, as time passed, became more and more pessimistic and more and more discouraging to them.

Mrs. Quinlan and the children were the first to conclude Karen should be removed from the respirator. Mrs. Quinlan, working at the local parish church, had ongoing talks with Father Trapasso, who supported her conclusion and indicated that it was a permissible practice within the tenets of Roman Catholic teachings.

Mr. Quinlan was slower in making his decision. His hope for recovery continued despite the disheartening medical reports. Neither his wife nor Father Trapasso made any attempt to influence him. A conflict existed between letting her natural body functioning control her life and the hope for recovery. Once having made the decision, he sought Father Trapasso's encouragement, which he received.

Father Trapasso based his support of the position taken by the Quinlans on the traditional, moral precepts of the Roman Catholic faith and upon a declaration by Pope Pius XII made on November 24, 1957. Father Trapasso acknowledges it is not a sinful act under the church teachings or the Papal statement to either continue extraordinary treatment or discontinue it. It is acknowledged to be a matter left optional to a Roman Catholic believer. Mr. Quinlan indicates that had Roman Catholic traditions and morals considered it a sin, he would not be seeking termination of the respiratorial support. Mr. Quinlan held that Karen's natural bodily functions should be allowed to operate free of the respirator. He states then if it is God's will to take her she can go on to life after death.

The Quinlans on July 31, 1975, signed the following statement:

> We authorize and direct Doctor Morse to discontinue all extraordinary measures, including the use of a respirator for our daughter Karen Quinlan.
>
> We acknowledge that the above named physician has thoroughly discussed the above with us and that the consequences have been fully explained to us. Therefore, we hereby RELEASE from any and all liability the above named physician, associates and assistants of his choice, Saint Clare's Hospital and its agents and employees.

The Quinlans, upon signing the release, considered the matter decided. Dr. Morse, however, felt he could not and would not agree to the cessation of the respirator assistance. He advised the Quinlans prior to the time of their signing the release that he wanted to check into the matter further before giving his approval. After checking on other medical case histories, he concluded that terminating the respirator would be a substantial deviation from medical tradition, that it involved ascertaining "quality of life", and that he would not do so.

Karen Quinlan was quoted as saying she never wanted to be kept alive by extraordinary means. The statements attributed to her by her mother, sister, and a friend are indicated to have been made essentially in relation to instances where close friends or relatives were terminally ill.

[Karen's father] urges the Court to act in Karen Quinlan's best interest by authorizing the cessation of the respirator. He asserts Karen Quinlan and her family have a constitutional right of privacy that lead to a right of self- determination which extends to the decision to terminate "futile use of extraordinary medical measures." He also asserts a constitutional right of free exercise of religious belief and freedom from cruel and unusual punishment as grounds for granting the sought relief.

The doctors and hospital essentially, contend, since Karen Quinlan is medically and legally alive, the Court should not authorize termination of the respirator, that to do so would be homicide and an act of euthanasia.

The doctors suggest the decision is one more appropriately made by doctors than by a court of law and that under the circumstances of this case a decision in favor of the parents would require ascertainment of quality of life standards to serve as future guidelines.

COMMENTARY

The New Jersey Supreme Court eventually ruled that Mr. Quinlan, as the guardian of Karen, had the authority to choose the physician responsible for her care. Although technically the physician could decide to continue the ventilator, Mr. Quinlan could dismiss any physician who made that choice, in effect, giving him the authority to terminate the ventilator.

Although this case confronted matters of law, crucial moral issues were at stake as well. Many of these question who has the authority to make medical treatment choices for incompetent patients. Strange as it may seem, many physicians believed that, once they had come to be in charge of a patient's treatment, they had the authority to continue treating even against the wishes of the patient or a valid surrogate. Dr. Morse believed he could base this decision on what he called "medical tradition," that is, the practices of his physician colleagues raising the question of whether that is a rational way to decide such issues. He also seemed to believe that deciding to stop treatment would involve a "quality of life" judgment, a task in which he was not willing to engage. Others might ask, however, whether the decision to continue support also involved such an assessment.

Other matters of controversy center on the role of parents, and others related to the patient, who are in a position to assume decision-making roles. It is not clear, for example, whether Karen's case should be decided based on her previously expressed wishes or on the basis of what her parents believe would be best for her. These questions of who should decide will be taken up in Chapter 18. Here our focus is on the substantive moral issue of whether stopping Karen's ventilator should be seen as active killing, which is viewed as immoral by many, or is more like not starting the treatment in the first place, which many, including leaders of Karen's own Roman Catholic Church consider acceptable.

The law makes a clear distinction between withdrawing life-sustaining treatment and active killing: treating killing as illegal while withdrawing treatment at the competent patient's request is treated as not only legal, but required. Although Karen Quinlan was incompetent at the time of the critical medical decisions, the record makes clear that she left some opinion of her wishes about refusing life support.

One approach to the problem is to view the decisions from the perspective of what the informed consent doctrine requires. Patients cannot be treated without consent, as we saw in the cases of Chapter 6. The autonomous patient has a right to agree or refuse to agree to any medical intervention. If Karen were conscious and competent while on a ventilator, she would have the legal right to refuse to permit the starting of a ventilator, even though it would mean her death. As we shall see, most people believe that people also have a moral right to refuse and that valid surrogates also have a right to make such choices on an incompetent person's behalf. The issue here, however, is whether, once Dr. Morse has started the treatment, he has a right to continue it even against the wishes of the patient or surrogate.

No rational consent would be open ended; no rational person would agree to the use of a drug or machine for ever and ever until death just because it seems to make sense for a time that it was started. In fact, many clinicians are recognizing that time-limited trials of possibly beneficial therapies often are more reasonable than some open-ended commitment that might lead caregivers to mistakenly believe that the patient's permission goes on forever. As we saw in Karen Quinlan's case, at first the parents and physicians retained hope that her need for the ventilator was temporary. In the use of medical treatments that will continue indefinitely, therefore, it is often wise to specify for how long the treatment will be tried. If no time limit is specified, the only reasonable conclusion is that if the patient has the authority to give permission to try a treatment, she also has the right to withdraw the permission and stop the treatment. Once the consent is withdrawn what else can the provider do but stop the treatment?

In addition to the moral basis for removing such treatments, a pragmatic argument has been given for this approach. If the rule were that once an authorization for treatment were given it could not be withdrawn, a strong incentive would exist not to try an intervention unless one were very sure it would work. It seems irrational to avoid trying possibly effective life-prolonging interventions unless they were sure to succeed. The alternative is to permit patients or their surrogates to withdraw permission once the trial treatment is found wanting.

While the consent doctrine can force a provider to stop a treatment just the way it can force the provider not to begin, it can never force the provider to actively intervene to kill the patient. From the point of view of the consent doctrine, withdrawing treatment is much more like withholding it than it is like active killing. Now most analysts including those in the medical profession reject the claim of the doctors in the Karen Quinlan case that stopping her ventilator would be the same as euthanasia. The American Medical Association's (AMA's) *Current Opinions*, for example, simply states, "There is no ethical distinction between withdrawing and withholding life-sustaining treatment."[5] Thus, the AMA has adopted a position similar to that of the Roman Catholic Church and the American courts.

DIRECT VERSUS INDIRECT KILLING

The distinction between active killing and forgoing treatment is sometimes confused with another distinction that has become important in deciding whether it is morally wrong to kill another human being. Roman Catholic moral theology has long distinguished between directly intended evil and evil that is not intended. Theologians within this tradition (and many people in the secular world as well) have held that there are certain evils that are intrinsically wrong (such as killing an innocent person) and that it is always wrong directly to intend such evils. They have long recognized, however, that sometimes what they consider to be evil may occur even though it is not intended. Sometimes the one causing the evil may have no reasonable way of knowing that the evil would result, as when a health professional produces a fatal anaphylactic reaction by giving penicillin to a patient who is not suspected to be allergic. Surely, there is a sense in which the one who gave the unexpectedly dangerous drug killed the patient and yet, just as certainly, the death was not intended. Health providers would have done anything to avoid such death, if only they could know the harm would occur. These "killings" are active killings, yet they are unintended; they are sometimes called *indirect killings*.

A more complicated case involves situations in which the evil is anticipated, but not desired. Some drugs are known to have undesirable side effects so that the health professional knows she is taking a risk by administering the drug. In some cases, she may even know for sure that the side effect will occur but consider the effect worth it. It may be known that giving an antihistamine will make the patient drowsy, but that, on balance, the antihistamine will benefit the patient. If it is given, we would not say that it was intended to make the patient drowsy; rather, it was foreseen and unavoidable, though not intended. The same distinction between intended and foreseen consequences is sometimes used in discussing the ethics of war when someone argues that an anticipated injuring of a civilian may be acceptable even if it is unacceptable to intend to injure the civilian.

Likewise, Catholic theologians have held that something as evil as a death may be morally tolerable if it is unintended, even if it is foreseen. If the patient dies from respiratory depression resulting from a heavy narcotic dose given to control pain, the death can be called an indirect killing, that is, one that, even though foreseen, is not intended.

Those who accept this distinction between directly intended and indirect killing hold that, even though direct (i.e., intended) killings are never acceptable, under certain circumstances indirect killings are morally acceptable. To be acceptable, the evil must not be intended. Also, the good that is done, such as the relieving of pain, must be at least as great as the evil. Finally, the evil cannot be the means to the good end.[6] This notion that unintended bad consequences are morally tolerable when these conditions are met is referred to as the principle of indirect or double effect.

Thus according to Catholics, who believe that abortion is evil, it is unacceptable to abort a fetus to produce the "good" of relieving a pregnant woman's anxiety about becoming pregnant because the evil (the abortion) would be the means to the good. This would be unacceptable even if, hypothetically, the pregnant woman were certain to commit suicide unless her pregnancy were terminated. However, it might be acceptable to remove a cancerous uterus even if the woman with the cancer happened to be pregnant at the time. In the case of the cancer, the death of the fetus would not be a means to removing the cancer; it would be a foreseen, but unintended side effect. Catholics and others who recognize these distinctions conclude that the removal of the uterus to save the pregnant woman's life is morally tolerable even though it will result in the death of the fetus because the death was merely foreseen and not intended. While some people do not accept this distinction, it has been the prevailing view in American law and in professional codes of ethics.

One of the most dramatic instances in which physicians consider proceeding with treatment even though it will produce terrible side effects involves the separating of conjoined twins who share common life-supporting organs. In some cases, such as the next one, we know that the only way to save one infant is to cut off the blood supply that is sustaining the other one. The question is whether this should count as an unintended, but foreseen consequence that is morally tolerable or as a directly intended killing of the infant who will not survive.[‡]

‡ This case is based on press and scholarly accounts: Wasserman, David. "Killing Mary to Save Jodie: Conjoined Twins and Individual Rights." *Philosophy and Public Policy Quarterly* 21 (No. 1, Winter 2001):9–14; Annas, George J. "Conjoined Twins—the Limits of Law at the Limits of Life." *New England Journal of Medicine* 344 (April 5, 2001):1104–1108; Dyer, Clare. "Siamese Twins to Be Separated against Parent's Will." *British Medical Journal* 321 (September 2, 2000):529; Dyer, Clare. "Parents of Siamese Twins Appeal against Separation." *British Medical Journal* 321 (September 9, 2000):589; Dyer, Clare. "Doctrine of Necessity Could Allow Separation of Twins." *British Medical Journal* 321 (September 16, 2000):653; Mallia, Pierre. "The Case of the Maltese Siamese Twins—When Moral Arguments Balance Out Should Parental Rights Come into Play." *Medicine, Health Care and Philosophy* 5 (2002):205–209; "Separation of Conjoined Twins." *Lancet* 356 (September 16, 2000):953.

========= **CASE 9-3** =========

Separating Conjoined Twins: An Unintended but Foreseen Killing?

Michelangelo and Rina Attard, living on the island of Gozo in Malta, were expecting to be parents. When they discovered Mrs. Attard was carrying conjoined twins, they traveled to Manchester, England, since no adequate facility to care for the babies existed at their home. The twins, given the fictional names of Jodie and Mary by the court, were born at St. Mary's Hospital in Manchester on August 8, 2000. The twins were joined at the abdomen. Jodie was described as bright and alert with an anatomically normal brain, heart, lungs, and liver. Mary, on the other hand, had significant brain pathology and relied on Jodie's heart and lungs for her blood supply. Separating the twins would mean the certain death of Mary, but Jodie had a good chance of survival with moderate physical impairment that would require further operations to correct. Without intervention to separate the twins, they would both die within 3–6 months.

The parents, Roman Catholics, said they wanted "God's will" to prevail and refused permission for the operation. They could not accept the idea of killing one by cutting off her blood supply in order for the other to survive. They were willing to accept the death of both, if necessary, but found intentional action that would end one of the lives to save the other unacceptable. While the main focus of their reported objection was the moral problem of sacrificing one for the benefit of the other, they were also quoted as expressing concern that neither they nor their home country would be able to provide the special care that Jodie would require. If medical treatment necessary to preserve life was "gravely burdensome" to the patient or others, Roman Catholicism has long recognized the legitimacy of forgoing life support.

The doctors at St. Mary's Hospital sought court authorization to perform the procedure against the parents' wishes, and the courts ultimately granted that request. The lower court attempted to claim that the operation that would lead to Mary's death was not a case of killing, but rather the withdrawal of nutrition and hydration by clamping off her blood supply. It was deemed "passive" euthanasia rather than active killing. The court acknowledged that the physicians felt they had a medical moral duty to preserve the life that could be preserved and their "collective medical conscience" would suffer if not authorized to proceed. When the parents appealed the lower court decision, the appeals court justices gave differing arguments but affirmed the right of the doctors to proceed. One appeals court judge rejected the claim that cutting off the blood supply was an omission of treatment rather than active killing. He argued that it cannot be claimed that the procedure was in Mary's best interest. Nevertheless, he endorsed it, claiming that Mary could be viewed as killing Jodie by her attachment to Jodie's blood supply. The action was thus labeled "self-defense" from Jodie's perspective.

A second appeals court justice frames his support of the intervention in what he called the "doctrine of necessity." He cites an analogy to a mountain climber justified in cutting the rope binding him to a companion who had fallen when, unless he frees himself, both will die.

The third justice concluded that remaining conjoined to Jodie would be of no benefit to Mary and would actually be to her disadvantage. He claims that the doctors' duties to Jodie and Mary are in conflict. He notes that the intent of the doctors was not to kill Mary, but to give each twin "bodily integrity" and that such independent existence was in the interest of each. He cites the conclusion of the physicians stating that "Highly skilled and conscientious doctors believe that the best course, in the interests of both twins, is to undertake elective surgery in order to separate them and save Jodie."

The procedure was performed on November 7, 2000. Mary died immediately when her blood vessels were cut. Jodie continued to survive with the expectation that she would need years of surgical care.

COMMENTARY

There is no question that Mary's death resulted from an active intervention that was known in advance certainly to be fatal. The moral issue is whether some justification can be provided for this action even though it will actively lead to Mary's death.

Some analysts bite the bullet and acknowledge that it is going to kill Mary to separate her from her sister, but claim that the alternative is needlessly tragic. It is a forced choice between one death and two. In such cases, it is better to save one life even if physicians must actively intervene in a way that will certainly lead to a patient's death. Consequentialists, including utilitarians, have relatively easy way of defending this action. The consequences will be worse, obviously worse they would claim, if both sisters die. Utilitarians, who focus on the consequences of actions, do not focus on the subtle difference between intended killings and unintended, but foreseen ones.

Some of the medical staff apparently believed that action that ended Mary's life would not only produce more good overall, but it would actually be better for Mary, given her bleak prognosis. These arguments amount to a defense of active, intentional killing (sometimes called "positive euthanasia") and would be accepted only by those favoring such decisions.

There were hints in some accounts of this case that perhaps the parents were defending on similar grounds their decision to refuse operation even though both children would die. It is more likely, however, that the parents were relying on the traditional Catholic distinction between active killing, which is unacceptable, and forgoing of life support, which can be justified when the burdens that result exceed the benefits. Parents who opposed active killing, but accepted the forgoing of disproportionally burdensome life support would have a basis for deciding to refuse surgical intervention as these parents did.

The most complex moral issue is whether Catholics and others who oppose directly intended active killings have a basis for accepting the proposed procedure as one in which the death of Mary is merely an indirect side effect of an effort to save Jodie's life. Thinking from the perspective of Jodie, the more healthy twin, her life literally requires that the "foreign" tissue be removed from her so that her body can function normally.

There are similar cases in which defenders of unintended, that is, indirect harmful effects have tolerated interventions that result in the death. The use of narcotic analgesia that has a side effect of respiratory depression and death may foreseeably lead to the death of the one taking the narcotic. If the benefit is seen as proportional to the harm, the death is morally acceptable. Even more closely analogous, those who oppose directly intended abortion have supported the removal of the uterus of a woman suffering from uterine cancer even though that woman happens to be pregnant at the time. Assuming that the fetus is not yet viable, the result is surely the death of the fetus, but, if that death is the side effect of a legitimate, medically appropriate procedure, then the death can be tolerated. Some have tried to argue that the death of Mary in our present case would be similar to the death of the innocent fetus—unintended though foreseen.[7] Others have rejected this indirect effect argument. Michel Therrien has argued that the surgery was a killing that was directly intended.[8] The claim is that, for a killing to be indirect there must be a "reasonable possibility" of saving Mary and an attempt to save her as well as Jodie must be made. Otherwise, Therrien claims, it is a fiction to say one did not directly kill Mary, but merely separated the blood supplies.

Whether one concludes that the killing of Mary was indirect, it seems clear that only by such a claim would Roman Catholic and other defenders of the indirect effect argument such as the twins' parents be satisfied that the killing was licit. They would not have the option of the more straightforward argument that it is a direct killing, but nevertheless acceptable as the lesser evil.

JUSTIFIABLE OMISSIONS: THE PROBLEM OF NUTRITION AND HYDRATION

The previous case suggested that for one reason or another many people believe that active killings are morally unacceptable, at least if they are directly intended. The distinction between active killing and omitting treatment (sometimes referred to as the commission–omission distinction or the active–passive distinction) has grown to great importance in the debate over the care of the terminally ill. That is why it has been so important to figure out whether withdrawing a treatment is more like withholding it or more like active killing. Even if some treatments may justifiably be omitted, clearly not all can. The next two cases raise the issue of what is necessary to justify omission of treatment. In particular, are there certain kinds of treatments that can be forgone even though others never can be or is the criterion for justifying an omission based on assessment of benefit and harms?

The problem arises because most of the early cases of decisions to forgo life support involved complex procedures or high-tech interventions. Karen Quinlan's case involved a ventilator. Others have involved refusal of a heart transplant (as in Case 6-2) or attempts at stem cell therapy as in Case 4-3. After it became well established that patients and their surrogates had the right to refuse complex medical procedures, the question began to be asked about simpler technologies and everyday, routine treatments such as antibiotics for infection, routine testing, and supplying nutrition and hydration by medical means.[9] People began asking whether some treatments were so common or routine that they must always be provided even in cases in which patients were refusing more exotic, burdensome treatments.

CASE 9-4

Claire Conroy: Are Medically Supplied Nutrition and Hydration Expendable?

In 1983, after many years of medical problems, Claire Conroy was eighty-four years old. She had long suffered from organic brain syndrome and had been legally incompetent since 1979. She was a resident at Parklane Nursing Home in Bloomfield, NJ. Her nephew, Thomas Whittemore, was her only living relative and her guardian. In July of 1982, her left foot was gangrenous and amputation was recommended. Mr. Whittemore refused consent for the amputation, claiming that Miss Conroy has always resisted medical involvement. It is testimony to the evolution of the right of patients and their surrogates to refuse medical treatment in the days since Karen Quinlan, that Mr. Whittemore's right to refuse on these grounds was not challenged legally even though the gangrene was a serious, possibly life-threatening condition.

While she was hospitalized in conjunction with the treatment of the gangrene, medical personnel noticed that Miss Conroy was not receiving adequate nourishment and placed a naso-gastric (NG) tube to provide better nutrition. By 1983, when the case became public, she was totally dependent on the tube for feeding.

Miss Conroy had many other medical problems. In addition to the severe organic brain syndrome, she had necrotic decubitus ulcers on her left foot, leg, and hip, a urinary tract infection, hypertension, arteriosclerotic heart disease, diabetes mellitus, and was unable to move except for minor movements of her head, neck, and arms. She did not speak. She laid in a fetal position, only sometimes followed people with her eyes, and her general physical appearance was very withered. She moaned when moved or touched. It was unclear whether she was capable of experiencing pain. She showed no signs of cognitive or volitional functioning.

Using reasoning similar to that in defending the refusal of the amputation, Mr. Whittemore now insisted that the NG tube be removed.

The doctors were reluctant to go along. They accepted the legitimacy of refusing ventilators or amputations, but considered provision of food and fluids as basic medical care, something they expected to provide to all patients who needed them.

COMMENTARY

Both secular and religious sources acknowledge that some treatments are so "extraordinary" that they are expendable.[10] We often think of high-technology treatments such as ventilators, dialysis machines, chemotherapy, or major surgical procedures as treatments that might be expendable because they are "extraordinary." But that seems to assume that a treatment is considered extraordinary because it is statistically unusual or technologically complex.

Those who traditionally used the term *extraordinary* did not really have in mind the unusualness or complexity of the treatment. After all, it does not make much sense to consider a treatment expendable simply because it is unusual or complex. Something may be very unusual but just right for a patient with an unusual condition. It may be high tech, but still very beneficial. The authorities that used to speak of extraordinary means of treatment now have tended to abandon that language because of this confusion. Instead they make clear that treatments are morally expendable or required based on consideration of the benefits and burdens.

If the benefits exceed the burdens, then the treatment is appropriate and should be provided; if they do not, then it makes no sense to require it. This notion of comparing the relative amount of benefits and burdens is now generally referred to as the *criterion of proportionality*.[11] If the burdens equal or exceed the benefits, then there is no moral necessity to provide the treatment. This is true for even simple treatments such as antibiotics, CPR, and routine nursing protocols such as those specifying when patients should be turned. The issue in the Conroy case is whether this benefits-burden approach (the criterion of proportionality) should be applied to medical means of supplying nutrition and hydration.

Many people now argue that even in the case of a feeding tube, such as that being used in Ms. Conroy's case, it is necessary to ask whether the treatment is serving any worthwhile purpose. Of course, almost all patients in a hospital get great benefit from receiving nutrition and hydration. If they cannot get adequate supply orally, then IVs and tube feedings are appropriate. In certain special cases, however, some people question the benefit of such treatments. This is particularly true in the case of permanently unconscious people. At least in such cases, one cannot appeal to the argument of the discomfort of being hungry or thirsty. Anyone who is unconscious cannot experience these. Even in the case of a conscious patient, it is conceivable that these treatments offer greater burden than benefit. This would especially be possible in the case of a patient who is inevitably dying if the patient suffered more when nutrition levels keep the patient more alert, increase respiratory secretions which make breathing more difficult and increase urine and stool output that can result in skin breakdown and discomfort. Increasingly, people are concluding that in such special cases, medically supplied nutrition and hydration are expendable because they do more harm than good.

Critics of this conclusion argue that supplying nutrition and hydration should not really be considered a "treatment." It is, they claim, simply basic care deserved by all human beings.[12] Others have argued that, even if medical means of supplying food and fluid do not provide medical benefit, they offer a symbol of our general commitment to the right of all human beings to receive basic nutrition and hydration.[13] In response, however, those who defend the use of the proportionality criterion in these cases claim it would be cruel to provide medically supplied nutrition and hydration that does not offer net benefit to the patient just because it is "basic" or because it symbolizes a commitment to the right of people to get fed. Thus, even those who are generally very wary of withholding life-prolonging treatment have recognized that there are special cases in which it may be withheld when it does not offer benefit.[14]

One remaining area of controversy is how these benefits and burdens are assessed. While some have traditionally believed that the benefits and the burdens can best be known by the physician, more recent commentaries have emphasized the subjective nature of these assessments. Hence, they have stressed that the physician has no special expertise in deciding whether an effect is a benefit and, if so, how beneficial it is. Likewise, the physician cannot have any special knowledge in deciding whether an effect is a harm, and, if so, how harmful it is.

The court in the case of Claire Conroy recognized three instances in which treatment (including medically supplied nutrition and hydration) can be omitted: (1) when it is clear that the particular patient would have refused the treatment, (2) when "there is some trustworthy evidence that the patient would have refused the treatment, and the decision-maker is satisfied that it is clear that the burdens of the patient's continued life with the treatment outweigh the benefits of that life," and (3) when "the net burdens of the patient's life with the treatment clearly and markedly outweigh the benefits that the patient derives from life so that the recurring, unavoidable, and severe pain of the patient's life with the treatment would render the life-sustaining treatment inhumane."[15] These are referred to as the subjective, limited objective, and pure objective standards, respectively.

These three criteria still leave us with some questions needing attention. The first criterion seems to pose few issues, but the second presents the problem of what should happen if there is some trustworthy evidence that the patient would have refused the treatment and it seems like the net burdens outweigh the benefits, but we cannot conclude that it is clear that the burdens outweigh the benefits. The second criterion seems to imply that a surrogate could not refuse the treatment even if there is some trustworthy basis for concluding the patient would have refused a treatment that seems to be harmful on balance as long as the judgment comparing burdens and benefits does not rise to the level of a clear difference. We are left with the question of why a surrogate should not have authority to refuse in such a case. Likewise, the third criterion raises the question of what a surrogate should do when the burdens seem clearly to outweigh the benefits, but the surrogate is unwilling to claim that the burden is so "markedly" greater that it is inhumane.

The need to determine which standard is appropriate for decisions about nutrition and hydration has arisen in the very famous case of Terri Schiavo.

CASE 9-5

Terri Schiavo: Choosing to Forgo Nutrition

Terri Schindler married Michael Schiavo on November 10, 1984.[16] They were apparently happy together living with her parents until February 25, 1990, when their lives changed dramatically. She suffered cardiac arrest resulting in massive brain damage before she was stabilized at the hospital. At the time a potassium imbalance was noted. Terri had a history of dieting and some suspected that her medical crisis was triggered by her eating behavior, but the actual cause was never determined. Although some later suggested abuse, no evidence related to abuse was ever uncovered.

In June of 1990 Michael was appointed as her legal guardian. He made efforts to find treatments that might restore normal brain function even taking Terri to California for experimental brain stimulator treatment and a thalamic stimulator implant. These efforts proved unsuccessful, and Terri was left severely compromised.

In 1992 Michael won a malpractice award resulting from claims related to inadequate treatment when she was first treated. A trust fund for Terri's care amounting to $750,000 and damages for Michael of $300,000 was established as a result. Perhaps related to disputes over the money and differences over Terri's treatment, Michael and his in-laws had a falling out.

By 1998 the tensions had crystallized focusing on whether it was appropriate to continue medically supplied nutrition and hydration for Terri. In May of that year, Michael petitioned the court to remove the feeding tube. Terri's parents opposed this action. This was only the first of many court reviews addressing the decision to forgo the feeding tube.

The court battles dealt with the question of whether Terri was in a persistent vegetative state (PVS) and therefore by this time presumably permanently unconscious and, if so, whether she would want the tube removed.

By the year 2000 the court had reviewed the findings of experts in neurology and had determined that Terri was indeed in PVS, thus agreeing with the majority of the experts. At this and other court reviews, two court-appointed temporary guardians also concurred with that finding. The court also concluded that Terri would want the feeding tube removed under these conditions.

During this time, Terri's parents, Bob and Mary Schindler disputed the find-ings both about Terri's wishes and about her mental state. They testified that she had not ever expressed wishes to forgo medically supplied nutrition, thus contradicting testimony of Michael, his brother, and his sister-in-law. They also insisted that she appeared to respond to them. Their views were supported by one physician who concurred in their judgment that she appeared aware of them at times. Nevertheless, after reviewing the evidence, the courts and the guardians all concluded she would not want the feeding tube under her present circumstances.

After many appeals in both state and federal courts and attempted interven-tions by the U.S. Congress and President George W. Bush, the original ruling autho-rizing the withholding of the feeding tube was sustained. It was removed for the final time on March 18, 2005. She died on March 31. The Schindlers continue to insist that she was not vegetative, had not expressed a desire to have the tube removed, and should not have had it removed.

COMMENTARY

It is not clear whether this case would have been as controversial if the treat-ment in question were a ventilator or some other complex piece of technol-ogy. It is also not clear what role the dispute over her mental status played. Perhaps the Schindlers would have insisted on maintaining life support no matter what the intervention and no matter if it were beyond dispute that she was permanently unconscious. The case at this point provides an opportunity to explore what difference these factors should make in decisions about forgoing life-supporting treatment.

Some states when first confronted with the question of forgoing nutri-tion and hydration made the assumption that these were somehow different from other, more complex interventions and that they should always be pro-vided even if other treatments had been refused by the patient while con-scious and competent. Only in the case of an explicit decision by the patient to refuse medically supplied nutrition and hydration would it be acceptable to omit them regardless of the agreement that a ventilator or dialysis machine was to be forgone. The courts did not dwell on the uniqueness of nutrition and hydration because they concluded that Terri's own wishes were known. Hence, the feeding tube could be withdrawn. In fact, it seems not to make any difference in those circumstances what the wishes of the next-of-kin or other relatives are.

What, however, if it had turned out that all could agree that the patient was not in PVS, but rather was in what is now sometimes called a minimally conscious state. In such a state, the patient might feel pain and otherwise be somewhat aware of the presence of family members. Many commentators seem to assume that if Terri had been found to be conscious, then the feeding tube should have been maintained. Others, however, find that survival for a long time in such a state might be worse than being unconscious. One could not express one's feelings, indicate perception of pain or other discomfort, or otherwise express oneself. What would be the appropriate decision, if it had been determined that Terri was minimally aware of those around her?

The other major issue in the case of Terri Schiavo is what role the husband and the parents should have played in the decision. That will be the main focus of the cases in Chapter 18, but some may wish to continue consideration now of that question. One issue that is unusual in the case of Terri Schiavo is the dispute between her husband and her parents over what she would have wanted. Some might argue that the benefit of the doubt should go to those who side on life, that is, the parents in this case. Others, however, empathize with the potential prolonged discomfort of being alive and uncommunicative for many years.

As a general rule, if the patient's wishes are known, the opinions of various family members are not critical, but, if they are not, the presumption of decision-making authority goes, as we shall see in Chapter 18, to the next-of-kin, that is, the husband in this case. The other family members, including the parents, would have the authority to challenge that decision, as Terri's parents did, but they are not the initial presumed surrogate. The fact that some eventually suspected the motivation of the husband raises an interesting problem. The presumed surrogate can be disqualified if he or she is found to have a conflict of interest, but we must also consider the possibility that, even if he did have a conflict of interest, he might be the most reliable source of information about her wishes. No doubt the court would have to take into account the potential influence of conflicts when deciding whether to rely on evidence the next-of-kin provides. The role of the various family members will be explored more thoroughly in Chapter 18.

VOLUNTARY AND INVOLUNTARY KILLING

In the previous cases we have seen that there is room for disagreement over whether some patients would be better off if they were dead. Those who focus exclusively on consequences would, logically, favor killing if they believed that the patient would be better off. However, those who accept that there is something inherently wrong with killing might continue to oppose active, direct killing even if they accepted the legitimacy of withholding or withdrawing treatment. There is one additional ethical principle that needs to be factored in. Especially if the decisions about what counts as a benefit or a harm are subjective, there may be good reasons to give moral weight to the autonomous choices of patients when it comes to deciding about whether to forgo life-sustaining treatment. In the following case, we shall explore the role of the autonomous choice of the patient in such decisions.

╔══════════════════ **CASE 9-6** ══════════════════╗

Assisted Suicide, Alzheimer's Disease, and Depression

Kathleen Rheel was a 56-year-old, married, former school teacher in the Oregon public schools who had retired from teaching five years previously because the daily grind had become too much for her. She had two years ago been diagnosed by Michael Carver, her internist, as showing the initial signs of Alzheimer's disease. She and her husband had never had children. She believed her friends had not realized her situation, but she had noticed an increasing inability to remember names, and her husband detected that she was forgetting birthdays and appointments. She feared her symptoms were getting worse. She and her husband had discussed a plan to hire a housekeeper anticipating the time when she would not be able to be left by herself. She had become increasingly distressed at these prospects. She wanted nothing to do with outside caregivers and did not want to be responsible for depleting the family's meager assets. She had always been a lover of knowledge. She read constantly, and she and her husband enjoyed attending adult education classes and local theatre. She hated the thought of a life without these basic pleasures. Her life was gradually becoming unbearable.

Ms. Rheel was horrified at the prospect of a gradual decline in her mental abilities and the economic impact on her husband if she would need care for a prolonged period. She explored the prognosis with Dr. Carver who indicated that he thought the disease was progressing, but that she would be quite capable of managing her own affairs and enjoying life for some years to come.

During one of her appointments with Dr. Carver, she asked about the terms of the Oregon law that permits physicians to assist in the suicide of terminally ill patients. Dr. Carver was reluctant to discuss it. He had originally been opposed to the law, believing that the physician's task is to promote health rather than cause the deaths of patients. Gradually, however, he had become convinced that some patients suffered terribly in spite of receiving the best medical care available. He believed in hospice care, but realized that some patients, such as Ms. Rheel, were not candidates. Her suffering was not physical. Even high-quality psychiatric and social work care were not going to address her increasing misery.

Dr. Carver knew that the Oregon assisted suicide law applied only to patients who were eighteen years of age, capable of making and communicating their own health care decisions, and had a terminal illness that would lead to death within six months. He explained that Ms. Rheel would not qualify since, although the Alzheimer's disease would likely eventually be related to her death, she did not have a terminal illness that would lead to death within six months.

Over the course of the next year, Ms. Rheel's condition worsened somewhat. Her depression became more pronounced although in Dr. Carver's opinion she was clearly still mentally competent. At an appointment with Dr. Carver, she pressed more aggressively. She informed him that she had decided that she did not want to live with her deteriorating condition. She and her husband had made all arrangements; her will had been reviewed, she had begun giving some of her possessions to friends and relatives, and she was now serious about discussing Dr. Carver's assistance. Dr. Carver strongly urged her to accept a referral to a psychiatrist, but she declined.

This continued for three additional appointments. It was clear to Dr. Carver that she was increasingly committed to ending her life. She had clearly thought through the decision carefully and would likely choose non-medical means if he did not cooperate. He was concerned that the Oregon law would not condone his prescribing of a lethal agent since his patient was not terminal according to the terms of the law. He reasoned, however, that, as she became increasingly suicidal without the hope of psychiatric care, she, in fact, would commit suicide within the next six months. He knew that the Oregon law left it up to the physician to determine whether the six-month criterion had been met. Fearing the bad consequences of her suicide using non-medical means, he seriously explored whether to write a prescription for barbiturates that would, with medical supervision, lead to her death. If he determined she met the terms of the law and remained mentally competent, he believed he could, with reluctance, write the prescription. Ms. Rheel died with her husband and Dr. Carver at her side. Her death was reported under the terms of the law.

COMMENTARY

There is increasing controversy over the role of the health professional in assisting a patient in bringing about his or her death. Physician killing on the persistent request of a competent patient is widely practiced in the Netherlands and is tolerated by the law.[17] Legislative and judicial efforts are underway in several states that would legalize physician efforts to end a dying patient's life actively and intentionally.[18] Until recently, Oregon was the one state that had explicitly legalized such assistance provided certain conditions are met.[19] One feature of these efforts, both in the Netherlands and in the United States, is that, if a physician is authorized to kill patients for a merciful motive or assist in a suicide, the plans carefully restrict such killing to patients who have made a voluntary request while they are mentally competent and, hence, able to make substantially autonomous choices.

The issue here is whether Ms. Rheel's request is voluntary, and, if so, whether that is a sufficient reason for Dr. Carver to cooperate. First, is Ms. Rheel capable of making a voluntary choice? If so, she would have to have the mental capacity to understand the nature of her choice and be substantially free from internal and external forces that would make her choice involuntary. Is she a substantially autonomous agent? What do you make of the fact that Dr. Carver has suggested that she seek consultation with a psychiatrist? Is that enough to make her incompetent to make a voluntary choice?

Assuming that she is substantially autonomous in her choice, does the principle of respect for autonomy provide a moral basis for overcoming our general reluctance to cooperate in active killing of another human being or does the moral prohibition on killing, insofar as there is one, carry over to cases in which the patient has made a conscious, voluntary choice to end her life? There are two separate issues here: whether autonomy provides a defense of suicide by autonomous persons and whether it provides a defense of the involvement of health professionals such as Dr. Carver. The principle of respect for autonomy holds that it is wrong to interfere with the actions of others who have made substantially autonomous choices based on their own life plans. Some would argue that this principle supports the choice of suicide by substantially autonomous people. Thus, those who hold this view would accept the right of Ms. Rheel to commit suicide. Even that conclusion is controversial. Some people have made commitments to others (such as their children) that they would be breaking if they ended their lives. The fact that Ms. Rheel has no children minimizes that concern here, although she might bear some responsibility to her husband to avoid ending her life in a way that would cause him a burden. In addition, if there is something inherently wrong with killing of humans, even self-killing might be seen as violating that notion. Religious people believe that their own lives are really not theirs to dispose of and that we are merely stewards of our lives. Secular people also sometimes believe self-killing is wrong.

Regardless, the principle of respect for autonomy cannot settle the question of whether someone else should cooperate in the killing. Ms. Rheel would be able to kill herself by taking prescribed medications, but, even in a state such as Oregon where assisted suicide might be legal, she would need a physician's assistance in providing information and writing a prescription. She would also need to have others involved, for example, a pharmacist who would fill the prescription.

Even if we conclude that Ms. Rheel has the right to kill herself, it does not necessarily follow that the physician has the moral right or duty to cooperate. Some would argue that even if, in theory, active mercy killing and suicide are legitimate, still health professionals ought not to be involved. They maintain that there is something about the role of being a health professional that is incompatible with killing even at the request of the patient and even if the killing is done for mercy. All parties recognize that Ms. Rheel, assuming she is competent, would have the right to insist that life-supporting interventions such as a ventilator be withdrawn. Ms. Rheel, however, has a condition from which a ventilator or other life-supporting equipment is unlikely to be needed and therefore cannot be refused. Most people also seem to agree that it is acceptable to give medication to make patients comfortable while they die, even if the medication hastens the death as a side effect. Ms. Rheel, however, is not likely to need any such medications. Is there any reason why, assuming she has voluntarily chosen the course, the prescription should not be written to end her life more directly?

The principles of avoidance of killing and respect for autonomy seem to pull us in different directions in this case. In order to resolve the matter we may have to appeal to our general theory of how to resolve conflict among principles. Does one of the two deserve priority such that it is ranked above the other permitting a ready formula for resolving the conflict? Or do both deserve consideration so that they are "balanced against each other" or in some other way combined to reach a final answer to the question of what Dr. Carver's duty is?

This problem of conflict among the major principles of bioethics arises in many areas of health care ethics. In Part 3 of this volume we will look at some of those areas to see how the principles can be integrated to resolve potential conflicts.

KILLING AS PUNISHMENT

Standard discussions of the ethics of killing usually include consideration of certain killing that is not done for merciful motive. They take up killing in war and police activity. They also include capital punishment. While most of these discussions are outside the realm of health professional ethics, capital punishment has emerged as a problem that health professionals must face. In the past decade many states have become troubled by the inhumaneness of traditional execution of criminals by electrocution, hanging, and other techniques increasingly seen as barbaric. They have moved to what they call *medical execution*, the use of lethal injection of barbiturates or other chemical agents intended to kill quickly and painlessly. Physicians, pharmacists, and other health professionals potentially can play a key role in the preparation of these agents and in determining the most effective dose regimens. Physicians are also called upon to pronounce death. Deciding whether ethically one can participate will be an issue facing every health professional, either as a direct participant or as a citizen debating state policy.

CASE 9-7

Physician Participation in Capital Punishment

Michael Angelo Morales was convicted by the California courts for the 1981 rape and murder of 17-year-old Terri Winchell and was sentenced to death. He had beaten her over the head with a hammer and stabbed her in the chest with a knife. He conspired in the murder with his cousin, Rick Ortega, who had been in a homosexual relation with another man who was concurrently dating Winchell. Ortega's jealousy was purportedly the motive for the attack on Winchell.

    For twenty-five years the conviction proceeded through the California courts until the much-postponed execution day of February 21, 2006 arrived. Mr. Morales was scheduled to be executed at 12:01 a.m. at San Quentin. U.S. District Judge Jeremy Fogel had ordered that, in order to avoid cruelty if the drugs to be used in the execution did not do their job properly, the prison had to have a medical professional present in the death chamber. Two anesthesiologists, whose identity has never been made public, were engaged for this purpose, but, under pressure from medical professional organizations, they withdrew two hours before the scheduled execution. The execution was indefinitely postponed. Morales expressed relief. Terri Winchell's mother described the news as "a blow in the stomach."

Those critical of the participation of the physicians in the execution cite the AMA's *Code of Medical Ethics,* which states, "A physician, as a member of a profession dedicated to preserving life when there is hope of doing so, should not be a participant in a legally authorized execution."[20] According to the AMA, this precludes selecting injection sites, starting IV lines, prescribing, preparing, administering, or supervising injection of lethal drugs. For the AMA, this does not extend to testifying about medical history, diagnosis, or mental state; certifying death; witnessing an execution in a totally non-medical capacity; or relieving the acute suffering of a condemned prisoner awaiting execution.

Defenders of physician participation claim that physicians, as licensed medical professionals, should be involved in order to assure that the state's commitment to avoiding unnecessarily cruel punishment is assured.

In California, following the postponement of the execution, competing bills were introduced into the legislature by physicians who were members of the California legislature. Sen. Sam Aenestad, a general anesthesiologist, introduced legislation to protect physicians who participate in executions from punishment or professional discipline. Meanwhile, Assemblymen Alan Nakanishi, an eye surgeon, and a colleague introduced a bill sponsored by the California Medical Association prohibiting physician participation. At issue is not only the general ethics of capital punishment but also the question of whether participation of physicians is compatible with their role as healers.§

COMMENTARY

The first issue raised by this case is whether capital punishment itself is ever morally justified. Many are increasingly critical, raising issues of whether it is too cruel and inhumane, even if done using a physically painless and certain medical method. Others argue that there seems to be something incongruous if a society punishes terrible crimes such as murder by committing another homicide. They are concerned that institutionalizing such a practice will corrupt the society, making it the kind of community that is not as noble as it could be. Still others point to the irreversibility of capital punishment and express fear

§ Based on the California state summary of the case available at http://caag.state.ca.us/victimservices/pdf/aamorales_presspack.pdf (accessed January 22, 2007); Finz, Stacy, Bob Egelko, Kevin Faga. "State Postpones Morales Execution Judge's New Order: Officials Refuse to Revise Method of Lethal Injection." *San Francisco Chronicle*, February 22, 2006. p. A-1; and .Lin, Judith. "Death Penalty Dilemma: For Some Legislators, Medicine and Politics Create a Quandary." *Sacramento Bee*, May 15, 2006, available at http://www.redorbit.com/news/health/504195/death_penalty_dilemma_for_some_legislators_medicine_and_politics_create/index.html (accessed January 22, 2007) that the inevitable erroneous convictions will eventually leave some innocent person dead. They point out that juries and courts cannot be infallible and that we can never be completely certain that those executed were really mentally capable of being responsible for their actions. They believe that the necessary doubt about the certainty of the criminal's responsibility should leave society with a way of reversing its judgment.

However, those defending capital punishment can point to the terrible crimes that have been committed. They argue either in terms of the general or specific deterrence of capital punishment or appeal to notions of retribution, claiming that the most vicious criminals, such as those who have taken innocent life should pay with their own lives.[21]

The position one takes on capital punishment will depend in part on one's interpretation of the principle of avoiding killing. If it is understood to mean that it is morally wrong to kill in all circumstances, that life is sacred to use the more religious language, then, capital punishment will be unacceptable. The most radical interpretation views killing even of those who have committed serious offense in war or civil life as unacceptable. If holders of such views are consistent, they are pacifists. Others interpret the principle of avoidance of killing to be only a *prima facie* duty, which can be offset by other principles. Certain interpretations of the principle of justice provide a basis for killing as retribution for the most serious wrongs. Some interpretations of beneficence might provide a basis for killing as a general or specific deterrence.

Even those who have moral objections to capital punishment may see the reason to make sure it is done humanely if it is to be done at all. It is conceivable one might claim that, even though capital punishment is unacceptable, society owes it to the criminal to see that the inevitable is done humanely and competently. This could lead to reluctant endorsement of the participation of health professionals. Of course, if one ends up concluding that, on balance, the deterrent or retributivist arguments in favor of the practice win out, then the issue of participation of physicians or other health professionals becomes an issue.

It is possible that one could conclude that a society has a right to execute its most evil criminals but that members of the healing professions cannot participate.[22] That could lead to the conclusion that, although capital punishment is acceptable, someone else will have to be the source of the knowledge needed to carry it out.

Some physicians have argued that their profession must separate itself from capital punishment because the practice is incompatible with the role of the healer.[23] However, if execution is to be accepted as appropriate public policy, someone will be needed who has the appropriate clinical and pharmacological skills.

The vigorous opposition by state and national medical associations raises a question at a deeper level: is it the role of the professional organization or of the society to decide whether physician participation is unethical? The courts in the Morales case seem to have concluded that the constitutional rights of the condemned prisoner require the involvement of health professionals skilled in the pharmacological and clinical questions raised. If the society acting through its government is the proper agent for deciding what constitutes proper moral conduct of physicians and other licensed health professionals, then it is within its rights to insist that a physician be present at the execution. To be consistent it would have to condone such participation and, following Senator Aenestad's view, avoid disciplinary actions against physicians who participate. On the other hand, if the medical professional organization retains authority to determine the moral conduct of its members, then it could pronounce such participation unethical and discipline members who are involved. This was the issue in Case 3-1 of Chapter 3. There is something inconsistent with a society that assumes the right to license health professionals and believes that physician participation in executions is needed, yet yields to the private professional organizations the authority to establish moral standards in this area.

These are very practical questions that will require considerations not only of the principle of avoidance of killing but also all the other principles discussed in this part of the book. Many other practices in which pharmacists may be asked to participate also raise questions that involve the careful balancing of two or more principles. Some of these areas are addressed in the chapters in Part 3.

NOTES

1 Rawls, John. "Two Concepts of Rules." *The Philosophical Review* 44 (1955):3–32; Lyons, David. *Forms and Limits of Utilitarianism.* Oxford: Oxford University Press, 1965; Ramsey, Paul. *Deeds and Rules in Christian Ethics.* New York: Charles Scribner's Sons, 1967; Brandt, Richard B. "Toward a Credible Form of Utilitarianism." In *Contemporary Utilitarianism.* Michael D. Bayles, editor. Garden City, NY: Doubleday & Company, 1968, pp. 143–186.

2 Ramsey. *Deeds and Rules in Christian Ethics.*

3 For example, see Kant, Immanuel. *Groundwork of the Metaphysic of Morals.* Trans. by H. J. Paton. New York: Harper and Row, 1964.

4 For a development of this view see Veatch, Robert M. *A Theory of Medical Ethics.* New York: Basic Books, 1981, pp. 227ff.

5 American Medical Association, Council on Ethical and Judicial Affairs. *Code of Medical Ethics: Current Opinions with Annotations*, Chicago, IL: American Medical Association, 1994, p. 70.

6 McCormick, Richard A. and Paul Ramsey, Editors. *Doing Evil to Achieve Good: Moral Choice in Conflict Situations.* Chicago, IL: Loyola University Press, 1978; Curran, Charles E. "Roman Catholicism." *Encyclopedia of Bioethics*, 2nd ed. Warren T. Reich, editor. New York: The Free Press, Vol. 4, 1995, pp. 2321–2330; for secular treatments of the indirect or double effect doctrine see Foot, Philippa. "The Problem of Abortion and the Doctrine of the Double Effect." *Oxford Review* 5 (1967):5–15; Graber, Glenn C. "Some Questions about Double Effect." *Ethics in Science and Medicine* 6 (No. 1, 1979):65–84.

[7] This argument was presented by Catherine Dominic, "Separating the Twins Jodie and Mary." *Ethics & Medicine* 26 (June 2001):3–4.

[8] Therrien, Michael. "Did the Principle of Double Effect Justify the Separation?" *National Catholic Bioethics Quarterly* 3 (Autumn 2001):417–427.

[9] Craig, Gillian. "Is Sedation Without Hydration or Nourishment in Terminal Care Lawful?" *Medico-Legal Journal* 62 (Part 4, 1994):198–201; Kenny, Nuala P. and Gerri, Frager. "Refractory Symptoms and Terminal Sedation of Children: Ethical Issues and Practical Management." *Journal of Palliative Care* 12 (3, 1996):40–45; Mount, Balfour. "Morphine Drips, Terminal Sedation, and Slow Euthanasia: Definitions and Facts, Not Anecdotes." *Journal of Palliative Care* 12 (4, 1996):31–37; Wilson, William C., Nicholas G. Smedira, Carol Fink, James A. McDowell, and John M. Luce. "Ordering and Administration of Sedatives and Analgesics During the Withholding and Withdrawal of life support from Critically Ill Patients." *Journal of the American Medical Association* 267 (7, 1992):949–953; Truog, Robert D., John H. Arnold, and Mark A. Rockoff. "Sedation before Ventilator Withdrawal: Medical and Ethical Considerations." *Journal of Clinical Ethics* 2 (2, 1991):127–129; Rietjens, J. A., J. J. van Delden, A. van der Heide, A. M. Vrakking, B. D. Onwuteake-Phillipsen, P. J. van der Maas, and G. van der Wal.. "Terminal Sedation and Euthanasia: A Comparison of Clinical Practices." *Archives of Internal Medicine* 166 (7, 2006):749–753.

[10] Pope Pius XII. "The Prolongation of Life: An Address of Pope Pius XII to an International Congress of Anesthesiologists." *The Pope Speaks* 4 (Spring 1958):393–398; President's Commission for the Study of Ethical Problems in Medicine and Biomedical and Behavioral Research. *Deciding to Forego Life-Sustaining Treatment: Ethical, Medical, and Legal Issues in Treatment Decisions.* Washington, DC: U.S. Government Printing Office, 1983.

[11] Congregation for the Doctrine of the Faith. *Declaration on Euthanasia.* Rome: The Sacred Congregation for the Doctrine of the Faith, May 5, 1980; Cf. President's Commission for the Study of Ethical Problems in Medicine and Biomedical and Behavioral Research. *Deciding to Forego Life-Sustaining Treatment,* p. 88.

[12] Meilaender, Gilbert. "On Removing Food and Water: Against the Stream." *The Hastings Center Report* 14 (No. 6, 1984):11–13.

[13] Callahan, Daniel. "On Feeding the Dying." *The Hastings Center Report* 13 (No. 5, 1983):22.

[14] May, William E., Robert Barry, Orville Griese, et al. "Feeding and Hydrating the Permanently Unconscious and Other Vulnerable Persons." *Issues in Law and Medicine* 3 (No. 3, 1987):203–217.

[15] In *re Conroy*, 98 N.J. 321, 486 A.2d 1209 (1985).

[16] This case is based on *re* "The Guardianship of Theresa Marie Schiavo, Incapacitated," File No. 90-2908GD-003, *Fla. 6th Judicial Circuit*, February 11, 2000; Report of Guardian Ad Litem, in *re* The Guardianship of Theresa Marie Schiavo, An Incapacitated Person, Case No. 90-2908GD-003; Cerminera, Kathy and Kenneth Goodman. "Schiavo Case Resources: Key Events in the Case of Theresa Marie Schiavo." University of Miami Ethics Programs. Available on the Internet at http://www6.miami.edu/ethics/schiavo/terri_schiavo_timeline.htm, accessed April 28, 2008.

[17] Van der Mass, Paul J., Johannes J. M. Van Delden, Loes Pijnenborg, and Casper W. N. Looman. "Euthanasia and Other Medical Decisions Concerning the End of Life." *The Lancet* 338 (September 14, 1991):669–674.

[18] Jonsen, Albert R. "Initiative 119: What Is at Stake?" *Commonweal* 118 (14, Supp, August 9, 1991):466–469; *Compassion in Dying v. Washington* No. 94-35534 D.C. No. CV-94–119-BJR, United States Court of Appeals for the Ninth Circuit; *Quill et al. v. Vacco et al.* Docket No. 95-7028, United States Court of Appeals for the Second Circuit.

[19] For information on the Oregon law see http://www.oregon.gov/DHS/ph/pas/faqs.shtml#whatis, accessed January 19, 2007.

[20] American Medical Association. *Code of Medical Ethics*, p. 18.

[21] For more thorough discussion of the ethics of capital punishment general analyses can be found in Grupp, Stanley E., ed. *Theories of Punishment*. Bloomington, IN: Indiana University, 1971; Berns, Walter. *For Capital Punishment: Crime and the Morality of the Death Penalty*. New York: Basic Books, 1979; Bedau, Hugo Adam. *Death Is Different*. Boston, MA: Northeastern University Press, 1987.

[22] For a discussion of the pharmacist's role see Brushwood, David B. "The Pharmacist and Execution by Lethal Injection." *U.S. Pharmacist*, September 1984, pp. 25–26, 28.

[23] American Medical Association, Council on Ethical and Judicial Affairs. *Code of Medical Ethics: Current Opinions with Annotations, 2004–2005 Edition*. Chicago, IL: American Medical Association, 2004, pp. 18–19.

PART 3

Special Problem Areas

CHAPTER 10

❧

Abortion, Sterilization, and Contraception

Other Cases Involving Abortion, Sterilization, or Contraception

One of the areas that has traditionally generated controversy in health care ethics is the set of problems surrounding obstetrics: abortion, sterilization, and contraception. All of the general moral themes represented by the principles discussed in Part 2 arise, but they do so in a dramatic and often emotionally charged setting. Moreover, these issues of obstetrical ethics pose a different kind of question: to whom do the basic principles of biomedical ethics apply? We need to determine, for example, whether a principle such as avoiding killing applies to fetuses or only humans after they are born. If it applies to fetuses, then we need to determine whether it applies to all fetuses or only those with certain properties such as those with consciousness, the ability to move in a way perceived by the pregnant woman (quickening), or the ability to survive independently outside the womb (viability). These issues also present a complex overlay of religious and philosophical notions about the duties and expectations of marriage, the role of natural law (a theory that grounds moral obligation in the ends for which beings were created), and the role of the state in controlling intimate, personal choices. The first group of cases examines the ethics of abortion and the role of health professionals in abortions.

ABORTION

Perhaps the most controversial and intractable issue in health care ethics is abortion.[1] The underlying issue is what moral status and moral claims should be attributed to embryos and fetuses after conception has taken place and prior to birth. Do the normal moral principles such as beneficence and avoiding killing apply and, if not, why not?

At least a major part of what is at stake is the moral standing of the early embryo and the fetus that it becomes. If the embryo or fetus is considered nothing more than a part of the pregnant woman's body, then there is little reason to doubt that she can do whatever she pleases with it including removing it. However, if it is considered to have the moral status of an independent human being with full moral standing, then the full range of principles we have been examining in this volume would apply to actions taken toward it. Not only would there be a *prima facie* duty to benefit and avoid harm but there would also be a duty to keep promises made, to provide a just share of resources, and to avoid killing.

It is true that some who are more liberal on abortion still grant the full standing of the fetus. They might argue that the pregnant woman's moral claims are enough to override the fetus's claim. Some argue that one can recognize the full moral standing of the embryo as early as implantation and still recognize that the moral standing of the pregnant woman could force an awful choice between the two in some circumstances. This is particularly true in cases such as rape in which the woman has in no way consented to taking the risk to become pregnant.

Holders of the most conservative position believe the embryo as well as the fetus has the full standing of other human beings from the moment of conception. The embryo already has whatever is necessary to give it such standing. That might be the unique genetic composition or the genetic potential to develop certain features thought necessary to be treated as having this full standing. These features might be certain capacities for brain function or circulation and respiration.

Increasingly, controversy is emerging over exactly what gives this standing. For example, some have suggested that the genetic code may not actually be fixed exactly at the moment of conception but may be capable of variation for some days thereafter. One Catholic bioethicist has suggested that the development of the so-called primitive streak signals the point at which a unique individual is established.[2] Others who are traditionally conservative have identified the latest point at which twinning can take place.[3] Still others may emphasize the development of more complex brain functions but hold that what is critical is the potential for these functions as signaled by the presence of the genetic information that will be necessary for their expression.

Others, more liberal on the ethics of abortion, believe that some other functions such as neurological integration, quickening, or the development of capacity for consciousness, must actually have appeared before the fetus has full moral standing. Of course, no one denies that from the moment of conception the embryo is made up of human cells. In that sense the tissues are "human." What is at stake is whether those tissues have moral claims against the rest of the human community. Some who hold these more liberal views would readily acknowledge that prior to the appearance of the feature they consider critical for full standing, there is some intermediate or lesser claim. Just as one might have an ethical duty to show respect for a human corpse after the death of an individual, so there might be a similar obligation to treat early embryos and fetuses with a certain degree of respect.

The matter of real controversy is whether full equality of moral claims comes from the moment of conception or at some later time. In theory one might identify that moment even after birth. Some extreme commentators hold, for example, that a newborn infant still lacks the key feature (such as the ability to reason or use language) that would give it a full claim against the human community. Most, however, recognize that at least by birth this full moral standing is present. The real controversy is whether it arises at conception or some later time and precisely what it is that is responsible for this standing.

Different reasons given for abortion raise these issues in different ways. For example, if someone proposed to abort a fetus because of a genetic abnormality, what would be at stake would be whether the key genetic characteristics are nevertheless present. Abortions proposed for other reasons, such as the health of the pregnant woman, rape, or socioeconomic reasons, would require some argument supporting the abortion even though the fetus presumably is genetically intact. The following cases all look at abortions for commonly proposed reasons.

Abortion for Medical Problems of the Fetus

One of the most commonly offered reasons for abortion is that the fetus has some genetic or other medical abnormality that justifies the abortion. This can happen on two different grounds. First, in some extreme cases the fetus might not be medically capable of surviving. A fetus prenatally diagnosed with anencephaly is one example. More often, the fetus unarguably has the capacity to survive, at least for some time, but still has enough of a medical problem that some might consider abortion justifiable. What is striking here is that the parents may, in general, be eager for a child. If they abort they will be deciding that this child is so compromised that the medical problem warrants the abortion. Health professionals working in facilities that do abortions face the question of whether they will cooperate in such abortions. The following case illustrates the problem.

=== CASE 10-1 ===

Abortion for Teratogenic Indications

After Sally Baltimore had her third child at age thirty-two, she and her husband Mort thought that they had completed their family. The Baltimores certainly did not live hand-to-mouth. They managed fairly well on Mort's construction worker's salary and what Sally could make as a substitute teacher. They were shocked when at forty-one Sally learned she was pregnant again. Sally was further shocked when she learned from her obstetrician, Sandra Benton, after a routine amniocentesis that the fetus had Down syndrome.

This was particularly distressing to Sally because her stepsister Judy had Down syndrome too. Sally had first-hand knowledge of what it meant to live in a family who had someone with this diagnosis. She knew that there would probably be multiple operations, hospital stays, and medications since the fetus showed signs of significant cardiac problems as well. She had watched Judy suffer after each admission to the hospital. What made it worse, is that Judy could not make any sense out of all of the trauma even as she reached an age when a "normal" person would have appreciated why the treatment and surgery was necessary. She also knew about the sacrifices that the whole family would have to make for many years to come to accommodate the needs of this child. She watched her stepmother and father struggle with Judy's care even though she was now in her late thirties. Judy would always need care. Given all of this, Sally and Mort thought they just could not put this child or their family through it. Terminating the pregnancy seemed like the best course of action.

COMMENTARY

There are at least two questions raised by this case. The first is substantive: is it legitimate to abort a fetus because it has Down syndrome and a related cardiac problem? The second is more procedural: What role should Dr. Benton play in providing information for the Baltimores? Clearly, the two are linked, but separate issues.

Serious genetic disorder is one of the reasons for abortion that has been found plausible even among those who object to abortion for more vague social and psychological reasons. The other "hard case" reasons include rape, which will be discussed in Case 10-2 and incest, as well as the life of the pregnant woman, which will be the subject of Case 10-3.

Terminating a pregnancy because of a genetic abnormality in the fetus is a controversial and complicated decision. Some prenatal genetic diagnoses show extremely serious problems with the fetus. For instance a diagnosis of Monosomy-18, the occurrence of only a single chromosome at the eighteenth position rather than the usual two chromosomes, forecasts a very bleak future for the fetus. Many are stillborn, and those born alive will be hospitalized, bedridden, and severely impaired before facing death usually after weeks or months. Many couples will choose to terminate pregnancies with this diagnosis. A diagnosis of Down syndrome is quite different. It is caused by having three chromosomes in the twenty-first position. Hence, it is sometimes called Trisomy-21. Children with this diagnosis have varying degrees of mental impairment, some severe and some mild. The extent of the impairment cannot be known during the fetal period.

Down syndrome (without considering the related cardiac anomaly) is not painful. Persons with Down syndrome can be quite happy unless caregivers make it unpleasant for them. Hence, it is now considered wrong to assume life with Down syndrome will be depressing, boring, or filled with suffering. The Baltimores should not assume that they should terminate the pregnancy to spare their child inevitable difficulties in life. If they decide to abort solely on the basis of a diagnosis of Down syndrome, they would almost have to be doing so on the basis of their interests rather than the interests of the fetus. While they are not financially in critical position, they had decided to complete their family several years earlier. No doubt having a child with Down syndrome would add complexity to their lives. Since some couples choose to terminate pregnancies with no known complications, some would feel justified in making such a decision in this case. Aborting for socioeconomic reasons and family convenience is the subject of Case 10-5. This case, if it did not involve an additional cardiac problem, would be a similar example of deciding about abortion based on family interests.

The diagnosis of a congenital cardiac anomaly complicates the analysis. There is a known association between Down syndrome and cardiac defects, such as openings in the septum separating the heart chambers. These will require surgical correction, perhaps many operations, and sometimes can have fatal outcomes. It is unlikely that the Baltimores or their medical consultants will know the extent of the operations that will be required at the time they need to decide about whether to end the pregnancy.

Many people believe that serious burdens to patients justify decisions not to treat. Even those who oppose abortion may accept such decisions. Others would consider the pain and suffering of the future medical procedures a justification for abortion as well, even if they would reject abortion for fetuses with Down syndrome but without the accompanying cardiac problems. Hence, the Baltimores face a decision that will incorporate fetus-based reasons as well as family-based ones.

Terminating the pregnancy would involve active and direct killing, something those who oppose abortion would find unacceptable. Even if they accept the moral legitimacy of forgoing life support (as discussed in the cases in Chapter 9), they would not agree to active, direct killing even if it would spare the child certain suffering before it died. Only if ending this pregnancy were somehow morally different from killing a postnatal human, would those who object to mercy killing agree to abortion.

Dr. Benton also faces difficult issues. She will have to provide information and counsel to the Baltimores. The Baltimores are in a position in which they may base their decision on their knowledge of one particular patient, Sally's stepsister. While that gives her direct, intense knowledge of one person with Down syndrome and a related cardiac problem, the Baltimores run the risk of generalizing from this one limited experience. Dr. Benton may be the one best positioned to help the Baltimores know the extensive variety of outcomes for persons with Down syndrome as well as those with cardiac anomalies.

In addition to providing factual information about Down syndrome and cardiac problems, Dr. Benton will have to face the question of whether she should counsel the Baltimores about the moral aspects of the abortion decision. Dr. Benton must first decide whether she considers the abortion plausible in this circumstance. Here her decision is similar to the Baltimores except she is deciding not to undergo the actual abortion, but rather to determine her role in providing information to her patient. Then she has to address the difficult question of determining the extent of her cooperation in a project that may be unacceptable to her. These include questions that Dr. Benton should have faced when choosing to become an obstetrician. If she categorically opposes abortion, she should make that fact known to patients who enter her practice. She may, however, accept some abortions, but not others. She may, for example, oppose abortions of fetuses whose only problem is a genetic predisposition to mental impairments that do not cause burdens to the individual. These issues should be faced in advance as much as possible, but she may not be able to anticipate all dimensions of the pregnancies of future patients. She may simply have to explain her moral reservations to the Baltimores if she has them. In that case, she may have to refer her patient to a competent colleague willing to cooperate with the Baltimores' decision.

The case becomes more complicated if Dr. Benton were to find it immoral to refer her patients for abortions that she, herself, opposes. Conscientious objection by a health professional raises unique problems beyond those that face all actions of conscience. Professional roles are publicly sanctioned roles that create fiduciary obligations to patients. Patients cannot be expected to know when a health professional is withholding information unless, at minimum, the professional informs them. In some cases, a professional may even be obliged to provide services that are a normal part of the role even when they violate conscience. For example, the courts have repeatedly ordered physicians to provide life-prolonging treatments to patients who want them even if the physician insists that it violates his or her conscience to do so.[4] There is considerable controversy over whether health professionals can legally refuse to provide information that could likely lead to abortion.[5]

Abortion Following Sexual Assault

Another major reason offered for abortion is that the pregnant woman was raped and, therefore, did not consent to the risk of getting pregnant. In such a case, however, as contrasted to the previous one, the fetus presumably is perfectly normal or at least not at significant medical risk. If the fetus is aborted, it is in order to serve the psychological well-being of the pregnant woman. Does the fact that the woman was exposed to pregnancy against her will justify aborting a presumably healthy fetus?

CASE 10-2

Postcoital Contraception or Abortion: Moral Choices Following a Rape

Twenty-seven-year-old Daniela Sackler and her husband of four years were attempting to conceive their second child. Both were graduate students doing research on doctoral dissertations. They had even arranged their schedules so that they both could share in the child care and household responsibilities while they both went to school. Daniela was studying sociology and conducting interview research that required one-on-one two-hour interviews of young adults. She usually offered to conduct the interviews in the homes of her research subjects. She had an interview schedule that had been approved by her university's institutional review board.

On a Tuesday evening she called on one of her subjects and initiated the interview. After about an hour, the subject, who indicated his wife was away for the evening, offered her coffee, which she gratefully accepted. Ms. Sackler noticed the subject became increasingly friendly. By the end of the interview, the subject turned on a CD and asked her to dance, an invitation she quickly refused indicating she had to leave. At that point he blocked her exit and raped her.

Upon returning home, she told her husband what had happened and called the police. She was taken to the hospital emergency room (ER). She told the ER staff that she and her husband were trying to conceive a child so she was not taking her birth control pills. She was almost exactly at the time of month at which conception would occur. In fact, if she had become pregnant this month, she would have no way of knowing whether her husband or the research subject turned rapist was the father of the child. After examination by the ER personnel, she was offered a "morning after" pill in case a conception had occurred.

COMMENTARY

In contrast to the previous case, the medical status of the fetus does not provide any moral basis for aborting this potential pregnancy. Two reasons might be given. First, while Ms. Sackler has no explicit physical health problems that lead her directly to seek to terminate any possible pregnancy, she might have mental-health concerns. Surely, the trauma of the rape can be psychologically agonizing. Having the reminder of that horrid event during the rest of Ms. Sackler's life could add to that trauma.

But if the woman's mental health is the basis for the abortion, Ms. Sackler and her husband would need more information before reaching a decision about how to respond. They would have to have some understanding about just how much mental trauma would be necessary to justify an abortion. Presumably any unwanted pregnancy is traumatic. If just any mental disturbance justified the abortion, then any woman who was upset with a pregnancy would be justified on these grounds. Case 10-5 in this chapter looks at abortion for social and economic reasons. Is there a significant difference between abortion for the mental stress of a pregnancy following rape, on the one hand, and abortion for the stress caused by social and economic reasons or for a woman who simply does not want to be pregnant, on the other? If the reasoning is based on mental health, is there some minimal level of psychological trauma that is necessary to make the abortion morally justified? For example, would a real risk of suicide be necessary as some conservatives on abortion would claim and, if so, what level of risk would be necessary? Or would any mental-health risk be sufficient as more liberally inclined commentators would suggest? Is there some level of mental suffering that would convince Ms. Sackler that her use of the medication would be tolerable? Would adoption help abate some of this trauma, making the abortion less defensible?

Abortion following rape seems to command more sympathy than other cases involving similar levels of mental trauma. Could it be that there is some other reason beyond the psychological stress standing behind such intuitions? Some have argued that the morally special feature of rape is that in no conceivable way was the woman agreeing to take the risk of getting pregnant by the rapist. Some philosophers have suggested that even if the fetus has the right to life in some strong sense, still a woman cannot be made to carry a pregnancy to term if she did not consent to the behavior that led to the pregnancy.[6] If it were technically possible, this could lead to the position that the fetus should be removed from the woman and incubated independently. Until such a procedure is technically possible, defenders of abortion following rape say that the woman has a right to remove the "intruding" fetus even if that results in the death of the fetus.

More conservative critics of abortion reject this reasoning pointing out that the end result is what, to them, is the evil of the death of the fetus. In the previous chapter, we discussed the Catholic doctrine of indirect or double-effect killing. This doctrine tolerates an evil if that evil is not intended even if the evil is foreseen. They consider that this could justify removing a cancerous uterus even if the woman with the cancer happens to be pregnant as long as the death of the fetus is not the purpose of the removal of the uterus and the abortion is not a means to the desired end (which it would not be).

By contrast, if the woman claimed that she simply desired to be able to lead her life nonpregnant as she was prior to the rape, the abortion would be the means to her desired end and, according to those who rely on the doctrine of indirect or double effect, the abortion would not be justified.

There is another issue in this case. Regardless of whether Ms. Sackler decides the abortion is justified, others also face important moral choices. Her husband will be impacted by the decision. She might involve him in the decision whether to take the morning after pill. If she has a child that is genetically the rapist's, her husband would potentially have the responsibility for that child. On the other hand, if the morning after pill is taken and it interrupts a pregnancy, it could end the life of an embryo or fetus that was fathered by the husband. Given that he might have fathered the child and has arranged his schedule to take a role in the nurturing and household tasks, he might claim a role in making the decision whether to end any pregnancy that resulted.

The hospital personnel also face moral questions. By positioning themselves to provide medical and psychological counsel for rape victims, they place themselves in a position in which, under the doctrine of informed consent examined in Chapter 17, to provide information about all options including presumably the morning after contraception or abortion. (The very choice of the term is controversial. If the drug blocks conception it would properly be a contraceptive, but if it blocks implantation or otherwise interrupts the development of an embryo after conception has occurred, it would function as an abortifacient.) Discussing the abortion option is not, and never has been, prohibited, but it would in this case violate the health professional's conscientiously held convictions. Insofar as the informed consent doctrine requires presenting the alternatives that the patient would reasonably want to know about, there is good reason to believe that discussion of the abortion option is required morally and legally as part of the consent process. If the medication offered to Ms. Sackler functions as an abortifacient, someone else would have the obligation to inform the patient about the treatment alternatives.

Some procedures would be such a dramatic violation of the conscience of the health provider that he or she would not be expected to discuss them and, in fact, might be expected to refuse to discuss them. For example, in some jurisdictions suicide is not illegal, and it could be considered a possible option for someone diagnosed as having a malignancy, yet no health professional is required or expected to discuss the suicide option as part of the consent process for the treatment of the cancer. Similarly, most analysts of professional ethics hold that a physician is usually not required to be a party to a procedure that violates his or her conscience. A physician or nurse might claim a conscientious right to refuse to suggest a morning after pill in this case. However, unless the professional can easily secure needed medical services by a colleague, the question is raised about the choice to be in obstetrics or gynecology (OB/GYN) in the first place; for these issues do arise with some frequency in OB/GYN.

In some situations the problem might be resolved by having the health professional ask a colleague to take on the task. There are two problems with that strategy, however. First, in some settings only one properly qualified person may be on duty capable of providing this information. Delaying until regular staff return would not meet Ms. Sackler's needs.

This suggests a second problem with the strategy of transferring responsibility to a colleague. If the ER professional really believes that the use of the morning after pill would constitute murder of the embryonic human being, does it make sense morally for that person to refer to someone else?

Abortion to Save the Life of the Pregnant Woman

In the previous case we considered whether a rape victim would be justified in terminating a pregnancy if she were so distraught that she were suicidal. That is a special case of the general problem of whether abortion is justified when the life of the pregnant woman is in jeopardy. That case does not happen as often in the era of advanced obstetrical care, but it does still occur, as, for example, in the case of a woman who with a history of a ruptured uterus who is again pregnant and shows a thin uterine wall likely to rupture. Even some ethics commentators known to be strongly opposed to abortion have been challenged to acknowledge an exception in such cases. One example of such as case is a pregnant woman with systemic lupus erythematosus (SLE).

CASE 10-3

Abortion to Save a Pregnant Woman's Life

At midnight, 19-year-old Emelina Pena, fourteen-weeks pregnant, was seen in a general hospital ER with complaints of dizziness, decreased urine output, and difficulty breathing. Ms. Pena was accompanied by her husband, Manuel, who reported that his wife had a history of SLE. Before her pregnancy, Ms. Pena had been hospitalized because of cardiac involvement and pleural effusion. She had been on high-dose corticosteroids prior to her pregnancy to control rheumatic flares. She had discontinued all of her medications when she found out she was pregnant. She had also avoided seeing her physician because, as she told her husband, "He will want me to be on those drugs and that is no good for the baby." The past few days, Ms. Pena had become sicker and sicker, so her husband decided to bring her to the ER. The ER physician diagnosed possible pericarditis, serious hypertension, and pending renal failure.

Roger Bishop, MD, the obstetrician on call, asked the care team to join him for a family conference regarding Ms. Pena's case. Dr. Bishop began the conference by stating, "The best treatment for your wife is delivery of the baby. At this stage of gestation, the baby will not survive. If we treat your wife with the proper medications to control her numerous systemic problems, the baby will most certainly be irreversibly harmed anyway." Mr. Pena responded, "So there is no way to save my Emelina and the baby?" Dr. Bishop replied, "I believe that the delivery of the baby is the only way to guarantee your wife's life." One of the other members of the health care team indicated he was extremely uncomfortable with what Dr. Bishop told Mr. Pena. He was opposed to abortion, but he knew that Ms. Pena could die from renal failure if a caesarean section was not performed soon.

COMMENTARY

The plan proposed by Dr. Bishop is to sacrifice the fetus in order to save the pregnant woman. This would constitute a directly intended killing of the fetus, something that we saw in Chapter 9 was unacceptable to many in both the religious and secular worlds. The killing would be the means of accomplishing an admittedly good end of saving the pregnant woman, but, as a means to a good end, the doctrine of double effect always considers the means intended. According to the double-effect doctrine, intended killing is morally unacceptable. If one believes, as the other health care team member apparently does, that intentional termination of the fetus's life is morally wrong, the proposed termination of the pregnancy becomes controversial. The most militant opponents of intended abortion hold that such abortion is always unacceptable, even if it is necessary to save the pregnant woman's life. Holders of this view claim that if failing to abort leads to the woman's death, this is nevertheless not a "killing." Rather it is thought of as letting an evil occur. The evil is foreseen, but not directly intended, a difference that holders of the double-effect doctrine consider crucial. Those who take the doctrine of double effect seriously may justify letting both die, if necessary, on the grounds that allowing a death—even two deaths—to occur is not the same as intentionally causing a death. They hold firmly to the view that what is wrong is not the death per se, but intentional human action that causes the death.

Some might argue that the intention is to save the mother's life, not to produce the death of the baby. That reasoning is unacceptable, however, to proponents of the doctrine of double effect. They claim that if one intends a good end (such as saving the woman's life) one also intends all actions taken to accomplish that end. The abortion is considered a means to saving the woman. In this case, they insist that one necessarily intends the fetus's death if the abortion is intended to save the woman. The only case in which an action that caused a fetus's death would be acceptable according to strict proponents of the doctrine would be situations such as removal of a cancerous uterus of a pregnant woman. Here they claim the hysterectomy is the normal treatment of the cancer and the killing of the fetus occurs only secondary to the hysterectomy, not as a means to treating the cancer. This is seen by the fact that the hysterectomy is exactly the procedure one would use for uterine cancer even if the woman were not pregnant. By contrast, in Ms. Pena's case, what Dr. Bishop proposes makes no sense if she is not pregnant. Killing the fetus is, according to defenders of the doctrine, a direct means to the good end and is therefore intended and morally unacceptable.

Of course, those who are liberal on abortion would not be as troubled by the plan of sacrificing the fetus to save the pregnant woman. They are willing to accept abortion for much lesser reasons. They might see the ending of the fetus's life as tragic, but morally tolerable to serve worthy purposes. Saving a woman's life would certainly in their eyes be a particularly worthy purpose.

The most interesting position is the intermediate one of those who are generally opposed to abortion, but are troubled by the choice of the death of the pregnant woman *and* the fetus, when termination of the pregnancy could save at least one. Not all who are generally opposed to abortion and who usually take the doctrine of double effect seriously will go to the wall in the kind of case presented here. They may view the case as a choice between one death and two and conclude that aborting to save the life of the pregnant woman is the one exception to the abortion prohibition.

The other member of the caregiving team apparently opposes the abortion. One plan he could consider would be pointing out to Dr. Bishop and Ms. Pena that there is a chance that with aggressive treatment both fetus and Ms. Pena could survive or at least maintain the pregnancy until the fetus is viable at approximately twenty-five weeks gestation. He would have to honestly disclose that the results of such attempts are not promising, but this option seems not to have been presented by Dr. Bishop to Ms. and Mr. Pena. Assuming a critic of abortion concludes that abortion in this circumstance would be unacceptable, what are his options beyond making sure that the option of attempting to save both the pregnant woman and the fetus needs to be presented?

Abortion and the Mentally Incapacitated Woman

Another difficult situation in which abortion might be considered involves women who become pregnant and who are not mentally competent to consent. In some ways the situation is like the rape. The pregnancy is not the result of a consensual act. In the case of the mentally incapacitated woman, however, she may not have resisted the sexual encounter. In fact, she may have voiced an approval albeit one that may not be truly voluntary.

This scenario poses another problem, however. If the woman is incompetent, she may not be capable of raising the child. Thus both the woman and the child may be at risk.

That suggests still another difference. In the case of rape, the victim is capable of making her own choices about terminating the pregnancy while in the case of the woman with severely diminished mental capacity, someone else will have to make the choice for her. In the following case, a health care team confronts the problem of whether to push for terminating a pregnancy in one of their incompetent patients.

=== **CASE 10-4** ===

Abortion for the Mentally Incapacitated Patient

A 17-year-old teenager, Karen Thomson, with previous admissions to the Crisis Unit, entered the psychiatric residential facility with symptoms of depression, suicidal ideation, and psychosis. She was known to be a prostitute and addicted to cocaine. During one month of individual and group treatment she was considered manipulative and frequently feigned symptoms, seeking attention. Karen's IQ, previously tested, was 69. Although interpretation of IQ scores is controversial, scores below 70 are often classified as indicating mental retardation, so Karen might be described as being at the top of the group of persons with mild retardation. Current medications were haloperidol and chlorpromazine. Serving as ex-officio guardian was her grandmother, Elsa Thomson. Tests confirmed pregnancy at about three months. Karen did not know the man responsible.

General assessment by her physicians was that she was not mentally fit to be a parent. Her mental disability was compounded by her addiction and medications. They considered her hazardous to the fetus. Some of the staff recommended abortion. Her grandmother concurred believing that the pregnancy was not in her granddaughter's interest and that the baby would not thrive. In addition, Elsa Thomson was not eager to take on the role of foster mother, living sparsely herself. No other family was known.

Karen preferred not to abort the pregnancy, but was not adamant; she tended to agree with the doctors' advice but was often not compliant with recommendations. Given that the physicians believed that abortion would be best and the grandmother concurred, is the abortion ethically acceptable? Would it make a difference whether the patient agreed?

COMMENTARY

This is a tragic case of a woman who has found herself pregnant, perhaps as a result of prostitution. There is no male acknowledging paternity. Karen is a minor and is suffering from serious mental and physical problems. She clearly cannot be considered a "mature minor." It is possible that she cannot even be adequately informed about the options including carrying the fetus to term and raising it, placing it for adoption, or ending the pregnancy.

In many jurisdictions minors can obtain abortions, but a parent or guardian must be notified. In some localities parental permission is needed unless a judge determines obtaining it would seriously jeopardize the minor's welfare. Guardian permission is not the issue here, however. Her grandmother seems inclined to support the abortion. The real problem is whether her approval is necessary and whether Karen can be informed adequately to make that choice.

Her limited intelligence may make her incapable of making such a momentous choice. Not all mentally ill persons are incompetent to nurture their children or to make health care decisions, but Karen's capacities seem quite limited. If she continues to desire to continue to pregnancy, should her grandmother and the physicians have the authority to override her views and choose the abortion anyway? If she is persuaded to change her mind, would that make any difference or is the guardian's judgment all that is relevant here?

The suggestion that those involved could try to persuade Karen to consent to the abortion seems to imply that she is competent to make her own choices.

If, in fact, she is not competent to make her own decisions—a presumption that is made for all minors and seems particularly plausible in this case, her choice is irrelevant. As presented, Karen is demonstrably incapable of taking care and being adequate for a child's needs for 18–21 years. The grandmother is the only family member available and her decision should be followed, according to surrogate laws.

Assuming that the grandmother with the concurrence of the medical staff decides in favor of abortion, is the justification based on the welfare of Karen, the child, the grandmother, or the community? Should this be treated like a case of a fetus with a potential genetic anomaly inherited from its mother or should the welfare of the child be based on the sort of nurturing environment that is anticipated? Does either provide a basis for terminating this pregnancy?

Abortion for Socioeconomic Reasons

The most controversial abortion cases are also very frequent. They are abortions desired by women who simply do not want to be pregnant—at least at the present time and circumstance. The woman is not ready to have children or cannot presently afford them. These abortions, illustrated in the following case, are frequently called abortions for socioeconomic reasons.

═══════════════ CASE 10-5 ═══════════════

Abortion for Socioeconomic Reasons

In March of 1970 Norma McCorvey was unmarried and pregnant, living in Dallas County, Texas. She signed an affidavit claiming she wished to terminate her pregnancy by an abortion. She wanted it done by a competent, licensed physician and under safe, clinical conditions. Although there has been some dispute about whether the affidavit stated her actual wishes, it stated she was distressed that her right of privacy was put in jeopardy because the Texas law was so vague that physicians might be reluctant to perform an abortion for a woman in her situation out of fear that it would be illegal.

Ms. McCorvey was a working class blue collar woman of twenty-four who thought of herself as tough-talking and of unrefined ways. She was raised as a poor Louisiana girl who had spent a good part of her childhood in reform schools. She ran away from home when she was ten, then supported herself with odd jobs as a carnival barker, waitress, cleaner of apartments, and construction worker. She had had three previous pregnancies, all of which had resulted in live births with the children placed for adoption. In one case, the removal of the child was against her will. She realized she did not meet the criterion of wanting to discontinue a pregnancy to save her life or prevent serious medical problems. She was simply at a point at which financially, psychologically, and emotionally she should not have more children.

James Hubert Hallford, who was a licensed physician in Texas, entered the case testifying that he, in fact, was sufficiently concerned about the vagueness of

the Texas law that he feared performing abortions. He had been arrested for performing them and had two prosecutions pending. He argued that he could not tell
whether his participation in an abortion for a patient like Norma McCorvey was
legal, that the law was too vague, and that it violated the privacy of the doctor–
patient relation and his own right to practice medicine.

This case became world famous when Ms. McCorvey was referred to as Jane
Roe of the 1973 Supreme Court decision, *Roe v. Wade*, that declared laws restricting
abortions unconstitutional. Now that abortion is legal, women like Ms. McCorvey
must make the ethical choice of whether an abortion for psychological and socioeconomic reasons like hers would be morally justified.[7]

COMMENTARY

If the fetus Norma McCorvey is carrying was considered to have the same
moral standing as postnatal humans, then ending the pregnancy for psychological or socioeconomic reasons would be indefensible. This can be seen by how
society would react if a mother proposed to kill one of her existing children
because of her psychological or financial situation. Almost certainly she would
not even consider such an idea, and if she acted on the thought, she would be
guilty of homicide. The fact that she was economically desperate would not
work as a justification.

Likewise, if someone believed that a fetus at this stage of development had
no moral standing whatsoever, the case would pose no problem. Others adopt
an intermediary position typical of many who have moderate views on abortion. They are willing to support abortion for serious reasons such as the health
of the pregnant woman or serious genetic anomaly. This strongly suggests that
they believe fetuses have some moral standing, but not the same standing as
that of postnatal children.

Many who hold this view end up trading off the interests of the fetus with
the interests of the pregnant woman (who wants to abort) and others who
also have an interest in the situation (such as her other children). This could
imply that the more serious the interest of the woman, the more justifiable
the abortion. However, those holding this view may also view moral standing
as increasing with fetal development, meaning that moderate interests of the
woman could justify abortion in the earliest days of the pregnancy while only
more serious interests would be sufficient in later stages of pregnancy. Is this
mode of reasoning an acceptable one for Norma McCorvey and Dr. Hallford
to adopt?

Assuming this approach is acceptable in principle, what should be the role
of the pregnant woman's finances in making these decisions? There seems to be
something questionable about forcing a low-income woman to make a choice
between her fetus and her other interests. In the case of a woman with other
children, she might be forced to choose between her fetus and the interests of

her other children based on finances. Some would argue that society should never put women in such a position, but, assuming it does, should the woman be able to base her abortion decision on these economic factors?

One option women considering abortion need to consider is adoption. Since maintaining a pregnancy and then placing the infant for adoption involves nine months or more psychological and economic impacts, some women might not find adoption acceptable. Still, society, and especially those who oppose abortion, should develop policies to minimize these constraints. It is likely, however, that many women will continue to find adoption to be an acceptable alternative.

As was suggested in the case description, Ms. McCorvey has claimed that she was pressured into signing an affidavit that led to the famous court case. Surely, no one can defend such pressure on her or other women to choose abortion. Regardless, of the facts of the original court case, Ms. McCorvey has since then come to reject abortion. She now is committed to actions opposing abortion.

STERILIZATION

Another intervention that has traditionally raised moral controversy in biomedical ethics is sterilization. Designed to permanently prohibit fertility, it has run afoul of Catholics and others who apply natural law reasoning to matters of medical morality.[8] They hold that there are certain "natural ends" of human beings that are associated with certain bodily organs and tissues. One of these natural ends of the human is said to be to procreate and that any directly intended interference with these functions violates the moral law.

Others, who may not share this natural law reasoning, also encounter moral problems related to sterilization. Other women have reported finding it extremely difficult to convince physicians to sterilize them, especially if they were not considered too young to permanently foreclose childbearing or had not already given birth to a number of children.[9] Low-income women have reported being pressured by health care professionals to consent to being sterilized out of a paternalistic concern by the providers that pregnancy would not be good for either the woman or her offspring as in the following case.

═══ CASE 10-6 ═══

Sterilization of an Economically Deprived Woman

Tilly Johnson lived with her two-year-old daughter in a small town in a southeastern state. She discovered that she was pregnant for the fourth time. At twenty-four years of age she was distressed. She had had three previous pregnancies. In addition to her daughter, she had a son when she had been married briefly to a man no longer in her life. The Department of Child Protection took custody of the baby. Last year she had had an abortion of a pregnancy that resulted from a brief relationship with another man. This time she decided she would keep the baby.

She was being seen at the clinic at the local hospital designed to provide prenatal care for women who might otherwise not receive any medical care prior to childbirth. She was being seen by Dr. Andrew Lacey. He had first seen her when she was six months pregnant. He realized she was unhappy with the pregnancy. He counseled her about the pregnancy and, during the visit at the seventh month, asked her to consider having her tubes tied as part of the delivery. Dr. Lacey was also a Southern Baptist. He had some concerns about sterilization, but believed it was appropriate for women who are not in a position to provide long-term support for their children.

Ms. Johnson was interested, but seemed ambivalent. She knew that two children would be all she could handle. Her Baptist upbringing did not explicitly oppose sterilization, but her church leaders had emphasized the importance of motherhood and expressed the importance of avoiding permanently foreclosing further pregnancies. She hoped that some day the right man would come into her life and she could be part of what she considered a normal family. On the other hand, she knew it would be economically and socially bad for her to have more children for the foreseeable future. She ended the conversation tentatively agreeing to having her tubes tied. Dr. Lacey indicated they would discuss it further at a future appointment.

Ms. Johnson was unable to return to the clinic until she was starting her eighth month of pregnancy when she unexpectedly went into labor. Dr. Lacey was surprised, realizing that he had not had a chance to obtain a signed consent for the tubal ligation, he asked the head resident to make sure Ms. Johnson still wanted her tubes tied. Ms. Johnson was quite uncomfortable by the time the resident came to her in the labor room. She wanted anesthetic. She signed the consent form before anesthesia was administered. Should Dr. Lacey perform the tubal ligation?

COMMENTARY

This case presents a complex combination of religious, medical, and personal issues for Tilly Johnson and Dr. Lacey. Focus first on the religious ethical issues about sterilization. One potential problem with sterilization is that it can be seen as a violation of the moral natural law. Surely, sterilization will permanently disrupt the reproductive function, considered by many, including many Catholics, to be a "primary end of marriage." Moreover, the disruption will come about by intentional interference with the natural body function.

Neither Dr. Lacey nor Ms. Johnson is Catholic; they are Baptists. Nothing in the case suggests they would have natural law reservations about sterilization. But there are other reasons why some people have traditionally objected to sterilizations. Some have reservations about sterilization because they realize that once a woman can no longer become pregnant, the social control on sexual relations outside of marriage resulting from fear of pregnancy are removed.

There are some, especially in conservative communities, who fear that sterilization will further promiscuity.

Especially among Protestant and liberal, secular thinkers, there is a belief that keeping one's options open is a good thing. Permanent loss of fertility has been seen as foreclosing options. Such objectors have a strong preference for temporary forms of birth control. Would the advantage of keeping options open be the reason why Dr. Lacey should refrain from tying Ms. Johnson's tubes?

This case also raises serious questions about the quality of Ms. Johnson's consent. The problem is not entirely Dr. Lacey's fault since he had only had one prenatal visit from her at which time they had explored sterilization and she had tentatively consented. He no doubt believed he would have further opportunity to discuss the matter with her before she went into labor. For a variety of reasons, he did not have that opportunity. Now he must decide how to proceed under circumstances in which Ms. Johnson cannot give a calm and reasoned response. She was under the stress of labor. She wanted relief from the discomfort. Given that no written consent was obtained prior to these events, one might argue that Dr. Lacey should avoid the irreversible procedure. On the other hand, it is much more convenient for the patient to have the tubal ligation as part of delivery. Given that Ms. Johnson's situation was such that further pregnancies would be a serious problem for her and she had tentatively consented at the six-month visit, Dr. Lacey chose to proceed. Was that the right choice?

CONTRACEPTION

The third area of moral concern related to fertility and birth is contraception. Until the 1930s, most of the major religious traditions had moral objections to efforts to control fertility through contraception. The techniques that were available were not very reliable and such efforts were seen as infringing on the traditional "duties of marriage" as well as posing a risk of promiscuity.

In 1930, the Lambeth Conference signaled the willingness of the Anglican tradition (the Episcopalians in the United States) to open the door cautiously to some fertility control. The other Protestant traditions soon followed,[10] but Catholic moral theology reinforced its traditional view that all sexual acts had to be open to procreation as well as expressing the unity of marriage.[11] The mainstream of Catholic thought acknowledged that the rhythm method of fertility control, which was considered "natural," might be acceptable, but no barrier methods were considered tolerable because they interfered with the natural ends of marriage.

By the 1960s some Catholics began to consider this strong prohibition unnecessary, becoming open to the use of the new oral contraceptives.[12] The majority of a Papal Commission considered such an opening acceptable, but with the Papal Encyclical *Humane Vitae* a condemnation of all except so-called natural methods was reaffirmed.[13] Similar disputes arose in the Jewish tradition with the Jewish commitment to the duty to procreate in conflict with more liberal acceptance of self-determination regarding fertility.[14]

There is increasing evidence that all people have underlying value commitments that will have influence on medical decisions. These will be manifest in decisions about birth control in which even those who are attempting to be fair and neutral may use language in ways that reflect their value commitments.[15] As seen in the next case, pharmaceutical care providers may find themselves in positions in which their often hidden values may come into play as they teach or counsel about fertility control.

=== CASE 10-7 ===

Biased Counseling: Teaching about Birth Control

Stanislaw Pokowski was in a four-person group practice in internal medicine. He had immigrated from Poland in 1990 soon after Poland's political changes. He had routinely explained to his female patients that he was morally opposed to abortion and would not counsel patients on the subject. Since others in his practice were willing to take such patients, this arrangement had never caused problems.

Dr. Pokowski was increasingly troubled by a related moral problem. He was regularly asked by his patients for prescriptions for contraception. He had provided prescriptions for them but was troubled by such requests from unmarried patients, especially from young women. He decided he would not ask that these patients transfer to a colleague in the practice, but would rather continue providing care for them. He would counsel them about the pharmacological effects of the pill.

His practice was to describe minor side effects first: light bleeding, skipped periods, nausea, weight change, bloating, increase in vaginal infections. He also mentioned a darkening of the skin on the face, which, he noted, may be permanent.

He then turned to cardiac problems noting the association of the pill with blood clots, heart attacks, and blood pressure increases, and strokes as well as effects of worsening migraines, gall bladder disease, and changes in blood levels of fatty acids.

On the subject of cancer he said that questions remain about the association of the pill with cancer and there was some evidence of association with liver cancer. He also said he was not convinced of an association between the pill and cervical cancer, but some studies have shown an increased risk of breast cancer.

Dr. Pokowski also opened conversation with his younger patients about the problems of bearing children while young and unmarried. He pointed out the enormous economic responsibility involved in having children and went on to connect this discussion with the fact that even with the best birth control pills pregnancies result. He also urged the patient to talk with her priest of minister about the issues of using chemicals that were not a natural way of limiting births.

If his patients insisted on a prescription for the pill, he would then write it.

COMMENTARY

It appears that all that Dr. Pokowski said about oral contraceptives was more or less true although one could argue that, overall, his message was unduly alarming. Two kinds of issues are raised by Dr. Pokowski. First, is he presenting biased counseling and, second, is oral contraception in a young, unmarried woman unethical?

Regarding whether his message, although truthful, was biased, he might have pointed out that many of the minor side effects—the break through bleeding, nausea, and weight changes, for example—can sometimes be eliminated by using a different pill. The cardiac problems are real, but occur only in a small number of women using the pill. While some studies have suggested a relation between oral contraceptives and breast cancer, others have found no increased risk. Moreover, the link with cervical cancer is not definitive, and the pill seems to prevent cancer of the ovaries and cancer of the endometrium (the lining of the uterus).

If Dr. Pokowski had said only these more positive things about oral contraceptives, he would also have been speaking the truth. The problem is getting a fair and unbiased balance between the positive and negative messages. One is tempted to say that Dr. Pokowski should simply state everything, but there are many things that could be said that are too technical, too trivial, or too uninteresting. The list of possible statements is virtually infinite. Moreover, each statement can be expressed in countless ways, some of which will be much more alarming than others. He could say that oral contraceptives fail only 1 percent of the time and that is often from improper use. Or he could say that, if a woman relied on the pill to prevent pregnancy for about eight years, chances are the pill would fail and she would have a child. These statements are different ways of saying the same thing, but carry very different messages.

Turning to the second issue, Dr. Pokowski's opening of social and ethical dimensions of oral contraception is also controversial. Most people consider it responsible for a physician to introduce social and ethical issues and many would agree that bearing children as an unmarried adolescent is irresponsible. Some would also agree that the use of chemical means to control pregnancy is unnatural and may even raise issues of moral violation. On the other hand, even the majority of the Roman Catholic birth control commission was open to the licitness of oral contraceptives before the Vatican expressed the finding that oral contraception violated the moral natural law.

The issues of this chapter, which traditionally arose in the context of abortion, sterilization, and contraception, are increasingly being seen in newer problems related to genetics and birth technologies designed to enhance fertility. The cases in the next chapter present some of the moral controversies related to these new technologies.

NOTES

[1] For further discussion of the ethics of abortion see Callahan, Daniel. *Abortion: Law, Choice and Morality*. New York: Macmillan, 1970; Feinberg, Joel, editor. *The Problem of Abortion*. Belmont, CA: Wadsworth Publishing Co. 1973; Bayles, Michael D. *Reproductive Ethics*. Englewood Cliffs, NJ: Prentice-Hall, 1984; and Noonan, John T. *The Morality of Abortion: Legal and Historical Perspectives*. Cambridge, MA: Harvard University Press, 1970; Dworkin, Ronald. *Life's Dominion: An Argument about Abortion, Euthanasia, and Individual Freedom*. New York: Vintage Books, 1994.

[2] McCormick, Richard A. "Who or What is the Preembryo?" *Kennedy Institute of Ethics Journal* 1 (1991):1–15, esp. 4, 9, 11–12.

[3] Hellegers, A. "Fetal Development," *Theological Studies* 31 (March, 1970):3–9.

[4] *In the Matter of Baby K*, 832 F.Supp. 1022 (E.D. Va. 1993); Veatch, Robert M. and Carol Mason Spicer. "Medically Futile Care: The Role of the Physician in Setting Limits. *American Journal of Law & Medicine* 18 (Nos. 1 & 2, 1992):15–36.

[5] Weinstein, Bruce D. "Do Pharmacists Have a Right to Refuse to Fill Prescriptions for Abortifacient Drugs?" *Law, Medicine and Health Care* 20 (3)(1992 Fall):220–223; Brushwood, David B. "Conscientious Objection and Abortifacient Drugs." *Clinical Therapeutics* 15 (1)(1993 Jan–Feb):204–212; Brushwood, David B. "Must a Catholic Hospital Inform a Rape Victim of the Availability of the "Morning-after Pill"?" *American Journal of Hospital Pharmacy* 47 (2)(1990 Feb):395–396.; Cantor, J. and K. Baum. "The Limits of Conscientious Objection—May Pharmacists Refuse to Fill Prescriptions for Emergency Contraception?" *NEJM* 351 (2004):2008–2012.

[6] Thomson, Judith Jarvis. "A Defense of Abortion," *Philosophy and Public Affairs* 1 (No. 1, Fall 1971):47–66.

[7] This case is based on Roe v. Wade, 410 U.S. 113, 93 S.Ct. 705, 1973; McCorvey, Norma and Gary Thomas. *Won by Love: Norma McCorvey, Jane Roe of Roe v. Wade, Speaks Out for the Unborn As She Shares Her New Conviction for Life*. Nashville, TN: Thomas Nelson, Inc., 1998; and Norma McCorvey's website, http://www.crossingoverministry.org/, accessed September 8, 2007.

[8] Ashley, Benedict M. and Kevin D. O'Rourke. *Healthcare Ethics: A Theological Analysis*, 3rd ed. St. Louis, MO: The Catholic Health Association of the United States, 1989.

[9] Scrimshaw, Susan C. and Bernard Pasquariella. "Obstacles to Sterilization in One Community." *Family Planning Perspectives* 2 (1970):40–42.

[10] Fagley, Richard M. *The Population Explosion and Christian Responsibility*. New York: Oxford University Press, 1960.

[11] Noonan, John T. *Contraception: A History of Its Treatment by the Catholic Theologians and Canonists*. Cambridge, MA.: Harvard University, 1966.

[12] Callahan, Daniel, editor. *The Catholic Case for Contraception*. New York: The Macmillan Company, 1969.

[13] Pope Paul VI. "Encyclical Letter on the Regulation of Births (July 25, 1968)." In *Medical Ethics: Sources of Catholic Teachings*. Kevin D. O'Rourke and Philip Boyle,

editors. St. Louis, MO: The Catholic Health Association of the United States, 1989, pp. 85–91.

[14] Feldman, David M. *Birth Control in Jewish Law.* New York: New York University Press, 1968.

[15] Veatch, Robert M. *Value-Freedom in Science and Technology.* Missoula, MT: Scholars Press, 1976.

CHAPTER 11

◦∽

Genetics, Birth, and the Biological Revolution

Other Cases Involving Genetics or Birth Technologies

2-3: Infertility Treatment: God's Will?
4-3: The Benefits and Harms of High-Risk Chemotherapy
9-3: Separating Conjoined Twins: An Unintended but Foreseen Killing?
15-3: The $300,000 Marginal Treatment
16-8: Waiving Consent for Future Research on Blood Samples

───────────

In addition to the moral problems related to contraception, sterilization, and abortion, which were addressed in Chapter 10, newer, more complex ethical questions are emerging connected with the process of conception, prenatal development, and birth.[1] Some issues are related to the increasing importance of the science of genetics. For many years we have had a vague idea that certain diseases were inherited, but only recently have we had the precise knowledge and ability to determine the chances that a disease will be transmitted and to counsel the prospective parents about intervention alternatives.

The first level of these issues involves counseling that requires assessing and informing parents whether a condition is inherited, and if so, how? It may now involve prenatal sampling of amniotic fluid or chorionic villi blood sampling that permits either chromosomal or biochemical determinations of whether a fetus, already gestating, is afflicted with a disease.[2] Other efforts are oriented toward genetic screening of larger populations at risk for conditions such as Tay-Sachs disease, so that individuals can be informed about whether they are at risk for conceiving an afflicted child and, if they are, what the chances are of a child being affected.[3] When one shifts to mass screening, additional moral problems—confidentiality, record keeping, statistical morality—come into play.

More recently, the technologies related to in vitro fertilization (IVF)—removing an egg from a woman and fertilizing it in the laboratory—have posed new and controversial problems.[4]

Once the technology to fertilize human eggs outside the woman's body is available, no technical reason exists why the fertilized egg needs to be returned to the woman from whom the egg was taken. Surrogate motherhood involves reimplanting the fertilized egg into some other woman, either so that she may bear the child and continue to be its social mother after the birth, or so that she may bear the child in order to return him or her for parenting to the woman who supplied the egg.[5] In theory, the egg could be obtained from one woman, gestated and delivered by a second, and parented by a third.

Still newer and more controversial is what is referred to as gene therapy or genetic engineering.[6] Efforts are under way to modify the actual genetic codes of patients suffering from genetic diseases. This has already been attempted to treat some conditions such as the enzyme deficiency, adenosine deaminase (ADA) deficiency, and research is developing rapidly to use similar technologies to treat other conditions. Initial attempts at the use of this technology have been made to treat HIV.[7]

The first efforts are designed to modify somatic cells (so that only the treated individual and not his or her offspring will have the genetic material changed). Eventually, similar technologies will probably be used to modify reproductive cells (so that the genetic change will be transmitted to the offspring).

Ethical problems arise at many levels with these birth technologies. Perhaps the most fundamental issue is whether tampering with the genetic and birth processes is "playing God" in an unacceptable way. Such technologies have the potential to change the nature of the human species.[8] While the species undoubtedly is already undergoing change, changes to date have been in a much slower, unplanned evolutionary fashion. The technologies under development have the potential for much more rapid change in the genetic character of the species, as well as in the basic biological processes such as reproduction. The first question raised is thus, whether such efforts extend beyond what humans should be permitted to do.

Even if one accepts the idea in principle of producing such fundamental changes, there will remain controversy over just which changes are ethically acceptable. This will, in turn, require judgments about what conditions in our species are unacceptable. Everyone might agree that a terrible disease such as Lesch-Nyhan syndrome—incompatible with life of more than a few months and dreadfully painful while the infant is alive—is a condition worth changing if we can; however, the same technologies are likely to permit us to intervene to modify conditions less obviously unacceptable. Color-blindness, for example, might be amenable to some of these technologies. Even conceiving an embryo of an undesired sex can be diagnosed prenatally and is, in principle, subject to interventions. The question is, "Does such a condition justify genetic interventions?"

Many other moral problems arise with these technologies: problems of identifying unexpected paternity, notifying other family members of the diagnosis of a genetic anomaly, and conflicts among parties over custody of a child. The cases in this chapter raise many of these issues.

GENETIC COUNSELING

Increasingly, patients are being counseled about the statistical risk of conceiving a child with a genetic anomaly.[9] Problems of concern could involve a genetic condition already present in a child, a parent, or some other member of the family. Or it could involve concern about a new genetic problem such as the risk of an older woman conceiving a child with trisomy 21 (Down syndrome). The following case illustrates the issues.

CASE 11-1

Statistical Morality: Prenatal Diagnosis of Colon Cancer

Harrison Merrik was a 38-year-old man who had been diagnosed with hereditary nonpolyposis colon cancer (HNPCC). It had taken his father's life when he was an adolescent. Mr. Merrik had been diagnosed in time to have his colon removed. Now he and his wife, Barbara, age thirty-two, were planning on having their first child. They had been told by their internist and by a genetic counselor that HNPCC results from a genetic mutation that is inherited in an autosomal dominant fashion.[10] This meant that, for anyone who had the mutation, each of his offspring had a 50 percent chance that each of his children would also have it. For that reason and because Mr. Merrik had been under medical treatment, he and his wife had hesitated to have children. They had decided that, if they could not be assured that their children would be free of the mutation causing the cancer, they would remain childless.

They were now told that tests with great accuracy could be performed that would tell them if any conception carried the gene. They had two options for testing. They could undergo IVF and have the resulting embryos tested using preimplantation genetic diagnosis (PGD). At about three days after fertilization a single cell would be removed and tested for the presence of the mutation. At that point they could choose from among the embryos free of the mutation a number to be implanted. Since not all implanted embryos would develop, typically two or three would be implanted hoping that at least one would survive to birth.

The Merriks were aware that it was a challenging and expensive option. Mrs. Merrik would have to be treated to make egg cells available that could be procured and fertilized with her husband's sperm. The cost could be upward of $25,000, depending on the number of cycles involved. They would face the daunting task of selecting from the embryos which would be chosen to survive, a task Mrs. Merrik thought would be like "playing God." Remaining healthy embryos as well as any with the HNPCC genetic mutation would be discarded unless they chose to donate them to another couple who was infertile or for research. Both choices were unacceptable to them.

Their second option for having a child that was genetically their own would be to conceive naturally and then have the fetus tested prenatally for the presence of the mutation. They would have to wait for 16–20 weeks and then have amniotic fluid withdrawn to have fetal cells recovered and tested. The risk of the amniocentesis was a small risk of interrupting the pregnancy (about 1 percent). They had a 50-50 chance that any offspring would not have the gene. If it did, they could choose abortion if they remained committed to avoiding children with the gene. This approach would require a more substantial medical procedure—a midterm abortion. It would also raise the moral issues of abortion for a serious but not uniformly fatal medical condition.

Adding to the complexity of their choice was the fact that not all people with the HNPCC mutation would get clinically significant colon cancer. About 80 percent of persons with the gene eventually develop it. For those developing the cancer, death will result without treatment, but removal of the colon and perhaps the rectum could provide a good chance of survival. This could result in the need for a colostomy, but the gene did not mean a certain death from this kind of cancer. The risk for other cancers would remain, just as in any other person.

They had the additional options of waiting to test the offspring postnatally, perhaps waiting until the child had matured to the point that he or she could decide about when to test, or having a child that was not carrying Mr. Merrik's genes— either through adoption or artificial insemination. Was prenatal testing through PGD or amniocentesis acceptable and, if so, was one of them morally preferable?

COMMENTARY

The Merriks here face some difficult choices. The strategy of IVF with PGD would be objectionable to those who oppose artificial manipulation of gametes and other so-called unnatural manipulations of sperm and egg cells. There is no reason to believe that the Merriks would object on those grounds, but some couples might. Even secular observers who have no religious objections might be concerned about the risks of removing cells from the embryo or the ominous responsibility for selecting which embryos to implant and which to discard.

If they choose a somewhat more traditional approach, they could conceive a child through natural means and then undertake the amniocentesis with which we now have some decades of experience. The approach would still pose some risk to the fetus and would require a decision to abort if they wanted to avoid any offspring with the HNPCC gene.

Either approach leaves the Merriks with the difficult responsibility of deciding that some of their offspring will not survive to birth. This is particularly difficult since some of these, even some with the gene responsible for the colon cancer, will not actually experience the disease. This is because the gene does not have complete "penetrance"; that is, sometimes the gene does not produce a clinically observable cancer. About 20 percent of the conceptions with the affected gene will not manifest clinical signs of the disease.

If the Merriks were to set out to calculate the potential benefits and harms of alternative courses of action, they would not only have to determine how much harm comes from destroying a three-day embryo or a twenty-week fetus, they would also have to decide how to count the destroying of the genetically abnormal embryos. Statistically, about 20 percent of the aborted fetuses would have been genetically normal with regard to HNPCC. (Of course, they would still face the same risk as others that they might have some other genetic anomaly.) Moreover, with IVF not only would any embryos with the anomaly be destroyed, but those known not to have would as well, if there were more embryos than they chose to implant.

The issue here, however, is whether this statistical approach is morally valid. Some parents and counselors might reason that if a normal fetus is aborted, a terrible wrong is done and that the wrong is not lessened at all by considering the probabilities. Many parents and counselors are willing to accept terminating pregnancies of fetuses diagnosed with great certainty to be afflicted with some terrible genetic condition incompatible with life; however, the diagnosis here only presents some degree of certainty. The only plausible way of parents justifying the possibility that they will terminate a normal pregnancy would seem to be discounting the harm by adjusting for the probability.

CASE 11-2

Dwarfism: When Is a Fetus Normal?

Obstetrician Elizabeth Whistler asked for a bioethics consultation to consider the request of Charles and Amanda Harrelson for genetic testing and a possible elective abortion. Mrs. Harrelson, who was pregnant for the first time, was three months into an apparently normal pregnancy. She and her husband were both achondroplastic dwarfs. They seemingly were financially comfortable and well adjusted to their physical conditions. They had requested testing of their developing fetus for evidence of achondroplasia.

Achondroplastic dwarfism is a bone growth disorder in which cartilage is not properly converted into bone. Adult males develop to an average height of about four feet, four inches; females average about three inches shorter. While trunk size is normal, arms and legs are short and the head is enlarged featuring a prominent forehead. Intelligence is generally normal. Physical problems include bouts of apnea (periods in which breathing stops), obesity, bowed legs, and abnormalities of the lower back. Back pain is common in older people with the condition.[11]

The condition results from a mutation in a single gene, the *FGFR3* (fibroblast growth factor 3) gene. It occurs once in every 15,000 to 40,000 births, but if both parents have the gene, one child in four will inherit two copies, which results in severe effects, usually stillbirth or death from respiratory failure soon after birth. One child in four will not inherit any copies and will not be affected. Two in four will inherit one copy and have dwarfism, the same characteristics as their parents.

Prenatal diagnosis for the presence of the abnormal gene is now possible. Since incidence is so rare, if neither parent has the condition, testing would not normally be carried out. If both parents are affected, then testing would become more plausible. Any fetus with two copies of the gene could be aborted.

Dr. Whistler was discussing the diagnostic procedure with Mr. and Mrs. Harrelson and helping them understand their options. It became apparent to her that their intention was not only to abort any fetus with two copies of the gene, but also any child with no copies. If the fetus was not achondroplastic, they would have the pregnancy aborted because they did not want to rear a child obviously different from themselves.

COMMENTARY

Dr. Whistler entered into counseling with Mr. and Mrs. Harrelson for reasons that seemed relatively uncontroversial. There is one chance in four that any offspring of the Harrelsons will have two copies of the *FGFR3* gene and will either be stillborn or will die soon after birth. Aborting such a pregnancy would be opposed by someone who categorically opposes all abortion, but would be one of the most likely cases in which parents might choose to terminate a pregnancy. Dr. Whistler cannot claim that such a decision would necessarily be the right one. She might attempt to present only the facts of the expected outcome and let the Harrelsons decide or she might, especially if asked, disclose her personal moral views about abortion under these circumstances.

This case gets more complicated for Dr. Whistler when she realizes that decisions will be made regarding the abortion of a fetus that has either one copy or no copies of the critical gene. She might have anticipated that a parent would consider a fetus with one copy of the gene to be "diseased" to the point that the pregnancy should be terminated. This would raise the question of whether the short stature of dwarfism and the associated respiratory and skeletal problems to be serious enough to justify ending the pregnancy.

Even those who are not opposed to abortion in principle must face the question of when a genetic abnormality is too trivial to justify an abortion. Aborting for hair color, polydactyly (having a sixth finger), color-blindness, or gender by themselves would surely be controversial. Even though some of these are real genetic anomalies, they could easily be considered differences without any negative connotation. Whether achondroplastic dwarfism is like these other conditions—a difference that carries little or no negative implications—would be the question that Dr. Whistler and the Harrelsons would then have to face.

Dr. Whistler was surprised when she realized that the Harrelsons might prefer the child with dwarfism and might even abort the child without the condition. That they could see the so-called normal child as less desirable could be surprising, but this view is connected with the realization that medical conditions are not "diseases" just because they are abnormal. Any condition, whether statistically normal or abnormal, can be evaluated by imposing a value judgment. While many would consider achondroplastic dwarfism something undesirable (particularly when physical problems in addition to short stature are taken into consideration), the evaluation can vary from person to person. Someone in a family in which both parents and possibly older siblings have dwarfism might place positive value on having a child with the condition. Couples with dwarfism have expressed concern about having a child that was different from them. One parent has been quoted as saying that a child with dwarfism would be "just precious." She asked, "What is life going to be like for [the child] when her parents are different than she is?"[12]

Achondroplastic dwarfism can be detected not only by prenatal screening of pregnant women but also by preimplantation diagnosis of embryos created through the process of IVF. In such cases, discussed more fully in Case 11-5, several embryos can be created in the laboratory and the most desirable one or ones chosen for implantation. This process would avoid the complications of pregnancy but would still raise the questions of selection based on an unusual set of genes. If the Harrelsons had created embryos by IVF, would they be more justified in choosing the one they preferred, even if it happened to include the gene for dwarfism?

GENETIC SCREENING

Sometimes genetic counseling arises in the context of community-based genetic screening programs. These differ from the previous cases in that the counselor or other health professional would be involved in decisions about a mass or group screening rather than one-on-one counseling. These efforts often take place in churches or community programs in which the professional staff really has no continuing contact with the people being screened. In some cases, governments are mandating screening, particularly of newborns. A World Health Organization conference in December of 1997[13] offered guidelines on ethical issues in medical genetics and genetic services that are often interpreted as supporting mandatory testing of newborns, when early diagnosis and treatment will provide benefit.[14] About the same time, an American National Institutes of Health (NIH) Consensus Conference on screening of newborns for sickle cell disease and other hemoglobinopathies explicitly endorsed "universal screening of newborns for sickle cell" and urged that state laws make such screening mandatory while permitting parental refusal.[15]

Sometimes these programs have racial or ethnic implications complicating the counseling. For example, proposals to screen for sickle cell disease, a blood disease affecting primarily persons of African origin, raises issues of whether the purpose is to discourage fertility among this group. The issue has arisen in programs to screen adults for carrier status prior to their decision to have children. One of the uses of this information could be to influence a decision about whether to have children. Although carrier status is often understood to pose no immediate threat to health, there are suggestions that some medical problems can arise and, in any case, those carriers run the risk of marrying other carriers who can then have children with the actual disease. The following case illustrates the issues.

CASE 11-3

Sickle Cell and Black Genocide

Wilbur Johnson and Mae Sanford, both black, had met while working on a community action project in a large Eastern city. After going together for a year, they decided to get married and have a family.

Mr. Johnson's physician, Lester Kettering, asked if Mr. Johnson knew his sickle cell status and explained that if both he and his future wife were carriers, they had one chance in four that a child born to them would have the disease. He further explained that they would also have two chances in four that a child would be a carrier, while in one of four births the offspring would carry no copies of the gene. Dr. Kettering also explained that it was state law that any children born would be routinely tested for sickle cell status, unless the parents registered their objection.

The disease itself is an inherited abnormality in the structure of hemoglobin, which at a minimum almost always severely handicaps its victims. Life expectancy now, as a result of better treatment, has increased, but average age of death is still in the forties. Sickle cell disease is autosomal recessive; that is, both parents must be carriers (heterozygotes) before there is a risk of producing children with the disease (homozygotes). When both parents are carriers, the risk of bearing such a child is 25 percent with each pregnancy. Carriers themselves are almost symptomless and may have no idea of their status unless they are screened.

Mr. Johnson's younger brother had died in adolescence from the disease, after many painful and debilitating attacks. He thus knew something about it, including the fact that there was a good possibility that he himself was a carrier. Mr. Johnson also knew that the trait is fairly common among black Americans, about one in twelve of them being a carrier, so that there was a good chance his fiancée was a carrier too. Ms. Sanford knows of no sickle cell disease in her immediate family, but she is in a racial group with this relatively high rate of carriers.

Mr. Johnson understands that, if both he and his future wife are carriers, they will face additional choices. Prenatal diagnosis is now available that will accurately determine if a fetus has sickle cell disease. The only intervention other than counseling available at that point, however, is the termination of the pregnancy. Their other option would be to continue the pregnancy until delivery, at which time routine testing will determine the sickle cell status. If the infant has the disease (i.e., two copies of the gene), treatment regimens are now considered sufficiently effective that identification of infants with the disease is mandated. For example, infections need to be suppressed using antibiotics.

Thus, two prospective parents who know they both are carriers have four options: they can risk a 25 percent chance of having a child with the disease itself with each pregnancy, living with the attendant anxiety; they can undergo prenatal diagnosis and abort affected fetuses; they can resort to artificial insemination with a noncarrier donor; or they can forgo childbearing altogether, perhaps adopting if the short supply of adoptable babies permits.

Mr. Johnson found each of these alternatives infuriatingly unacceptable. He feared that the offer of premarital screening of blacks for the sickle cell trait, which is not a clinical condition and about which nothing can be done, was just another government attempt to cripple black reproductive capability. In the context of black history, he viewed it as an attempt by white society to control his fecundity in the beneficent guise of providing medical options. All of their options seemed to inhibit childbearing either because they would limit births (abortion and forgoing children altogether) or because they were expensive (prenatal testing or artificial insemination). The choices were all unattractive and would inhibit his and his wife's normal family development. Since the information would produce anxiety and would inhibit childbearing, he came to doubt that screening for carrier status was defensible. He was also annoyed that while the state rushed in to mandate screening of newborns—screening which might suggest that blacks should have no children—it paid little attention to the need for counseling connected with that screening which would help those identified as having a sickle cell trait to understand their situation and the alternatives for having children. He was more disturbed that, while the state mandated testing, it did not mandate health insurance that would be necessary to cover the costs of intervention if their child turned out to have sickle cell.

Ms. Sanford did not feel so strongly, but she agreed that there was a danger whenever the state mandated screening for a disease that primarily affected black families.

COMMENTARY

Routine or mandatory screening programs for either adult carrier status or the presence of actual genetic disease have been controversial. They have been resisted widely. Identifying someone as having a genetic disease can be stigmatizing and can impact access to employment and health insurance. When the genetic disease is associated with a particular ethnic or religious group, the problems can be even more severe. It is not uncommon to perceive efforts to identify genetic disease or carrier status with attempts to discourage fertility of the group involved. Thus, Mr. Johnson and Ms. Sanford have some grounds for concern.

Even the identification of carrier status, the end result of the test being offered to Mr. Johnson, can pose problems. The broader society may confuse carrier status with the presence of the actual disease and discriminate unfairly against those who are carriers. Psychologically, there is a tendency for those with carrier status to think of themselves as "ill" or "defective" even if their single abnormal gene can have no impact on their health whatsoever. It is easy to see that Mr. Johnson and Ms. Sanford would be seriously affected if one or both turned out to be carriers. Mr. Johnson already has a high probability of being a carrier, since he had a brother with the disease. Ms. Sanford's risk is not as high since she knows of no sickle cell disease in her family, but she still has a significant chance of being a carrier.

There are additional risks of screening of newborns that couples and their physicians may not anticipate. If, for example, their child tests positive with the disease and one presumed parent is not a carrier, then it becomes evident that that person is not really the parent. Similar "surprises" can arise if mandatory screening identifies an infant with carrier status when both parents have tested negative for carrier status.

Since routine or mandatory screening of adults for carrier status and of infants for disease can raise so many complex questions, a right to refuse screening has been recognized widely, but such refusal can leave infants vulnerable to serious diseases such as phenylketonuria (PKU) or sickle cell disease. Assuming that Mr. Johnson and Ms. Sanford have a legal right to refuse to be screened to determine if they are carriers, do they still have a moral right to do so? Do they also have a right to refuse to let their offspring be screened?

IN VITRO FERTILIZATION AND SURROGATE MOTHERHOOD

Some of the most exotic and controversial developments in biomedical ethics involve our new-found capacity to manipulate the human egg and sperm cells in the laboratory, in ways that permit the actual creation of human life in the "test tube."[16] These technologies were originally designed to help couples suffering from certain kinds of female infertility, such as blockage of the oviduct, to bypass the cause of the infertility. They involve removal of one or more egg cells from the ovary, followed by fertilization mechanically in the clinic.

Some of the ethical problems have actually been with us for a long time. These newer technologies replicate what we have long been able to do through artificial insemination. Some, especially within the Roman Catholic tradition, consider such manipulations "artificial," which is taken to mean "immoral."[17] Others see the moral issues not so much in the physical manipulation of the gametes per se but in the risks of injury that are involved. Still others are concerned primarily about the more exotic uses of these technologies, which would permit conception of a child in ways that involve more than a married couple: first through artificial insemination by a donor and, more recently, through surrogate motherhood and schemes whereby a woman who wanted to bear a child that was genetically hers could engage another woman to carry the fetus through the pregnancy. The following case illustrates the issues.

CASE 11-4

Surrogate Motherhood: The Case of Baby M

Mary Beth Whitehead and her husband Rick Whitehead lived in New Jersey with their two children. In 1984, Mary Beth responded to an advertisement placed in a local newspaper asking for women who would like to help couples who are unable to have children themselves. Ms. Whitehead responded to the advertisement and was matched-up by the New York based Infertility Center with Elizabeth and William Stern. The Sterns, who also lived in New Jersey, wanted very badly to have a child of their own. Mrs. Stern had multiple sclerosis and had been advised that pregnancy could be medically dangerous for her. The Sterns and Ms. Whitehead signed a contract that stipulated that Mary Beth Whitehead would be artificially inseminated with William Stern's sperm and that, after the birth of the resulting child, the Sterns would obtain custody and parental rights while Ms. Whitehead would be paid $10,000 in compensation.

The Sterns and the Whiteheads remained on relatively good terms through-out the pregnancy. However, shortly before she was due to give birth, Ms. Whitehead began to have serious doubts about the agreement. In her own words, she began "to resent the idea that [Elizabeth Stern] had rented my body to produce a child."[18] On March 27, 1986, Mary Beth Whitehead gave birth to a baby girl. She immediately began to bond with the child and named her Sara. The Sterns were equally thrilled to see the beautiful healthy baby at the hospital and named her Melissa.

Several days later, when Ms. Whitehead and Sara/Melissa were ready to leave the hospital, the Sterns took Sara/Melissa home with them. Mary Beth Whitehead went home that night in great emotional distress and decided that she wanted Sara back. She went the next day to the Sterns and asked if she could take Sara/Melissa for a week to have some time with her. The Sterns agreed and Sara/Melissa went home with Ms. Whitehead. A little over a week later, the Sterns came to collect the baby but Mary Beth and Rick Whitehead had decided that they were going to keep Sara permanently. Elizabeth Stern demanded the child and William Stern broke into tears. Finally, they left Melissa with the Whiteheads.

A month later, the Sterns returned to the Whitehead house with a court order and police in tow. The police demanded that the Whiteheads hand over Melissa Stern, but they replied that the only baby in the house was named Sara Whitehead. There was some confusion during which the Whiteheads conferred with each other and decided that they should make a run for it. Rick Whitehead sneaked out of the house with Sara. The next day, the entire Whitehead family and Sara/Melissa fled to Ms. Whitehead's parent's house in Florida. Soon after, the police found them and took Melissa back to the Sterns. The battle for Sara/Melissa now moved from the homes of the two families to the courtrooms of New Jersey.

The Sterns wanted to ensure that they had permanent custody of Melissa so they initiated a court hearing. The Whiteheads challenged them, claiming that the baby should be brought up by her biological mother. The court called Sara/Melissa "Baby M" since neither Sara nor Melissa was acceptable to both parties. The trial went on for months and was subject to enormous media coverage. On March 31,

1987, exactly one year after Ms. Whitehead left the hospital and first parted with her baby, Judge Harvey Sorkow issued a ruling that granted the Sterns custody of Baby M and allowed Elizabeth Stern to legally adopt Baby M. This ruling amounted to a legal statement that Mary Beth was not the mother of Baby M.

The Whiteheads appealed the court's ruling to the New Jersey Supreme Court. On February 3, 1988, the court ruled that although the Sterns should maintain custody of Baby M, Mary Beth's parental rights cannot be terminated. The Supreme Court held that the surrogacy contract between Ms. Whitehead and the Sterns was not legally binding because a biological mother can only consent to give a child up for adoption after the child is born. This ruling allowed Mary Beth Whitehead the legal possibility of parental visitation rights. [19]

Today, Baby M goes by the name Melissa Stern. She is a successful university student who is thinking of studying to become a minister. She remarked to one journalist that it was very strange to have to study her own case in an ethics class.[20] When she turned eighteen several years ago, she chose to formally adopt Elizabeth Stern as her mother.

COMMENTARY

The Whiteheads and Sterns were in the middle of some of the most controversial and complex moral issues in health care today. Like artificial insemination for a previous generation, surrogate motherhood raises issues of whether it is unethical to manipulate the conception process and whether there is an "artificiality" about it that makes it unethical.

Mary Beth Whitehead was inseminated artificially with sperm from Bill Stern so the issues of manipulating the gametes were similar to the classic artificial insemination cases. Had Mrs. Stern provided the egg cell for an IVF, another layer of controversy would have been added. IVF is ethically even more complex. Especially in the early days, there were serious questions of the risk to the offspring as well as to the woman. Now many of the basic safety issues appear to have been resolved, but other questions remain.

For the Whiteheads and the Sterns, the moral issues did not involve IVF but surrogacy. Surrogate motherhood raises many of the ethical issues of IVF for a couple within a marriage but adds additional problems to consider. Some surrogates are volunteers, often relatives of a woman who is unable to bear children herself. Sisters, mothers, and other relations offer to bear a child as an act of familial kindness. Other surrogates may also act out of charity, but if they are strangers to the infertile couple, it seems only fair for the surrogate to be compensated, at least for medical expenses. Most assume that it is also reasonable to compensate for the time and inconvenience involved. Some states have considered a policy of prohibiting paid surrogacies, while permitting those that are voluntary. What would be different if Mary Beth Whitehead had been a volunteer surrogate rather than a paid one?

One of the central concerns with surrogacy is the disruption of traditional patterns of marriage and family. Three separate functions are often identified: contribution of the genetic information, gestation, and nurturing. In most cases of childbirth, all three are provided by the same woman who is unquestionably the mother. In some cases of surrogacy, such as that of Mary Beth Whitehead, a woman engaged as a surrogate who initially commits to gestating an infant plans to turn over the infant to another set of parents. Sometimes, as in this case, the male has provided the sperm while the surrogate mother provides the egg cell. In other cases, the egg can come from the woman who expects to receive the infant from the surrogate mother. An embryo can be created in vitro (in the laboratory) for purposes of implantation. What difference would it have made in this case if Mary Beth Whitehead had been carrying a fetus that was genetically derived from both Mrs. Stern and her husband?

When Mary Beth Whitehead experienced her pregnancy, the emotional experience, to her surprise, led to bonding that she had not anticipated. In such cases, should the surrogate be able to retain custody of the infant she bore or is the initial promise to return the infant to the couple that conceived the child morally binding? Would it make a difference whether the surrogate mother or the woman who was initially planning to be the nurturing mother provided the egg?

An underlying argument among those who are critical of surrogate motherhood is that women cannot be expected to anticipate the psychological and physiological effects of pregnancy and therefore should not be bound by contracts or promises made prior to the pregnancy. Even if a woman agrees in advance to give up the infant at the end of the pregnancy, according to these critics, she cannot be bound by such a commitment.

Defenders of surrogacy contracts, however, claim that this, in effect, reduces women to second class status. The argument suggests that because of psychology and physiology unique to women, at least in this one area they cannot be permitted to make binding contracts the way male adults can. Does Mary Beth Whitehead's claim that she did not anticipate that she would bond with the fetus she was carrying provide a basis for permitting surrogate mother's the right to negate surrogacy contracts? Should Mr. Stern have to engage in a custody battle with the surrogate mother to determine who should have custody of the resulting child or should these matters be decided by the terms of the initial contract?

PREIMPLANTATION DIAGNOSIS

Once the idea of genetic testing emerged, people began thinking about choosing to maintain pregnancies based on that information. With the development of IVF, determining the genetic makeup of the embryro prior to implantation became a goal of some in the new field of birth technologies. Removing a small sample to analyze for the presence of certain genes became possible.

This technique, known as preimplantation genetic diagnosis (PGD), has raised many ethical issues. Which genetic characteristics justify decisions to reject or select an embryo has become a question of great importance, as we see in the following case.

CASE 11-5

Embryo Biopsy

It was only a few months after an IVF procedure was approved at Midwest Medical Center that a proposal was presented to the Ethics Committee for discussion and approval of a new procedure that would expand on IVF. The procedure, referred to as embryo biopsy, allows for PGD for simple gene defects such as Huntington disease and cystic fibrosis (CF) in embryos.[21] For couples who have had a CF child in the past and are worried about having another, physicians could offer standard IVF protocol with the following additional steps. The sample used to infer genetic composition includes polar bodies removed on day one after fertilization and one or two blastomeres on day three of cleavage-stage embryo development (the six- to eight-cell stage).[22] The embryos that do not have the defect would be implanted in the mother's womb ensuring that their child or children would not have the gene nor be able to pass the gene on to their children.

Dr. Thomas Sobeira, a member of the ethics committee, had deep concerns about this proposal for "embryo biopsy." He was concerned about how accurate the test was and the potential for misdiagnosis. Even though the prevention of CF seemed an admirable goal, he was also concerned about opening the door to separating fetuses we wish to develop from those we wish to discontinue. In addition, a child with CF is not doomed to death in infancy. The median age for survival for CF patients is 36.8 years and there is no intellectual or behavioral impairment. Gene therapy offers great promise for treatment. In the meantime, however, the child is likely to be chronically ill and require repeated hospitalizations.

COMMENTARY

In addition to the moral issues raised by IVF, Dr. Sobeira must deal with another issue: qualitative judgment in choosing which embryos to implant and which to discard. The process of embryo biopsy and assessment also poses a potential additional risk to the fetus that is implanted, beyond the risks of the IVF itself. In Case 11-4, however, even though some embryos might be discarded, the selection process seemed to be more nearly random. No judgment was made based on actual genetic testing to determine which embryos were "better." In this case, the selection will be a function of someone's judgment about the quality of the life to be lived.

Even though in the case of CF, it seems that choosing between those embryos with and without the disease would be uncontroversial, the general idea of qualitative selection could be very controversial. The potential already exists to select embryos of a particular sex. Soon it could be possible to biopsy and select for traits most would consider trivial such as hair color, height, or color-blindness. Does permitting biopsy and selection to avoid CF start Dr. Sobeira down the road to qualitative evaluation and selection of embryos? Is that a road he should avoid?

GENE THERAPY

The future of innovative genetic technologies is in interventions undertaken intentionally to change the genetic code. Some of these changes will occur in human gene therapy.[23] If a gene is missing, for example, a gene that is responsible for producing a necessary enzyme, incorporating that gene can, at least in theory, correct the deficiency. One such disease is ADA deficiency, the disease that causes severe combined immunodeficiency such as that of children who have lived their early lives in "bubbles" to protect them from infection. Other efforts are attempting to use gene therapy to switch off the gene for Huntington disease and to treat the blood disorder thalassemia, CF, sickle cell disease, HIV, and some cancers.[24]

Several technologies are potentially available to transmit genetic material. The use of viruses to pick up and transmit genetic material into cells is one such technology. For some diseases, the transfer of recombined or "recombinant" DNA can take place outside the body by removing bone marrow, making the transfer in the laboratory, and then reimplanting the modified marrow. Among the issues raised by these new technologies are the potential risks of the processes themselves.[25] If the virus transfers the genetic material incorrectly or to the wrong cells, there is the potential for serious harm. For patients with life-threatening illness such as ADA deficiency the risks may be worth it, but some recombinant DNA transfer will eventually be considered for more minor medical problems, and it is not only the sick patients who could be affected by the genetic changes.

The direct risks are not the only concern raised by these technologies. Some changes that at first appear to be beneficial may later in life produce indirect effects that are unattractive. Some are concerned that the remaking of the human genetic code will change the underlying fabric of the culture. While we used to assume that the nature of the human was fixed permanently, increasingly, it may be seen as temporary and subject to human manipulation. We are remanufacturing ourselves.

The same technologies that permit adding a critical missing enzyme might permit adding additional production of some substances. In a competitive world, genetic engineering may eventually permit improvement on the normal average functioning of humans so that users of the technologies get "unnatural" advantages. If everyone else begins using the technologies to gain an advantage, nonusers will be at a disadvantage much like an athlete competing against opponents who are on steroids.

Similar technologies permit modifying animal or plant species, in some cases making possible production of new drugs and biologicals. In the following cases, health professionals confront the ethical implications of gene modification and transfer in an attempt to produce outside the human body a new biological product that might have therapeutic uses. In this case, the interests of a critical ill patient clash with the orderly process of doing scientific research and development.

CASE 11-6

Using Genes to Treat Brain Cancer

A California woman, whose name has been kept confidential, was suffering from a glioblastoma, a fatal, rapidly growing form of brain cancer.[26] She had had two previous brain operations, the most recent of which involved the removal of her entire right temporal lobe. She had also undergone three rounds of chemotherapy, radiation treatment, and an experimental monoclonal antibody treatment. All have failed to improve her situation. Her doctors had given her just weeks to live.

Dr. Ivor Royston of the San Diego Regional Cancer Center asked the NIH Recombinant DNA Advisory Committee for a "compassionate waiver" that would allow him to treat this woman with an unapproved, experimental gene therapy. A compassionate use waiver would permit the use of an experimental agent outside the normal research protocol and approval process.

Dr. Royston's plan was to inject the woman with her own cells altered genetically to contain interleukin 2 in an attempt to stimulate the woman's immune response to the cancer. This would require that the woman be injected with the cells in progressively larger doses every two weeks.

At the time of the proposal to treat this woman, the United States Government had a Recombinant DNA Advisory Committee (RAC), which had to review and approve all therapeutic use of gene therapy involving recombination of genetic DNA. It had not reviewed this procedure.

Royston and the woman's husband had obtained a review from the Food and Drug Administration. It had concluded that the therapy was, in all likelihood, not harmful. There was, however, no evidence that the therapy would be effective. It had not been proven effective on animals and had never before been attempted in humans.

In an ideal world in which a patient had time to wait for the orderly development of a new drug or biological product, a patient would wait for testing in nonhuman animals as well as humans. This woman did not have that time to wait.

Dr. Bernadine Healy, then the Director of the National Institutes of Health, had the authority to make the final decision. She originally rejected the request.

Then Senator Tom Harkin of Iowa requested that the NIH create a system whereby the RAC could expedite compassionate use hearings for patients dying of terminal diseases. Senator Harkin wrote to Healy requesting that she create guidelines for expedited hearings in special cases.

Dr. Healy had denied his request stating that there was simply not enough information available on this therapy to justify its use, even as a compassionate exemption. She also stated that since many patients would qualify for this consideration, it would be impossible to decide which should be granted waivers. Healy later reversed her decision citing the woman's short life expectancy.

This reversal prompted much speculation and anger among members of the RAC who were not consulted before Healy ultimately granted the exemption. Members of the RAC expressed concern that such a precedent, involving the premature use of experimental therapies, was potentially dangerous. The Committee members speculated about Senator Harkin's role in the decision noting that he heads the Senate subcommittee on appropriations, which allocates funds for the NIH. Harkin was initially made aware of the woman's plight by her husband, whose sister had worked on Harkin's successful senatorial campaign.

COMMENTARY

This political confrontation, which occurred in 1993, was one of the first attempts to use genetic modification therapeutically. It differed from later developments in that it did not use gene transfer to change the human genetic code. It merely exposed human cells that had been removed from the body to genetic manipulation in order to turn them into a kind of biological medicine. It used genetic engineering to attach the interleukin 2 molecule to the cells with the hope that the interleukin could thereby enter the body and establish an immune response.

The highly unusual effort to obtain a compassionate use exemption was an attempt to bypass the normal methodical channels of medical science in which data would accumulate slowly using studies in nonhuman animals and laboratory procedures and then gradually begin studies in humans testing for safety using small exposures followed by carefully planned and controlled attempts at therapy. Since these developments are under the control of the Food and Drug Administration, a special exemption would be required to use a new product in human therapy outside this careful, slow process.

Those who defended the woman's right of access offered libertarian arguments, claiming that an adequately informed adult, especially one who has a terminal illness and has tried all other available therapies, ought to be able to decide to take the risk. She had little to lose.

Therapies relying on recombinant DNA, however, introduce a new layer of controversy. The viral vectors used to recombine the genetic material could, in theory, produce effects other than the intended ones. Even though they would be used in carefully controlled environments, some worry that the vectors could get loose and affect other bodily processes or other people. There is a social dimension to the risk usually not present in other medical therapies.

In this case, Dr. Healy presented the RAC with the interim policy she devised for accommodating compassionate use requests until formal policy is adopted. The policy called for the NIH to respond in a timely manner to requests for compassionate use by gathering evidence on the safety of the procedure and on the particulars of the patient's case. All decisions would have to be approved by the FDA and the local IRB, but the RAC would not have to meet as a committee in order to rule on such requests.

At the RAC meeting on January 14, 1993, the vote was 9 to 3 with one abstention in favor of allowing compassionate use approvals.

NOTES

[1] Cohen, Cynthia B. "Reproductive Technologies: viii. Ethical Issues." In *Encyclopedia of Bioethics*. 3rd ed. Stephen G. Post, editor. New York: Macmillan Reference USA: Thomson/Gale; 2004, pp. 2298–2307; Hall, Mark A., Mary Anne Bobinski, and David Orentlicher. "Reproductive Rights and Genetic Technologies." In their *Health Care Law and Ethics*, 6th ed. New York: Aspect Publishers; 2003, pp. 663–781; Arras, John D. "Reproductive Technology." In *A Companion to Applied Ethics*. R. G. Frey and Christopher Heath Wellman, editors. Malden, MA: Blackwell Publishing, 2003, pp. 342–355.

[2] Murray, Robert F. "Genetic Counseling, Ethical Issues In." In *Encyclopedia of Bioethics*, 948–952; Matthews, Anne L. "Genetic Counseling." In *Encyclopedia of Ethical, Legal, Policy Issues in Biotechnology*, 2 vols. Thomas H. Murray and Maxwell J. Mehlman, editors. New York: John Wiley & Sons; 2000, pp. 342–352; Wright, Rollin M., John A. Balint, Ian H. Porter, and Wayne N. Shelton. "Ethical Issues in Genetic Research, Testing, Counseling, and Therapy." In *Advances in Bioethics: Bioethics for Medical Education*. Rem B. Edwards and E. Edwards Bittar, editors. Greenwich, CT: JAI Press; 1999: 171–213; Clarke, Angus. "Genetic Counseling." In *Principles of Health Care Ethics*. Richard E. Ashcroft, Angus Dawson, Heather Draper, and John R. McMillan, editors. Chichester, England: Wiley, 2007, pp. 427–434.

[3] Ford, Norman M. "Ethical Aspects of Prenatal Screening and Diagnosis." In: Magill, Gerard, ed. *Genetics and Ethics: An Interdisciplinary Study*. Saint Louis, MO: Saint Louis University Press, 2004, pp. 197–215; Juengst, Eric T. "Genetic Testing and Screening." In *Encyclopedia of Bioethics*, pp. 1007–1016.

[4] Bonnicksen, Andrea L. "Reproductive Technologies: Ix. In Vitro Fertilization and Embryo Transfer." In *Encyclopedia of Bioethics*, pp. 2307–2311; Lin, Olivia. "Rehabilitating Bioethics: Recontextualizing In Vitro Fertilization Outside Contractual Autonomy." *Duke Law Journal* 54 (November 2004):485–511; Schotsmans, Paul T. "In Vitro Fertilization and Ethics." In Henkten Have

and Bert Gordijn, eds. *Bioethics in a European Perspective.* Boston, MA: Kluwer Academic Publishers, 2001, pp. 295–308; Steinberg, Avraham. "In-Vitro Fertilization." In his *Encyclopedia of Jewish Medical Ethics: A Compilation of Jewish Medical Law on all Topics of Medical Interest.* Nanuet, NY: Feldheim Publishers; 2003, pp. 571–586.

5 Gostin, Larry, editor. *Surrogate Motherhood: Politics and Privacy.* Bloomington, IN: Indiana University Press, 1990; Lincoln, David H. "Surrogate Motherhood." In *Life and Death Responsibilities in Jewish Biomedical Ethics.* Aaron L. Mackler, editor. New York: The Louis Finkelstein Institute, The Jewish Theological Seminary of America; 2000, pp. 188–192; Tong, Rosemarie. "Surrogate Motherhood." In *A Companion to Applied Ethics.* Malden, MA: Blackwell Publishing, 2003, pp. 369–381.

6 Resnik, David B. "Genetic Engineering, Human." In *Encyclopedia of Bioethics*, 959–966; Brock, Dan W. "Genetic Engineering." In *A Companion to Applied Ethics*, pp. 356–365; Gert, Bernard. "Genetic Engineering." In *Encyclopedia of Ethics*, 2nd ed. Lawrence C. Becker and Charlotte B. Becker, editors. New York: Routledge, 2001, pp. 602–606.

7 Bruce L. Levine, Laurent M. Humeau, Jean Boyer, Rob-Roy MacGregor, Tessio Rebello, Xiaobin Lu, Gwendolyn K. Binder, Vladimir Slepushkin, Franck Lemiale, John R. Mascola, Frederic D. Bushman, Boro Dropulic, and Carl H. June. "Gene Transfer in Humans Using a Conditionally Replicating Lentiviral Vector." *PNAS* 103 (November 14, 2006):17372-17377.

8 Baillie, Harold W. "Genetic Engineering and Our Human Nature." In *Genetic Prospects: Essays on Biotechnology, Ethics, and Public Policy.* Verna V.Gehring, editor. Lanham, MD: Rowman and Littlefield Publishers; 2003, pp. 43–50.

9 President's Commission for the Study of Ethical Problems in Medicine and Biomedical and Behavioral Research. *Screening and Counseling for Genetic Conditions: The Ethical, Social, and Legal Implications of Genetic Screening, Counseling, and Education Programs.* Washington, DC: U.S. Government Printing Office, 1983

10 For general information about HNPCC the NIH website provides a good introduction. See http://ghr.nlm.nih.gov/condition=hereditarynonpolyposiscolorectalcancer/.

Another genetic form of colon cancer resulting from familial adenomatous polyposis (FAP) also poses similar questions about preimplantation genetic diagnosis and selective abortion, but raises somewhat different genetic and clinical issues. See http://ghr.nlm.nih.gov/condition=familialadenomatouspolyposis. For references to scientific papers see http://www.cancer.gov/cancertopics/pdq/genetics/colorectal/HealthProfessional/page5#Section_468.

11 For details of the characteristics of achondroplastic dwarfism see the National Institutes of Heatlh website at http://ghr.nlm.nih.gov/condition=achondroplasia (accessed July 17, 2007).

12 Sanghavi, Darshap. "Wanting Babies Like Themselves, Some Parents Choose Genetic Defects." *The New York Times*, Dec. 5, 2006. [available on the Internet at http://www.nytimes.com/2006/12/05/health/05essa.html?ex=1184817600&en=afb46fff1fcf3410&ei=5070, accessed July 18, 2007.

13 World Health Organization (WHO), *Proposed International Guidelines on Ethical Issues in Medical Genetics and Genetic Services*, Geneva, December 15 and 16, 1997, available on the Internet at: http://whqlibdoc.who.int/hq/1998/WHO_HGN_GL_ETH_98.1.pdf (accessed Oct. 16, 2007).

14 Avard, Denise, Linda Kharaboyan, and Bartha Knoppers. "Newborn Screening for Sickle Cell Disease: Socio-Ethical Implications." In *First Do No Harm: Law, Ethics and Healthcare*. Sheila McLean, editor. Aldershot, England ; Burlington, VT: Ashgate, 2006, p. 493 [pp. 493–507].

15 NIH Consensus Development Program, *Newborn Screening for Sickle Cell Disease and Other Hemoglobinopathies: National Institutes of Health Consensus Development Conference Statement*, April 6–8, 1987, available on the Internet at http://www.ncbi.nlm.nih.gov/books/bv.fcgi?rid=hstat4.section.3076, accessed October 16, 2007.

16 For the classic statement of the ethical issues see Ramsey, Paul. *Fabricated Man*. New Haven, CT: Yale University Press, 1970. For recent discussions see Robertson, John A. *Children of Choice: Freedom and the New Reproductive Technologies* Princeton, NJ: Princeton University Press, 1994; President's Council on Bioethics. *Reproduction & Responsibility: The Regulation of New Biotechnologies*. Washington, DC: The Council, 2004; and Murray, Thomas. "Limits to Reproductive Liberty." In *Principles of Health Care Ethics*, pp. 409–413.

17 Sacred Congregation for the Doctrine of the Faith. "Instruction on Respect for Human Life in Its Origin and on the Dignity of Procreation." *Origins* 16 (No. 40, March 19, 1987):698–711.

18 Whitehead, Mary Beth and Schwartz-Nobel, Loretta. "My Fight for Baby M." *Family Circle* 102 (No. 3, February 1989):100–102, 175–178.

19 In *re* Baby M. 109 N.J. 396, 537 A.2d 1277 (1988).

20 Anon. "Now It's Melissa's Time," *New Jersey Monthly*, March 3, 2007, retrieved from the World Wide Web on July 18, 2007 at http://www.njmonthly.com/issues/2007/03-Mar/babym.htm.

21 Verlinsky, Y., J. Cohen, S. Munne, L. Gianaroli, J. L. Simpson, A. P. Ferrareti, et al. "Over a Decade Experience with Preimplantation Genetic Diagnosis: A Multicenter Report." *Fertility and Sterility* 82 (2004):292–294.

22 S. J. McArthur, D. Leigh, J. T. Marshall, K. A. de Boer, R. P. Jansen. "Pregnancies and Live Births after Trophectoderm Biopsy and Preimplantation Genetic Testing of Human Blastocysts." *Fertility and Sterility* 84 (6, 2005):1628–1636.

23 President's Council on Bioethics. *Reproduction & Responsibility*, pp. 105–119.

24 See http://www.ornl.gov/sci/techresources/Human_Genome/medicine/genetherapy.shtml#status, accessed November 7, 2006.

25 For additional information on the ethics of genetic engineering see Wivel, Nelson A. and Walters LeRoy. "Germ-Line Gene Modification and Disease Prevention: Some Medical and Ethical Perspectives." *Science*, 262 (22 October 1993):533–538; Medical Research Council of Canada. *Guidelines for Research on Somatic Cell Gene Therapy in Humans*. Ottawa: Minister of Supply and Services, 1990; John C. Fletcher and W. French Anderson. "Germ-Line Gene Therapy: A New Stage of Debate." *Law, Medicine & Health Care* 30 (1–2, Spring/Summer 1992):26–39; and Eric T. Juengst and Hannah Grankvist. "Ethical Issues in

Human Gene Transfer: A Historical Overview." In *Principles of Health Care Ethics*, pp. 789–796.

26 This case is based in part on the minutes of the Recombinant DNA Advisory Committee. Department of Health and Human Services, National Institutes of Health, Recombinant DNA Advisory Committee, Minutes of Meeting, January 14, 1993. Minutes are available on the Internet at http://www4.od.nih.gov/oba/rac/minutes/193rac.pdf, accessed July 18, 2007.

CHAPTER 12

✦

Mental Health and Behavior Control

Psychiatry and other forms of study and modification of human behavior raise many ethical problems in the health professions.[1] When we say that many people *suffer* from behavior disorders, we imply that they are harmed or injured by these conditions. To the extent that care givers can assist in relieving that suffering or in modifying undesired behaviors, the traditional ethics of health care professions that focuses on doing what will benefit the patient, requires attempting to intervene. At the same time, we may lack consensus on whether the condition is really one requiring intervention. In the case of organically based illnesses we can normally ask the patient or surrogate whether he or she wants help in attempting to change the condition. In the case of behavioral problems, however, there is often doubt whether the patient is capable of making an informed and rational choice. It is the "consenting organ" itself that may be "diseased." If we rely on surrogates, significant conflicts of interest may exist between the surrogate decision-maker and the patient. The behavior of the patient may not bother the patient but can create inconvenience or embarrassment to the surrogate. Some of the most difficult ethical problems in the health care professions can arise in mental health and the behavioral sciences. In this chapter we look at cases raising these problems.

The first problem in dealing with mental health is with the concept of mental health itself.[2] Traditionally, many mentally abnormal behaviors have been viewed as problems of religion or of criminality. Only in the twentieth century did we begin to view these behaviors within the medical model. In the first section of this chapter, we look at a case that raises the issue of the concept of mental health and whether mental problems should be deemed "deviant behavior choices" or "medical problems."

In the second section, we take up one of the classical ethical problems in the mental health professions—whether patients with mental health problems should be viewed as having sufficient autonomy that they can be asked to consent or refuse consent to treatment the way we would for organic medical treatments. The third section deals with the conflicts of interests that arise between the mental health patient and other parties—other patients, families, work colleagues, or other members of the society. The problems here involve confidentiality, loyalty to the patient, and the trade-offs between patient interests and those of the others potentially affected by the patient's behavior.

Finally, in the fourth section of this chapter, we focus on a controversial type of therapy—aversion therapy.

THE CONCEPT OF MENTAL HEALTH

Human behavior is complex. It has been interpreted over the centuries in many different ways.[3] In traditional religious world views, members of the community who manifest unusual or strange behaviors might be thought to have been possessed by demons or to have been the victims of magical spells. We can say that the behavior is interpreted as religiously influenced deviance. The same behavior in another culture, also in a religious framework, might be interpreted as being sinful—as a violation of the will of God. While both are religious cultures, there is an important difference. While the view that sees the behavior as the result of demon possession, or spells, might imply that the behavior was not the "fault" of the individual (who could be called a "victim"), the behavior of the "sinner" is usually seen as somehow within the voluntary control of the actor.

In other cultures, the behavior may be seen as simply an unusual lifestyle choice, not carrying any of the religious implications. Such behaviors may be interpreted as unusual, but acceptable. However, they may be seen as socially unacceptable and in need of control. Especially, if they harm others, they may be interpreted within a criminal model in which the behavior is illegal and worthy of social sanction.[4]

In still other interpretations, the behavior is seen in what is called a "medical model." According to this now-dominant view, many unusual behaviors are believed to be caused by some medical condition. The convulsions we associate with epilepsy are now thought to have an organic medical cause; they are not the result of demon possession, the wrath of God, or sinful lifestyle. If a behavior is believed to have an organic cause, it still remains a question whether that behavior is acceptable or should be the target of efforts to change it. Most would agree that even though epilepsy has an organic cause, it still produces undesirable consequences for the person who has epilepsy. For other conditions, controversy rages over whether the behavior is merely unusual, but acceptable, or should be modified. Many people increasingly view the gay lifestyle as having a biochemical or genetic cause. Some conclude that, once one assumes such a basis for the behavior, one should recognize that there is no reason to attempt to change it. Others, while acknowledging the organic cause, still believe there is something wrong or dysfunctional or unpleasant about the behavior and, like epilepsy, try to use pharmacological or other medical means to try to change it. This latter group would consider the gay lifestyle a "disease" while the former would not.

While we have fully medicalized some conditions such as epilepsy that were once thought of in other terms, other behaviors are less clearly medical. Alcoholism, for instance, is believed by some to be a disease, while others continue to see it as a sin. Still others may interpret it as nothing more than a lifestyle choice. The medicalization of human behavior has very important and controversial implications.[5] The choice of a "model" for interpretation of behavior does important work. It conveys an implied understanding of the source of the behavior, whether one is "responsible" for it, what experts or authorities should be consulted to deal with the behavior, and what interventions are to be used in attempting to modify the behavior.

The "medical model" in its pure form implies that there is an important "medical" (usually organic) element in the cause of the behavior.[6] It often implies that the individual manifesting the behavior is not volitionally responsible for it and is thus exempted from blame. It also implies that a medical professional is an appropriate expert for dealing with the behavior if one wants to change it. Many of the most interesting and difficult ethical problems for those working in mental health arise at the point of classifying the patient's behavior as fitting in the medical model. The following case shows how health professionals may find themselves dealing with patients whose classification as medical is controversial.

═══════════ **CASE 12-1** ═══════════

Guilt over Suicidal Thoughts

Lilly Wong was a 44-year-old married woman of Chinese American heritage. She had been seeing psychiatrist Gilbert DeVita now for a month, attempting to resolve intense feelings of guilt related to her persistent suicidal thoughts. She acknowledged to Dr. DeVita that for the past two years she had had thoughts of ending her life. She had developed deep feelings that included her more and more firm resolve to commit suicide, but simultaneously felt very guilty that she would be abandoning her responsibilities to her family and her community were she to do so.

Dr. DeVita had learned over the course of the four sessions he had had with her that she was married to a Caucasian American with a history of alcoholism and abuse of his wife. Most of the abuse was mental. He criticized her constantly, complaining about the way she kept house and prepared meals. Dr. DeVita had gotten her to reveal that on at least two occasions he had struck her; once, a year ago, it had resulted in a trip to the hospital emergency room. That was the most recent physical attack that Dr. DeVita was able to elicit from Ms. Wong.

Over the years Ms. Wong had studied the history of Chinese thought and the culture of her parents who had immigrated from China when Ms. Wong was a child. This Chinese cultural history, with its Confucian influences, was the closest thing Ms. Wong had to a religion. From it she had come to understand that those in her heritage had sometimes chosen suicide as a way to end a difficult life situation. She had decided that her marriage was hopeless and that ending her life was her way out. At the same time, from her American culture she had absorbed the idea that suicide was immoral and was in her words, "running away from the problem."

Dr. DeVita sympathized with Ms. Wong's plight, but had real doubts about the wisdom of her chosen course. He was in a difficult position if she was asking him to help her overcome her guilt in order to free herself from the constraints that would help her pursue the course she had chosen. At the same time, he was not sure what his role should be. He knew that spousal abuse could be reported, but Ms. Wong pleaded that he not disclose those problems. The physical aspects of the abuse had ceased, at least for the time being, and the mental cruelty was, in her view, not something she wanted to address. Dr. DeVita offered to begin a course of therapy to overcome what he took to be a depression related to her feeling of hopelessness in her marriage. She asked some questions as if she were interested in that approach, but then quickly said that that was not what she wanted. Should Dr. DeVita attempt to treat her depression, perhaps having Ms. Wong committed as dangerous to herself, should he report the abuse and attempt to have her husband confronted, or should he help Ms. Wong overcome her guilt as she is asking?

COMMENTARY

Ms. Wong is under great tension with several options available to her as well as several explanations of her problems. The most straightforward response of Dr. DeVita might be to use his psychiatric skills to help Ms. Wong get over her guilt feelings so that she can continue in her plan to commit suicide. This approach might view her guilt as the psychiatric problem. Most psychiatrists would not accept this strategy, however. Another resolution would be to focus on her suicidal ideation as the problem. Dr. DeVita might use his psychiatric skills to attempt to overcome her desire to end her life and adjust to her life situation. He might also attempt to intervene to advance another option: getting Ms. Wong out of a destructive and possibly dangerous marriage. Each of these approaches identifies some element of the situation as the "problem" to be solved, some strategy for resolving the tension.

Dr. DeVita might also ask whether Ms. Wong's problem is a medical one or, alternatively, whether her problem is religious, cultural, or moral. Deciding she is mentally ill is a complex and controversial decision. The concepts of illness and disease are more complex than many people realize. Sometimes the term *disease* is used to refer strictly to the objective manifestations while *illness* is used to refer to the psychological components of suffering, stress, and *dis*-ease. The problem arises, however, when we realize that some conditions that are very distressing have no discernable objective, organic cause. To make matters more complicated, even though they appear to have no objective, organic cause, they may nevertheless respond to medication, an operation, or other medical intervention.

Imagine two people who have identical behavioral manifestations that are dissatisfying to care givers (and perhaps to the patient as well). In one case, the behavior may be related to a clear organic factor that seems like the cause; the patient may have some chemical imbalance making her depressed. In the other, the depression cannot be related to any organic element that can be said to cause it. For example, the patient may simply feel she is in a hopeless situation. Ms. Wong may have such feelings related to her unhappy marriage. If both depressions are the same in all relevant aspects—both distress the patient to the same extent—and if both are equally amenable to modification by the use of medication, is there any moral reason why the patients do not have an equal claim on the medication? Does the fact that the behavior has an apparent organic cause in one case make the use of medication more acceptable?

Calling a condition medical may have important implications. If a person is seen as having a significant medical problem, he or she is less likely to be blamed for the behavior. He will be seen as a "patient" to be treated by a psychiatrist, occupational therapist, or social worker. Medication may be more easily justified. The causal force that makes the patient depressed will be seen as organic or psychological rather than merely a persistent unhappiness or as resulting from some external source.

A person's behavior will be seen as "medical" if its cause is some organic lesion or chemical imbalance, especially if the lesion or imbalance was not the result of what is taken to be a voluntary choice on the patient's part. If there is a brain lesion or a tumor causing abnormal hormonal secretions that cause the peculiar behavior, it is unreasonable to blame the person. Moreover, what the patient needs will be seen as within the medical realm. A health care professional who has specialized knowledge capable of addressing the problems will be seen as the appropriate expert.

Classifying the individual's behavior within the medical model will be seen by some not only as mistaken but also as offensive. If, for example, the individual is interpreted as rebelling against an immorally oppressive society or bad marriage, someone who labels him or her as having a "disease" will be seen as ignoring the real cause of the patient's condition—feelings that could be interpreted as morally appropriate rebellion. If the patient is perceived as being punished by God or as having inherited bad karma from a previous life, then the behavior will be seen in an entirely different causal framework. Persons may be held accountable for their actions: either praised for rejecting societal oppression or blamed for past deeds that condemned him or her to the present fate. Different kinds of expertise will be seen as appropriate: the clergy or the police, perhaps. If the individual is seen as responding appropriately to an oppressive society, perhaps no professional expertise will be seen as needed at all. In fact, he or she could be viewed as a saint, or martyr, or hero. (Consider whether Gandhi, Malcolm X, Jesus, or Stalin could be classified as mentally ill.)

One issue raised by this case is what it takes for a person to be classified as a patient, as one in need of the services of health care professionals. One condition seems to be that something bad is happening. Only if the patient's behavior is interpreted as inappropriate and negative will he or she be seen as in need of therapy. But more than that will be needed. The behavior usually must be seen as having a significant organic (or psychological) component. If evil spirits, divine forces, or freely chosen lifestyle causes them to act the way they are acting, the behavior will be seen as less likely to fit the medical model. If there is believed to be a significant medical (organic–psychological) component causing the behavior, then it is more likely that those with the appropriate medical or psychological expertise will be seen as having something to offer. Finally, if the behavior is beyond these persons' control (even if perhaps he or she was in some way originally responsible for the events that led to it), it is less likely they will be seen as blameworthy.

Even if Dr. DeVita decides that Ms. Wong's situation justifies the attention of a psychiatrist, he will still face the question of what the treatment objective should be. Accepting Ms. Wong's formulation of needing help to overcome her guilt is not the only goal Dr. DeVita may choose to pursue. He might also strive to help her grow to accept her situation or, more plausibly, grow to realize that she may find life more worth living if she changes her situation perhaps by leaving her husband. The issue is whether the psychiatrist's role includes picking among these treatment objectives.

MENTAL ILLNESS AND AUTONOMOUS BEHAVIOR

Once we have reached agreement that the patient's condition is appropriately classified as a medical or health problem and therefore the appropriate concern of those in the mental health profession, the next issue to be confronted is whether the patient can be sufficiently autonomous to consent or refuse consent for medical treatment.

As we discussed in Chapter 6, autonomy is both a psychological and a moral concept. One is said to be *psychologically* autonomous if one has substantial capacity to form a life plan and make choices in accord with it. Individual actions are autonomous to the extent that they are made in accord with such a life plan. Seen in this light, it becomes apparent that no person and no personal action can be said to be totally autonomous. Individual actions can be more or less autonomous, depending on the degree to which the individual generates a decision based on his or her life plan.

Autonomy is also a *moral* concept. We saw in Chapter 6 that respect for autonomy as a moral principle states that actions are morally right to the extent that they respect the autonomous choices of individuals. We saw that informed consent as a moral requirement is grounded largely in the moral principle of autonomy.

In order for respect for autonomy to come into play, however, the individual must be deemed to be a substantially autonomous agent. For many patients this decision is relatively easy. Minors generally are presumed not to have sufficient autonomy to make their own medical choices, except in special circumstance. In special cases minors may be found to be mature and granted both the moral and legal right to consent to treatment on their own.[7] Some adults are so severely retarded or comatose that it is obvious they also are not significantly autonomous agents. However, most adults are sufficiently autonomous that they will clearly be treated as autonomous for purposes of making medical decisions. Even some people who are seeking mental health services are autonomous. The courts have determined that it is possible that a patient might be committed for mental treatment and still sufficiently autonomous that he or she is deemed mentally competent for purposes of consenting to or refusing treatment.[8] This is particularly true for certain critical medical treatments including electroconvulsive therapy.[9]

While autonomy is a moral and psychological category, competence is a legal category. Only a court can make a legal finding that a patient is incompetent to consent or refuse consent for treatment.

Nevertheless, a significant number of patients receiving mental health services present serious problems at the borders of autonomy. For these cases, autonomy must be viewed as a threshold concept.[10] A patient must be deemed either sufficiently autonomous that his or her own judgments will be accepted or as below the threshold of sufficient autonomy, in which case some surrogate will have to be designated for that purpose. The following cases pose problems at the borderline of assessing autonomy in mental health treatment.

CASE 12-2

"Ain't Nobody Gonna Cut on My Head"

A 56-year-old farmer, Wilber Williams, accompanied by his wife, Nellie, consulted the Neurology Service of the Veterans Hospital because of memory difficulty. For two years the patient had experienced increasing trouble with the technical aspects of his work. More recently he had been talking about his brother, George, as if he were alive although he had died six years earlier. He identified his own age as 48 and the year as "1994...er, no, 2000." Examination revealed that the patient walked with a wide-based gait, a standard sign of brain pathology, and had a decreased cerebral function but was otherwise normal. The patient had no difficulty with simple coin problems and could repeat six digits.

Pleading pressing business, the patient declined hospitalization to determine the cause of his decreasing cerebral function. His wife tried to persuade him to enter the hospital, but when the physician suggested that she might assume guardianship of her husband through court action, she declined.

Six months later the patient's condition had worsened. Through the urging of the county agent, the patient had leased most of his farmland to his neighbors and now did no farm work. His gait had become so wide-based that acquaintances mistakenly thought him inebriated. He urinated in his pants about once a week but seemed not to care. He sat watching television all day but paid no attention to the program content.

A medical examination showed an apparently alert man without speech difficulty but with considerable mental deterioration. This time the patient gave his age as 38, the year as 1973, the president as Clinton, and the location as a drugstore in his home town. He failed to recognize the name George W. Bush, but upon hearing the name Dick Cheney, he spontaneously volunteered an opinion on the war in Iraq. The patient could not subtract 20 cents from a dollar but could name the number of nickels in a quarter He could recite the months of the year and could, upon request from his wife, give fairly long quotations from the Bible.

The resident and the attending physician urged hospitalization. They told the patient that they could evaluate him for treatable causes of mental deterioration and memory deficit. In view of his wide-based gait and urinary incontinence in association with dementia, it was likely he had occult hydrocephalus. It was explained to the couple that this disorder causes decreased mental abilities by interference with the absorption of cerebrospinal fluid. The mental deterioration in such patients is partially reversible, as in his case at the present time, or completely reversible, as in his case six months ago when first seen. The treatment was to place a plastic tube through the skull to drain the cerebrospinal fluid from the brain to the vascular system, which was explained to the patient with diagrams. The patient immediately rejected the operation, summarizing his thoughts with the words, "Ain't nobody gonna cut on my head."

The patient's wife again attempted to persuade the patient to accept hospitalization and, if tests confirmed the clinical impression, an operation. The attending physician argued to the wife that the patient did not have the mental competence to decide his own fate and that the wife should become the patient's legal guardian through court action and force his hospitalization. The wife politely but vigorously rejected this course of action, pointing out that in her family the husband made all important decisions. In addition, she expressed horror at forcing this kind of invasive procedure on her husband.

The resident and the attending physician differed in opinions at this point. The resident thought the patient should be followed in the outpatient clinic until he perhaps changed his mind. The resident pointed out that though the patient had decreased mental abilities, he still retained enough intelligence to decide his own fate. The attending physician wished for court action to make the patient the ward of one of his relatives or, if necessary, the temporary ward of the hospital and forcing hospitalization and therapy.

COMMENTARY

One of the firm conclusions of the moral debate about health care in the last half of the twentieth century is that competent patients have the moral and legal right to refuse any medical treatment, provided that treatment is offered for the patient's own good. We saw in Chapter 6 that the moral principle of respect for autonomy affirms the right of such patients to make their own choices even if they turn out to be bad decisions. In Chapter 18 we will see that this right to refuse treatment is widely believed to hold, even in cases in which the result of the refusal is likely to be death.

If Mr. Williams were clearly competent, those who defend the right of competent patients to refuse treatment would permit him to make unusual lifestyle choices even if those choices seem unattractive to the rest of us. However, were he clearly incompetent and unable to understand the nature of his choices, most would favor having a guardian appointed for him who would make choices that are in his interest. Mr. Williams, however, does not completely fit either category.

It makes little sense to talk of people being *completely* competent. Nevertheless, most adults are what can be called *substantially* competent; we treat them as if they were autonomous agents capable of understanding enough about the decisions they make and free enough to be said to be making free choices. However, most people are not totally incompetent either. Even children understand choices to some degree and have some capacity to choose freely, even if that freedom is quite constrained.

Mr. Williams appears to be some place in between. The moral issue that the physicians must confront is what moral offense is committed if they make a mistake about Mr. Williams' competency. Members of the healing professions traditionally have given highest priority to beneficence and nonmaleficence. They are committed to benefiting the patient (even if it sometimes involves violating the patient's autonomy). They should admit that if they presume the patient is incompetent when he really is competent, Mr. Williams will be further upset. That should count in their calculation of benefits and harms. Traditional physicians, for whom violations of autonomy are not morally critical, will therefore be inclined to presume incompetence and strive to benefit the patient even at the risk of acting paternalistically.

Physicians who incorporate a principle of respect for autonomy into their moral framework will have to be concerned about the possibility that such paternalistic action could violate the autonomy principle. For them the error of violating autonomy is worse morally than the error of failing to do what is best. Which kind of error should these physicians risk?

The question of mental competence sometimes arises outside of the context of medical treatment. In the following two cases, a person has offered to make a large gift to a stranger, an act of altruism that we might normally consider praiseworthy, but, if the one making the gift is under psychological constraints when making it, the nature of the gift can be called into question. It is possible that the mental condition of the donor makes the gift not truly voluntary. A psychiatrist here is asked to determine whether the gift should proceed.

CASE 12-3

The Jesus Christian Transplant: Brainwashed into Donating a Kidney?

Ash Falkingham, a 22-year-old man from Sydney, Australia, wanted to donate one of his kidneys to a stranger as an act of kindness. Legal complications prevented him from making the gift in Australia so he traveled to Toronto, Canada. Through the Internet he met Sandi Sabloff who needed a kidney transplant. One of her kidneys had failed completely and the second was failing as well.

Prior to coming to Canada, he had been interviewed by telephone by a committee. It included a psychiatrist, a social worker, and a bioethicist. On March 19, 2007, he arrived at Toronto General Hospital where the organ procurement was planned. He had further evaluation including meetings with the committee and medical compatibility testing. Following the screening, the hospital sent a letter to Ms. Sabloff indicating the transplant would occur on April 30.

Some days later the hospital began reassessing its decision. Mr. Falkingham's mother and stepfather, Kate and Nick Croft, had urged the hospital to review the case further. They claimed he had been unduly pressured into donating by the religious group, the Jesus Christians. It is a group that believes it can act on its Christian faith by donating a kidney to a stranger as an act of kindness. About half of the thirty members of the group have donated including its leader David McKay, who had donated one of his kidneys at the Mayo Clinic in 2003.

Mr. Falkingham's stepfather was quoted by the *National Post* newspaper as saying, "I'm certain that the pressure to donate a kidney is one of the many pressures involved in being a member of this group ... I would say it's a cult. I would say it's a sect. I would say it's a madness."[11] They claimed that the group coerced members into giving kidneys as a way of gaining publicity. Meanwhile, the group claims it is their way of expressing spiritual devotion and Christian charity. Mr. Falkingham said he was sent to a forensic psychiatrist with a specialty related to brainwashing and undue influence.

After some five weeks of waiting, the hospital announced that it was canceling the operation. Robert Bell, the CEO of University Health Network, the parent of Toronto General, was quoted by the Toronto-based *Globe and Mail* newspaper as saying, "We need to make sure the [donor] has informed consent for what this is all about, without any evidence of coercion and without any evidence of value consideration being given to the donation of the tissue."[12]

Is it appropriate for a health professional, a psychiatrist, social worker, or a bioethicist to block an altruistic action by an adult on grounds that he is being coerced or brainwashed?

CASE 12-4

A Kidney to Turn a Life Around

Adam Taylor, age thirty-three, had lived a tough life. He started drinking in high school and was an alcoholic by the time he was twenty-one. His marriage failed after two years. His wife won custody of his two children and now will not let him see them. He had been employed with various construction firms, but his alcoholism had cost him those well-paying jobs.

After a decade lost in the haze of drugs and alcohol, he entered a treatment program at age thirty-one. It began with a four-week inpatient program followed by intensive group, outpatient therapy. He had now been sober for eighteen months. He had joined the church of his girl friend and was working steadily at a local fast-food restaurant. His life was beginning to improve.

Mr. Taylor read in the local newspaper that the organ procurement organization (OPO) was accepting, on a trial basis, people who wanted to altruistically donate a kidney to a stranger. No one was actively recruited for the program, but the OPO would accept donor-initiated requests. Following a rigorous work-up, those who passed the medical and psychiatric screen would enter a hospital in the area to have a kidney removed. Those who called the OPO were told that the removal of the kidney was a major operation that would require about a week's hospitalization followed by a month's recovery. Healthy people should be able to function well for the rest of their lives with one kidney. The procedure is the same one now used routinely by family members who donate a kidney to a loved one. The only difference in the case of an altruistic donor to a stranger is that the kidney, once procured, would be allocated according to the standard algorithm for organs procured from newly deceased donors.

Mr. Taylor passed the medical screen. There was no sign of infectious disease related to his history of drug use. His psychiatric evaluation was conducted by Ann Buchanan, who was under contract with the OPO for such evaluations. She had to certify that the potential donor was mentally able to give an adequate consent to the donation and was not under undue influence. Dr. Buchanan spent more than the usual amount of time with Mr. Taylor because of his medical and lifestyle history. She came to believe that Mr. Taylor wished to donate a kidney as a symbol that he was leading a new life, that he had turned his life around. No doubt, he had serious problems in the past, but she could find no mental issues except for the historical problems. Her problem was whether she should certify that he was mentally fit to consent to donation when she recognized that this was his way of symbolizing a life change.

COMMENTARY

These two cases are similar not only in dealing with organ donation, but also in raising questions about the voluntariness of the donation. It is widely assumed that substantially autonomous persons (including most adults) have the right to offer a kidney to those who need one. Normally, this gift is given to a family member or close friend, but now the gift of a kidney is sometimes being accepted from strangers who will donate to someone chosen by the organ procurement organization based on the same allocation algorithm that is used when kidneys are obtained from those who have died. This is called "altruistic" or "stranger" donation. In order to donate, certain requirements must be met. The donor cannot receive compensation and must pass medical and psychological screens to assure that he or she understands what is involved and is making the gift voluntarily.

In both Case 12-3 and Case 12-4, donations to strangers are contemplated and the potential donors are undergoing the screening to see that their gift is adequately free and voluntary. Case 12-3 that of Ash Falkingham (his real name and information since this case has been made public), raises questions about whether the religious group, the Jesus Christians, has exerted undue pressure on him to the point that he is not making his gift freely. His parents claim he has been "brainwashed." Case 12-4, that of Adam Taylor (a fictional name referring to a real case that has been modified to provide anonymity), raises questions because his life has been so chaotic that the screeners wonder whether he is mentally stable enough to offer an adequately free consent.

"Brainwashing" is a complex and controversial issue.[13] The Jesus Christians claim to manifest Christian love in a radical way. A significant number, including their leader, have donated kidneys to strangers. No doubt, Mr. Falkingham feels some desire to conform to the norms of his religious group. Here the issue is whether such desire, especially when it is within an organized religious group, constitute such limits on human autonomous choice that he should be disqualified from organ donation.

Adam Taylor is not under pressure from any outside group. In fact, the organ procurement organization goes to some lengths to attempt to discourage him from donating. In his case, the issue is whether his life is sufficiently stable that he can make a substantially autonomous choice to make a gift of a body part that will irrevocably change his organ function capacity. In both cases, the standard belief is that adults with normal kidney function can exist quite well with only one kidney. The donors will suffer the usual risks of a major operation—including side effects of anesthesia and the postoperative pain. They will be restricted in their activity while they recover—for a period of a few weeks—but are believed to suffer no long-term consequences. If you were a member of the group screening these potential donors, would you agree that their actions would be sufficiently autonomous to accept their gifts?

MENTAL ILLNESS AND THIRD-PARTY INTERESTS

The decisions in the previous section of this chapter posed traditional medical ethical questions of the conflict between benefiting the patient and protecting the patient's autonomy to the extent that it exists. Patients receiving mental health treatment also pose the newer ethical problems of conflict between the interests of the patient and the interests of others in the society. These can arise in the context of confidentiality. (See Chapter 13 for additional cases involving the general problem of breaking confidence in order to protect the interests of others.) Additional conflicts between the interests of mental health patients and others include situations in which providing good care for the patient will necessarily jeopardize the care that can be given to others. Sometimes these problems arise because of the shortage of resources. These issues are sometimes reflected in controversies over insurance coverage. They can be especially controversial in cases involving mental health therapies. The following two cases are examples.

CASE 12-5

Posttraumatic Stress Disorder: Funding Therapy for a Preexisting Condition

James Schultz, a soldier who had served in Iraq, had been involved in a combat operation in which three of his comrades were killed by an IED (Improvised Explosive Device). He had been on that same road just prior to the explosion. He deeply grieved their deaths; subsequently, he spoke with an Army psychologist about his "survivor guilt."

He returned to the United States and to his previous job. Ironically, within six months he was involved in a car accident in which the other driver was killed. Then he developed frequent flashbacks to his war losses, affecting his ability to concentrate, to say the least. While under therapy with a psychiatrist, Lucille Bell, he heard from a friend that "Eye Movement Desensitization and Reprocessing" (EMDR) treatment had been used successfully in such cases. However, when he sought treatment from Dr. Bell, he learned that his insurance company considered his problem as a "preexisting condition" and denied coverage.

CASE 12-6

Insurance Coverage for Psychoanalysis

Doris Palmer, a 42-year-old woman with a history of panic attacks, obsessive-compulsive rituals, and inability to maintain employment sought consultation at the outpatient psychiatric clinic at the County Hospital. She tried short-term therapy in the form of cognitive-behavioral treatments, with only moderate improvement in her problems.

On the basis of a friend's suggestion about analysis being helpful to him, she consulted Dr. Steven Melby, a psychoanalyst in private practice. Dr. Melby noted the complexity and long-standing nature of her problems as well as her capacity for insightful reflection. Given these, he recommended intensive treatment requiring four weekly appointments for an extended period of time.

She then discovered that her health insurance plan covered only twenty sessions per year. Although a new federal mental health parity law prohibits unequal co-payments and lifetime caps on mental and physical conditions, it does not prohibit limiting the number of visits per year.

COMMENTARY

The patients in these two cases both face significant mental health problems. In both cases, therapists, apparently in good faith, are willing to provide therapy that is potentially beneficial. One issue that could cause controversy is whether the therapies under consideration are really likely to be beneficial. There is debate over whether EMDR is effective for various kinds of stress-related disorders and, if so, what its mechanism of action is and whether eye movement is actually an essential element in producing the effect.[14] Similarly, people argue over the effectiveness and rationale for psychoanalysis. Of course, if the insurer is unconvinced that the therapy is effective, it would have reason not to provide coverage. Since the controversy over the effectiveness of therapies, especially mental health therapies, can incorporate culturally sensitive beliefs and values, insurers will necessarily have to set the policies regarding coverage in ways that cannot avoid entering these disputes. Psychoanalysis, for example, especially in previous decades has been criticized by feminists for its gender stereotypes. Controversies over innovative and disputed therapies such as EMDR may raise issues over the standards for determining that a therapy has been proven effective.

Assuming that the insurer is convinced that these therapies are effective, it must still deal with the question of whether there are legitimate limits on the amount of resources that should be devoted to them. One aspect of this controversy involves coverage for preexisting conditions, the issue raised in Case 12-5. It is common for insurers to exclude preexisting conditions. That is the only way that the insurance industry can permit people to start insurance coverage without creating the problem of adverse selection, the decision by people who already suffer from some medical condition to sign up for an insurance policy that is known to provide good coverage for their problem.

Part of the problem Mr. Schultz faces in Case 12-5 is that his current condition is a result of a combination of his military trauma, clearly a preexisting condition, and his more recent automobile accident, which presumably occurred after he had subscribed to his present insurance. Without both events, Mr. Schultz would not be in need of the therapy under consideration. Surely, someone should cover his care. Assuming the EMDR is known to be effective for his condition, either the Veterans' Administration or his present insurer should be responsible. If neither will accept responsibility and Dr. Bell agrees that the EMDR has a reasonable chance of working, should she provide the therapy *pro bono* (free of charge), while she tries to get the two possible insurers to accept responsibility?

Doris Palmer's situation in Case 12-6 is similar. There is potential controversy over the legitimacy of the therapy, but even if we assume it is an effective therapy, we still must face the question of whether an insurer can legitimately place financial limits on the amount of resources to be devoted to a patient's problems. It is not uncommon for insurers to place limits on the number of psychotherapy sessions per year that will be covered. They may also limit the kinds of therapy, limiting patients to psychiatric social workers, for example.

Dr. Melby, the psychoanalyst in this case, has recommended four sessions per week for an extended period of time. This could last for months or years. If we assume that he billed the insurer at a rate of $100 per session, this would amount to $20,000 per year. That is far in excess of what other therapeutic strategies might cost. He obviously has a financial interest in seeing these sessions funded, but Ms. Palmer also has an interest in receiving effective therapy. Should insurers be permitted to place such limits on their coverage and, if so, how should these policies be adopted given that both the insurer and the therapist have financial conflicts of interest?

Conflict between the interests of the patient and those of the broader society can also arise when society has an interest in treating someone who does not want to be treated. The two cases that follow pose such problems, first in a situation in which society may wish to treat a mentally ill patient in order to make him well enough to stand trial and, second, in the extreme conditions of a military prison, the U.S. detention facility at Guantanamo Bay in Cuba, where the military has an interest in using psychological strategies to maximize the possibility that potentially dangerous terrorists will disclose information critical for protecting innocent citizens.

CASE 12-7

Treating in Order to Stand Trial

Until 1997, Charles Sell worked as a dentist in St. Louis, Missouri. He had a history of treatment for mental illness involving several episodes of strange delusions. Despite these delusional episodes, he seemed to function fairly well on a day-to-day basis. In 1997, Dr. Sell was arrested by federal agents for allegedly making numerous fraudulent Medicaid claims. One of Sell's dental assistants, Jane Alderman, testified that Sell had altered dental x-rays to show work that he had not in fact performed.

After an initial hearing, Dr. Sell was released on bail and, due to his history of mental illness, the court ordered a mental competency evaluation. The competency evaluation determined that Dr. Sell was competent to stand trial but noted that if he were to have a psychotic episode he might cease to be competent.

Through a strange coincidence, the office of the psychiatrist that Dr. Sell was ordered to visit for his competency evaluation was located in the same building where Jane Alderman now worked for a different dentist. On January 21, 1998, Ms. Alderman told the FBI agent Anthony Box that she saw Dr. Sell outside her dental office using his fingers to make the shape of a gun. She interpreted this as a death threat, and, in response to this allegation, the federal prosecutors added the charge of threatening a witness to the original fraud charges.

A hearing was immediately held to deal with the new charge. During this hearing, Dr. Sell was quite upset and began shouting insults including racial slurs at Agent Box, who was African American. The judge ordered Dr. Sell to be removed from the courtroom to a holding cell. She then held the hearing in front of the cell. Dr. Sell asked for his lawyer and after the judge refused he spit in her face. The judge then revoked his bail and sent him to jail.

Later, another former employee of Sell's began working with the FBI to attempt to entice Sell into hiring a hit man to kill Box and Alderman. From the recorded conversations between this employee and Dr. Sell it seems that Dr. Sell was interested in proving Mr. Box and Ms. Alderman to be liars but did not want to kill them. Nevertheless, the federal prosecutor added two counts of conspiracy to murder to the list of charges against Dr. Sell.

At this point, the court was asked to reconsider his mental competency. He was sent to a prison medical center where he was deemed to be mentally incompetent. The judge then ordered that he be given appropriate medical treatment for his mental illness. The medical center staff recommended that he be put on antipsychotic medication. Dr. Sell refused the medication claiming that his previous experience with such medication had been negative. The medical center claimed that the medication should be forcibly administered, both because the medication was necessary to prevent Dr. Sell from becoming dangerous and also because the medication was needed to render him competent to stand trial. The claim of dangerousness was not sustained; the court agreed that Dr. Sell could be forcibly medicated in order to make him competent to stand trial. While the order for medication was later overturned, in part because Dr. Sell had already been in jail for so long that the time exceeded his maximum possible sentence, the question remains whether the public, in the interest of pursuing the prosecution of a defendant, can medicate that person in order to make him competent to stand trial and, if so, whether psychiatric personnel in a prison medical system should cooperate.[15]

COMMENTARY

The public has an interest in prosecuting potential Medicaid fraud, witness intimidation, and conspiracy. At the same time, a well-recognized legal principle prohibits putting people on trial when they are not mentally competent, even if they may have been competent at the time when they committed their alleged crimes.

We can well imagine that a prosecutor in these circumstances would be highly motivated to make Dr. Sell competent to stand trial. That is the prosecutor's role. The interesting medical ethical issue is what role the medical facility psychiatrist and associated psychiatric personnel should play in pursuing this end.

The traditional Hippocratic ethic required the health professional to work always and only for the benefit of the patient. While normally that would require working to improve the patient's health, including his mental health, in this case Dr. Sell may not have an interest in becoming healthy. It could lead to his trial and potentially a bad outcome for him. Thus, if the Hippocratic ethic is applied and is interpreted as requiring promotion of the patient's total well-being (as opposed to his medical or mental well-being), the psychiatrist and associated nurses, social workers, and other caregivers may have a duty to keep him sick enough to avoid trial and potential prison time. If, however, the goal of the medical personnel should be to promote the patient's medical and psychological well-being, they could be required to treat him. In a purely Hippocratic world in which consent is not an issue, this could lead to forced treatment of Dr. Sell even against his protest. The choice would depend on whether the psychiatric professionals pursue his total well-being or his psychological well-being.

Still thinking only of the consequences, if the total consequences of their behavior for all parties are what should guide the actions of medical personnel, then they should consider not only Dr. Sell's interests, but the interests of the society. If the medical personnel are in the employment of the state's prison medical facility, loyalty to their employer would seem to require serving the institution's goals, which would include facilitating a fair trial of a mentally competent defendant.

One might be inclined to suggest that the mental health professionals should ask their clients what role they want them to play in such a situation based on the assumption that there is a contractual professional/patient relationship that relies on the consent of the patient before treatment is provided. There are two problems with this suggestion, however. First, Dr. Sell has been deemed incompetent to stand trial and may also be incompetent for the purposes of directing his medical care. Thus, even if the choice were the patient's, in this case the patient is not competent to make it. Second, there is good reason to doubt that, in a setting of a prison medical center in which the patient has been ordered to therapy by a court, the medical professionals have a traditional professional–patient relationship that is based solely on the consent of the patient.

CASE 12-8

The Interrogation of Guantanamo Prisoner Mohammed al-Qahtani

In August 2001, Mohammed al-Qahtani arrived in the Orlando Florida Airport, allegedly to join the group of men who would go on to hijack the planes on September 11. However, an observant interviewer was suspicious of Mr. al-Qahtani's story and deported him back to Saudi Arabia. During the American invasion of Afghanistan in 2002, American soldiers captured Mr. al-Qahtani, and transferred him to the detention center at Guantanamo Bay. Once, authorities realized that he may have been directly involved with the 9/11 hijackers, he was labeled a "high-value detainee."

In 2002, Former Secretary of Defense Donald Rumsfeld authorized extraordinary interrogation techniques for high-value detainees. He also mandated that these interrogations be subject to oversight by health professionals. To implement these policies, special teams were created to work on interrogations called, Behavioral Science Consultation Teams (BSCTs). These teams were headed by a psychologist or psychiatrist. Their job was not simply to monitor interrogations but to employ their knowledge of human psychology to better exploit a prisoner's psychological and cultural vulnerabilities for the purposes of extracting information.

Under the new interrogation guidelines, Mr. al-Qahtani was interrogated using very aggressive and controversial techniques. These included being deprived of sleep for more than a week at a time, having hypothermia induced by air conditioning, being exposed to barking, growling dogs to which the prisoner had a phobia, being forced to take many bags of intravenous fluid and then to urinate on himself, and being forced to violate various Islamic religious obligations and prohibitions.

Throughout Mr. al-Qahtani's interrogation, he was monitored daily by physicians. Although the physicians were officially not involved in the interrogation itself but only in ensuring the prisoners continued health, they were in frequent contact with the prisoner during the ongoing interrogation. They helped to facilitate these tactics by approving the continuation of interrogation immediately after Mr. al-Qahtani had been treated for severe hypothermia. On at least one occasion a medical professional was involved in the administration of large amounts of intravenous fluid to the prisoner against his will for the purpose of causing discomfort and humiliation.

The involvement of the BSCT psychologist in the interrogation tactics was even more extensive. An army investigation revealed that the BSCT psychologist witnessed and possibly encouraged the use of growling and barking dogs to terrify the prisoner. A log which details a two-month period of Mr. al-Qahtani's interrogation revealed that a BSCT psychologist later identified as Major John Leso was present during the interrogation sessions. The log notes two instances where Major Leso directly encouraged controversial psychological tactics. In the first instance, Major Leso suggested that the prisoner be placed in a swivel chair so that he could be prevented from focusing his eyes on one spot. In the second instance, after days of allowing the prisoner no sleep other than brief naps while shackled to the interrogation chair, Mr. al-Qahtani requested that he be allowed to sleep in a room other than the interrogation room. When interrogators consulted Major Leso, he said that "the detainee was only trying to run an approach on the control and gain sympathy."[16]

In addition to these two instances of psychologist's encouragement of controversial tactics, there is evidence of numerous other ways in which the BSCT may have advised interrogators on how to harmfully manipulate the prisoner's emotions and beliefs. Interrogators systematically violated various Islamic prohibitions. For example, a female interrogator would seductively touch the prisoner. The interrogators disrespectfully handled the Quran. They shaved his head and beard, and repeatedly refused to allow him to pray. Further, they employed dehumanizing techniques such as leashing the prisoner like a dog and making him bark, and remarking that the prisoner's life was worse than that of the rats inhabiting the compound.[17]

COMMENTARY

The professional associations for both psychiatry and psychology in the United States have raised questions about the role of members of their professions in such interrogations. The American Psychiatric Association condemned such involvement in a May 2006 resolution. It held that:

Psychiatrists providing medical care to individual detainees owe their primary obligation to the well-being of their patients, including advocating for their patients, and should not participate or assist in any way, whether directly or indirectly, overtly or covertly, in the interrogation of their patients on behalf of military or civilian agencies or law enforcement authorities

No psychiatrist should participate directly in the interrogation of persons held in custody by military or civilian investigative or law enforcement authorities, whether in the United States or elsewhere.

Direct participation includes being present in the interrogation room, asking or suggesting questions, or advising authorities on the use of specific techniques of interrogation with particular detainees.[18]

Meanwhile, the American Psychological Association was slower to take a position. At its August 2007 meeting it reaffirmed earlier condemnations of psychologist participation saying[19]:

> BE IT RESOLVED that the American Psychological Association unequivocally condemns torture and cruel, inhuman, or degrading treatment or punishment, under any and all conditions, including detention and interrogations of both lawful and unlawful enemy combatants....

It went on to say any member engaging in such activity will be disciplined:

> BE IT RESOLVED that the American Psychological Association asserts that any APA member with knowledge that a psychologist, whether an APA member or non-member, has engaged in torture or cruel, inhuman, or degrading treatment or punishment, including the specific behaviors listed above, has an ethical responsibility to abide by Ethical Standard 1.05, Reporting Ethical Violations, in the Ethical Principles of Psychologists and Code of Conduct (2002) and directs the Ethics Committee to take appropriate action based upon such information, and encourages psychologists who are not APA members also to adhere to Ethical Standard 1.05....

At the point at which the American Psychiatric Association had condemned involvement of its members, but while the American Psychological Association had not spoken, Guantanamo officials chose to use psychologists, such as Major Leso, so that they would not be contravening the articulated ethical position of the professional group with which the personnel were associated.

This raises the issue of whether psychiatrists and psychologists should be involved in such controversial roles and whether their professional associations should have authority in such matters. Of course, the first and most basic question in this case is whether the interrogation tactics themselves are morally offensive and violate international law. In analyzing the medical ethical dimensions of this case, however, the more direct question is whether psychiatrists and psychologists can contribute their expertise to achieving ends seen by a government as crucially important to protecting the interests of its citizens.

There seems to be no way that such involvement would be consistent with the Hippocratic ethic of having health professionals work only for the benefit of patients and to protect them from harm. Many clinical psychologists as well as physicians have historically accepted this ethical mandate to work for the benefit of their patients. This would seem to require having Major Leso and any psychiatrists and psychologists involved extend maximum effort to stop the mental and physical suffering involved.

More recent medical ethics, however, emphasizes the responsibility of health professionals to promote the interests of the community as well as those of patients. This suggests that there may be some role for psychiatric and psychological professionals in facilitating societal benefits, at least to the point that abuse does not occur.

This case is most provocative if we assume for purposes of discussion that governmental military authorities have made the decision that whatever harm and abuse is experienced by prisoners, it is justified by the critical public interest at stake. That seems to be the judgment made by government officials in this case, even if that judgment may not square with international law.

Assuming that is the case, may health professionals contribute to this societal benefit by using their professional skills to facilitate disclosure of this crucial information by detainees? The two professional associations seem to believe that they have the authority to articulate positions that should govern the conduct of their members and perhaps others in the professions who are not members of the associations. Moreover, the government seemed to accept this authority of the professional group when it excluded psychiatrists from any role in interrogation while relying on psychologists, that is, those whose professional association had not condemned their involvement.

There are, to be sure, questions at stake requiring the professional expertise of psychiatrists and psychologists, and we would expect the professional groups to contribute authoritatively to answering those questions. For example, professional associations may judge, based on their scientific expertise, that information extracted under psychological duress is likely to be faulty. Also, Congress has passed a law banning torture, defining torture as interrogation tactics that cause lasting harm. It is within the realm of professional expertise to determine what sort of techniques cause lasting psychological harm. These more technical questions are certainly issues to which professionals and professional groups can make special contributions. These are, however, different from the moral question of whether psychiatrists and psychologists may use their special skills to assist in bringing more effective pressure on detainees when doing so is important to a societal interest.

We are thus left with a substantive question—may psychiatrists and psychologists participate in interrogations by using their professional skills to make it more likely that reluctant detainees will disclose critical information—as well as a procedural metaethical question—should the profession or the broader society be the one that determines whether it is incompatible with a professional role to participate in such activities. Major Leso is also psychologist Dr. Leso. Does his identification either as a military officer or as a member of the profession of psychologists determine whether he should continue to participate in these interrogation activities?

OTHER BEHAVIOR-CONTROLLING THERAPIES

The ethical problems in mental health arise not only in clinical psychology; they must be faced in other behavior-controlling interventions as well. Neurological interventions including psychosurgery and electroconvulsive therapy (ECT) require judgments about the concept of mental health.[20] They require judgments about when a patient is autonomous; they require moral trade-offs between the welfare of the patient and that of other parties.[21]

Other behavior-modifying therapies in the future are likely to involve interventions that will force health professionals to face important ethical questions. One such area is aversive conditioning. These are therapies in which interventions are used to punish persons or to provide "negative reinforcement" when individuals engage in unacceptable behavior. The following case illustrates the problem.

CASE 12-9

Starving an Adolescent to Shape Him Up

Kathleen Barthells has enjoyed her new position for the last two months as an occupational therapist on the adolescent psychiatry unit. She feels fortunate to have gotten the job, because the hospital is nationally known and the occupational therapy program is well established. She is involved in care conferences on all of the patients. Her input is valued because of her honesty and insight into the problems of her adolescent patients.

At a unit meeting, the chief psychiatrist informs the groups that he is going to begin using a new type of behavior modification with his patients whose behavior had been diagnosed as an "adjustment disorder with mixed disturbance of emotions and conduct." He is vague as to the exact type of treatment he plans to use, but he has a solid reputation in the community and the hospital, hence the rest of the staff supports him. He admits the majority of inpatients on the unit and is therefore quite valuable to the hospital.

Two weeks later, Ms. Barthells sits in a care conference on a new adolescent male patient admitted to the facility by a foster parent. The nurse reads the case history. The patient has a history of running away from foster homes, extended absences from school, possible drug use, and a violent temper. He is fourteen years old. The chief psychiatrist is his attending physician. The patient has been in an isolation room for the past two days because of aggressive behavior shortly after his admission. The psychiatrist says, "I have been withholding food and water from him and intend to continue with this behavior modification until he is willing to comply with the rules and regulations on the unit."

Ms. Barthells is not sure if she heard him correctly. She asks for clarification. The psychiatrist replies, "This is a new type of behavior modification therapy that has proved quite effective for recalcitrant youths. He is healthy and a few days without food and water won't hurt him." The psychiatrist leaves the group to make rounds. The rest of the care team discusses what has happened. A staff colleague asks, "What do you think of all this? Is it right?"[22]

COMMENTARY

Aversive conditioning poses the issue of coercion and its closely related behavior-controlling strategies of manipulation and irresistibly attractive offers. It also illustrates how health professionals other than physicians are called into account for their participation in ethically controversial therapies.

Ms. Barthells is taken aback by the psychiatrist's therapeutic strategy, probably because it relies on what might be considered unacceptable means to force an adolescent into more appropriate behavior. Actually, several strategies for controlling behavior are invoked—a hospitalization without the patient's consent or approval, forced confinement to an isolation room, and now intentional withholding of food and water.

A 14-year-old, especially one with significant mental problems, is not an autonomous agent to begin with. He was brought to the facility by a foster parent who had legal responsibility for his welfare, but he cannot be said to be consenting to his treatment. He has not received conventional psychotherapies, either counseling or drug therapies. He has, however, been confined to an institution, then to an isolation room, and now to strong incentive that he will not get to eat or drink unless his behavior changes.

Coercion is morally suspect in medicine, even when it is used for seriously ill patients who cannot be said to be autonomous agents. Consider, for example, the coerciveness of a restraint system such as the old-fashioned wrist and leg restraints or its modern less-confining variant, the Posey belt. These are designed to force the patient to refrain from violent acting out. They raise moral issues in that they rely on force, but many would consider them justified in extreme circumstances when necessary to protect the patient or others.

The isolation room has a greater physically coercive element to it than the forced hospitalization, but is not normally seen as an attempt to coerce a behavior change. It uses physical force to confine the patient, but does not immobilize him to the same degree as the "four point" restraints.

Ms. Barthells seems particularly concerned about the withholding of food and water. She needs to determine what the moral difference is between the earlier efforts at confinement, which she seemed to accept, and the new proposal for aversive therapy. Is the difference that the confinement was presumably to keep the patient safe rather than change his behavior? If so, should she view the withholding of food as a negative incentive or as coercion used to change behavior? Some might argue that even labeling the strategy as a "negative" incentive is controversial. It could be said that the approach is one of rewarding him for good behavior by giving him food. Would that formulation make the therapy more acceptable? The difference is one of whether the baseline starting point for describing the events is a confined patient who will be rewarded with food for good behavior or one who will be punished by withholding food for bad behavior.

Ms. Barthells may also be concerned about the physical risks to the patient from withholding food and water. It is usually agreed that patients can safely go for many days without food, but withholding water for more than a day or two could be dangerous. Is it the risk of physical harm from dehydration that underlies her worry? If so, would her moral concerns be solved if food were withheld according to the psychiatrist's plan but adequate fluid was provided?

These problems of conflicts between infringements on patient freedom and promotion of patient welfare as well as the conflicts between patient welfare and societal welfare that arose in earlier cases of this chapter arise not only in mental health settings but also in disputes over the duty to preserve confidentiality. It is to those cases that we now turn.

NOTES

1 Roberts, Laura Weiss and Dyer, Allen R. *Concise Guide to Ethics in Mental Health Care.* Washington, DC: American Psychiatric Press [APA], 2004; American Psychiatric Association Ethics Committee. *Ethics Primer of the American Psychiatric Association.* Washington, DC: American Psychiatric Association, 2001; American Psychiatric Association [APA] *Opinions of the Ethics Committee on the Principles of Medical Ethics with Annotations Especially Applicable to Psychiatry.* Washington, DC: American Psychiatric Association [APA], 2001; Bloch, Sidney, Paul Chodoff, and Stephen A. Green, eds. *Psychiatric Ethics*, 3rd ed. Oxford, England/New York: Oxford University Press, 1999.

2 Englebretsen, George "The Concept of Mental Health." *APA [American Philosophical Association] Newsletter* 2001 Spring 00(2): 162–164.

3 Caplan, Arthur L., James J. McCartney and Dominic A. Sisti, eds. *Health, Disease, and Illness. Concepts in Medicine.* Washington, DC: Georgetown University Press, 2004.

4 Flew, Antony. "Disease and Mental Illness." In *Crime or Disease?* London: Macmillan Press, Ltd., 1973, pp. 38–48.

5 Conrad, Peter. "The Discovery of Hyperkinesis: Notes on the Medicalization of Deviant Behavior." In *Health, Disease, and Illness*, pp. 153–162.

6 Veatch, Robert M. "The Medical Model: Its Nature and Problems." *Hastings Center Studies* 1 (No. 3, 1973):59–76. Also see Parsons, Talcott. *The Social System.* New York: Free Press, 1951, chapter 9.

7 Goldstein, Joseph. "Medical Care for the Child at Risk: On State Supervention of Parental Authority." *Yale Law Journal* 86 (1977):669–670 [645–670].

8 In *re Maida Yetter*, 62 Pa.D. and C.2d 619 (1973).

9 New York City Health and Hospitals Corporation v. Stein. 335 N.Y.S.2d 461 (1972).

10 Faden, Ruth, and Tom L. Beauchamp in collaboration with Nancy N. P. King. *A History and Theory of Informed Consent.* New York: Oxford University Press, 1986, pp. 235–269.

11 Boswell, Randy. A Toronto Hospital Rejects Kidney from >Cult= Donor.@ *National Post* June 4, 2007, accessed on the Internet at: http://www.canada.com/nationalpost/news/story.html?id=088014cb-4349-4932-8402-f80646f2b2ad&k=54375

12 Hartley, Matt. Donor Wasn't Brainwashed, Patient Says,@ [Toronto] *Globe and Mail*, June 6, 2007, accessed on the Internet at http://www.theglobeandmail. com/servlet/story/RTGAM.20070606.wkidney06/BNStory/Entertainment/

13 Bromley, David G. and James T. Richardson, eds. *The Brainwashing/Deprogramming Controversy: Sociological, Psychological, Legal and Historical Perspectives*. New York: Edwin Mellen Press, 1983; Winn, Denise. *The Manipulated Mind: Brainwashing, Conditioning and Indoctrination*. London: Octagon Press, 1983; Hyde, Margaret O. *Brainwashing and Other Forms of Mind Control*. New York: McGraw-Hill, 1977; Galanter, Marc. *Cults: Faith, Healing and Coercion*. New York: Oxford University Press, 1999.

14 Devilly, G. J. "Eye Movement Desensitization and Reprocessing: A Chronology of Its Development and Scientific Standing." *Scientific Review of Mental Health Practice* 1 (2002): 113–138.

15 This case is based on Tuft, Carolyn, "No-Contest Plea Will Get Dentist Out of Jail." *St. Louis Post-Dispatch*, April 16, 2005, p. 10, available on the Internet at http://infoweb.newsbank.com/iw-search/we/InfoWeb?p_action=doc&p_docid= 1098708F6DB599E8&p_docnum=36&p_queryname=5&p_ product=AWNB&p_theme=aggregated4&p_nbid=V70Y5CHTMTE4ODMy ODk2My4xMzUxNToxOjE0OjE0MS4xNjEuMTIxLjcw, accessed August 28, 2007; Tuft, Carolyn, "Judge Rejects Sell's Request for Trial." *Association of American Physicians and Surgeons*, December 22, 2004. Online at http://www.aapsonline.org/ judicial/sell-tuft-1122.htm, accessed August 28, 2007; Tuft, Carolyn, "Dentist Wins Round––Judge Orders Tapes of Alleged Abuse by Guards." *St. Louis Post-Dispatch*, May 20, 2004, p. C1, available on the Internet at http://infoweb.newsbank.com/ iw-search/we/InfoWeb?p_action=doc&p_docid=102B55DF36F1AA52&p_ docnum=2&p_queryname=7&p_product=AWNB&p_theme=aggregated4&p_n bid=V70Y5CHTMTE4ODMyODk2My4xMzUxNToxOjE0OjE0MS4xNj EuMTIxLjcw, accessed August 28, 2007; Tuft, Carolyn, "Witnesses Against Dentist Lied in Other Cases––Three Had Fabricated Their Testimony in Previous Instances, Records Show." *St. Louis Post-Dispatch* March 21, 2004, p. C1, available on the Internet at http://infoweb.newsbank.com/iw-search/we/ InfoWeb?p_action=doc&p_docid=1017816D0C9DDBAA&p_docnum=1&p_ queryname=8&p_product=AWNB&p_theme=aggregated4&p_nbid=V70Y5C HTMTE4ODMyODk2My4xMzUxNToxOjE0OjE0MS4xNjEuMTIxLjcw; Annas, George J. "Forcible Medication for Courtroom Competence—the Case of Charles Sell." *New England Journal of Medicine* 250 (22, May 27, 2004): 2297– 2301; Klein, Dora W. "Curiouser and Curiouser: Involuntary Medications and Incompetent Criminal Defendants After *Sell v. United States*." *William & Mary Bill of Rights Journal* 13 (2004–2005):897–921.

16 *Secret ORCON Interrogation Log Detainee 063: Interrogation Log of al-Qahtani (Week 3): 07 December 2002*, available on the Internet at http://humanrights.ucdavis.edu/ projects/the-guantanamo-testimonials-project/testimonies/testimony-of-an- interrogation-log/interrogation-log-of-al-qahtani-week-3, accessed September 18, 2007.

17 This case was researched and written by Avi Craimer, Ph.D. candidate, Georgetown University, Department of Philosophy. The account is based on Miles, Steven.

"Medical Ethics and the Interrogation of Guantanamo 063." *American Journal of Bioethics* 7 (4, 2007):5; Bloche, Gregg and Jonathan Marks. "Doctors and Interrogators at Guantanamo Bay." *New England Journal of Medicine* 353(1, July 7, 2005): 6–8; Zagorin, Adam, Michael Duffy, Brian Bennett, Timothy J. Burger, Sally B. Donnelly, and Viveca Novak. "Inside the Interrogation of Detainee 063." *Time* 165 (25, June 20, 2005): 26–33; *Secret ORCON Interrogation Log Detainee 063: Interrogation Log of al-Qahtani (Week 3): 07 December 2002*, available on the Internet at http://humanrights.ucdavis.edu/projects/the-guantanamo-testimonials-project/testimonies/testimony-of-an-interrogation-log/interrogation-log-of-al-qahtani-week-3, accessed September 18, 2007.

[18] Available on the website of the American Psychiatric Association at http://www.psych.org/edu/other_res/lib_archives/archives/200601.pdf, accessed September 11, 2007.

[19] http://www.apa.org/governance/resolutions/councilres0807.html, accessed September 11, 2007, See also Benjamin, Mark. August 21, 2007. "Will Psychologists Still Abet Torture?" *Salon.com.* Online at http://www.salon.com/news/feature/2007/08/21/psychologists/index_np.html; Vedantam, Shankar. "APA Rules on Interrogation Abuse." *Washington Post*, August 20, 2007, p. A03.

[20] Faden and Beauchamp. *A History and Theory of Informed Consent.*

[21] Merskey, Harold. "Ethical Aspects of the Physical Manipulation of the Brain." In *Psychiatric Ethics*, pp. 275–299.

[22] This case is adapted from Haddad, Amy. "Teaching Ethical Analysis in Occupational Therapy." *American Journal of Occupational Therapy* 42 (5, 1988):300–304.

CHAPTER 13

✦⟋◦

Confidentiality: Ethical Disclosure
of Medical Information

Other Cases Involving Confidentiality

4-6: Intentional Exposure of Unknowing Sexual Partners to HIV
16-4: Surveying Illegal Immigrants
16-5: Homicide in Research: A Duty to Breach Confidentiality?

Confidentiality is one of the oldest issues of medical ethics. It is often assumed the health professional has an exceptionless duty to keep medical information confidential. It is obvious that details of a patient's medical condition should not be repeated as cocktail party gossip or for entertainment. The ethically interesting cases are those in which disclosing a patient's information may be needed to benefit someone. The benefit may come to the patient or to others. Of course, disclosure can potentially do harm as well. It may at least upset the patient if that patient does not want his or her medical information revealed. Others could be harmed as well.

Disclosing that a woman has HIV, for example, could not only harm her but could also raise questions about the HIV status of her sexual partner. If a married woman's HIV positive status is revealed and her husband tests negative, embarrassing questions may be raised. Nevertheless, sexual partners have a clear interest in knowing about HIV status in order to protect themselves. The cases in this chapter examine the ethics of whether normally confidential information may ethically be disclosed if the benefits of disclosure are expected to exceed the harms.

The rule that confidential information should not be disclosed is sometimes seen as being grounded in the more general duty of the health professional to benefit the patient. Since disclosure of medical information can be embarrassing and can discourage a patient from seeking further medical assistance, a rule requiring that information be kept confidential could be a specification of the general duty to benefit the patient.

The problem with that justification is that sometimes disclosure may actually be seen as benefiting the patient. In other cases it can benefit third parties. Thus, the moral problem is whether the confidentiality rule should provide for exceptions in such cases.

In normal human interaction, a premise of confidentiality is often not assumed. If we see a stranger's or even a friend's behavior, we are not automatically expected to refrain from describing it to others. The professional-client relation seems to be special in this regard. Whether the relation is between a lay person and a lawyer or a priest or a physician, an expectation of confidentiality is presumed. However, since either the patient or others may benefit from disclosure in certain cases, a flat rule requiring confidentiality cannot be presumed. Assuming that expectation cannot automatically be grounded in the ethical principle of beneficence, in what principle might it be based? Some would say it comes from promises—implicit or explicit—that professionals make to their clients. They would make such promises in order to achieve important ends of their practice—such as promoting and restoring health. If a flat promise of confidentiality cannot be assumed, then it will be critical to look at exactly what is promised.

The codes of ethics in health care are actually remarkably different on the question of when, if ever, confidences may be broken. Some, such as the Declaration of Geneva of the World Medical Association, contain an apparently exceptionless rule regarding confidentiality. The Declaration of Geneva states simply, "I will respect the secrets which are confided in me, even after the patient has died."[1]

Others would permit exceptions under certain circumstances. The Declaration of Geneva is a modern paraphrase of the Hippocratic Oath and, as such, usually follows the Oath closely; however, while the Declaration of Geneva would permit no exceptions, the original Hippocratic Oath seems to envision them on occasion. It says, "What I may see or hear in the course of the treatment or even outside of the treatment in regard to the life of men, which on no account one must spread abroad, I will keep to myself holding such things shameful to be spoken about."[2] While this commits the Hippocratic health professional to certain confidences, it also implies that some things should be "spoken abroad."

Typical modern interpretations determine what should be disclosed by applying the core Hippocratic principle that the clinician should always work for the benefit of the patient according to his or her ability and judgment. This would permit breaking of confidences whenever the clinician believes the patient would benefit. Such a provision can be called the "paternalistic exception" because it provides an exception for the good of the patient.

The codes of ethics of the various health professions have taken significantly different positions on the question of breaking confidence in order to benefit a patient. The code of the American Pharmaceutical Association (now called the American Pharmacists Association [APhA]) prior to 1995 clearly incorporated the paternalistic exception to the confidentiality rule as well as authorizing disclosures required by law. That code stated that, "A Pharmacist should respect the confidential and personal nature of professional records; except where the best interest of the patient requires or the law demands, a pharmacist should not disclose such information to anyone without proper patient authorization."[3] As we shall see, this provision was modified after 1995.

Other codes in the sister health professions contained similar paternalistic exceptions. The American Nurses Association (ANA) generally requires that nurses hold medical information in confidence, but appears to make an exception for the welfare of the patient, at least if the disclosure is to those involved in the patient's care. It also makes clear that information can be shared among other members of the caregiving team (apparently with no requirement that the patient agree):

> The standard of nursing practice and the nurse's responsibility to provide quality care require that relevant data be shared with those members of the health care team who have a need to know. Only information pertinent to a patient's treatment and welfare is disclosed, and only to those directly involved with the patient's care.[4]

Another provision of the ANA code seems to permit disclosures to protect innocent third parties and when "mandatory," presumably referring to legal requirements for disclosure.[5]

The American Dental Association is less direct when it comes to its position on confidentiality. It holds that patient records should be maintained in a manner consistent with the welfare of the patient[6] but goes on to state that dentists shall provide information upon request of a patient or another dental practitioner when disclosure will be beneficial for further treatment. Perhaps dentists can only disclose when the purpose is aiding the patient's treatment. At the same time, it appears that the patient need not be asked before information is disclosed in response to another dentist's request.

The American Medical Association (AMA) has changed its position on confidentiality quite dramatically. Prior to 1980, the AMA permitted disclosure when it would benefit the patient, when it would benefit others, or when the law required. Thus, even without patient approval, physicians following the AMA could breach confidence not only for the patient's welfare but also for the welfare of others:

> A physician may not reveal the confidences entrusted to him in the course of medical attendance, or the deficiencies he may observe in the character of his patients, unless he is required to do so by law or unless it becomes necessary in order to protect the welfare of the individual or of the society.[7]

Thus the AMA accepted not only the Hippocratic paternalistic exception to a confidentiality rule so that a physician could break confidence to benefit the patient; it also permitted breaking confidence to benefit society, a position not envisioned in Hippocratic ethics.

BREAKING CONFIDENCE TO BENEFIT THE PATIENT

Beginning in the 1970s, commentators on medical ethics began to question whether it was acceptable to break confidence in order to benefit the patient when the patient did not want the information disclosed. Sometimes a health professional comes to believe that the patient very much needs to have someone else know some important, but perhaps embarrassing or controversial, fact. If the patient agrees to the disclosure there is no problem, but what happens if that patient refuses to agree? The debate was triggered by an important British case that is the first case of this chapter.

CASE 13-1

Warning: Premarital Sex May Be Dangerous to Your Health

The British General Medical Council's Disciplinary Committee was charged in 1971 with the task of deciding whether or not a physician was guilty of "serious professional misconduct," whereupon it made the following report:

> The Committee next inquired into the charge against Dr. Robert John Denis Browne of Birmingham, that he had disclosed to the father of a Miss X that an oral contraceptive had been prescribed for her by the Birmingham Brook Advisory Centre, notwithstanding that he had been given the information in confidence by the centre and that he had neither sought nor received her permission to make the disclosure.

The complainant was the Birmingham Brook Advisory Centre, which was represented by Mr. G. S. Jonas, Solicitor...

Mr. Jonas said that it was only after the most anxious thought and deliberation, including meetings with Dr. Browne, that the matter had been brought before the Disciplinary Committee. Dr. Browne had practiced in Birmingham since 1941 and was highly regarded by his patients. Mr. Jonas alleged that in his capacity as a doctor he had received confidential information about one of his patients and quite deliberately and for no valid medical reason had betrayed that confidence by telling the patient's father what he had been told.

At the time Miss X called at the centre she was just over 16, a highly intelligent, attractive, and mature young woman. Mr. Jonas told the Committee that when an oral contraceptive was prescribed it was the practice of the clinic to inform the family doctor unless the patient specifically forbade it. In this instance Miss X agreed to her doctor being informed.

Dr. Browne had informed the girl's father that she was on the pill. No effort had been made by Dr. Browne to discuss the matter with his patient, and the patient's consent to this disclosure was neither sought nor obtained...Dr. Browne had said he would have to do the same again in every case that came to his notice, and the only situation he could see was that the centre should never again inform him if one of his patients came to see them. He had said it was all very well for the clinic prescribing the pill but if anything went wrong he would have to deal with the problem. The burden of the complaint was that the doctor let his views interfere with the objectivity demanded of a professional man.

The press had said the issue was important for doctors, and also to patients, but in Mr. Jonas's submission it was primarily important to patients, whose confidence must be kept. The confidence was always with the patient, it was never that of the doctor.

[A clinic physician testified that he] felt it important that the general practitioner should be informed so that if there were any side effect the doctor would have knowledge that the girl was taking oral contraceptives...

Mr. R. Alexander, Counsel... for Dr. Browne submitted that this was not in any sense a test case. The sole issue was whether this respected doctor had been guilty of the offense of serious professional misconduct. There were three issues: first, could one doctor unilaterally impose a confidence on another, and by unilaterally he meant could he do so without seeking the consent of the other doctor; second, what was the position with regard to the duty or right of a doctor to tell the parents of a child who had not reached the age of majority of the medical treatment that child was receiving; and the third issue was that medical confidence existed for the benefit of the patient. If the doctor believed it to be in the interests of the patient to reveal the confidence to a third party, then he was entitled to do so...

Dr. Browne, in evidence, said that he was sixty-three years of age and was married with three children, including a girl of eighteen. He had qualified in 1941 and had been in practice in Birmingham for about thirty years. The parents of the girl had been his patients for many years and he had been their doctor at the time of her birth. She had been his patient all her life. She still was his patient, and he had seen her professionally quite recently.

When he had received the letter from the Brook Centre it sounded an alarm bell in his mind. He was concerned that a girl only just 16 had been placed on a contraceptive pill without prior knowledge or consultation with the family doctor. It was a stable family with the daughter living at home. He had discussed the matter, which gave him great anxiety, with professional colleagues. He tried to get an estimate of the situation without mentioning anyone's name and considered the problem carefully.

The girl's father happened to come to the surgery shortly after this, and he asked him if his daughter was getting married. The father said that she was not, but that she had a steady boy friend and was still at school. Dr. Browne said he thought hard and then made up his mind—bearing in mind the girl's best interests, and for that reason solely—and handed the father a copy of the letter from the centre and explained what it meant...

Dr. Browne said that he had had two motives in informing the parents. One was the physical hazards of the pill, and second were the moral and psychological hazards. He was not standing in judgment, but with his knowledge of the home background, and knowing the parents were sympathetic and kindly and could handle the situation with care and tact, he considered they were the best people to counsel her in their own way. He also saw psychological hazards, for if she were keeping a secret she might have a sense of guilt, which could have a harmful effect on her emotionally. He pointed out that it would have been difficult for him to contact the girl without arousing parental suspicion. The episode did not appear to have impaired his relationship with Miss X.

In reply to cross-examination by Mr. Jonas, Dr. Browne said that his interests were primarily for the patient and for her alone. He had no other interest except what was best for her. His patient was being placed on a dangerous drug without his prior knowledge or consent with all the hazards that might involve—and steroid drugs were a particular hazard...

Dr. Walter Woolley, ex-Chairman of the Central Ethical Committee of the British Medical Association, told the Committee he had been a family doctor since 1933. In his view a third party could not fetter the right of the doctor—for instance, by a letter such as the one from the Brook Centre—to exercise his own judgment.

Dame Amis Gillie said that she had had thirty-eight years' experience in general practice, and in her view professional secrecy existed in the interest of the patient. She considered that there could be situations in which the benefit of the patient meant that a confidence must be disclosed. Every case should be judged on its own merits by the practitioner involved...

The final witness was Dr. J. C. Cameron, Chairman of the General Medical Services Committee of the British Medical Association (BMA). He had been in general practice for many years, and considered that a long-standing knowledge of a patient was of great advantage in forming an assessment of a situation. He would have preferred that, if possible, the girl's consent should have been sought prior to the disclosure to her parents, but there might be circumstances in which this was impracticable...

After consideration in camera the President said:

> The Committee has found proved that the information you received from the Birmingham Brook Advisory Centre was in confidence, and that you had neither sought nor received the patient's permission to make the disclosure; but in the particular circumstances of this case...the Committee do not regard your action in disclosing the information referred to in the charge as improper. The Committee therefore has not found that the whole of the facts alleged in the charge, including the word 'improperly,' have been proved. It has accordingly recorded a finding that you are not guilty of serious professional misconduct.

COMMENTARY

The BMA principle of confidentiality as adopted by the Representative Body in 1959 was in effect at the time of the Browne case. It stated clearly that "the overriding consideration must be adoption of a line of conduct that will benefit the patient, or protect his interests." Dr. Browne was claiming that his patient's interests required the disclosure to her parents. Furthermore, he was arguing from what is normally considered to be an enlightened broad conception of health that includes social and psychological considerations. Sex for the single girl, according to his considered "medical" judgment, was unhealthy, which he felt obliged him to disclose the information.

In light of the Browne case, the BMA in 1971 adopted an amendment to its principle of confidentiality, which in effect rejects the "patient's interest" grounds for violating confidentiality. The physician, according to the revised principle, cannot ethically second-guess the patient's judgment of his or her own best interest and must respect the patient's refusal to allow information to be given to a third party.

The AMA Code in effect in the 1970s held that confidences may be broken to protect the welfare of the individual patient.[8] The paternalistic exception was not abandoned until the major revision of the AMA Code that was adopted in 1980 and published the following year when the new provision simply stated that "the physician shall . . . safeguard patient confidences within the constraints of the law" dropping the authorization to disclose when the physician believed it would be beneficial to the patient.[9]

When the APhA approved its revised code in June of 1995, it appears to have dropped the patient-benefit exception clause as well. Now its view is that, "A pharmacist promotes the good of every patient in a caring, compassionate, and confidential manner."[10] There may be, however, some doubt about whether this is really an abandonment of the traditional paternalism, because this sentence is in a paragraph that begins with a commitment to promote "the good of every patient."

BREAKING CONFIDENCE TO BENEFIT OTHERS

Other codes contain another kind of exception (or add to the paternalistic one). They would permit confidences to be broken when doing so would benefit third parties. We could call this the "other-benefiting exception." This is a clear abandonment of Hippocratic ethics, which requires the physician to work for the benefit of the patient, but it is the feature of most newer codes, those written since the 1970s.

While breaking confidence paternalistically, in order to benefit the patient, is one of the traditional justifications for disclosure, serving the welfare of other parties is also put forward as a reason why a health professional might reveal information about a patient. According to a rigid application of the traditional Hippocratic ethic, all actions of the physician should be solely for the welfare of the patient. Of course, this means that any action for the purpose of serving other individuals or the society as a whole would be unethical. This would not only make public health interventions, research medicine, and cost containment unethical, but would also make it unethical to disclose confidential information for the benefit of another. Since at least some of these concerns are increasingly seen as a legitimate part of medicine, including others as part of the physician's concern is more commonly becoming accepted.

The interests of various third parties might be served by disclosure of confidential patient information. The cases in this section consider breaking confidence to protect an identified third party from serious threat of bodily harm, to help in the capturing of a person wanted for criminal behavior, to protect the public from a dangerous motorist, and to inform relatives of a risk of a genetic affliction.

One of the most widely cited cases raising these issues involved a college student who conveyed to a school psychologist that he was contemplating killing a former girl friend. The case, decided by the California courts, poses the ethical as well as legal question of whether the therapist has a duty to warn the intended victim.

CASE 13-2

The Murder of Tatiana Tarasoff: The Therapist's Duty to Warn

Prosenjit Poddar, a graduate student at the University of California, had a romantic interest in a fellow student named Tatiana Tarasoff. She did not reciprocate that interest, which led to Mr. Poddar's depression. He eventually sought the assistance of the Dr. Lawrence Moore, a psychologist at the Cowell Memorial Hospital at the university. Mr. Poddar confided his intention to kill Tatiana.[11]

That Dr. Moore took the threat seriously is confirmed by his notifying the campus police who briefly detained him, but soon released him when he appeared rational to them. Dr. Moore's supervisor, Dr. Harvey Powelson, directed that no further action be taken. Ms. Tarasoff was out of the country visiting an aunt in Brazil. Neither Ms. Tarasoff nor her parents were warned of the threat. When the young woman returned Mr. Poddar began stalking her and eventually stabbed her to death.

Ms. Tarasoff's parents sued Dr. Moore, Dr. Powelson, the campus police, and the university, alleging that they failed to warn Tatiana or her parents and failed to see that Mr. Poddar was confined.

Many psychiatrists, psychologists, and police came to the defense of their colleagues in this case. Their professional associations entered the case on their behalf. Those focusing on the health professional's duty argued that danger to others is not accurately predictable, but even if it were, the duty of the psychologist or psychiatrist in this case is to the patient, not to third parties. Furthermore, they contended that a policy requiring a duty to warn would dissuade potential patients from seeking professional assistance thus eliminating a potential benefit to the one in danger.

Those supporting the parents argued that the duty of a professional cannot be limited to the patient when the health professional has knowledge of a serious and credible threat of grave bodily harm.

The police were found according to state law to be immune from liability and had no duty to warn. The medical personnel were immune from failing to confine Mr. Poddar, but concluded they could face charges of failure to warn. The court concluded:

> When a therapist determines, or pursuant to the standards of his profession should determine, that his patient presents a serious danger of violence to another, he incurs an obligation to use reasonable care to protect the intended victim against such danger. The discharge of this duty may require the therapist to take one or more of various steps, depending upon the nature of the case. Thus it may call for him to warn the intended victim or others likely to apprise the victim of the danger, to notify the policy, or to take whatever others steps are reasonably necessary under the circumstances.[12]

While a court case determines only what the law in that jurisdiction requires, it is also important to ask what was ethically appropriate and whether the legal conclusion is, in fact, an appropriate resolution or whether the law should be changed. When physicians or psychotherapists conclude that a person poses a credible threat of serious bodily harm to another, should the confidential information be disclosed by taking action to warn?

COMMENTARY

The claim that Dr. Moore should be expected to take action to protect Tatiana Tarasoff by warning her or her parents of the risk can be defended on at least two separate grounds. Many traditional health professionals claim that they have a special and limited set of duties—to work for the welfare of the patient. While normally that is consistent with keeping patient information confidential, in this case it could be argued that Mr. Poddar would have been much better off if something had been done to prevent him from carrying out his threat. Dr. Moore clearly took his threat seriously. He even accepted the breach of confidentiality involved in notifying the campus police. He could have taken further action to prevent it by disclosing the content of the normally confidential communication to Ms. Tarasoff or her family.

The second ground on which disclosure might be defended abandons the Hippocratic, patient-centered commitment. While patient communication should normally be kept confidential, according to this view there are also other interests that must be protected. As the court pointed out, physicians already have a duty to report diagnoses of infectious diseases for the purpose of protecting the public. Here an analogous public risk is at stake. As long as the threat is both credible and serious, the argument is that limits must be placed on the duty of confidentiality.

A counterargument is that one way to protect Ms. Tarasoff would be to assure that Mr. Poddar gets the therapy he needs and that opening the door to breaches of confidentiality would dissuade other potential patients from seeking help. One way to guard against this risk would be to state boldly an exceptionless promise of confidentiality such as is found in the Declaration of Geneva.

After the publicity surrounding this case, the AMA and other professional organizations rewrote their confidentiality rule making it appear to conform with the court's position. It reads:

> The obligation to safeguard patient confidences is subject to certain exceptions which are ethically and legally justified because of overriding social considerations. Where a patient threatens to inflict serious bodily harm to another person or to him or herself and there is a reasonable probability that the patient may carry out the threat, the physician should take reasonable precautions for the protection of the intended victim, including notification of law enforcement authorities. Also, communicable diseases and gun shot and knife wounds should be reported as required by applicable statutes or ordinances.[13]

This raises the question of what role, if any, a professional organization should have in deciding the ethics and legality of physician conduct in such cases. It could be argued that physicians are a biased party in this discussion since they have historically been oriented to the welfare of the patient. Since this kind of case requires a trade-off between the interests of the patient and others (just as law enforcement officers might be), they must yield to the public assessment of the relative claims. As the court put it, this is a matter of social policy, not professional expertise.

BREAKING CONFIDENCE AS REQUIRED BY LAW

In the previous case, the psychologist and psychiatrist were in a position to warn a specific person against whom a patient had made a concrete and credible threat. The issues of confidentiality can also arise when a physician or other health care professional is in a position to have confidential information that could benefit society more generally. In some of these cases, the law requires physicians and others to benefit society by reporting certain patients.

CASE 13-3

The Required State Psychiatric Diagnosis Record

For Andrew Gorly it was the second admission to the Brooklyn Psychiatric Clinic. The patient had been subdued on the corner of Rose and Belmont Streets. He claimed that the Nazis were infiltrating the Political Science Department of the university where he was a graduate student. The patient had, that afternoon, assaulted three innocent passersby, whom he accused of being part of the conspiracy. Mr. Gorly was scheduled to take his doctoral examination the coming Tuesday. He had been up for three consecutive nights reading modern European political history, cramming for one of his exams. After completing the exams and writing his dissertation, the patient was planning on a career in the foreign service. His professors had always thought of him as a bit strange but considered him one of the bright young scholars in the department. They had tried to persuade him to go into teaching, but he was an activist; he still had faith that hard-working, intelligent foreign service officers could do something to change American foreign policy.

His parents brought him to the Brooklyn Psychiatric Clinic late that evening. The diagnosis was an acute paranoid schizophrenic break. Dr. Andrew Lyons, the psychiatrist on call, understood the extreme pressure of the exams. He confided to the parents that he thought the prognosis was good. Hopefully, a short stay as an inpatient would get their son through the crisis.

The doctor administered 20 mg Ziprasidone intramuscularly and made appropriate notations on the chart. The patient, who was still present, insisted on knowing what was being written. Dr. Lyons explained. The doctor then picked up the Admission Form. Mr. Gorly insisted on seeing the form, and Dr. Lyons obligingly gave him a blank copy. It was a standardized, computerized form giving the patient's name, address, social security number, occupation, and psychiatric history. It also included religion, education, weekly family income, a "problem appraisal," and most significantly, the psychiatric diagnosis written as the code.

"You mean you are going to fill out this entire form so my whole life can be fed into a computer?" the patient asked. "Where does the duplicate copy go?" he demanded.

"To the Department of Mental Hygiene in the state capital," was the reply.

"Do you realize what this does to my foreign service career when this reaches the government computer?"

Dr. Lyons said he was sure that the records were treated with strict confidence. The records were needed for statistical purposes only. Certainly they would not be turned over to the foreign service.

"And why do my name, address, and social security number go on the form if it is only for statistical purposes?" the patient asked. "You can't just send my name in. It violates my right to confidentiality."

"The law says I have to send in the form. It is part of a multi-state information system for psychiatric patients," was the reply.

COMMENTARY

It is unlikely that Mr. Gorly will benefit in any direct sense from the reporting of his diagnosis to the state mental hygiene department. It is of course possible that, through the accumulation of statistics on acute paranoid schizophrenic breaks, treatment or preventive measures might be developed that would benefit the patient, but almost certainly this is not the justification of the reporting, and such a rationalization is best left out of the argument. Our society might possibly benefit from the reporting by accumulating masses of statistics that could contribute to the knowledge of mental illness. Whether society would benefit by having direct knowledge of Mr. Gorly's psychiatric condition, however, is questionable. One might argue that society would benefit by keeping him out of a sensitive foreign service assignment, but the connection is tenuous. If such an argument is made, it must also weigh the harm done by creating a surveillance system that infringes on personal freedom and probably prevents many persons from making constructive contributions to society.

The extent to which the medical condition of the patient is directly a threat to society may be one of the ethically significant factors in deciding whether a confidence should be broken. In Mr. Gorly's case, the medical condition is a threat in only an indirect and tenuous way at best. In another type of case, the patient's medical condition is of direct concern to society. For example, the physician's obligation is to report a patient with a contagious disease, venereal disease, or clearly present homicidal psychiatric illness. In still another type of case, the medical condition of the patient is clearly not a threat, but he poses other threats to society.

In opposition to these concerns, society also has an interest in making sure patients such as Mr. Gorly get into therapy and remain in it. Some would doubt the ability of society to provide an adequate guaranty that the patient would comply and remain in follow-up, but that would surely be in society's interest. It is apparent that he finds the required reporting alarming. Minimizing such reports, removing identifiers, and, perhaps eliminating them entirely would further society's interest in getting such patients the help they need.

CASE 13-4

Reporting the Motorist with Epilepsy

A young man was brought into a private hospital seizure clinic, where the following record was kept on him over the next four days:

3/22 9:47 A.M. Admitted to seizure clinic from ER. Reported seizure while walking to work...Patient reports one previous seizure "just like this one" approximately four years ago...Rx diphenylhydantoin O.IGm. No.21 sig: i tid.

3/24 EEG confirms suspicion of grand mal. Patient pleads not to report case to Motor Vehicle Department. Says he only drives 2 times a month-to care for mother who lives alone on the family farm. Says distance is "about 10 miles." Will consult hospital attorney, but consider primary responsibility is to patient and patient's mother.

3/25 Attorney says law in California requires report of all seizure diagnoses. But does this conflict with medical ethics?

COMMENTARY

The person who wrote in the chart a question about whether a law requiring the reporting of a diagnosis of epilepsy conflicts with "medical ethics" may wonder whether his or her professional association would approve of such reporting. As we have seen, the AMA codification has endorsed conforming to legal reporting requirements. The more difficult question is what difference the AMA's endorsement would make to answering the question of whether it is ethical for the physician to report. It is unlikely that such reporting would be done to serve the patient's interests (although one could imagine that reporting would eventually lead to preventing this patient from the limited driving he is presently doing). More than likely the justification for reporting is to protect other parties, a goal consistent with a more social ethic even if it is inconsistent with the Hippocratic ideal of working so as to benefit the patient.

The excerpt from the record does not indicate the physician's professional relationship with the epileptic patient's mother for whom he intermittently cares. Suppose that he or she is in fact the family physician and has cared for the mother as well as the son for many years. Is this ethically relevant? Does the physician then have a special moral obligation to see that the mother is cared for or is the situation the same ethically if the physician has never seen the mother before?

If the same case arises in a hospital in another city where there is no law requiring the reporting of epileptic diagnoses to the Department of Motor Vehicles, how does this change the physician's ethical obligations?

How does the physician's obligation to report a diagnosis differ ethically if he or she is treating a patient with a venereal disease, food poisoning from a college food service, or a gunshot wound?

CASE 13-5

Medicine in the Service of the FBI

The following notice appeared in the "News and Notes" section of a leading dermatology journal. It is an exact reproduction of an FBI poster:

Wanted by the FBI

A Federal Grand Jury at Tucson, Ariz., indicted _____ for conspiring with another individual in an act which involved the interstate transportation and unregistered possession of 120 sticks of dynamite, 30 electric blasting caps, 20 fuse caps, and 50 feet of fuse.... _____ using the name William Allen Friedman, allegedly drove from Venice, Calif., to Tucson, Ariz., purchased the explosives and fuse, and returned to Venice, Calif.

CAUTION: _____ HAS BEEN KNOWN TO ASSOCIATE WITH INDIVIDUALS WHO ADVOCATE THE USE OF EXPLOSIVES AND SHE HERSELF

HAS ACQUIRED EXPLOSIVES IN THE PAST. SHE REPORTEDLY MAY HAVE ACQUIRED FIRE-ARMS AND SHOULD BE CONSIDERED DANGEROUS.

_____ is known to be afflicted with a skin condition known as acne vulgaris, which has been described as being acute and recurrent. The recurrent aspect of this skin condition could necessitate treatment by a dermatologist.

_____ is also known to frequently wear prescription eyeglasses or contact lenses, which are required for her to operate an automobile.

Notify the FBI

Any person having information which may assist in locating this fugitive is requested to immediately notify the nearest FBI field office, the telephone number of which appears on the first page of most local telephone directories.

COMMENTARY

The notice produced a major dispute about the possible necessity for the physician who sees this notice and then is asked to care for the patient to violate the assumed confidential relationship. Physicians and others critical of the notice in a medical journal argued that the obligation of the physician is to health, specifically to the health of his patient, and that the obligations to society must be subordinated when these conflict with the right of the patient to health care. According to this position, physicians, when they are in their medical role, should work for ends "internal" to medicine, that is, ends consistent with the objective of promoting or restoring health.[14] Objectives outside of the medical arena are not legitimately included.

The problem with that position is that sometimes society has important non-medical ends that require the skill of those trained in medicine to achieve. Physicians are asked to use their skills to assist in industry, scientific research, the military, the judicial system, and individual life enhancement. Such activities as assuring occupational safety, exploring space, preparing troops for battle, monitoring capital punishment, and assisting individuals in cosmetic surgery are all undertaken to achieve non-medical ends, but require skilled medical professionals to do well. Their defenders hold that it must be acceptable to use physicians and other health professionals for worthwhile non-medical social purposes.

If society is justified in using its licensed professionals to achieve worthwhile purposes outside of medicine, then why should it not be permitted to ask physicians for their assistance in finding a fugitive from justice? Surely, that is a worthwhile social purpose.

One difference between the FBI poster and these other non-medical objectives may be that medical skill is not inherently necessary to track down a wanted person; it is using the medical context in a way that is not essential.

Moreover, the patient may not reasonably be expected to understand that being identified to the FBI is one of the risks of seeking medical attention.

If a physician recognizing this person is to cooperate with the FBI, the disclosure would be a breach of confidentiality. If it is justified, it would have to be on the basis of the benefit to society. Has the criminal forfeited her right of confidentiality by engaging in illegal activities?

The physician may determine that he has a duty to society as a citizen that precludes maintaining confidential the fact that the fugitive-patient was in his or her office. If one generalized to other situations where wanted criminals could be apprehended by alerting members of a professional group who might be especially likely to come into contact with them, one might make a case that general duties as a citizen to report such criminals may take precedence over special role-related duties such as a promise of confidentiality. A journalist, for example, might believe he has a duty to report a criminal even if it means violating a duty generally recognized by his profession to maintain confidentiality.

The physician who identifies this person in the course of medical treatment may not even have a conflict between his general duty to report and his special medical duty as a physician to keep confidences. As we have seen in previous cases, the AMA's *Code of Medical Ethics* states that

> When a patient threatens to inflict serious physical harm to another person or to him or herself and there is a reasonable probability that the patient may carry out the threat, the physician should take reasonable precautions for the protection of the intended victim, which may include notification of law enforcement authorities.

That would seem to put the AMA on the side of those wanting to use a physician to obtain a tip about the fugitive. Nevertheless, since the danger is unrelated to the medical condition the physician would be asked to treat, some would argue that confidentiality should be preserved.

CONFLICT BETWEEN CONFIDENTIALITY
AND OTHER DUTIES

The issues of confidentiality can arise in situations in which a physician is committed to maintain the promise to keep information confidential until he or she discovers that he has also made a commitment that will require breaking confidence. The problem can be especially acute if the promise has been made to another patient as in the classic case that first appeared in the *Hastings Center Report*.[15]

CASE 13-6

The Case of the Homosexual Husband

David Moss, the oldest of three children, was the son of a well-to-do manufacturer. David's father valued physical prowess and athletic accomplishments, areas in which David showed little interest. When David was twelve or thirteen years old, conflicts with his father resulted in almost nightly arguments. It was evident that David's father had become concerned about David's mannerisms and considered them to be effeminate.

David's schoolwork deteriorated considerably, and he became withdrawn. His father decided to send him to military school, but he remained there for only six months. By this time, David had told his parents that he was a homosexual, and had engaged in, and was engaging in, homosexual practices. He came home and completed his high school studies, but did not go on to college and continued to live at home.

Before he was even twenty years old, he had been treated for gonorrhea, asthma, and infectious hepatitis. At the age of twenty-one, to gain exemption from the draft, his physician attested to the fact that he was a homosexual.

Five years later, another patient, Joan Gibbens, visited her family physician for a premarital serological exam. The physician was the same physician who had treated Mr. Moss. She was twenty-four years old and had been under this physician's care since the age of fourteen. A close and warm relationship had developed between the physician and Joan's family, and it was normal, then, for the physician to ask about her fiancé. When he did, he learned that she was about to marry David Moss. She had known him only briefly, but well enough, she felt, to be certain about her choice. Nothing more was said at the time.

David and Joan were married shortly thereafter and lived together for a period of six months. The marriage was annulled on the basis of nonconsummation. David told Joan that he was homosexually oriented, and she learned as well that not only did they share a physician but also that the physician was aware of Mr. Moss's homosexuality. She subsequently suffered a depression as a result of this experience and was angry that her physician had remained silent. She felt that she could have been spared this horrible episode in her life and that it was her physician's duty to inform her. His failure to do so was an act of negligence resulting in deep emotional scars.

To whom did the physician owe primary allegiance? Does the interest of one patient prevail over the requirements of confidentiality surrounding another's case?

COMMENTARY

Physicians setting out in Hippocratic fashion to benefit their "patient" will be taken aback by this case. Doing what would plausibly benefit the young woman who is a patient will almost certainly cause harm to the other patient. One might try to argue that it would also be in the interest of the man to force the disclosure on his fiancée because it would head-off a disastrous marriage. Or one might try to argue that it is not really in the woman's interest to know, since possibly her future husband could pull off this marriage and make it work. Neither of these is terribly plausible, however. It is hard to know in advance that this marriage would fail and equally hard to predict that the marriage could succeed. The rule to "benefit the patient" simply leaves the physician asking which patient.

The problem in this case seems to arise from the fact that the physician has made two implicit and vague promises—to benefit his patient and to protect confidentiality. Such an implicit, unexamined set of promises can, in rare cases, come into conflict as they have here.

It is conceivable that the physician has taken steps to make the implicit promises somewhat more explicit. For example, he might have displayed on his waiting room wall a copy of the Hippocratic Oath promising to work to benefit the patient and protect the patient from harm. He might also have the Declaration of Geneva posted, which promises confidentiality without specifying any limits. If that were true, the physician has displayed two promises that in this case come into conflict. It would be impossible to fulfill both commitments simultaneously.

The solution would appear to be offering only more precise and carefully crafted commitments. The physician could have promised to benefit the patient unless doing so violated a promise of confidentiality. Alternatively, he could have promised confidentiality unless it was necessary to break confidence in order to protect some third party from harm.

It would be unreasonable to hedge the promise of confidentiality so that it could be broken whenever even minimal harm to a third party could be avoided. The AMA's current promise, with an exception if necessary to protect third parties from "serious physical harm," is more reasonable. If that were the content of the physician's commitment, he would at least have avoided a conflict. He would then have to determine whether the risk to the woman constituted a threat of "serious physical harm" and act accordingly. His alternative would be to promise to benefit his patient unless doing so violated duties owed to others. That would provide grounds for keeping the information confidential.

Similar problems of conflict between benefiting the patient and fulfilling duties owed to the patient or others constitute the central issues of medical ethics. These kinds of problems arise regularly in the care of patients.

NOTES

[1] World Medical Association. "Declaration of Geneva." *World Medical Journal* 3 (1956).

[2] Edelstein, Ludwig. "The Hippocratic Oath: Text, Translation and Interpretation." *Ancient Medicine: Selected Papers of Ludwig Edelstein.* Owsei Temkin and C. Lilian Temkin, editors. Baltimore, MD: The Johns Hopkins Press, 1967, p. 6.

[3] American Pharmaceutical Association. *Code of Ethics.* Washington, DC: American Pharmaceutical Association, 1981.

⁴ American Nurses Association. *Code of Ethics for Nurses with Interpretive Statements*. Washington, DC: The Association, 2001, p. 12.

⁵ Ibid.

⁶ American Dental Association, Council on Ethics, Bylaws and Judicial Affairs. *Principles of Ethics and Code of Professional Conduct, with Advisory Opinions Reviewed January 2004*. Chicago, IL: American Dental Association, 2004.

⁷ American Medical Association. *Judicial Council Opinions and Reports*. Chicago, IL: American Medical Association, 1971, p. 53.

⁸ Ibid.

⁹ American Medical Association. *Current Opinion of the Judicial Council of the American Medical Association*. Chicago, IL: American Medical Association, 1981, ix.

¹⁰ American Pharmaceutical Association. *Code of Ethics for Pharmacists*. Washington, DC: American Pharmaceutical Association, 1995.

¹¹ This case is based upon Tarasoff v. Regents of the University of California Supreme Court of California, 1974 13 Cal. 3d 177 (1974); and Tarasoff v. Regents of University of California, 17C.3d 425, 131 Cal. Rptr. 14, 551 P.2d 334.

¹² *Tarasoff v. Regents of University of California*. 17C.3d 425, 131 Cal. Rptr. 14, 551 P.2d 334, p. 340.

¹³ American Medical Association. Council on Ethical and Judicial Affairs. *Code of Medical Ethics: Current Opinions with Annotations, 2006-2007*. Chicago, IL: AMA Press, 2006, accessible on-line at http://www.ama-assn.org/ama/pub/category/8353.html [accessed May 7, 2007].

¹⁴ Pellegrino, Edmund D. "The Internal Morality of Clinical Medicine: A Paradigm for the Ethics of the Helping and Healing Professions." *Journal of Medicine and Philosophy* 26 (No. 6, 2001):559–579.

¹⁵ ©The Hastings Center. Reprinted by permission. This case originally appeared in the *Hastings Center Report*. vol 7, no. 2 (1977).

CHAPTER 14

✎⌒

Organ Transplants

Other Cases Involving Organ Transplantation

4-5: Blocking Transplant for an HMO Patient with Liver Cancer: Serving the Patient and Serving the Community

5-5: Allocating Livers for Transplant

12-3: The Jesus Christian Transplant: Brainwashed into Donating a Kidney?

12-4: A Kidney to Turn a Life Around

The transplantation of solid organs into humans was first attempted over a century ago when kidneys from a sheep and a dog were placed into two patients who were suffering from kidney failure.[1] It was, however, not until 1954 that the first successful kidney transplant occurred. That involved an organ from an identical twin, thus avoiding rejection problems. In the early 1960s, success was first reported in the transplantation of cadaveric kidneys, livers, and lungs. Then on December 3, 1967, when Louis Washkansky volunteered to subject himself to the scalpel of South African surgeon Christiaan Barnard, he became the first successful recipient of a transplanted heart. The heart was obtained from Denise Darvall. When it beat, it was a sound heard throughout the world. The era of organ transplant captured the public's fascination. It also introduced serious controversies in medical ethics.

When organs—hearts or kidneys or livers—are transplanted, they are the scarce and invaluable resources that stand between imminent death or serious morbidity and a thread of hope for life. Organ transplant poses a series of ethical problems that can be divided into two major groups. First, organs need to be obtained, either from people who have just died or, in the case of organs, such as kidneys, that are not essential to maintaining life, from willing living donors. The cases in the first part of this chapter deal with problems of procuring organs. The second half of the chapter is devoted to the other category of problems: allocating organs once procured. Hearts, kidneys, livers, and other critical organs have become the archetype of scarce medical resources in the public policy debates over what constitutes a just distribution of medical resources.

PROCURING ORGANS

Many organs for transplantation are obtained from cadavers. Some traditions raise questions about the mutilation of the corpse for transplant purposes, but when a life can be saved by retrieving a cadaver heart or kidney, most would not object. Even Orthodox Jews, who normally would be opposed to manipulating the dead body, support, even require, procuring organs that could save lives.[2] Most of the controversy has been over what permissions, if any, are needed to procure organs and whether organs can be procured before the death of the one from whom the organs can be taken.

Generally, procurement is based on the "dead donor rule," which holds that life-prolonging organs can only be procured after the one from whom the organ is taken is dead. Organs, tissues, and organ parts that are not essential for preserving life are, however, procured from people while they are still alive, provided appropriate permission is obtained. Thus, a single kidney, a liver lobe, or tissue including blood can come from living donors.

Donation versus Salvaging

The initial ethical question of organ procurement is whether the organs must be donated by the one from whom they are taken or can be "salvaged" without obtaining permission. In the early days of organ transplant, this was referred to as the controversy between the donation and salvaging models.[3] There are recent proposals to "conscript" the dead body to procure organs,[4] that is, take organs routinely without obtaining any permission or approval, but most controversy today pits donation by the deceased or next-of-kin against other strategies such as payment of financial incentives and presuming consent for procurement (with an "opt-out" provision so that organs will not be taken from those who have registered their objection while they were living).[5]

=== CASE 14-1 ===

Donation, Salvaging, and Incentives for Transplantable Organs

In April of 2006, the U.S. President's Council on Bioethics held a meeting to consider strategies for increasing the procurement of organs for transplantation. At the time, approximately 90,000 people were waiting for solid organs in the United States. In the previous decade, about 60,000 people had died while waiting for an organ. The waiting time for a kidney, for example, was typically as long as five years. The existing approach had been based on the National Organ Transplantation Act (1984). Organs from the newly dead could be obtained only if the deceased had donated his or her organs while alive or, absent objection from the deceased, if the next-of-kin donates them. This approach is referred to as the donation or "opting-in" model.

The President's Council was asked to consider alternative approaches including the routine procurement of organs unless there is a known objection from the deceased or the next-of-kin. This approach, sometimes called the "opting-out" model, assumes organs can be taken unless an objection is recorded.

Another approach the Council was asked to consider involved payment of incentives, usually financial, for those willing to donate. A small payment (such as a $10.00 income tax deduction) could be provided for those willing to sign a donor card. Other proposals would pay the estate of the deceased if organs are actually procured. Still other proposals would permit people to be paid for supplying a kidney (and possibly a liver lobe), while the one supplying the organ is still alive. Some versions of the incentive proposals would not pay directly for organs but would provide for funeral expenses or for expenses for family.

Some defenders of these alternatives argued that they would save hundreds, perhaps thousands of lives per year. No one would be forced to provide organs against his or her will. These defenders argued that many people are not opposed in principle to providing organs but simply have not taken the time to think about an unpleasant subject or at least have not taken the step to actually make a donation. They would rely on free-market mechanisms to encourage people to become suppliers of life-saving body parts.

The critics of the proposals were concerned that routine salvaging, even with an opt-out, would radically revise the relation of the individual and society. They would, in effect, say that the individual's body is the property of the state rather than something that should remain under individual control. Permitting financial incentives would, they fear, result in a "commodification" of the body—rendering it a commercial product—and generate unfair pressures on the poor.

Should the Council endorse either routine procurement financial incentives or remain with the donation model?

COMMENTARY

The debate among the members of the President's Council recapitulates a controversy that has taken place over the past two decades. The prevailing approach, especially in English-speaking countries of the Western world, has been to begin with the presumption that organs belong in some sense to the one in whose body they reside. They have not been considered personal property like other possessions, but individuals have been said to have a "quasi-property right" in their body parts and that right has transferred to the next-of-kin when an individual dies. The possessor of that right has had the right and responsibility for disposing of the body properly. Traditionally, that meant burial, cremation, or perhaps donation for medical research. That this is not a normal property right can be seen in the limits placed on how the body can be treated. It must be disposed of properly, and there are limits on how this is done. For example, it could not be sold for commercial manufacturing purposes. At the same time, we have acknowledged since the time of the Greeks (consider the play Antigone by Sophocles) that the state cannot automatically use the body for society's purposes. This notion that the individual has rights and responsibilities over the disposition of the dead body and that the state is constrained in accessing the body stands behind the commitment to the donation mode of procuring organs.

Utilitarian ethics opts for the policy that will produce the greatest possible net benefit to the community as a whole. Some human bodies, if they are otherwise healthy at the time of death, have the potential of doing a great deal of good. As many as six or seven lives—perhaps more—could be saved from transplant of heart, liver, pancreas, lung, and sometimes other organs such as stomach and small bowel. Even kidneys are increasingly being seen as life saving since patients with kidney disease do much better following transplant than they do on dialysis. At the same time, taking one's organs after death does the deceased no harm. The worst that can be envisioned is a psychological distress among the living who would not want their organs procured. Given the dramatic benefits and the minimal harm that could come from routine procurement of organs, utilitarians often defend routine salvaging policies.

Those who defend the donation model (and those who generally defend the rights of individuals against the interests of society) usually do so on moral grounds other than utilitarianism. They claim that individuals are the bearers of rights and this includes the right to consent or refuse consent for the use of one's body for social purposes, even important ones like saving the lives of others. They see the integrity of the individual threatened by routine salvaging proposals. They ask, "If the state can take one's body parts after death, what else can it take?" Some critics of utilitarian reasoning point out that even more good could come from taking body parts from people while they are still alive. Some people, such as those contemplating suicide, might not object. Body parts from prisoners condemned to execution might also be salvaged.

Both those who would defend routine salvaging and those who would oppose it should compare public policy regarding organ procurement with policies authorizing autopsy on the dead bodies of those whose deaths might have involved foul play. Normally, autopsy requires consent of the deceased or family, but laws authorize autopsy without consent if needed to investigate a crime. If the state can invade the body without consent for this reason, should it also be allowed to procure organs when it serves the societal interest?

Sometimes policies for routine salvaging are referred to as "presumed consent" laws. This is a controversial term, however. In fact, many European countries have laws authorizing the state to take organs unless there has been an opt-out. None of these laws technically presume consent.[6] There is an important difference, at least philosophically, between claiming that organs can be taken because consent can be presumed and claiming that they can be taken regardless of whether the individual would have consented. Since we know that a significant minority of people oppose organ procurement and would not consent if asked, it is hard to justify routine salvaging on grounds that consent can be presumed. It must rest on a belief that the state has a right to take regardless of consent.

The proposals for financial incentives appeal to a different moral principle. The advocates of incentives appear to agree with the defenders of donation in holding that the organs of the deceased are not the state's for the taking. The deceased when he or she was still alive (or the next-of-kin) must be induced to provide the organs. Unlike the defenders of donation, however, the advocates of incentives are skeptical of arguments that place limits on the property rights in the body. Incentive schemes seem to imply that the organs are property of the deceased or the next-of-kin and they can be sold as well as given away. They are attractive to defenders of free-market exchanges. Often these are libertarians, people who give first priority to the ethical principle of autonomy rather than utility.[7]

If a restriction on organ procurement that requires actual donation by the deceased or the next-of-kin can be defended, it will probably have to be based on an appeal to some moral principle other than utility or autonomy. The most plausible candidate would appear to be some notion of justice, concern about unfair pressure on the poor, or individual rights that preserve grounds for the individual to prohibit the use of organs even when their use would save lives.

Diseased and Poor-Quality Organs

More specific ethical problems in organ procurement arise regardless of whether organs are procured via donation, salvaging, or market mechanisms. The first of these problems is how the transplant system should handle cases in which the potential organ procurement involves organs of questionable quality—organs from older people, organs with poorer function, and those that run the risk of transmitting HIV, cancer, or other disease.

CASE 14-2

Tainted Organs: Donors with High-Risk Lifestyles

Carol Weekley, the Director of Gift of Life, the organ procurement organization for an east coast metropolitan area, received a phone call that a patient at City Hospital had met preliminary criteria for brain death and was a potential source of organs. Joel Williams, a 25-year-old Caucasian male, had succumbed to a gun shot wound to the head, apparently in retaliation for a drug deal that had gone bad. Physicians at City Hospital had done all they could to save his life but did not succeed. The family was now asking about the possibility of donating his organs for transplant.

A young, previously healthy person who suddenly receives a fatal gunshot wound is, in many ways, an ideal source of organs, but Williams had a long history of IV drug abuse and evidence of bad heart valves probably related to his drug use. That meant that his heart or its valves would not be usable, but other organs were potentially of usable quality. Preliminary tests had shown good liver and kidney function. Williams's mother wanted something good to come from his death, which she considered a terrible waste of what had once been a promising son.

A history of IV drug abuse is a warning sign in transplantation. IV drug use is one of the major sources of HIV infection. Williams had screened negative for HIV, but there was some chance he had not seroconverted, that he was actually carrying a recently acquired HIV infection. Transplanting organs from an infected person posed a danger of transmission of HIV. Organs would be perfused to remove as much of Williams's blood as possible, but the virus could still be present in the organs.

At one time, organs from those with high-risk lifestyle including homosexual men and IV drug abusers were routinely disqualified as donors. Now, however, thousands were dying while on the waiting list for organs and transplant community professionals were questioning whether such organs should always be discarded. The chance of such persons being infected was very low and a transplant might not transmit an infection. (Since surgeons would never intentionally transplant an organ from someone with known HIV infection, experience was too limited to determine the likelihood of transmission.)

The problem was made more complicated by the fact that having HIV no longer disqualifies one from being listed for transplant. People who need organs for reasons that may be unrelated to their HIV receive organs using the standard allocation system. Ms. Weekley realized that she could offer Mr. Williams's organs to those on the list who are already HIV+. This might theoretically increase their risk by adding copies of the virus, possibly introducing a new strain that could make the disease worse. On the other hand, some of these candidates on the list might be suffering significantly for need of an organ—perhaps declining toward death. For the kidneys, the wait can be five years for a normal organ, a waiting time that could be unattractive to potential recipients. It had even been suggested that those with HIV might find solidarity with a donor who shares the disease or a risk of it.

Should Ms. Weekley offer the organs to those on the waiting list with a history of HIV? Would there be circumstances under which she should offer it to those without such a history?

COMMENTARY

The problem posed by Mr. Williams's high-risk lifestyle combined with a negative initial screening is part of a larger problem sometimes referred to as the "tainted organ" problem. Organs from those with infectious disease or cancer often may be of good quality except they pose a risk of transmission of disease. Organs with poorer function or those from older persons pose issues of whether they should be offered to potential recipients and, if so, what should be said about their condition? The transplant community sometimes refers to these as "extended criteria donors," ECDs.

If organs are to be transplanted that are known to pose quality issues, one approach would be to ask those on the waiting list whether they would be willing to accept such organs. Since these are complex decisions that would require some thought, one strategy would be to ask those on the waiting list in advance whether they would potentially accept extended criteria organs. The kind and degree of risk vary, and recipients' conditions change, so those maintaining the waiting list would probably have to note whether those on the list would generally be willing to consider such organs. Then at the time an offer can be made, the recipient would have to decide whether to accept a particular offer.

Some might be concerned that surgeons would resist having to operate to procure and transplant an organ associated with a risk of infection such as HIV. Surgeons, however, have considerable experience with precautions such as double or triple gloving to minimize their own exposure. Their real objection may be that they have historically been committed to protecting patients and avoiding direct harm to them. The thought that they could be responsible for placing a virus or a cancer into their patient is repugnant. Some surgeons object even in cases in which the risk is low and the choice of the candidate for a transplant could be considered rational considering their options. This raises the question of whether surgeons should retain the right to refuse to operate in cases in which the use of tainted organs poses a health risk to the recipient, but the recipient has been informed and consented to that risk.

If it is reasonable to procure organs from patients like Mr. Williams who test HIV negative but have a history of a high-risk lifestyle and may not have seroconverted, this raises the question of whether it would ever be acceptable to intentionally procure and transplant an organ from someone known to have HIV or cancer. Recipients on the waiting list with these conditions may at least want to consider accepting such organs. Conceivably, someone facing eminent death from liver failure, for example, might consider such an offer a good risk considering the alternative. Should organs from people with infectious disease, cancer, old age, or poor organ function be offered to those on the waiting list who could be adequately informed of the risks?

Donation after Cardiac Death

Another special group of organs pose problems in procurement. There was a time when life-saving organs could be procured under the "dead donor rule" only after the one who might provide the organs had died, as measured by the traditional mode of an irreversible cardiac arrest. Beginning in 1968, a new definition of death based on loss of brain function began to be explored.[8] It was first adopted in American law in 1970. (The debate over this definition is explored further in Case 18-1.) Soon thereafter, almost all organs were procured from people who were pronounced dead, based on brain criteria. Since heart function remained, organs were preserved in better condition.

With the serious shortage of organs, transplant personnel developed a rekindled interest in people who die based on measurement of loss of heart function from heart attacks, for example, or from decisions of terminally ill people to withdraw life support. Many more people die that way, and there is potentially a large number of organs that could be procured. These cases, however, raise ethical questions about whether, in the case of heart attack victims, maximal effort will be made to resuscitate the patient, and, in the case of withdrawal of life support, whether death will be pronounced too quickly in order to obtain organs.

CASE 14-3

Donation after Cardiac Death: Starting Procurement without Consent

Michael Horton, a 33-year-old healthy Caucasian man, was at work in a large American city when he suddenly collapsed and lay unconscious on the floor. The rescue squad arrived in eight minutes and began cardiopulmonary resuscitation (CPR). He was transported to the level-1 trauma center at City Hospital Center where attempts to start heart function were unsuccessful. He was pronounced dead by the emergency room (ER) attending physician.

City Hospital was the leading transplant center in the city. Mr. Horton was a potential source of organs, but no record of donation (on a driver's license or other document) could be located. No measurement of brain function was taken. He was pronounced dead, based on traditional cardiac criteria. The transplant team initiated efforts to contact family and engage in the delicate process of telling them of the death of Mr. Horton and then asking for permission to procure organs by a process that is now referred to as donation after cardiac death (DCD). Unfortunately, Mr. Horton's wife could not be located quickly. Organs deteriorate rapidly when the body is warm and blood is not flowing, a condition known as warm ischemia. Transplant surgeons prefer that organs be transplanted with no more than thirty minutes of warm ischemia time. If, however, the body is perfused with a cold perfusate solution, the transplant team has a longer time, about four hours.

Two controversies emerged. First, now that procurement typically follows death pronounced by brain criteria, is it still acceptable to procure organs from people pronounced dead by cardiac criteria? If so, exactly when can the procurement begin? Second, in cases in which the next-of-kin cannot be located, would it be permissible to cool the body using cold perfusate thus giving the team a longer time to locate family and attempt to gain permission to obtain organs?

COMMENTARY

In the beginning days of organ transplants, no deaths were pronounced based on brain criteria. All organs were procured following death based on cardiac criteria. Now death based on brain criteria is the predominant mode of obtaining organs. Increasingly, theorists are convinced that people really die when their brains irreversibly lose function regardless of the status of the heart. Thus, in cases in which a full set of brain function measurements are not performed (usually taking six or more hours), the absence of heart function may not really guarantee that brain function has been lost.

It is clear that people are not dead as soon as their hearts stop beating. People regularly suffer temporary cardiac arrests (sometimes mistakenly called "clinical death" by clinicians) and their hearts can be started again. In those cases, brain function may not have been destroyed. If, however, the heart has stopped for a long enough time for the brain tissue to die from lack of oxygen, then the stoppage of the heart can be used as an indirect measure that brain function is irreversibly lost. The issue is, how long the heart must be stopped in order to pronounce death?

Donation after cardiac death can occur in two different ways. The first is referred to as "uncontrolled" or "unplanned" arrests. Mr. Horton's case is an example. Mr. Horton suffered a cardiac arrest in an uncontrolled environment. The initial goal of the health care team is to resuscitate him and preserve his life, if possible. Only when the clinical team concludes that resuscitation will not be possible will organ procurement be on the agenda. In these cases, the first moral issue is the separation of the rescue activities from the procurement. Normally, this requires a separation of the two functions, with the procurement team kept separate and restricted from their activities until the rescue team has decided more effort will be fruitless and death has been pronounced.

Organs can also be procured following death based on cardiac criteria when the death is planned or controlled. This can occur in the case of a critically ill patient for whom life support is being stopped based on the patient's advanced directive or the decision of the familial surrogate. Some of these patients, including trauma victims, may have usable organs, and the patients or their surrogates may actually have initiated a request to procure organs. In these cases, the problem of when to stop a resuscitation attempt does not arise. The problem of how long to wait after cardiac arrest may be more severe, however, since the organ procurement team would like to obtain the organs as soon as death is pronounced.

The University of Pittsburgh, which pioneered the procuring of organs from people pronounced dead by cardiac criteria following planned arrests, originally proposed waiting two minutes after asystole (absence of heart beat) on the grounds that at that point the heart cannot spontaneously begin beating again. Since planned arrests do not raise the issue of whether to resuscitate, it can be argued that the heart stoppage is irreversible even though the heart tissues are not actually dead after two minutes, and the heart could be started again if someone were authorized to intervene. Most programs, however, insist on waiting longer, at least five minutes before pronouncing death.

In unplanned arrests such as Mr. Horton's case, two minutes of asystole is clearly not a basis for pronouncing death. The resuscitation efforts will continue perhaps for an hour or more. During that time blood will be circulating if external means are applied. Then the question is how long to wait before pronouncing death after the decision has been made that the patient's heart cannot be started to beat spontaneously.

For both planned and unplanned arrests, waiting at least five minutes makes sense. At that point, the heart function will be lost. That is the recommendation of the Institute of Medicine.[9] If, however, one insists that death is really based on irreversible loss of all brain function, five minutes of asystole may not be sufficient to guarantee that brain tissue is actually destroyed. Whether the arrest was planned or unplanned, the decision has been made that the heart will not or cannot be started again so the brain tissue will be destroyed very soon. Deciding how long to wait after the last blood flow will depend on whether one actually wants to insist that the brain is dead.

In Mr. Horton's case, waiting five minutes or more will not be the main issue. The problem is that the transplant team would like to procure organs as soon as possible and would like to see the body cooled quickly if organs cannot be procured immediately. Procurement from Mr. Horton without permission of the next-of-kin is ruled out by anyone who insist on actual donation. Since there is no record of Mr. Horton's donation, this means waiting until the next-of-kin is located and gives permission. Then the issue is whether the body can be cooled while the team waits to attempt to locate the relative. This would require cannulating an artery in the thigh and removing the body's blood, replacing it with a cooled fluid designed for this purpose. That would give the team several more hours to locate the next-of-kin and get permission. If permission is refused, the cannula would be removed, leaving the body intact except for a tiny cut in the skin of the thigh where the cannula had been placed.

The moral problem is that the law prohibits conducting procedures on a dead body for the purposes of benefiting others, whether for transplant, research, or teaching purposes without permission, so it seems we would need the next-of-kin's permission to cannulate and cool the body. If, however, the next-of-kin of Mr. Horton can be reached, this procedure would not be needed.

One approach would be to pass legislation to permit the limited intervention to cool the body and preserve the option of donation. This has been done, for example, in the District of Columbia. This means that, in theory, someone who had moral or religious objections to manipulating a dead body could be perfused prior to contacting relatives to learn of this objection. On the other hand, it means that the option of donation is preserved. The alternatives would be to perfuse without consent or lose the possibility of transplanting the organs.

Preserving the Organs of the Dying

Patients such as those who are potential donors following cardiac arrest, as well as those who are approaching death by brain criteria, should be given the full attention of the medical team. Normally, organ procurement is a subject that comes up only after the death of the patient. In some cases, however, the patient or family may initiate a conversation about organ donation asking whether this altruistic gift might be possible.

If the patient or family has indicated a clear desire to donate organs, a new problem arises. In order to preserve the option of donation, drugs such as heparin (a blood thinner) or ventilation might have to be administered. This would not be for the benefit of the patient, but rather to preserve the organs. In certain cases, these treatments could even hasten the death of the patient or, in the case of a ventilator, risk stabilizing the patient in a severely compromised state. The moral issue in the following case is whether these activities can be undertaken to preserve organs before the death of the patient and, if so, whether the hastening of the death would constitute an illegal and unethical killing.

CASE 14-4

Treating Donors to Optimize Organ Quality

Peter Hendershott was transported to Provincial Hospital in a large Canadian city following a serious auto accident in which he suffered massive head injury. Soon it became clear that he would not recover and, in fact, was progressing toward brain death.

In his possession at the time of the accident was an organ donor card indicating he would want to be a donor in the event of such an accident. His family had been with him for three days and was now resigned to the fact that he would not recover. They initiated a conversation with the personnel in the intensive care unit (ICU) that they knew he was an organ donor. They stated clearly that they wanted something good to come from this tragedy.

The patient had been tested for brain function. He presently did not meet brain criteria for pronouncing death. The ICU attending physician explained the options. They could maintain maximal life support (but acknowledged that he would never recover consciousness). They could withdraw all life support and allow him to die. They expected that withdrawal of a ventilator would probably result in death based on stoppage of heart function over the course of the next day or so.

When the family again raised the question of organ donation, the ICU team indicated that might be possible but were concerned that prolonged deterioration would make DCD unlikely and waiting for brain death criteria to be met might take so long that organs would no longer be usable.

The attending physician was aware of another possibility. They could medicate him using vasopressor and heparin not for Mr. Hendershott's benefit, but in order to preserve the organs for transplant. Their concern, however, was that these drugs could pose a slight risk of hastening the death. This might happen, for example, if Mr. Hendershott had a slow internal bleed that would be made worse by the heparin. They also expressed concern of another kind. Maintaining Mr. Hendershott on a ventilator could pose the possibility that he would stabilize and never progress to brain death. He could remain in a coma and not die even if the ventilator were

disconnected. Since the physicians and family were in agreement that it was not serving Mr. Hendershott's interest to preserve his life any longer, the physician believed
that stabilizing him in a coma that could last for months or even years would actually
be a bad outcome for him. Since the attending physician in the ICU believed his sole
duty was to work for Mr. Hendershott's interest and not to promote the agenda
of the transplant team, he felt that he could, in good conscience, neither administer vasopressors and heparin, which could count as actively killing the patient, nor
maintain the ventilator, which could inappropriately preserve his life.

The family still insisted that Mr. Hendershott would want everything done to
make his organs transplantable, especially since he would not suffer in any way from
the drugs or the ventilator.

COMMENTARY

The normal rule in cases of patients who are approaching death and potential
candidates for organ donation is that the caregiving team responsible for the
patient must pursue single-mindedly the medical welfare of the patient. The
possibility of organ procurement is isolated from that and should arise only at
the point that death has occurred. Normally, this involves a shift to a different
team of health personnel who are no longer expected to benefit the terminally
ill patient, but to pursue organ transplant (with appropriate permissions from
the deceased and relatives).

This case challenges this moral division of labor. Mr. Hendershott has made
a clear commitment to become an organ donor and his family actively supports
that goal. In such a case, the interests of the patient cannot be completely isolated from organ procurement. Advancing organ procurement is at the same
time advancing the patient's interest as expressed when he was competent.

Thus the possibility of interventions—vasopressors and heparin as well
as a ventilator—arises. The patient and family may not only consent to these
treatments, they may demand them even if the result is the slight possibility
of hastening death (with the drugs) or inappropriately prolonging life (with
the ventilator). The physician may perceive the administering of the drugs as
risking active killing, something that is normally illegal. He may perceive the
ventilator as oddly contrary to his patient's interest.

Although actively administering a drug that kills is normally illegal and
considered immoral by most physicians, special cases exist that we encountered
in Chapter 9 when we considered indirect killing. Administration of drugs
can occur for good, defensible purposes even though they pose a risk of side
effects, even death. Such a killing would be classified as "indirect," that is,
not the intention of the one administering the drugs. If certain conditions are
met, indirect evil effects are often considered morally tolerable. The good end,
not the evil one, must be intended even if the evil can be anticipated as a side
effect. The good must be proportional and the evil must not be a means to

the good end. For example, those accepting the double effect doctrine would permit administering doses of narcotic necessary to relieve pain even though a risk of respiratory depression and death was recognized.

Some have argued that, using this double effect reasoning, drugs such as heparin may be administered in order to preserve organs for transplant even though the risk of hastening death is understood as a slight risk. The benefit in this case is not for the patient (unless fulfilling his wish to be a donor counts as a benefit to him). The purpose is to help others who desperately need organs. Nevertheless, it is clear that the intention is not to give heparin to hasten death; the intention is to preserve organs. The hastening of death is an unlikely side effect. It is less clear whether the hastening of death is a means to achieving the good end. Many would argue that it is not. For these reasons, many have concluded that administering the drug is acceptable.

Applying this reasoning to the ventilator requires a similar analysis. It would first require sharing the physician's conviction that delaying death significantly by stabilizing the patient would count as a harm, not a benefit. If it is a harm, however, it is surely not intended. As long as the benefit of preserving organs is proportional to the harm, it could be deemed ethical.

There is one more dimension to this case. If the risk of the ventilator is stabilizing the patient and keeping alive in a coma for months or years, the physician and family would need to consider their options before deciding to take this "risk." In Case 9-4, we considered a case of withdrawing nutrition and hydration from a terminally ill patient in order to let the dying process continue. A patient who becomes stable in a coma as a result of a ventilator is a potential candidate for withdrawing nutrition and hydration. If the family considered this an acceptable response to the unexpected but possible outcome of stabilizing the patient in a coma, then the patient would not face a future of months or years in a coma. If consent were withdrawn to provide nutrition and hydration, the patient would die within days. This would, of course, make organ procurement impossible, but would avoid the outcome of prolonged coma perceived to be a harm.

Socially Directed Organ Donation

Another kind of problem that can arise in procuring organs is what is referred to as socially directed organ donation. The law has long recognized the right of someone donating an organ to direct the organ to some friend or relative. If a man is in an auto accident and is left brain dead so that the family has to make a decision to donate his organs, that family may know of another family member who is in need of a kidney or other organ. They have the legal right to specify who will receive that organ. It can be directed to a named individual.

Now the problem occasionally arises that the patient or family wishes to direct the donation not to a named individual, but rather to a social class of potential recipients. The organ can be directed to a group defined by religious affiliation, gender, sexual orientation, race, or other social group. These socially directed gifts raise problems of justice that usually do not seem troubling when the gift is directed to another family member.

CASE14-5

Whites Only: The KKK and Socially Directed Donation

Thomas Simons was assaulted in a $5 robbery in Manatee County Florida. He was struck in the head and sustained massive brain damage that completely destroyed his brain function. His family was approached about donating organs. The family was willing to donate, but with a restriction.

Simons was a leader of the Ku Klux Klan. Knowing his beliefs, his father agreed to donate "to white recipients only."

The organ procurement organization tried unsuccessfully to persuade the family to make an unrestricted donation. The procurement team understood that these organs were in a relatively young man who was healthy before the assault—an ideal source of organs. Those organs could potentially save the lives of several people on the waiting list. A heart, liver, lungs, and pancreas could be procured as well as kidneys. If they were needed, stomach and small intestine could also be procured as well as corneas and bone.

When the family refused to modify the conditions under which the donation would be made, the procurement team, having to make a rapid decision, accepted the restriction, and procured the organs.

Following these events a national debate occurred. Lawyers raised the point that organ procurement in the United States is part of a public system administered by the Organ Procurement and Transplant Network under the supervision of the United Network for Organ Sharing. Should the organs have been accepted under these restrictions?[10]

COMMENTARY

Clearly, the conditions under which the Simons family is willing to donate Thomas Simons's organs are discriminatory. The organ procurement team will object if it is trying to run a fair system with equal access regardless of race. Nevertheless, the procuring personnel had to make a rapid decision and could be tempted to tolerate the discrimination in order to gain several life-saving organs. They could insist that any organs procured be distributed according to the current allocation algorithm, which would not take race into account. That option would lead to a refusal to procure even though there were many people on the waiting list who were Caucasian. Those who were first priority might, in fact, have been Caucasian, but they might not be. Insisting that the allocation algorithm be followed would mean the organs would not be donated, and some people would go without what we can presume were good organs for transplant. Their alternative was to accept the conditions specified by the family even though this would discriminate.

Defenders of utilitarianism would ask which option would do the most good, taking into account all parties affected. They point out that no one would have any less access to an organ (when compared to the alternative of declining the Simons's offer) and some would gain.[11] Since someone needing a heart or a liver could very easily die if the organs are refused and others, including those who could get Mr. Simons's kidneys, would have a significantly better life, it is easy to see how utilitarians would swallow hard and accept the organs with the conditions attached.

Those committed to a principle of justice as a basis for allocating organs would insist that the pattern of allocation was what was morally critical. They would insist on fairness even though it could mean that some valuable organs would be wasted.[12]

Some sophisticated utilitarians might look for more subtle consequences that would support refusal of the donation with strings attached. They might point to the long-term consequences for the transplant system as a whole if it became known that the program accepts such discriminatory restrictions. If, for example, two families are sufficiently offended that they withhold consent for donation of a family member's organs, the net result would be a loss of organs. Thus, utilitarians could also support a policy of refusing the organs. On the other hand, some nonutilitarians might identify arguments on which they could tolerate discriminatory allocation. For example, if the organs were accepted and the highest priority recipient were a non-Caucasian who was willing to consent to passing the otherwise wasted organ on to the highest Caucasian on the list, the freely given consent might be seen as adding moral complexity to the choice.

Lawyers have argued that, since the national transplant program is a public program, it must conform to laws prohibiting discrimination. Since the law seems to prohibit discrimination, utilitarians might imagine arguments concluding that accepting such organs could actually have negative consequences; the nonutilitarian justice concerns are so conspicuous, the transplant program now refuses organs directed to social groups such as those based on race. This poses the question of whether there are any other social groups for which directed donation would be tolerable morally. Examples have been cited of people wishing to donate to recipients of a certain religion, gender, sexual orientation, or age group. Would a directed donation restricted to go first to children be acceptable?

Living Donor/Deceased Donor Organ Swaps

Since the organ shortage is so severe, more and more people are relying on living donors of kidneys. Donors are usually family members or close friends. If someone volunteers to consider donating a kidney, that person is screened medically and psychologically. Tests are performed to determine whether the potential donor has a well-functioning and compatible kidney.

In some cases, a willing donor turns out to be incompatible because of a blood-type mismatch, the presence of incompatible antibodies, or problems with organ size. Until recently, these donors were simply turned away. Now, however, plans are being explored to permit this potential donor to swap his or her incompatible organ for one from the cadaveric pool of transplantable organs. The living donor's organ is given to the person who is next in line on the waiting list and, in exchange, the donor's paired recipient goes to the front of the line on the waiting list for the next suitable cadaveric organ.

CASE 14-6

Is an Organ Swap Unfair?

Thirty-seven-year-old Serena Goolsby had suffered from hypertension that led to kidney failure. She had been on dialysis for two years and had found it a very difficult experience. She had been listed for a kidney transplant, but at the center at which she was listed she could expect to wait at least three more years before she rose to the top of the waiting list.

Her husband, Frank, had discussed with her over the past year the possibility that he donate a kidney to her as a living donor. Such procedures are increasingly common and pose a very low risk although occasionally some serious complication can arise. The evidence is that an adult with normal kidney function can do quite well with only one kidney.

Receiving a living donor transplant would be a substantial advantage to Mrs. Goolsby. The kidney would have a somewhat better chance of functioning well and she would avoid the three-year wait with the potentially resulting medical problems. Mr. Goolsby eventually is tested to be a donor. His kidneys were fine, but, he was of B-blood type and Mrs. Goolsby had O-blood. She could only receive an O-blood organ.

The organ procurement organization in their area was experimenting with a new policy that would permit "organ swapping." The arrangement had been approved on a pilot basis by UNOS, the national transplant network. Mr. Goolsby's organ could be procured and donated to the person who ranked highest on the waiting list for an organ that normally would come from someone after he or she had died. (That recipient would be someone of B-blood type.) In exchange, Mrs. Goolsby would be moved to the top of the list for the next compatible organ procured from a deceased donor. That donor would have to be of O-blood type, and the organ would not be quite as good statistically as a living donor, but it would be much better for Mrs. Goolsby than waiting three years or so for her name to come to the top of the list. There was controversy within the organ procurement organization about whether such swaps between living and deceased donor organs were ethical. Should it be permitted?

COMMENTARY

Swapping of living donor kidneys for a deceased donor organ is one of the innovative strategies being tested to attempt to meet the serious shortage of organs. These swaps, in essence, add an organ to the system. An otherwise unusable living donor organ can be procured and transplanted. The person on the waiting list for a deceased donor organ who gets Mr. Goolsby's living donor kidney gets a substantial benefit. He or she gets the organ a bit earlier than otherwise and gets a living donor organ, which is a real advantage.

Another advantage is that an additional person is removed from the wait list. Mrs. Goolsby would otherwise have been in the ever-increasing pool of those waiting for organs. Thus, it seems like both recipients are helped and the pool of those waiting for a kidney is as well. Mr. Goolsby would, of course, suffer the consequences of becoming an organ donor, but presumably he was already open to that decision when he first agreed to be screened as a potential donor to his wife. From a utilitarian point of view, this seems like a win all around.

There is a problem, however. The people who will need to swap organs in this way will usually be recipients of O-blood type. Those of O-blood type who need a transplant and have an incompatible family member as a potential donor will be the most likely to need to swap. Since they can only use O-organs, this means those O-organs will be the most likely to be removed from the pool of deceased donor organs. Moreover, those of O-blood type on the waiting list are already experiencing the longest waits because they can only use O-organs. This means that the swap that helps both of the recipients who get the organs and shortens the overall wait list will also make those on the wait list who are already waiting the longest wait even longer. Mrs. Goolsby will, in effect, jump over those who had been waiting longer.

This creates a classic justice problem: the plan that maximizes overall benefits does so by hurting the group who is already worst off. For these reasons those who would give first priority to the ethical principle of justice will be skeptical about such swaps even if utilitarians will find the swap justified.[13] Should the organ procurement organization cooperate in providing the exchange of Mr. Goolsby's kidney for one from the deceased donor wait list that is of O-blood type?

Children as Living Organ Sources

If living kidney donors are sometimes the best arrangement when someone in the family needs an organ and the waiting time for a deceased donor organ is a problem, cases will inevitably emerge in which no adult family members are suitable donors. At that point, the question arises of whether children can ever provide a kidney. The medical risk is very low, but children cannot give an informed consent for the procedure undertaken to benefit another person. If they are to provide the kidney, they therefore cannot really be "donors." They could be called an "organ source" with the parents or other guardians being the ones making the decision. The issues are illustrated in the following case.

CASE 14-7

The Child as the Source of a Kidney

Diane and Dione DeLeon were identical twins born eight years ago. Dione was now suffering from a progressively serious kidney disease, hemolytic uremic syndrome. In December she began hemodialysis along with other treatments. By the next February her kidney was biopsied for a second time because of the onset of malignant type of blood pressure elevation. The decision was made that the kidneys had to be removed.

Both Dione's parents volunteered to donate kidneys for transplant but were rejected because of a tissue incompatibility. No other related donors were available except Diane who, being an identical twin, would make the ideal source for an organ. There is virtually no risk of failure for transplants from identical twins, but for transplants from an unrelated cadaver source, which is the only other possibility, the rejection risk remains real.

Mr. and Mrs. DeLeon were horrified at the decision they had to make. They agonized with the alternatives in a long counseling session with their minister. He thought that authorizing the transplant between the twin daughters was a morally sound decision. Pressured by knowledge that Dione's condition was deteriorating rapidly, the parents, together with the physicians, decided they should obtain a declaratory judgment from the court to authorize the donation.

The court appointed an independent guardian for Diane who, after spending a great deal of time talking with the child, concluded that she understood to the limits of her age and agreed with what was being asked of her. The guardian consented to the donation. A psychiatrist examined Diane and found that she had a strong identification with her sister and apparently desired to help her without having received undue pressure from the others in the family.

There had been previous cases involving minor identical twin donations, but these involved teenage minors who had a great deal more capacity to understand the procedure. There had also been a case involving a mentally retarded twin donor. He, however, was twenty-eight years old and so utterly dependent on the brother needing the kidney that a strong case was made that he would benefit more by keeping his brother alive than by keeping the second kidney. In this case while some possible benefit to Diane was recognized, all agreed that it was not a major consideration. The problem facing the judge was whether to permit the parents to approve the transplant, which would be of immense benefit to the recipient, but of some risk and limited benefit to her sister, who was not herself competent to consent.

COMMENTARY

Kidney donation by a minor or a mentally incompetent individual raises many of the same issues as does the consent for medical treatment of those who cannot consent on experimentation that does not benefit the subject. This kind of case raises several critical issues. First, should it be assumed that the one who provides the organ will not benefit, or can it be argued that the donors might reasonably benefit? Diane DeLeon might benefit because of the psychological risk from damaging the close relation with her twin sister.

In another legal case, the possible harm to the donor brother was considered the critical factor in justifying the donation. Tommy Strunk, a 28-year-old employee of the Penn State Railroad and a part-time student at the University of Cincinnati, was suffering from a fatal kidney disease. He was being maintained on a kidney machine, but according to the physician's opinion, the treatment could not be continued much longer.[14] Cadaver transplant was considered, but his 27-year-old brother Jerry had a highly compatible tissue match. Both parents and collateral relatives were ruled out as medically unacceptable. Jerry, however, had been committed to the Frankfort State Hospital and School, an institution maintained for the "feebleminded". He had an IQ of approximately thirty-five—the mental age of approximately six years. He could not communicate well with those not well acquainted with him, yet he was the ideal kidney donor.

The Department of Mental Health evaluated the case and made the following report:

> Jerry Strunk, a mental defective, has emotions and reactions on a scale comparable to that of a normal person. He identifies with his brother Tom; Tom is his model, his tie with his family. Tom's life is vital to the continuity of Jerry's improvement at Frankfort State Hospital and School. The testimony of the hospital representative reflected the importance to Jerry of his visits with his family and the constant inquiries Jerry made about Tom's coming to see him. Jerry is aware he plays a role in the relief of this tension. We the Department of Mental Health must take all possible steps to prevent the occurrence of any guilt feelings Jerry would have if Tom were to die.[15]

The necessity of Tom's life to Jerry's treatment and eventual rehabilitation is clearer in view of the fact that Tom is his only living sibling and, at the death of their parents, now in their fifties, Jerry will have no concerned, intimate communication so necessary to his stability and optimal functioning.

This case represents the extreme of the claim that the donor might benefit from the donation. Questions remain, however: Must there be a benefit to the donor to justify the transplant? Can a legitimate case be made for a benefit in the case Diane DeLeon? Would it be more honest to argue for the moral possibility of the donation authorization even without the grounds of benefit to the one providing the organ? If so, should such a decision be made simply by the parents or should it be reviewed by some other authority, such as a court or a transplant review committee?

A second issue in this case is the problematic consent of the one providing the organ. What should her role be? Is it possible for her to give a meaningful, voluntary, and informed consent in any sense?

In contrast with the DeLeons, in the first twin transplant cases involving minors, the minors were teenagers, nineteen in one case and fourteen in two others. Can one rely on their consent for the procedure independent of the benefit to them? If so, what is the difference between their cases and the DeLeons, where the twins were eight years old? What should be the response, for instance, if a child of five or six says no to the operation even though the parents, psychiatric consultants, social workers, and courts all determine that the child does not comprehend his choice and will in the long run seriously regret it?

ALLOCATING ORGANS

Once an organ is obtained, if it is not directed to a loved one, it must be allocated to the person with moral priority. The problem is identifying the ethical basis for doing that allocation. This is a special case of the resource allocation issues examined in the cases of Chapters 4 and 5. The difference is that, in organ allocation, it is not only money and professional time that is scarce, it is also the organs. They are inherently in a limited supply, so only some on the waiting list will be able to obtain one and, among those who can, there must be a priority established.

Maximizing Benefits and Distributing Organs Fairly

The ethical principles that govern organ allocation, like all resource allocation problems, are utility (beneficence and nonmaleficence), justice, and, in some cases, respect for autonomy. The most common allocation problem is the conflict between utility and justice. It is often found that one allocation will predictably offer the most benefit while another seems more fair. That was the issue in Case 5-5 in Chapter 5. In that case, surgeons and United Network for Organ Sharing (UNOS) officials who defended local allocation made a good case that more benefit would come from the limited supply of organs if they were kept locally. Even if it turns out that donation rates are not higher with local allocation, the cold ischemia time is a problem with transporting livers, and it is possible that, at least in some cases, more good would be done in the long run giving the livers to somewhat healthier patients.

The claims about doing greater good with local allocation will depend on exactly how one quantifies benefits. In transplantation, benefit is usually measured in terms of years of life added per transplant. Sometimes these years are adjusted for the quality of the lives lived, thus producing a unit called the "quality-adjusted life year [QALY]." The case for greater good seems plausible, however.

The moral conflict is over whether such an allocation is fair. The Department of Health and Human Services issued a regulation that required livers to be allocated more equitably by moving livers beyond the local level when people in another area were sicker and needed organs more urgently. The moral principle of justice requires that resources be allocated to create patterns of distribution of benefit that treats similarly situated people equally. There seems to be no doubt that equally sick people in different geographical areas were not being treated equally. Some very sick patients had a much better chance of getting an organ than others. In some regions with relatively few people in very serious liver failure, all those patients could be transplanted and there were still enough livers left over to give many of them to healthier patients who had months or years before they would be as ill as some in other geographical areas who were unable to be transplanted.

Many contemporary theories of justice give content to the notion that similarly situated people should be treated equally by insisting that resources should be targeted so as to benefit the worst off people. While it cannot be denied that people in the early stages of liver failure may eventually deteriorate to very sick status if they do not get transplanted, their need is less urgent and less certain. In medicine we often define the worst off as those who are in most urgent need. There is an impulse to rescue those in immediate need first. This is supported by the claim that the less ill may not actually deteriorate and, in any case, will have a longer time to get an organ. Hence, those committed to just allocation rather than utility-maximizing allocation have tended to support the government effort to get organs allocated over a wider area.

When Voluntary Risks Cause a Need for Organs

Many organ allocations will be based on the conflict between the utility-maximizing principles (beneficence and nonmaleficence). Sometimes the ethical principle of autonomy also comes into play. An obvious case is one in which a person who is critically ill comes to the top of the list for organ allocation and decides to refuse the transplant. If respect for autonomy is one of the relevant moral principles, we recognize the right of patients to consent or refuse consent to treatment, including transplant. Refusal of treatment by competent patients is one of the rights derived from this principle.

A second, and more controversial, way in which autonomy comes into play in organ allocation is in respecting the freedom of persons to choose lifestyles they prefer—even if those choices are not necessarily best for their health. If we respect freedom of individuals, we tolerate, at least for competent adults, choices to smoke, eat junk food, live a sedentary life, and consume alcohol, even though these are not healthful decisions.

This respect for autonomy impacts organ allocation when people need transplants as a result of the lifestyle choices they have made. Some argue that, if someone has voluntarily chosen a lifestyle with a known risk of damaging an organ, then that person deserves a lower priority for an organ, at least in a world in which organs are scarce resources.

For this position to be defensible, some assumptions will need to be made. The lifestyle choices involved are complex. They result from habits formed early in life, before one is a substantially autonomous adult. Some may have a genetic component beyond voluntary control of the individual. In order to consider a policy in which voluntary, health-risky lifestyle choices come into play, one must assume that there is, in fact, a voluntary component in the behaviors in question. If there is at least some voluntary element, then asking whether this voluntary element is relevant to organ allocation becomes a legitimate question. A debate in the UNOS Ethics Committee some years ago illustrates the problem.

CASE 14-8

Patients with Alcohol Dependency and Their Rights to Livers for Transplant

The United Network for Organ Sharing, the national Organ Procurement and Transplant Network created by the U.S. Congress to run the transplant program of the United States has an Ethics Committee that addresses policy questions having an ethical component. In the mid-1990s, the committee took up the controversial question of whether a history of alcoholism should come into play in allocating livers.

Liver failure can result from many causes. Some patients have failing livers as a result of an in-born condition called biliary atresia, a blockage in the liver that causes liver failure. Surely, neither the small children nor their parents are in any way responsible for this type of liver failure. Other causes involve more problematic behaviors—exposure to toxic chemicals and abusable drugs. Those damaging their livers in this way may have no advance knowledge of the risk. They may not even voluntarily choose to be exposed.

Alcohol consumption is a major cause of liver failure and the need for transplant. It is notoriously difficult to determine the extent to which alcoholism involves a voluntary component. The issue debated in the UNOS Ethic Committee was whether a history of alcoholism should play a role in allocating livers and, if so, what role it should play.

The committee staked out four positions. Theoretically, one could have a full and equal claim to a liver even if one were an active alcoholic. No one on the committee took that position. Everyone agreed that there must be evidence that the alcoholic was to some degree recovered. Most thought that at least six months of abstinence, preferably a year, was needed to show a likelihood that the patient would not return to drinking and damage the new liver the way he or she had damaged the original one.

At the other extreme, one could take the view that, since the choice to consume alcohol damaged what was presumably a perfectly good liver, the alcoholic patient had no entitlement to a liver for transplant at all. This view might lead to the conclusion that even if there were extra livers available, the alcoholic patient did not deserve one. No one on the committee took this view either.

The real debate was between two intermediate positions. One group, made up largely of surgeons, took the position that the role of UNOS was to produce as much benefit as possible from the limited supply of livers available. The cause of the liver failure was not relevant; what mattered was whether a transplant would help. As long as there was some assurance that the alcoholic was recovered, the question was whether a transplant would help. The data showed that alcoholics do quite well with a transplant. Since that was the case, these committee members believed the alcoholics deserved full and equal consideration in the liver allocation. The history of the patient did not matter; only the probability of benefit.

The other group on the committee was not convinced. They believed that history was morally relevant. If some people had had the opportunity to have good livers and others had not, those who clearly had no role in their liver failure deserved more consideration than those who might have voluntarily jeopardized theirs. This led to advocating some differential between those whose livers failed without their involvement, such as the biliary atresia cases, and those that failed with a possible voluntary lifestyle choice involved.

Since any justifiable organ allocation system will be multifactorial, this final approach would not give an absolute priority to those without the history of alcoholism (or other voluntary health-risky behavior), but it would justify a small negative consideration, enough at least to break ties.

Since livers are allocated on the point system called a MELD score (see the previous case discussion), this could be accomplished by subtracting one or more points from the score if one has a history of alcoholism. The number of points subtracted would be an indication of how relevant the alcoholism history was in comparison to the risk of mortality, which is the main factor measured by the MELD score. The issue before the committee, then, was whether to propose subtracting one or more points as an indicator that a history of voluntary behavior leading to the need for a transplant was a fair way of allocating organs.

COMMENTARY

This case adds the dimension of voluntary behavior to the debate about organ allocation. The general issue is whether voluntary lifestyle choices are relevant in deciding who gets an organ. The first problem, of course, is determining what behavior is voluntary. Rather than sorting all behaviors into either the voluntary or involuntary category, it probably makes sense to view choices on a continuum from involuntary to extensively voluntary. One must consider biological causes (genetic and others) and social and psychological forces that shape human conduct and physical limits. Many lifestyle choices that have an impact on health are in a gray zone in which there seems to be many nonvoluntary contributing factors, but some residual voluntary choice as well. We behave as if smoking, consumption of fatty foods, and alcohol intake have at least some voluntary component. Those who reject that conclusion would not recognize this case as posing a moral issue at all.

For those who believe there is enough of a voluntary component to the decision to consume alcohol over a long enough time period to pose a risk to the liver, the issue is whether that voluntary choice is to be a factor in allocating livers. Utilitarians, like the surgeons on the UNOS Ethics Committee, believed the history of alcoholism was not relevant. They were only concerned about how much good they could do for the people on the waiting list for livers. Since alcoholics had been shown to do as well as others on the list, as long as they were not ruled out as being actively alcoholic and continuing to pose a risk to their new liver, they deserved exactly the same consideration as anyone else on the list.

Those on the other side gave greater weight to the principle of justice. They wanted equals to be treated equally, but considered a history of a voluntary choice that damaged their otherwise good liver to be relevant in deciding alcoholics (and others who voluntarily damaged their liver, for example, through choosing to use drugs that were known to cause liver damage) deserved some degree of lower priority.

Since many other factors were also morally relevant, such as the mortality risk the patients were facing, the history of alcoholism would not be an all-or-none factor ruling out alcoholics. Especially, since there remained considerable doubt about how voluntary the choices were that led to alcohol consumption; the history of alcoholism would warrant, according to this group, only a marginal negative consideration—a point or so subtracted from the MELD score.

Multiple Organs and Special Priority for Special People

One final case presents two more ethical problems in organ allocation. Some patients need transplantation of more than one organ. They typically can need a kidney and a pancreas or, less often, a liver and small bowel, for example. Some need two organs either of which could be life saving for some other candidate on the waiting list. Giving the person who needs two of these means that two other people will go without. Especially, in the case of two organs necessary for life, the moral dilemma is dramatic. If each organ is in short supply, as in the following case, this means two people will die in order to save one who needs both organs.

The next case also poses another moral issue of allocation. The case involves a famous public figure, a state governor. (All details are real. The case is based exclusively on public information to avoid problems of confidentiality.) Some have suggested that this figure received special consideration and was moved to the head of the list because of his fame or because of his unusual responsibility for the welfare of many other people. The issues here, then, are whether one person deserves two life-saving organs and, if so, whether fame or responsibility ever command special consideration in allocating organs

---

===== **CASE 14-9** =====

Multiple Organs for a Famous Governor

Robert P. (Bob) Casey, Sr., was governor of Pennsylvania from 1987 until 1995. He was a union-backed Democrat famed for his opposition to abortion that led to a major Supreme Court decision, *Planned Parenthood v. Casey*, which upheld provisions for parental notification in the case of minors and a twenty-four-hour waiting period.[16]

Although unknown to his constituents, Gov. Casey was diagnosed in 1990 with a rare genetic disease, Appalachian familiar amyloidosis, in which production of amyloid was destroying his organs.[17] On June 14, 1993, just a few days after his disease was announced to the public, he received a rare combined heart–liver transplant. There was dispute about whether he received preferential treatment because of his public status as governor. Some claim he was moved to the head of the waiting list. Others say he had actually been on the waiting list for a year.

There were no clear rules for how allocation should be handled in the case of such a rare combination of organs. It is generally agreed that when more than one organ needs to be transplanted, they should be done simultaneously in order to avoid the trauma of two operations. Normally the organs would be obtained from the same donor. A case can be made that, if all the organs that are needed for a multiple-organ procedure are available, they should go to someone who needs them both, at least if that person is at the top of the waiting list for one of the organs.

Given that no clear rules were in place and that Gov. Casey needed a multiple-organ transplant, there are reasons to move him to the head of the line independent of whether he was a prominent figure. The fact that he was responsible for the welfare of all the citizens of Pennsylvania suggests an additional reason why he might be given special status. On the other hand, a multiple-organ transplant consumes two life-saving organs—a heart and a liver—both of which are so scarce that a person on the waiting list will die because he or she will not receive them. Thus, two people will go without transplant if the multiple-organ procedure is carried out. Should one person be entitled to two life-prolonging organs when two other people also need them? If that is acceptable, should Gov. Casey have been given any additional special consideration because of his important public responsibility?

COMMENTARY

This case presents two issues: allocating organs to those who need more than one and giving special consideration to those with fame or special responsibility.

Let us consider the multiple-organ problem first. This is more complicated than it may appear. For example, some people need multiple organs, but some of the organs they need are not in short supply. Danny Canal was a youngster who suffered a twisting of his intestine that eventually damaged his stomach, liver, and pancreas as well. He received a four-organ transplant in 1998. When those organs failed, he received another four-organ set, and then a third, all within the space of about two months.

Several of those organs were, however, not a scarce resource. The second set were transplanted as an emergency, using organs that were known in advance to be of poor quality. They were transplanted as a temporary bridge until good organs could be found and would not have been used otherwise. Moreover, intestines and stomachs are not really in much demand so only four organs of the twelve were really valuable, scarce resources. When the first two were put in, there was every reason to hope they would not fail so that decision involved only two valuable organs, the same that Gov. Casey received.

Some would argue that retransplant—in Danny Canal's case, the third round of transplant involving two scarce organs—liver and pancreas—should get lower priority. There are both utility and justice reasons. On grounds of utility, patients getting organs for retransplant do not do quite as well. On justice grounds, some people believe that the patient has already had a turn and now others deserve consideration. "No one should get seconds until everyone has had firsts" is roughly the idea here.

Both the utilitarian and justice arguments are controversial, however. If we always gave organs to those who predictably would do somewhat better, many people would be disqualified for their first transplant as well as retransplants. The justice argument raises the question of whether a patient like Danny Canal, whose first organs fail, deserves any lower priority than someone like him in need of a first transplant. The failure was clearly not his fault. If retransplant deserved lower priority there would be an incentive to make sure the first set were as good as possible. People would be reluctant to take less than perfect organs. For these reasons, the UNOS Ethics Committee adopted the position that retransplant per se was not a reason to lower allocation priority.

What, however, of the fact that multiple transplant uses up two life-prolonging organs when two people each of whom needed only one organ could otherwise be saved? Utilitarians might see this as an easy call. The payoff for single transplants would be twice as great as giving two organs to someone like Gov. Casey. As in the case of the retransplant, however, if we always gave priority to the arrangement that predictably would have the greatest payoff, many people would be excluded from transplant who, through no fault of their own, had a lower calculated net benefit. Older people, for example, would be excluded since they might not live as long with the transplant. Patients with harder-to-treat conditions might be excluded. Those with antibodies or antigens that increase the chance of rejection would be excluded—in some cases even if these factors only slightly decreased the calculated expected benefit. We have generally resisted using utilitarian arguments to allocate organs in the most efficient way possible. Gov. Casey or others needing multiple organs would get equal consideration if the utility-maximizing calculations were rejected.

Now, what about the fact that Gov. Casey is a famous governor with responsibility for the welfare of many citizens? Two slightly different issues need to be distinguished here. First, mere fame by itself could give people enough attention that they get special consideration. The famous baseball player, Mickey Mantle, needed a liver transplant and received an organ about twenty-four hours after being listed in spite of the fact that about 4,000 people nationally were listed ahead of him. Many people took that as a favoritism resulting from Mantle's fame. In fact, once one knows the algorithm for allocating livers, it seems unlikely that he really got any special favors. At the time, livers were allocated within the local OPO first. (See Case 5–5 for the debate that changed this policy to allocate livers more on a regional basis.) That meant he was competing against a much smaller pool, closer to 140 people. Then, there is a rule that people of O-blood type get first crack at organs from O-blood group donors—about half of all donors. Mantle was of O-blood type so he was really competing with only about seventy people. Then at that time, an available liver should have gone first to patients in the ICU, which is normally about half of 1 percent of the total. Mantle was not in the ICU but was in the hospital. In order for him to get an organ, there should have been no one in the ICU. Statistically, one-half of 1 percent of seventy people suggest that it was reasonable that no one was in the ICU. Organs would go next to the 1.5 percent of the people on the list who are in the hospital. Mantle should have gotten the first O-organ if he was the only one in the hospital. Statistically, one or two people (1.5 percent of seventy) should have been in the hospital, so if he were the only one, it would not be surprising. Nevertheless, most people would conclude that if he did get any favors solely because of his fame, then that would be unfair.

Gov. Casey's case is a bit different. It would not be his fame, per se, that generated a claim for priority, but his special responsibility as governor of a state. While it might seem plausible to give special consideration to people with special responsibility, trying to put such a policy into operation could be very difficult. It would require some agreed upon scale of who had greater responsibility. Would a single mother of four, for example, deserve consideration? Would the executive of a large, but controversial corporation charged with Enron-type corruption be given positive or negative consideration? Most of those who have thought about this problem conclude that the problems of ranking people on this basis would be too overwhelming. They would simply exclude all consideration of special status for special responsibility. That would mean that Gov. Casey's heart–liver allocation would be fair only if he rose to the top of the line the same way anyone else could—because of his time on the waiting list or because those needing multiple organs get special priority without regard to their fame or special responsibility.

Allocation of organs for transplant is a special case of the more general problem of allocating scarce resources. These more general problems involve the reconciliation of conflicts between utility and justice—the issues of Chapters 4 and 5. They arise in the real world of health care in the decisions that have to be made by health insurers and in health system planning, issues to which we now turn.

NOTES

[1] A nice brief history of organ transplantation and its relation to changes in the definition of death is provided by a team headed by the Cuban neurology, Calixto Machado. This summary is based, in part, on their work. See Machado, Calixto, Julius Korein, Yazmina Ferrer, Liana Portela, Maria de la C. Garcia, and José M. Manea. "The Concept of Brain Death Did Not Evolve to Benefit Organ Transplants." *Journal of Medical Ethics* 33 (2007):197–200.

[2] Rosner, Fred. "Organ Transplantation in Jewish Law." In *Jewish Bioethics*. Fred Rosner and J. David Bleich, editors. New York: Sanhedrin Press, 1979, pp. 358–374.

[3] See Ramsey, Paul. "Giving or Taking Cadaver Organs for Transplant." In *The Patient as Person*. New Haven, CT: Yale University Press, 1970, pp. 188–197; Dukeminier, Jesse and David Sanders. "Organ Transplantation: A Proposal for Routine Salvaging of Cadaver Organs." *New England Journal of Medicine* 279 (1968):413–419.

[4] Spital, A. and C. A. Erin "Conscription of Cadaveric Organs for Transplantation: Let's At Least Talk About It." *American Journal of Kidney Disease* 39 (2002):611–615.

[5] For a summary of the arguments see Institute of Medicine (U.S.). Committee on Increasing Rates of Organ Donation, Board on Health Sciences Policy. Childress, James F. and Catharyn T. Liverman, eds. *Organ Donation: Opportunities for Action*. Washington, DC: National Academies Press, 2006.

[6] Veatch, Robert M. and J. B. Pitt. "The Myth of Presumed Consent: Ethical Problems in New Organ Procurement Strategies." *Transplantation Proceedings* 27 (April 1995, No. 2):1888–1892.

[7] Taylor, James Stacey. *Stakes and Kidneys : Why Markets in Human Body Parts Are Morally Imperative*. Aldershot, England; Burlington, VT: Ashgate Pub., 2005; Cherry, Mark. *Kidney for Sale by Owner: Human Organs, Transplantation, and the Market*. Washington, DC: Georgetown University Press, 2005; Hippen, Benjamin. "In Defense of a Regulated Market in Kidney from Living Donors." *Journal of Medicine and Philosophy* 30 (2006):593–626.

[8] Harvard Medical School Ad Hoc Committee. "A Definition of Irreversible Coma. Report of the Ad Hoc Committee of the Harvard Medical School to Examine the Definition of Brain Death." *Journal of the American Medical Association* 205 (1968):337–340. See the cases in Chapter 18.

[9] Institute of Medicine (U.S.). Committee on Increasing Rates of Organ Donation, Board on Health Sciences Policy. Childress and Liverman. *Organ Donation*.

[10] The events of this case were reported by Testerman, Jeff. "Should Donors Say Who Gets Organs?" *St. Petersburg [FL] Times.* January 9, 1994.

[11] Callender, Clive. "Testimony of Group 13." Presented at Increasing Organ Donation Liver Allocation December 10, 11, 12, 1996. Bethesda, MD: Natcher Center, National Institutes of Health; Wilkinson, T. M. "Racist Organ Donors and Saving Lives." *Bioethics* 21 (2007, No. 2):63–74.

[12] Fox, Mark D. "Directed Organ Donation: Donor Autonomy and Community Values." In *Organ and Tissue Donation: Ethical, Legal, and Policy Issues.* Bethany Spielman, editor. Carbondale, IL: Southern Illinois University Press; 1996, pp. 43–50, 163; Arnason, Wayne B. "Directed Donation: the Relevance of Race." *Hastings Center Report* 21 (6)(1991, Nov.–Dec.):13–19; Veatch, Robert M. "Directed Donation of Organs for Transplant: Egalitarian and Maximin Approaches." In his *Transplantation Ethics.* Washington, DC: Georgetown University Press, 2000, pp. 388–401.

[13] Ackerman, Paul D., J. Richard Thistlethwaite, Jr., and Lainie Friedman Ross. "Attitudes of Minority Patients with End-Stage Renal Disease Regarding ABO-Incompatible List-Paired Exchanges." *American Journal of Transplantation* 6 (2006):83–88.

[14] Strunk v. Strunk. Ky., 445 S.W.2d 145 (1969).

[15] Ibid.

[16] Planned Parenthood of Southeastern Pennsylvania v. Casey, 505 U.S. 833 (1992).

[17] Kyle, Robert A. "Amyloidosis: A Convoluted Story," *British Journal of Haematology* 114 (No. 3, 2001):529–538.

CHAPTER 15

❧

Health Insurance, Health System Planning, and Rationing

Other Cases Involving Health Insurance

5-1: Under the Gun: Staying on Schedule in the HMO

8-1: Keeping a Patient Waiting

8-3: Continuing Treatment of a Patient Who Will Not Pay Her Bills

12-5: Posttraumatic Stress Disorder: Funding Therapy for a Preexisting Condition

12-6: Insurance Coverage for Psychoanalysis

In the United States, the total national expenditure on health care reached two trillion dollars in 2005, the last year for which statistics are available. That is $6,697 per person, up 6.9 percent from the previous year. That is a smaller increase than we had been experiencing in previous years but double the amount spent in 1993 and up from a mere $148 per person in 1960. Even allowing for inflation of the dollar, these are huge increases. The percentage of gross domestic product (GDP) spent on health care has risen from 5.2 to 16.0 percent in this forty-five-year period.[1]

With this expenditure the health of Americans has improved. During that same forty-five-year period, the average life expectancy at birth has increased by seven years (from 69.7 to 77.8 years).[2] Some of that has come from improvements in sanitation and lifestyle choices, but part comes from the advances in health care services. Additional years are being purchased at higher and higher costs.

Just as troublesome, there are enormous differences among different income and racial groups. The most recent numbers show life expectancy for black males in the United States to be 69.5 years; for white females it is 80.4 years.[3] Large numbers—around 45 million in the United States in 2005—go without health insurance for at least part of any given year.[4] To make matters more complicated, some of the expenditures are on medical services that are very expensive yet do little or no good for patients. Some others such as some diagnostic tests, though cheap individually, generate enormous costs when provided millions of times a year. Others are for services that patients may not want in the first place—ventilators for persistently vegetative patients, life support for anencephalic infants, and aggressive chemotherapy with little documented chance of success.

The continual growth in expenditures and percentage of GDP cannot be sustained. It comes at the price of constraining other important projects—education, the arts, and public safety, for example. Moreover, some of the expenditures provide unconscionable profits for private corporations and individuals. Insurance generates complex incentives so that individual patients and professional providers tend to perceive the treatment as "free" in the sense that it costs the patient nothing extra beyond the hidden insurance premium costs. The cases in this chapter present various problems we encounter in attempting to gain control of these health expenditures.

THE PROBLEM OF SMALL, INCREMENTAL BENEFITS

As health care costs began their conspicuous rise in the last decades of the twentieth century, analysts of health care costs realized that there were ever-increasing ideas for medical therapies. Some of these were unproven, but promising; some were clearly beneficial, but only offering very marginal benefits in comparison to costs; some offered more dramatic benefits but at extremely high costs. For many people, a classic publication in the *New England Journal of Medicine* in 1975 elevated the problem to their consciousness. The following case is based on that publication.

CASE 15-1

The Sixth Stool Guaiac: A Classic Cost-Containment Case

By the 1970s, a standard test to screen patients for the possibility of colorectal cancer was being used. Called the Greegor screening protocol for testing of stool for occult blood, it provides a preliminary indication that the patient has a risk for the disease that needs further workup. One problem with the test is that each time the test is performed, it finds 91 percent of true positive incidents of blood in the stool. Thus it is possible to repeat the test on a second sample and catch some of the cases that were missed in the previous test. The same problem exists with the second test: a few more cases will be identified if the test is repeated a third time. In 1974 the American Cancer Society endorsed a protocol of six sequential tests.

This led to a provocative paper in the *New England Journal of Medicine* by Duncan Neuhauser and Ann Lewicki that calculated the cost per case identified for each occurrence of the test.[5] Their calculations were based on the empirical evidence that the incidence rate of colorectal cancer was 7,200 per million in the population. Since 91 percent of these cases would be found on the first testing, theoretically a total of 6,594 cases would be identified on that first testing. The cost per case found was determined to be $1,175, surely a wise investment since interventions could be undertaken to greatly reduce the consequences to those patients. The problem was that out of each million people tested, 606 cases would be missed that could perhaps be caught if the test were repeated. On the second testing, however, there would, in theory, be only 606 cases of colorectal cancer remaining per million people tested so the cost per case found would be much higher.

The following table indicates, based on Neuhauser and Lewicki's estimates, the number of cases found per million people and the cost per case found:

Test number	Cases found per million	Marginal cost/case found
1	6,594	$1,175
2	7,144	$5,492
3	7,190	$49,150
4	7,193	$469,534
5	7,194.17	$4,724,695
6	7,194.20	$47,107,214

The numbers indicate that, if the American Cancer Society recommendations are followed, it would cost $47 million to find a single case when the sixth test is performed. The costs become extremely high because so many tests have to be performed to find a case because, by the time the sixth test is performed, most of the true positives have already been identified and many more tests have to be conducted to find the smaller and smaller number of cases remaining. Moreover, at that point about six cases per million population still would be missed. The test could be repeated a seventh time, at which point it would cost about a half billion dollars to find a case and so on and on.

Neuhauser and Lewicki suggest, and most observers have agreed, that it is not plausible to spend $47 million to find the marginal case. Of course, to the person whose case is identified, any amount of money may seem worthwhile, but that same amount of money spent on other medical or non-medical life-saving efforts—better road construction, for example—would save many, many more lives. There are not enough resources in the world to make all the medical and social interventions that could save lives at a price of $47 million per life saved. The question then is: how many times should the test be repeated? Knowing that no matter how many times it is conducted, there will be some small number of missed cases, when should we draw the line and say we have conducted the test a reasonable number of times?

COMMENTARY

This early case in the era of cost containment reveals how complex the decisions will be when we set out to control the costs of health care. Viewed from the perspective of the Hippocratic physician whose only goal is to do what will benefit the patient, it seems that this test should be repeated over and over again, at least the six times recommended by the clinicians advising the American Cancer Society. The only limits from the patient-centered Hippocratic perspective on the number of times the test should be repeated would be any risks and inconvenience involved. Since the risks are negligible, a doctor might be inclined to repeat the test up to the point that the patient refused to cooperate any further.

If the patient were paying the costs of each test, which amount to a few dollars, he or she would probably insist on stopping before six tests were performed. The patient might accept the current clinical consensus that three tests is about right. On the other hand, the choice of three tests is, in effect, saying that it is worth spending about $50,000 to identify a case. While that is the consensus view of the value of finding a case from the eyes of a clinician committed to pursuing medical well-being of patients, it may not be exactly how a patient would want to spend marginal dollars. Perhaps only two tests would be acceptable; perhaps for some particularly worried patients, four tests would be defensible.

Since the costs of these tests are normally not borne directly by the insured patient, the people managing the insurance decisions end up being the ones who make the call. If the insurer is a private, profit-making entity, it might authorize a low number of tests in order to maximize profits. Even if the insurer is a public agency (such as Medicare or Medicaid), there will be incentives to avoid spending money foolishly. After all, the money saved belongs, indirectly, to the people. If there is an insurer making the decision about how many tests to fund, that insurer presumably would tolerate patients who choose to perform fewer than the number of approved tests. (Doing so may increase the costs to the community of those insured in the long run, but we normally do not require diagnostic testing of unwilling patients even when doing so would save money.) The insurer would reasonably set an upper limit on the number of tests that can be performed in order to avoid investing the commonly held insurance assets unwisely in tests that have too low a predicted payoff. In the end, some number of approved tests will have to be chosen by the insurer. Three seems like a reasonable number, but there is no principled reason for picking that number unless we insist on some cap on the amount an insurer should spend to save a life or diagnose a disease. The decision-makers must decide whether about $50,000 per case found is the reasonable limit in this case.

LIMITS ON UNPROVED THERAPIES

In the previous case, documented benefit could be obtained from each test performed. The problem was that as more and more tests were conducted, the benefit got smaller and smaller. Another kind of resource allocation problem arises for insurers and others making health resource allocation decisions when the treatment being considered is of unproven value.

One of the most troublesome problems in deciding about health insurance coverage is the challenge of new and unproven therapies. They are often expensive and many have unknown side effects when they emerge and come to the attention of physicians or patients. It is natural to want to try the newest therapies. Especially when a patient faces a critical illness, these therapies are tempting even if they are unproven. It is also true that they are often aggressively promoted by the pharmaceutical industry sales force.

One version of this problem is so-called off-label use. Some drugs have labeling approved by the FDA for particular uses based on adequate scientific evidence of safety and effectiveness for those uses, but they may also be plausible drugs for other uses that have not been reviewed and approved by the FDA. In some cases, the number of patients who would likely use the drug is so small that it is not economically attractive for a manufacturer to do the testing to establish safety and effectiveness, even though it seems reasonable that the drug would be appropriate. In such cases, the question arises whether a physician should recommend and a patient should decide to use the drug for the off-label use. The following case comes from the records of the Medicare Rights Center (MRC), which represented the patient in the case.

CASE 15-2

Insuring Off-Label Pain Relief

Mr. H, a Medicare beneficiary and veteran of the U.S. Navy, was severely injured in a tornado on March 29, 1997. He suffered severe craniofacial trauma for which he underwent removal of his left eye, removal of portions of the left frontal lobe of his brain, and extensive cranial facial reconstruction. At the time of the injury, he was diagnosed with organic brain disease that causes him to suffer from severe migraines. Shortly thereafter, he became eligible for Medicare on account of his disability. Since the tornado, Mr. H has required pain medication to manage the incapacitating headaches that cause seizures when left untreated. As a result, he has developed a tolerance to pain medications, causing most pain killers to be ineffective in managing his acute migraines. For six years, Mr. H was using Actiq, which is indicated by the FDA to treat breakthrough pain in cancer patients, to manage his migraines and reduce the risk of seizing. Before the enactment of Medicare Part D, Mr. H received coverage of his Actiq prescription under the state Medicaid program, TennCare. Initially, when Medicare Part D was enacted and Mr. H was forced to enroll in a Medicare prescription drug plan, Humana covered his Actiq prescription. In October 2006, however, Mr. H was suddenly told by his pharmacist that Humana was denying coverage. Mr. H did not receive notice that his coverage would change nor did he receive a transitional supply. Because he could not afford to pay for his Actiq prescription out-of-pocket, Mr. H's prescribing physician, Dr. B, prescribed Fentora, which is also indicated by the FDA to treat breakthrough pain in cancer patients, as a replacement for the Actiq. Fentora has also proven to successfully ease Mr. H's pain. Initially, Humana provided coverage of Mr. H's Fentora prescription, but in January 2007, ended this coverage without prior notification or transition fill. Because his Fentora prescription costs approximately $1,500 a month, Mr. H cannot afford to pay for it out-of-pocket. As a result, he visits the emergency room (ER) on a biweekly basis so that he can receive the medication at the hospital and avoid suffering from a seizure caused by his extremely severe pain. Maximus Federal Services has denied his appeal for Part D coverage and MRC is representing him in his appeal for review by an Administrative Law Judge.[6]

COMMENTARY

Once a drug is on the market for some use, in this case cancer pain, a physician may legally prescribe it for other uses. That is what Mr. Horrigan's physician did. One might assume that if Fentora has labeling that indicates approval for relief of cancer pain, it would also be a reasonable drug for other severe pain. In general, one cannot make such an assumption. Just because a drug has been shown to be adequately safe and effective for one group of patients with one diagnosis, that does not establish it is either safe or effective for other patients with other conditions.

It makes sense that insurers—private or governmental—would want to avoid paying for treatments that have not been demonstrated to be safe and effective. This evidence needs to meet adequate standards of good science, not merely anecdotes from patients who claim the medication is effective. The reasons to resist paying for unproven therapy are particularly strong for a drug such as Fentora that is so expensive. This is an $18,000 a year decision just for Mr. Horrigan. Multiplied by the number of patients who would like to use Fentora for noncancer pain, this is a significant financial issue.

A plausible strategy for handling special cases of requests for off-label use would be to establish an independent review group to evaluate the special needs of the patient and whether there are other plausible alternatives. Maximus Federal Services is the national independent entity chosen by the Center for Medicare and Medicare Services to conduct external reviews of Medicare claim denials. It is the group that denied Mr. Horrigan's appeal. This group must make judgment calls trading off the interests of the citizens in using Medicare funds responsibly and assuring that patients with unusual needs are spared unnecessary burden.

MARGINALLY BENEFICIAL, EXPENSIVE THERAPY

Another kind of insurance decision raises moral concern. In the case of the off-label use, the problem is not knowing whether the drug is safe and effective. Other treatments are documented to be effective and are adequately safe, but they offer very modest benefits in comparison with the costs. Does the certainty of the benefit justify an obligation of the insurer to pay the costs, regardless of what they are?

CASE 15-3

The $300,000 Marginal Treatment[7]

Marvin Watts, MD, the Medical Director of American Ins. Co. for the past seven years, is reviewing newly approved drugs. Recently, there has been an increase in the approval of biotechnological drugs that target niche disease states such as hemophilia. A newly approved orphan drug, Elaprase, is currently under his review. Elaprase is FDA approved for patients with mucopolysaccharidosis II (MPS II), also known as Hunter Syndrome. Package labeling concludes the following: "Elaprase is indicated for patients with Hunter Syndrome (MPS II). Elaprase has been shown to improve walking capacity in these patients."

Hunter Syndrome is an inherited X-linked recessive genetic disorder where the enzyme responsible for the breakdown of glycosaminoglycans (GAG) is malfunctioning or absent. Signs and symptoms of MPSII include but are not limited to the following: retarded growth, hearing impairment, hypertension and blood vessel obstruction, respiratory difficulties, coarse facial features, joint rigidity, diarrhea, and a distended abdomen (due to organ enlargement). Produced by recombinant DNA technology, Elaprase is designed to serve as an enzyme replacement therapy (ERT).

Review of the medical literature on Elaprase reveals that the single largest study that reviewed safety and efficacy of Elaprase included ninety-six patients with a diagnosis of Hunter Syndrome. Primary efficacy of the drug was based on a statistically significant two-component composite score that focused on the following: Change from baseline in distance walked during a six-minute walk test (6-MWT) and respiratory change in percent-predicted forced vital capacity (FVC). Results of the study found that when compared to placebo, patients in the weekly Elaprase treated group experienced a 35-meter mean increase in distance walked in six minutes. The change in percent-predicted FVC was not statistically significant. Pharmacodynamics of Elaprase was assessed through effects of Elaprase on Hunter Syndrome related organ enlargement and excess urinary GAG levels. Liver and spleen volume reductions were sustained in the Elaprase weekly treated population. Urinary GAG levels were also reduced in the Elaprase weekly treated group, but half of the population had GAG levels that remained above the upper limit of normal even after fifty-three weeks of therapy.

Warnings with Elaprase include potentially life-threatening hypersensitivity reactions that can occur with infusion. Thus, medical support should be readily available with each administration of Elaprase. In addition, Dr. Watts noted that 51 percent of the weekly treated patients developed anti-idursulfase IgG antibodies, which correlated with an increased incidence of infusion related reactions, including hypersensitivity reactions.

Lastly, Dr. Watts reviewed the cost of the drug. Since Elaprase is dosed based on kilogram body weight, the cost of the drug is typically over $300,000 a year, which increases as patients gain weight.

Dr. Watts will recommend against the addition of this product to the formulary. His decision was made based on many factors that include but were not limited to the following:

1. The baseline distance walked before weekly therapy was approximately 400 meters in six minutes. What is the significance of a 35-meter increase based on this baseline?

2. While the treatment group realized a sustained reduction in liver and spleen volume, what is the clinical significance of this pharmacodynamic effect?

3. Urinary GAG levels were reduced in the Elaprase treatment arm, but what is the overall clinical effect of this reduction?

4. With potentially life-threatening reactions that require medical support to be readily available during infusion, what are the additional direct and indirect medical costs associated with this therapy?

5. Does an indication of improvement in walking capacity justify the use and cost of Elaprase?

Dr. Watts recognizes that Elaprase ERT is the only product approved as therapy for Hunter Syndrome. He also acknowledges that it appears to show promise in reducing organ enlargement and urinary GAG, but he questions how these reductions are clinically significant. Unfortunately, Elaprase does not appear to be the magic bullet, or cure, for Hunter Syndrome. Has Dr. Watts made the right decision?

COMMENTARY

Elaprase has been approved for use for a serious condition, Hunter Syndrome. That does not necessarily mean that American Insurance Co. has to cover the drug. Some treatments are recognized as effective, but still offer benefits so marginal that they raise questions about the appropriateness of coverage. In this case, the mobility benefits and other acknowledged benefits are of questionable clinical significance. Moreover, there are significant side effects—hypersensitivity reactions that can be life threatening. On top of these concerns, the cost of the drug will be $300,000 or more per patient per year.

One of the more puzzling features of this case is that a medical director of an insurance company is in a position to make the decision. On the one hand, as a physician, his traditional medical ethical perspective should be to benefit the patient. Patients will evaluate the potential benefits and compare them with the risks. Assuming some patients see the benefits as outweighing the harm, they will want the treatment. They will perceive it in their interest. Dr. Watts should have no patient-based reason for disagreeing. He is, however, also the medical director of a private insurance company. He has responsibility for the welfare of the company. Approving a $300,000 a year drug is certainly contrary to the company's interest. It would only support such an expenditure if the public relations costs of excluding coverage forced them to. The fact that the benefits are so marginal may give him the leverage he needs to defend his decision to decline to include coverage.

It would be interesting to compare this private insurance decision with the choice the medical administrator of a public insurance system would have to make. If, for example, it were the Medicare administrator facing this question, he would have loyalty not to a group of shareholders, but to the tax-paying citizens who contribute to the Medicare program. As such he is a custodian of these common, public assets. Dr. Watts in that case might still decide that use of the common resource for this purpose had to be subordinated to other higher-priority uses. He surely knows that even a public insurance system cannot fund every marginal benefit for every covered patient regardless of how marginal and how expensive it is.

If the task of the manager of a public insurance system is to allocate common assets responsibly, we may need to ask whether Dr. Watts, as a medical director, is in the best position to allocate the scarce resources of the insurance fund according to the values shared by the larger community. It is possible that Dr. Watts might let his traditional professional values influence his allocation decisions—perhaps deciding to fund the expensive, marginal benefit—in cases in which the broader community might make some other allocation.

If there are not enough funds for the insurance company to pay for every benefit that any patient would like, on what grounds should the scarce funds be allocated? If it is a private insurer, how much of the pool of assets should be reserved for profit?

VALUED CARE THAT IS NOT COST-WORTHY

In the previous section we examined how an insurer might deal with a treatment that is expensive but only marginally beneficial. A related problem that such companies face involves expensive treatments for which a patient may plausibly have a strong desire, while the benefit is viewed by others as limited. Providing life-prolonging interventions for the very elderly poses such a problem.

=== **CASE 15-4** ===

Too Old for Bypass?

Hannah Krauss was a 92-year-old patient at the nursing facility of a retirement home. She was a Medicare patient who had for many years been a member of an

HMO. She was under the care of David Kniceley, a cardiologist with a contract with the HMO. She had suffered from a debilitating stroke, arteriosclerotic heart disease, and diabetes. Together they had left her semi-mobile. She was, however, mentally lucid and able to understand her situation. She was now complaining of intermittent chest pain.

She had heard that bypass surgery might address her chest pain. Dr. Kniceley was not supportive of the idea. He explained the risks in a 92-year-old and that she might not survive the operation.

Mrs. Krauss listened carefully and, after some hesitation, decided she wanted the procedure. She pointed out that if she did not survive the surgical attempt, it would not be the worst possible outcome. She was more concerned about the continual chest pain.

Should Dr. Kniceley agree to perform the operation? Should he take into account in his decision that, in addition to the risks to her, the procedure would generate considerable costs for the HMO? Dr. Kniceley consulted the medical director of the HMO. Should the medical director take into account the costs to the HMO in deciding whether to authorize the CABG (coronary artery bypass graft)?

COMMENTARY

A physician does not always have an obligation to perform a procedure requested or demanded by a patient. Some requests make no sense or cannot deliver what the patient is seeking. Mrs. Krauss's request for bypass surgery is not completely irrational, however. She has chest pain that may respond to such intervention. Dr. Kniceley presumably would have endorsed the procedure for a younger, healthier patient. He has two potential kinds of reservations. First, there are real risks to Mrs. Krauss that are more serious than what would be faced by a younger patient. Moreover, the benefits, given her immobility and advanced age could be seen as less valuable and less enduring. Dr. Kniceley might conclude that the harms from the operation outweigh the risks. If that is his conclusion and he acted on it by refusing to endorse the operation, he would be acting paternalistically; he would be imposing his judgment about what is in her interest on her even though his conclusion would not be consistent with her own. Moreover, since there is no evidence that her illness or advanced age make her mentally incompetent, he would be acting in a strongly paternalistic way.

Second, Dr. Kniceley could take into account the interests of the HMO and the other subscribers to the HMO in deciding that even if Mrs. Krauss is correct about the procedure being in her interest, the anticipated benefit does not justify using the considerable resources of the HMO for this purpose. If this is Dr. Kniceley's concern, he is moving beyond his Hippocratic, patient-centered focus to consider the interests of other parties—the HMO and the other subscribers.

In regard to this second dimension, Dr. Kniceley's duty to Mrs. Krauss should be compared with that of the medical director. The medical director does not have direct patient care responsibility for Mrs. Krauss. He is acting as an agent for the HMO and for the total group of patients in the HMO. Perhaps a moral division of labor is called for in this case. Dr. Kniceley, as the caregiver for Mrs. Krauss, may have a duty to focus only on her interests and her rights. If he refuses to provide the operative intervention, he would do so on paternalistic grounds, not out of concern for the HMO or other patients. By contrast, the medical director might have the responsibility of placing limits on Dr. Kniceley and his patient when the interests of others in the HMO require it. Since the primary scarce resource in this case is money, then the issue is whether the pool for funds in the HMO devoted to patient care should be used for the benefit Mrs. Krauss is pursuing or whether they should be reserved for other patients who could gain more benefit from them.

FUNDING CARE THAT PATIENTS HAVE REFUSED

In contemporary health care, the insurance company is often cast in the role of denying payment for services sought by physicians and desired by patients. Occasionally, however, insurers have an opportunity to weigh in on the side of the patient. Once in a great while, the insurer commits to paying bills for treatments desired by patients or their surrogates even though a provider insists that the treatment is unnecessary. That occurred, for example, in the well-known case of Baby K, an anencephalic infant whose mother insisted on life support against the wishes of her physicians.[8] An easier opportunity for insurers to support patient decisions arises when patients are treated against their consent. Such treatments are illegal and widely rejected as unethical, yet in previous decades such treatment was widely ordered and delivered by physicians. Although physicians and hospitals stood to gain financially from delivering such services, they often did so out of a moral commitment that their duty was to preserve life, even against the explicit instructions of patients. It is in this context that insurers have an opportunity, as in the following case, to support patients' rights while serving their own financial interests.

===== **CASE 15-5** =====

Promoting Patients' Rights by Denying Insurance Coverage

An 88-year-old man, Cletis Bumgartner, was admitted to the hospital, in a coma due to cerebral hemorrhage. Despite a DNAR (do-not-attempt-resuscitation) form signed by his daughter, the consultant pulmonologist, Dennis Havens, administered CPR (cardiopulmonary resuscitation). Mr. Bumgartner was admitted to intensive care. The primary care physician and consultant neurologist authorized extubation and removal of the respirator but then declined to insist on this because of the pulmonologist's insistence that Mr. Bumgartner was not "brain dead." Without any change in his condition, Mr. Bumgartner died three days later.

Horton Pickering was the case reviewer for the insurance company, which was part of an HMO system. He refused to pay the costs for the three days of "extended care" because of the valid DNAR on the chart. Mr. Pickering claimed that the patient should not have been admitted to intensive care and that overuse of facilities and services were not the responsibility of the HMO.

COMMENTARY

The consulting pulmonologist, Dennis Havens, insisted on treatment in spite of an explicit refusal of attempted resuscitation signed by Mr. Bumgartner's daughter. There was no reason to doubt the validity of this refusal of resuscitation so Dr. Havens seems clearly to be in the wrong. Why he insisted is not clear. He may have been doing so to gain compensation, but it seems more likely that he really believed this was necessary and appropriate care of the patient. It is morally more interesting if that was his basis for acting.

Clinicians might see this as presenting the problem of whether the consultant or the primary care physician was really in charge. There are good reasons why one person needs to have definitive authority in such cases and that person is, by custom, usually the attending physician. It seems that the primary care physician was the attending physician, and he allowed a consultant, Dr. Havens, to overrule his evaluation and decision to discontinue pulmonary support. Disagreement among physicians is not uncommon, especially in estimates of prognosis, but the role of consultants is advisory only, unless the care of a patient is relinquished by the attending. Thus, this can be seen as a case in which a patient received inappropriate treatment because the attending physician was intimidated by the consultant to refuse to block the inappropriate treatment.

Horton Pickering's role in this case was also important. As the case reviewer for the HMO, he is often cast as the ogre denying important medical treatment. In this case, however, he was able to enter the case in a way that would tend to support the patient's interest as represented by his daughter. Whether Dr. Havens sent the patient to intensive care for reasons of personal financial gain or, more likely, because he believed it was the right thing to do, the decision seems clearly wrong. Agents for insurers have an opportunity to encourage more responsible behavior in the future by refusing to pay for any treatments that were clearly and appropriately refused by patients or their surrogates. Refusing to reimburse in such cases will not only save the insurance company money, it will also inspire overzealous providers to show greater respect for the rights of patients.

An additional action that could further encourage such respect could come from patients and their families. They might consider law suits not only for costs involved but also for any physical and mental suffering endured by patients and loved ones. Such law suits have been infrequent and with limited success, but the results in the future may be different and, in any case, such actions should get the attention of overzealous providers.

PHARMACEUTICAL MANUFACTURERS VERSUS INSURERS

Another aspect of the ethical tensions involving health insurance includes the relation of insurance companies to pharmaceutical manufacturers. It is in the interest of manufacturers to get insurers to pay for their products. The new Medicare Part D program is designed to pay the costs of pharmaceuticals. Other patients outside of Medicare also rely on their HMOs or insurers to cover the potentially enormous cost of prescription drugs. Often the insurer is the only one in a position to exercise effective restraint to the charges that are made for pharmaceuticals. Insurers and HMOs may negotiate contracts to obtain prescription drugs at reduced prices. They may also confront, as in the following case, controversial practices that increase the costs of the care of patients in ways that do not always maximize patient welfare. In the case that follows, a manufacturer has developed a complex strategy to increase its sales and gather data about a new product. The case is based on a real set of events, but the name of the company is fictional.

=== **CASE 15-6** ===

Drug Companies versus Insurance Companies: The Costs of Postmarketing Clinical Trials

The marketing departments of drug companies have become increasingly sophisticated in their strategies to promote their products. Advance Pharmaceuticals has recently received FDA approval of a new oral antidiabetic agent that shows promise for providing superior blood glucose control with minimal side effects. The only concern with the drug is that there have been reports of liver toxicity in a small minority of patients including at least three deaths reported.

The drug was beginning to penetrate the large market with some leading nephrologists adopting the drug. Although the drug was more expensive than its competitors, insurers were paying for the prescriptions.

The marketing department at Advanced proposed to the medical department that the company launch a large-scale, phase 4 clinical trial. Phase 4 trials are postapproval studies, normally on a nonrandomized basis without placebo controls for the presumed purpose of gathering data on clinicians' impressions of efficacy and side effects of newly approved pharmaceuticals. The design also has the advantage of permitting a manufacturer to pay certain clinicians fees for gathering data if they use the new product with their patients.

Advanced had data that identified the top 10 percent of physicians in the United States based on the frequency with which they prescribed oral antidiabetic agents. They also had data on which physicians within that group were already prescribing the newly approved product made by Advanced. The marketing department proposed that the medical director launch a phase 4 trial. They would use the company's 900 "detail" people (manufacturer's representatives who spend their time visiting doctors to educate them about the company's products) to approach the physicians in the top group of prescribers who are not already using their oral antidiabetic agent. Each physician would be paid $300 per patient for gathering information about each patient placed on the drug. Insurance companies would be billed for the clinical visits and for the normal retail price of the prescription, which would be filled at local pharmacies. The proposal was for the "detail" people to recruit up to 5,000 physicians to administer the drug to up to twenty patients each. Although this strategy would generate income of $6,000 per physician if each physician switched twenty of his or her patients, the recruiting would clearly state that the payment was not to get physicians to switch their patients (which would be illegal); it would be for the time spent in gathering and reporting the data on the results.

Insurance companies would bear the normal costs for clinical visits. Their added costs would come from coverage of the new pharmaceutical, which was more costly than other available agents. How should the insurance companies and physicians respond to this arrangement?

COMMENTARY

This case presents some complicated issues. No doubt, the data gathered by the medical department of Advanced Pharmaceuticals will be useful in gaining a better understanding of the benefits and side effects of the drug. No doubt, it is also a strategy that stands to entice thousands of high-prescribing physicians to switch patients to the new product. In the process, they will gain experience with the drug, and some will no doubt continue to prescribe it outside of the phase 4 trial. Targeting high prescribers of oral antidiabetic agents has the advantage of gathering data quickly as well as introducing this group of physicians to the new agent.

One of the controversial elements of the design is that it exposes patients to being switched by their doctors even though they may be doing well on their medication already. There is a risk that the payment, though labeled as compensation for gathering data, will actually induce physicians to switch patients for whom there is no good reason to change.

Since insurers are already paying for their new and expensive drug—presumably for patients who were not doing well on alternative drugs—the company may not have a way of identifying those who are switched even though they could continue to do well with their existing medication. Patients are not in a good position to understand that they may be manipulated onto a new drug. The insurer may be the only one with an incentive to place limits on this practice of phase 4 trials that stimulate use of new drugs. The insurer could insist that it will only pay for the new agent when there is documentation that the patient was not doing well on some older, cheaper but efficacious drug. Insurers usually are cautious about questioning the clinician's judgment about what is the best treatment. In this case, should they attempt to limit the use of the new drug? If so, should they do so on grounds that the new agent is more expensive or that it is an unnecessary change in the patient's treatment plan.

INSURANCE AND THE UNINSURED

One final problem arises with private health insurance. In almost all developed countries of the world some form of universal health insurance or health care service is available. In the United States, as many as 47 million people are without coverage.[9] Some are not eligible for Medicaid, the state-based programs receiving federal funding to provide medical care for low-income citizens. Some young adults make the calculation that, with insurance costs so high, they should gamble that they will not need health care to any significant degree.

Until recently, the uninsured were cared for at local hospitals and clinics as charity cases. The institution would charge enough to paying customers (including those with insurance) that they could reserve some surplus to provide for care for the uninsured sometimes called cost shifting. The rationalizing of health care costs has led to insurers forcing hospitals to lower their costs so that no surplus is generated. This leaves the uninsured without a source of medical care. The following case illustrates the problem.

=== **CASE 15-7** ===

Hospital Bureaucracy and the Uninsured

Loretta and Fidel Cardosa were migrant workers living in temporary camp facilities near Ruskin, Florida, south of Tampa, during the tomato season harvest. While they went grocery shopping, Loretta's 15-year-old brother took care of the younger children. Lorie Ann, 4 and a half, was missing when they returned. While looking for her, Mrs. Cardosa noticed an old, abandoned refrigerator. She was quoted in a news story describing what happened next. "I ran over then, opened the door, and there she was curled on the bottom....I was afraid to touch her. I was afraid she was cold dead."

When removed from the refrigerator, the child was limp. Someone began mouth-to-mouth resuscitation producing some response from the child. At 10:52

p.m. the rescue squad received the first call. When the emergency responders arrived, they placed Lorie on a heart monitor. The ambulance rushed Lori and her parents to Memorial Hospital, which was the designated emergency hospital for this area. Mrs. Cardosa was not permitted to ride with her daughter.

When Lorie arrived at the ER, Dr. Rumburger initiated resuscitation. He decided the child needed to be transported to Tampa General Hospital. At 1:06 a.m. Sunday morning Lorie was transported by ambulance to Tampa General.

Mrs. Cardosa had to wait to find some one to drive her to Tampa. She couldn't get transportation for two hours. A stranger offered to drive, but at that moment a nurse informed Mrs. Cardosa by phone that Lorie was being transferred from Tampa General to St. Petersburg.

After leaving for Tampa General, Memorial Hospital was notified that she would not be admitted at Tampa General. The director of the hospital later explained that she would have had to have administrative clearance to be admitted. The decision was attributed to a policy of the Florida Medical Association. Unfortunately, the ambulance was not notified that admission would be denied. It arrived at Tampa General fifty-six minutes later when it was directed to All Children's Hospital in St. Petersburg, across Tampa Bay.

The ambulance reached All Children's in St. Petersburg at 2:48 a.m. only to find that the ER was not open. Bayfront Medical Center, next door, was the next destination. As the ambulance technicians took Lorie Ann through a tunnel, she suffered a severe seizure. An hour later she was dead, some five hours after Mrs. Cardosa opened the refrigerator door.[10]

COMMENTARY

This tragic story reflects the chaos that exists in the fragmented, disorganized health care system, or nonsystem, in the United States. The case was probably exacerbated by the fact that the Cardosas did not have health insurance and did not have a relationship with a physician or an HMO that could immediately take charge of directing the girl's emergency care. There is good reason to fear that the runaround this child received and the demand for "administrative clearance" was bureaucracy's way of attempting to avoid accepting responsibility for what could amount to costly long-term care for a child without insurance.

The public policy issue is how our society should respond to this deficiency. Should hospitals and providers be required to accept emergency cases such as this? That is the legal requirement of the EMTALA (Emergency Medical Treatment and Active Labor Act), although hospitals have often found ways around this requirement—for example, by claiming they are not equipped to handle the case or are at the limits of their capacity. If each hospital is required to accept all emergency cases in its catchment area, then those institutions attempting to serve the poor by locating in low-income neighborhoods will be overrun with cases. Some strategy is needed to assure that such hospitals are reimbursed fairly or that equally equipped hospitals "take turns" when feasible in handling these types of cases in which no reimbursement for services is likely. Short of universal insurance with adequate coverage for emergency care, what can be done to prevent the death of patients such as Lorie Ann Cardosa?

NOTES

[1] Data from U.S. Department of Health and Human Services, Centers for Medicare and Medicaid Services, NHE Web Tables, "Table 1: National Health Expenditures Aggregate, Per Capita Amounts, Percent Distribution, and Average Annual Percent Growth, by Source of Funds: Selected Calendar Years 1960–2005." http://www.cms.hhs.gov/NationalHealthExpendData/downloads/tables.pdf, accessed August 2, 2007.

[2] http://www.cdc.gov/nchs/data/hus/hus06.pdf#027, accessed August 2, 2007.

[3] Ibid.

[4] Center for Budget and Policy Priorities. "The Number of Uninsured Americans Is at an All-Time High." August 29, 2006, available at http://www.cbpp.org/8–29–06health.htm, accessed August 2, 2007.

[5] Neuhauser, Duncan, and Ann M. Lewicki. "What Do We Gain from the Sixth Stool Guaiac?" *New England Journal of Medicine* 293 (No. 5, July 31, 1975):226–228.

[6] This case is taken from "Statement for the Record of Robert M. Hayes, President, Medicare Rights Center," at the Hearing on "The Medicare Prescription Drug Benefit: Monitoring Early Experiences" Before the United States Senate Committee on Finance, May 2, 2007, and is used with permission.

[7] We are grateful to Lee Handke, Pharm.D. and Bill Karolski., Pharm.D., for their assistance in providing information about this case.

[8] In the Matter of Baby K, 1993 WL 343557 (E.D. Va.).

[9] Carmen DeNavas-Walt, Carmen, Bernadette D. Proctor, and Jessica Smith. *Income, Poverty, and Health Insurance Coverage in the United States: 2006.* Washington, DC: U.S. Census Bureau. U.S. Department of Commerce, 2007, available on the Internet at http://www.census.gov/prod/2007pubs/p60–233.pdf, accessed September 11, 2007.

[10] This case is based on newspaper accounts in the *St. Petersburg Times* and on Hoffman, Pat. "The 12 Year Struggle of the United Farm Workers Union," *Sojourners*, July 1977, available on the Internet at http://www.farmworkermovement.org/essays/essays/eleven/06%20-%20GAINING%20JUSTICE%20GROUND.pdf, accessed October 3, 2007.

CHAPTER 16

⚬

Experimentation on Human Subjects

Other Cases Involving Human Experimentation

3-4: The Eager Research Subject: Justifying External Moral Standards
6-3: Readdicting a Heroin User: Are Prisoners Free to Consent to Research?
15-6: Drug Companies versus Insurance Companies: The Costs
of Postmarketing Clinical Trials

═══════════

Many of the great controversies in health care ethics have focused on problems in research involving human subjects. The research done by the Nazis gave rise to the Nuremberg trials, which exposed to all humankind the outrageous things that could be done in the name of medical science. Those trials gave rise to the Nuremberg Code,[1] the first international document from public sources setting out an ethic for research on human subjects.

It may come as a surprise to some that, taken literally, the Hippocratic ethic does not permit research on human subjects, at least if research is defined as activity designed to gain knowledge rather than to help a specific patient. The Hippocratic code says that everything a health care worker does should be to benefit the patient, according to the clinician's ability and judgment. It is the very nature of medical research that the purpose is not to benefit the individual subject but to produce generalizable knowledge for the benefit of the future of the people as a whole. (Some people distinguish between "therapeutic" and "nontherapeutic" research, in which the former refers to research on treatments that can potentially benefit a patient, but even in these cases, all of the research procedures—the randomization and data gathering—are undertaken to produce knowledge, not to benefit the patient.)

The various codes of ethics of the health professions differ considerably on these matters. Some follow the Hippocratic Oath in pledging commitment to the welfare of the individual patient. Others follow more traditional religious and secular ethics from outside medicine, focusing on the rights of subjects, as well as their benefit, and opening the door to consideration of the common good and the welfare of others beyond the individual.

Health professionals have, of course, faced difficult situations in which known therapies were not successful. In some of these cases, they might, in desperation, try something new, hoping it would help. Sometimes that might be called "experimenting," but it is not medical research as we now know it. Trying something new on a patient is what can be called "innovative therapy." It is used precisely as with any other therapy, because it is believed, everything considered, to be the best thing to do for the patient. Even a Hippocratic health professional could accept such innovation.

Medical research in a more formal sense is quite different. It often involves randomization between two or more therapies. The therapies are chosen precisely because it is not known which is better. The process of randomization and many of the tests performed on the subjects are not done to benefit the patient; they are done to produce knowledge for the welfare of society. Some of these experiments on human subjects may even involve normal subjects or patients who are not suffering from the condition being studied. These subjects surely are not involved for their personal medical benefit. None of these research interventions could be justified in advance as being best for the individuals; none could be justified under the traditional Hippocratic ethic or any health profession code that requires its members to work solely for the welfare of the individual patient.

During the Nuremberg trials, a critical choice had to be made. Either the medical community could return to the Hippocratic notion that every intervention had to be for the benefit of the patient (thus eliminating randomized trials, systematic data gathering, and the use of normal subjects), or it could modify the Hippocratic tradition, providing exceptions in the case of medical research that would justify some actions by health professionals not based on the good of the immediate patient but rather on the welfare of the community or of other individuals.

The health care community, and the world public, took the latter course. It developed an ethic that permitted "use" of human beings under certain carefully defined conditions. The Nuremberg Code spells out one version of these conditions. For one, the good being sought must be important to people with medical needs and not obtainable by other means.[2] This requirement necessitates calculating the risks and benefits of the research proposal, a set of issues we shall take up in section one of this chapter. That would provide some protection but not nearly enough. Theoretically, the Nazi experiments could have been designed to produce really important information not obtainable by other means. In fact, some have claimed that at least some of the Nazi research was pursuing some important research questions.[3]

In order to provide further protection, the writers of the Nuremberg Code placed, as the first and perhaps most important new requirement, the provision that the consent of the subject be obtained. The code called voluntary consent "absolutely essential."[4] This provision, as we saw in Chapter 6, is grounded in the ethical principle of respect for autonomy. Informed consent in research will be taken up in the last section of this chapter, preparing the way for additional cases raising consent issues that will be covered in Chapter 17.

Other provisions in the Nuremberg Code include protection of privacy and confidentiality (to be explored in section two of this chapter) and equity in subject selection (to be taken up in section three).

In examining the ethics of research on human subjects, other professional and public codes that have emerged since the events of Nuremberg will be important to consider. The World Medical Association developed its Helsinki Declaration in 1964. The Declaration of Helsinki was revised and extended by the Twenty-Ninth World Health Assembly in Tokyo in 1975 and again in Venice in 1983, in Hong Kong in 1989, in South Africa in 1996, and in Edinburgh, Scotland, in 2000.[5] While covering many of the same requirements of Nuremberg, it is a professionally generated code, written by the world association of medical societies. In some ways it differs from Nuremberg, not only in its origins, but also in its content. For example, while Nuremberg insists on the autonomous informed consent of all subjects, the Declaration of Helsinki recognizes that in some cases it is necessary to do research on infants, children, the severely retarded, or critically ill, who are not mentally capable of consenting. The notion of surrogate or guardian consent, and the moral limits of such consent, are introduced in the Helsinki Declaration.[6]

In the United States, the American Medical Association (AMA) adopted a specific code for research on human subjects in 1966.[7] In the public arena, the federal government of the United States has long been concerned about protection of human subjects but increased its level of attention in the 1960s. By 1970, the first federal guidelines designed to protect human subjects were issued by the Department of Health, Education, and Welfare (DHEW, now called the Department of Health and Human Services).[8] With several dramatic cases involving alleged abuse of human subjects in the 1970s and 1980s, more formal regulations emerged, including requirements that all research funded by the Department of Health and Human Services be reviewed by local institutional review boards (IRBs) made up of health professionals and lay people capable of assuring that the welfare and rights of human subjects were adequately protected.[9] These were revised and extended to cover virtually all federal government research in 1991.[10] Several minor revisions have occurred since then, most recently in June 23, 2005. Other countries similarly have codes governing research with human subjects.[11] The following cases reveal some of the major problems raised in assessing the ethics of such research.

CALCULATING RISKS AND BENEFITS

The earliest efforts to protect human subjects focused on assessment of risks and benefits. As was fitting the earlier, more Hippocratic ethic focusing on benefiting patients and protecting them from harm, the primary attention of those reviewing research was directed to research posing significant risks. Reviewers were not as concerned about protecting the rights of subjects who were involved in research with little or no risk. They, for example, were not focused on the possible inequity of a research project conducted exclusively on low-income patients as long as they were not at substantial risk. They were not concerned about whether potential subjects gave their informed consent to be studied, as long as they were not going to be placed at much risk of injury. By way of contrast, more recent codes, including the federal government's, pay attention to at least some of these issues of rights of subjects as well as simply making sure the subjects are not injured.[12] This includes matters of honesty, confidentiality, plagiarism, and fraud.

Assessing the benefits and harms and determining how the risks to the subjects should be related to the benefits envisioned for the society was the central task in the early years of human subject research. The following case reveals some of the problems in making such assessments.

CASE 16-1

Chemotherapy Risks: Is Going Without Chemotherapy a Benefit?

Laurie DeSoto, a 16-year-old girl who had recently been diagnosed with leukemia, came to the Pediatric Oncology Clinic with her mother to discuss treatment options with Dr. Elizabeth Holmes, the oncologist who had assumed responsibility for her care when she was referred to the clinic. Several different chemotherapy regimens were under consideration, but Dr. Holmes thought Laurie might be an ideal candidate for a research protocol now under way at the clinic.

The protocol involved a standard four-drug regimen that had been used successfully for Laurie's type of leukemia for several years. The original regimen required patients to be on the drugs for five years. After considerable experience with this drug schedule, oncologists began to suspect that the patients on it did not need to continue the drug for five years. The data from long experience showed that three years was just as effective as judged by the percentage of patients who remained leukemia free for five years. The three-year regimen was now the standard. It was used widely in oncology programs throughout the United States and elsewhere.

On the basis of that experience, Dr. Holmes and several colleagues began to wonder whether two years on the regimen might be as effective. They realized that the adolescents taking the drug had to endure the side effects of the chemotherapy, the nausea, hair loss, and other effects, and would appreciate having to stay on the regimen only two years rather than three. On the other hand, if they were wrong, it would mean that some patients taken off the regimen after the shorter period might have recurrence of their disease—a terrible, potentially fatal result.

Dr. Holmes had become the principal investigator of a new research protocol that would randomize patients to receiving either the now-standard three-year regimen or to an experimental group that received exactly the same drug combination, but received it for only two years. It included preliminary evidence from several clinical cases in which, for various reasons, patients had stopped the treatment after two years and had not had recurrence of their leukemia. The protocol had to be approved by the hospital IRB, the group charged with protecting human subjects of research. One of the criteria for approval was that the risks to subjects were reasonable and were justified by the potential benefits. The review board, after considerable discussion, voted, by a eight to two margin, that the risks were reasonably balanced. In other words, the majority of the board thought that the small risk of greater chance of recurrence of the leukemia was justified by the benefits to the youngsters who received the shorter two-year regimen.

Dr. Holmes now decided to present the opportunity to enter this protocol to Laurie DeSoto and her mother. If they agreed to enter the study, Laurie would be assigned randomly to either a standard three-year regimen or an experimental two-year treatment. Although subjects of research are normally "blinded," that is, kept ignorant of which treatment arm they enter, in this case, that would not be possible since patients and physicians would clearly know whether they were receiving the treatment for three years or two. If the investigators and the IRB believe that the risks and benefits are more or less equally balanced between the two groups, such randomization is considered morally acceptable. When two treatment arms in a research protocol are perceived as being equally balanced in their risks and benefits, the study is said to be in equipoise.[13] Since Dr. Holmes and the IRB agreed that the risks were evenly balanced, they considered the offer to be randomized morally justified.

Dr. Holmes presented the study to Laurie and her mother including the fact that, if they agreed to enter the study, they would be randomly assigned to either three years or two years of treatment. After being given an opportunity to ask any questions, Mrs. DeSoto signed the consent form on behalf of Laurie. Laurie, as a minor, could not give her own consent, but was nevertheless asked to give her "assent," which she gave. This amounts to approval even though it is not based on a level of understanding and voluntariness that we would expect from an adult.

Dr. Holmes, having received documented consent, left the room and soon returned with the news that Laurie had been randomly assigned to the three-year arm, that is, the existing standard treatment. To her surprise, Laurie burst into tears. When asked, she explained she really wanted the two-year treatment course. She hated the thought of the side effects, especially the hair loss. She did not want to look strange for any longer than necessary. She sobbed in her mother's arms as Dr. Holmes looked on. Had Dr. Holmes and the IRB assessed the risks and benefits properly?

COMMENTARY

The concern of IRBs in the early years of research review was to avoid exposing subjects to serious risks. We had gone through a period in which poorly educated African American men with syphilis were purposely left untreated for research purposes, live cancer cells had been injected into patients without their knowledge, humans had been exposed to radiation for studying its impact, and women had been given placebos in place of birth control pills to see if the side effects of the pill were merely in the imagination of the patients.

An IRB will typically ask whether the risks involved are more than minimal. If only minimal, a more expedited review process may be in order, but quite clearly this is not a minimal risk experiment. The IRB is supposed to assure that the risks to the subject are minimized and that they are "reasonable in relation to anticipated benefits, if any, to subjects and the importance of the knowledge that may reasonably be expected to result."[14]

In deciding to approve this protocol, the IRB members faced some interesting questions. The major risk of the protocol was an increased risk of recurrence of leukemia in the patients receiving the two-year course of treatment. Unfortunately, neither Dr. Holmes nor the IRB know in advance exactly what that risk is. They have only informal clinical cases to go by. Of course, they must believe it is very small, but they cannot know how small.

They must also compare that uncertain risk with the value of the potential benefits. The primary benefit is the avoidance of the side effects of the chemotherapy during the third year. These benefits are very subjective. They are almost impossible to quantify. Moreover, they must then compare the unknown risk of leukemia recurrence with a very different kind of benefit. At best they can make an intuitive judgment that they are more or less equal. Although these kinds of comparisons are subjective, physicians and researchers must make them daily. There is no reason to doubt that when Dr. Holmes and the IRB members concluded that the risks were in balance with the potential benefits, they were acting in good faith. They apparently believed that the two treatment arms were in "equipoise," that the risks and benefits were close enough to being balanced that it would be ethical to randomize subjects.

Then what can be said about Laurie DeSoto's response when she was told she had been assigned to the three-year arm? If the benefit–risk considerations were more or less equally balanced in the two treatments, why should she be so upset when she learns she is getting the three-year arm? She avoids the possibility of an extra recurrence that might occur if she got the chemotherapy for only two years.

The benefit and risks of each treatment arm are not only subjective; they involve subjective judgments that vary from person to person. There is no reason to doubt that the investigators and IRB members really believed that the benefit–risk packages in the two treatments were equally balanced. If they had entered the protocol, they presumably would not care to which treatment arm they were assigned. If the benefits were equally attractive in the two groups after taking into account the risks, they would have no reason to care which treatment they received.

Just because oncologists and IRB members were indifferent between the two treatments, however, it does not mean that a 16-year-old girl would also be indifferent. Laurie had interests and psychological concerns about hair loss that she apparently evaluated differently. She had the time perspective of a teenager and the feeling of invincibility of one as well. There is no reason why she should compare the risks and benefits of the treatments the same way the medical scientists do. Oncologists who have given their lives to fighting death from cancer cannot be said to be typical in their attitudes about death. Apparently, they gave more weight to the risk of the two-year arm than Laurie did. She was clearly not in equipoise even if the investigators were.

The outcome in this case poses another issue. It appears that Laurie and her mother may not have understood the choices before them. If they had refused consent to be randomized in the protocol, Laurie would have been assigned to the standard three-year treatment. While that is not what she wanted, she and her mother would have had the option of withdrawing from treatment after two years, thus getting exactly what Laurie wanted. It appears that not only was Laurie not in equipoise; she and her mother did not really give an adequately informed consent either.

The unique values of the potential subject need to be taken into account. This suggests that deciding the benefits and harms of research will be a very difficult task for the IRB and investigators as well as subjects. The main responsibility of an IRB might be making sure that investigators and subjects understand exactly what is being proposed and what the risks are. In addition, the IRB must attempt to assure that the other criteria of adequate research including protection of confidentiality, equity, minimizing conflict of interest, and adequately informed consent are satisfied.

These additional criteria for ethically acceptable research suggest that IRBs have responsibilities even in the case of minimal risk research, such as in the following case.

CASE 16-2

Research to Develop Screening Techniques for HIV-Infected Blood

Dr. Michael Willey, the director of the blood bank at a major inner-city hospital, was interested in developing better techniques for screening blood for viral infections such as HIV. He wanted to do a large-scale trial of new tests that eventually could permit him to screen blood more quickly and cheaply. He was also interested in identifying high-risk blood sources so that, if necessary, extra precautions could be taken with blood obtained through certain clinics and from certain sociological groups.

To conduct this research he needed a large number of samples of fresh blood. He would not need large samples, just enough to perform one of his experimental tests and run the more traditional screens to provide a basis for seeing if his new techniques were accurate. He would not need to know the names of those providing the blood, but he would want some general background information—the clinic from which the sample was obtained, the age, race, and admitting diagnosis of the patient from whom it was obtained.

Rather than impose on a large number of patients to contribute the samples for these initial tests, he proposed to take the "remaindered" or left-over blood from routine laboratory studies. This blood was normally discarded but would be perfectly suited for his research. He therefore proposed to the IRB that, when his lab was finished with blood samples, the remaindered blood be transferred to the research technician with names and identifying numbers removed. Only the clinic, age, race, and diagnosis would be retained. He would like to obtain a thousand such samples for his research. Since the lab would not know which samples would provide enough blood until the clinically required tests had been completed and, at that point, the patients would be hard to track down to obtain consent, the investigator proposed that the consent requirement be waived. He pointed out that such left-over blood had been used for research for years without consent of the patients.

The IRB received this protocol and determined that there was no plausible risk to the subjects and that there was no risk of confidentiality being breached since critical identifying information would not even be retained. Technically, such research could be deemed "exempt" from IRB review. The regulations state that research is exempt if it is

Research involving the collection or study of existing data, documents, records, pathological specimens, or diagnostic specimens, if these sources are publicly available or if the information is recorded by the investigator in such a manner that subjects cannot be identified, directly or through identifiers linked to the subjects.[15]

Although this research might meet federal requirements for an exemption, the IRB chose not to grant the exemption. It was concerned that, even if the research were risk-free and posed no chance of a breach of confidentiality, there were elements of the research that could raise concern. Subjects might be interested in the fact that the research involved HIV and they were contributing to a project that could eventually stereotype certain clinics, races, or diagnoses. For these reasons the IRB retained jurisdiction over the research proposal. For the same reasons it refused to review the research on an expedited basis, a procedure whereby one member of the IRB could conduct the review and report back to the IRB at its next meeting.

Some members of the IRB insisted that most patients would not be concerned about these matters. Given the absence of risk, the impossibility of a confidentiality breach, and the difficulty in getting consent, they favored granting the investigator's request for access to the remaindered blood without consent. Others, however, objected. While they found the research worthwhile and essentially risk-free, they believed some subjects would want to consent before contributing to this research. Should the IRB grant approval?

COMMENTARY

It seems reasonable to conclude that this research poses no direct risk to the subjects. Their blood would only be discarded if not used for research. Furthermore, it does not present a confidentiality problem. Historically, such research would not even trigger IRB review and, even today, it may be deemed exempt by the IRB so that no further scrutiny would be given.

Nevertheless, the current regulations impose certain criteria for acceptable research that may raise questions in this study. First, the regulations require that, as part of the consent process, the subjects be informed of the purpose of the research. It is conceivable that even with risk-free research that can pose no confidentiality issue, a subject may object to the purpose of the study. Research is sometimes undertaken for controversial purposes—historically, studies have included testing LSD for use in military settings, attempting to correlate race and intelligence, and studying the psychology of women refusing abortion for the purpose of determining if their mental state led to their decision. Some research is conducted to advance the interests of private drug companies, government agencies, or researchers. Subjects might object to contributing to the advancement of these interests. For this reason, the regulations require disclosure of the purpose of the research. IRBs have routinely required disclosure of the funding source, especially if that source is controversial (the Central Intelligence Agency, for example).

It is possible that some subjects may not want to contribute to these studies. They may have developed hostility to the hospital or even the lab involved, or they may be nervous about the sensitivity of the hypotheses related to social correlates of blood-born viruses. Even if they cannot be harmed directly or identified, they may have reasons to object.

On the other hand, most subjects probably would not object and tracking them down to gain consent would be difficult. Should these facts lead to approval of the study? One strategy proposed to deal with these issues is to ask whether a reasonable potential subject would want to be asked whether his or her blood should be used in this way. The investigator could even conduct a preliminary study asking potential subjects whether they would have objections to the use of their left-over blood and whether they would want to be asked first.

This poses an interesting theoretical question. Suppose that the majority said they would not object, but a minority indicated they would want to be asked first. One could argue that this minority would have its rights violated if the IRB approved the proposal without a consent provision. This raises the question of what percentage would have to object before an explicit documented consent would have to be obtained. Surely, a simple majority approving would not be sufficient since that would mean to as many as almost half of the subjects would be objectors. Their right to consent would be violated. On the other hand, if we insisted that there be no objectors, then the research could not be done because, no matter how many consecutive cases of approval were documented, the next person could always be the one who objected.

It seems that some small percentage of objectors would have to be tolerated if an IRB is ever to approve a waiver of consent in these cases. If, for example, no more than 5 percent of potential subjects objected when asked, one might argue that this is a sufficiently small chance of violating the subject's right to consent that the risk would be tolerable. If 5 percent is not the correct number what would be—1 percent, 10 percent, no objectors at all? Does the fact that subjects may object to the purpose or the sponsor of apparently risk-free research justify an IRB refusal to grant a waiver or an exemption in this case?

PRIVACY AND CONFIDENTIALITY

A second major issue in the ethics of research involving human subjects is protection of privacy and confidentiality. The general issues of confidentiality were examined in Chapter 13. There we saw that one moral basis for the requirement that medical professionals maintain confidentiality is an implied promise to do so. If that is the basis, then the underlying moral principle is fidelity or promise-keeping. The key then is what is promised.

Traditional Hippocratic ethics would permit breaking of confidences when the clinician believed doing so would benefit the patient. Sometimes, of course, the patient might not agree with that judgment. Newer codes, those reflecting a more "patients' rights" approach, include a stronger confidentiality requirement. According to those, if the clinician believes that the patient could be benefited by disclosure of confidential medical information, he or she must ask the patient. If the patient agrees, there is no problem, but if the patient insists that the confidence be kept, then it must be.

The second basis for breaking confidence involves situations in which the clinician believes that disclosure will benefit not the patient, but others in society. That disclosure may be to other specific individuals or to law enforcement authorities. Many codes now accept the need to break confidence if there is a serious threat of bodily harm to others. That is the current position of the AMA.[16]

Confidentiality becomes a critical issue in research involving human subjects when medical information in a patient's chart could be useful in the research enterprise. Sometimes the risk is that others will be able to identify the patient as a subject of a study. In other cases, the problem is that the investigators themselves will obtain information that the patient does not want disclosed to strangers, even if the ones getting the information happen to be legitimate researchers.

Some researchers assume that it is acceptable to search a patient's medical records for research purposes provided that the patient is not identifiable in the published study. Others hold that even if the patient is not identifiable, the fact that investigators are entering the medical record itself constitutes a breach of confidentiality unless the patient has given permission. The following case reveals how confidentiality can arise in the research setting.

CASE 16-3

Abortion and Psychopathology: Research on Medical Records

Dr. Victor Ripley was concerned that many of the adolescent girls he saw in the hospital's prenatal clinic were clearly unprepared for motherhood. As the psychiatrist, he met with a patient, whenever asked by the obstetrician, to rule out major psychiatric problems incompatible with the parental role. He observed many high-school-aged, unmarried girls with no source of income, poor educational background, and no ongoing relationship with the father of the children.

He decided to begin preparation for research on the choices made by this group of patients. In his view, the only rational course was to abort the pregnancy and yet very large numbers of the patients, particularly inner-city patients from minority groups, were not making that choice. He suspected that psychologically these girls had a desperate need to be placed in the maternal role to demonstrate their capacity and to establish a close bond that they otherwise lacked.

He prepared to develop his research by doing a pilot project in which he would review the medical records of one hundred patients in the clinic. Most of them he had not seen as patients, but, as the attending psychiatrist in the clinic, he had access to all the records. He would review the records for evidence of psychological problems of those who chose to carry their pregnancies to term and compare them with those who chose to abort. No intervention with the patients was planned. It would merely involve record review.

In presenting the project to the IRB, he asked for an exemption on the grounds that there was no risk to the subjects and no identifiers would be collected. He pointed out that since his research would be limited to first-time pregnancies, there was no way that any of the subjects of the records could even be affected by the findings of the research.

COMMENTARY

Underlying this case is a viewpoint of a psychiatrist that is controversial to say the least. He appears to believe that any unmarried young woman, especially one of low socioeconomic status, who refuses to abort a pregnancy must have some mental problem. It is not clear, however, what an IRB should do with that aspect of this case. The IRB is asked to exempt this research from its review or, alternatively, to approve the research use of the medical records.

As we saw in Case 16-2, research that poses no risk to subjects, including medical records review, is potentially exempt from IRB review provided it does not collect identifying data as part of the review. There is no reason why Dr. Ripley would not be able to meet these requirements.

Nevertheless, IRBs are not required to grant exemptions. This is a good example of a proposal for which the IRB might wish to retain jurisdiction. Not only is the investigator potentially biased, but the subject of his research is extremely controversial. It seems reasonable that the subjects, the young women whose records would be searched, might be concerned about the purpose of the research. They may also feel that their confidentiality has been violated by having someone not involved in their clinical care searching their medical records.

Even though Dr. Ripley is a clinician on the service where these patients have been seen clinically, his agenda is not their care. It is a research project, one that at least some of the patients could find offensive. The subject matter of the records that Dr. Ripley would review is delicate, private information. Even if none of the patients were known personally by Dr. Ripley, they might object to having a stranger reviewing their records.

The same regulations that would permit an IRB to classify this research as exempt from IRB review also requires that IRBs must assure that "When appropriate, there are adequate provisions to protect the privacy of subjects and to maintain the confidentiality of data."[17] One test that an IRB can use, in a case like this, is to ask whether subjects would reasonably object to having their private medical information searched for the purposes of this research. Perhaps some would not object but surely some would. In such cases, consent for the use of the private medical information seems to be in order.

The problem of protection of subject confidentiality is not limited to medical information. Social scientists also collect sensitive information, sometimes from medical records and other times through surveys outside of the medical context. The next case poses such a problem in the context of gathering data connected with an illegal activity.

=============================== **CASE 16-4** ===============================

Surveying Illegal Immigrants

Dr. Yvonne Dacosta was an economist at State University who specialized in the economic and social impacts of undocumented and illegal immigrants to the United States. She was conducting research on the interactions of these residents with the relatives in their home countries. Her hypothesis was that economic relations between the subjects of the study and their relatives predict the socialization of the immigrants and their economic patterns within the United States.

She proposed to conduct a survey of a sample of these immigrants by recruiting them at sites where day-laborers gathered to find work and at ethnic grocery stores where she knew they would shop. She understood that collecting identifiable data on them could pose a risk, so she designed a research instrument that would not involve collecting the subject's name or address. For her research, however, she needed to know the country of origin, the age, gender, and education level of the subjects. She also needed an approximate indicator of their residence, for which she would collect the subject's zip code. She would also collect data on how long the persons had been in the United States and whether they had documents making their immigration legal.

She proposed to obtain oral consent of each subject and submitted a script that would explain her study, the fact that she was not collecting names and addresses, and that she promised to keep her data in a locked storage cabinet. She disclosed that the research was funded by her academic department research fund and did not involve any governmental or immigration officials.

Following university requirements, Dr. Dacosta submitted her protocol to the IRB for review and approval. One of the federal criteria for review of research was that "When appropriate, there are adequate provisions to protect the privacy of subjects and to maintain the confidentiality of data."[18] One of the IRB members expressed concern that many of Dr. Dacosta's subjects were engaging in an illegal activity that was potentially of interest to the governmental immigration authorities. While it was unlikely that any attempt would be made to examine the data, the possibility existed that, even though names and addresses were not collected, sophisticated analysis of the background data could identify people at the employment and shopping locations who were engaging in illegal activity. Moreover, it was established that research records were subject to subpoena even against the wishes of the investigator. This IRB member pressed for a specific plan to protect the identity of these subjects.

Should the IRB approve this research, and, if so, under what requirements?

COMMENTARY

This study involves normal procedures for consent for research. Subjects would be asked to complete a survey. They would clearly know they were giving information to a researcher. They might not, however, understand that the information focuses on the legal status of the immigrant and poses a potential, if remote, risk that the data could be pursued by immigration officials and used to identify them.

The investigator might defend her project by insisting that she promises confidentiality and even will go so far as to keep her records in a locked cabinet. The problem with that, however, is that the good will of the investigator does not protect the information from the pursuit of government officials. They may request the information and, if refused, subpoena it.

Federal regulations permit application to the National Institutes of Health for a "Certificate of Confidentiality" that would protect data such as Dr. Dacosta's. If such a certificate were obtained, an investigator could not be "compelled in any Federal, State, or local civil, criminal, administrative, legislative, or other proceedings" to identify subjects.[19]

If such a certificate were obtained, Dr. Dacosta could not be compelled to reveal data. The certificates, however, do not require an investigator to protect the confidentiality of her data. Normally, an investigator with integrity would do so, but in some cases, such as the following one, the investigator might feel morally obliged to identify a subject.

CASE 16-5

Homicide in Research: A Duty to Breach Confidentiality?

Dr. Margaret Carstens was part of a large, multicenter study to attempt to protect the health and welfare of high-risk infants with a history of a previous cardiac or respiratory arrest. The study involved the use of twenty-four-hour electronic monitors placed on infants that would provide around the clock recordings of the infant's heart rate, blood pressure, respiratory rate, and other clinical indicators. The goal was to identify markers that could eventually be used to predict which infants were at high risk for cardiac or respiratory arrest.

Parents signed a standard consent form that explained the nature and purpose of the experiment, the funder, and the potential risks, which were considered minimal. The monitoring equipment had been well tested and was deemed safe from electrical and mechanical risk to the infants. The consent form also contained the standard promise of confidentiality of the medical data.

Unfortunately, one of the infants on the monitor died during the study. This was not entirely unexpected since all the infants were at high risk. It was discovered, however, that this infant had had an older sibling who also had died, and in the case of the earlier death, there was some suspicion that the death may not have been a natural occurrence. A psychological condition known as Munchausen-by-proxy involves a parent who induces a medical crisis in a child apparently for the purpose of generating attention that satisfies some psychological need of the parent. One method of accomplishing this is temporary suffocation of the child followed by a call for rescue. While the purpose is not to kill the child, the risk exists of a miscalculation that can actually cause the child's death.

The medical examiner in the case of the death of the infant who was the subject of the study began to suspect Munchausen-by-proxy and, when he learned the infant was part of a study involving twenty-four-hour monitoring, asked to see the research records. The records would have included data on the infant with a high potential of revealing the nature of the death including the possibility of identifying abnormal activity consistent with an assault. Dr. Carstens realized that she might have the evidence that a homicide had taken place, indeed, a homicide in a family that had previously experienced the unexpected death of an infant. She realized the importance of discovering the truth about the events. She also realized she had promised confidentiality of the medical records from the research.

COMMENTARY

It is not clear from this case whether Dr. Carstens had asked for and received a certificate of confidentiality that would guarantee her the legal right to protect her data from discovery by a prosecutor in this case. The interesting moral question is whether she should attempt to protect the information. The certificate of confidentiality permits, but does not require, the investigator to protect the data. Only her promise made as part of the consent process would obligate her morally. If she did not obtain a certificate of confidentiality, which she might not have since the research did not suggest the probability of illegal behavior, she would not even have a legal basis for refusing to provide the information.

Most clinicians and investigators would presume a commitment to confidentiality for private medical information obtained from patients or subjects. In special cases, however, there may be a duty to disclose that overrides this presumption. We saw in the cases of Chapter 13, particularly the Tarasoff case, that health professionals sometimes have a duty to breach confidentiality, especially when there is a credible threat of serious harm to another party.

That same moral reasoning would appear to apply in the case of Dr. Carstens. The society has a clear interest in protecting children and in prosecuting adults guilty of serious child abuse. Thus, there are good reasons why a researcher might feel compelled to make an exception in a case like this one. It is possible that the mother had murdered two of her children and might be at risk to murder others. Society also has an interest in prosecuting criminals even if there were some assurance that they would never repeat their crimes. Does the promise of confidentiality as part of the consent process require non-cooperation? If so, does Dr. Carstens have to contemplate civil disobedience in the form of refusal to respond to the subpoena or should she decide that, in this case, there are such compelling, unexpected reasons that her promise of confidentiality must be broken? Would this case have been different if her consent commitment had acknowledged that she would not be able to keep information confidential if there were a serious public interest requiring disclosure?

EQUITY IN RESEARCH

In the previous cases, we saw that the ethical principles of fidelity and autonomy might be relevant in assessing research protocols. Another ethical principle that can sometimes place limits on pursuit of social benefits of research is the principle of justice.

The importance of the principle of justice in assessing medical research involving human subjects has been discovered quite recently. A federal government commission report, called the Belmont Report, was the first to mention justice with regard to research.[20]

There are two areas in which questions of justice can arise in research involving human subjects. The one that has received the most attention is subject selection. We have begun to realize that certain groups of people have tended to be particularly vulnerable to being asked to be research subjects. These are often persons who are oppressed: the lower-income, ward patients who have very limited options in getting care, or prisoners who have even fewer options. In some cases, the subjects are from countries other than that of the sponsor of the research. These countries may make research easier because they have less rigorous standards for review of research. In other cases, the subjects suffering from the disease being studied may not have the economic means to afford the therapy if it proves successful. This raises problems in equity in subject selection.

More recently, questions of justice or equity have been raised in the design and conduct of the research. If worst off people are recruited as subjects (perhaps because they are the only ones who have the condition being studied), some people are claiming that they also have claims of justice to make sure that the research is designed in ways that are as beneficial as possible to them. For example, in the next case, instead of making seriously ill patients come to the hospital for tests needed in a protocol, justice may require sending a nurse to their homes, making it as easy as possible for them to participate. Some studies have even had their designs modified—reducing the number of tests or the length of the study—to help protect particularly ill research subjects. The case in this section poses the question of the ethics of equity in subject selection.

=== **CASE 16-6** ===

Justice in Research Design: Being Fair to the Critically Ill

Cancer researchers at a major medical center wanted to conduct a pilot study of a five-drug combination using high doses of chemotherapeutic agents. The drugs were cyclophosphamide, adriamycin, VP-16-213, vincristine, and methotrexate. The first four were drugs long known to researchers. The side effects anticipated included nausea, vomiting, myelosuppression, stomatitis, alopecia, and cardiomyopathy. The patients to receive these were seriously ill with tumors that were resistant to standard therapies.

The fifth drug, methotrexate, also posed the risk of side effects including myelosuppression, stomatitis, occasional hepatitis, nephrotoxicity, and neurotoxicity. These were of particular concern when the drug was given in high doses. The proposed study would administer 1.0 g/M², a relatively high dose. The toxic effects would be neutralized by administering leucovorin intravenously twenty-four hours later followed by three days of oral administration. This strategy would permit administering higher doses of the methotrexate. It was referred to as "methotrexate with leucovorin rescue." The protocol called for administering the drugs on a twenty-one-day cycle with methotrexate given on the fifteenth day. All drugs were to be administered on an outpatient basis, except that the methotrexate and intra-venous leucovorin would be administered on an inpatient basis, thus keeping the patients in the hospital for twenty-four hours out of every three weeks.

The IRB reviewed the protocol focusing first on the traditional questions of the risks and benefits of the five drugs. The debate soon focused on the methotrex-ate and leucovorin. Some IRB members were concerned that the oral leucovorin would be given to the patients to take at home. Given the severity of the patient's illness and the general propensity of patients to miss doses of medication, the IRB members were concerned that some patients might forget their rescue medication, which would result in death. It was noted that a patient could even intentionally omit the oral leucovorin leaving an exposure to a potential lethal result. It would amount to suicide by drug refusal. These IRB members proposed that it would be safer for patients to remain in the hospital for the three days to assure they received their leucovorin rescue appropriately.

A second contingent of the IRB membership expressed a different concern, one shared by the investigators. They feared that requiring patients to remain in the hospital for three days out of every twenty-one would tax the resources of the research ward of the hospital. Other research projects might have to be put on hold while the research beds were devoted to this use. Concern was expressed not only about the costs, but also about the burden on personnel. They also pointed out that the goal of the research was to develop a regimen that could be used widely. Administration of the oral leucovorin at home was a more plausible strategy con-sidering the overall costs and benefits.

A third group in the IRB focused not on the protection of patients or the impact on the institution, but on two other ethical concerns. First, they observed that some patients might find the original protocol with oral leucovorin taken at home too burdensome, while others might find being hospitalized for three out of every twenty-one days too much to ask. Since these were critically ill patients who were probably dying, this would mean asking them to spend as much as one-seventh of the rest of their lives in the hospital when they really did not need to be there. This group proposed modifying the protocol to permit patients to choose either inpatient or outpatient administration of the oral leucovorin depending on which method the patients wanted.

The research design purists were unhappy with this proposal. It meant intro-ducing another variable into the study. They preferred that all patients be treated identically. To this the defenders of the patient choice provision introduced another argument thus raising a new moral principle. They observed that in this protocol, the patients who could become subjects were very severely ill with drug-resistant tumors. They were probably going to die soon even with the treatment. Thus they could be said to be among the worst off in society. It raised the question of how much researchers could ask of this especially vulnerable and burdened group. They proposed that the modification of the protocol was particularly called for in this case because the potential subjects were among the worst off patients, and they had a special claim of justice to be burdened as little as possible by the research. Since they were the only patients who had the cancers that were appropriate for this risky research, it was appropriate to ask them to be subjects, but in design-ing the research, the patients had a right to expect that the protocol would be as attractive to them as possible. This, they claimed, required modifying the protocol to give this group of patients the choice of where they should receive the oral leucovorin even if it meant that the costs were going to be greater than the original outpatient design and even if the research design was not as clean as it would have been with all patients receiving exactly the same treatment.

The IRB faced the choice: should patient medical benefit be maximized by requiring all to receive the leucovorin in the hospital, should total social benefit be used to justify the original home-based administration, or should respect for patient autonomy and justice require permitting this group of patients to choose, even though the costs would be greater than exclusive home-based administration and the research design would be slightly inferior.[21]

COMMENTARY

The three groups within this IRB chose different ethical principles upon which to base their evaluation of the protocol. The first group took seriously the assignment of the IRB to protect human subjects from risk of harm by focusing on protecting patients from medical risks by administering the oral leucovorin in the hospital, thus assuring that the full medication would be provided and that any side effects could be monitored. They were classic Hippocratic utilitarians, committed to maximizing the net benefit but limiting their attention to patient benefit and particularly medical benefit.

The second group of IRB members was made up of classic social utilitarians. They asked which version of the protocol would predictably maximize the benefits, considering all interests of all parties affected. The extra costs of hospitalization were made up for by the belief that even more good would come if the hospital's resources were used in some different way.

The third group took a very different perspective. They emphasized the principles of autonomy and justice. First, they introduced patient autonomy by recognizing that different patients might be differently affected by home and in-hospital administration of the leucovorin. Patients, they argued, should be permitted to choose the option that was best for them. Then they introduced a defense of giving these options. Even though the costs would be greater than home administration and the research design would be less clean, they defended the choice for this particular group of subjects by noting that they were among the worst off members of the society who had a special justice-based claim to having the protocol be as beneficial to them as possible.

In cases in which researchers have recruited subjects who have low levels of well-being—ward patients, prisoners, or low-income people—merely for the convenience of the investigators, a problem of justice or equity in subject selection is raised. Since the Belmont Report, standards for ethical research have mandated that subject selection be equitable and that no protocol be targeted exclusively for vulnerable groups simply because it is cheap or convenient to do so.

This protocol is different. It is justifiable to target this research exclusively for very sick, dying patients because they are the only ones with the condition being studied. By the same reasoning, other vulnerable groups such as prisoners can be targeted for research that only is relevant to that group—experiments in cell design or punishment strategies, for example. The novel feature of this case is that the principle of justice is introduced not only at the point of subject selection but also in the design of the protocol itself. The group making this appeal held that somewhat less clean and more expensive research design is called for if necessary to make the research as beneficial as possible for the worst off group—the patients with the drug-resistant cancers being studied.

CONFLICTS OF INTEREST IN RESEARCH

While much traditional discussion of the ethics of research involving human subjects has focused on the conduct of the investigator vis-à-vis the subject, increasing attention is being given to the moral status of the investigator and his or her relation to the funder of the research. This moral relation is, in a way, independent of the problems addressed thus far: assessment of benefits and harms, confidentiality, and equity. It is also independent of the consent issues to which we turn in the final section of this chapter.

The essence of being an investigator conducting scholarly research is what used to be called objectivity or neutrality. Today, we are beginning to recognize that pure objectivity or neutrality is an impossibility. We will always be influenced by our cultural, religious, familial, and economic interests. Nevertheless, we still maintain the goal of minimizing the distortion that can come from letting outside agendas and loyalties shape research. It has been a serious enough problem for the investigator to resolve the conflicts between his or her research goals and loyalty to the subject as patient. When strong influence from funding agents or others claiming loyalty penetrates the research enterprise, the problem of the investigator becoming a "double agent" can become overwhelming. Still, a source of support is inevitable, and that funding agent will have an agenda that will come into play. Investigators may try to hold these outside influences at bay, but, as we see in the following case, that may be a difficult task.

CASE 16-7

Paying Clinicians to Recruit Research Subjects

Officials of a major pharmaceutical company believed they had a financial blockbuster, a drug for type-2 diabetes that, in clinical trials, outperformed those on the market and promised to shift revenues to the company if even a fraction of adults using oral drugs for the type of diabetes that used to be referred to as "adult onset." Oral insulin products were a major revenue source. Sometimes they were not effective.

Compound 17392, as the manufacturer referred to it, had now been approved for clinical use. Some early adopting physicians were already using it, especially for their patients who had problems with the earlier generation agents. Now that the drug had FDA approval, marketing and postmarketing surveillance was heavy on the minds of both the research and marketing departments.

The two departments began a collaboration to follow the adoption of the new drug. Marketing was eager to have high-volume prescribers adopt the product, and the research department wanted to follow early reports of potential liver toxicity. Together they came up with a plan.

Marketing already had access to the prescribing practices of all physicians in the United States who saw patients for type-2 diabetes. It proposed a phase-4 clinical trial, the industry term for postmarketing studies to get prescribing physicians to report their experience with new pharmaceuticals. Years ago, pharmaceutical manufacturers simply paid physicians to try new products with their patients. Now, however, that was avoided since it appeared to interfere with the physician's clinical judgment and duty to prescribe what he or she believed best for patients.

The current plan would identify those physicians who were among the top 10 percent of prescribers for type-2 diabetes. From among that group, several hundred physicians would be recruited to enter their patients into a trial for whom the clinician had made a judgment that Compound 17392 was appropriate. Physicians who were already prescribing would not be invited (since the manufacturer wanted each clinician to feel free to choose whether to enter a patient into the trial). Following a protocol designed by the research department, these physicians would report on a regular basis the results of the use of the drug, reported side effects, and both patient and physician subjective evaluations.

Physicians who were in the identified pool of prescribers would be invited to a two-day meeting to be introduced to the protocol. The meeting would be held in Palm Beach at an elegant hotel with golf privileges included with the room. Those who were interested in the research would be paid $300 for every patient entered into the study with an additional payment of $300 for every patient who completed the one-year follow-up. The payment was not a "finder's fee" but rather compensation for the time and effort involved in following the patients and filing reports. No physicians who owned stock in the manufacturer would be allowed to participate (although ownership through mutual funds was acceptable).

Dr. Carlos Carera is a diabetologist with a large practice in New York City. He received an invitation in the mail to attend a two-day meeting in Palm Beach, California, to learn about a phase-4 clinical trial of a newly approved oral antidiabetic agent. He was not sure why he was selected, but he had a large practice involving adults newly diagnosed with diabetes. Since some of his patients were not doing well on the available drugs or could not tolerate them well, he was interested in these developments and was considering whether to attend the meeting. If Dr. Carera accepts $600 for his labor involved in recruiting and entering patients into this trial, is his objectivity compromised?

COMMENTARY

Research, development, and marketing of new pharmaceuticals is a very large business. These new agents have revolutionized medicine, generating large costs for the drugs, but significantly improving health of patients and reducing costs for hospitalizations and other treatments.

The pharmaceutical manufacturer in this case is following a common practice of postmarketing surveillance for the purpose of documenting risks and benefits of the agents. At the time a new drug is approved, data may exist on only a few thousand patients. It is quite possible that rare side effects will not be caught by this time so phase-4 trials are important. They are also a potential way for manufacturers to encourage physicians to adopt their new products.

This manufacturer has targeted high-volume prescribers who are not yet using their new drug. This makes sense medically since it would be inefficient to recruit physicians who do not see patients who could use the drug and recruiting those already using it might produce a bias. Doing so might also decrease the likelihood of getting new physicians to use the product.

It is now recognized that it would be an unethical conflict of interest to pay physicians to convert from the drugs they are currently using to the manufacturer's new competing product. Postmarketing studies have the advantage of simultaneously meeting a legitimate need for collecting large amounts of data and encouraging more widespread use of the product without overtly bribing doctors to switch.

The arrangement in this case looks rather like paying clinicians to enter their patients into the trial. On the other hand, the gathering of information about a new drug after FDA approval is surely a worthwhile project, and clinicians cannot be expected to spend the time to do extra tests and file reports on the drug without compensation for their time.

One problem with this design is that it pays an additional fee for each patient who completes the trial. This could easily provide a financial incentive for physicians to keep their patients on the drug even if some problems arise. Presumably, most physicians would have the integrity to stop the use of the drug if a serious problem arose, but it is hard to determine whether the extra $300 payment would tip the balance in more borderline cases.

Researchers are now required to report any financial conflicts of interest including payments from drug manufacturers for participation in speakers' bureaus, consulting fees, and stock ownership. What, however, about the fees paid in this case and the initial offer of what sounds like a golfing trip at a luxury resort at the drug company's expense? Is there any thing that could be done to eliminate the conflict of interest in phase-4 trials like this?

INFORMED CONSENT IN RESEARCH

In earlier cases in this chapter, the requirements of confidentiality and equity in subject selection, grounded in the principles of fidelity to promises and justice, provided reasons why some would place limits on research even if it is believed to be well designed and is likely to produce significant benefits for society. These two ethical principles not focusing on maximizing good consequences potentially could hold social beneficence in check, protecting the rights of patients even though societal benefits might be lost in the process.

Another way in which societal interests come into conflict with the moral requirements of other principles of ethics is when they jeopardize individual autonomy. A final way in which societal interests may conflict with other moral requirements arises in the area of informed consent. As we saw in Chapter 6, the consent requirement is often grounded in respect for autonomy rather than utility. Consent is required according to the principle of autonomy, even if the health professional believes that more benefit to the patient or society might result if the consent requirements were ignored.

This conflict between autonomy and social benefit arises frequently in cases in which investigators believe that the consent should be waived or modified in order to assure greater benefit for society from the research. The next case, which continues the events described in Case 16-7, illustrates the problem.

CASE 16-8

Waiving Consent for Future Research on Blood Samples

In Case 16-7 a manufacturer recruited high-prescribing clinicians to enter their appropriate patients into a postmarketing (phase-4) clinical trial that would follow the use of Compound 17392, a new oral antidiabetic (hypoglycemic) agent. Clinicians would recruit their patients, prescribe the new drug, and follow the effectiveness of the drug as well as the side effects. Patients would be given a detailed written informed consent describing the risks and benefits of the drug, potential side effects, any additional tests to be performed for purposes of gathering research data (as opposed to tests needed for routine clinical care), and any additional burdens. The subjects would also be told the purpose of the study, how confidentiality would be protected, and what compensation, if any, would be provided for patients injured during the research.

One of the concerns of the drug company was that a small group of patients using Compound 17392 were showing abnormal liver function. Sometimes these problems were self-correcting, but in some cases, liver toxicity was great enough that patients had to be withdrawn from the drug.

Since only a small percentage of patients showed any liver problems, investigators wanted to see if they could understand the pathology. They began to suspect that a small group of patients metabolized the drug atypically, perhaps as a result of some rare genetic variant producing a modification in the metabolism. The research department at the drug company designed an additional study that would look at genetic markers in a blood sample from the patients. They also decided to store the additional blood for future research at a later time.

This research, like almost all clinical trials, must be reviewed and approved by an IRB. The board that was reviewing this study came to the consent document and faced a number of issues. Explaining the known risks including the slight chance of liver toxicity was straightforward. Similarly, alternatives to entering the research must be explained. Since this was not a randomized trial, the IRB could avoid having to make sure the randomization process was explained adequately. Standard "boiler-plate" language about the patient's right to withdraw, compensation for injury, and confidentiality were incorporated. Two issues presented a problem for the IRB.

First, what should be said about the complicated financial arrangement between the physician and the drug company? Patients could be told that their physician was being paid to enter them into the trial and to have them complete the trial. That could include the amount the physician was paid or merely a statement that a fee was provided.

Second, the collection of the blood samples presented challenging consent issues. Subjects would be told that a blood sample would be taken. This would include standard language about the risks of venipuncture as well as a statement that additional blood would be taken for research purposes. The problem was what to tell the patient/subjects about the tests and their results.

Standard research consent includes a statement that subjects will be told of any new developments that could be meaningful to them during the study, including new findings. In this case, however, since the liver pathology was poorly understood, it was not clear what could be said about testing. Moreover, samples were being stored for future testing, which could occur at a time well after the patient had completed the trial, perhaps even after the patient had stopped seeing the clinician involved.

It was assumed that nothing clinically meaningful would come from these tests, but there was always a chance that the genetic tests could identify a gene carried by a small group of people that was responsible for the liver toxicity. Patients would surely want to know if they were carrying such a gene. It could be meaningful in future drug decisions. On the other hand, learning that one has a gene responsible for unusual medical problems is potentially stigmatizing and could even lead to jeopardizing employment and insurance. Would health and life insurance companies, for instance, have a right to know of the identification of such genes?

Not only was the disclosure of findings from these blood studies problematic, it was also potentially very difficult to carry out. If the findings occurred soon after completion of the study, the researchers could notify the clinicians who could inform and educate the patients, but some of these studies could occur years later when the doctor–patient relation no longer existed.

COMMENTARY

Informed consent is a central part of the ethics of research involving human subjects. It was the central innovation in the Nuremburg Code designed to permit physicians and other researchers to do things to humans that are not specifically designed to benefit the patient. The full range of issues of informed consent will be discussed in the cases of the next chapter. Here our attention should focus on the specific issues related to the research context.

We have already seen in Case 16-7 that problems of potential financial conflicts of interests of investigators can arise in research. One of the special issues of research consent is making sure that subjects are adequately informed of the financial arrangements between the patient's physician and the drug company sponsoring the research. Similarly, other kinds of conflict of interest should be disclosed, including how the investigator might benefit from successful completion of the research.

Consent for research clearly needs to include an adequate account of risks and benefits, alternative therapies that may be available, procedures for protection of confidentiality, availability of compensation, the right to withdraw from the study, and a person to contact. In this study, special compensation arrangements for the clinician that posed a potential conflict of interest would also have to be disclosed. The most challenging feature of this study, however, is the collection of blood samples for possible future genetic and pharmacodynamic studies. Some investigators assume that, because there is no further risk from these studies, nothing more needs to be said, but reasonable subjects may still want to know about this future research. The problem is that the investigators themselves may not know what studies will be conducted.

One strategy is to inform the patients that they will not receive the results of any future genetic and pharmacodynamic studies. That would simultaneously avoid the logistic problems and difficulties for patients who might learn of damaging information. It could also, however, keep from them information with true life-saving potential. Although it seemed unlikely, the studies conducted in the future could identify a marker for the liver toxicity that would be important for avoiding some class of drugs similar to the agent now being tested. Given that some subjects might really want the results of future studies and others might just as fervently not want them, one strategy is to give people a chance in the initial consent to indicate whether they would like to learn of future results. If subjects indicate a desire for this information, then some arrangement must be made for contact. In the case of genetic information, that may require committing to providing someone with sophistication in genetic counseling to explain the nature of the findings. Since subjects cannot know in advance whether they would find these future findings meaningful, it is hard for subjects reasonably to waive their right of access. On the other hand, if researchers commit to providing any future findings, they may not be able to deliver if they cannot locate subjects and, even if they can, subjects may find the information distressing or harmful to their employment and insurance interests. Consenting to research, especially research that involves open-ended approval of future studies that have not yet been defined, poses challenging issues in addition to the standard moral problems of consent. It is to those more traditional issues of consent for therapy to which we now turn.

NOTES

[1] "Nuremberg Code." http://www.hhs.gov/ohrp/references/nurcode.htm.

[2] "Nuremberg Code." http://www.hhs.gov/ohrp/references/nurcode.htm, point 2 of code.

[3] Caplan, Arthur L., editor. *When Medicine Went Mad: Bioethics and the Holocaust.* Totowa, NJ: Humana Press, 1992; Annas, George J., Michael A. Grodin, Editors. *The Nazi Doctors and the Nuremberg Code: Human Rights in Human Experimentation.* New York: Oxford University Press, 1992.

[4] "Nuremberg Code." http://www.hhs.gov/ohrp/references/nurcode.htm, point 1 of code.

[5] The current version of the Declaration of Helsinki as well as some of the history is now available on the website of the World Medical Association, http://www.wma.net/e/policy/b3.htm (accessed June 2, 2006).

[6] Declaration of Helsinki, points 24–26.

[7] American Medical Association. "Ethical Guidelines for Clinical Investigation." In *Encyclopedia of Bioethics*, Vol. 4. Warren T. Reich, editor. New York: The Free Press, 1978, pp. 1773–1774.

[8] U.S. Department of Health, Education, and Welfare. *The Institutional Guide to DHEW Policy on Protection of Human Subjects.* Washington, DC: U.S. Government Printing Office, 1971.

[9] U.S. Department of Health and Human Services. "Final Regulations Amending Basic HHS Policy for the Protection of Human Research Subjects: Final Rule: 45 CFR 46." *Federal Register: Rules and Regulations* 46 (No. 16, January 26, 1981):8366–8392.

[10] U.S. Department of Health and Human Services. "Federal Policy for the Protection of Human Subjects; Notices and Rules." *Federal Register* 46 (No. 117, June 18, 1991):28001–28032.

[11] United States. Department of Health and Human Services [HHS]. Office for Human Research Protections [OHRP] *International Compilation of Human Subject Research Protections*, 2nd ed. Washington, DC: Office for Human Research Protections, 2005 October 1. Available: http://www.hhs.gov/ohrp/international/HSPCompilation.pdf [2005 October 5] Second edition.

[12] U.S. Department of Health and Human Services. "Federal Policy for the Protection of Human Subjects." *Code of Federal Regulations* 45 Part 46, Revised June 18, 1991, reprinted March 15, 1994, revised June 23, 2005.

[13] Freedman, Benjamin. "Equipoise and the Ethics of Clinical Research." *New England Journal of Medicine* 317 (1987):141–145.

[14] U.S. Department of Health and Human Services, National Institutes of Health, Office of Protection from Research Risks. "Protection of Human Subjects." *Code of Federal Regulations* 45 Part 46, Revised June 23, 2005.

[15] U.S. Department of Health and Human Services. "Protection of Human Subjects." §46.101.

[16] [Principle II]; American Medical Association, Council on Ethical and Judicial Affairs. *Code of Medical Ethics: Current Opinions with Annotations, 2004–2005 Edition.* Chicago, IL: American Medical Association, 2004.

[17] U.S. Department of Health and Human Services, National Institutes of Health, Office of Protection from Research Risks. "Protection of Human Subjects." §46.111 (a) (7).

[18] Ibid.

[19] Office for Human Research Protections (OHRP), Department of Health and Human Services (HHS), *Guidance on Certificates of Confidentiality*, February 25, 2003, available on the web at http://www.hhs.gov/ohrp/humansubjects/guidance/certconf.htm (accessed May 10, 2007).

[20] National Commission for the Protection of Human Subjects of Biomedical and Behavioral Research. *The Belmont Report: Ethical Principles and Guidelines for the Protection of Human Subjects of Research.* Washington, DC: U.S. Government Printing Office, 1978.

[21] This case is based on an earlier version of this account that appeared as Veatch, Robert M. "Case Study: Risk-Taking in Cancer Chemotherapy." *IRB* 1 (No. 5, August/September, 1979):4–6.

CHAPTER 17

Consent and the Right to Refuse Treatment

Other Cases Involving Consent

6-1: Borderline Competency: Deciding About Major Heart Surgery
6-2: A Mature 12-Year-Old Who Refuses a Heart Transplant
6-4: A Diabetic Who Refuses Treatment for an Infection
6-6: Ignoring a Daughter's Do-Not-Resuscitate (DNR) Request
7-1: A Routine Mole or an Early Case of Skin Cancer: The Duty to Disclose Doubtful Information
7-6: A Clash of Cultures: A Japanese Family Asks that Their Father Not Be Told of Cancer
7-7: Disclosing Cancer to a Mentally Compromised Patient
8-5: Profiting from Unnecessary Angioplasty
10-6: Sterilization of an Economically Deprived Woman
10-7: Biased Counseling: Teaching about Birth Control
11-6: Using Genes to Treat Brain Cancer
12-2: "Ain't Nobody Gonna Cut on My Head"
14-7: The Child as the Source of a Kidney
15-5: Promoting Patients' Rights by Denying Insurance Coverage
16-1: Chemotherapy Risks: Is Going Without Chemotherapy a Benefit?
16-2: Research to Develop Screening Techniques for HIV-Infected Blood
16-3: Abortion and Psychopathology: Research on Medical Records
16-4: Surveying Illegal Immigrants
16-8: Waiving Consent for Future Research on Blood Samples
18-2: Ambiguous Advance Directives: Who Interprets?
18-3: The Cruzan Case: Whether to Forgo Nutrition Based on a Patient's Views
18-7: The Case of the Suspect Surrogates

Issues of informed consent that arise in medical research were discussed in the final case of the previous chapter. Informed consent has also emerged as a central issue in therapeutic medicine, at least in the last half of the twentieth century.[1] Recent literature on informed consent reveals its increasing importance.[2]

It is striking that the Hippocratic ethical tradition has no provision for consent of the patient for any treatment. Its central ethical approach was to assume that the health professional could figure out what was in the interest of the patient and act accordingly. The Hippocratic Oath actually prohibits the health care professional from sharing any medical knowledge with patients.[3]

It was not until the twentieth century that consent of the patient became morally important. Its moral foundation is generally not in the moral principles of doing good and protecting from harm, but in the key principle of Western political philosophy: self-determination or autonomy. As we saw in Chapter 6, respect for autonomy as a moral principle requires that people be allowed to make life choices according to self-generated life plans. In health care this means choosing alternatives that fit with one's own goals and purposes.

The realization that different health care choices will be appropriate for different life plans and that the patient should be permitted to choose among them is one of the most revolutionary ideas in the health care ethics of the twentieth century. At first, the only requirement was that the patient actually agrees to the treatment proposed by the physician. A key legal case in 1914 summarized the emerging notion saying, "Every human being of adult years and sound mind has a right to determine what shall be done with his own body; and a surgeon who performs an operation without his patient's consent commits an assault, for which he is liable in damages."[4]

We gradually began to realize that it was possible for a patient to consent to treatment and still not be informed about the choices being made. It was not until the 1950s that concern began to emerge that consent be informed and voluntary.[5] That introduced several important questions in the discussion of consent. In the first section of this chapter we look at what can be called the *elements of consent*, that is, the types of information that need to be transmitted for a consent to be adequately informed. In the second section, we look at cases involving questions of the *standards of consent*. This refers to the question of what standard of reference should be used in determining whether a sufficient amount of a particular type of information has been transmitted. In the third section we examine the questions of whether the information transmitted is comprehended and whether the consent is adequately voluntary. Finally, in the fourth section we address whether incompetent patients can be expected to consent and what role parents, guardians, and other surrogates can play in giving approval of medical treatments for those who are legally incompetent to do so themselves.

THE ELEMENTS OF A CONSENT

An adequate consent to treatment must be informed. For it to be informed, it must contain several types of information (sometimes called "elements"[6]);

for example, information not only about the benefits and harms but also their probabilities of occurring as well as information about treatment alternatives. There may be other kinds of information that patients would desire as well including information about the costs of the treatment, inconvenience, the time consumed, risks relating to confidentiality breaches, any changes in lifestyle that will or could result from treatment, and the competence of the provider. In some situations, patients might want to know about the funding source or about fees researchers will receive for recruiting subjects. The following cases show problems arise in deciding whether patients have been given enough information for their consent to be adequately informed.

CASE 17-1

Therapeutic Privilege: Scaring the Patient to Death with News about Risks

The patient, Steven Mendos, was a 55-year-old white male with a history of complex heart problems, hypertension, and unstable ventricular arrhythmias. He complained of cramping pain in his legs and intermittent limping. The physician, Susan Therapides, suspected a block in his abdominal aorta and recommended translumbar aortography to locate the block. She needed to inject a dye, sodium urokon.

Dr. Therapides knew that this was a procedure that exposed the patient to some risk. The injection can cause an anaphylatic response and, in rare cases, paralysis or even death. The standard procedure called for informing the patient of these risks and obtaining a written consent for the test. But Dr. Therapides was concerned about getting the consent. The patient was very frightened about his condition, he was apprehensive, and, had serious heart disease, with hypertension. She came to the hospital ethics committee (HEC) with the problem. She argued, "If you frighten him further, you have a problem which you have created. If I mention the risk of paralysis to him, I think it might be a terrible mistake." She claimed that she should have a "therapeutic privilege" to omit getting the consent for the procedure.

COMMENTARY

The traditional ethic of medicine commits the health professional to doing what will benefit the patient according to the professional's ability and judgment. That is what was required in the Hippocratic Oath. That was a culture in which patients were never told what medication they were receiving. The use of benevolent deception for the patient's good was a rather common practice. For example, placebo medications were prescribed for patients when the physician believed that the patient's complaint was only in the patient's mind.

Physicians would dishonestly tell patients they were receiving some specified drug, when they were actually receiving sugar pills. In other cases, they would not be told of the risks if the physician believed that the procedure was in the patient's interest and the explanation of the risks would serve no useful purpose or would even cause harm.

That surely is what the physician, Dr. Therapides, had in mind when she proposed avoiding mention of the risks of the sodium urokon. This approach, in which a deception or an omission is used therapeutically, had been referred to as a *therapeutic privilege*. It is supported by an ethic in which the only moral goal is the welfare of the patient.

In recent years, that ethic has been challenged. One reason for the challenge has come from a commitment to the moral principle of respect for autonomy in which the patient is given the right to be informed of the medication he or she is receiving and to decide whether to agree to the proposed treatment course.

In many cases, we now believe that it is in the patient's interest to be informed. In a mobile society, it is often for the good of the patient that he or she knows the name of the medication being taken, details about his or her diagnosis, and other aspects of the treatment plan and future possibilities. That means that even those committed to the traditional paternalistic ethic of patient benefit would usually now support disclosing the name of the medication to the patient, the clinical side effects that could interfere with driving or other potentially dangerous tasks, and aspects of the prognosis relevant to patient planning. They might even insist that the patient understand the therapeutic rationale, the future course of the disease, research being conducted, or other dimensions of the illness that could be involved in patient cooperation in treatment.

In rare cases, however, physicians and other health professionals remain convinced that providing reasonable information about the diagnosis, the treatment alternatives, name of the medication, and the therapeutic strategy may not be in the patient's interest. That seems to be Dr. Theripides's attitude in this case. Others may not be completely convinced that omitting the information about the risks is in the patient's interest. Thus, they might even object to Dr. Theripides's strategy on more traditional Hippocratic grounds. They might have another concern, however. They might acknowledge that the information could be upsetting to the patient, but still have ethical concerns about the nondisclosure. For example, they could be concerned that it violated the principle of autonomy or other aspects of respect for persons. They could believe that he has a right to be treated as an autonomous agent with a right to be informed about the essential features of the treatment plan. This could force them to the conclusion that there was no way to follow this treatment plan without telling the patient about the risks, including the potentially disturbing ones, the diagnosis, and the prognosis.

Just what kinds of information must be disclosed in order for a consent to be adequately informed? The kinds of information that must be disclosed are sometimes called the *elements* of consent. Sometimes patients may be interested in additional information beyond the risks and the benefits. One kind of information that is often included is the alternative therapies available. In this case, the alternatives might include doing the imaging without the dye and not doing the testing at all as well as explaining to Mr. Mendos the risks in a calm and reassuring manner.

Among the other elements of a consent that might need to be transmitted are the costs of the alternative treatments, other professionals who might be involved, which treatments are covered by insurance and which are not, and the extent of disagreement, if any, among health professionals about the feasibility of the treatment. In this case, it would probably be important for Mr. Mendos to know how important the imaging is in developing treatment options.

In some special cases there may be additional information as well. If a physician is receiving some incentive from a manufacturer to use the therapy involved, patients would probably want to know about it. Information about special funding, the name of the manufacturer, and so forth may sometimes be information that is relevant to the patient in deciding whether to consent to the therapy being proposed.

In the doctrine of informed consent, the key criterion for deciding which kinds of information are to be included in the disclosure is what would reasonably be meaningful or useful information to the patient in deciding whether to agree to the proposed therapy, and then deciding that the consent was adequately informed. No rational person would want to be "fully informed." It is not even clear what that could mean since there is an infinite amount of information that one theoretically could provide about any medication: its chemical formula, the details of the manufacturing process, the complete details of all clinical trials, and so on. It is conceptually impossible for anyone to be fully informed, and we would cease to find the information relevant or interesting long before we ran out of things that could be said. The goal is "adequate" information for the patient to make a reasonable choice. Deciding which elements must be included for a consent to be so informed is the issue of the next case.

CASE 17-2

Disclosing the Experience of a Surgeon

Angus McBride had recently retired from a career working on an assembly line in a Michigan auto factory. He had long been bothered by gastroesophogeal reflux disease (GERD). Reflux of gastric acid produced an unpleasant sensation resulting from an improperly functioning sphincter between the stomach and the esophagus that permits the upward flow of stomach contents, especially gastric acid.

Mr. McBride's internist, William Arnold, had monitored the esophageal problems for several years. Treatment had included antacids, histamine blockers (ranitidine or Zantac), and proton pump inhibitors including esomeprazole (Nexium). Dr. Arnold had noted increasing irritation of the lining of the esophagus and the emergence of a condition known as Barrett's esophagus, in which some of its lining is modified with cells resembling intestinal cells replacing the normal tissue. This, in itself, is not harmful, but is associated with the development of esophageal adeno-carcinoma. The risk of the cancer is between 30 and 105 percent higher in people with Barrett's esophagus.

Mr. McBride's risk of getting adenocarcinoma remained small, less than 1 per-cent, but the consequences would be severe. Dr. Arnold referred Mr. McBride to Dr. Rachel Herbert, the chair of Laparoscopic Surgery at the city's most prestigious teaching hospital. Dr. Herbert agreed with Dr. Arnold's diagnosis. When the condi-tion worsened, she recommended the removal of the portion of the esophagus that manifest the abnormal cells. This would reduce the risk of the cells becoming can-cerous. This was a major operation but should result in the elimination or reduction of the risks associated with Barrett's esophagus. She explained the risks and benefits. She proposed to do the procedure laparoscopically, that is, using instruments that could be passed through small slits in the skin thereby making the intervention much less invasive. Dr. Herbert was one of the country's most experienced laparoscropic surgeons, having pioneered the techniques for several laparoscopic procedures.

Two issues related to the consent were on Dr. Herbert's mind. First, she knew that the standard treatment for Barrett's esophagus was a procedure in which the thoracic cavity was opened, involving extensive trauma to the ribs and associated tissues. She explained to Mr. McBride that the laparoscopic approach would be much less traumatic and would involve a much shorter recovery period. She knew, however, that at other hospitals the standard procedure would be performed, pri-marily because the laparoscopic procedure was new and only a small number of surgeons were prepared to perform it. She also knew that laparoscopy posed dif-ferent risks: that visualization through the scope necessary to operate posed some risk of having the instruments accidentally cut surrounding tissues including the aorta, which passed dangerously close to the esophagus.

To her knowledge, no serious injury of this kind had ever been reported, but this was a new procedure, so not many attempts had been made. She won-dered whether she should explain this undocumented hypothetical serious risk and whether a patient would rather consider the open procedure because of this risk. Since she did only laparoscopic operations at this point in her career, she also won-dered whether she should have a more traditional thoracic surgeon present the case for the open procedure.

Her second concern was more awkward for her. Although she was a world-class laparoscopic surgeon, most of her experience was on intestinal procedures and in sterilization of women who wanted their tubes tied using the laparoscopic technique. She had only performed two previous esophageal procedures laparo-scopically. Thus, although she was a leading surgeon, she was relatively new at this particular procedure. She feared that telling Mr. McBride this would alarm him and could even drive him to consider the traditional open procedure, which she was convinced was not in Mr. McBride's interest. In reviewing the elements of an adequately informed consent, should Dr. Herbert explain the risks and benefits of the open procedure and should she explain her relative inexperience? Also, should she ask another surgeon to explain the options from the perspective of one who performed the open procedure?

COMMENTARY

Dr. Herbert has no difficulty with the most obvious elements of an informed consent. She will be as clear and thorough as she can about the risks and benefits of the procedure that she proposes as well as the alternative open procedure. She is more troubled, however, about whether she would be biased in supporting the newer technology, which she sees as obviously preferable. In fact, she may believe that the invasiveness and long recovery period related to the open procedure make it so inferior that Mr. McBride would not seriously entertain that option. Nevertheless, a surgeon less focused on laparoscopy might tell the story differently.

The more troublesome issue is whether her relative lack of experience with esophageal laparoscopy is something she should explain to Mr. McBride. Especially, since she is one of the world's leading laparoscopic surgeons, how does she convey accurately her experience when she has performed this particular procedure only twice before?

The problem of including physician experience as part of the consent process is much more extensive. All physicians begin their careers with limited experience. That lack of experience could be alarming to patients but is plausibly relevant to their decision whether to work with this physician or seek out someone else. Moreover, even if it is clear that physicians should reveal that this is their first time trying some procedure, they will face a similar problem the next time when they could state that they had done the procedure only once before. In Dr. Herbert's case, she had done countless laparoscopies but only two esophageal procedures. She would have to decide at what point she had done enough of them that her experience is no longer worth mentioning. Even then, however, she may know that no matter how skilled she is, there may be some other surgeon who has an even better reputation. Does the fact that another surgeon in town or in some other town has a better reputation have to be included in the consent information?

Once the categories or elements of information are understood, there still remains the question of just how much of each kind of information must be provided. This requires assessment of the alternative standards for consent.

THE STANDARDS FOR CONSENT

In the previous section we saw that there were several elements of information that could be part of a consent (such as the competence of the provider) that are normally not told to patients but nevertheless are potentially very important in some cases. When there is doubt about what information to disclose, some standard of reference is needed to establish exactly what to disclose. One approach is for a physician to rely on a judgment about what colleagues in similar situations would disclose. This raises an important question: should the consensus of one's colleagues be the standard for deciding what must be disclosed?

Deciding what to disclose based on what one's colleagues would disclose is what is called the *professional standard*. Traditional legal and moral practice relied on the professional standard for determining what must be disclosed.

Beginning about 1970 our standard began to change. What is now called the *reasonable-person standard* emerged as an alternative.[7] It replaced the idea that one is required to disclose what one's colleagues similarly situated would have disclosed with the idea that one is required to disclose what the reasonable person would want or need to know in order to make an informed choice for or against the proposed treatment.

The argument behind this shift is that if the goal is to give information needed in order to make autonomous choices, then it really is not decisive what professional colleagues similarly situated would disclose. They may also have developed a practice that does not provide the patient with everything he or she would want or need to know. Only telling what one needs to know will do the job.

The reasonable-person standard makes a controversial presumption: that what the "reasonable person" would need is what a particular patient would need. But what about the patient who is unique, who would like some information that the typical reasonable person would not want? Or what about the patient who is unique in not wanting some information that the typical reasonable person would need? Some are now proposing a *subjective standard*.[8] It would require disclosing what the actual patient would want or need to know rather than either what professional colleagues would disclose or what the reasonable person would need to know. The following case requires a hospital clinic to choose which of these three standards is appropriate.

CASE 17-3

Disclosing the Risks of Dilantin to Seizure Clinic Patients: How Much to State

Physicians in the Seizure Disorder Clinic of an East Coast Hospital were in the process of developing an information sheet that would be provided to adult patients receiving a common medication for epileptic and other seizures. They set out to explain in lay language the benefits and risks of the medication and alternative treatments. The group preparing the information was committed to providing information to patients as background for their agreement to recommended therapies. The group was concerned, however, that providing too much information could include items that were unimportant to patients, potentially disturbing, or possibly confusing to them.

They had information available from an empirical study done some years ago at the Johns Hopkins Hospital Seizure Clinic and Walter Reed Army Hospital.[9] The investigators prepared a list of five potential benefits and sixteen possible risks of the drug. They asked neurologists familiar with the drug which of the effects they told patients about. Then they asked patients which of the side effects they would want to be told about. The study involved both adult patients and the parents of pediatric patients, but only the adult patient data were relevant here. The data on risks were the focus of concern.

The physicians of adult patients, the ones most relevant to the clinic that was writing the information sheet, indicated a range of behaviors ranging from 86 percent who mentioned gingival hypertrophy (enlargement of the gums) to 3.2 percent who would mention a small risk of hyperglycemia (high blood sugar). Only three other side effects were mentioned by at least 50 percent of the physicians. These were dose-related ataxia, dose-related sedation, and skin rash. Smaller percentages mentioned such effects as hirsutism (hair growth) (45.5 percent), hematologic changes (33.7 percent), hepatitis (9.3 percent), and drug-related mortality (7.5 percent). The problem was how this list of responses could be converted into items on the information sheet and which should be included.

Before making those decisions, the group also looked at what the patients said they would want to be told about Dilantin. Large majorities wanted to know about each of the sixteen side effects, for example, dose-related ataxia (98.0 percent), hyperglycemia (77.4 percent), down to the lowest percentage for drug-related mortality (71.4 percent).

Given this information, the group set out to write the information sheet. Should they rely on the physicians' views or the patients' views? Since at least some physicians presented each of the sixteen side effects, but a majority presented only four, how would they use this information in deciding which side effects to present to patients? At least some patients would not want to be told about each of the side effects, yet a majority wanted to know about each of them. Which, if any, should be omitted?[9]

COMMENTARY

Assuming that one has an estimate (or in this case hard data) on what clinicians tend to disclose and what patients say they would want to be told, the intriguing question is what standard should be used in determining what counts as a morally or legally adequate disclosure. One option would be to be guided by the consensus of physician colleagues. This is called the "professional standard."

Assuming the professional standard was used, there remains a question of just what percentage of one's colleagues would have to favor disclosure before it became a standard. Would it be 50 percent, 95 percent, or what? The professional standard also can be problematic because it is quite uncommon for medical professionals to know the standard practice of more than a few of their colleagues.

A moral and legal duty to get an informed consent exists in such cases. Physicians must realize that they cannot tell patients literally everything about any drug. There are virtually infinite effects that could occur, many of which patients clearly would not be interested in learning about. There are trivial and irrelevant details about the research that went on leading to approval of drug labeling, manufacturing processes, and extremely rare and trivial side effects. There is no way they can tell *everything*. Knowing what to disclose depends on which standard is appropriate. According to the traditional professional standard, clinicians need tell only what their colleagues similarly situated would have claimed. The data suggest, however, that some physicians would not have disclosed each of the sixteen named side effects of the medication, while others would have. One approach would be to disclose only what a majority of physicians would have disclosed, that is, the four effects getting the highest positive responses: dose-related ataxia, dose-related sedation, gingival hypertrophy, and skin rash. Perhaps physicians should have the option of disclosing additional items, but should not be required to do so.

The reasonable-person standard holds that the physician must tell what the reasonable person would want to know before consenting. The patients at the clinic studied by the researchers apparently had a strong desire for substantial information. A majority expressed a desire to know about each of the side effects mentioned. That, of course, does not imply they want to know "everything." If there are countless things that could be said about any pharmaceutical, some of them are surely so trivial or irrelevant that learning about them would not be worth the time and energy required.

The moral principle behind this reasonable-person standard is respect for autonomy: the patient must be told what he or she needs to know to make an informed choice even if the information will be upsetting. Concern about patient adherence to regimen or about fear of side effects dissuading the patient from needed medication may not be definitive according to the principle of respect for autonomy. That was what we saw in the cases of Chapter 6. A potential asymmetry exists: omitting needed information could violate the principle of autonomy, but providing too much information may only be upsetting. It may only violate the principle of nonmaleficence.

Some patients may have unusual desires when it comes to what they are told. Some may want to know less than the typical patient. If the patient says he or she has been told enough, then is that sufficient to satisfy the ethical principle of autonomy? What about the patient who wants to know more than the typical patient? Some people are now advocating what is called the *subjective standard*, whereby a patient should be told information that fits his or her needs. This would seem to conform to the principle of respect for autonomy even better than the reasonable-person standard.

There is a problem with this subjective standard, however. How can the clinician know what the individual patient's need for information is? In some cases, clinicians may know or have reason to know that the patient's needs are atypical. The patient may be in a profession where predictably she would have special concerns about injury to hands or legs or certain mental functions. Some are now arguing that if the clinician knows or has reason to know that the patient's needs are atypical, because of what is known about the patient or what the patient discloses, then information must be disclosed according to the subjective standard, but that, otherwise, the reasonable-person standard should be used.

The reasonable-person standard poses some problems of its own, however. Just as with the professional standard, one problem is just what percentage of patients desiring information would count as evidence that the "reasonable patient" would want to know? Would it be justifiable to disclose only those items which more than 50 percent wanted to know? If so, that suggests that up to 50 percent of the patients would not be given information that they desired. That could mean that 50 percent of the time a patient's autonomy would be violated, what many would take to be a high rate of moral error.

We might try to remedy this problem by telling any information that only a small percentage of patient's would want to know, say, 5 percent or 10 percent. That policy, however, would still leave some patients not getting certain pieces of information they would want for them to make an informed choice. There will always be some information-hungry patient who wants to know more. There would be no way of guaranteeing that a patient got every last piece of information relevant to making his or her decision without disclosing everything—a task we have already suggested is impossible. The logic of the principle of autonomy implies that a clinician should withhold information only if he or she has strong reason to believe that the patient would not want it. This can be expressed in terms of what percent chance one would be willing to take of withholding a piece of information necessary for the patient to decide autonomously about consenting to the drug. Defenders of autonomy claim that they would not be willing to take a 50 percent risk or even a 20 percent or 10 percent risk. Would a 5 percent error in assuming the patient would not want the information be tolerable or should it be more or less than this chance?

These concerns about figuring out what patients would want to know have led to suggestion of a combined standard. Under it, patients would have to be told information according to the reasonable-person standard, adjusted by what the clinician knows or has reason to know is unique about the patient's interests.

COMPREHENSION AND VOLUNTARINESS

It is not enough that the patient be adequately informed, if the consent is to satisfy the requirements of the principle of respect for autonomy. The information must also be understood, and the consent must be voluntary. Consent may be constrained either because the information, though communicated, was not understood or because the individual's choice was somehow not sufficiently free.

Understanding is jeopardized when the words cannot be comprehended because they are unfamiliar, either because the patient is not a native speaker or the terms are simply too complex. Psychological factors, such as stress from an illness, may also make the information incomprehensible.

Even if the patient understands, the consent may not be voluntary. The patient can be constrained externally by undue physical or psychological pressures or internally by mental illness or compulsion.[10] The following cases raise the problem of whether a consent is based on adequate comprehension and voluntariness.

CASE 17-4

Consenting to Admission to a Psychiatric Unit

Otis Garvey had brought his 56-year-old wife, Donna, to the hospital emergency room for the second time in a week. She had been under enormous stress from a family crisis and had been taking Xanax, a benzodiazapine, to help her get some sleep. Over the past two months, she had become more and more depressed and agitated. She was now sleeping very little and acting more and more strangely, and was seriously out of control at this point. She even attempted to get out of the moving car on the way to the hospital.

In the emergency room, the triage nurse recognized the seriousness of Mrs. Garvey's condition and brought her and her husband almost immediately to an examining room. There her bizarre behavior continued. She wanted to leave the hospital, but her husband persuaded her to remain. She was given additional drugs to calm her down while she awaited the psychiatrist.

The psychiatrist's diagnosis was agitated depression with a possible relation to bipolar disorder. Given that she had been unsuccessfully treated as an outpatient and that her behavior was getting more dangerous, the psychiatrist proposed admission to the psychiatric unit for what would probably be a few days to attempt to stabilize her medication and overcome the acute crisis.

While in the unit she would be seen by the admitting psychiatrist, nurses, social workers, and others attempting to manage her acute crisis. The psychiatrist's hope was that she could be stabilized on oral medication and return home in a few days, perhaps a week or so at the most.

To be admitted to the psychiatric unit she would either have to sign herself in voluntarily or be committed. Since the car door opening episode had occurred, it could be claimed she was dangerous to herself so that she could be committed against her will. On the other hand, Mrs. Garvey understood that she was not well and was open to the suggestion of a short-term voluntary admission. One problem with the voluntary admission, however, was that it made no sense to get her to consent to the admission if she was not competent to do so. Being of danger to herself was not necessarily enough to have her declared incompetent, but the logic of consent requires a judgment that the patient is competent enough to make an informed and rational choice. The psychiatrist was not sure Mrs. Garvey was either informed or rational.

COMMENTARY

Mrs. Garvey is being considered for admission to the psychiatric floor of the hospital because of serious, persistent depression and agitation that could be related to a bipolar disorder. It might be assumed that she is not mentally competent to be informed about the options she has and the drug she is being given because of her mental illness. It does not make sense to rely on her consent if, in fact, she is not capable of understanding and making a free and informed decision. This is not necessarily the case, however. Just because she is being admitted to a mental institution it does not necessarily mean that she cannot give a legally effective consent to treatment. In fact, many people sign themselves into such institutions. They realize they need such help. Clinicians routinely take such signing in as effective consent to treatment. The law does not automatically assume a lack of competence just because one is in a mental institution.

If she were deemed incompetent, she could be admitted by psychiatrists following the laws of most states based on the claim that she was dangerous to herself or others. She could be held for a time. If she objected, a judicial proceeding would be required to review her case and determine whether she lacked competency to refuse the treatment being offered.

Even if she were deemed incompetent, that would not settle the issue of whether she has a right to be informed. There are good reasons to inform people of certain side effects of medications even if one assumes the patient is not competent to give or withhold consent to treatment. We routinely inform small children of the effects of an injection ("This may sting a bit."). We might want to alert an incompetent adult to report certain effects if they are experienced. Doing so, of course, increases the risk that the patient will report the effects, perhaps even if they are not actually experienced, but in various cases there are good reasons to inform a patient even if she is not competent to consent.

In this case there seems to be uncertainty over the patient's mental state and whether she is competent to consent to treatment. Health professionals have a duty to assess the capacity of a patient to render judgments in such situations, but they do not have the legal authority to declare incompetence. Only a court can do that. This leaves clinicians, such as the psychiatrist in this case, in an awkward position. They cannot legally treat without an effective consent and consents from incompetent patients are not effective consents, yet they do not have the authority to declare the patient legally incompetent even if she is institutionalized for her mental condition.

Adults are presumed to be substantially autonomous agents with the capacity to consent until proven otherwise. Yet it would be terribly dangerous for health professionals to presume all adults in fact have such capacity. The duty of the professionals is to make an initial assessment, seeking outside consultation if that seems necessary. Some patients are so clearly lacking in capacity that little formal assessment is needed. Others, such as Mrs. Garvey, may be sufficiently near the threshold of adequate capacity that drawing the line can be extremely difficult.

One strategy is to make the assessment and then, if the health professional believes that the patient lacks capacity, ask if the patient would be willing to let a surrogate act on her behalf. The surrogate might be the next-of-kin or someone else appropriate for the surrogate role. In a number of states, the next-of-kin is now designated by law to have the authority to act on behalf of an incompetent adult. If the patient concurs in transferring the decision-making authority, most would accept this as adequate. There may be no explicit legal authority for such transfer, but it is routinely done and absent ill-will on the part of the people involved has apparently never caused any legal trouble. Likewise, if the patient is so incoherent that she cannot object, it is generally presumed that the transfer of authority to the surrogate is appropriate. If Mrs. Garvey is believed by the admitting psychiatrist to be incompetent, this is one approach which could be used.

If the clinicians believe the patient lacks capacity but the patient herself insists she should be her own decision-maker, then a more serious problem arises. The clinicians lack the authority to declare her incompetent. In a case such as this one, there may even be dispute among the caregiving professionals about whether she is competent. The law permits temporary confinement to protect the safety of the patient or others, but the only safe course legally is to seek judicial review if the patient and the caregivers cannot reach agreement.

The other possibility is that the clinicians believe that she possesses the capacity to give an adequately effective consent. Since the patient is an adult, that would be the initial presumption. Of course, even the competent patient possesses the right to ask significant others for assistance in reaching a decision. Assuming Mrs. Garvey approved, there would be no barrier to transferring the decision-making authority to her husband, even if the clinicians believed her to be competent to consent.

CASE 17-5

Ambivalent Consent: Adequately Voluntary?

The surgeon, Stuart Clark, had an uneasy feeling about the patient, Marybeth Rich, a 56-year-old female with a localized breast mass. After careful evaluation, excisional biopsy was indicated, and he carefully discussed with her the seriousness of obtaining the diagnosis with this operative procedure. She seemed to understand the situation accurately and agreed to having the biopsy. At her request, he called the referring physician, 65 miles away. Then she insisted on the surgeon calling her sister, her niece, her neighbor, and her minister to inform them about the proposed treatment. Dr. Clark complied with the request but noticed that each of the people he talked to on the patient's behalf seemed confused as to why he called. Then she was scheduled for the operation.

The patient returned in 10 days for pre-op exam and further details of preparation. She then asked that a different neighbor be called about her situation. The surgeon realized another round of calls would be requested; he not only had little time for this but believed serious behavioral problems awaited. He canceled the operation and shared his concerns with her, then called the referring physician with the story and the need for further evaluation now, despite the real possibility of malignant disease. He was not interested in being her physician under these conditions. Was the surgeon correct in removing himself from the patient's case?

COMMENTARY

This case raises issues of voluntariness in a way that differs from Case 17-4. In that case the patient was manifesting overt signs of mental incapacity. She was being admitted to a psychiatric floor of the hospital. In this case, the patient's diagnosis is unrelated to mental illness and the physician involved was a surgeon, one not particularly prepared to make complicated psychiatric diagnoses. The case also suggests the necessity for surgeons to refuse to be mere technicians and raises questions about the right of the physician to be a party to the consent process.

For a consent to be adequately free and informed, the patient must make an adequately decisive choice that the surgeon can proceed. The procedure being considered was relatively straightforward. The patient seemed to show unusual hesitation. Does that hesitation amount to a pathological ambiguity and, if so, does a momentary concurrence with the surgeon's proposed plan constitute a sufficient consent for him to proceed?

We normally think of consent as something given by the patient—an act of the will following adequate understanding and deliberation in which one chooses to agree to a course of action affirming that it is consistent with one's goals, values, and life plan. Occasionally, medical professionals speak crudely of "consenting a patient," by which they mean going through the process of getting the patient's consent. That terminology is frowned upon because it implies that "consent" is something done by the health professional rather than the patient.

While that affirmation of the patient as the one who actively gives the consent is important, we should not overlook the fact that consent is also something that needs to be given by the health professional. Consent is an act of mutual pledging and agreement, a meeting of the minds about a course of action to be undertaken jointly. In this case not only must Marybeth Rich choose whether to agree to the operation, but Dr. Clark must also decide whether to participate. In the case of Ms. Rich, the issue is whether she is mentally sufficiently free to make a voluntary choice. In the case of Dr. Clark, the issue is whether he wants to be involved in a procedure that, in his estimation, threatens to pose problems for him down the road. His patient may remain ambivalent even after the operation, may complain about the outcome, and may even grow to regret having had the procedure, leading to hostility and perhaps even to a law suit.

Most contracts require a mutual set of commitments in which either party may refuse to be a party to the agreement. In professions such as medicine, however, the professional is not always free simply to refuse to be involved. Generally, in Anglo-American culture, health professionals are deemed to be free to refuse to take a case. Even then, there are limits. A physician on duty in an emergency room, for example, cannot refuse a patient who arrives with an urgent medical problem. Once a physician has taken a case, a further set of obligations is established including the moral and legal duty not to abandon the patient.

By the time Dr. Clark has discovered Ms. Rich's ambivalence, certainly a doctor–patient relation has been established. Furthermore, Dr. Clark seems to have no doubt that Ms. Rich needs the biopsy. This raises the question of whether he retains the right to refuse to be a party to the consent process. It is widely agreed that a physician has the right to opt out of a case if a competent colleague willing to take the case can be found. It is quite likely, however, that if Dr. Clark discloses his dilemma to a colleague who might be asked to take the case, that colleague might refuse. At that point Dr. Clark is in a bind. He knows Ms. Rich needs the biopsy. Refusing would constitute abandonment, but he may honestly believe he cannot get an adequately free consent from her to proceed. If Ms. Rich were truly incompetent, the procedure would be for Dr. Clark to get her declared incompetent and have a guardian appointed, but it is not clear Ms. Rich really is incompetent, and if Dr. Clark attempts to get her so declared, she might feel insulted. If Ms. Rich can be brought to agree to the biopsy, is her consent adequately voluntary? If Dr. Clark decides he does not wish to be a party to the procedure, is he free to refuse to consent to performing the procedure?

In the previous two cases, the mental capacity of the patient made the consent problematic. In other cases, such as the one that follows, it is the constraints on the choices available to the patient that call the quality of the consent into question. Some people may have the mental capacity to assess the choice they are making but still raise questions about whether they are making a substantially voluntary choice to agree to a therapeutic intervention. They may be lacking adequate information or, as in the following case, they may have been given a reasonable amount of information. If their choice is constrained by external circumstances of confinement or other limits on their options, some are inclined to say that the choice is "coerced" and therefore not free or voluntary. Is it possible for a prisoner in this case to make a voluntary choice to agree to the proposed medication?

=== CASE 17-6 ===

Chemical Castration or Prison: Is There Really a Choice?

"So I'm damned if I do and damned if I don't. That about sums it up doesn't it, Doc?" James Ginter flatly stated to Hal Mason, Pharm.D., Director of Pharmacy in the

Regional Correctional Facility. Dr. Mason watched as Mr. Ginter paced in the small counseling area of the prison infirmary. Mr. Ginter had been convicted of first degree criminal sexual assault. His charges arose from acts of sexual intercourse with his 12-year-old stepdaughter. Mr. Ginter had already been convicted once before for child molestation and placed on probation. He received behavior modification after the first incident. For this second offense, Mr. Ginter was sentenced to fifteen years in prison to be served in the Regional Correctional Facility plus a $25,000 fine, reduced to one year with four years probation if the prisoner agrees to castration by chemical means and psychotherapy. Dr. Mason was asked to explain the action, side effects, and adverse reactions of the most commonly used hormone for this purpose—medroxyprogesterone acetate (MPA)—to Mr. Ginter. Dr. Mason explained,

> MPA has been shown to be effective in the treatment of sex offenders. We aren't really sure how it lowers libido, but it does. There also seems to be a sort of tranquilizing effect on the brain. The drug is given either by weekly injections or a depot form of injection that can be given every 3 months. The side effects include weight gain, mild lethargy, cold sweats, hot flashes, nightmares, hypertension, elevated blood sugar, shortness of breath, and lessened testes size.[11]

Mr. Ginter asked, "Will these side effects go away if I quit taking the drug?"

Dr. Mason replied, "As far as we know, yes. If you take the drug with some form of psychotherapy, the success rate is good."

"I hate shots," Mr. Ginter shuddered.

> It seems to me that this is too harsh of a punishment. I mean they're going to be putting something in my body that will work all sorts of ways. From what you've said, I probably won't be able to have any kind of sex, even the legal kind with an adult. If I don't agree to these shots, then I'm locked up for four-teen more years. Some choice.

Dr. Mason knew that there were several programs in other jurisdictions in which imprisoned paraphilias, or sexual deviants, were voluntarily participating in the study of MPA, talk therapies, and control groups. It appeared that the MPA groups were significantly less likely to re-offend. However, Mr. Ginter was not being asked to participate in a study. He was being asked to choose between two unap-pealing alternatives: chemical castration or prison.

COMMENTARY

It appears that Dr. Mason, the pharmacist in this case, has given Mr. Ginter substantial and fair information about the medication being proposed and that Mr. Ginter has the mental capacity to understand the choice. In fact, he may understand all too well that he either takes the medication and has a chance of being released from prison, or he refuses and remains incarcerated for fourteen more years. But is Mr. Ginter free to consent or refuse the medication? Is he being coerced by the forced choice between two unattractive options and, if so, does that negate the voluntariness of his consent?

Mr. Ginter is not being physically coerced in the sense of being held down while the medication is injected against his will. He seems to have a real opportunity to accept or decline the offer. But one is tempted to say that the alternative (fourteen years in jail) is so awful that he is de facto forced to agree to the drug. The issue seems to be one of whether one can be said to be coerced when the only available alternative is very unattractive. By comparison, some might say that MPA is "coercively attractive" even if it presents potential side effects that Mr. Ginter finds very unpleasant.

Sometimes people are forced into choices through circumstances beyond their control. When one of the options seems traumatic, but nevertheless much better than the other, we might say the choice is forced. If a parent is asked to consent to a liver lobe donation after being told by a transplant surgeon that a live donation is the only way that his or her child's life can be saved, for many the choice presents no real option. The donation is so attractive compared with the death of the child that there is no doubt in the mind of the parent that the donation must be made.

But the overwhelming power of the option should not be taken to imply that the parent's autonomy is being violated. The surgeon offering to procure a liver lobe seems to have no other alternatives to present. We tend to exonerate the surgeon if there is no other alternative available to him as a solution to the problem. The choice of the parent can be said to be autonomous if it fits with the parent's consistent life plan. Assuming this is a loving parent who has previously made sacrifices for his or her child, it is perfectly understandable that the donation of a liver lobe fits the parent's life plan. It can be a forced choice and an autonomous one at the same time.

Dr. Mason presents Mr. Ginter with what may be a forced choice that is very attractive compared with the alternative. His case differs from the surgeon who offers the parent the chance to donate, in that there may be other options open. The society could choose other punishments; it could simply forgive Mr. Ginter, but those do not seem terribly plausible or morally defensible. Moreover, these are options that are probably not within Dr. Mason's control, such as restricted residency arrangements. He seems to be giving Mr. Ginter a choice between the only two options available to him. We certainly would not see Mr. Ginter as more free if chemical castration is removed as an option. In the context of a legitimate incarceration, it is not even clear whether maximizing Mr. Ginter's freedom is relevant.

If additional plausible options were available to Dr. Mason and he chose to withhold them, say, because he wanted to conduct a clinical trial of the medroxyprogesterone and needed more subjects, then Dr. Mason might be said to be guilty of unethical manipulation of the consent process by withholding legitimate options, but in this case that does not seem to have happened. Does it make sense to say someone is free to choose and can act autonomously in these circumstances?

There is still another kind of case raising problems about comprehension and voluntariness of consent. In the two previous cases, the patients were adults and were, at least initially, presumed to be competent to consent or withhold consent to treatment. The issues were the mental capacity of the patient (Case 17-4 and Case 17-5) and the constraints on choice created by a prison environment (Case 17-6). There is another kind of problem with comprehension and voluntariness. Minors are presumed to be incompetent. Their parents are their presumed surrogates for making decisions in medicine and many other important aspects of daily living. Unless they are found to be negligent or malicious, they are usually assumed to speak for their children. In the following case, however, a child's wishes challenge the legitimacy of the parent's role.

CASE 17-7

An Adolescent Refusing a Blood Transfusion

Brian and Melissa Tracy were the parents of 17-year-old, Tammy. The parents were Jehovah's Witnesses who had raised their daughter in the religion, which has, as one of its tenets, opposition to transfusion of blood. On the basis of their interpretation of the Bible, any consumption of blood is forbidden and most Jehovah's Witnesses believe that this prohibits transfusion.[12] The result would be eternal damnation and, in some cases, an end to the acceptance of the person in the religious community.

When Tammy was diagnosed with leukemia at age sixteen their family physician, Dr. Stephen Erwin, anticipated that the family's opposition to transfusion could be a problem. Soon after her seventeenth birthday, Tammy had to be hospitalized for septicemia, anemia, and fatigue. Dr. Erwin knew that for a patient without religious objections, a blood transfusion would be standard treatment for the anemia. He discussed the issue with Mr. and Mrs. Tracy, who steadfastly insisted that their daughter be treated without blood. He also discussed the problem with Tammy, who, at first, appeared confused about what was at stake, but eventually seemed to have a very clear understanding of the situation. She hesitatingly expressed her agreement with her parents' position.

He explored the possibility of using blood substitutes. Some provide blood volume without raising issues of using actual blood products. These are acceptable to Jehovah's Witnesses, but would not help in Tammy's case since she needed red blood cells. After a delay of several days, Dr. Erwin was becoming worried. He was aware that hospital attorneys could get a court order for blood for minors against the wishes of parents when a transfusion was potentially a life-and-death matter. He also knew that some minors are considered "mature" and are given authority to consent on their own behalf even if their parents object to medical treatment.

Dr. Erwin, after consultation with the hospital ethics committee and hospital attorneys, determined that he had at least five options:

(1) Seek a court order attempting to override the parents' refusal.
(2) Claim she was a mature minor and attempt to persuade Tammy to consent to the transfusion.

(3) Give her a transfusion without getting consent after giving her medication so she would sleep through the procedure.

(4) Accept her parents' refusal.

(5) Accept her refusal if she cannot be persuaded to consent as a mature minor.

COMMENTARY

Minor children are assumed to be subject to significant limits in their capacity to make autonomous choices. They may lack the capacity to understand the nature of alternatives, or they may lack the capacity to be sufficiently oriented to their long-term interests that they cannot make free choices. Parents are presumed to be the legitimate and authorized agents to act on their children's behalf, with a duty to act in their best interest. This presumption extends to choices in health care, including the right to consent or withhold consent for medical procedures for the minor including blood transfusions.

This case adds complexities that challenge these presumptions. First, Tammy seems to have a reasonably mature understanding of the choice before her. At first she is confused by the situation, but eventually comes to understand what is at stake. We recognize that the initial presupposition that minors are incompetent and adults competent is, at best, a crude rule-of-thumb. There is no magic transition point when a youngster reaches the age of majority (eighteen in most jurisdictions). For this reason, adults, while initially presumed competent, can be declared incompetent by a court. That was a possibility in some of the earlier cases in this chapter. It is also true that for some decisions those below the age of majority can be deemed competent. The law recognizes four instances in which minors will be treated as having the authority to consent on their own behalf. First, according to the *emancipated minor* rule, minors who are married or living substantially on their own may be deemed to have the authority to consent to medical treatment without parental involvement. Tammy, however, is not emancipated.

Second, according to the *mature minor* rule, some minors may be found competent to make substantially autonomous choices. This option is normally reserved for older adolescents who can demonstrate that they have a substantial understanding of the nature of the choices to be made and sufficient autonomy to make a choice consistent with a developed life plan. A mature minor might, as a substantially autonomous person, have the same authority to consent to treatments (or refuse consent) as an adult. There is controversy over whether clinicians such as Dr. Erwin have the authority to declare minors mature for purposes of consenting to treatments. Some clinicians believe they have such authority, but, since courts are the only agents with the authority to declare adults incompetent, it seems to follow that they should be the only ones with authority to declare minors competent. Clinicians wanting to play it safe will seek judicial approval before acting on the basis of the consent of a mature minor. That is especially true when a parent is actively objecting to the proposed choice of her daughter and would retain the capacity to press charges against the physician, but it might also be a reasonable policy in cases like this one in which a life-and-death decision is to be made. Especially for a 17-year-old like Tammy, classifying her as a mature minor capable of consenting or refusing consent on her own and independent of her parents' views is a possibility. It would be unacceptable, however, for Dr. Erwin to go "fishing" for the answer that he is seeking and accept her as mature if she were to decide to consent against her parents wishes.[13] Here the critical question is whether Tammy is deemed to be under the influence of her parents that she is not thinking independently, in which case getting a court order to treat might be an option, or, alternatively, she is believed to be sufficiently mature in her thinking that her judgment is the one that should prevail regardless of whether her parents' influence was the source of her beliefs.

There is a third set of circumstances in which minors are deemed capable of authorizing treatment without parental permission. In many jurisdictions, state laws authorize minors to obtain certain treatments without parental consent. These often include treatments for venereal diseases, birth control, and, in some jurisdictions, abortion. The reasoning behind these laws is somewhat obscure. There is no reason to believe that a minor is any more capable of making substantially autonomous choices about these treatments than about any others. Moreover, there is no reason to assume that all minors are mature in such matters.

One explanation might be that parents in their wisdom have come to believe that for certain treatments it is best for their children if they give "blanket approval" for treatment without explicit parental consent or even knowledge. Parents might reason that, if the minor had to get parental consent for treatment of venereal disease, that requirement might dissuade the minor from seeking treatment. Parents may believe that it is better in the long run for their minor to be treated than to insist on waiting for parental permission. If so, this is a special case in which the law permits treatment of minors who are not deemed necessarily mature or emancipated without parental permission, because it is seen as what is best for the minor.

Whatever one thinks about such a policy, it does not seem to apply in our case of a potential blood transfusion. The fourth grounds on which a minor might make medical choices that warrant respect involves choices that are too trivial to make much difference. Even if a minor is not competent to make momentous life-and-death choices, she might well be given the authority to choose among options when either seems about equally plausible: which are in which to receive an injection, which of two equally effective drugs, or whether to have therapy at one time of day or another. Entry of a minor into a research protocol, as we saw in Case 16-1, often poses such a choice. In randomized trials, the moral premise that permits randomization is that each treatment arm is more or less equally attractive. This is called the condition of equipoise. If, however, each treatment arm is deemed equally attractive, then nothing would be lost (in terms of the child's well-being) by letting the child pick among the treatments. In particular, nothing is lost by letting a child refuse to agree to enter a randomized clinical trial of this sort. For this reason, children are asked to "assent" to entry, even if they are not sufficiently mature to comprehend at the level needed to give a "consent."[14]

Whatever one thinks about these grounds for permitting minors to make their own medical choices, the only one that could plausibly apply in our case is the mature minor rule. If Tammy is deemed sufficiently mature to make her own decisions, she should have the right given to any adequately competent decision-maker to accept or refuse the treatments proposed for her. This would be grounds either for providing the transfusion or omitting it, depending on Tammy's eventual decision. This is particularly important if Dr. Erwin and those advising him conclude that Tammy's parents may not have the discretion to refuse a transfusion for their daughter. In this case, it is possible that an adequately mature minor has a right of refusal that exceeds that of a parent, whose discretion in medical choices is constrained.

Many of the most controversial informed consent cases involve consent or refusal of consent for treatment for critical or terminal illness. Patients may refuse consent, knowing that they may be at risk for dying. In fact, they may actually want to die, when they refuse the consent. These issues arise in the cases in Chapter 18.

NOTES

[1] President's Commission for the Study of Ethical Problems in Medicine and Biomedical and Behavioral Research. *Making Health Care Decisions: A Report on the Ethical and Legal Implications of Informed Consent in the Patient-Practitioner Relationship*, Vol. 1. Washington, DC: U.S. Government Printing Office, 1982; Faden, Ruth, and Tom L. Beauchamp in collaboration with Nancy N. P. King. *A History and Theory of Informed Consent*. New York: Oxford University Press, 1986; Katz, Jay. *The Silent World of Doctor and Patient*. New York: The Free Press, 1984; Beauchamp, Tom L. and Ruth R. Faden. "Informed Consent: I. History of Informed Consent." In *Encyclopedia of Bioethics*. 3rd ed. Stephen G. Post, editor. New York: Macmillan Reference USA: Thomson/Gale; 2004, pp. 1271–1277.

[2] Katz, Jay and Angela Roddey Holder. "Informed Consent: V. Legal and Ethical Issues of Consent in Healthcare." In *Encyclopedia of Bioethics*, pp. 1296–1306; Evans, Martyn "The Autonomy of the Patient: Informed Consent." In *Bioethics in a European Perspective*. Henk ten Have and Bert Gordijn, editors. Boston, MA: Kluwer Academic Publishers; 2001, pp. 83–91.

[3] Edelstein, Ludwig. "The Hippocratic Oath: Text, Translation and Interpretation." In *Ancient Medicine: Selected Papers of Ludwig Edelstein*. Owsei Temkin and C. Lilian Temkin, editors. Baltimore, MD: The Johns Hopkins Press, 1967, p. 6.

[4] *Schloendorff v. New York Hospital* (1914). In *Experimentation with Human Beings: The Authority of the Investigator, Subject, Professions, and State in the Human*

Experimentation Process. Jay Katz editor. New York: Russell Sage Foundation, 1972, p. 526.

5 Salgo v. Leland Stanford, Jr. University Board of Trustees, 317 P.2d 170 (1957).

6 Beauchamp, Tom L. and Ruth R. Faden. "Informed Consent: II. Meaning and Elements." In *Encyclopedia of Bioethics*, pp. 1277–1280.

7 *Berkey v. Anderson*, 1 Cal. App. 3d 790. 82 Cal. Rptr. 67 (1969); *Cobbs v. Grant*, 502 P.2d 1 (Cal. 1972); *Canterbury v. Spence*, United States Court of Appeals, District of Columbia, 1972, 464 F.2d 772, 150 U.S.App.D.C. 263.

8 President's Commission for the Study of Ethical Problems in Medicine and Biomedical and Behavioral Research. *Making Health Care Decisions*, p. 43.

9 Faden, Ruth R., Catherine Becker, Carol Lewis, John Freeman, and Alan I. Faden. "Disclosure of Information to Patients in Medical Care." *Medical Care* 19 (No. 7, July 19, 1981):718–733.

10 Brown, Alan P., Troyen A. Brennan, Lisa S. Parker, and Kamran Samakar. "Informed Consent: VI. Issues of Consent in Mental Healthcare." In *Encyclopedia of Bioethics*, pp. 1307–1313; Schwartz, Harold I., David M. Mack. "Informed Consent and Competency." In Richard Rosner, editor. *Principles and Practice of Forensic Psychiatry*, 2nd ed. London: Arnold; New York: Oxford University Press; 2003, pp. 97–106.

11 Drugdex Editorial Staff. "Medroxyprogesterone (monograph)." In *Drugdex(R) Information System*. C. R. Gelman and B. H. Rumack, editors. Englewood, CO: Micromedex, Inc., 1996.

12 Smith, Martin L. "Jehovah's Witness Refusal of Blood Products." In *Encyclopedia of Bioethics*, pp. 1341–1354; Singelenberg, Richard. "The Blood Transfusion Taboo of Jehovah's Witnesses: Origin, Development and Function of a Controversial Doctrine." *Social Science & Medicine* 31 (No. 4, 1990):515–523; For the Jehovah's Witness position on blood see "Showing Respect for Life and Blood" on the official Jehovah's Witness website, http://www.watchtower.org/e/rq/index.htm?article=article_12.htm, accessed September 28, 2007.

13 Catlin, Anita. "The Dilemma of Jehovah's Witness Children Who Need Blood to Survive." *HEC (Healthcare Ethics Committee) Forum* 8 (No. 4, July 1996):195–207.

14 U.S. Department of Health and Human Services. "Additional Protections for Children Involved as Subjects in Research." *Federal Register* 48 (46, March 8, 1983):9814–9820.

CHAPTER 18

❧

Death and Dying

Other Cases Involving Death and Dying

The informed consent issues raised in the previous chapter often arise in the care of terminally and critically ill patients. In the consent process, patients must be told of the treatment alternatives. With terminally ill patients, sometimes doing nothing to attempt a cure is among the plausible alternatives. The terminally ill patient (or his or her surrogate) may decline the treatment offered in favor of letting nature take its course. While this is sometimes referred to as doing nothing at all, in fact it normally involves continuing to care for the patient while forgoing efforts to cure. The pioneering medical ethicist, Paul Ramsey, was one who stressed the distinction between curing and caring and the appropriateness of continuing to care when cure becomes impossible.[1] He and others have summarized the moral issues related to terminal care decisions.[2] Often health professionals, family members, and other caregivers will have responsibilities for continuing to care for the dying patient in order to make him or her comfortable by providing pain-relieving medication, adequate and appetizing nutrition, and compassionate engagement.

In the cases of Chapter 9, the problems surrounding the ethics of killing and letting die were examined. Some traditional medical ethics, such as Orthodox Judaism, include the belief that health professionals always have a duty to preserve life.[3] We saw in Chapter 9, however, that many medical ethical traditions, including those in the health care professions[4] as well as U.S. law,[5] often distinguish between active killing, which is prohibited, and forgoing treatment, which can legitimately be chosen by the patient or surrogate under certain circumstances. We also saw that deciding what was ethical to forgo is often based on assessment of benefits and harms expected. The doctrine of proportionality holds that treatments are ethically expendable when the benefits expected do not exceed the expected harms to the patient. While some people consider withholding of life-sustaining treatments morally more acceptable than withdrawing treatments that have begun, the dominant view today is that there is no morally significant difference between withholding and withdrawing. Thus, those who consider all behaviors that will result in death to be immoral will condemn both withholding and withdrawing (as well as active killing); whereas those who find withholding treatments on the grounds that there is not a proportional benefit expected will likely consider withdrawing treatments acceptable on the same grounds. A treatment may be started because it is believed that expected benefits justify any necessary risks of harm. If, however, the treatment turns out not to offer the benefit originally expected, a patient or surrogate may withdraw the consent to the treatment leading to a justifiable withdrawal. These issues of deciding to accept or refuse treatment are explored in the cases of Chapter 9.

Many of the critical moral decisions related to the care of the terminally and critically ill actually involve the ethical issues of informed consent or the refusal and withdrawal of consent. Both law and most ethical theories consider the moral principle of (respect for) autonomy to take priority over paternalism. If this is true, then it is acceptable for the substantially autonomous patient to decline or withdraw consent, thus forgoing treatment even for life-sustaining situations.

Some additional problems related to care of the terminally ill patient are taken up in this chapter. These are problems that cannot be resolved solely by figuring out the relation among the duties to benefit the patient, respect autonomy, and avoid killing. The first section focuses on the problems of the definition of death. Then, in succeeding sections, the cases deal with decisions by surrogates for terminally or critically ill patients who are not competent to make their own choices about care, looking first at formerly competent patients, then at those who have never been competent. In the final section, the issues are new controversies over limiting care to the terminally ill in order to conserve scarce medical resources.

THE DEFINITION OF DEATH

Until the late 1960s, there had been a millennia-old general understanding of what it meant to be dead. With the development of cardiopulmonary resuscitation (CPR), ventilators, and better understanding of pulmonary and cardiac physiology, we have gained greater capacity to intervene in the dying process. We were able to uncouple a series of events that, until then, had always been connected. Now, for the first time, it was possible and feasible to maintain cardiac and respiratory function even after brain function had been destroyed.

During this same period, the first human heart transplant took place, and society developed a profound interest in the viable organs that might be taken from dead patients. At this time we asked whether people could be considered dead if their heart and lung functions continued but they had irreversibly lost the capacity for bodily integration.[6] These patients have lost brain function known to be responsible for bodily integration. If such patients could be considered dead, then organs with life-saving potential could be procured. These developments gave rise to what is now thought of as the brain-oriented definition of death. According to it:

> An individual who has sustained either (1) irreversible cessation of circulatory and respiratory functions, or (2) irreversible cessation of all functions of the entire brain, including the brain stem, is dead. A determination of death must be made in accordance with accepted medical standards.

This incorporates what is called the "whole-brain" definition of death. It makes clear that someone can be pronounced dead based on loss of all brain function even if the heart is still beating. To make matters more complicated, some scholars have suggested a third possible definition of death based on irreversible loss of only certain "higher" brain functions, usually referring to brain activities related to consciousness. Although no jurisdiction has adopted this third view for legal purposes, it is important to distinguish it from the "whole-brain" view. This "higher-brain" definition of death would consider people dead when they have permanently loss of consciousness, including people in a coma and people like Terri Schiavo, the woman discussed in Chapter 9, who are in what is called a persistent vegetative state (PVS).

Sometimes health professionals must confront cases that force them to determine exactly what it means for a patient to be dead. In this case, we see that the now-fashionable definition based on irreversible loss of all brain function (the so-called whole-brain-oriented definition) poses problems for clinicians who must struggle with their own and others' tendencies to rely on the older, heart-oriented definition of death.

CASE 18-1

The Dying of Pelle Lindbergh: His Brain Is Gone, But Is He Dead?

At 5:41 a.m. Sunday morning, November 10, 1985, Philadelphia Flyers star goal tender, Pelle Lindbergh slammed his 1985 Porsche into a cement wall of a Somerdale,

New Jersey, elementary school. The following summary is excerpted from reports from *Washington Post* staff writer David Sell.[7] While all details may not be accurate or conceptually clear, they all reflect statements that can commonly be heard in clinical contexts when discussing patients with severe brain injuries.

Flyers Goalie Lindbergh is Declared Brain Dead

Philadelphia, Nov. 10[Sunday]—Philadelphia Flyers goaltender Pelle Lindbergh was hovering near death tonight in a suburban Philadelphia hospital after he suffered severe brain and spinal cord injuries. Lindbergh was listed in critical condition in the intensive care unit of John F. Kennedy Hospital in Stratford, N.J. The brain damage was compounded by the fact that Lindbergh went without breathing for approximately 15 minutes as rescuers tried to free him from the wreckage.

Somerdale detective Charles Pope said he arrived at the crash site five minutes after the accident occurred. "He was more or less all mangled up under the steering wheel," said Pope. He said that after Lindbergh was removed from the car his heart stopped beating and CPR was administered.

Referring to his parents, who were called from Sweden to be at his side, Vicki Santoro, nursing supervisor at the hospital said, "They were just devastated."

Flyers' team physician Edward Viner said that if Lindbergh's situation does not improve, the family will be left with a decision about how long to leave him on the respirator.

"He's a person that loves life," [flyers Coach Mike] Keenan said of Lindbergh.

Stratford, NJ Nov. 11[Monday]—The injuries to Lindbergh...left the goalie brain dead. With cardiac stimulants and fluid replacement to keep his blood pressure up, Lindbergh was still alive tonight, but with no chance to survive.

"We simply now work with the family to decide how far they want to go in sustaining his biological life," said Dr. Lewis Gallo, one of the hospital doctors assigned to the case. Without a respirator, Gallo added, Lindbergh would stop breathing "in a matter of minutes."

Viner said the respirator keeping Lindbergh alive would be disconnected "as soon as they can come to grips with this as a family.... I'm concerned about the father's own health. He's not well and I understand he has a significant heart condition."

Stratford, NJ, Nov. 12 [Tuesday]—Pelle Lindbergh, the Philadelphia Flyers goalie who had been brain dead since a car crash early Sunday morning, was declared dead tonight after surgeons removed all his vital organs for possible transplantation.

Lindbergh, 26, who suffered extensive brain and spinal injuries, was officially declared clinically dead Monday morning while his heart and lungs were kept functioning only through the use of a respirator.

Team Captain Dave Poulin said, "If his organs can be donated that will help others and Pelle will live on."

COMMENTARY

Anyone reading this summary of these tragic events has a right to be confused. Pelle Lindbergh, we are told, was brain dead on Sunday, clinically dead on Monday, and was "declared dead" Tuesday night after surgeons removed his vital organs. Nevertheless, according to team captain, Dave Poulin, Pelle will live on. The family and the community have a right to know exactly when he died and whether removing his organs caused his death, the legal charge for which would be homicide.

The first distinction that is critical in this case is between having a brain in which all the tissues have died, that is, having a "dead brain," and being an individual who is dead. It appears that Pelle Lindbergh's brain was determined to be dead on Monday. The fifteen-minute period without oxygen that occurred on Sunday immediately after the accident is enough to have destroyed all the tissues so it makes sense to say on Tuesday that Pelle Lindbergh "had been brain dead since a car crash early Sunday morning." It is also true, however, that it could not be determined with certainty that the tissue was all irreversibly destroyed until all the tests have been completed. Depending on which tests are relied on, this can take from six to twenty-four hours, so it is appropriate that the news stories could not state that his brain was dead until Monday, the day after the accident.

The more complicated question is whether Pelle Lindbergh is deceased—dead—just because his brain has died. By law in the United States, and in most jurisdictions throughout the world, if the brain is confirmed to have irreversibly ceased all of its functions, then death shall be pronounced. The individual is no longer with us. Case law in New Jersey as early as 1983 accepted that if the brain was dead, then the person was dead.[8]

At the time of Pelle Lindbergh's accident, New Jersey had not passed a statute accepting death based on brain criteria, it has since passed such a law. That state is unique in permitting people who have religious objections to declaring death based on brain criteria to execute a document that will require that, for their own case, death not be pronounced until the heart function has irreversibly ceased.[9] Lindbergh had not executed such a document, so on Monday, according to the law in New Jersey and most other places, if his brain was dead, he was dead—regardless of what his physicians or family believed.

Then what does it mean to say that on Monday morning he was "was officially declared clinically dead"? Perhaps this was a confusion in the newspaper account or perhaps it was a confusion on the part of Lindbergh's physicians. The statement has no real meaning unless it was noting that he was officially declared "dead" on Monday because it was at that point that it was determined that his brain had lost all of its functions and that they would never again be restored. The term "clinically dead" is heard in hospitals, but has no real meaning. People are either dead or alive, not partially dead or clinically dead. Sometimes clinicians use the term to mean that certain critical bodily functions have stopped and that, unless they are started again soon, the individual will be dead. A temporary cardiac arrest is, thus, sometimes referred to as "clinical death," but that is a confusing and mistaken way to talk. What is really meant is that heart function has stopped and, if someone does not intervene quickly with CPR, the individual will become dead. In Lindbergh's case, on Monday apparently his heart continued to beat because cardiac stimulants and fluids kept his blood pressure up and presumably a ventilator continued to supply oxygen. If, in fact, his brain function was completely lost, he was breathing only because lung function was being maintained on a ventilator. Nevertheless, once brain function was determined to be lost, he was dead. It was therefore wrong to say that he was "still alive" on Monday night but had "no chance to survive."

Then what happened on Tuesday? The newspaper account states that he was declared dead Tuesday night "after surgeons removed all his vital organs for possible transplantation." One possibility is that, even though his brain had been known to be dead for over twenty-four hours and the law required that he be pronounced dead, he, in fact, was not so declared until Tuesday after the vital organs were removed. If that is what happened, the "dead donor rule" was violated. This is the rule that prohibits removing life-prolonging organs until after death is pronounced. Technically, then, the surgeon who removed the organs might be said to have killed him, that is, caused the loss of function even though death had not been pronounced. The other possibility is that he was really pronounced dead on Monday, and the still-viable organs were removed on Tuesday from the body of the recently deceased patient.

We are still left with the perplexing question: did Pelle Lindbergh die on Sunday, when his brain functions were lost, never to return again; on Monday, when it could be first measured that those functions were gone and someone (physician or reporter) called him "clinically dead"; or on Tuesday, when all vital functions had ceased because organs had been removed and the ventilator turned off?

Several sets of tests can be used to determine that brain function has been lost irreversibly. The first of these, referred to as the Harvard Criteria, developed by the Harvard Ad Hoc Committee,[10] calls for repeating of tests over a twenty-four hour period. The Medical Consultants to the President's Commission recommend a period of observation of "at least twelve hours."[11] Except in New Jersey when a document has been signed by the individual involved, if some such set of tests is satisfied, according to the law, death has occurred regardless of whether the heart and lung function have stopped and regardless of whether the individuals involved accept that this is the proper meaning of the concept of death.

While the issues in dispute in the Lindbergh case center on whether he should be treated as dead or alive, most disputes, in the care of the terminally ill, involve patients who are clearly alive by anyone's view. The issue in these cases, to which we now turn, is whether it is ever acceptable to forgo life support and let the patient die.

COMPETENT AND FORMERLY
COMPETENT PATIENTS

The cases of Chapters 6 and 17 address the ethical principle of respect for autonomy and informed consent, which is usually seen as protecting autonomy. Those of Chapter 9 address the ethics of killing and letting patients die. Those cases examined whether refusals of life-sustaining treatments are ethical and, if so, under what circumstances. Most commentators now generally agree that if a mentally competent patient wants to refuse medical treatment, he or she has the legal and perhaps also the moral right to do so.

In order to attempt to avoid certain unwanted treatments, some people are now writing advance directives specifying which treatments they want and which ones they want to refuse.[12] Federal law requires that all patients, upon admission to a hospital or any health facility or care delivery program such as a long-term care facility or home care who receive Medicare or Medicaid funding be offered information on advance directives.[13]

If the patient remains conscious and competent to confirm the advance directive at the time of crisis, normally the patient's wishes will be followed, but most critically ill patients are so ill that they lapse into incompetence. Health professionals worry that the patient's wishes may not be adequately clear or that the patient may have changed his or her mind. The following case illustrates the problem.

═══ CASE 18-2 ═══

Ambiguous Advance Directives:
Who Interprets?

The following case was presented to a hospital ethics committee. The patient, Molly Murton, is a 74-year-old female first admitted to the hospital in June with an acute cerebral vascular accident and currently has a diagnosis of "multi-infarct dementia." She has deteriorated since her first admission and is now very weak, not coherent, and has to be spoon fed by the nursing staff. She swallows poorly. The patient was transferred to the acute hospital because of swallowing difficulties and aspiration pneumonia on three occasions in the past year. Two years ago, the patient made out a Durable Power of Attorney for Health Care (DPAHC) naming her daughter, Helen, as the agent but making no other comments on the form.

A year later, one year before the present admission, she made out another DPAHC, with a skilled care facility ombudsman in attendance, in which she again named her daughter as agent but also added on the form that she wanted no efforts made to prolong her life, no CPR, and no feeding tubes inserted. The patient was presumably considered competent when she signed the second DPAHC. Her daughter was not in attendance at the time.

Subsequently, no feeding tubes were inserted despite three admissions for aspiration pneumonia. Now that she is having severe difficulty with oral nutrition, her daughter, unwilling to see her mother suffer, has decided she wants a gastrostomy tube inserted to decrease the likelihood of aspiration. She also indicated that if her mother develops pneumonia or another potential fatal complication, she does not want her transferred to the acute hospital. She wants her to be given comfort care in the skilled care facility. The physician fully agreed with the daughter's decision. However, the administrator of the skilled care facility was uncertain that it was legal or ethical for the daughter to go against her mother's expressly stated wishes not to have a feeding tube inserted. The insertion of the tube would be for the purposes of comfort and avoidance of aspiration pneumonia but might potentially prolong her life, which had been objected to by the mother. What should the ethics committee say to the skilled care facility administrator in response to his concerns?

COMMENTARY

Patients are urged to complete advance directives indicating their desires about critical medical care should they ever become incompetent to express their own wishes. These advance directives come in two forms, substantive directives and proxy directives. A substantive directive indicates which treatments a patient would want or reject under specified circumstances. A proxy directive indicates who the patient would want to make medical decisions if the patient is unable to do so. Often these two forms of directives are combined in a single document.

This patient had first prepared a proxy directive naming her daughter as her surrogate to make medical choices on her behalf. Had that been her only effort in this regard, the situation would have been relatively simple. When she had her cerebral vascular accident and became unable to consume sufficient nutrition orally, her daughter would have been asked to render a judgment about what her mother would have wanted. If she could not determine what she would want under the circumstances, she would try to decide what was in her best interest. That presumably would have included authorization of the feeding tube to avoid aspiration and a refusal of authorization to transfer her to an acute care hospital.

The problem in this case, however, was that the patient also completed, at the urging of the hospital ombudsman, a second advance directive that was a combination substantive and proxy directive. Her substantive wishes were not to have a feeding tube or other efforts to prolong her life. Her second advance directive reaffirmed her desire for her daughter to act as her surrogate. Since new advance directives supersede older ones, presumably the second one is binding.

The problem is that the plan her daughter would choose if she were operating freely under the first directive seems to be foreclosed by the second directive with its substantive instruction to avoid a feeding tube. Moreover, it seems unlikely that the patient thought carefully about the exact implications of the second directive when she signed it, including the refusal of the feeding tube. More than likely, she was given a standard form by the ombudsman with blanks to fill in and boxes to check indicating whether she wanted a feeding tube. Probably, she was not asked whether she would want to make an exception to the refusal of the feeding tube if her daughter believed it would make her more comfortable or prevent unnecessary difficulties with aspiration.

This case illustrates the difficulty with substantive directives that cannot possibly anticipate the exact circumstances under which various treatments would be considered. One option would be to sign a stand-alone proxy directive, particularly if one has a trusted relative or friend to whom one could give complete discretion. Often, however, patients want to provide some general guidance, at least indicating whether they generally would like aggressive life prolongation or more conservative palliative care. Many states require that, if medically supplied nutrition and hydration are to be omitted, the advance directive must explicitly say so. Hence, the form may have been written to give the patient this explicit option.

The moral mandate to a proxy administering an advance directive of this sort is to pursue what she believes the patient would want under the circumstances within the framework of the substantive content of the written instructions as well as any orally expressed desires. What is unclear in this case is whether the patient would want her surrogate to take the second directive literally as refusing any feeding tube under any circumstances, or more loosely, as refusing feeding tubes designed to prolong life rather than prevent avoidable complications and make the patient more comfortable.

Some people prefer advance directives to be interpreted literally, others more loosely. Commentators now recommend that advance directives indicate how much discretion the surrogate should have in interpreting the document. In this case, with no such guidance, a case can be made that the patient's wishes can best be understood by encouraging the daughter to use her judgment about what she thinks her mother meant. She should not be free to override the directive, but could be given discretion in interpreting it. If this is the approach taken, the named surrogate would be given latitude within reason, not to decide what is best, but to decide what the patient really meant when she wrote the document. The patient could give this latitude to anyone, but there is some evidence that family members are better at figuring out what patients would want than clinicians are.[14] Other writers of advance directives might indicate that they want their words taken literally, leaving to the surrogate's judgment only those questions about which the directive provides no guidance.

Some cases involving formerly competent patients are more complex because the patient has never written any advance directive at all. The patient may have been the victim of a sudden accident or simply never gotten around to reducing his or her views to writing. The following case is a real one, the first death and dying forgoing treatment case to go to the U.S. Supreme Court.

It requires evaluation of a patient's orally, but somewhat vaguely, expressed wishes and raises the question of how certain we must be of the patient's views before relying on them as a basis for forgoing life support.

CASE 18-3

The Cruzan Case: Whether to Forgo Nutrition Based on a Patient's Views

At 12:54 a.m., January 11, 1983, police were called to the scene of a single car accident. They arrived six minutes later and found Nancy Cruzan lying face down in a ditch 35 feet from her car without detectable cardiac or respiratory function. At 1:12 a.m., spontaneous cardiac and respiratory function was restored, but there had been significant anoxia for as much as 12–14 minutes.

Nancy was left with permanent brain damage, in a coma for 3 weeks. A gastrostomy was performed on February 7, consented to by her (then) husband. Since then she had been at Mount Vernon State Hospital, fed entirely by gastrostomy tube. At the time of review of the case, she was not on ventilator, was oblivious to her environment except for reflexive responses to sound and perhaps painful stimuli, and had a massive enlargement of the ventricles of her brain that were filling with cerebrospinal fluid. The finding was that cerebral cortical atrophy is irreversible, permanent, progressive, and ongoing.

The highest cognitive brain function is exhibited by her grimacing, perhaps in recognition of ordinarily painful stimuli, indicating the experience of pain and apparent response to sound. She was described as a spastic quadriplegic with irreversible muscular contracture and tendon damage in all extremities, no cognitive or reflexive ability to swallow food or water to maintain her daily essential needs. She was alive but in a PVS. She could live for decades in this condition.

Before the accident she had expressed, "in somewhat serious conversation" that if sick or injured she would not want to continue her life unless should could live "halfway normally." Her parents, Lester and Joyce, took over role of guardian and asked the Missouri courts for permission to terminate artificial hydration and nutrition.

The lower court supported their request, but the Missouri Supreme Court reversed, arguing the state has an unqualified interest in life without regard to quality. This interest took two forms: (1) prolongation of life of individual patient and (2) interest in sanctity of life itself. Moreover, the case raises the question of how certain we must be of the patient's wishes. In this case, Nancy had not explicitly stated she would refuse nutrition and hydration medically supplied. The state noted how this case differs from other famous cases in that Nancy was not a competent patient contemporaneously refusing treatment; she did not have an advance directive, she was not terminal, the treatment could not be a burden to her (since she was in a vegetative state), and this case involved nutrition and hydration rather than more complex treatments.[15]

COMMENTARY

This case received a great deal of attention and posed several important questions. The state appeared to be claiming that it had an interest in preserving life not only to protect the interest of the specific patient, but also to protect a general interest in human life. Taken in its most robust form, this would seem to count against all decisions to refuse life support, even those offered by competent patients imminently dying and are well informed about the choice they are facing. At the same time, by pointing out that Nancy is not making a contemporaneous refusal as a competent patient, there seems to be an implication that the state's claim is more restricted. The right of the competent patient to refuse life support seems secure and is affirmed by the U.S. Supreme Court action in this case.

In this case, the patient is, of course, not presently competent. Prior to the accident, however, she was, and she had expressed some views on terminal care at the time. One of the key issues is whether her expressed wishes were expressed clearly enough to govern. Most states accept previously expressed wishes if they are understandable by some minimal standard (such as the "preponderance of the evidence"), but some states, including Missouri, insist that the expression must meet a higher "clear and convincing" standard. This case went to the U.S. Supreme Court to determine if this higher standard is legally acceptable. The court acknowledged that a state can impose this higher standard if it chooses. When the case was returned to the state, additional evidence of Nancy's wishes were presented that the court found sufficient, thus providing the basis for the order to withdraw the nutrition and hydration, the decision that eventually led to Nancy's death in spite of continuing protests by those who found this unacceptable.

Embedded in this debate was a series of additional questions including that of whether withdrawal of medically supplied nutrition and hydration is somehow special. The issue is whether nutrition and hydration are so basic that they must be provided even if other life-extending technologies are to be forgone. Of course, if the nutrition and hydration are serving a useful purpose, they should be provided, but the problem arises when someone concludes that they are useless or are providing a net burden for the patient. Most, but not all, commentators recognize that, even if nutrition and hydration are special, they may be omitted on the same grounds as other interventions when they are useless or burdensome. In Nancy Cruzan's case, once it was determined that her wishes were known at an adequate level of certainty, there was no special restriction to withdrawing the nutrition and hydration.

Since the case was finally determined on the basis of Nancy's previously expressed wishes, a more complicated question did not get addressed: what should happen if her own views could not be determined at an adequate level of certainty. If the patient's own wishes are the only basis for forgoing life support, this would mean that infants, children, the mentally incapacitated, and the senile who have not previously expressed their wishes would be forced to undergo every life-prolonging intervention including those that almost all reasonable people have consistently refused. In the next group of cases, we face this problem of decision-making for those who have left no record of their views expressed while they were competent.

NEVER COMPETENT PATIENTS

The previous cases involved patients, once mentally competent, who had formulated a view about their terminal care. One had a written advance directive. The issue was whether physicians, family, or others had the right to interpret the directive and who should interpret the directive when it was unclear. In the Cruzan case, the patient had expressed her views even though they were not written down in an advance directive. Many patients, however, have never been sufficiently autonomous to formulate a plan about their terminal care. They are children, significantly retarded, or otherwise incapacitated. (Other patients were once competent and could have formulated their plans, but they have left no available evidence that they did. For purposes of making medical decisions, these patients are as if they had never been competent and will be treated in this section.) In such cases, patient autonomy is an impossibility. Some other appeal is necessary. This is often expressed as the standard of patient *best interest*. Someone has to be designated as the surrogate for the patient, perhaps by court designation of a guardian.

Never Competent Persons without Available Family

Of the cases involving patients who have never left any record of their wishes about terminal care, the most difficult ones are people who have no family or friends available who can provide assistance. These can be thought of as cases in which there is no candidate for a surrogate with a preexisting psychological bond with the patient. They may be elderly persons who have outlived all their relatives, street people living in isolation, or those who have otherwise lost all contact with relatives. They are the most vulnerable group of patients we will encounter. They are alone, dying, and out of control, unable to take responsibility for their own medical decisions. One such case, involving a severely mentally impaired man named Joseph Saikewicz, was one of the most important early cases in the debate over decision-making for the terminally ill. What appears here is based on the court record.[16]

======== **CASE 18-4** ========

Joseph Saikewicz: Withholding Chemotherapy for an Impaired Patient

Joseph Saikewicz, a 67-year-old white male, was reported to have an IQ of 10 and mental age of approximately two years, eight months, but was otherwise in good health, strong, and well built. He was not able to communicate verbally, using grunts and gestures instead. He had been institutionalized in a state school since 1923 and at the Belchertown State School in Massachusetts since 1928. His only known family was two sisters who lived in California.

On April 19, 1976, Mr. Saikewicz was diagnosed as suffering from acute myeloblastic monocytic leukemia. His physician proposed chemotherapy. It was believed that, with chemotherapy, he had a remission chance of 30–50 percent. If remission does occur it will typically last for 2–13 months, possibly longer. The side effects include nausea, bladder irritation, numbness and tingling of extremities, loss of hair, and bone marrow depression. He would die in a matter of weeks or months without the chemotherapy. He was not in pain.

It was agreed that most competent patients would elect to undergo chemotherapy, but Mr. Saikewicz was unable to understand what would be done with him. The medical personnel envisioned that they would have to use orderlies to hold him down on his bed while the chemotherapy and blood transfusions were administered. Thus, even though mentally normal people would choose the therapy because they could understand the rationale, for Mr. Saikewicz it would appear that his caregivers had turned on him and were inflicting an unkind and painful assault.

For these reasons, his physician recommended that the chemotherapy be omitted. It would offer, for him, more burden than benefit. The administrator of the school was not certain this was ethical or legal. In order to resolve the conflict, they asked for a judicial opinion on what to do.

Perhaps because in the early part of the twentieth century, families were advised not to visit or bond with those placed in institutional facilities, they chose not to attend the hearing. Mr. Saikewicz was thus without any family or friends to assist except for the administrative and health care staff of the school. The issue was whether it was in Mr. Saikewicz's interest, given his unique mental capacity, to receive the chemotherapy and blood transfusion.

The Massachusetts Supreme Judicial Court rendered an opinion that called into question the role of doctors, family, and hospital committees in making these decisions stating: "We take a dim view of any attempt to shift the ultimate decision-making responsibility away from the duly established courts of proper jurisdiction to … the attending doctors, family, or hospital ethics committees."

Given these circumstances, what should be done for Mr. Saikewicz and who should make the choice?

COMMENTARY

Mr. Saikewicz clearly has never been competent enough to form an opinion on whether he should receive chemotherapy and blood transfusions. Although he had sisters who theoretically could have served as his surrogate in making these choices, the sisters had had no involvement in Mr. Saikewicz's life. It is sad that advice to avoid institutionalized retarded persons was once given to family members, but little can be done about that now. Thus, in effect, Mr. Saikewicz is alone; no family member or friend is available except perhaps the physician and administrator of the school. Since they disagree about the best possible course, the court has been asked to help resolve the conflict.

We know that some (but presumably not all) competent persons would accept chemotherapy in similar circumstances, but they are facing somewhat different facts. They are not mentally impaired and can be made to understand why some temporarily painful and unpleasant interventions are being proposed.

The first issue debated in this case was whether the mental retardation should play a role in the decision. Some may have suggested that the benefits of the treatment were somehow less because they would prolong the life of someone in an impaired state. Critics, however, have rejected the claim that the life of someone with mental retardation is any less valuable. In fact, the court rejected any premise that Mr. Saikewicz's life had less value.

There is another way in which his mental state could be relevant. His impairment may not make the benefits of treatment any less, but they seem to make the burdens greater. His inability to understand means the burdens of the proposed treatment will be significantly greater for him than they would be for a mentally competent patient.

The court's confusing warning that it takes a dim view of decision-making by physicians, family, or ethics committees needs some clarification. This seemed to be a direct attack on the New Jersey decision in the case of Karen Quinlan, which gave all three of these a role in the decision.[17] Technically, the court had assigned the physician the task of deciding whether treatment should be rendered. It had, however, given to Karen Quinlan's father the role of picking the physician (and presumably dismissing that physician if that person made a choice that did not square with her parents' views). Assuming that the physician decided to stop the treatment, the decision was to be reviewed by an "ethics committee." The only task assigned to that committee, however, was to confirm that she was in a PVS. No review of the morality of the decision to forgo made by the physician (but really under the control of the parent acting as surrogate) was envisioned.

Thus the Massachusetts court in Mr. Saikewicz's case seemed to attack this by claiming that neither physician, family, nor ethics committee could make the ethical choice to forgo treatment. However, neither the physician nor the committee really had ultimate control in the Quinlan case in the first place. The court in Massachusetts was, at most, questioning the family's role. All it said, however, was that the court must remain under the ultimate jurisdiction (ultimate decision-making responsibility), something that the New Jersey court no doubt would not deny. In fact, the Massachusetts court would soon make clear that family members working with physicians can make decisions to forgo without having the court explicitly review the decision.[18]

The critical difference in the Saikewicz case was that no family member was in a position to make any choices. The only family members available were two sisters who had never bonded with their brother and chose not to become involved. That left only the school administrator and the physician as potential surrogates, neither of whom had any basis for claiming discretion in making the choice. Since they disagreed about what was best for Mr. Saikewicz, the only option seemed to be going to court. Was there any other approach that could have avoided a judicial review?

CASE 18-5

Homicide and Forgoing Life Support

Millie Shaw was an 82-year-old woman who had been a resident at the Mountain View Nursing Home for six years. She had Alzheimer's disease for at least fifteen-years duration and was now clearly incompetent. She had no living relatives.

In a dispute with another resident one afternoon Ms. Shaw is pushed and strikes her head. She is left unconscious and taken to the emergency room (ER) where cerebral aneurism is suspected. An emergency operation was only partially successful. She has now been hospitalized postoperatively for one month. The neurologist says she is in a PVS, on a ventilator.

The attending physician, Dr. Harry Winston, wants to write a do-not-attempt-resuscitation (DNAR) order. With no relatives to get permission from, he asks the ethics committee for permission. How should they advise him?

COMMENTARY

Millie Shaw, like Mr. Saikewicz, is clearly not competent to make her own decisions about refusing medical treatment. There are several important differences in the two cases. The problem is deciding which of them is morally relevant. Millie Shaw is persistently vegetative, but is not dying in the sense of being inevitably declining rapidly toward death, whereas one could argue that is Mr. Saikewicz's situation. Some believe that one must be in the dying process to have justification for forgoing life support.

Millie Shaw is vegetative while Mr. Saikewicz is not. This means that Mr. Saikewicz can be burdened by the treatment in a way that Ms. Shaw cannot be. If Dr. Winston is to be justified in forgoing life support for his patient, it would have to be on the grounds that it is useless to continue the life of one in PVS.

There is another difference between these two cases. Millie Shaw is in PVS because of an assault. Mr. Saikewicz was a victim of leukemia. If Millie Shaw dies, a homicide was committed by the person who attacked her. In all likelihood that person was not mentally competent and probably would be treated lightly by prosecutors, but that person's legal fate hangs on whether Ms. Shaw lives or dies. This raises the question of whether her treatment should be affected by the potential legal implications for the person who assaulted her. A case can be made that the right choice for her care should not be shaped by the legal consequences for others.

Finally, one might question why Dr. Winston is contemplating a DNAR order but not a decision to forgo the ventilator or medically supplied nutrition and hydration. If a relatively simple and temporarily life-prolonging CPR is deemed to serve no worthwhile purpose for Ms. Shaw, is there a reason to conclude that the ventilator and other supporting interventions are any different?

Assume for purposes of discussion that Millie Shaw's care is best served by writing the DNAR order or forgoing the ventilator. The issue then is who should have the authority to make that decision? We have seen that the Massachusetts court in the Saikewicz case was skeptical about physicians and ethics committees making these choices. Presumably, that is because the question of what is best for Ms. Shaw is a moral choice about which people might differ and there is no reason to assume that the physician or the committee has any special expertise in making that choice. If Dr. Winston is not an authoritative decision-maker and there are no family members to participate, who else might be asked? Is this a case in which a guardian should be appointed by the court as it was in Mr. Saikewicz's case? Those who are incompetent for whom a decision is made that will lead to death are particularly vulnerable. Even those who generally wish to keep the courts out of cases may feel it is necessary to maximize due process protections before authorizing a decision that will lead to death.

Never Competent Persons with Available Family

The two previous cases involved patients for whom we have no information about their preferences for terminal care and no family were available to help determine what the patient would have wanted or what is best. When family is available, these cases can become even more complicated. Sometimes the family may disagree among themselves; in other cases, the family draws on its idiosyncratic religious or cultural values to make choices that deviate from what most reasonable people would choose. The next case presents a particularly unusual combination of these problems.

CASE 18-6

Picking Parents to Make Good Medical Choices

Phillip Becker was twelve years old in 1978 when critical medical problems arose in his care. He had been born on October 16, 1966. He was determined to have Down syndrome, a congenital heart defect (a ventricular septal defect), and elevated pulmonary blood pressure. With these problems he will suffer progressive loss of energy and vitality until he is forced to lead a bed-to-chair existence.

For reasons that are unknown, when Phillip was an infant no action was taken to correct his septal defect. In 1977, Dr. Gathman, a pediatric cardiologist, recommended catheterization to determine if an operation would be appropriate at this late point for the septal defect. Phillip was referred to second cardiologist who is less convinced than Dr. Gathman that the procedure would help.

Phillip's parents were told that the mortality risk from an operation was between 5 and 10 percent and that children with Down syndrome have higher than average risk. Without the operation he will face severe incapacitation. The longer the wait, the more risky the procedure will become. The heart must work three times harder than normal to supply blood. Without the operation he may live twenty more years. With it—if it is successful—he will live the life of a normal Down syndrome child, which, they were told, is less than a normal life span but clearly longer than twenty years.

Considering all of the risks and benefits, Phillip's parents refused the operation. They gave a range of arguments based on the welfare of child including the risk of immediate mortality, the pain and suffering from the surgery, and the concern that they were responsible for Phillip's welfare and that, if he outlived them, he could suffer from neglect from whoever would end up caring for him. The court accepted the parental refusal on these grounds.

Although it had not been emphasized during the original court deliberations, Phillip had been transferred to a residential facility called the We-Care facility in 1972. It was claimed that the parents had been advised not to remain emotionally close to Phillip in order to spare him the trauma of not being with them.

A volunteer named Patsy Heath became involved and began to develop a bond with Phillip. Eventually, he began making overnight visits to the Heath household and was accepted as part of their family. The Heaths were awarded guardianship on August 7, 1981, on the grounds that the Heaths were, de facto, the psychological parents and should have custody. In doing so the second court was aware that the Heaths wanted Philip to undergo the operation.

Given that the Beckers thought surgical correction was not in Phillip's interest and the Heaths thought it was, should custody be determined on the basis of which adults are making the most defensible choice for Phillip? [19]

COMMENTARY

Phillip Becker is a mentally incapacitated youngster with some complicating medical problems. It is not clear why he was not operated on as soon as the cardiac defect was discovered, but by the time he was twelve, all parties had become aware of the oversight and recognized a decision needed to be made. The physician began with the assumption that his biological parents were Phillip's guardians and that they needed to consent to the exploratory catheterization. The only reason for that procedure was to go ahead and correct the septal defect if that proved feasible. There was agreement that by this time there were serious problems. The mortality risk was not insignificant. The operation would certainly produce pain and suffering. To these considerations the Beckers added the controversial judgment that it might not be in Phillip's interest to live longer than they do.

Comparing these concerns to the benefits of a longer life (albeit shorter than for someone without these medical problems) is necessarily a subjective judgment. There is no definitive way to make the comparison. Nevertheless, it was agreed that most people probably would choose to have the exploratory catheterization followed by the heart operation if it was feasible. The issue before the first court was whether parents were entitled to make a different judgment for their child.

The first court, in 1979, accepted the idea that parents making subjective choices about what is best for their children do not need to conform to exactly what others in society might choose. The family is a fundamental unit in our society and it needs some space to function well. Families, like individuals, have some autonomy to choose beliefs and values on which they can operate. This includes the values that they will impose on their children through medical and other choices made on their behalf.

At the same time, there are limits on how much discretion parents and other family decision-makers can exercise. Some choices—such as refusal of life-saving blood transfusions—are so far beyond reason that society must intervene and take custody of the incompetent one for the purpose of ordering a more reasonable way of serving that person's best interest. The first Becker court concluded that his parents were close enough to being reasonable that the court should not intervene.

Once it became clear that Phillip was no longer living at home and had developed a family-like bond with Patsy Heath and her family, the story became more complicated. Eventually, the Heaths made the argument—successfully—that they were the "psychological parents" of Phillip and should be granted custody for the purpose of making medical choices including the choice to elect surgical repair.

In 1983 a second court, considering these new issues, awarded the Heaths custody. One explanation is that the Heaths had made a more reasonable choice about what was in Phillip's interest. The problem with that explanation, however, is that very frequently someone other than parents may be said to have a more reasonable view about what is in a child's interest. We do not want to have a society in which any friend, neighbor, teacher, or activist can claim to be entitled to custody of a child just because they have a more reasonable view about what is best for the child. The courts would spend all their time adjudicating disputes about which adults are making the best choices for children.

The "psychological parenthood" argument provides an alternative, narrower explanation. Only rarely could people like the Heaths make a plausible case that they are de facto in the parental role and that the biological parents have stepped aside. When the facts support such a claim, as they do in Phillip Becker's case, then the court can mediate an unusual version of a custody dispute and, if appropriate, award custody to someone other than the biological parent. Once that is done, the "new parent" can proceed as usual to make medical choices. As long as those choices are not beyond reason, the society can then accept those decisions even if they turn out not to be the best possible choices for a child. The difference between the "best interest" and what is "within reason" provides a basis for keeping the courts and other societal powers out of most familial decisions.

CASE 18-7

The Case of the Suspect Surrogates

Two weeks before the Ethics Committee consultation at a hospital in Philadelphia, a 76-year-old woman was admitted to the hospital's ER, some three hours after having fallen and found to be unconscious. Only fragmentary history could be obtained. The family later was found to be a local ex-husband, a sister with whom the patient lived, a daughter in Boston, and a daughter in Ohio. CAT scan of the head showed a subdural hematoma. The patient was taken to the operating room after a delay of a couple of hours due to lack of available room in the OR. During the operation, both a fresh subdural hematoma and a chronic subdural hematoma were removed. Postoperatively, the patient has remained unconscious, attached to a ventilator through an endotracheal tube and fed by nasogastric tube (N-G tube). Though the patient has remained comatose, by eleven days postoperatively the patient was able to be weaned off the ventilator and was breathing on her own through the endotracheal tube.

The attending physician was able to get some additional history from the daughter in Ohio. She indicated that the patient was disabled since a left craniotomy fifteen years earlier for an auto-accident head injury. It is not clear to what extent she was disabled; however, beginning in January 1998, six months before the admission to the hospital, the patient was said to have begun failing, became confused and stopped reading newspapers and watching television. According to the Ohio daughter, the patient has been living with her sister who is said to be a drug addict and to have physically abused the patient. The Ethics consultation was called because of a conflict about what to do next. The pulmonary consultant had advised that a tracheostomy be performed so that the endotracheal tube could be removed. Also, consideration was being given to replacement of the N-G tube with a gastrostomy tube for long-term nutrition. The attending physician had talked with the neurosurgeon who felt that the patient would wake up. The neurosurgeon, however, did not indicate what he thought would be the patient's functional deficit upon awakening. The attending physician then called and explained this information to the daughter in Ohio. She expressed a strong desire directing the attending physician that no further treatment be given toward maintaining her mother's life, including tracheostomy and tube feedings, if she were to remain in a vegetative state. She indicated that her sister in Boston would agree with her decision. The attending physician tended to agree with the daughter's feelings but was concerned about the ethical issues involved.

The patient had no Living Will or Durable Power of Attorney for Health Care. There was no evidence of the patient's own wishes. The ex-husband apparently appeared once shortly after admission as a "courtesy call." The patient's sister did not visit or communicate with the doctors. Neither of the two daughters traveled to the patient's bedside. In fact, the daughter in Boston could not be reached. The attending physician was aware that the Ohio daughter had not seen her mother in at least three months; she did not come now when her mother was critically ill and did not remove her from the patient's sister, about whom the Ohio daughter herself had said was physically abusive to her.

Is there a valid surrogate? Who? What do you think the ethics committee should say to the attending physician? Should the tracheostomy be performed and the G-tube inserted?

COMMENTARY

It is critical that medical decisions be made for this patient and soon. Since she left no expression of her own wishes, the family members are the first option for the role of surrogate. A sister, two daughters, and an ex-husband are all candidates. The general rule in such cases is that the next-of-kin is the initial candidate for that role. Each state has its own order of degrees of kinship. If no one has been named as a durable power of attorney, the spouse is usually considered to be the closest relative, but a divorced ex-spouse is not given that role (unless he were named by the patient). The adult children, in this case the daughters in Ohio and Boston, are next in line, followed by siblings. If two people are of equal degree of kinship, they could jointly assume this role.

Thus, in this case neither the ex-spouse nor the sister is a primary candidate for decision-making (although the decision-maker could consult them, if appropriate). That means the person reportedly abusing the patient (and herself) is not someone that should be seen by the physician as the primary decision-maker. The two daughters are the ones to whom the physician can turn unless they are disqualified because they are unwilling to serve or appear not to have the patient's interest at heart.

Is there any reason for the physician to question the role of the daughters? The daughter in Ohio has taken a position that is surely within reason. The only concern is that she has not traveled to be with her mother and has not intervened to remove her mother from the oversight of the sister. That could potentially be a reason to fear that the daughter in Ohio is lacking in commitment but does not necessarily require that the daughter's role be challenged.

The physician does not have the authority on his own to remove the daughter from the next-of-kin role. Assuming that the daughter does not voluntarily remove herself, and there is no evidence she intends to do so, an unpleasant legal challenge might be required.

The other issue is whether the second daughter in Boston needs to be involved directly. The Ohio daughter indicates her sister would agree with the decision to forgo the tube feeding, but it would seem to be a safer course to consult with that daughter directly, at least by phone. That surrogate could express approval or convey that her sister could make further decisions. Should the two sisters disagree on the course to be followed, the physician would potentially be in a bind and might have to get a court to clarify the situation. If, however, they agree that the feeding should stop, there seems to be no need for further review unless the physician is concerned that the daughters are not adequately committed to their mother's welfare. In that case, it would surely be time to ask for help from the court in clarifying who has the power to speak for this woman.

FUTILE CARE AND LIMITS BASED ON THE INTERESTS OF OTHERS

All of the cases in this chapter examined thus far work in what can be called a "patient-centered" framework. They focus on patient benefit or patient autonomy. Either way, the goal is to center on the patient. We saw, however, in Chapters 4 and 5 that some of the most important ethical conflicts today involve tensions between the patient and others in the society. The principle of social beneficence that underlies utilitarian reasoning holds that actions tend toward being right when they produce the most good overall, considering both the good for the patient and others.

That is a controversial notion, often rejected in health care ethics in favor of a more exclusive focus on the welfare of the patient. But in Chapter 5 we saw that there is another way that the interests of others can enter the picture. The principle of justice holds that actions tend toward being right if they distribute goods to those who have special claims. Egalitarian justice, which dominates modern nonutilitarian thinking about justice, usually interprets this to mean distributing health care on the basis of need.

Since terminally ill patients would normally be thought of as being in great need, they might, according to egalitarian interpretations of justice, have claims to resources that cannot be sustained solely on the more utilitarian notion of maximizing total benefit to the society. Terminally ill patients often require extremely expensive treatments, and those treatments often do not have much chance of producing substantial benefits. If we calculate expected benefit by multiplying the possible benefit times the probability of that benefit, the expected benefit can be very small. Hence, increasingly there are controversies over the ethics of allocating expensive treatments to the terminally ill. The last two cases in this chapter introduce what may be one of the most critical issues of health care ethics of the future. The health professionals here have both patient-centered and social reasons for stopping treatment even though the result may be the death of the patient.

CASE 18-8

Demands for Futile Care

William MacArthur was a 74-year-old black male who had been a widower for six years after a long, very happy marriage. He had had a long career as a business executive running a financially successful printing business. He now suffered from end-stage renal disease. He had been on dialysis for four years and tolerated it well. Now, however, his disease had progressed to the point that he needed a blood transfusion to survive. He said he wanted to live, but he was a Jehovah's Witness and was a classical blood refuser. He had cardiac arrest twice and had been resuscitated.

Dr. Edmund Harvey, the attending clinician, is morally uncomfortable with Mr. MacArthur's refusal of the blood. He knows he could save Mr. MacArthur's life with a simple transfusion with very little risk or discomfort, but he understands the patient's right of refusal and accepts that his patient may refuse even if it will mean certain, rapid death. He asks the patient to accept DNAR status on the grounds that there is no further treatment he has to offer the patient.

Mr. MacArthur refuses to accept the DNAR status saying he wants to live as long as possible. He realizes that the repeated resuscitations will be a burden and that they will likely fail within a short time.

Dr. Harvey brings the case to the hospital ethics committee. He claims further resuscitation is futile and a waste of medical resources. Moreover, he claims that continuing to provide CPR on such a patient with the pain and suffering it entails violates his notion of the good practice of medicine and offends his conscience.

COMMENTARY

In an earlier era, the moral controversy in this case would focus on the refusal of the blood transfusion. Many physicians would have objected, claiming that they had a right and a duty to prolong the life of Mr. MacArthur with a relatively safe and simple therapy. We now recognize the right of Mr. MacArthur to refuse the blood based on his well-formed and sincere religious belief.[20] Now the problem is whether Mr. MacArthur can have access to repeated CPR when he has suffered two cardiac arrests brought on by his refusal of blood. Physicians like Dr. Harvey are demanding the right to place limits on treatments that they perceive as futile. If the physician is permitted to omit repeated CPR, it is not in order to serve Mr. MacArthur's interest; it is for one of two other reasons.

First, some are concerned that in an era of scarce medical resources it seems odd to permit hospital personnel to spend their time and energy performing an effort at CPR that is eventually bound to fail. It seems odd that hospital and insurance company resources are used in this way. Some physicians are insisting they have a right, indeed a duty, to protect precious resources to make sure they are used for patients who will really benefit. We may have reached the point at which the traditional Hippocratic mandate that the physician should work only for the benefit of the patient has to be replaced with some consideration of the interests of others. If we are ever to place limits on the use of resources in the name of serving the interests of others, it would seem that treatments such as Mr. MacArthur's repeated CPRs that are bound to fail should be the easiest targets for resource conservation.

Limiting inefficient, expensive, and ultimately useless treatment is going to be necessary in the era of scarce medical resources. The deeper issue is whether this is legitimately on the agenda of Dr. Harvey, the primary physician with unique responsibility for Mr. MacArthur. Some would argue that, when limits must be placed in order to preserve scarce resources, clinicians with primary responsibility for one of the patients involved should exclude themselves from decisions that place limits on care in the name of serving the interests of others. They have special, role-specific duties to the patients to whom they have pledged loyalty. Moreover, given their historical psychological commitment to their patients, they may well make rationing decisions in a way that unfairly favors their own patients at the expense of others. Since the physicians are not necessarily in a position to know what the alternative uses of the resources might be, it is better, so the argument goes, to have other persons—administrators, ethics committees, or hospital boards—set the policies for rationing limits and have supervising clinicians make actual case-by-case decisions. Thus, if Mr. MacArthur's CPR should be limited for these reasons to protect the interests of other patients, it is argued that someone in Dr. Harvey's role ought to be excluded from the decision process.

Dr. Harvey's concern may not be one of scarce resources, however. The second reason he may be concerned is that he may have an understanding of the way he should practice medicine that excludes delivering treatments such as Mr. MacArthur's CPR that will soon fail. He may believe that medicine has the end of healing or relieving suffering or some goal beyond merely pumping a few extra hours of life into an inevitably dying patient. Many physicians who have come through the era when physicians tried to preserve life at all costs have developed a more realistic idea of what medicine can and should accomplish. They feel that their professional integrity is violated if patients are given the right to demand and receive treatments that cannot achieve anything more than temporary life preservation that comes at the price of added burden to the patient. These physicians are demanding the right to use their professional judgment to decide that the treatment provides no benefit. The controversy is referred to as the "futile care" debate.[21]

The problem with this view, however, is that, as we have seen in the cases of Chapters 2 and 4, deciding the value of medical outcomes is essentially a subjective judgment. While many physicians (and many lay people) have come to see no point in mere temporary life preservation by repeated CPR that is doomed to fail, some patients and some physicians continue to see value in such outcomes. When a treatment under consideration will produce some real change in the patient's condition (even if it is only a temporary delay in an inevitable death), people will evaluate those changes differently. Some, like Mr. MacArthur, may see value in even a short period of life preservation. They may want additional hours of life because a relative is traveling to say a final good-bye or simply because they view each moment of life as precious and to be preserved (as long as it can be done without violating important moral norms). Deciding the value of those extra moments is essentially a value question, not one that can be answered with special expertise by a medical professional.

That still leaves open the question of why a physician should be forced to deliver such treatment against his conscientious objection. It cannot be that patient autonomy gives the patient the right of access. Autonomy gives the patient the right to refuse (including the right to refuse the blood transfusion), but it does not give the patient the right to force the doctor to deliver a treatment that he finds objectionable.

If there is a duty to continue the CPR, it must come from some other moral source. One place to look is to the promises made by the physician. Physicians, when they take patients, promise loyalty to them. Patients cannot be abandoned by their physicians without an effort by the physician to make alternative arrangements. That does not mean that the doctor must do everything that the patient demands, but it does require staying with the patient.

Also at stake are the promises made by physicians as part of the agreement for professional licensure. Physicians gain a monopoly privilege to practice medicine, including using medical technologies in ways that no other citizens are permitted to do. If society is going to restrict the use of medical procedures to those who are licensed to practice medicine, and society understands that some of its members may want access to life-prolonging technologies, then it is possible that it would require of licensed professionals that they use those technologies for their patients, with whom they have a doctor–patient relation, when the patient wants the intervention and it will be effective in providing some fundamental service such as prolonging life or relieving pain.

Cases like that of Mr. MacArthur force on society a choice between requiring a physician to provide a treatment that he does not want to provide and arranging health care so that patients will die when they do not want to and do not need to. The choice is not an easy one. In Mr. MacArthur's case, he was conscious and competent to express his views about the value of the treatment under consideration and whether the burdens of the CPR are offset by the value of the extra life added. Futile care cases are more complicated when the patient is conscious and may suffer from the treatment in question, but the patient is not competent to voice an opinion about whether the burdens of that treatment are worth it. That is the problem in the final case of this volume.

CASE 18-9

Emilio Gonzales: Is His Care Futile in Texas?

Emilio Gonzales was born on November 3, 2005, at Brackenridge Hospital in Austin, Texas. His mother, Catarina Gonzales, had a C-section at thirty-five-weeks gestation.[22] Emilio was moved immediately to the neonatal intensive care unit because of apnea and feeding difficulties. He eventually was found to have extreme loss of vision, bilateral auditory neuropathy, and abnormal seizure activity. He was diagnosed as potentially having Leigh's syndrome, a rare metabolic condition involving neurological degeneration. In December of 2006 he suffered a setback, perhaps related to a viral illness and was transferred to the pediatric intensive care unit of Children's Hospital of Austin where his condition continued to worsen. His MRI results were consistent with an inherited metabolic disease called Leigh's syndrome, which effects the nervous system and usually results in death within 2–3 years. Emilio was at this point ventilator dependent. Consultation with colleagues led to agreement with the diagnosis and poor prognosis. He was now semi-conscious. It was unclear whether he could perceive pain. His treatment consisted of ventilation and feeding via a naso-jejunal tube. His condition was described as irreversible with continuation of brain atrophy.

On February 19, 2007, a meeting of the Neonatal/Pediatric Ethics Committee was held. His attending physician, Dr. Alexandra Wilson, believed he was experiencing pain. He could not gag, was experiencing collapse of his lungs, and was having seizures. MRIs showed progressive loss of brain tissue. He was now too ill to survive anywhere but in an intensive care setting.

A second meeting of the ethics committee was held on March 9, 2007. At the time, Dr. Wilson and other members of the patient care team believed that Emilio was suffering and that the burdens of his current treatment far outweighed any benefits. Catarina Gonzales continued to request that Emilio be maintained on a ventilator and provided with medical support.

The ethics committee concluded that aggressive care measures including ventilation were "medically inappropriate" and recommended "only comfort measures" such as pain control. It concluded that Emilio's code status be changed to "do not resuscitate."

In 1999 a Texas law was passed permitting attending physicians to forgo life support on patients such as Emilio even against the wishes of the patient's family ten days after a hospital-based ethics committee endorses the physician's decision.[23]

Emilio's life support was to be terminated after the ten-day period, during which Ms. Gonzales could attempt to find another facility to take her son. She was unable to locate another doctor or hospital, but near the end of the time period, state legislators and the Texas Right to Life organization held a press conference highlighting Emilio's situation. Shortly later, the hospital granted an additional ten-day period. On April 4, a federal judge refused to grant Catarina Gonzales a restraining order forcing the hospital to continue treatment any longer. The hospital nevertheless did not withdraw the ventilator. Some days later the court did extend the requirement of treatment until May 8 when a new court hearing was to take place, but that hearing was rescheduled for May 30 because several of its witnesses were unavailable. Emilio Gonzales died May 19, 2007, while the parties were awaiting further judicial review.

Later that year Senator Bob Duell introduced into the Texas legislature a bill to extend the waiting period from ten to twenty-one days, but the bill was not acted upon before the legislature adjourned.

COMMENTARY

This case is in many ways similar to that of Mr. MacArthur, the patient in the previous case. In both cases, the physician believed that the treatment was doing no good, that it was "futile," but the patient or the patient's agent wanted the treatment and believed it would do good. In both cases, the health care providers would have to acknowledge that the desired treatment would extend the patient's life, at least for a while. It was not "physiologically futile." The controversy was over whether the added days or weeks of life were of any value given the patient's inevitably fatal condition.

Critics of the position such as that of the Texas law claim that physicians cannot claim to be experts on deciding whether a treatment that effectively changes the dying of a patient—at least at the margin—offers benefits that justify the burdens and the costs. Defenders of policies like that of the Texas law, at least those who acknowledge that physicians cannot claim expertise on the value of the effects of the treatment, claim either that the treatments use scarce resources better left for other patients or that physicians are professionals whose integrity is threatened if they are forced to provide treatments, even effective treatments, that violate their judgment about what counts as appropriate use of professional skills.

We have seen in earlier chapters that the argument over the use of scarce resources raises issues of justice and social utility that take us well beyond these cases. Many, in fact, argue that individual physicians should be excluded from decisions that are based on the alternative uses of resources since the physicians are not in a good position to evaluate all the alternatives and they have a fiduciary duty to remain loyal to their patient.

The core question is whether physicians should have the unilateral authority (or authority after review by an ethics committee) to stop treatments that patients or their surrogates see as offering valued benefits. If professional integrity should prevail in these circumstances, then they presumably should have the right to refuse to provide the treatment being sought. If, on the other hand, the health professional is viewed as someone who is licensed by the state to perform functions that society considers important and society wants patients to get treatments that effectively produce what the patient desires, at least when the patient's interest involves life and death, then society might claim that, as a condition of licensure, physicians should provide the desired and effective service when no one else is available who is competent to provide it and that the treatment will actually achieve the end sought such as preservation of life or relief of significant suffering. Critics claim that requiring them to try to find alternative sources of the treatment places an unfair burden on the patient and his or her supporters. They say that extending that period does not adequately address the core problem of needing a licensed health professional to achieve the basic goal of preserving life. They argue that licensed physicians are in a position different from that of an ordinary citizen. The ordinary citizen has certain autonomy-based rights to refuse to participate in practices that violate his or her conscience. The licensed professional, on the other hand, is given control over technologies that literally mean life and death to the patient. These technologies are too complicated for every patient to be given unfettered access. Therefore, the critics claim, we should impose on professionals as a condition of the privileges of licensure that they have a duty to use these services when they will extend life, even if the individual practitioner does not think there is any value in doing so.

There is one important difference that is worth noting between Mr. MacArthur's case and that of Emilio Gonzales. In Mr. MacArthur's case, he was mentally competent to decide that, for him, the burdens of CPR following cardiac arrest were worth it in order to achieve the brief addition to his life. In Emilio Gonzales' case, however, it is not he, but his mother, who is making the judgment. Since it was believed that he was conscious enough to feel the pain and other burdens of his treatment, the physicians could have opted for a different course other than invoking of the Texas futility law. Dr. Wilson and the ethics committee could have recommended asking for judicial review to determine if the burdens faced by Emilio were so great in comparison to any good achieved that his mother, Ms. Gonzales, was, in effect, guilty of abuse or neglect in insisting on the continuation. That is the grounds on which parental decisions about refusal of blood and other life-sustaining treatments are challenged. The physicians in Emilio's case had available to them a more direct means of addressing their problem than appeal to futility. They could have claimed that since Emilio apparently was conscious enough to suffer pain, his mother was making a significantly wrong choice. Courts regularly make determinations of whether parents' choices are so mistaken that they, in effect, constitute neglect or abuse, even if there is no doubt that their choices are made in good faith.

At the present time, unless the Texas law is amended, physicians in that state (and perhaps some others including Virginia) have a legal right to unilaterally forgo life support, once certain legal requirements are met. Several courts have made decisions in other states that imply that patients and their surrogates have a right of access in these cases. The central remaining issue is whether individual physicians have the right to unilaterally decide to withhold life support in cases in which the patient or surrogate wants the life support, and it will, at least for a while, be effective. Either the physician's right to practice medicine as he or she sees fit or the patient's right to live when life can continue will have to give way. This may well be one of the most difficult issues that is unresolved in the cases of medical ethics.

NOTES

[1] Ramsey, Paul. *The Patient as Person*. New Haven, CT: Yale University Press, 1970.

[2] Ramsey, Paul. *Ethics at the Edges of Life*. New Haven, CT: Yale University Press, 1978; Cohen, Cynthia, editor. *Casebook on the Termination of Life-Sustaining Treatment and the Care of the Dying*. Bloomington, IN: Indiana University Press, 1988; Veatch, Robert M. *Death, Dying, and the Biological Revolution*, rev. ed. New Haven, CT: Yale University Press, 1989.

[3] Bleich, J. David. "The Obligation to Heal in the Judaic Tradition: A Comparative Analysis." In *Jewish Bioethics*. Fred Rosner and J. David Bleich, editors. New York: Sanhedrin Press, 1979, pp. 1–44.

[4] American Medical Association. *Council on Ethical and Judicial Affairs, Code of Medical Ethics: Current Opinions with Annotations, 2004-2005*. Chicago, IL: American Medical Association, 2004.

[5] President's Commission for the Study of Ethical Problems in Medicine and Biomedical and Behavioral Research. *Deciding to Forego Life-Sustaining Treatment: Ethical, Medical, and Legal Issues in Treatment Decisions*. Washington, DC: U.S. Government Printing Office, 1983; Meisel, Alan. "The Legal Consensus about Forgoing Life-Sustaining Treatment: Its Status and Its Prospects." *Kennedy Institute of Ethics Journal* 2 (1992):309–345.

[6] Gervais, Karen G. "Death, Definition and Determination of: III. Philosophical and Theological Perspectives." In *Encyclopedia of Bioethics*. 3rd ed. Stephen G. Post, editor. New York: Macmillan Reference USA: Thomson/Gale, 2004, pp. 615–626; Youngner, Stuart J., Robert M. Arnold, and Renie Schapiro, editors. *The Definition of Death: Contemporary Controversies*. Baltimore, MD: Johns Hopkins University Press, 1999; Wijdicks, Eelco F. M., editor. *Brain Death*. Baltimore, MD: Lippincott Williams & Wilkins, 2001; Potts, Michael, Paul A. Byrne, and Richard G. Nilges. *Beyond Brain Death: The Case against Brain Based Criteria for Human Death*. Dordrecht/Boston: Kluwer Academic, 2000.

[7] Sell, David. "Flyers Goalie Lindbergh Is Declared Brain Dead." *The Washington Post* November 11, 1985, pp. D1, D13; Sell, David. "Lindbergh Was Legally Drunk." *The Washington Post* November 12, 1985, pp. D1, D4; Sell, Dave. "Flyers' Lindbergh Is Declared Dead." *The Washington Post* November 13, 1985, pp. D1, D8.

[8] State v. Watson, 191 N.J.Super. 464, 467 A.2d 590, 1983.

9 New Jersey Declaration of Death Act (1991). *New Jersey Statutes Annotated*. Title 26, 6A-1 to 6A; Olick, Robert S. "Brain Death, Religious Freedom, and Public Policy." *Kennedy Institute of Ethics Journal* 1 (December 1991):275–288.

10 Harvard Medical School Ad Hoc Committee. "A Definition of Irreversible Coma. Report of the Ad Hoc Committee of the Harvard Medical School to Examine the Definition of Brain Death." *Journal of the American Medical Association* 205 (1968):337–340.

11 President's Commission for the Study of Ethical Problems in Medicine and Biomedical and Behavioral Research. *Defining Death: Medical, Legal and Ethical Issues in the Definition of Death*. Washington, DC: U.S. Government Printing Office, 1981.

12 For a sample of an advance directive see the following websites: www.agingwith-dignity.org; www.gundluth.org; www.midbio.org; www.critical-conditions.org; www.hardchoices.com; http://fidelitywisdomandlove.org; Cantor, Norman L. "My Annotated Living Will." *Law, Medicine & Health Care* 18 (Spring–Summer 1990):114–122; Bok, Sissela. "Personal Directions for Care at the End of Life." *New England Journal of Medicine* 295 (1976):367–369; The Catholic Hospital Association. "Christian Affirmation of Life." St. Louis, MO: The Catholic Hospital Association, 1982; Concern for Dying. "A Living Will." No date; and Veatch, Robert M. *Death, Dying, and the Biological Revolution*, pp. 154–155. For discussions of the ethics of advanced directives see Dyck, Arthur J. "Living Wills and Mercy Killing: An Ethical Assessment." In *Bioethics and Human Rights: A Reader for Health Professionals*. Bertram Bandman and Elsie Bandman, editors. Boston, MA: Little, Brown, 1978, pp. 132–138; Buchanan, Allen. "Advance Directives and Personal Identity Problem." *Philosophy and Public Affairs* 17 (No. 4, Fall 1988):277–302; and Buchanan, Allen E., and Dan W. Brock. *Deciding for Others: The Ethics of Surrogate Decision Making*. Cambridge: Cambridge University Press, 1989.

13 McCloskey, Elizabeth Leibold. "The Patient Self-Determination Act." *Kennedy Institute of Ethics Journal* 1 (June 1991):163–169.

14 Uhlmann, Richard F., Robert A. Pearlman, and Kevin C. Cain. "Physicians' and Spouses' Predictions of Elderly Patients' Resuscitation Preferences." *Journal of Gerontology: Medical Sciences* 43 (No. 8, 1988):M1115–M1121; Hare, Jan, Clara Pratt, and Carrie Nelson. "Agreement between Patients and Their Self-Selected Surrogates on Difficult Medical Decisions." *Archives Internal Medicine* 12 (May 1992):1049–1054; SUPPORT Principal Investigators. "A Controlled Trail to Improve Care for Seriously Ill Hospitalized Patients." *Journal of the American Medical Association* 274 (November 22/29, 1995):1591–1598.

15 This case is based on the various court records including Cruzan, by Cruzan v. Harmon, 760 S.W.2d 408 (Mo.banc 1988) and Cruzan v. Director, Missouri Dept. of Health, 110 S.Ct. 2841 (1990).

16 Superintendent of Belchertown State School v. Saikewicz, 373 Mass. 728, 370 NE 2d 417 (1977

17 In re Quinlan, 70 N.J. 10, 355 A. 2d 647 (1976), *cert. denied* sub nom., Garger v. New Jersey, 429 U.S. 922 (1976), overruled in part, In re Conroy, 98 NJ 321, 486 A.2d 1209 (1985

18 *In re* Dinnerstein, 6 Mass. App. Ct. 466, 380 N.E.2d 134 (App. Ct. 1978).

[19] In the matter of Phillip Becker, 92 Cal. App. 3d 796, 156 Cal Rptr. 48 (1979), Cert. denied sub nom. Bothman v. Warren B., 445 U.S. 949 (1980); and Guardianship of Phillip Becker, No. 101-981, at 4 (Cal. Super. Ct., August 7, 1981), aff'd., 139 Cal. App.3d 407, 420, 199 Cal.1Rptr. 781, 789 (1983).

[20] Moore, Maureen L. "Their Life is in the Blood: Jehovah's Witnesses, Blood Transfusions and the Courts." *Northern Kentucky Law Review* 10 (No. 2, 1983):281–304.

[21] Miles, Steven H. "Informed Demand for 'Non-Beneficial' Medical Treatment." *New England Journal of Medicine* 325 (1991):512–515; Veatch, Robert M. and Carol Mason Spicer. "Medically Futile Care: The Role of the Physician in Setting Limits." *American Journal of Law & Medicine* 18 (Nos. 1&2, 1992):15–36; Jecker, Nancy S. and Lawrence J. Schneiderman. "Medical Futility: The Duty Not to Treat." *Cambridge Quarterly of Healthcare Ethics* 2 (1993):151–159.

[22] This case is based on Moreno, Sylvia. "Case Puts Texas Futile-Treatment Law under a Microscope: Statue Allows for Deadline on Care." April 11, 2007. *Washington Post.* Accessed April 2, 2008, at <http://www.washingtonpost.com/wp-dyn/content/article/2007/04/10/AR2007041001620.html; and Sheppard, Nancy: Co-Chair, Pediatric Ethics Committee. "Ethics Committee Report Form; Seton HealthCare Network Neonatal/Pediatric Ethics Committee— Patient: Emilio Gonzales." Date of Consult: March 9, 2007. Austin, Texas, accessed on the Internet at <http://www.northcountygazette.org/documents/PediEthicsCommitteeReport.doc>.

[23] Texas Statutes Health & Safety Code, §166.046: Advance Directives. Accessed April 2, 2008. <http://www.tlo2.tlc.state.tx.us/statues/docs/HS/content/htm/hs.002.00.000166.00.htm>

APPENDIX: CODES OF ETHICS

Many people seek guidance in evaluating difficult medical ethics cases by turning to various codes of ethics written by professional, religious, governmental, and voluntary organizations. Four of the most well-known are reproduced in this appendix. Others are readily available from the websites of the sponsoring organizations. The web addresses of some of the most important are presented here.

American Dental Association Principles of Ethics and Code of Professional Conduct:
http://www.ada.org/prof/prac/law/code/index.asp

American Nurses Association: Code of Ethics for Nurses with Intepretative Statements
http://www.nursingworld.org/MainMenuCategories/ThePracticeofProfessionalNursing/EthicsStandards/CodeofEthics.aspx

American Pharmacists Association: Code of Ethics for Pharmacists:
http://www.pharmacist.com/AM/Template.cfm?Section=Search1&template=/CM/HTMLDisplay.cfm&ContentID=2903

American Hospital Association, Patient Care Partnership (replacing the Patients Bill of Rights)
http://www.aha.org/aha/issues/Communicating-With-Patients/pt-care-partnership.html

Council of Europe: Convention on Human Rights and Biomedicine:
http://www.bioethics.nih.gov/international/declarat/conv.htm

United States Conference of Catholic Bishops, Ethical and Religious Directives for Catholic Health Care Services:
http://www.usccb.org/bishops/directives.shtml

Oath of Maimonides
http://www.library.dal.ca/kellogg/Bioethics/codes/maimonides.htm

Oath of a Muslim Physician
http://www.islam-usa.com/im2.html

THE HIPPOCRATIC OATH[1]

The Hippocratic Oath was written in around the fourth century before the common era. It appears to have been used by a school of physicians that was related, at least to some extent, by Pythagorean thought. Although no medical schools administer the Oath to their students in this original form, the Oath is still seen by some as a symbol that the physician should act ethically. The Oath has increasingly been seen as morally controversial and potentially in conflict with other systems of ethics for professional conduct.

I swear by Apollo Physician and Asclepius and Hygieia and Panaceia and all the gods and goddesses, making them my witnesses, that I fulfill according to my ability and judgment this oath and this covenant:

To hold him who has taught me this art as equal to my parents and to live my life in partnership with him, and if he is in need of money to give him a share of mine, and to regard his offspring as equal to my brothers in male lineage and to teach them this art if they desire to learn it without fee and covenant; to give a share of precepts and oral instruction and all the other learning to my sons and to the sons of him who has instructed me and to pupils who have signed the covenant and have taken an oath according to the medical law, but to no one else.

I will apply dietetic measures for the benefit of the sick according to my ability and judgment; I will keep them from harm and injustice.

I will never give a deadly drug to anybody if asked for it, nor will I make a suggestion to this effect. Similarly I will not give to a woman an abortive remedy. In purity and holiness I will guard my life and my art.

I will not use the knife, not even on sufferers from stone, but will withdraw in favor of such men as are engaged in work.

Whatever houses I may visit, I will come for the benefit of the sick, remaining free of all intentional injustice, of all mischief, and in particular, of sexual relations with both female and male persons, be they free or slaves.

What I may see or hear in the course of the treatment or even outside of the treatment in regard to the life of men, which on no account one must spread abroad, I shall keep to myself holding such things shameful to be spoken about.

If I fulfill this oath and do not violate it, may it be granted to me to enjoy life and art, being honored with fame among all men for all time to come; if I transgress it and swear falsely, may the opposite of all this be my lot.

WORLD MEDICAL ASSOCIATION, DECLARATION OF GENEVA

Adopted by the 2nd General Assembly of the World Medical Association, Geneva, Switzerland, September 1948, and revised most recently at the 173rd

Council Session, Divonne-les-Bains, France, May 2006. The World Medical Association is made up of national medical associations.

AT THE TIME OF BEING ADMITTED AS A MEMBER OF
 THE MEDICAL PROFESSION:

I SOLEMNLY PLEDGE to consecrate my life to the service of
 humanity;

I WILL GIVE to my teachers the respect and gratitude that is their due;

I WILL PRACTISE my profession with conscience and dignity;

THE HEALTH OF MY PATIENT will be my first consideration;

I WILL RESPECT the secrets that are confided in me, even after the
 patient has died;

I WILL MAINTAIN by all the means in my power, the honour and
 the noble traditions of the medical profession;

MY COLLEAGUES will be my sisters and brothers;

I WILL NOT PERMIT considerations of age, disease or disability,
 creed, ethnic origin, gender, nationality, political affiliation, race,
 sexual orientation, social standing or any other factor to intervene
 between my duty and my patient;

I WILL MAINTAIN the utmost respect for human life;

I WILL NOT USE my medical knowledge to violate human rights
 and civil liberties, even under threat;

I MAKE THESE PROMISES solemnly, freely and upon my honour.

14.10.2006

THE AMERICAN MEDICAL ASSOCIATION, PRINCIPLES OF MEDICAL ETHICS

The American Medical Association (AMA) adopted its first code of ethics in 1847 at the time of its founding. The code, currently referred to as the "Principles of Medical Ethics," has been revised many times since then. A major revision in 1980 included the first mention of rights in a professional code of physicians, committed physicians to honesty, opened the door to accepting some disclosures of confidential information for the purpose of protecting third parties, and continued the AMA's commitment to working for the benefit of society as well as patients. In 2001, modest revisions shifted attention back to treating responsibility to the patient as paramount.

Preamble

The medical profession has long subscribed to a body of ethical statements developed primarily for the benefit of the patient. As a member of this profession, a physician must recognize responsibility to patients first and foremost, as well as to society, to other health professionals, and to self. The following Principles adopted by the AMA are not laws, but standards of conduct that define the essentials of honorable behavior for the physician.

Principles of Medical Ethics

A physician shall be dedicated to providing competent medical care, with compassion and respect for human dignity and rights.

A physician shall uphold the standards of professionalism, be honest in all professional interactions, and strive to report physicians deficient in character or competence, or engaging in fraud or deception, to appropriate entities.

A physician shall respect the law and also recognize a responsibility to seek changes in those requirements that are contrary to the best interests of the patient.

A physician shall respect the rights of patients, colleagues, and other health professionals, and shall safeguard patient confidences and privacy within the constraints of the law.

A physician shall continue to study, apply, and advance scientific knowledge, maintain a commitment to medical education, make relevant information available to patients, colleagues, and the public, obtain consultation, and use the talents of other health professionals when indicated.

A physician shall, in the provision of appropriate patient care, except in emergencies, be free to choose whom to serve, with whom to associate, and the environment in which to provide medical care.

A physician shall recognize a responsibility to participate in activities contributing to the improvement of the community and the betterment of public health.

A physician shall, while caring for a patient, regard responsibility to the patient as paramount.

A physician shall support access to medical care for all people.

Adopted by the AMA's House of Delegates June 17, 2001.

UNIVERSAL DECLARATION ON BIOETHICS AND HUMAN RIGHTS[2]

On October 19, 2005, the General Conference of the United Nations Economic, Scientific, and Cultural Organization adopted the following declaration. It is the first codification of bioethics principles adopted by a public agency that is intended to speak for all countries of the world. The document begins with an extensive statement of clauses stating the reason for the adoption of these principles and providing the history of the declaration.

The General Conference

Proclaims the principles that follow and adopts the present Declaration.

General Provisions

Article 1—Scope

1. This Declaration addresses ethical issues related to medicine, life sciences and associated technologies as applied to human beings, taking into account their social, legal and environmental dimensions.
2. This Declaration is addressed to States. As appropriate and relevant, it also provides guidance to decisions or practices of individuals, groups, communities, institutions and corporations, public and private.

Article 2—Aims

The aims of this Declaration are

- to provide a universal framework of principles and procedures to guide States in the formulation of their legislation, policies or other instruments in the field of bioethics;
- to guide the actions of individuals, groups, communities, institutions and corporations, public and private;
- to promote respect for human dignity and protect human rights, by ensuring respect for the life of human beings, and fundamental freedoms, consistent with international human rights law;
- to recognize the importance of freedom of scientific research and the benefits derived from scientific and technological developments, while stressing the need for such research and developments to occur within the framework of ethical principles set out in this Declaration and to respect human dignity, human rights and fundamental freedoms;
- to foster multidisciplinary and pluralistic dialogue about bioethical issues between all stakeholders and within society as a whole;
- to promote equitable access to medical, scientific and technological developments as well as the greatest possible flow and the rapid sharing of knowledge concerning those developments and the sharing of benefits, with particular attention to the needs of developing countries;
- to safeguard and promote the interests of the present and future generations;
- to underline the importance of biodiversity and its conservation as a common concern of humankind.

Principles
Within the scope of this Declaration, in decisions or practices taken or carried out by those to whom it is addressed, the following principles are to be respected.

Article 3—Human dignity and human rights

1. Human dignity, human rights and fundamental freedoms are to be fully respected.

2. The interests and welfare of the individual should have priority over the sole interest of science or society.

Article 4—Benefit and harm

In applying and advancing scientific knowledge, medical practice and associated technologies, direct and indirect benefits to patients, research participants and other affected individuals should be maximized and any possible harm to such individuals should be minimized.

Article 5—Autonomy and individual responsibility

The autonomy of persons to make decisions, while taking responsibility for those decisions and respecting the autonomy of others, is to be respected. For persons who are not capable of exercising autonomy, special measures are to be taken to protect their rights and interests.

Article 6—Consent

1. Any preventive, diagnostic and therapeutic medical intervention is only to be carried out with the prior, free and informed consent of the person concerned, based on adequate information. The consent should, where appropriate, be expressed and may be withdrawn by the person concerned at any time and for any reason without disadvantage or prejudice.
2. Scientific research should only be carried out with the prior, free, expressed and informed consent of the person concerned. The information should be adequate, provided in a comprehensible form and should include modalities for withdrawal of consent. Consent may be withdrawn by the person concerned at any time and for any reason without any disadvantage or prejudice. Exceptions to this principle should be made only in accordance with ethical and legal standards adopted by States, consistent with the principles and provisions set out in this Declaration, in particular in Article 27, and international human rights law.
3. In appropriate cases of research carried out on a group of persons or a community, additional agreement of the legal representatives of the group or community concerned may be sought. In no case should a collective community agreement or the consent of a community leader or other authority substitute for an individual's informed consent.

Article 7—Persons without the capacity to consent

In accordance with domestic law, special protection is to be given to persons who do not have the capacity to consent:

> authorization for research and medical practice should be obtained in accordance with the best interest of the person concerned and

in accordance with domestic law. However, the person concerned should be involved to the greatest extent possible in the decision-making process of consent, as well as that of withdrawing consent; research should only be carried out for his or her direct health benefit, subject to the authorization and the protective conditions prescribed by law, and if there is no research alternative of comparable effectiveness with research participants able to consent. Research which does not have potential direct health benefit should only be undertaken by way of exception, with the utmost restraint, exposing the person only to a minimal risk and minimal burden and, if the research is expected to contribute to the health benefit of other persons in the same category, subject to the conditions prescribed by law and compatible with the protection of the individual's human rights. Refusal of such persons to take part in research should be respected.

Article 8—Respect for human vulnerability and personal integrity

In applying and advancing scientific knowledge, medical practice and associated technologies, human vulnerability should be taken into account. Individuals and groups of special vulnerability should be protected and the personal integrity of such individuals respected.

Article 9—Privacy and confidentiality

The privacy of the persons concerned and the confidentiality of their personal information should be respected. To the greatest extent possible, such information should not be used or disclosed for purposes other than those for which it was collected or consented to, consistent with international law, in particular international human rights law.

Article 10—Equality, justice and equity

The fundamental equality of all human beings in dignity and rights is to be respected so that they are treated justly and equitably.

Article 11—Non-discrimination and non-stigmatization

No individual or group should be discriminated against or stigmatized on any grounds, in violation of human dignity, human rights and fundamental freedoms.

Article 12—Respect for cultural diversity and pluralism

The importance of cultural diversity and pluralism should be given due regard. However, such considerations are not to be invoked to infringe upon human dignity, human rights and fundamental freedoms, nor upon the principles set out in this Declaration, nor to limit their scope.

Article 13—Solidarity and cooperation

Solidarity among human beings and international cooperation towards that end are to be encouraged.

Article 14—Social responsibility and health

1. The promotion of health and social development for their people is a central purpose of governments that all sectors of society share.
2. Taking into account that the enjoyment of the highest attainable standard of health is one of the fundamental rights of every human being without distinction of race, religion, political belief, economic or social condition, progress in science and technology should advance:

   access to quality health care and essential medicines, especially for the health of women and children, because health is essential to life itself and must be considered to be a social and human good;
   access to adequate nutrition and water;
   improvement of living conditions and the environment;
   elimination of the marginalization and the exclusion of persons on the basis of any grounds;
   reduction of poverty and illiteracy.

Article 15—Sharing of benefits

1. Benefits resulting from any scientific research and its applications should be shared with society as a whole and within the international community, in particular with developing countries. In giving effect to this principle, benefits may take any of the following forms:

   special and sustainable assistance to, and acknowledgment of, the persons and groups that have taken part in the research;
   access to quality health care;
   provision of new diagnostic and therapeutic modalities or products stemming from research;
   support for health services;
   access to scientific and technological knowledge;
   capacity-building facilities for research purposes;

other forms of benefit consistent with the principles set out in this Declaration.

2. Benefits should not constitute improper inducements to participate in research.

Article 16—Protecting future generations

The impact of life sciences on future generations, including on their genetic constitution, should be given due regard.

Article 17—Protection of the environment, the biosphere and biodiversity

Due regard is to be given to the interconnection between human beings and other forms of life, to the importance of appropriate access and utilization of biological and genetic resources, to respect for traditional knowledge and to the role of human beings in the protection of the environment, the biosphere and biodiversity.

Application of the principles

Article 18—Decision-making and addressing bioethical issues

1. Professionalism, honesty, integrity and transparency in decision-making should be promoted, in particular declarations of all conflicts of interest and appropriate sharing of knowledge. Every endeavour should be made to use the best available scientific knowledge and methodology in addressing and periodically reviewing bioethical issues.
2. Persons and professionals concerned and society as a whole should be engaged in dialogue on a regular basis.
3. Opportunities for informed pluralistic public debate, seeking the expression of all relevant opinions, should be promoted.

Article 19—Ethics committees

Independent, multidisciplinary and pluralist ethics committees should be established, promoted and supported at the appropriate level in order to

assess the relevant ethical, legal, scientific and social issues related to research projects involving human beings;

provide advice on ethical problems in clinical settings;

assess scientific and technological developments, formulate recommendations and contribute to the preparation of guidelines on issues within the scope of this Declaration;

foster debate, education and public awareness of, and engagement in, bioethics.

Article 20—Risk assessment and management

Appropriate assessment and adequate management of risk related to medicine, life sciences and associated technologies should be promoted.

Article 21—Transnational practices

1. States, public and private institutions, and professionals associated with transnational activities should endeavour to ensure that any activity within the scope of this Declaration, undertaken, funded or otherwise pursued in whole or in part in different States, is consistent with the principles set out in this Declaration.
2. When research is undertaken or otherwise pursued in one or more States (the host State(s)) and funded by a source in another State, such research should be the object of an appropriate level of ethical review in the host State(s) and the State in which the funder is located. This review should be based on ethical and legal standards that are consistent with the principles set out in this Declaration.
3. Transnational health research should be responsive to the needs of host countries, and the importance of research contributing to the alleviation of urgent global health problems should be recognized.
4. When negotiating a research agreement, terms for collaboration and agreement on the benefits of research should be established with equal participation by those party to the negotiation.
5. States should take appropriate measures, both at the national and international levels, to combat bioterrorism and illicit traffic in organs, tissues, samples, genetic resources and genetic-related materials.

Promotion of the Declaration

Article 22—Role of States

1. States should take all appropriate measures, whether of a legislative, administrative or other character, to give effect to the principles set out in this Declaration in accordance with international human rights law. Such measures should be supported by action in the spheres of education, training and public information.
2. States should encourage the establishment of independent, multidisciplinary and pluralist ethics committees, as set out in Article 19.

Article 23—Bioethics education, training and information

1. In order to promote the principles set out in this Declaration and to achieve a better understanding of the ethical implications of scientific and technological developments, in particular for young people, States should endeavour

to foster bioethics education and training at all levels as well as to encourage information and knowledge dissemination programmes about bioethics.

2. States should encourage the participation of international and regional intergovernmental organizations and international, regional and national non-governmental organizations in this endeavour.

Article 24—International cooperation

1. States should foster international dissemination of scientific information and encourage the free flow and sharing of scientific and technological knowledge.

2. Within the framework of international cooperation, States should promote cultural and scientific cooperation and enter into bilateral and multilateral agreements enabling developing countries to build up their capacity to participate in generating and sharing scientific knowledge, the related know-how and the benefits thereof.

3. States should respect and promote solidarity between and among States, as well as individuals, families, groups and communities, with special regard for those rendered vulnerable by disease or disability or other personal, societal or environmental conditions and those with the most limited resources.

Article 25—Follow-up action by UNESCO

1. UNESCO shall promote and disseminate the principles set out in this Declaration. In doing so, UNESCO should seek the help and assistance of the Intergovernmental Bioethics Committee (IGBC) and the International Bioethics Committee (IBC).

2. UNESCO shall reaffirm its commitment to dealing with bioethics and to promoting collaboration between IGBC and IBC.

Final provisions

Article 26—Interrelation and complementarity of the principles

This Declaration is to be understood as a whole and the principles are to be understood as complementary and interrelated. Each principle is to be considered in the context of the other principles, as appropriate and relevant in the circumstances.

Article 27—Limitations on the application of the principles

If the application of the principles of this Declaration is to be limited, it should be by law, including laws in the interests of public safety, for the investigation, detection and prosecution of criminal offences, for the protection of public health or for the protection of the rights and freedoms of others. Any such law needs to be consistent with international human rights law.

Article 28—Denial of acts contrary to human rights, fundamental freedoms and human dignity

Nothing in this Declaration may be interpreted as implying for any State, group or person any claim to engage in any activity or to perform any act contrary to human rights, fundamental freedoms and human dignity.

NOTES

[1] Taken from Edelstein, Ludwig. "The Hippocratic Oath: Text, Translation and Interpretation." Supplements to the Bulletin of the History of Medicine, no. 1, 1943, p. 3. © 1943. The Johns Hopkins Press. Used by permission.

[2] This Declaration was adopted by the General Conference of UNESCO at its 33rd session in 2005. The full text is available on the UNESCO website: http://portal.unesco.org/en/ev.php-URL_ID=31058&URL_DO=DO_TOPIC&URL_SECTION=201.html, accessed October 30, 2007.

GLOSSARY[1]

A priori.   Derived from self-evident proposition.

Act-based theory.   A kind of action theory in which principles are applied directly to individual actions.

Action theory.   A theory of right action in which general principles are articulated, sometimes through the use of rules, to make moral evaluations of actions (rather than the character of the actors); cf. virtue theory.

Antinomianism.   The position that ethical actions must be evaluated in each situation without the use of any rules or guidelines; cf. legalism, rules of practice, situationalism.

Autonomy.   The governing of oneself according to one's own system of morals and beliefs or life plan.

Beneficence.   The state of doing or producing good; cf. nonmaleficence. Also the moral principle that actions are right insofar as they produce good.

Best interest standard.   Judgment based on an idea of what would be most beneficial to a patient; cf. substituted judgment standard.

Collegiality.   The quality of relationships among similarly situated individuals, in this case professionals, which may influence or reinforce their values, function, and self-regulatory discipline.

Consequentialism.   The normative theory that the rightness or wrongness of actions is determined by anticipated or known consequences; cf. deontologism.

Contract.   A term sometimes used to describe the fiduciary relationship in professional ethics grounded in promises or pledges.

Covenant.   A solemn agreement between two or more parties that, as related to health care, emphasizes the moral and social character of the bond between professional and patient.

Cultural relativism.   The claim that moral judgments are grounded only in each culture's collective opinion.

De facto.   In reality, actual; cf. de jure.

De jure.   By right, by law; cf. de facto.

Deontologism.   A theory according to which actions are judged right or wrong based on inherent right-making characteristics or principles rather than on their consequences.

Descriptive relativism. The claim that different cultures have differing views as to which matters are believed to be moral.

Distributive justice. The just allocation of society's benefits and burdens.

Double effect, the doctrine of. The theory that an evil effect is morally acceptable provided a proportional good effect will accrue, evil is not intended, the evil effect is not the means to the good, and the action is not intrinsically evil.

Due process criterion of paternalism. A criterion sometimes used to justify paternalism by which the individual who coerces paternalistically must have observed proper procedure and have proper authorization.

Duty proper. A duty decided after taking into account all relevant principles and applying some theory on how to reconcile conflict among principles.

Egalitarianism. A social philosophy or principle that advocates human equality.

Ethical. An evaluation of actions, rules, or the character of people, especially as it refers to the examination of a systematic theory of rightness or wrongness at the ultimate level.

Fidelity. The state of being faithful, including obligations of loyalty and keeping promises and commitments. Also the principle that actions are right insofar as they demonstrate such loyalty.

Fiduciary relationship. A relationship based on trust and confidence that commitments made between parties will be honored.

Human immunodeficiency virus (HIV). A retrovirus responsible for acquired immune deficiency syndrome (AIDS).

Legalism. The position that ethical action consists in strict conformity to law or rules; cf. antinomianism, rules of practice, situationalism.

Macroallocation. The process of allocation, with reference to issues of justice, of total societal resources to a particular area, for example, dentistry.

Metaethics. The branch of ethics having to do with the meaning, justification, or grounding of ethical claims; cf. normative.

Microallocation. Distribution of resources on a small scale.

Moral. An evaluation of actions or the character of people, especially as it refers to ad hoc judgments by individuals or society.

Neutralism. A characteristic of moral or ethical evaluations in which there is general application not favoring one party.

Nonmaleficence. The state of not doing harm or evil; cf. beneficence. Also the moral principle that actions are right insofar as they avoid producing harm or evil.

Nontherapeutic. Something that does not serve the purposes of benefiting an individual patient.

Normative ethics. The branch of ethics having to do with which actions are right or wrong, which states are valuable, or which character traits of people are praiseworthy; cf. metaethics.

Normative relativism. The claim that there is no single universal foundation of moral judgments.

Ordering. A characteristic of moral or ethical evaluations on which a set of principles, rules, or character assessments provides a basis for ranking conflicting claims.

Paternalism. The system of action in which one person treats another the way a father treats a child, striving to promote the other's good even against the other's wishes.

Personal relativism. The claim that a behavior or character is good or right if it conforms to one's personal standard of goodness or rightness.

***Prima facie* duty**. A duty based on consideration of a single moral dimension of an action represented by one moral principle; cf. duty proper.

Profession. An occupation that is oriented toward service to others based on a fiduciary relationship with its clients, that requires extensive specialized knowledge, and that is self-regulating with respect to issues of entry education and collegial discipline.

Professional standard for consent. The standard that health professionals must disclose all information that their professional colleagues similarly situated would disclose about a proposed procedure; cf. reasonable person standard, subjective standard.

Publicity. A characteristic of moral or ethical evaluations in which one must be willing to state the evaluation publicly and the basis on which it is made.

Reasonable person standard of consent. The duty of health professionals to disclose all information that a reasonable person would find meaningful in making a decision whether to consent to a proposed procedure; cf. professional standard, subjective standard.

Rule-based theory. A kind of action theory in which rules, rather than acts, are used to apply principles to individual actions.

Rules of practice. Rules that define general practices in a society; the position that ethical action must be judged by such rules rather than by direct assessment of individual cases; cf. antinomianism, legalism, situationalism.

Secular ethics. Theories of what is good and bad, or right or wrong, based on criteria other than religious doctrine.

Situationalism. The position that ethical action must be judged in each situation guided by, but not directly determined by, rules; cf. antinomianism, rules of practice.

Strong paternalism. The provision of treatment for the good of an individual against the wishes of the individual who is known to be substantially autonomous.

Subjective standard of consent. The standard that health professionals must disclose the information that the individual patient would desire in order to know whether to consent to a proposed procedure; cf. professional standard, reasonable person standard.

Substituted judgment standard. Judgment based on an idea of what the patient would have wanted considering his or her beliefs and values; cf. best interest standard.

Two-tiered medicine. A dual-level system of health care in which tier 1 offers coverage of basic and catastrophic health needs through required societal resources and tier 2 provides other health needs and preferences through voluntary private coverage.

Ultimacy. A characteristic of moral or ethical evaluations that they are grounded in the highest standard by which one might judge.

Universality. A characteristic of moral or ethical evaluations in which an action or character trait should be evaluated the same by all people.

Utilitarianism. The view that an action is deemed morally acceptable because it produces the greatest balance of good over evil, taking into account all individuals affected.

Utility. The state of being useful or producing good.

Value theory. A theory in which objects or states are rationally desirable; what counts as a good or a harm.

Virtue theory. A theory that focuses on the character traits of the actor rather than the ethics of the behavior itself; cf. action theory.

Weak paternalism. The provision of treatment against the wishes of individuals whose autonomy is or may be compromised.

NOTE

[1] This glossary is adapted from Rule, James T. and Robert M. Veatch. *Ethical Questions in Dentistry,* 2nd ed. Chicago: Quintessence Books, 2004, and is used with permission of the publisher.

LIST OF CASES FROM PUBLIC SOURCES

The following cases included in this volume are from sources available publically. They are listed in the order in which they appear in the book. Names and places for these cases are real. Other cases in this volume are from private sources. While these cases are based on real-life events, names and other details of such cases have been changed to provide anonymity and clarity of issues.

Case Number	Patient's Name	Source
4-4	Dr. Jim Witcher	This case is based on the PBS documentary, "On Our Own Terms: Moyers on Dying," which first aired September 10–13, 2000. More information and a study guide are available at http://www.pbs.org/wnet/onourownterms/about/index.html (accessed September 19, 2007).
4-6	Nushawn J Williams	http://query.nytimes.com/gst/fullpage.html?res=9B06E1DC173AF93AA15752C0A96E958260&sec=health&pagewanted=print
9-2	Karen Quinlan	In *re* Quinlan, 137 N.J. super 227 (1975). While that court ruled that the physicians could continue life support against the parents' wishes, that opinion was later overturned by the New Jersey Supreme Court: In *re* Quinlan, 70 N.J. 10, 355 A. 2d 647 (1976), *cert. denied* sub nom., Garger v. New Jersey, 429 U.S. 922 (1976), overruled in part, in *re* Conroy, 98 N.J. 321, 486 A.2d 1209 (1985). See also Quinlan, Joseph and Julia with Phyllis Battelle. *Karen Ann*. Garden City, New York: Doubleday, 1977.

(*continued*)

Case Number	Patient's Name	Source
9-3	Jodie and Mary Attard (court-assigned pseudonymns)	Wasserman, David. "Killing Mary to Save Jodie: Conjoined Twins and Individual Rights." *Philosophy and Public Policy Quarterly.* 21 (No. 1, Winter 2001):9–14; Annas, George J. "Conjoined Twins—the Limits of Law at the Limits of Life." *New England Journal of Medicine* 344 (April 5, 2001):1104–1108; Clare Dyer. "Siamese Twins to Be Separated Against Parent's Will." *British Medical Journal* 321 (Sept. 2, 2000):529; Clare Dyer. "Parents of Siamese Twins Appeal Against Separation." *British Medical Journal* 321 (Sept. 9, 2000):589; Dyer, Clare. "Doctrine of Necessity Could Allow Separation of Twins." *British Medical Journal* 321 (Sept. 16, 2000):653; Mallia, Pierre. "The Case of the Maltese Siamese Twins—When Moral Arguments Balance Out Should Parental Rights Come into Play." *Medicine, Health Care and Philosophy* 5 (2002):205–209; "Separation of Conjoined Twins." *Lancet* 356 (Sept. 16, 2000):953
9-4	Claire Conroy	In the Matter of Claire C. Conroy, Superior Court of New Jersey, Chancery Division, Essex County, Docket No. P-19083E, Decided February 2, 1983. In the Matter of Claire C. Conroy, Superior Court of New Jersey, Appellate Division, Docket No. A-2483-892 T1, Decided July 8, 1983.
10-5	Norma McCorvey	Roe v. Wade, 410 U.S. 113, 93 S.Ct. 705, 1973; McCorvey, Norma, and Gary Thomas. *Won by Love: Norma McCorvey, Jane Roe of Roe v. Wade, Speaks Out for the Unborn as She Shares Her New Conviction for Life.* Nashville, TN: Thomas Nelson, Inc., 1998; and Norma McCorvey's website, http://www.crossingoverministry.org/, accessed September 8, 2007.
11-4	Mary Beth Whitehead; Bill and Elizabeth Stern	In *re* Baby M. 109 N.J. 396, 537 A.2d 1277 (1988); Whitehead, Mary Beth and Schwartz-Nobel, Loretta, "My Fight for Baby M." *Family Circle* 102(No. 3, Feb. 1989):100–102, 175–178.

(*continued*)

Case Number	Patient's Name	Source
12-3	Ash Falkingham	Boswell, Randy. AToronto Hospital Rejects Kidney from >Cult= Donor.@ National Post June 4, 2007. Accessed on the Internet at: http://www.canada.com/nationalpost/news/story.html?id=088014cb-4349-4932-8402-f80646f2b2ad&k=54375; Hartley, Matt. Donor Wasn't Brainwashed, Patient Says,@ [Toronto] *Globe and Mail*, June 6, 2007, accessed on the web at http://www.theglobeandmail.com/servlet/story/RTGAM.20070606.wkidney06/BNStory/Entertainment/
13-1	Anonymous (Dr. Robert John Denis Browne)	General Medical Council: Disciplinary Committee. *British Medical Journal Supplement* (No. 3442, March 20, 1971):79–80.
13-2	Prosenjit Poddar; Tatiana Tarasoff	Tarasoff v. Regents of the University of California Supreme Court of California, 1974 13 Cal. 3d 177 (1974); and Tarasoff v. Regents of University of California. 17C.3d 425, 131 Cal. Rptr. 14, 551 P.2d 334; Tarasoff v. Regents of University of California. 17C.3d 425, 131 Cal. Rptr. 14, 551 P.2d 334, p. 340.
14-5	Thomas Simons	Testerman, Jeff. "Should Donors Say Who Gets Organs?" *St. Petersburg [FL] Times.* January 9, 1994.
14-10	Pennsylvania Governor Bob Casey	Colburn, Don. "Gov. Casey's Quick Double Transplant: How Did He Jump to the Top of the Waiting List?" *Washington Post Health* 9 (June 22, 1993):8–9; "Controversy about Allocation of Organs for Transplantation: The Case of Governor Casey." *BioLaw Update* (October 1993):U:303–304.
15-7	Lori Ann Cardosa	This case is based on newspaper accounts in the *St. Petersburg Times* and on Hoffman, Pat. "The 12 Year Struggle of the United Farm Workers Union," *Sojourners*, July 1977, available on the Internet at http://www.farmworker-movement.org/essays/essays/eleven/06%20-%20GAINING%20JUSTICE%20GROUND.pdf, accessed October 3, 2007.

(continued)

Case Number	Patient's Name	Source
18-1	Pelle Lindbergh	Sell, David. "Flyers Goalie Lindbergh Is Declared Brain Dead." *The Washington Post* November 11, 1985, pp. D1, D13; Sell, David. "Lindbergh Was Legally Drunk." *The Washington Post* November 12, 1985, pp. D1, D4; Sell, Dave. "Flyers' Lindbergh Is Declared Dead." *The Washington Post* November 13, 1985, pp. D1, D8
18-3	Nancy Cruzan	Cruzan, by Cruzan v. Harmon, 760 S.W.2d 408 (Mo.banc 1988) and Cruzan v. Director, Missouri Dept. of Health, 110 S.Ct. 2841 (1990)
18-4	Joseph Saikewicz	Superintendent of Belchertown State School v. Saikewicz, 373 Mass. 728, 370 NE 2d 417 (1977)
18-6	Phillip Becker	In the matter of Phillip Becker, 92 Cal. App. 3d 796, 156 Cal Rptr. 48 (1979), Cert. denied sub nom. Bothman v. Warren B., 445 U.S. 949 (1980); and Guardianship of Phillip Becker, No. 101–981, at 4 (Cal. Super. Ct., August 7, 1981), aff'd., 139 Cal. App.3d 407, 420, 199 Cal.1Rptr. 781, 789 (1983).

INDEX